Corporate
and Tax Aspects
of
Closely Held
Corporations

are all clearly treated. Chapter 8 deals with the corporate and tax aspects of "selling" the corporation, embracing mergers, consolidations, stock and asset sales and other reorganizations, with special attention to the structure of tax free acquisitions.

Following the chapters on the dissolution and sale of a close corporation is one on "going public". Advantages, prior steps, registration procedures, and considerations of state law are all explained together with the implications of the proposals of the Wheat Report and the SEC's proposed Rule 144. Fringe benefits are outlined with appropriate references to the Internal Revenue Code (including the Tax Reform Act of 1969) and current substantive law developments. In the last chapter legislation from key close corporation states like Delaware, New York, New Jersey, Pennsylvania, Florida, and others are detailed. Back matter includes Appendices, Checklists, Tables of Cases, Regulations and Rulings, and a thoroughly developed Index.

William H. Painter, after graduation from Harvard Law School in 1954, joined the New York law firm of Debevoise, Plimpton, et al. where he practiced for four years. Subsequently, he returned to Harvard Law School as a Teaching Fellow for one year and then joined the Villanova School of Law faculty where he taught until 1965. After serving as Visiting Professor at the University of Michigan Law School for a semester, he was appointed Professor of Law at the University of Missouri – Kansas City, School of Law, a position he now holds.

In addition to being a featured speaker at numerous professional meetings and a regular contributor of articles in the areas of corporate law, taxation, and securities regulation, Professor Painter is the author of FEDERAL REGULATION OF INSIDER TRADING (1968).

Corporate
and Tax Aspects
of
Closely Held
Corporations

WILLIAM H. PAINTER

Professor of Law, University of Missouri–Kansas City

LITTLE, BROWN AND COMPANY
BOSTON   TORONTO

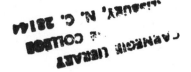

LIBRARY OF CONGRESS CATALOG CARD NO. 71–138949
57 BBI–02/71

FIRST PRINTING

Published simultaneously in Canada
by Little, Brown & Company (Canada) Limited

PRINTED IN THE UNITED STATES OF AMERICA

For
M.H.P., R.W.P. and E.H.P.

Preface

Recent years have seen an increasing recognition that problems of business law cannot be broken down into the neat classical categories of corporate law, tax law, securities regulation, labor law, antitrust law and so forth. In the law schools this has resulted in widespread popularity of "problems" courses such as Business Planning. In part this has been an attempt to approximate more closely the context in which the practicing attorney is likely to encounter problems. Many large law firms continue to have a departmentalized structure, with partners who specialize in tax work, estate planning, financing, labor law, antitrust law and other matters, but even these firms have recognized the need for a well-rounded background before entering a specialty and for the capacity to interrelate the component parts of a complex business problem.

Although much recent attention in business circles has been focused on the increasing significance of the federal securities laws in the affairs of both publicly and closely held corporations, and on the gradual development of what has been called a "federal corporation law," the need to prepare lawyers to deal with the traditional corporate, tax and other legal problems of the smaller closely held enterprise continues to be a vital one. Notwithstanding the desirability of a more integrated approach, most texts and other writings have tended to perpetuate the classical compartmentalized perspective. Thus one may find excellent treatises on corporate aspects of closely held corporations (such as that of Professor O'Neal) and exhaustive treatments of the tax aspects (such as the outstanding work of Professors Bittker and Eustice), but, aside from lengthier works such as those of Hornstein and Cavitch, it is difficult to find a concise treatment of tax and corporate (including securities law) aspects of closely held corporations. It is hoped that this book will make a small contribution toward filling this need.

Consistent with this approach, primary stress has been placed upon collecting information hitherto available only in several separate sources, organizing it and presenting it in a way which will be most meaningful to both student and practitioner in dealing with problems of closely held corporations. Thus, with a few exceptions, the author has not served as creator or innovator but rather has performed the more modest function of collector and organizer. Although every effort has been made to discuss each topic as comprehensively as possible, it is obviously not feasible, within the confines of a single volume, to refer to all the pertinent authorities, mention each case or discuss every detail however obscure. Rather, the main outlines of various areas have been explored and reference has been made throughout to more exhaustive treatments of particular topics, such as the various treatises already referred to. Thus it is hoped that this book will be a useful guide to the entire area and that the researcher, bent upon unearthing more authorities on a particular point of law, will have no great difficulty in locating further helpful source materials.

I wish to express my indebtedness to the School of Law of the University of Missouri–Kansas City, to its Law Foundation, and to the Office of Research Administration of the School of Graduate Studies for valuable assistance in the typing and preparation of the manuscript. I am also indebted to my family, which continues in its patient (albeit baffled) understanding of the eccentricities of authorship. Although the content of the book may prove to them elusive—if not entirely obscure—they may still sense that the father has again given birth and join with him in the fond hope that the child will not be stillborn but will flourish.

WILLIAM H. PAINTER

Kansas City, Missouri
September 1, 1970

Summary of Contents

Contents

Corporate
and Tax Aspects
of
Closely Held
Corporations

I   Alternatives to the Close Corporation

A useful preliminary to any discussion of the close corporation is an examination of the significant characteristics, including tax aspects, of doing business in other forms. Since the two principal ways of doing business other than in the corporate form are the sole proprietorship and the partnership, we shall concentrate on these and contrast each of them with the close corporation.

1.1   SOLE PROPRIETORSHIP

In the sole proprietorship the business is typically owned and operated by a single individual who employs others to assist him in the conduct of the business. The income of the business is his and is taxable to him. This means, of course, that such income is taxed at varying rates depending upon the owner's particular tax bracket and whether he files a joint or separate return. He owns or leases the assets and is entitled to deduct depreciation on depreciable properties or rental payments on leased properties. Similarly, he may deduct all other ordinary and necessary business expenses, including reasonable salaries or compensation paid to his employees.[1] He is fully liable on business obligations and bears the entire loss if the business should fail. Such losses are deductible from his income as business losses.[2] He is entitled to run the business as he sees fit, delegating responsibilities to others if he chooses. If he should die or become disabled, the business might well terminate.

Interestingly enough, the sole proprietorship is, numerically speaking, the most popular form of business organization. For example, in 1963 there were approximately 9.1 million sole proprietorships with a net profit of $23.8 billion. This compares to a total of approximately 924 thousand part-

---

[1] Int. Rev. Code of 1954, §162. For an excellent discussion of the various advantages and disadvantages of various business forms, see J. Crane and A. Bromberg, Partnership 123–136 (1968). For other discussions, see id. at 134 n.87.
[2] Int. Rev. Code of 1954, §165(c).

nerships and 1.3 million corporations, with net profits of $8.7 billion and $54.3 billion, respectively.[3]

The sole proprietorship is, as one might expect, suitable primarily for the small business. Almost invariably the owner's income is relatively modest. As his income grows and as the business becomes more profitable, the greater is the advantage of incorporation, where the total tax on net income is limited to 22 percent of the first $25,000 and 48 percent of income in excess of $25,000. In the case of married individuals filing joint returns, the advantage becomes apparent when the taxable income of the business, together with all other taxable income of the married couple, exceeds $44,000 (based on 1970 tax rate schedules). For single taxpayers (other than heads of households), the advantage of incorporating emerges when such income exceeds $32,000. This is equally true in the case of partnerships. The major difference is that a partner is taxed on only his distributive share of partnership profits.[4] In most cases the distributive share will depend upon the terms of the partnership agreement.[5] The sole proprietor is, as has been said, taxed on all business income remaining after deductions.

Aside from tax aspects, the major advantages and disadvantages of the sole proprietorship may be summarized as follows. First, and perhaps foremost, the sole proprietorship is the simplest way of doing business. There is no need for preparing a partnership agreement, articles of incorporation, bylaws or other documents. Aside from statutory requirements imposing licensing for various occupations, or registration of trade or fictitious names, there is no need for filing or registration with state or local officials.[6] Another advantage is the fact that the owner of the business has sole control; he need not obtain the consent of partners, directors or shareholders to engage in various business activities.

A major disadvantage of the sole proprietorship is the exposure of the individual's personal assets to business risks. This is also true of partnerships other than limited partnerships. The sole proprietor or general partner, in

---

[3] J. Crane and A. Bromberg, id. at 9, tabulating statistics obtained from U.S. Treasury Department, Internal Revenue Service sources.

[4] Int. Rev. Code of 1954, §702. For a fairly extensive arithmetical illustration of the tax impact of doing business as a sole proprietorship in contrast to a corporation, see 3 Z. Cavitch, Business Organizations §68.01[2] (1968). Section 1348 of the Code, added by the Tax Reform Act of 1969, lessens to some extent the advantage of incorporating in that it provides for a maximum tax on earned income of 60 percent in 1971 and 50 percent in 1972 and thereafter. However, the maximum tax applies only to earned income and thus does not benefit the individual who has income from other sources. Moreover, in computing earned income eligible for the maximum tax, income from so-called tax preference sources, such as accelerated depreciation, qualified stock options, depletion and capital gains, must be subtracted to the extent that such tax preference income exceeds $30,000. See Int. Rev. Code of 1954, §§56–58 and 1348.

[5] Id. §704(a).

[6] 1 Z. Cavitch, id. §4.02.

the event of business catastrophe, may lose his home, bank account and other investments. The failure of the business may result in his personal bankruptcy. Stemming from this is another disadvantage—the business is able to obtain financing only if the individual's credit rating qualifies for loans. In the case of partnerships, eligibility for financing will depend on the credit rating of the other partners along with the size of their capital contributions to the partnership as well as on the partnership's overall profit history. Although financing for corporations, particularly closely held ones, may depend, in part, on the credit standing of major shareholders or officers who may be required to guarantee corporate borrowing, the corporation may be better able to obtain funds from outside sources. Thus it may sell new issues of common or preferred stock, or bonds or debentures convertible into common or preferred. Partnerships may, of course, admit new partners, but only with the consent of all the partners or otherwise in accordance with the partnership agreement.[7] And obtaining new partners may at times be difficult in view of the unlimited liability imposed on general partners.[8] Limited partnership interests may be obtained where available and the liability of a limited partner may be satisfied only out of his contribution to the partnership.[9] The sole proprietorship has the least flexibility of all of these various forms of business organization when it comes to obtaining financing. By and large, the matter resolves itself into a loan application by the sole proprietor. His credit rating is the paramount consideration, although the profits and assets of the business are obviously crucial in determining the availability of credit.

Aside from the foregoing, another major disadvantage of the sole proprietorship is its status on the death of the sole proprietor. Unless there is someone, typically a member of the family, to continue the business, or unless a purchaser can be found, the enterprise will be discontinued, resulting in loss of "going concern" value and in many instances the sale of business assets at sacrifice prices. Although a partnership may in theory "dissolve" on the death of any general partner,[10] the more modern view is that the partnership continues where this is provided for in the partnership agreement. Most modern partnerships operate in this fashion, making suitable provision for purchasing or otherwise disposing of the deceased partner's interest.[11] The ultimate in longevity or immortality is, of course,

[7] Uniform Partnership Act §18(g).

[8] A person entering an existing partnership is liable for all partnership obligations subsequently incurred and is also liable for obligations arising before his admission except that the latter liability may be satisfied only out of his partnership contribution. Id. §17.

[9] Uniform Limited Partnership Act §7. This is so only if he does not take part in the control of the business. Also he may be liable as a general partner if his name appears in the partnership name. Id. §5.

[10] Uniform Partnership Act §31(4).

[11] J. Crane and A. Bromberg, Partnership 418, 432–434 (1968).

the corporation. Unless the articles of incorporation provide for a limited corporate life, a corporation continues until its dissolution. Thus it may be perpetual.

In summary, then, the sole proprietorship is suitable primarily for small businesses with relatively low profits where the owner is taxed at modest rates and has little outside income. In addition, such enterprises involve comparably small amounts of risk and require only minimal financing. Unless there is a purchaser or someone capable of continuing the business, the enterprise terminates on the death of the owner. A prime advantage of the sole proprietorship is its simplicity and the ease with which the owner may run the business free from restraints of other owners or outsiders.

1.2 PARTNERSHIP

A partnership, as defined in the Uniform Partnership Act, is "an association of two or more persons to carry on as co-owners a business for profit." [12] Unlike the sole proprietorship, the property of the business belongs to no one individual; rather, it belongs to the partnership.[13] Business decisions are made by the partners in accordance with the manner prescribed by the partnership agreement, whether it be by majority rule, unanimous consent or some other method. All general partners are each jointly liable for debts and other obligations of the partnership, and jointly and severally liable for torts, such as fraud or misappropriation of property of others.[14] As previously stated, profits of the partnership are taxable to the individual partners in accordance with their distributive shares as determined under the partnership agreement.[15] This is true whether or not the profits are actually received by a particular partner. A partner may deduct his share of partnership losses to the extent of his "basis" in the firm, which will generally correspond to the basis of any property he has contributed to the partnership plus his money contributions—adjusted upwards or downwards in accordance with such items as partnership income previously taxed but unreceived by him, or losses which have already been made available to him as deductions.[16] As far as the death of a partner is concerned, it has already been seen that, although the traditional view is that the firm dissolves, the partnership agreement may, and generally does, provide that the partnership continues, often under the name of the surviving partners.[17] Partnership interests may be transferred to others, or other partners ad-

[12] Uniform Partnership Act §6.
[13] Id. §8.
[14] Id. §15.
[15] Int. Rev. Code of 1954, §704(a).
[16] Id. §§704(d), 705.
[17] See note 11 *supra*.

mitted, if permitted by the partnership agreement, but this may require the unanimous consent of all the partners.[18]

There are only a few advantages to the partnership which do not also pertain to the sole proprietorship. The very fact of partnership implies the availability of additional capital by way of the investment made by copartners. Since the business is apt to be larger and perhaps more prosperous than the sole proprietorship, it may encounter less difficulty in obtaining outside financing. Much depends upon the profitability of the business, its assets, other liabilities and the credit standing and reputation of the various partners. If additional capital is required, new partners can be admitted to the partnership if suitable candidates can be found. Those who do not wish to incur the risk of personal liability for partnership debts may either lend money to the partnership or purchase limited partnership interests.

Aside from having greater ease and flexibility of financing, the partnership is a convenient means of mixing a variety of talents and management skills, as well as delegating responsibility for running various aspects of a business. The sole proprietor, although he is always free to hire management help, is ultimately responsible for all phases of his enterprise. Thus he must combine skills of production, supply and marketing, along with routine office administration. In a partnership these duties may be split up and delegated to those best equipped to handle particular areas. Hence the business is more likely to be run efficiently. This is particularly important as a business grows in size. In most situations there will come a time when one man either cannot or should not take responsibility for the entire business. This will be the time when it will be wise to consider either a partnership or a corporation.

There are a few tax advantages in doing business in the partnership form as compared with the sole proprietorship. Since a partnership is, in some respects, treated as an entity for tax purposes, a partner may sell or lease property to a partnership. This may be of some benefit since, in the event of sale, he may realize a deductible loss on the property, or, if the property is sold at a gain, the partnership may obtain a "stepped-up" basis for the purpose of computing subsequent depreciation and gain on resale. If the property is leased, the firm is entitled to deduct rental payments and the lessor-partner is entitled to deduct depreciation. Although the rentals are included in the lessor-partner's income for tax purposes, such payments (deductible by the partnership) reduce his distributive share of partnership income and in that respect his taxes. One hazard which must be guarded against in the event of a sale of property between a partner and his firm is the provision

[18] Although a partner may assign his interest in the profits of the partnership to a third party, or his rights in the event of dissolution of the partnership, the assignee may not become a partner without the consent of the other members of the firm, except in accordance with the provisions of the partnership agreement. Uniform Partnership Act §§18(g), 27.

disallowing loss deductions where the selling partner owns, directly or indirectly, more than 50 percent of the capital interest, or the profits interest, in the partnership.[19] A similar rule applies to gains on sales between a partner and a firm in which he owns, directly or indirectly, more than 80 percent of the capital interest or profits interest. Such gains are taxed at ordinary income rates.[20]

Enough has already been said to suggest the major disadvantages of the partnership in contrast to the sole proprietorship. By entering into a partnership an owner relinquishes sole control of the venture. He now must consult with his partners and often must obtain their affirmative consent before undertaking certain basic matters, such as expanding or changing the nature of the business, seeking new financing, entering new lines of endeavor, disposing of major assets or otherwise engaging in anything other than routine business activity.[21] Of course, much will depend upon the terms of the partnership agreement. Often a former sole proprietor will reserve power to make major business decisions, but his very association with others implies a loss of personal freedom to make all decisions on his own. Yet this constitutes a positive gain rather than a detriment as the business grows and new management skills are needed, and where the partnership offers a reservoir of differing talents and responsibilities. Furthermore, a sole proprietor, with advancing age, may feel these things more keenly. Although he may be loath to surrender his former powers, he must eventually realize that he is no longer capable of running the entire business, particularly if it should grow in size. Often a partnership is a useful method whereby the transition is made between generations; children, other relatives and outsiders may be brought into the business, spreading responsibility and providing continuity in the event of the retirement or death of the founder.

In summary, then, the partnership is a collective way of doing business and resembles the sole proprietorship in that partners are liable for partnership debts, partnership profits and losses are taxed or deducted by the partners in accordance with their distributive shares under the partnership agreement, and the enterprise *may* terminate by the death or retirement of a partner. But it lacks some of the flexibility of the sole proprietorship in

[19] Int. Rev. Code of 1954, §707(b). The rule also applies to sales between partnerships in which the same persons own, directly or indirectly, more than 50 percent of the capital interest or profits interest. In determining ownership, the constructive ownership rules of §267(c) are applicable. Id. §707(b)(3). Thus a partner is deemed to own not only his personal interest in the firm but also that of his spouse, brothers, sisters, ancestors and lineal descendants. The practical effect of this provision is to disallow losses on transactions between firm members and a family partnership in many instances.

[20] Id. §707(b)(2). The rule also applies to transactions between firms in which the same persons own, directly or indirectly, more than 80 percent of the capital interests or profits interests. As in the loss situation, the constructive ownership rules of §267(c) apply.

[21] J. Crane and A. Bromberg, Partnership 381–382 (1968).

that a partner, unlike a sole proprietor, may not transfer his interest to another except in accordance with the partnership agreement, and in that the agreement will doubtless contain restrictions as to how business decisions are to be made, whether by majority vote or in some other manner. Thus when a person enters a partnership with others he gains the advantages of their capital contributions and skills but must sacrifice the freedom of operation which he would have had as a sole proprietor.

1.3 CORPORATIONS—LIMITED LIABILITY; TAX ADVANTAGES AND DISADVANTAGES

Perhaps the most significant aspect of the corporation, in contrast to the sole proprietorship or partnership, is that it is legally treated as a separate "entity" or person, and this is also true for tax purposes. Thus the profits of the enterprise are taxed to the corporation—not, as a general rule, to its shareholders.[22] Corporate losses are deductible by the corporation in computing its taxable income. Another very significant feature is that the corporation, and not its shareholders, is responsible for corporate obligations. Hence, two main advantages of incorporating are the avoidance of taxation on any profits of the enterprise which have not actually been distributed to the shareholder (as salary, as dividend or in some other manner) and the avoidance of liability for business obligations. The shareholder's risk is limited to the amount of capital he has put into the corporation. If the enterprise fails, his shares may become worthless but he will suffer no further financial loss. Thus the corporate form of doing business is especially attractive to individuals who wish to limit their risk, not exposing their other personal assets to liability for business debts. Additionally, it is attractive to those who, perhaps having substantial nonbusiness income from other sources which places them in high tax brackets, do not wish to be taxed on business income as long as they elect not to receive it. The profits of the business may thus be ploughed back into the corporation, increasing the value of the shares. If the shares should later be sold, the gain will be taxable at the lower capital gain rates. Any amounts which the shareholders wish to take out of the corporation may, within certain limitations of reasonableness, be paid as salaries rather than as dividends. If the salaries are reasonable in amount, they are deductible as business expenses by the corporation in figuring its tax liability. The same is true in the case of rentals paid on leased property or interest payments on loans made by shareholders to their corporation. Here, as will be discussed later in greater detail,[23] one must be sure that the loan is bona fide, that it is not in substance a contribu-

---

[22] The exception is Int. Rev. Code of 1954, Subchapter S, discussed in text accompanying note 84 *infra*.
[23] Ch. II, text accompanying notes 67–102.

tion to capital and that the capital structure is not excessively "thin" (i.e., that there is a reasonable relationship of debt to equity, preferably no greater than 50–50).

A further tax advantage to corporateness is greater flexibility in fringe benefits for employees. Of primary importance are qualified pension, profit-sharing and stock bonus plans[24] as well as qualified stock options and employee stock purchase plans.[25] Although pension plans may now be established by self-employed individuals, there are several restrictions on such plans which do not apply to qualified pension plans established by corporations. For example, deductions for amounts contributed to a pension plan for self-employed individuals are limited to the lesser of 10 percent of the individual's earned income from trade or business, or $2500. In addition, there is no capital gains treatment for lump sum distributions from the fund and these are subject to a five-year averaging formula.[26] The major tax advantages of qualified pension plans are that contributions to the pension fund by the employer corporation are tax-deductible to it and are not taxed as compensation to employees, income of the pension trust is not subject to tax and distributions from the fund may be subject to more favorable tax treatment.[27]

✗The advantages of qualified stock options and employee stock purchase plans are well known. Briefly, they enable the executive or employee to receive options to purchase stock of the employer with no tax consequence at the time the option is granted or exercised (other than possible imposition of a 10 percent tax on so-called tax preference income, which includes income from the exercise of qualified stock options, as required by Section 56 of the Code, added by the Tax Reform Act of 1969; the tax is imposed only if tax preference income exceeds $30,000). If the stock is held for a minimum period and the other restrictions imposed on such plans are met, the only tax is on subsequent sale of the stock, and here the employee is taxed at capital gains rates. Fortunes have been made in this fashion.

Two further tax advantages of the corporate form of business might be mentioned: One is the fact that dividends received from *other* corporations are entitled to a dividends-received credit of at least 85 percent and, in the

---

[24] Int. Rev. Code of 1954, §§401–407.

[25] Id. §§421–423. Due to the difficulty of valuing stock precisely in a close corporation, stock option or purchase plans are less frequently used. The matter is discussed in detail in Ch. X. For a listing of further fringe benefits available for corporate employees, see Ch. X (tax-free accident and health benefits, group insurance plans, a $5000 exclusion for employee death benefit payments, and salary continuation plans in the event of illness or disability).

[26] Int. Rev. Code of 1954, §§401(e)(1)(B)(iii), 402(a)(2), 1301–1304. The discrepancy between the two has been lessened as a result of the Tax Reform Act of 1969, which imposes a tax on lump sum distributions from qualified plans of corporations under a complex seven-year "forward-averaging" formula, rather than at a capital gains rate, as formerly. See id. §§402(a)(5) and 72(n)(4).

[27] Id. §§401–405, 501. See also §72.

case of dividends received from an "affiliated" corporation (i.e., one in which the recipient corporation has at least 80 percent ownership), a credit of 100 percent.[28] A further advantage is the ability of a corporation to "time" its income distributions to shareholders. For example, all income received by a partnership is automatically "passed through" to the firm members and is includible in their respective gross incomes. Corporate income may be withheld, subject to the rule against excess accumulations, discussed below, and conveyed to shareholders in a later year in the form of dividends or salaries. This provides for greater flexibility and aids in tax planning.

⋇There are several tax disadvantages to incorporating. Among the primary disadvantages is the so-called double taxation of any corporate earnings which are distributed to shareholders in the form of dividends. As already pointed out, the corporation, an entity for tax purposes, pays a tax on its earnings and such earnings are again taxed at the shareholder level if they are distributed as dividends. The tax is imposed only to the extent that the corporation has earnings and profits either of the current taxable year or accumulated since February 28, 1913.[29] Recipients of dividends are generally entitled to a small dividend exclusion of $100 for individuals and $200 on a joint return.[30] We have already seen how double taxation may to a certain degree be avoided by distribution of earnings in the form of reasonable salaries, interest on indebtedness, or rental payments on leased property. Also, consideration should be given to an election under Subchapter S, discussed later in this chapter.

A further tax disadvantage, closely related to the double taxation point, is the fact that earnings of the corporation which are distributed to shareholders do not retain their original character. Thus amounts received by a corporation from the sale of a capital asset and taxed to it at capital gains rates are taxed at ordinary rates when distributed to shareholders in the form of dividends, salaries or interest. In sharp contrast, capital gains of partnerships are passed through and taxed to members of the firm at favorable rates. We have already seen how losses are similarly treated in the case of partnerships (i.e., passed through and deductible by a partner to the extent of his basis in the firm).[31]

[28] Id. §243. A few more relatively minor tax advantages might be mentioned: A corporation has a separate charitable contribution deduction of 5 percent of its taxable income and also may amortize its organizational expenses over a period of not less than sixty months. Id. §§170(b), 248. Also sale of stock in a corporation which has substantially appreciated inventory or unrealized receivables will not give rise to ordinary income, as is the case in a partnership. Id. §751. The same problem exists as regards the death or retirement of a partner.

[29] Id. §316.

[30] Id. §116.

[31] Id. §§702(b), 704(d). It should also be noted that capital gains may be taxed at a higher rate to a corporation (30 percent) than to an individual, who may in effect pay a tax at half his normal rate, if that is less than 25 percent. Note, however, that the Tax Reform Act of 1969 amended Section 1201 of the Code to provide

Since the corporation is a tax entity, amounts transferred to it may result in a tax to the transferor, or in certain cases a deductible loss. Similarly, the liquidation of a corporation will generally result in capital gain or loss for any amounts distributed to shareholders in partial or complete termination of the enterprise.[32] Some tax relief is available as regards the formation of corporations if there is careful compliance with Section 351 of the Code, discussed in greater detail in the following chapter. Since the partnership, at least in this respect, is not an entity for tax purposes, amounts contributed to it either on its formation or subsequently do not give rise to taxable gain or deductible loss.[33] Similarly, with a few exceptions, distributions from the partnership, whether or not in liquidation of its affairs, do not give rise to gain or loss.[34] It may be readily seen, then, that the corporate form of doing business lacks a certain flexibility characteristic of partnerships when it comes to transferring amounts in and out of the business. Such amounts may be moved in or out of the partnership with little or no tax effect, at least as a general rule. This is not true of the corporation.

Another way in which the corporation differs from a partnership in the tax sense is the method by which losses are handled. As already indicated, losses are deductible by the corporation and not, as in the partnership, passed through to the investors. On the failure of the enterprise, a shareholder is entitled to a deduction for worthless securities at the less favorable capital loss rate.[35] The exception to this is the so-called small business corporation, where shareholders may, within certain limits, deduct their investment losses as ordinary losses.[36] The significant advantages of small business corporations will be discussed in the following chapter.

There are some special Code provisions applicable only to corporations which may result in significantly higher taxes in certain situations. For example, closely held corporations may run afoul of the provision imposing a penalty tax of 70 percent on "undistributed personal holding company income." Briefly, a personal holding company is a corporation in which more than 50 percent in value of the stock is held, directly or indirectly, by or for

---

that only $50,000 of an individual's long-term capital gains will qualify for taxation at the 25 percent maximum rate. Thus the 25 percent alternative tax is repealed as regards capital gains in excess of $50,000, which are subjected to a maximum tax of $32\frac{1}{2}$ percent for 1971 and 35 percent thereafter. In addition, Section 56 of the Code, added by the Tax Reform Act of 1969, may result in a 10 percent additional tax on 50 percent of the excess of net long-term capital gain over net short-term capital loss, since this must be included as an item of tax preference income.

[32] Id. §331. A limited exception is the so-called one-month elective liquidation provision. Id. §333.

[33] Id. §721.

[34] Id. §§731, 751. See also §736. Among the significant exceptions are the realization of gain where a distribution of money (not property) exceeds the recipient's basis in the firm and certain disproportionate distributions where the firm has unrealized receivables or substantially appreciated inventory.

[35] Id. §165(g).

[36] Id. §1244.

not more than five individuals.[37] Personal holding company income is, in general, income of a "passive" variety (i.e., not from operations), such as dividends, rents, royalties and income from personal service contracts.[38] Unlike a partnership, there is a limit to which a corporation may accumulate its earnings without paying the same out in dividends, salaries, interest and so forth. Although every corporation is permitted to accumulate $100,-000 without the imposition of the penalty tax on excess accumulations, amounts in excess of that figure must be justified as not having been accumulated for the purpose of avoiding income tax with respect to the shareholders. A corporation is, however, permitted to accumulate such amounts as are necessary for the "reasonable needs of the business," which includes reasonably anticipated needs.[39] Special rules apply to distributions and sales of stock in so-called collapsible corporations. These are situations where taxpayers sell stock in or liquidate a corporation prematurely with a view to realizing profits at capital gains rates which would otherwise be taxed at ordinary income rates. For example, a corporation might be formed to construct houses and the corporation liquidated before the houses are sold. In these cases the gain, if it falls within the collapsible corporation rules, is taxed at ordinary rates, thereby frustrating the taxpayer's purpose to achieve a lesser tax at capital gains rates.[40] Thus any enterprise which is likely to be short-lived, and which might therefore fall within the collapsible corporation rules, might consider the advantages of doing business as a partnership. The same might be said for enterprises where a large amount of income is likely to be of a passive sort (i.e., personal holding company income).

One commentator has pointed out two further ways in which a partnership may have some tax advantages over a corporation: Where there is a change in membership in the firm, the firm may adjust its tax basis, often permitting a step-up to a higher basis for depreciation purposes. Such an adjustment is not permitted to a corporation merely because there has been a transfer of shares.[41] Furthermore, the partnership form permits agreements among partners allocating income and expense items. Such agreements are valid for tax purposes if their principal purpose is not the avoidance or evasion of tax.[42] Thus a partner who contributes property with a high basis may be allocated a larger share of the firm's depreciation deduc-

---

[37] Id. §542(a)(2). Constructive ownership rules apply in determining the number of persons so that, for example, an individual is deemed to own stock owned by his brothers, sisters, spouse, ancestors and lineal descendants. Id. §544. For further discussion see Ch. V.

[38] Int. Rev. Code of 1954, §543.

[39] Id. §§531–537. For further discussion see Ch. V, text accompanying notes 69–132.

[40] Int. Rev. Code of 1954, §341. For discussion of collapsible corporations, see Ch. V, text accompanying notes 167–188.

[41] See 1 Z. Cavitch, Business Organizations §§3.01[10], 8.02 (1968).

[42] See 1 id. §3.01[12], and Int. Rev. Code of 1954, §704(b).

tion, attributable to the high basis, or of the loss realized on sale of the property. Such allocations are not permissible in corporations since the income, expense and loss items are not passed through to the shareholders.

1.4   CORPORATIONS—OTHER NONTAX ADVANTAGES AND DISADVANTAGES

We have already seen how a major nontax advantage of the corporation is limited liability. There are other advantages as well. One such advantage is ease of management. Although in some respects the partnership is a relatively flexible method of doing business, in other ways it may prove clumsy and troublesome. In a firm composed of an even number of partners, the members may equally divide and disagree on some proposed course of action, producing a deadlock. A similar impasse is possible in those situations where, in accordance with the partnership agreement or otherwise, the unanimous consent of the partners is required.[43] Although it would be misleading to assume that there may never be a deadlock in a corporation, particularly a closely held one,[44] the corporate organizational structure, being more monolithic than a partnership, lends itself to more precise lines of authority. Thus at the top of the pyramid of command, directly under the board of directors, is the company's chief executive officer, whether he is designated by president, chairman of the board or some other title. Underneath him fall various executives and subordinates, ranging from divisional vice-presidents to managers and department heads. Disagreements are resolved by committee vote or, if this fails, by reference to the next higher person or group in the chain of command. Although there is always a distinct possibility of deadlock among directors or shareholders, particularly in the close corporation, the structural arrangement of authority tends to a more predictable method of resolving disputes within the business.

Some reference has already been made to the fact that the corporation may encounter less difficulty in obtaining new financing than a partnership or sole proprietorship. Although there may be little difference in practice between a partnership and a closely held corporation when it comes to obtaining bank loans, a corporation may obtain additional funds through the sale of stock under circumstances where, if the enterprise were doing business as a partnership, it might be difficult to find persons who were willing and able to become general or even limited partners. This advantage is tied to another, namely, greater liquidity of investment when shares are used instead of partnership interests. As previously stated, although a partner

[43] Uniform Partnership Act §9.
[44] See Ch. VII. If there is a deadlock in a corporation, the consequences may be more serious than in a partnership, since those who hold minority interests cannot always withdraw and dissolve the firm. Thus they may be more vulnerable to oppressive tactics and "squeeze-out" plays on the part of majority owners. See Ch. IV.

may assign his interest in the profits of the firm, and his rights on liquidation, outsiders may not become members of the firm without the consent of the other partners. In view of this, a partnership interest lacks the liquidity which pertains to shares of stock. The latter are freely transferable in the absence of a stock transfer restriction. Even if transfer of the shares is restricted, as is often the case in a close corporation, the restriction frequently takes the form of a so-called right of first refusal, an option giving the corporation or the remaining shareholders the right to purchase the shares.[45] Thus, if a shareholder wishes to sell his shares to an outsider, he is assured that they will be purchased by *someone,* whether it be the outsider or the corporation. Although it is true that a partner is technically entitled to dissolve the firm of which he is a member at any time, he may do so only at the risk of being held liable in damages unless there is a provision in the partnership agreement whereby he may be released as a partner and paid for his interest.[46] Hence, although shares in a close corporation may be difficult to market or may be subject to a restriction, they may still have greater liquidity than a partnership interest.

Another advantage of the corporate form of business is its perpetual existence. Although this has at times been overrated, particularly in view of the modern tendency of partnerships to provide for continuation in the event of death, retirement or disability of a partner,[47] the corporate form may offer a more convenient vehicle for planning for those contingencies. The most popular scheme, although by no means the only one, is a buy-and-sell agreement between the corporation and each shareholder whereby the purchase price of the shares is funded by a life insurance policy taken out by the corporation, which is also the beneficiary.[48]

Finally, we should consider some of the nontax disadvantages of incorporating. These can generally be summarized under the headings of additional expense and formalities incurred in forming and running the corporation. Thus on its organization, aside from legal fees, possible accounting fees and the cost of printing or engraving stock certificates, there are inevitably filing fees and organization taxes of various varieties imposed by the state in which a corporation is formed. In addition, unlike a partnership or sole proprietorship, a corporation must formally qualify to do business in states other than the state of its domicile. This may entail additional legal expense, filing fees and the preparation of forms for initial qualification as well as annual or periodic reports for the payment of franchise taxes, etc.

As far as the formalities of corporate life are concerned, although these may at times be irksome, they should not be thought of as a major obstacle. Aside from the formalities of the incorporation process itself—the

[45] See Ch. III, text accompanying notes 1–82.
[46] Uniform Partnership Act §31(2).
[47] See note 11 *supra.*
[48] See Ch. VI, text accompanying notes 140–191.

signing and filing of articles of incorporation, the preparation of bylaws, minutes of first meeting of incorporators and directors, and so forth—there must be at least one annual meeting of shareholders and also periodic directors' meetings. Although several states now provide for so-called informal action without a meeting of shareholders or directors if there is unanimous written consent to the action proposed to be taken,[49] a properly run corporation will of necessity entail more formalities than a partnership, which can be as informally run as the partners choose.

Although the closely held corporation is not likely to encounter substantial problems with federal, or even state, securities regulation, any public offering of shares is likely to require registration under both the Securities Act of 1933 and the various state Blue Sky laws, unless some exemption can be found, as is often the case.[50] Also, it should not be forgotten that the much discussed rule 10b-5 promulgated by the SEC under the Securities Exchange Act of 1934 [51] applies to a purchase or sale by *any* person of shares in *any* corporation, whether or not publicly held. The current extension of rule 10b-5, and the extent of implied liabilities possible under it, indicate that the rights of minority shareholders will receive a substantial amount of protection on the federal level. This is, of course, not true in the case of a partnership, where rights are protected only in the state courts.

When an enterprise is incorporated, those who as shareholders are said to own it may be less capable of withdrawing from the firm. Although a partnership may be dissolved by any member of the firm at any time, subject to contractual liability for breach of the partnership agreement, a corporation is not as easily dissolved, particularly by minority shareholders, unless they are able to show that the acts of the majority are oppressive or fraudulent. If the shares are not readily marketable, as is so often the case in the closely held concern, the minority shareholder may find himself "locked in."

1.5 THE DECISION TO INCORPORATE

It has been said, "When in doubt, don't incorporate." [52] For the small, new firm, particularly the closely held one, a partnership may be more desirable. Our survey of the various advantages and disadvantages of the sole proprietorship, partnership and corporation should indicate some of the plus and minus factors which go into any decision to incorporate. Rather than recapitulate the several matters which have already been discussed, it

---

[49] E.g., Del. Gen. Corp. Law §§141(f), 228 (1967).

[50] Thus an exemption is available for so-called intrastate offerings under Section 2(a)(11) of the Securities Act of 1933 and also an exemption under Section 3(b) for small offerings of not more than $300,000 annually. State laws commonly exempt offerings to small numbers of persons, or so-called isolated transactions. See Ch. IX.

[51] 17 C.F.R. §240.10b–5 (1942) (formerly known as rule X-10B-5).

[52] G. Seward, Basic Corporate Practice 8 (1966).

may suffice to mention some of the more important considerations, particularly from the standpoint of the small, new enterprise. Since incorporation is seldom justified if merely for tax reasons, it may be appropriate to consider the nontax factors first.

Limited liability is often uppermost in the minds of persons wishing to incorporate. Frequently overlooked, however, is the fact that adequate provision for tort liability can often be had through insurance of one form or another. As far as contractual liability is concerned, lenders often require the signature of major shareholders in close corporations to guarantee the payment of corporate indebtedness. Thus, although the advantage of limited liability should not be ignored, it should not be overstated. Naturally there may be situations, such as businesses involving an unusually high degree of risk, where limited liability is of singular importance. However, it is only a very unusual risk that cannot be adequately covered by insurance, and even if a corporation were formed, insurance would probably be a necessity.

Enough has already been said about the greater ease and flexibility of financing which the corporate form offers. Although the partnership way of doing business should suffice for the small enterprise, which can subsist on relatively modest bank loans, more substantial financing needs which emerge as the business grows may suggest the use of bonds, debentures and stock of various types. These offer the widest possible market acceptance and permit transfer and readjustment of the various interests of those who own the business. This is particularly useful for estate planning. As we shall see in a later chapter,[53] preferred stock is a useful device in estate planning and in preparing for the retirement and eventual demise of a major shareholder.

The cost of incorporating has also been mentioned. This may be broken down into initial cost, such as filing fees, organization taxes, etc., and continuing expense, such as franchise taxes and other fees exacted for the privilege of continuing to do business in various states, including the state of domicile. Although it is doubtful that initial cost of incorporating should be a decisive factor in any decision not to incorporate, this, along with other factors, including the continuing expense of doing business, may indicate the inadvisability of small businesses with modest profits forming a corporation unless there is some pressing reason to do so.

Of obvious relevance to the decision to incorporate is the number of persons likely to be involved in running the business. If the number is great, a partnership may prove to be a clumsy organizational structure within which to allocate responsibilities and powers. As we have seen, a corporation, with its monolithic, pyramidal scheme, is well adapted to the more elaborate and complex requirements of a business involving large numbers of people.

The foregoing analysis may be easily summarized as follows: If the busi-

[53] Ch. VI.

ness is small, with modest profits, has little need for substantial financing and requires relatively few persons to run it, a partnership or sole proprietorship may be indicated. This, of course, ignores the vitally important tax aspects yet to be considered.

Among the various tax factors influencing the decision of whether or not to incorporate, perhaps the most important are the individual's income level and the anticipated profits or losses in the years immediately following the proposed incorporation. We have already seen how incorporation becomes more and more advantageous as the individual's taxable income rises.[54] Against the advantage of having business profits taxed at rates lower than the individual's tax rate must be weighed the disadvantages of any double taxation which would result from a distribution of earnings in the form of dividends. As already pointed out, much double taxation may be avoided by the payment of reasonable salaries, interest on shareholder loans and rentals on leased property. And an election under Subchapter S, to be discussed shortly, avoids double taxation almost entirely. Accordingly, although the double taxation aspect is important, it should not be overemphasized, particularly for small businesses which are closely held.

If the business should operate at a loss in its early years, it may well be advantageous to conduct it as a partnership, which permits pass-through loss treatment. Similar advantages are also available under Subchapter S, however. If the owner of a business should have losses from nonbusiness sources, incorporation will result in his inability to balance these losses against business income. Carry-overs of capital losses are also handled differently for a corporation, which is permitted a deduction of carried-over capital loss only against capital gain, than for an individual, who is permitted to deduct carried-over loss from $1000 of his ordinary income to the extent capital losses exceed his capital gain.[55]

It is likely that, *from the tax viewpoint,* the decision of whether or not to incorporate will depend largely upon a weighing of the above factors as they apply to a particular fact situation. The outcome will often be apparent from an arithmetical computation of the tax result under each alternative. Stress has been placed upon the words "from the tax viewpoint" in view of the importance of not choosing a particular business form *solely* for tax reasons. As we have seen, the differences are not that clear-cut, as in the avoidance of double taxation through the use of reasonable salaries, etc., or an election under Subchapter S, which also allows a pass through of losses. The differences are of equal subtlety in the nontax area. In view of the practice of requiring shareholder guarantees of corporate indebtedness in the closely held enterprise, limited liability may not be all its name implies,

[54] See text accompanying note 4 *supra.*

[55] Int. Rev. Code of 1954, §§1211–1212. Note, however, that the Tax Reform Act of 1969 amended Section 1211(b) of the Code so as to provide that long-term capital losses must be first reduced by 50 percent before becoming available as an offset against ordinary income.

and, in addition, considerable protection can be achieved through insurance in the case of a partnership. The advantages of perpetual duration commonly identified with the corporate form may be achieved through a properly drafted partnership agreement providing for continuation of the firm in the event of the death, retirement or disability of a partner. Thus, although it would be wrong to assume that the contrast, tax or nontax, between one form and another is sharp and clear, it would be equally misleading to overlook the very real differences, particularly in some fact situations. For example, it seems safe to say that profitable businesses owned by persons in relatively high income tax brackets should be incorporated and the converse is probably true as well.

It should be apparent from our discussion that a decision to incorporate should not be made on a trial-and-error basis. This is particularly true in view of the cost involved in the incorporation process and the fact that property may not normally be moved in and out of the corporation tax free. Thus, as has been pointed out, liquidation of the corporation will frequently involve the realization of capital gain or loss. Similarly, corporate profits may not always be withdrawn under the guise of tax deductible salaries if to do so would make the salaries unreasonable. The formation of a corporation hence implies a commitment of a fairly permanent character. It may be more appropriate to a fairly mature and growing business than a struggling new one.

There are, of course, other tax benefits to incorporation, and these have been previously discussed (e.g., the wide array of fringe benefits available for corporate employees, the corporation's ability to time distributions of earnings to suit the tax plans of shareholders and the 85 percent credit for dividends received from other corporations). It is doubtful that such benefits, except in an unusual case, should serve as the primary tax motive, much less the sole motive, for incorporating. But once the decision to incorporate has been made, such tax factors serve to reinforce its desirability.

The foregoing discussion of tax and other differences between sole proprietorships, partnerships and corporations is summarized in tabular form as Appendix A, The Decision to Incorporate, at the end of this volume.

1.6 CORPORATE AND TAX PROBLEMS IN CHANGING FROM PARTNERSHIP OR SOLE PROPRIETORSHIP TO CORPORATION

Once the decision has been made to incorporate, there are several problems of a more or less preliminary nature which should be considered. The matters of whether and how to take advantage of the Code provisions permitting tax-free incorporation will be left to the following chapter.

The questions of where to incorporate and how to do it from a mechanical standpoint can be dealt with relatively briefly. The simplest and probably the most satisfactory answer to the first question is that, in most instances, the wisest choice of a domiciliary state will be that jurisdiction wherein the business is primarily located and where most of its chief shareholders reside. This is not because of any requirement that shareholders, or even directors, be residents of the state of incorporation but because it is generally less expensive, and certainly more convenient, to incorporate locally. If some other jurisdiction is selected, it is necessary to pay not only organization fees and taxes in that state but one must also qualify the corporation to do business in the state wherein it might have incorporated if it had done so locally. This will entail the filing of more papers and the payment of further fees and taxes. Thus, unless there is some pressing reason to do so, it is not advisable to incorporate in a foreign jurisdiction. However, certain states, notably Delaware, Maryland, New York, New Jersey, North Carolina, Pennsylvania and South Carolina, have enacted statutes which are particularly well adapted to the needs of the close corporation, and if, for some reason, the statutory options available in the home state are unsatisfactory, some thought should be given to incorporating elsewhere. Although the matter will be discussed fully in a later chapter,[56] an example or two may suffice. Delaware has one of the most liberal and modern statutes as far as close corporations are concerned. One of its more significant provisions states that

> No written agreement among stockholders of a close corporation, nor any provision of the certificate of incorporation or of the by-laws of the corporation, which agreement or provision relates to any phase of the affairs of such corporation, including but not limited to the management of its business or declaration and payment of dividends or other division of profits or the election of directors or officers or the employment of stockholders by the corporation or the arbitration of disputes, shall be invalid on the ground that it is an attempt by the parties to the agreement or by the stockholders of the corporation to treat the corporation as if it were a partnership or to arrange relations among the stockholders or between stockholders and the corporation in a manner that would be appropriate only among partners.[57]

The above provision, along with another which expressly permits shareholders to enter into agreements which restrict or interfere with the discretion of the board of directors,[58] permits much greater latitude for shareholder agreements than is available in most states. Thus shareholders may agree as to who shall be officers of the corporation and their maximum or minimum salaries, how much of the net profits of the business shall be retained and how much paid out in dividends, and a host of other matters which normally fall within the discretion of the directors. In fact, if the

[56] See Ch. XI.
[57] Del. Gen. Corp. Law §354 (1967).
[58] Id. §350.

certificate of incorporation so provides, the board of directors may be entirely eliminated and the business managed by the shareholders.[59] This makes a good deal of sense for the relatively small, closely held concern and permits the shareholders to agree on matters which would lie beyond their powers in most other jurisdictions. Further possibilities for control arrangements are suggested by another provision which permits so-called consent-type stock transfer restrictions. These prohibit the transfer of shares without the consent of the board of directors or the other shareholders, or forbid the transfer of shares to designated persons or classes of persons. In most states such restrictions are invalid,[60] but in Delaware they are expressly allowed.[61]

Despite the allure of foreign states such as Delaware, the resourceful and creative draftsman will find that most problems can be successfully resolved in his home state. It is only the somewhat unusual situation which will justify the expense and additional paperwork entailed in incorporating elsewhere.

The mechanics of incorporating are surprisingly simple and are familiar to most practitioners and even the neophyte law student. All that need be said, perhaps, is to emphasize the importance of *literal compliance* with the statute. To do otherwise is to invite subsequent litigation and to enter the shadowy realm of the so-called de facto corporation, with all of its uncertainties and unsatisfactory conceptualism.[62] Thus care should be taken to see that the requisite number of incorporators are obtained,[63] that they are of proper age and otherwise qualified, and that the certificate of incorporation is properly signed, verified or acknowledged (using the statutory form for doing so where provided), that the document sets forth all of the matters required by statute and such other matters as are considered appropriate, and that it is filed in the various offices provided by law, together with the payment of the requisite filing fees. In most instances a statutory minimum capital must be paid in before the corporation may commence business.[64] And other formalities must generally be met, such as a first meeting of shareholders or directors, before the existence of the corporation may be said to have been "perfected." [65]

If for some reason it is not feasible or desirable to file the incorporation

---

[59] Id. §351.

[60] See Ch. III, text accompanying note 10.

[61] Del. Gen. Corp. Law §202 (1967).

[62] See, e.g., Robertson v. Levy, 197 A.2d 443 (D.C. App. 1964).

[63] The trend in recently enacted statutes is to require only one incorporator. See, e.g., Del. Gen. Corp. Law §101 (1967).

[64] The minimum capital requirements vary from $200 to $1000, the most common being either the latter or $500. See 3 Z. Cavitch, Business Organizations §62.06 (1968). In the most recent statutory revision, the old Delaware requirement of $1000 minimum capital was eliminated since it was considered insufficient to protect creditors, who currently rely on other aspects of the business. Del. Gen. Corp. Law §102(a)(4).

[65] See, e.g., Beck v. Stimmel, 39 Ohio App. 510, 177 N.E. 920 (1931).

papers immediately, some thought should be given to reserving the right to use the corporate name, both in the state of incorporation and in those states wherein it is planned to qualify the corporation to do business. Many states have procedures for reserving the name for a prescribed period on the payment of a fee.[66] Needless to say, it is always advisable to inquire in advance as to the availability of the name sought to be used in order that it not be rejected as deceptively similar to the name of another corporation already on file.

An important consideration is the selection of the fiscal year for federal and state tax purposes. Although most corporations will wish to use either a calendar year or a year ending June 30, any twelve-month period ending on the last day of a month will do. The first fiscal year must, however, begin on the date of incorporation. Thus, if a corporation is formed on June 15, 1971, its first fiscal year will begin on that date and must end at the close of any month beginning with June 30, 1971, and ending with May 31, 1972. This permits a so-called short taxable year for the first period of reporting.[67] For example, our hypothetical corporation might select a calendar year as its method of reporting. In such case its first taxable year would run from June 15, 1971, until December 31, 1971. Use of a short taxable year is an effective means of limiting tax liability for the first year of operations. For example, the taxable year can be selected so as to include a period when the corporation's taxable income amounts to $25,000 or less, thus permitting taxation of the profits at the lower tax rate of 22 percent. For businesses of a seasonal nature it is often desirable to end the taxable year in an off-season so as to permit a return which accurately reflects a full season's operations and to allow a more convenient audit of the company's books when inventories are at a low ebb. The end of the first fiscal year is elected by the filing of a tax return. If no election is made, the corporation is placed on a calendar-year basis.

1.7 PREINCORPORATION AGREEMENTS

Some attorneys have the principal parties who form a corporation sign a preincorporation agreement prior to the time when articles of incorporation are actually filed. This is not legally necessary and often agreements of this type are dispensed with. However, they may be of some utility where there is to be some delay in the actual formation of the corporation. In such situations it is advisable that the parties crystallize their thinking about their future relations into a written agreement.

Since a corporation cannot be legally bound prior to its formation, such agreements may also serve to commit the various parties to future financing

---

[66] See 1 G. Hornstein, Corporation Law and Practice §105 (1959).
[67] Int. Rev. Code of 1954, §§441, 443; Treas. Reg. §§1.441–1, 1.443–1(a).

of the business, employment agreements to be entered into, buy-and-sell agreements regarding stock to be issued or other arrangements covering death, retirement or disability of shareholders or employees, transfer restrictions to be imposed on stock, insurance to be obtained by the company or shareholders (such as to fund a buy-and-sell agreement), pension plans or other fringe benefits to be established by the corporation, agreements among shareholders as to future voting of their shares so as to maintain control of the corporation (so-called pooling agreements), and any other matters which might not be covered expressly in the articles of incorporation or bylaws.[68]

It may be helpful to distinguish between a preincorporation agreement, a promoters' contract and a shareholders' pooling agreement. A promoters' contract is a preincorporation agreement of limited scope. It generally covers such matters as the number of shares to be authorized and issued, the various subscribers and the number of shares to be subscribed for by each, the manner of payment for shares, the place, manner and time of formation of the corporation and the major provisions to be included in its articles of incorporation and bylaws. Obviously a promoters' contract relates to the period prior to the formation of the corporation and after that time it becomes obsolete, having been replaced by the articles of incorporation and bylaws.[69] As already pointed out, however, some preincorporation agreements contain provisions which extend beyond the time of incorporation and relate to matters which are not covered in the articles of incorporation and bylaws (such as, for example, insurance, buy-and-sell agreements, fringe benefits and so forth). In such situations it is helpful to have the corporation "adopt" the preincorporation agreement once it has been formed. This formality, which can be accomplished by a simple directors' resolution, assures that the corporation will be bound by the agreement. Only in England or one or two states is the adoption idea not recognized, making it necessary for a new agreement to be drawn up and executed by the proper corporate officers.[70]

A preincorporation agreement may, as already pointed out, contain provisions relating to how the shares shall be voted so as to insure that control of the corporation is maintained in the hands of a particular shareholder group. Such an agreement survives the incorporation process and becomes a shareholders' pooling agreement. The corporation need not be a party since it cannot vote its own shares[71] and is theoretically indifferent to the way in

---

[68] See 1 F. O'Neal, Close Corporations 77–81 (1958); 1 G. Hornstein, id. §§91–96; C. Israels, Corporate Practice 49–79, 367–380 (1963). All of the authorities cited contain useful forms for preincorporation agreements.

[69] See 1 F. O'Neal, id. at 79.

[70] For the English authorities and some Massachusetts cases following the English view, see W. Cary, Cases and Materials on Corporations 103 (4th ed. unabr. 1969).

[71] See Model Bus. Corp. Act §33.

which control is maintained.[72] Such agreements are generally recognized as valid, although problems may arise as to the manner in which they are enforced.[73] As one commentator has pointed out,[74] it is wise to have the agreement contain the usual provision binding the successors and assigns of the various parties, and specifically any executor or administrator. In addition, the parties might revise their wills so as to instruct their executors to abide by the terms of the agreement.

1.8 TREATMENT OF LIABILITIES

When a sole proprietorship or partnership incorporates, the sole proprietor or former partners remain liable on obligations incurred prior to incorporation. Their release from liability may be accomplished only with the consent of the creditor or obligee. Such consent may be either express or implied. Although it is doubtful that the mere adoption by the corporation of a contract entered into between a promoter and a third party is sufficient to constitute a novation, an agreement to enter into a novation may be implied from the terms of the contract.[75] However, where a going business is incorporated, it is unlikely that a novation will be implied as to most claims against the predecessor business. Hence, the former partners or the sole proprietor continues liable in the absence of an express agreement releasing them.

A former partner or sole proprietor may be liable for debts of the business incurred subsequent to incorporation in several situations. First, the corporation may have been defectively formed. If one of the statutory conditions precedent to incorporation has not been satisfied, the enterprise may not qualify as a de facto or de jure corporation, in which case the *status quo ante* may govern to determine the persons who should be liable on claims arising against the business.[76] Hence the importance of literal and complete compliance with the statutory formalities and all the other requirements for perfecting the corporate existence.[77]

[72] Cf. Hoover v. Allen, 241 F. Supp. 213 (S.D.N.Y. 1965).

[73] See Ch. III, text accompanying notes 128–155.

[74] See 1 F. O'Neal, id. at 81.

[75] See Frazier v. Ash, 234 F.2d 320 (5th Cir. 1956), *cert. denied*, 352 U.S. 893 (1956); Restatement of Agency Second §326, and H. Henn, Handbook of the Law of Corporations 185 (2d ed. 1970).

[76] See, e.g., Harrill v. Davis, 168 F.2d 187 (8th Cir. 1909). The conflicting views on the question of whether partnership liability should be imposed on shareholders in all cases of defective incorporation are discussed in W. Cary, Cases and Materials on Corporations 79–80 (4th ed. unabr. 1969). For a good contrast *compare* Dodd, Partnership Liability of Stockholders in Defective Corporations, 40 Harv. L. Rev. 521 (1927), *with* Magruder, A Note on Partnership Liability of Stockholders in Defective Corporations, id. at 733.

[77] See text accompanying note 62 *supra*.

Another possibility is that creditors doing business with the predecessor firm may not have been properly notified that the firm has been dissolved and a corporation substituted in its place. If they continue to advance credit in the honest belief that they are dealing with a partnership or sole proprietorship, those who mislead creditors may not deny their continuing responsibility.[78] In the case of partnerships, those who extended credit to the firm prior to its dissolution are entitled to receive actual notice of the dissolution of the firm and formation of the corporation. All others who knew of the firm prior to its dissolution should be notified by newspaper publication in the place or places at which the partnership business was regularly carried on.[79] Similar notification rules should be followed in the case of a sole proprietorship.

When we come to consider the liability of the corporation for business debts incurred prior to its formation, the general rule is that the corporation is not liable in the absence of an express or implied adoption by it of pre-existing claims. But the receipt of benefits under a contract entered into prior to incorporation and a continuing course of conduct indicating acquiescence, such as the payment for goods ordered or services rendered prior to incorporation, may result in liability, either as an implied adoption or possibly in quasi contract.[80] It is therefore important that a corporation's directors assess the status of all contracts and other business arrangements existing at the time the corporation is formed and notify any who have contracts or business dealings with the predecessor business as to whether the corporation wishes to be bound. In most situations it will be advisable for the corporation to inherit the obligations of its predecessor, for these will in a very real sense constitute its business and livelihood. If there is any doubt about the corporation's liability, however, the situation had best be clarified in order to avoid misunderstanding.

1.9   ASSUMPTION OF LIABILITIES—TAX ASPECTS

If the sole proprietorship or partnership has been run on the cash basis of accounting and there are unpaid expenses or unrealized losses which have not been deducted, although the assumption of these liabilities by the corporation will not necessarily cause the transfer of properties to be treated as

---

[78] The liability here is not technically based on estoppel but on failure to comply with the notification requirements of the Uniform Partnership Act §35. See Painter, Partnership by Estoppel, 16 Vand. L. Rev. 327, 340 (1963). However, there may be a collateral liability imposed on an estoppel theory of "holding out." See Uniform Partnership Act §§35(4), 16.

[79] Id. §35.

[80] See Morgan v. Bon Bon Co., 222 N.Y. 22, 118 N.E. 205 (1917). Ballantine indicates that the weight of authority is against imposing liability on a quasi-contractual basis for preliminary expenses and organization services. H. Ballantine, Corporations §39 (1946).

a taxable transaction,[81] the subsequent payment by the corporation of the expense items of its predecessor will not entitle it to a deduction. The reason for this is that the corporate payment of the expense is viewed as part of its cost of acquiring the properties which have been transferred to it. Thus the expense should be capitalized and not deducted.[82] Accordingly, it has been suggested that it is vitally important for the transferor to withhold sufficient cash to discharge its own liabilities. This will entitle it to a deduction for its final taxable year and the deduction will thus be preserved.[83]

1.10   SUBCHAPTER S

The provisions of Sections 1371 to 1379 of the Internal Revenue Code, referred to as Subchapter S, are of considerable importance to anyone faced with the problem of whether to incorporate. In a sense they offer advantages which are *sui generis,* lying somewhere between partnership and corporation, a third form of business organization which should always be considered among the various options which are available. Occasionally these provisions are inaccurately described as "allowing a corporation to be taxed as a partnership." Although this may convey the general feeling of Subchapter S, it hardly does justice to the statutory scheme. As we shall see, there are several important ways in which Subchapter S treatment differs from partnership taxation and there are numerous traps which lie in wait for the person who blandly assumes that the two are equivalent to one another.

Subchapter S is designed to provide certain advantages to shareholders in a so-called small business corporation. Generally speaking, these advantages may be described as permitting shareholders to be taxed on corporate income on a pass-through basis, thus permitting corporate profits to be taxed at lower rates where shareholders are in relatively low tax brackets, eliminating the threat of double taxation and also the troublesome problems encountered by many closely held concerns in justifying salary payments to shareholder employees under a "reasonableness" test so as to permit deductibility.[84] In addition, pass-through treatment is permitted for corporate losses to a certain extent. This may be of considerable value for those who wish to engage in a new, untried venture which is likely to have considerable start-up costs and losses in its first few years of operation.

---

[81] Int. Rev. Code of 1954, §357(a). See, however, §357(c), taxing as capital gain the excess of the sum of the liabilities assumed, plus the liabilities to which the property is subject, over the total of the adjusted basis of the property transferred.

[82] Holdcroft Trans. Co. v. Commissioner, 153 F.2d 323 (8th Cir. 1946) and other cases cited in B. Bittker and J. Eustice, Federal Income Taxation of Corporations and Shareholders 99 n.48 (1966).

[83] See 3 Z. Cavitch, Business Organizations §68.05[4] (1968).

[84] Int. Rev. Code of 1954, §162(a)(1).

Subchapter S is an elective provision. All the shareholders of a small business corporation, as defined by the Code, must consent to the special tax treatment.[85] A small business corporation is one which has no more than ten shareholders, is not a member of an "affiliated group" of corporations, as defined in Section 1504 of the Code, has only one class of stock, and does not have as a shareholder a person (other than an estate) who is not an individual (e.g., a trust or corporation) or a nonresident alien.[86] If the corporation qualifies, and if the consent of all the shareholders has been obtained, it may file its election for Subchapter S treatment at any time during the first month of the taxable year (or the month preceding that month).[87] The election terminates if anyone becomes a shareholder and does not, within thirty days of purchasing his stock, consent to the special tax treatment.[88] It may also be terminated upon the consent of *all* the shareholders, or if the corporation ceases to be a small business corporation, as already described (e.g., if it should have more than ten shareholders or if there should be more than one class of stock).[89] A further reason for terminating the election is if the corporation derives more than 80 percent of its gross receipts from sources outside the United States, or if more than 20 percent of its gross receipts is composed of passive investment income (e.g., dividends, interest, rents, royalties, annuities and sales or exchanges of stock or securities).[90] Once terminated the election cannot be invoked for five years without the consent of the Treasury Department.[91] An important exception to the percentage requirement as to passive investment income is a provision which permits a corporation, during the first or second taxable year in which it commenced the active conduct of a trade or business, to have more than 20 percent of its gross receipts in the form of passive investment income if the amount of passive income is less than $3000.[92] This permits a corporation to elect Subchapter S during its early years when its operating receipts are low or nonexistent and where its primary income may come from passive sources. In addition, it should be noted that the 20 percent test refers to the corporation's "gross receipts" in contrast to its "gross income." Losses, then, need not be taken into account in computing gross receipts and a corporation may still qualify under the percentage test even though it may be operating at a loss.

The actual mechanics of pass-through tax treatment and the computation of the shareholder's tax liability under Subchapter S are somewhat com-

---

[85] Id. §1372(a).

[86] Id. §1371(a). Stock held by husband and wife as community property or in joint tenancy is considered as held by one shareholder for the purpose of determining the number of shareholders. Id. §1371(c).

[87] Id. §1372(c).

[88] Id. §1372(e)(1).

[89] Id. §§1372(e)(2) and 1372(e)(3).

[90] Id. §§1372(e)(4) and 1372(e)(5). See note 132 *infra*.

[91] Id. §1372(f).

[92] Id. §1372(e)(5)(B).

plex. They may be more easily understood by keeping in mind the fact that Subchapter S does not, as already pointed out, provide for partnership type tax treatment in the fullest sense; rather it retains the overall corporate scheme of taxation and exempts the corporation from paying a tax under certain conditions, treating the shareholder as having received all of the corporate profits in the form of dividends. Since all dividends actually distributed would be taxed to shareholders to the extent of corporate earnings and profits, a basic concept of this pass-through treatment is that of "undistributed taxable income." Briefly, this undistributed taxable income is included in the gross income of the shareholders to the extent that it would have been so included if it had been distributed as a dividend by the corporation on the last day of the corporation's taxable year.[93] It should be noted that only income which, if distributed, would have been out of corporate earnings and profits, is included within the concept of undistributed taxable income. In addition, the amount of "taxable income" (for computing undistributed taxable income) is equivalent to what would have been the taxable income of the corporation absent the Subchapter S election, except that various deductions cannot be used, i.e., the deduction for net operating loss carry-overs, the deduction of partially tax exempt interest and the deduction for dividends received from other corporations.[94]

Once the undistributed taxable income has been subjected to tax at the shareholder level, there must be some means whereby subsequent distributions of such income are not subjected to a second tax. This is done by an upwards adjustment to the basis of the shareholder's stock in the corporation to the extent of the undistributed income previously taxed to him.[95] The next step is to permit distribution of these amounts (in the form of money, not property) without dividend tax treatment. Such distribution reduces the basis in the shareholder's stock. Distribution of amounts in excess of basis produces capital gain.[96]

It is important to note that only money (i.e., not property) distributions qualify for dividend-free tax treatment. In addition, all of the earnings and profits for the current taxable year must have been distributed before a dividend-free distribution may be made.[97] To this limited extent, previously taxed earnings are, in a sense, "frozen in" and can be "unthawed" only if certain conditions are met. If not unthawed and distributed they may be

[93] Id. §1373(b).

[94] Id. §1373(d). See also B. Bittker and J. Eustice, Federal Income Taxation of Corporations and Shareholders 722–724 (1966), for illustrations of the method of computation. The discussion (at 709–739) is an invaluable guide to the complexities of Subchapter S.

[95] Int. Rev. Code of 1954, §1376(a).

[96] Treas. Reg. §1.1375–4.

[97] Id. §§1.1373–1(d) and (e). One court recently held that the regulations were invalid insofar as they prevent property other than money from qualifying as a distribution of previously taxed income. De Treville v. United States, 312 F. Supp. 362 (D.S.C. 1969).

lost entirely. For example, they may be reduced by subsequent net operating losses of the corporation, which are passed through and allowed as deductions on the shareholder level. Termination of the Subchapter S election will result in forfeiture of the right to receive these amounts free of tax and the situation will revert to the *status quo ante* (i.e., all further corporate distributions will be taxed as dividends to the extent of either current or post February 28, 1913, earnings and profits).[98] Finally, transfers of stock, even to those who consent to the Subchapter S election, may create real difficulties. Although the transferor is entitled to retain his right to receive his share of all previously taxed but undistributed income free of tax if he continues to hold *any* stock in the corporation, his transferee does not acquire any rights to tax-free treatment other than for undistributed income accruing after he acquires his stock.[99]

In view of the partially frozen-in character of undistributed previously taxed earnings, it is desirable for a Subchapter S corporation to distribute as much of its current earnings as possible rather than to subject them to uncertain tax treatment in future years. If the corporation needs cash for operational purposes, a possible solution to the dilemma may be for it to distribute the requisite amounts and then have the shareholders loan them back to the company. As at least one commentator has pointed out, this technique may be hazardous in that this may be viewed as the distribution of a corporate obligation rather than money.[100] Since only cash distributions reduce the corporation's undistributed taxable income, the tactic would fail to reach its objective. In addition, the obligation might possibly be viewed as a second class of stock, resulting in a termination of the entire Subchapter S election.[101]

In those instances where it is possible to distribute earnings, some tax relief has been provided for the frequent situation where it is not possible to determine accurately the amount of income by December 31 or the close of the taxable year. Thus any distribution of money within two and one-half months following the close of the taxable year to a person who was a shareholder at the close of the taxable year is treated as a distribution of the corporation's undistributed taxable income for that year.[102]

Before turning to the subject of pass-through loss treatment, a final word should be said regarding gains. In a Subchapter S corporation, unlike a partnership, all income which has been passed through is treated as dividend income (with no dividend exclusion, however) with one exception, namely, that any excess of net long-term capital gain over net short-term capital loss is passed through as long-term capital gain, but only to the extent that it constitutes a distribution which is not in excess of the corpora-

[98] See B. Bittker and J. Eustice, id. at 732–734.
[99] Id. at 732.
[100] Id. at 734.
[101] Ibid.
[102] Int. Rev. Code of 1954, §1375(f).

tion's taxable income and which is out of earnings and profits for its current taxable year.[103] However, to forestall to a limited extent certain "one-shot elections" (i.e., Subchapter S elections made for the sole purpose of attaining pass-through treatment for a substantial capital gain expected for a particular taxable year), there is a provision which imposes a tax at the corporate level, at a 25 percent rate, on the amount by which the excess of net long-term capital gain over net short-term capital loss exceeds $25,000. The tax applies only if this excess is greater than 50 percent of the corporation's taxable income for the year, and then only if such taxable income exceeds $25,000.[104] A further exception is applicable in the case of a corporation which has had a Subchapter S election in effect for the three immediately preceding taxable years (i.e., the election has been continuous and not on a one-shot basis) and in the case of certain new corporations (those which have been in existence for less than four taxable years and the Subchapter S election has been in effect for each of those years).[105] Even if the corporation is subject to the 25 percent tax, there may be a limited advantage in a one-shot election since the first $25,000 of passed-through capital gain is not subject to tax on the corporate level.[106]

As previously indicated, net operating losses are passed through to shareholders and may be deducted by them as a loss attributable to a trade or business, but only to the extent that the losses exceed the shareholder's basis in stock and any claims (i.e., debt) which he may hold against the corporation.[107] As far as the determination of the amount of loss passed through to each shareholder is concerned, this is computed on a daily basis, and the shareholder is given a loss pass-through which corresponds to his pro rata share of the corporation's net operating loss attributable to the period when he held stock in the corporation.[108] Thus, if a shareholder sold his stock halfway through the taxable year he would be allowed one half of the loss which he would have received had he held the stock for the full year. The purchaser of the stock is entitled to the remaining portion of the loss. This method of determining the amount of losses passed through is sharply different from that used in determining the shareholder's portion of undistributed taxable income, where the person who owns shares at the end of the fiscal year is charged with all the undistributed taxable income for the year attributable to those shares. It should also be observed that the pass-through treatment is confined to net operating losses of the corporation. Capital losses go to offset corporate capital gains, and any excess is carried over for the succeeding five taxable years.

Having set forth the general outlines of Subchapter S, it is now time to

[103] Id. §1375(a).
[104] Id. §1378.
[105] Id. §1378(c).
[106] See B. Bittker and J. Eustice, Federal Income Taxation of Corporations and Shareholders 728 (1966).
[107] Int. Rev. Code of 1954, §1374(c)(2).
[108] Id. §1374(c)(1).

consider more specifically some of the traps which lie in wait for those who elect it.

Among the principal hazards of the Subchapter S election is the danger of its involuntary termination. This may occur if stock is transferred to a shareholder who does not consent to the election within thirty days, if the corporation ceases (for one of several possible reasons) to qualify as a small business corporation or if the 80 percent or 20 percent tests on foreign and passive investment income, respectively, are no longer met.

A transfer of stock to a nonconsenting shareholder may be either accidental or intentional. Transfers could occur by sale or gift, as where a father gives his interest to his son or other relative. They could also occur on death. Although an estate may own shares in a Subchapter S corporation, a trust may not. Thus, if a testator were to leave his shares in trust, the election would terminate at his death. This might also occur if he were to give or leave his shares to more than one person so as to increase the number of shareholders in the corporation to more than the allowable maximum of ten. Even if the number of shareholders were not increased, those receiving the shares would have to file an election to receive Subchapter S treatment within thirty days of the date the shares were transferred to them.[109] If a Subchapter S shareholder were to remarry after the death or divorce of his spouse, then the consent of the new wife to the election must be obtained if the shares are to be held in joint tenancy or tenancy by the entirety with her.[110] And there is always the possibility that the former wife might not surrender her interest in the shares, in which case the election might terminate if the ten shareholder maximum is exceeded; for since she is no longer the "wife," shares held by her in joint tenancy with her former husband will not qualify as being held by one shareholder.[111] Hence, the former wife would have considerable bargaining power concerning the terms of the divorce settlement.

The possibility of an intentional termination of the election by a transfer to a nonconsenting shareholder is distasteful and probably runs counter to the policy of another provision in the Code which requires the consent of all the shareholders for a valid revocation of the election.[112] Thus it is possible that a court might find a transfer made with the express intention of terminating an election invalid, or treat the nonconsenting new shareholder as somehow the agent of the transferor.[113] But the matter is not free

[109] If the new shareholder is an estate, the thirty-day period does not begin to run until the executor or administrator has qualified under local law to perform his duties, but the period must begin no later than thirty days after the close of the taxable year of the corporation in which the estate became a shareholder. Treas. Reg. §1.1372–3(b).

[110] See Id. §1.1372–3(a).

[111] The provisions of the Int. Rev. Code of 1954, §1371(c), apply only to a husband and wife—not to any joint tenancy or tenancy in common.

[112] Id. §1372(e)(2).

[113] See B. Bittker and J. Eustice, *Federal Income Taxation of Corporations and Shareholders* 717 n.16 (1966). Several years ago the American Bar Association rec-

from doubt. Thus it is imperative to have some form of stock transfer restriction in Subchapter S corporations. The restriction might take the form of a prohibition against transfer to nonconsenting shareholders, a prohibition against transfer without the consent of either the corporation's directors, the other shareholders, or both, or a so-called first refusal restraint, which gives the others (including the corporation) an option to purchase the shares before an effective transfer may be made. As we shall see,[114] the law on the validity of the above restrictions is unclear, with the exception of the first refusal restriction, which is unquestionably valid if reasonable. Although it is possible that many state courts would uphold a more rigid consent-type restraint if it were reasonably justified by the need to preserve the Subchapter S election, this too is unclear. However, one statute expressly validates such restraints, stating that any restriction imposed for the purpose of maintaining Subchapter S status is "conclusively presumed to be for a reasonable purpose." [115]

Regardless of the form of the restriction, it is obviously important that it be effective on the death of the shareholder and bind his executor, administrator or legatee. As previously suggested, the shareholder's will should be revised to provide that the executor or administrator shall file his consent to the Subchapter S election within thirty days after his qualification or the close of the corporation's taxable year, whichever shall be earlier.[116]

There are several ways in which a corporation may inadvertently cease to qualify as a small business corporation. As we have seen, this may happen if the corporation should have more than ten shareholders, have as a shareholder someone other than a person or estate (such as a corporation or trust) or someone who is a nonresident alien. Also the corporation would cease to qualify if it were to become a member of an "affiliated group" (i.e., a group of corporations under 80 percent common control) or if it were to have more than one class of stock. What has been said about the need for stock transfer restrictions to prevent transfers to nonconsenting shareholders applies equally to the need for preventing a transfer to more than one individual if the transfer causes the ten shareholder limit to be exceeded. Obviously the transfer restriction should also cover any transfer to a corporation, trust or nonresident alien.

It would not seem difficult to avoid a corporation's having more than one class of stock, since the articles of incorporation can provide that only one class may be issued. However, due to the manner in which the term "class"

---

ommended that the statute be changed so that termination would occur only if a new shareholder filed a refusal to consent to the election. See H.R. 11450, 89th Cong., 1st Sess. §64 (1965), and ABA, Explanation of H.R. 11450 (Ways and Means Committee Print 1965).

[114] See Ch. III, text accompanying notes 1–82.
[115] Del. Gen. Corp. Law §202(d) (1967).
[116] See text accompanying note 74 *supra*.

has been interpreted by the Treasury Department, there are serious problems in particular areas. Thus:

> If the outstanding shares of stock of the corporation are not identical with respect to the rights and interest which they convey in the control, profits, and assets of the corporation, then the corporation is considered to have more than one class of stock. Thus a difference as to voting rights, dividend rights, or liquidation preferences of outstanding stock will disqualify a corporation. However, if two or more groups of shares are identical in every respect except that each group has the right to elect members of the board of directors in a number proportionate to the number of shares in each group, they are considered one class of stock.[117]

Note, however, that a corporation having one "group" of 1000 shares entitled to vote for two directors and another of 750 shares entitled to vote for one director would not qualify since the voting rights would not be spread between the groups in proportion to the number of shares in each. Thus the second group would have to contain only 500 shares to qualify as being the same class as the shares in the first group.

But the problem of defining a class does not rest there. A very serious difficulty results from what may be an overly restrictive view set forth in a ruling to the effect that *any* voting agreement, irrevocable proxy, voting trust or veto provision in the articles of incorporation which gives one or more shareholders disproportionate voting power, dividend or liquidation rights will be considered as having created a second class of stock.[118]

There seems to be little justification for such a rigid view. The reason for the one-class requirement appears to be its simplicity, avoiding difficulties of allocating income and losses between shareholders of several classes.[119] It is hard to see how voting agreements among shareholders in a class of common stock, or veto powers, such as a requirement of unanimity for certain types of corporate action (e.g., mergers, asset sales, issuances of more stock, etc.), or a voting trust complicate the problem of allocating income and losses. Thus such agreements should not prevent the corporation from having a single class. This is particularly so in view of their great utility in preserving control and protecting minority shareholders in closely held corporations.[120] The persistence of this interpretation of the term "class" by the Treasury Department is a significant limitation on the ability of those

---

[117] Treas. Reg. §1.1371–1(g). For an application of the regulation in a situation involving disproportionate voting power among four groups of stock, see Samuel Pollack, 47 T.C. 92 (1966), *aff'd*, Pollack v. Commissioner, 392 F.2d 409 (5th Cir. 1968). The court did not question the Treasury Department's authority to issue the regulation or whether it was in accord with the intent of the statute.

[118] Rev. Rul. 63–226, 1963–2 Cum. Bull. 341.

[119] See B. Bittker and J. Eustice, Federal Income Taxation of Corporations and Shareholders 714 (1966). See also Note, Stockholder Agreements and Subchapter S Corporations, 19 Tax L. Rev. 391 (1964).

[120] See Ch. III.

who form a Subchapter S corporation to engage in intelligent business planning.[121]

A further difficulty with the single class concept is the possibility that shareholder-held debt may be viewed as another class of stock. Here the regulations state that

> Obligations which purport to represent debt but which actually represent equity capital will generally constitute a second class of stock. However, if such purported debt obligations are owned solely by the owners of the nominal stock of the corporation in substantially the same proportion as they own such nominal stock, such purported debt obligations will be treated as contributions to capital rather than a second class of stock. But, if an issuance, redemption, sale, or other transfer of nominal stock, or of purported debt obligations which actually represent equity capital, results in a change in a shareholder's proportionate share of nominal stock or his proportionate share of such purported debt, a new determination shall be made as to whether the corporation has more than one class of stock as of the time of such change.[122]

In interpreting the above regulation there are really two problems: First, when does an obligation which purports to represent debt "actually represent" equity capital; second, when does such equity capital constitute a second class of stock? To put the matter differently, is all shareholder-held debt equity capital, and is *all* such equity capital a second class of stock?

It seems clear from the cases and even from the regulation itself that all shareholder-held debt is not equity capital. Thus in two of the leading cases on the point[123] the court, in finding that the debt there constituted a capital contribution, emphasized the facts that the shareholder-"creditors" made no effort to enforce repayment of the debt and waived interest due on notes evidencing it. Also, in both cases there was a high debt-equity ratio and the capital was probably inadequate for carrying on the business as it was being operated. Although the court in the earlier case[124] refused to rule that the fact that debt is held in the same proportion as the stock is dispositive of the

---

[121] In Catalina Homes, Inc., 23 CCH Tax Ct. Mem. 1361, 1368 (1964), the court, without passing on the issue, expressed doubt as to whether the Treasury's position regarding voting trusts, as a disqualifying factor in Subchapter S, was a reasonable interpretation of the statute or the Congressional intent behind it. The taxpayer argued that, since a voting trust is not a taxable entity, the election should not be invalid because of the prohibition against a trust holding stock in a Subchapter S corporation, as the Commissioner appeared to be urging. The court did not rule on the point. For a recent holding expressly repudiating the Treasury Department's view that a voting trust terminates a Subchapter S election, see A & N Furniture & Appliance Co. v. United States, 271 F. Supp. 40 (D. Ohio 1967).

[122] Treas. Reg. §1.1371–1(g). See James L. Stinnett, Jr., 54 T.C. 221 (1970), invalidating the regulation in part and permitting debt to be held disproportionately to equity without classification as a second class of stock. For discussion see Note, Shareholder Lending and Tax Avoidance in the Subchapter S Corporation, 67 Colum. L. Rev. 495 (1967).

[123] W. C. Gammon, 46 T.C. 1 (1966); Catalina Homes, Inc., 23 CCH Tax Ct. Mem. 1361, 1368 (1964).

[124] Catalina Homes, Inc., 23 CCH Tax Ct. Mem. 1361, 1367 (1968).

question, this was relied on in the later case to conclude that the debt there was really stock.[125] The upshot of all this is that if the parties behave as if the debt is really debt, if the debt is not held pro rata proportionately with the stock, if principal and interest payments are met, if the debt is evidenced by some instrument and is not mere open-account indebtedness or if it is secured,[126] and if the debt-equity ratio of the corporation is not excessive,[127] then shareholder-held debt will not be considered stock even in a Subchapter S context.

Assuming, however, that the facts of the case are such that loans are classified as stock, are they always a *second* class of stock? Prior to *W. C. Gammon,* it appeared that the Treasury Department was urging this view. The *Gammon* case criticized this interpretation as arbitrary and not in accord with the Congressional intent.[128] Shortly thereafter the regulation was amended to concede that, if the debt and equity are held in substantially the same proportion, the former will not be considered to be a second class of stock. But if, as a result of transfers, redemptions and the like, the proportion changes, then "a new determination shall be made as to whether the corporation has more than one class of stock as of the time of such change." [129] Presumably the factors to be considered in such a determination would be whether the "debt-stock" was given any preferential rights and whether these rights were intended to be or were enforced. Thus the court in the *Gammon* case emphasized that the taxpayers

> placed little, if any, reliance on the rights and preferences granted them by the notes in making their advances to the corporation. It is likely that in the event of bankruptcy of the corporation a bankruptcy court would have subordinated their claims to those of common creditors.[130]

But where open-account advances were preferred over the no-par common stock so that dividends could not be paid on the latter unless the advances,

---

[125] W. C. Gammon, 46 T.C. 1, 9 (1966) (although the court was also addressing itself to the second question, namely, was the stock a second *class* of stock?).

[126] See Comment, Tax Planning with Subchapter S in 1967: Problems and Prospects, 53 Va. L. Rev. 1161, 1172 (1967), a very useful discussion of the whole area.

[127] As seen in Ch. II, a ratio of shareholder-held debt to equity of 50–50 is probably not excessive.

[128] See W. C. Gammon, 46 T.C. 1, 8 (1966).

[129] Treas. Reg. §1.1371–1(g), quoted in text accompanying note 122 *supra.* Query whether the addition of substantial outside debt at the time the shareholders make pro rata advances will make the language in the regulation (which refers to the "purported debt obligations" being owned "solely" by the shareholders) inapplicable. For an affirmative answer see Comment, 53 Va. L. Rev. 1161, 1176, n.78 (1967). Recently the Tax Court held that the regulation was invalid if construed to characterize installment notes, which were non-interest-bearing and subordinated to outside debt, as a second class of stock merely because they were held by shareholders in amounts which were disproportionate to their equity interests. James L. Stinnett, Jr., 54 T.C. 221 (1970) (reviewed by the Tax Court). See Braverman, Subchapter S Situations—Regulations Run Rampant, 114 U. Pa. L. Rev. 680, 681 (1966).

[130] W. C. Gammon, 46 T.C. 1, 9 (1966).

plus 5 percent interest, were fully paid, then the preference was sufficient to support a finding of a second class of stock despite the fact that no demand was ever made that the loans be repaid.[131]

In summary, then, debt may be held by shareholders in proportion to their stockholdings, but any transfers, redemptions or further issuances of stock which change the proportion in which the stock is held in relation to the debt entail a risk that the debt will be considered a second class of stock. Unless the terms of the debt are such that no preferential rights are intended or enforced, there will be at least two classes of stock and the corporation will be disqualified under Subchapter S.

As mentioned before, another cause of involuntary termination of the Subchapter S election is where more than 80 percent of a corporation's gross receipts come from foreign sources or where more than 20 percent of its gross receipts constitute passive investment income. Although these tests may be met initially, when the corporation files its election for Subchapter S treatment, they may cease to be met if there is a substantial change in the company's operations which alters the character of its gross receipts. Suppose, for example, that reduced sales lower operating revenues. If the company already receives substantial amounts of income from passive sources, then the 20 percent limit may be exceeded. Another possibility might be a sale of a capital asset which gives rise to substantial amounts of "imputed interest" under Section 483 of the Code.[132]

The consequences of termination of the election can be extremely serious. Since the corporation will resume its taxable status, all undistributed previously taxed income which has been frozen in to the corporation may no longer be distributed free of tax. Thus a second tax will be imposed if such income is distributed as dividends when the corporation has earnings and profits. For this reason it is advisable to withdraw all previously taxed undistributed income prior to the election's termination, but this may not be possible if the termination is inadvertent and discovered at a later date.

As we have seen, the sale of Subchapter S stock will give rise to unexpected tax consequences. If a shareholder should sell all his stock, he thereby loses his right to withdraw his share of undistributed previously taxed income free of tax (although he does not lose the right to do so if he retains *any* of his stock).[133] Although he may be compensated in part for this by having his capital gain on the sale of the stock reduced due to the

---

[131] Catalina Homes, Inc., 23 CCH Tax Ct. Mem. 1361, 1367 (1964).

[132] Cf. O'Sullivan Rubber Co. v. Commissioner, 120 F.2d 845, 847–848 (2d Cir. 1941) (sale of assets giving rise to personal holding company income). See also Lansing Broadcasting Co., 52 T.C. 299 (1969), *aff'd*, 427 F.2d 1014 (6th Cir. 1970) (capital gains on liquidation of other corporation); Bramlette Building Corp., 52 T.C. 200 (1969), *aff'd*, 424 F.2d 751 (5th Cir. 1970) (rents); Temple N. Joyce, 42 T.C. 628 (1964) (sale of stock).

[133] See text accompanying note 99 *supra*.

relatively high basis resulting from his undistributed previously taxed income, he will still lose to the extent that such income could have been withdrawn from the corporation free of tax at *ordinary* rates as opposed to a reduction in his capital gain. Since the purchaser of the stock will not acquire the right to withdraw free of tax the transferor's share of previously taxed undistributed income, no allowance can be made for this in the purchase price of the stock. Thus the transferor had best withdraw his share of income prior to transfer if he disposes of all his stock.

A person who buys into a Subchapter S corporation may suffer unexpected tax consequences. As already pointed out, he does not "purchase" the transferor's right to undistributed previously taxed income. However, the purchaser will be charged with all the undistributed income of the taxable year in which the purchase is made even though he should hold the stock for only part of that year, since undistributed taxable income is computed as of the year's end.[134] Moreover, since operating loss pass-through is computed on a daily basis, the purchaser will be entitled to only so much of the operating loss as accrues subsequent to his purchase, the transferor being entitled to the remaining portion. The latter tax effects should be taken into account in determining the purchase price of the stock.[135]

If a shareholder in a Subchapter S corporation should die, his estate is not entitled to receive previously taxed undistributed income free of tax. This is also true where the shares are held in joint tenancy or tenancy by the entirety with the wife. On the death of the husband, the wife is not entitled to withdraw the husband's share of undistributed previously taxed income free of tax.[136] In this sense death is a classic example of accidental termination, for there are few who would be so tax minded as to plan for their imminent demise by making corporate withdrawals.

Various other disadvantages of Subchapter S involve the treament of losses. As we have seen,[137] only operating losses and not capital losses pass through to the shareholders. Furthermore, since pass-through treatment is permitted only to the extent of a shareholder's basis in stock and corporate indebtedness to him, his share of the operating loss will be wasted if his basis reaches zero[138] and of course the operating loss may not be deducted on the corporate level. Unless the shareholder raises his basis through the contribution or loan of funds to the corporation, the loss deduction will be wasted. The same might be said for net operating loss carry-overs from years prior to the year the election is made. Unless the election is terminated before the expiration of the loss carry-over period, the deduction will be

---

[134] Int. Rev. Code of 1954, §1373(b).

[135] See text accompanying note 108 *supra.*

[136] Rev. Rul. 66–172, 1966–1 Cum. Bull. 198. See also Comment, 53 Va. L. Rev. 1161, 1179 (1967).

[137] See text accompanying note 108 *supra.*

[138] See Byrne v. Commissioner, 361 F.2d 939 (7th Cir. 1966).

wasted, since it cannot be passed through to the shareholders and the corporation may not take advantage of the carry-over while the election is in effect.

If a new corporation experiences losses in its early years and the shareholders do not have income against which to deduct losses passed through to them, the loss deduction will be wasted unless the Subchapter S election is revoked. Since the losses may exceed their corporate salaries (assuming the shareholders are employees, which may not be true with all of them), unless they have income from other sources sufficient to absorb the losses, the Subchapter S election will be disadvantageous.

Net operating losses must be offset against capital gains of the corporation before such gains are passed through to the shareholders. Thus, instead of passing through the operating loss and the capital gain separately, the one must first offset the other. This may be disadvantageous, as illustrated in *Byrne v. Commissioner*,[139] where the taxpayer attempted to pass though net long-term capital gain of $8567.83 and net operating loss of $1858.38. Instead of being able to report these items separately, he was required to offset them against one another and report capital gain in the amount of the difference, $6709.45.

Troublesome problems also arise in connection with the withdrawal of undistributed, previously taxed income. In addition to those which have already been pointed out,[140] one must remember that such income may be withdrawn only in cash (i.e., not property).[141] Many corporations may not wish to impair their cash position to do this, and, as we have seen, withdrawing cash and then "lending" it back may be hazardous.[142] Moreover, before a tax-free withdrawal may be made, all current income of the corporation must be distributed. Even so, if previously taxed income is not distributed promptly, it may be lost if reduced by subsequent losses.

Subchapter S has a provision similar to that which governs certain family partnerships[143] whereby, to prevent tax avoidance through income splitting among members of a family who render little or no services to the corporation, the Commissioner is empowered to reallocate income to reflect fairly the value of the services rendered by each family member. Thus, if a Subchapter S corporation were owned 50 percent by a father and 50 percent by a son and the son rendered no services, the father rendering services reasonably worth $30,000, and if the father should receive only $10,000 in compensation, a dividend distribution of $35,000 to the father and $35,000

---

[139] Ibid.

[140] See text accompanying note 133 *supra*. See also Braverman, Subchapter S Situations—Regulations Run Rampant, 114 U. Pa. L. Rev. 680, 689–693 (1966).

[141] See text accompanying note 97 *supra*. See also Treas. Reg. §1.1375–4(g), Ex. (4).

[142] See text accompanying note 100 *supra*.

[143] Int. Rev. Code of 1954, §1375(c). The provision dealing with family partnerships is id. §704(e).

to the son could be reallocated so as to treat $10,000 of each $35,000 distribution as additional salary to the father. The father would then have $30,000 in compensation and the son and father would each have only $25,000 in dividend income.[144] Although these Subchapter S and partnership reallocation provisions are similar in most respects, there are differences. Thus the partnership allocation rules apply only to services rendered by the person who either gave or sold the stock to the family member whose income is being reallocated, whereas the Subchapter S rules allow reallocation where the family member received his stock from some other party. Unlike the partnership rules, the Subchapter S rules permit reallocation only among members of a family.[145]

Aside from the foregoing tax traps which lie in wait for those who make the Subchapter S election, it should be pointed out that where the electing shareholders are in different tax brackets, their interests may diverge enough to produce considerable friction in the business. Thus an election may be highly advantageous for a taxpayer in a relatively low bracket who is receiving a salary from the corporation. However, a taxpayer in a high tax bracket who is not an employee may find himself paying high taxes on corporate income which has never been distributed. If the corporation needs to retain considerable funds for growth and expansion, dividend payments may be held to a minimum, in which case the high bracket taxpayer, receiving no salary, has nothing to show for his added tax liability but a high basis for his stock. If he is a minority shareholder the Subchapter S machinery can be an exquisite means of torture in the tax sense, leading to "squeeze-out" opportunities for the majority shareholders.[146] Although the high bracket taxpayer may, in desperation, seek to terminate the election by transferring his stock to a nonconsenting shareholder, he may not do so if there is a valid stock transfer restriction and, even if there were not, the device might not work for reasons already mentioned.[147] He may thus be effectively locked in and at the mercy of his colleagues, creating dissension and leading to possible dissolution of the corporation in extreme cases.[148]

A final discouraging feature of Subchapter S is its complexity. The mechanics of pass-through treatment of net operating losses and capital gains have been sufficiently explored to indicate to the reader that one should not attempt a Subchapter S election without the aid of a competent tax accountant as well as an attorney to advise on the proper method and time for making distributions and to be alert to the ever-present dangers of premature termination of the election. This entails added cost.

It would be misleading, however, to close this discussion of Subchapter S

---

[144] Treas. Reg. §1.1375–3(c). See Walter J. Roob, 50 T.C. 891 (1968).

[145] See B. Bittker and J. Eustice, Federal Income Taxation of Corporations and Shareholders 725–726 (1966).

[146] See Ch. IV.

[147] See text accompanying note 113 *supra*.

[148] See Ch. VII.

without recapitulating some of the major advantages already discussed and listing some additional ones. The election is especially useful to avoid double taxation, permitting pass-through treatment for net operating losses and capital gains, and eliminating any question as to the reasonableness of corporate salaries for deduction purposes.[149] Although there are other methods of avoiding double taxation, such as the use of shareholder-held debt, with corporate earnings being paid out in the form of interest, they may entail risks of litigation, as where the corporate structure is held to be excessively thin.[150] If an election under Subchapter S is made, these hazards are removed. This will be particularly advantageous if most of the corporate profits would be distributed to the shareholders in any event. If, on the other hand, substantial profits are to be retained for growth or expansion purposes, as is so often the case, and there are few losses, the election will be disadvantageous, particularly to the high bracket taxpayer who is not a corporate employee.

There are some more subtle uses of Subchapter S as well. Due to what has been termed a "curious lack of correlation" between Subchapter S and the collapsible corporation provisions,[151] pass-through treatment of capital gain in a Subchapter S context does not fall within the sweep of Section 341 of the Code, which might otherwise tax the gain at ordinary rates. Thus a collapsible corporation may avoid Section 341 treatment by making a Subchapter S election, selling its property at a capital gain and passing through the gain to its shareholders.[152] The special rule taxing the corporation on certain one-shot elections may, however, diminish the usefulness of this device. It has also been pointed out that Subchapter S constitutes a useful alternative to Section 337 of the Code in certain situations where a corporation sells one or more assets before liquidating and distributing the proceeds to its shareholders.[153] Although Section 337 permits this to be done without the imposition of tax on the corporate level, there must be a complete liquidation and its other provisions must be rigidly complied with.[154] The Subchapter S election avoids tax on the corporate level and permits pass-through treatment for the gain. In addition, the passed-through gain on the sale of the assets may be reported under the installment method of Section 453.[155]

Among the other advantages of Subchapter S are the availability of fringe benefits open to corporations generally, such as qualified pension

[149] See text accompanying note 84 *supra*.

[150] See Ch. II, text accompanying notes 67–102.

[151] See B. Bittker and J. Eustice, Federal Income Taxation of Corporations and Shareholders 735 (1966). See also, however, the restrictions on so-called "one-shot" elections discussed in text accompanying note 104 *supra*.

[152] Id. at 735–736. For discussion of collapsible corporations, see Ch. V, text accompanying notes 167–188.

[153] Id. at 736.

[154] See Ch. VII, text accompanying notes 144–163.

[155] See B. Bittker and J. Eustice, id. at 736.

plans,[156] stock options, employee death benefits, group term life insurance and accident and health plans. Also, since a shareholder's portion of undistributed taxable income is calculated as of the end of the corporation's taxable year and is includible in his taxable year in which the corporation's taxable year ends,[157] some advantage may be gained through the adoption of a corporate taxable year which will effectively postpone tax liability for the shareholder for up to a year. Thus if a shareholder reports his income on a calendar-year basis, the corporation's first taxable year may be planned to end on January 31 of the following year. Finally, where a corporation plans to sell a capital asset, the advantages of one-shot elections have already been discussed. The availability of the one-shot technique is somewhat sharply curtailed by the extra tax imposed by Section 1378, and yet that section has its exceptions. Even if it applies, the overall tax may be slightly lower than the total tax incurred if Subchapter S is not used. Subchapter S may thus be employed where a corporation wishes to sell a substantial part of its property and distribute the proceeds and yet does not wish to liquidate completely, so that an election under Section 337 is unfeasible.

[156] Rev. Rul. 66–218, 1966–2 Cum. Bull. 120. Note, however, that the Tax Reform Act of 1969, by adding Section 1379 to Subchapter S, in effect restricted the maximum contribution of a Subchapter S corporation to the lesser of 10 percent of compensation received by shareholder-employees or $2500, which is the same amount which may be contributed to pension plans by the self-employed. Contributions in excess of this amount result in a tax on the employee in the year of contribution.

[157] Int. Rev. Code of 1954, §§1372(b)(2), 1373(b).

II   Setting Up the Close Corporation

2.1   ADVANTAGES AND DISADVANTAGES OF TAX-FREE AND TAXABLE TRANSFERS

Although a corporation may be formed without the imposition of income tax on the transfer of properties to it by qualifying the transfer under Section 351 of the Code, there are situations where it is advisable to make the transaction taxable. This is primarily where the transferor is in a relatively low tax bracket or has losses for the taxable year which will counterbalance gains recognized on the transfer, and thus will pay a relatively low tax "cost" for achieving a so-called stepped-up basis for the corporation. For example, if the fair value of the property transferred is $20,000 and the taxpayer's basis in the property is $15,000, he will pay a tax on the $5000 of recognized gain but the corporation will take as its basis its cost, or $20,000, instead of the taxpayer's former basis of $15,000.[1] With its basis thus increased, the corporation's ability to deduct depreciation will be enhanced, as well as its gain diminished if it should ever sell the property. A principal problem with this approach is that the so-called depreciation recapture provisions of Sections 1245 and 1250 may convert what might otherwise be capital gain on the transfer into ordinary income. There may be situations, however, where the recapture rules will not pose a threat, as where buildings have been held for more than two hundred months or have depreciated on a straight-line basis.[2] In such cases, and in the situation already mentioned where the tax cost of achieving the stepped-up basis is low because of the taxpayer's losses or his relatively low level of income for the taxable year of the transfer, it may be desirable to avoid the "tax-free" provisions of Section 351.

---

[1] Int. Rev. Code of 1954, §1012. For a good, general treatment of problems in this area, see Ellis, Tax Problems in Sales to Controlled Corporations, 21 Vand. L. Rev. 196 (1968).

[2] Int. Rev. Code of 1954, §§1250(a), 1250(b)(1). The Tax Reform Act of 1969 amendments to Section 1250(a)(1)(C) of the Code provide for a 1 percent reduction of the amount of depreciation recapture for each month during which new residential housing is held after the expiration of an initial period of one hundred months.

An additional possibility for use of a "taxable" exchange is where the asset involved is a capital asset in the hands of the transferor but will be held for sale to customers by the corporation and thus taxed to it at ordinary rates. In this case the transferor may be willing to pay a tax at capital gain rates on the increased value of the property over his basis if this will lessen the corporation's ordinary income on its sale of the property because of a stepped-up basis.

There is one further hazard, however. If *any* depreciable property (not merely Section 1245 or 1250 property) is transferred to a corporation in which the transferor (and his wife, minor children and grandchildren) own more than 80 percent in value of the outstanding stock, gain which otherwise would be treated as capital or Section 1231 gain is taxed at ordinary rates.[3] Thus a transferor of depreciable property should avoid ownership of 80 percent in value in himself or family unless he is prepared to pay the tax cost of ordinary income on the transfer.

It may be that a transferor wishes to recognize a loss on a transfer when the corporation is formed. Here the corporation would receive a "stepped-down" basis and thus have lower depreciation deductions in future years, together with greater gain or less loss on resale of the property. These disadvantages to the corporation will often make the recognition of loss inadvisable, but there may be situations where the taxpayer is willing to have the corporation suffer the detriment of a low basis because of his need to use the loss to offset other income. Here again, however, there is a provision which must be carefully watched. Section 267 disallows losses on sales or exchanges of property between an individual and a corporation more than 50 percent in value of the outstanding stock of which is owned, directly or indirectly, by or for him. In computing the 50 percent ownership requirement there are constructive ownership rules whereby an individual is deemed to own stock owned directly or indirectly by or for his brothers and sisters, wife, ancestors and lineal descendants. In addition, an individual owning stock in a corporation (other than by virtue of the family ownership attribution rule just described) is deemed to own stock owned, directly or indirectly, by his partner. This effectively precludes recognition of losses where the property is transferred to a corporation from a partnership.[4] Further complications arise from the fact that stock owned directly or indirectly by or for a corporation, partnership, estate or trust is considered as owned proportionately by or for its shareholders, partners or beneficiaries. And "constructive" ownership arising from the latter rule may be treated as "actual" ownership for the purpose of applying the other constructive ownership rules. Thus there may be a form of "double" attribution (although such double attribution may not be had by twice applying or combining the family attribution rule and the rule which attributes ownership from one

[3] Id. §1239.
[4] Treas. Reg. §1.267(c)–1(b), Ex. (2).

partner to another).[5] Suffice it to say that where any of the transferors of property are related to one another, or were previously associated together in some business enterprise, losses on transfers will probably be disallowed. If such losses are disallowed, the loss disappears and thus is not available for a deduction at a later time. The corporation comes out of the transaction with its lower stepped-down basis and the transferor of property takes as his basis in the stock received on the transfer the cost of the stock, or fair value of the properties transferred, which will be lower than his former basis in the properties. As a result, both the corporation and the shareholder will have a relatively low basis, certainly a highly undesirable state of affairs. There is some slight tax relief available to the corporation by virtue of Section 267(d) which provides that, if the corporation sells the property later at a gain, it will not be taxed except to the extent that the gain on the sale exceeds the loss previously disallowed to the transferor. Thus, if a person were to have a basis of $8000 on property which he sold to a 51 percent owned corporation for $5000, and the corporation were later to sell the property for $10,000, only $2000 of the gain would be recognized (the excess of the corporation's $5000 gain over the $3000 loss previously disallowed).[6]

One of the main disadvantages to a taxable transfer is that, as already mentioned, any transfer of property which is subject to the depreciation recapture provisions of Sections 1245 and 1250 (e.g., depreciable personal or tangible property used as an integral part of manufacturing, production, extraction, research, storage, etc., or depreciable real property) is likely to give rise to gain taxable at ordinary rates. Unless the transferor has losses or substantial deductions to offset the Sections 1245 and 1250 income, his tax cost of getting a stepped-up basis for his corporation is likely to be unduly high. Furthermore, in valuing the "amount realized" on the transfer (i.e., the stock, securities and other consideration paid by the corporation for the properties transferred to it) for the purpose of computing the transferor's gain on the exchange, intangible assets, such as good will, franchises and

[5] Int. Rev. Code of 1954, §267(c). See also Treas. Reg. §1.267(c)–1(b), Ex. (1).

[6] See id. §1.267(d)–1(a), Ex. (1). For a further possibility that losses on certain transfers may be disallowed even though they may not fall literally within the terms of Section 267, see Higgins v. Smith, 308 U.S. 473 (1940) (suggesting that a court may look at the entire factual situation to determine whether loss should be disallowed). For extensive discussion of the area, see Harley, Dealings Between Closely Held Corporations and Their Stockholders, 25 Tax L. Rev. 403 (1970). Note particularly the problems which may be encountered by one who holds approximately 49 percent of the shares. If ownership of the other shares is dispersed among several individuals, the 49 percent block will constitute effective control and thus be worth more than 49 percent of the net worth of the corporation or book value of the outstanding stock. Thus, as the author suggests (at 407), Section 267 may apply since it relates to the comparative *value* of the shares held and not merely to the percentage of the outstanding shares.

the like, will have to be taken into account.[7] If the business is based primarily on services or depends substantially upon customer relationships, good will may constitute a relatively large part of its value. Thus the transferor must pay a tax at capital gains rates on the good will as well as a tax at ordinary rates on the value of any covenant not to compete which he may enter into to assure that the corporation will be able to take full advantage of the good will it has acquired.[8]

As to the various methods of arranging a taxable exchange, a transfer may be made taxable either by avoiding Section 351, (as where the transferors of property fail to have the requisite 80 percent control immediately after the exchange) or by arranging to receive so-called boot (i.e., cash, short-term notes or property other than stock or securities). As we shall see, gain on the exchange will be recognized to the extent of the boot received even though the transaction otherwise qualifies under Section 351. However, Section 351(b) expressly provides that this method may not be used for loss recognition. A third method is for the transferors to sell property to their corporation after it has been formed under Section 351. The advantages of this approach are that loss can be recognized, if the disallowance provisions of Section 267 are avoided, the "sale" may be made on the installment method, with any gain reported as payments are made by the corporation, and various assets can be selected for taxable treatment, with the rest having been conveyed to the corporation in a prior Section 351 exchange free of tax. However, if this technique is used, one should be extremely cautious to avoid having the Section 351 transfer and the subsequent taxable exchange take place under circumstances which suggest that the two are really interdependent parts of a single scheme. If this should happen, then the transfer of property would be treated as an additional contribution to capital and the consideration for the sale, if in property other than stock or securities, would be treated as Section 351(b) boot, or possibly as a dividend. Although gain will be recognized to the extent of the boot, there will be no

---

[7] See Note, Tax Treatment of Covenants Not to Compete: A Problem of Purchase Price Allocation, 67 Yale L.J. 1261 (1958). See also Rev. Proc. 69–19, 1969–2 Cum. Bull. 301 (circumstances under which the Internal Revenue Service will rule as to whether the transfer of "know-how" will qualify as the transfer of "property" for the purpose of tax-free treatment under Section 351 of the Code).

[8] Note, 67 Yale L.J. 1261 (1958). As the writer indicates, if part of the "amount realized" must be allocated to a covenant not to compete, the interests of the transferor and transferee diverge, as far as determining how much is to be allocated to which item. The transferor will wish to maximize his capital gain by having as much as possible of the price allocated to good will rather than have it taxed at ordinary rates if allocated to the covenant not to compete. Conversely, since good will is not a depreciable item in the hands of the transferee, the latter will wish to allocate a larger share of the purchase price to the covenant not to compete, which may then be amortized if it can be shown to have a limited life. See also Eustice, Contract Rights, Capital Gain, and Assignment of Income—The Ferrer Case, 20 Tax L. Rev. 1 (1964); Rev. Rul. 69–643, 1969–2 Cum. Bull. 10; Rev. Rul. 64–56, 1964–1 (Part 1) Cum. Bull. 133.

loss recognition. Furthermore, the transferor may not be able to use the installment method for reporting gain.

2.2 TAX-FREE FORMATION OF CORPORATIONS

The underlying theory of the Code provision which permits tax-free formation of a corporation is that the transfer of assets or a going business to a corporation in exchange for stock or securities generally involves only a change in the business form. If the transferor retains his stock or securities, he continues to have a proprietary interest, albeit one which is described in terms of stock, or a long-term claim against the corporation. Although there may be some situations where the transition from one form to another produces a more or less radical change in the former owner's interest in the assets,[9] and a tax might arguably be imposed to commemorate the event, the overall tax policy appears to be to postpone the tax unless the former owner parts with his interest on terms which indicate a sale or other complete severance of his former relationship with the assets transferred.

The key provision for providing tax-free treatment of the transfer is Section 351 of the Code:

> Sec. 351. *Transfer to Corporation Controlled by Transferor*
> (a) General Rule.—No gain or loss shall be recognized if property is transferred to a corporation (including, in the case of transfers made on or before June 30, 1967, an investment company) by one or more persons solely in exchange for stock or securities in such corporation and immediately after the exchange such person or persons are in control (as defined in Section 368(c)) of the corporation. For purposes of this section, stock or securities issued for services shall not be considered as issued in return for property.
> (b) Receipt of Property.—If subsection (a) would apply to an exchange but for the fact that there is received, in addition to the stock or securities permitted to be received under subsection (a), other property or money, then—
> (1) gain (if any) to such recipient shall be recognized, but not in excess of—
> (A) the amount of money received, plus
> (B) the fair market value of such other property received; and
> (2) no loss to such recipient shall be recognized.

[9] One of the best discussions of this point may be found in B. Bittker and J. Eustice, Federal Income Taxation of Corporations and Shareholders 64–69 (1966). Among the possible situations which might qualify for taxable treatment is a transfer by a comparatively large number of independent grocerymen, each owning a corner store, of their businesses to a newly formed entity whose stock is publicly traded. Id. at 67. Another might be a transfer by A and B of assets where A receives all the stock (tax free) and B receives solely securities—i.e., bonds or notes (taxable?). Id. at 68. The two transactions appear to fit literally within the terms of Section 351 of the Code and tax-free treatment might for that reason be provided. However, there has been a relatively radical change in the economic perspective of some of the transferors; the difference is not merely one of form.

(c) Special Rule.—In determining control, for purposes of this section, the fact that any corporate transferor distributes part or all of the stock which it receives in the exchange to its shareholders shall not be taken into account.

In emphasizing the importance of literal compliance with Section 351 in order to achieve tax-free treatment, attention should be directed to a few key words in subsection (a):

First, "property" must be transferred to a corporation by one or more persons. Although the term "property" includes money,[10] it does not include services. This is expressly indicated in the last sentence of subsection (a). Where "stock" is "issued for services," at least several things should be noted. First, unless the stock is subject to a restriction which has a significant effect on its value,[11] its receipt will always give rise to compensation income, taxable at ordinary rates.[12] Secondly, since a person who receives stock solely for services is not a transferor of property, tax-free incorporation under Section 351 will not be available for *any* of those who form the corporation (i.e., whether or not property is transferred by others) if more than 20 percent of any class of stock is issued solely for services. This is because the issuance of more than 20 percent prevents those who do transfer property from receiving the requisite 80 percent to constitute "control" within the statutory definition.[13] However, if someone subscribes for stock by paying cash or transferring property and also receives stock for services, *all* of the stock received by him may be counted in determining control unless the stock issued for property is of relatively small value in comparison to the stock received for services.[14] For example, if A, B and C subscribe for stock of a corporation and C receives his stock solely for services, A and B receiving their stock for property, the transaction will be taxable to all parties if C receives more than 20 percent of any class of stock. If, however, C pays for his stock with both property and services, all stock received by C may be counted along with that received by A and B for determining control, unless C made merely a nominal payment in property in order to qualify the transfer by A and B as tax free. Regardless of the outcome, any stock received by C for services will be taxed as compensation

[10] Portland Oil Co. v. Commissioner, 109 F.2d 479 (1st Cir. 1940), *cert. denied*, 310 U.S. 650 (1940); George M. Holstein, 23 T.C. 923 (1955).

[11] Cf. Treas. Reg. §1.421–6(a)(2) (receipt of stock option subject to restriction). See also Section 83 of the Code, added by the Tax Reform Act of 1969, which governs the taxability of so-called restricted property. For a detailed discussion see Ch. X, text accompanying note 74.

[12] United States v. Frazell, 335 F.2d 487, 490 (5th Cir. 1964), *cert. denied*, 380 U.S. 961 (1965). For a discussion of the advantages of using senior securities in order to diminish the amount of compensation income, see text accompanying note 145 *infra*.

[13] For an extensive discussion, see Herwitz, Allocation of Stock Between Services and Capital in the Organization of a Close Corporation, 75 Harv. L. Rev. 1098 (1962).

[14] See Treas. Reg. §1.351–1(a)(1)(ii).

income unless it is subject to a restriction which has a significant effect on its value. Since stock in a close corporation is frequently difficult to sell to persons outside of the corporation, the usual "first refusal" type restriction, giving the corporation or the other shareholders the right to purchase in the event of a proposed sale, may very well not have a significant effect on the value of the stock.[15] Hence, the likelihood is that any stock received for services in a close corporation context will be taxed as compensation income.

In some situations it may be possible for a person to qualify as a transferor of property if the property was paid for by services rendered prior to its transfer. Thus in *Roberts Co., Inc.,*[16] a firm of attorneys was held to have acquired an equitable interest in certain lands belonging to an estate in return for their services in settling the affairs of a decedent. When the lands were subsequently conveyed to a corporation, the stock received by the attorneys was held to have been issued in exchange for property and could therefore be included for purposes of computing control.[17] However, where a father and son entered into an agreement that the latter would acquire a one-half interest in the business if he remained with it and continued to operate the plant, and where three years later a corporation was organized with the son and father receiving 1176 and 1181 shares, respectively, it was argued that the son, by virtue of the earlier agreement, had acquired an equitable one-half interest in the property, thus making him eligible for inclusion in the group of "transferors" for the purpose of determining control. This contention was rejected by the Circuit Court as "not borne out by the evidence," with no discussion or citation of authority, apparently overlooking the earlier *Roberts Co.* case.[18] In both situations the question of whether or not the transfer was taxable arose later in connection with determining the proper method of computing the basis of the property in the hands of the corporation, the latter arguing that it had received a stepped-up basis because the transfer was taxable. Since the problem presented was whether there had been an "equitable assignment" of an interest in the property being transferred to the corporation, and the two courts arrived at opposite conclusions on the point, this suggests that the matter might have been simplified if there had been an actual transfer of property prior to incorporation. Thus, where a father agrees that a son is to receive a one-half interest in the business in return for his services, a transfer to the son of his portion of the property prior to the subsequent transfer to the corporation in return for stock might eliminate any doubt as to the tax-free character of the exchange. If the tax objective is not to get a stepped-up basis but to achieve a tax-free transfer, this is obviously a better way of structuring the transaction. Conversely, if a stepped-up basis is de-

15 See Herwitz, *supra,* at 1117.

16 5 T.C. 1 (1945), *acquiesced in,* 1945 Cum. Bull. 6.

17 Cf. United States v. Frazell, 335 F.2d 487, 490 (5th Cir. 1964) (dictum), *cert. denied,* 380 U.S. 961 (1965).

18 Fahs v. Florida Machine & Foundry Co., 168 F.2d 957, 959 (5th Cir. 1948).

sired, the agreement should specify that the son is not to receive any interest in the father's property, but is to receive a portion of the stock in return for his services. This essentially was the situation in *Mojonnier & Sons, Inc.,*[19] where a husband and wife induced their son, son-in-law and a foreman to work for the business in return for being issued stock later on when the business was incorporated. The stock was issued directly to the sons and foreman and it was held that the corporation received a stepped-up basis for the properties transferred to it, for the exchange was taxable. The Commissioner urged that the two sons had received the stock subsequent to incorporation as a gift, but this was rejected, the court finding that the stock had been issued directly by the corporation for services performed in the past.[20] However, if the parties had chosen to do so, they could have structured the transaction in this way. Hence a transferor might elect to receive all of the stock and then later transfer it to others in satisfaction of a preexisting claim for salary. Thus in *G. & W. H. Corson, Inc.,*[21] the court found that the later transfer was a "subsequent independent step and not a part of the transaction constituting the original exchange." [22]

The foregoing cases involve not only the question of whether property has been transferred by those receiving stock (i.e., whether the stock was issued for property which, in turn, was earned through services, or whether the stock was issued directly for services), but also the interpretation of the requirement of Section 351 that the transferors of property have control "immediately after" the exchange. A leading case on this point is *American Bantam Car Co. v. Commissioner.*[23] There, certain associates transferred assets to a newly formed corporation in exchange for all of its common stock. Shortly thereafter, an issue of preferred stock was sold to the public by underwriters who were to receive from the associates, in addition to underwriting discounts and commissions, various amounts of common stock in accordance with a schedule, depending upon the amounts of preferred sold by them to the public. The underwriting agreement was signed five days after the assets were transferred by the associates to the newly formed corporation in exchange for all its outstanding stock. Approximately two months later the common stock received by the associates was escrowed until the public offering of preferred was completed, at which time the stock was to be surrendered to the associates for distribution to the under-

---

[19] 12 T.C. 837 (1949), *nonacquiesced in,* 1949–2 Cum. Bull. 4.

[20] For an opposite result, holding that the transferor received control and then gave a portion of his stock away, see Wilgard Realty Co. v. Commissioner, 127 F.2d 514 (2d Cir. 1942), *cert. denied,* 317 U.S. 655 (1942).

[21] 12 CCH Tax Ct. Mem. 753 (1953).

[22] 12 CCH Tax Ct. Mem. at 756. See also Wilgard Realty Co. v. Commissioner, 127 F.2d 514 (2d Cir. 1942), *cert. denied,* 317 U.S. 655 (1942), and O'Connor v. Commissioner, 16 CCH Tax Ct. Mem. 213 (1957), *aff'd,* 260 F.2d 358 (6th Cir. 1958), *cert. denied,* 359 U.S. 910 (1959).

[23] 11 T.C. 397 (1948), *aff'd per curiam,* 177 F.2d 513 (3d Cir. 1949), *cert. denied,* 339 U.S. 920 (1950).

writers in accordance with the number of shares of preferred sold. Over a year later, 87,900 of the 300,000 shares of common were transferred to the underwriters and 1008 of the shares so transferred were resold to the public. The question was whether, immediately after the assets were transferred to the corporation in exchange for its stock, the associates had control (i.e., at least 80 percent ownership). The taxpayer corporation, arguing that the transaction was taxable because of its wish to have a stepped-up basis in the assets it received, urged that the entire series of steps be considered as parts of an integrated whole. Thus it argued that the court should consider the net effect of the entire scheme, which would lead to the conclusion that the associates, because of their surrender of the 87,900 shares of common (and the sale of the preferred by the underwriters, each preferred share carrying three votes in contrast to one vote for each share of common) did not have the requisite 80 percent control. The court, in reaching the opposite conclusion, namely that there was control immediately after the transfer, stated that

> Among the factors considered are the intent of the parties, the time element, and the pragmatic test of the ultimate result. An important test is that of mutual interdependence. Were the steps so interdependent that the legal relations created by one transaction would have been fruitless without a completion of the series? [24]

The court emphasized the fact that no written agreement, obligating the associates to surrender any part of the stock they received to outsiders, had been in existence at the time the associates transferred the assets. At most there was "an informal oral understanding of a general plan" and the written agreement was not entered into until five days later. Even then the obligation to surrender the shares to the underwriters was contingent upon how many shares of preferred were later sold to the public. Thus the court distinguished two other cases on the ground that in those situations

> there was a written contract prior both to the organization of the new corporation and the exchange of assets for stock which bound the transferors unconditionally to assign part of the stock acquired to third parties after the exchange. Thus, at the moment of the exchange the recipient of the stock did not own it, but held it subject to a binding contractual obligation to transfer a portion.[25]

More broadly speaking, the court found that the underwriting of the preferred stock was not a *sine qua non* of the entire scheme, without which the corporation would not have been formed nor the assets transferred in exchange for the common, observing that "While the incorporation and exchange of assets would have been purposeless one without the other yet

---

[24] 11 T.C. at 405.
[25] 11 T.C. at 405–406.

both would have been carried out even though the contemplated method of marketing the preferred stock might fail." [26]

Although the court in *American Bantam* appeared to stress the fact that no *written* agreement had been entered into with the underwriters prior to the time the assets were transferred to the corporation in exchange for stock, a sounder approach would consider whether, at the time of transfer, there was a firm obligation, written or not, to resell part of the stock to others. Even then, it should be considered whether the obligation so incurred was an interdependent feature of the entire transaction. For example, if A and B transfer assets in exchange for stock and prior to the transfer A agrees to surrender one half of his shares to a third party in payment of a preexisting debt, it may well be that if A's agreement is not an interdependent part of forming and financing the corporation, the fact that it predated the transfer should not prevent qualification under Section 351.[27] Putting the matter another way, if A receives legal title to the stock, he should be able to dispose of it as he wishes; thus a subsequent gift to others should not prevent his being in control immediately after the transfer.[28] He should also be able to use part of the stock to discharge an outstanding debt. If this is so, should the whole transaction be taxable merely because he agrees with his creditor to do so in advance? However, if the arrangement with the creditor is somehow related to the financing of the corporation, then the result might well be different if the arrangement were an interdependent part of the whole process. As far as corporate planning is concerned, the wisest course of action is to avoid entering into any agreement regarding the stock prior to forming the corporation. In addition, the transferor of property should receive the stock himself, rather than receive only part of the stock with the remainder being issued to a third party.[29] Even though the difference is merely one of form, it is better to have the form of the transac-

[26] 11 T.C. at 406–407. For a similar case see Commissioner v. National Bellas Hess, Inc., 220 F.2d 415 (8th Cir. 1955). Query whether stock issued for cash to the public might not be included in the control group since cash (which is property, as indicated *supra* note 10) has been transferred. This point, ignored in both the *American Bantam* and *National Bellas Hess* cases, raises the broader question of whether Section 351 was meant to apply to a transfer of cash (or any property for that matter) by a large group of previously unrelated individuals. For a discussion, see D. Herwitz, Business Planning 91 (1966), and B. Bittker and J. Eustice, Federal Income Taxation of Corporations and Shareholders 67–68 (1966). The latter, at 89–94, contains a good discussion of the whole problem of determining when the "immediately after" requirement has been met. For a collection of other cases and authorities, see id. at 94 n.39.

[27] The illustration is taken from id. at 92–93.

[28] See Wilgard Realty Co. v. Commissioner, 127 F.2d 514 (2d Cir. 1942), *cert. denied,* 317 U.S. 655 (1942).

[29] *Compare* Fahs v. Florida Machine & Foundry Co., 168 F.2d 957, 959 (5th Cir. 1948) (stock issued directly to donee, transferor held not to have control), *with* O'Connor v. Commissioner, 16 CCH Tax Ct. Mem. 213 (1957), *aff'd,* 260 F.2d 358 (6th Cir. 1958), *cert. denied,* 359 U.S. 910 (1959) (stock issued directly to transferor's creditors, transferor held to have control).

tion correspond with the concept of the transferor's control immediately after the exchange unless there are pressing reasons for not doing so.

Having explored the meaning of control immediately after the exchange, some mention should be made of the definition of "control." Section 368(c) defines control as "ownership of stock possessing at least 80 percent of the total combined voting power of all classes of stock entitled to vote and at least 80 percent of the total number of shares of all other classes of stock of the corporation." Not only must the 80 percent requirement be met both with respect to the "total combined voting power" and the total number of all other shares, but the Internal Revenue Service has interpreted the provision to require 80 percent ownership of *each* class of stock.[30] Although there may in some instances be difficulties of determining which classes of stock should be considered "entitled to vote," [31] and also when one or more transferors have 80 percent of the total combined voting power of such classes,[32] the matter will be clear enough in most cases. If the Internal Revenue Service's additional requirement of 80 percent ownership of *each* class of stock whether or not entitled to vote is met, it is highly unlikely that a court would find control lacking on some more technical ground, since the Internal Revenue Service's interpretation appears, if anything, too strict in view of the statutory language.

Prior to the enactment of the 1954 Code, the predecessor of Section 351 required that where two or more persons transfer property, the stock or securities received by each must be "substantially in proportion to his interest in the property prior to the exchange." [33] This is no longer required. However, the interests of the various parties can be "realigned" if the circumstances appear to require it. Thus, according to the regulations:

> the entire transaction will be given tax effect in accordance with its true nature, and in appropriate cases the transaction may be treated as if the

[30] Rev. Rul. 59–259, 1959–2 Cum. Bull. 115.

[31] Although B. Bittker and J. Eustice, id. at 86, raises a question as to preferred stock with contingent voting rights, it seems unlikely that such stock would be held "entitled to vote" in the absence of a default on the preferred stock dividend requirements. If the transferor has 80 percent ownership of each other class of stock, as required by the ruling already mentioned, resolution of the precise status of contingent voting rights would appear unnecessary.

[32] Query as to the effect of shareholder pooling agreements, irrevocable proxies and so forth. As we have seen, such arrangements which alter the balance of voting power have prevented Subchapter S corporations from qualifying under the one class of stock requirement. See Ch. I, text accompanying note 118. For discussion of this see B. Bittker and J. Eustice, id. at 86. Although, as the authors state, "the question is not foreclosed by case law or rulings," if the transferors own 80 percent of *each* other class of stock, as called for in the ruling, it is difficult to see how voting power could be shifted sufficiently to destroy control in any but the most unusual situation. However, to be on the safe side, one should avoid giving irrevocable proxies to pledgees or other creditors until after the transfer has been completed and even then not as an interdependent part of the tax-free exchange. See text accompanying note 26 *supra*.

[33] Int. Rev. Code of 1939, §112(b)(5).

stock and securities had first been received in proportion and then some of such stock and securities had been used to make gifts . . . to pay compensation . . . or to satisfy obligations of the transferor of any kind.[34]

To illustrate this, suppose that a father and son organize a corporation with one hundred shares of common stock. The father transfers property worth $800,000 in exchange for twenty shares of stock and the son transfers property worth $200,000 in exchange for eighty shares of stock. Although the transfers of property will qualify under Section 351, the father may be found to have made a gift to the son of sixty shares, if the circumstances suggest a gift. If so a gift tax would be due on the $600,000 worth of stock. Similarly, part or all of the stock might be treated as compensation for services rendered by the son to the father, in which case, although the transfer of the properties to the corporation would as before be free from tax, the son would receive compensation income to the extent of the fair value of the shares treated as compensation. The father would realize short- or long-term capital gain on the transfer of the shares to the son equal to the difference between the basis of the shares to him and their fair market value at the time of the exchange. However, he would also, it would seem, be entitled to a deduction under Sections 162 or 212 for compensation paid if the same were reasonable in amount.[35] If shares are realigned in the above fashion, it may be that in some situations the computation of who is in control immediately after the exchange may be affected since persons will be deemed to have constructively received additional stock before transferring it to others.[36]

Since Section 351(a) requires that the property be transferred to a corporation "solely in exchange for stock or securities," some attention should be given to the meaning of the term "securities." In general, the intent of this language is to draw a rough line between transactions which are in reality "sales," albeit with a deferred payment of the purchase price, and transfers of property in exchange for a long-term obligation of the corporation. There are really two questions here. First, is a purported corporate obligation really debt? As we shall see,[37] there are circumstances where the capital of a corporation is held to be excessively "thin" and shareholder-held debt is considered to be in substance a contribution to capital.[38] But assuming that the debt is really debt, there is a further question of whether it is eligible for classification as a security. Here the main consideration appears to be the duration of the obligation. The general rule of thumb is that notes or other obligations maturing within five years of issuance are not

[34] Treas. Reg. §1.351–1(b)(1).
[35] See id. §1.351–1(b)(2), Ex. (1).
[36] See B. Bittker and J. Eustice, Federal Income Taxation of Corporations and Shareholders 88 (1966).
[37] See text accompanying notes 67–102 *infra.*
[38] The same problem was discussed in connection with Subchapter S. See Ch. I, text accompanying note 123.

securities and those maturing later than ten years are securities. Those falling in the middle ground between five and ten years may be eligible for security classification depending on the facts of each case.[39] However, time is not the sole consideration. As one court put it:

> Though time is an important factor, the controlling consideration is an over-all evaluation of the nature of the debt, degree of participation and continuing interest in the business, the extent of proprietary interest compared with the similarity of the note to a cash payment, the purpose of the advances, etc.[40]

Particularly puzzling problems may arise where property is transferred to a corporation in exchange for an installment obligation. At first blush there would appear to be little difference between a corporation's ten-year sinking fund note and an installment contract whereby it agrees to pay the "purchase price" of an asset over a period of ten years. If a ten-year note would qualify as a security and thus be eligible for tax-free treatment, arguably an installment contract should be treated no differently. However, several cases have cast considerable doubt on whether an installment obligation can ever qualify as a security.[41] One possible result of this is to treat the security as boot if it is received as part of a transaction which otherwise would be under Section 351. Another possibility would be to isolate the transaction whereby the property was "sold" to the corporation on a deferred payment basis, treating the transaction as separate from an earlier Section 351 exchange. If this route is followed, then the question of whether the installment obligation is a security does not arise, for the sale is treated as not falling within Section 351, with the result that the seller either reports a gain on the difference between the basis of the property sold and the fair value of the installment obligation, or, more likely, if the transaction qualifies under Section 453 of the Code, he will report the gain on the installment method, spreading it out over the period in which the payments are received. The question of whether a Section 351 exchange and a subsequent sale of assets on the installment method should be integrated is essentially one of fact, depending on whether the two are interdependent parts of the same financing.[42] Obviously the farther apart the two transactions

[39] See B. Bittker and J. Eustice, id. at 73 n.10 (collecting cases).

[40] Camp Wolters Enterprises, Inc., 22 T.C. 737, 751 (1954), *aff'd*, 230 F.2d 555 (5th Cir. 1956), *cert. denied*, 352 U.S. 826 (1956). For a somewhat unusual case holding six-month equipment notes to be securities where it was intended that they be eventually transformed into preferred stock, see Prentis v. United States, 273 F. Supp. 460 (S.D.N.Y. 1967), on remand from a reversal by the Circuit Court of an earlier decision. See Turner Construction Co. v. United States, 364 F.2d 525 (2d Cir. 1966). See also D. Herwitz, Business Planning 116–117 (1966).

[41] See, e.g., Warren H. Brown, 27 T.C. 27 (1956). See also D. Herwitz, id. at 117–118, and B. Bittker and J. Eustice, Federal Income Taxation of Corporations and Shareholders 103 n.57 (1966).

[42] Cf. Houck v. Hinds, 215 F.2d 673 (10th Cir. 1954); American Bantam Car Co. v. Commissioner, 11 T.C. 397 (1948), *aff'd per curiam*, 177 F.2d 513 (3d Cir. 1949), *cert. denied*, 339 U.S. 920 (1950).

are in time, the less the likelihood of integration, although time should not be the sole factor. If there is integration, then, as previously stated, the installment sale contract may not qualify as a security with the result that it becomes boot and gain on the overall exchange (the two transactions being treated as one) is recognized to the extent of the boot. Furthermore, there is serious question whether under such circumstances the gain may be reported under the installment method. Needless to say, no loss can be recognized because of the express provision to that effect in Section 351(b). Although there appears to have been a suggestion in some relatively recent cases that if a transfer for an installment obligation is a "bona fide sale," then it cannot fall within the sweep of Section 351,[43] the better approach, and certainly the one which merits the attention of the cautious planner, is whether, factually speaking, the installment sale should be integrated with an earlier Section 351 transaction if it is interdependent with it. In addition, at least one case has indicated that, if the sales proceeds, including the face amount of the installment obligation, exceed the fair market value of the property transferred, the difference may be treated as a dividend, taxed at ordinary rates to the extent of corporate earnings and profits.[44]

Frequently the property will be transferred to the corporation subject to liabilities, such as a mortgage, which may be expressly assumed by the transferee. The question then becomes one of whether the transfer, and *a fortiori* the assumption of the liability, should be treated as equivalent to the receipt of boot by the transferor, thereby permitting recognition of gain. Section 357 provides in effect that boot is not received in this situation except in two cases: First, if it appears that "the principal purpose" of the taxpayer was either a purpose to avoid federal income tax or was not a "bona fide business purpose," then the total liabilities assumed or acquired by the corporation are treated as money received by the taxpayer. In this regard the taxpayer has the burden of showing lack of a tax avoidance purpose or the presence of a business purpose by a clear preponderance of the evidence.[45] Furthermore, the tax returns of the transferor and transferee corporation must state the corporate business reason for the assumption of liability.[46] If the burden of proof is not met with respect to any item of assumed liability, then *all* of the assumed liabilities are treated as money received.[47] A typical tax avoidance situation might be if the transferor, holding property free from liability, were to desire cash in the process of incorporating. Rather than transferring the property free from liability to

[43] Charles E. Curry, 43 T.C. 667 (1965), *acquiesced in*, 1965–2 Cum. Bull. 4; Harry F. Shannon, 29 T.C. 702 (1958).

[44] Arthur M. Rosenthal, 24 CCH Tax Ct. Mem. 1373 (1965). See also B. Bittker and J. Eustice, id. at 103 n.57, and Treas. Reg. §1.301–1(j).

[45] Int. Rev. Code of 1954, §357(b).

[46] Treas. Reg. §§1.351–3(a)(6)(iii) and (b)(7)(iii).

[47] For a criticism see B. Bittker and J. Eustice, id. at 82–83 n.26. See also Burke and Chisholm, Section 357: A Hidden Trap in Tax-Free Incorporations, 25 Tax L. Rev. 211 (1970).

the corporation, having the latter mortgage the property and remit the cash to the transferor, the transferor might mortgage the property immediately prior to the transfer, receive the cash himself and have the corporation assume the mortgage. Another possible tax avoidance scheme might be the assumption by the corporation of personal obligations of the taxpayer (e.g., rent on an apartment, druggist bills, etc.) where there is no business purpose for doing so.[48]

A further exception to the general rule that assumption of liability on a Section 351 exchange will not result in boot is Section 357(c). This provides that if the *total* liabilities assumed or existing on the property exceed the *total* adjusted basis of *all* property transferred pursuant to the exchange, then such excess is considered as either capital or ordinary gain (depending on the nature of the particular assets), regardless of whether there is in fact gain realized on the exchange. Several things should be noted here. First, the *total* liabilities on the property are compared to the *total* adjusted basis of all property transferred (whether or not subject to a liability). Thus a high basis on nonliability property may alleviate or eliminate the possibility of gain recognition. Secondly, unlike Section 351(b) which states that the receipt of boot will lead to gain recognition *if* there is gain on the overall exchange (and to that extent), Section 357(c) states that an excess of total liabilities over total basis *always* leads to gain recognition. If more than one kind of property is transferred (i.e., capital assets, ordinary assets, Section 1231, 1245 or 1250 property), than the gain recognized is presumably allocated among the properties in accordance with their relative fair market values.[49] If there happens to be more than one transferor, it would seem that Section 357(c) should be applied on a person-by-person basis, rather than having the properties transferred by everyone considered collectively.[50] If in a particular case Section 357(c) applies, and also Section 357(b), because there is a tax avoidance purpose or no bona fide business purpose, then Section 357(b) treatment will be given and all of the liabilities will be considered as money received, resulting in recognition of gain, but (unlike Section 357(c)) only if there happens to be gain on the exchange (and to that extent).

It is clear that a corporation realizes no gain on the issuance of its stock, or a sale of its treasury stock, for money or other property.[51] This also applies to an issuance of stock for services.[52] In the latter situation the corporation will receive a deduction as a Section 162 business expense if the

---

[48] The illustration is suggested by B. Bittker and J. Eustice, id. at 82.

[49] Id. at 84. Note a potential tax trap where a cash basis taxpayer has a zero basis in uncollected accounts receivable. The basis of the other properties transferred may be less than the total liabilities assumed, etc. See Comment, Section 357(c) and the Cash Basis Taxpayer, 115 U. Pa. L. Rev. 1154 (1967).

[50] B. Bittker and J. Eustice, id. at 84.

[51] Int. Rev. Code of 1954, §1032.

[52] Treas. Reg. §1.1032–1(a).

payment of cash rather than stock would have qualified for a deduction (i.e., if the amount of compensation is reasonable).[53] Similarly, where shares are issued in payment for a corporate debt there is no gain, as if money had been used to pay the debt and then returned to the corporation in payment for the shares.[54] However, if a corporation sells its stock on a deferred payment basis, it may realize "imputed" interest under Section 483.[55]

2.3 COMPUTATION OF BASIS

If the exchange is taxable, the transferor's basis for the stock, securities or other property received by him is cost, equivalent to the fair market value of the property given up.[56] In the case of the corporation, its basis in the assets transferred to it is also cost, or the fair value of the stock, securities or other property given to the transferor. In an arm's-length transaction, and where it is difficult to establish precisely the value of the stock, securities, etc., because they are not readily marketable, one may assume that the cost of the assets transferred to the corporation is roughly equivalent to their fair market value at the time of transfer.[57]

If the transaction qualifies for tax-free treatment under Section 351, the basis of the stock, securities and other property received by the transferor is controlled by Section 358; the basis of the assets in the hands of the corporation is controlled by Section 362.

First, as regards the transferor, the following computation must be made: Beginning with the basis of the property *transferred* to the corporation, subtract the fair market value of any boot (i.e., "other property") and money received, and add the amount of gain which was *recognized* to the transferor (or any amount which may have been treated as a dividend).[58] The result is then allocated among the stock and securities in accordance with their respective fair market values.[59] The boot (other property) receives a basis equivalent to its fair market value.[60]

Suppose, for example, that a transferor surrendered property with a basis to him of $9000 and a fair market value of $15,500 in exchange for $2500 in cash, $1000 fair market value of boot, and stock and securities worth

---

[53] Rev. Rul. 62–217, 1962–2 Cum. Bull. 59.

[54] Commissioner v. Fender Sales, Inc., 338 F.2d 924 (9th Cir. 1964), *cert. denied,* 382 U.S. 813 (1965).

[55] Treas. Reg. §1.483–1(b)(6), Ex. 6.

[56] Int. Rev. Code of 1954, §1012.

[57] Cf. Philadelphia Park Amusement Co. v. United States, 126 F. Supp. 184 (Ct. Cl. 1954).

[58] Int. Rev. Code of 1954, §358(a).

[59] Id. §358(b). Treas. Reg. §1.358–2(b)(2).

[60] Int. Rev. Code of 1954, §358(a)(2).

$12,000. Suppose that the securities were worth twice as much as the stock. The basis of the stock and securities would be determined as follows:

Basis of property given up	$9000
Less boot	− 1000
Less cash	− 2500
Subtotal	$5500
Plus gain recognized on the exchange	+ 3500
Basis of stock and securities	$9000
Allocated as follows:	
Stock	3000
Securities	6000

Since the transferor surrendered property with a basis of $9000 and received a total of $15,500 in cash, boot, stock and securities, he realized a gain of $6500, of which $3500 was recognized (i.e., the total of the $2500 cash and the $1000 fair market value of the boot). The boot receives as its basis an amount equivalent to its fair market value—$1000.

Suppose that, in the above example, the property was transferred subject to a mortgage of $3000. In this case Section 358(d) provides that the liability, whether or not assumed by the corporation, is treated as "money received" by the transferor. The effect of this is to change the above calculation as follows:

Basis of property given up	$9000
Less boot	− 1000
Less money received	− 5500
Subtotal	$2500
Plus gain recognized on the exchange	+ 3500
Basis of stock and securities	$6000
Allocated as follows:	
Stock	2000
Securities	4000

It should be observed that, in the above example, the assumption of liability by the corporation did not give rise to taxable gain, since the liability was not in excess of the basis of the property transferred, nor did we assume that there was any tax avoidance motive or lack of a business purpose.[61] In the absence of such somewhat unusual factors, then, assumption of liability will not give rise to taxable gain, but it must nevertheless be considered as "money received" for the purpose of determining basis, requiring a downward adjustment. If the transferor is later called upon to discharge the liability because of the corporation's inability to do so, he would probably be

[61] See text accompanying note 45 *supra*.

entitled to increase the basis of his stock by the amount he pays, or take a deduction under Sections 165 or 166. If he sells the stock prior to discharging the debt, then his loss on payment would probably be considered as a capital loss.[62]

If the transferor subsequently sells the stock or securities he received in the Section 351 exchange, he is permitted to "tack" the holding period of any property he transferred which was either a Section 1231 asset or a capital asset onto the period during which he held stock or securities received on the exchange which were attributable to such assets. Since some of the assets transferred will fall into this category and others not, the consideration received for the assets must be allocated among them. As we shall see, the allocation will be made in accordance with the respective fair market values of the various assets.[63]

It is worth examining in detail a relatively recent revenue ruling[64] which sets forth the method of allocating the consideration received for assets transferred in a Section 351 exchange among the various assets for the purpose of determining the amount and character of gain on each asset where the presence of cash or boot causes gain to be recognized. Suppose that X and Y transfer properties to a corporation as follows: X transfers $20,000 in exchange for stock having a fair market value of $20,000, and Y transfers three separate assets in exchange for stock having a fair market value of $100,000 plus cash of $10,000. Suppose that if Y had sold the three assets instead of exchanging them tax free, he would have realized gain and loss of each asset as follows:

	Asset I	*Asset II*	*Asset III*
Character of asset	Capital asset held more than 6 months	Capital asset held less than 6 months	Section 1245 property
Fair market value	$22,000	$33,000	$55,000
Adjusted basis	40,000	20,000	25,000
Gain (or loss)	($18,000)	$13,000	$30,000
Character of gain or loss	Long-term capital loss	Short-term capital gain	Ordinary income

Since $10,000 in cash was received by Y on the Section 351 exchange, gain is recognized to that extent. To determine the way in which gain is to be recognized, each asset transferred should be considered separately and there

---

[62] See B. Bittker and J. Eustice, Federal Income Taxation of Corporations and Shareholders 97 (1966).

[63] Int. Rev. Code of 1954, §1223(1), and B. Bittker and J. Eustice, id. at 98. See also Rev. Rul. 68–55, 1968–1 Cum. Bull. 140.

[64] Rev. Rul. 68–55, 1968–1 Cum. Bull. 140.

is no netting of gains and losses, since the basis for the various assets transferred will not be aggregated and matched with the fair market value of the total consideration received on the exchange.[65] Each category of consideration received must be separately allocated to the transferred assets in proportion to the relative fair market values of each asset as follows:

	Total	Asset I	Asset II	Asset III
Fair market value of asset transferred	$110,000	$22,000	$33,000	$55,000
Percent of total fair market value	—	20%	30%	50%
Fair market value of stock received in exchange	$100,000	$20,000	$30,000	$50,000
Cash received in exchange	10,000	2,000	3,000	5,000
Amount realized	$110,000	$22,000	$33,000	$55,000
Adjusted basis	—	40,000	20,000	25,000
Gain (loss) realized		($18,000)	$13,000	$30,000
Gain recognized			3,000	5,000
Character of gain			short-term capital gain	ordinary income

Since Section 351(b)(2) provides that no loss is recognized despite the fact that cash or boot is received, the $18,000 loss on the first asset may not be used to offset the gains recognized on the second and third assets.

Turning now to the problem of determining the basis of the property in the hands of the transferee corporation, Section 362(b) provides that the basis is the same as the transferor's former basis for the assets, increased in the amount of gain recognized to the transferor on the exchange. As in determining the transferor's gain, we should consider the basis of each asset to carry over to the corporation, and if there is gain recognized because of the transferor's receipt of money or boot, then the gain is allocated to the various assets in accordance with their respective fair market values. Although this method seems more in accord with the revenue ruling previously discussed, a better approach might be to allocate the gain among the various assets in proportion to each asset's actual increase in value above basis.[66] This method could also be used for determining the character of gain recognized to the transferor. Under the method followed by the revenue ruling, odd results can frequently occur. Thus, suppose that inventory and a capital asset, having bases of $5000 and $30,000, respectively, are transferred to a corporation in exchange for stock, having a value of $36,000, and cash, in the amount of $1500 as follows:

[65] Ibid. Cf. Rev. Rul. 68–23, 1968–1 Cum. Bull. 144. See Rabinovitz, Allocating Boot in Section 351 Exchanges, 24 Tax L. Rev. 337 (1969).

[66] See B. Bittker and J. Eustice, id. at 100.

	Basis	Fair Market Values
Inventory	$ 5,000	$12,500
Capital asset	30,000	25,000
Total	$35,000	$37,500

Since the receipt of the $1500 cash will give rise to the recognition of gain, if we apportion the gain among the two assets in accordance with their fair market values, the capital asset, being worth twice as much as the inventory, will receive twice as much gain, or $1000, with the remaining $500 being assigned to the inventory. Since a comparison of the basis and fair market value of the capital asset reflects a loss, and, as we have seen, the loss is not recognized, it seems incongruous to assign most of the cash to it rather than to the inventory, which is responsible for virtually all of the gain on the exchange. If we were to use the second method rather than the one approved in the revenue ruling, we would assign the entire $1500 in recognized gain to the inventory and tax it as ordinary income. The basis of the inventory in the hands of the corporation would then be stepped up by that amount. The basis of the capital asset in the hands of the corporation would be the same as in the hands of the transferor, i.e., $30,000.

2.4 THIN CAPITAL STRUCTURES

Among the hazards which beset the close corporation is the possibility that its capital structure may be held to be excessively "thin," i.e., that shareholder-held debt is, in substance, nothing more than equity. The consequences of this are relatively serious. We have already seen how, in the Subchapter S situation, classification of debt as stock may lead to the termination of a Subchapter S election on the ground that there is more than one class of stock.[67] Aside from Subchapter S, however, there are many other disadvantages. One of the more significant of these is that if the debt is stock, "interest" payments by the corporation will be disallowed as deductions.[68] The retirement of "debt" will give rise to no tax ordinarily, being merely the repayment of a loan, or if the debt was acquired for less than face value and fully paid off, the gain will be taxed at capital gains rates, except for so-called original issue discount.[69] In sharp contrast, if the debt

[67] See Ch. I, text accompanying note 117.
[68] Int. Rev. Code of 1954, §163. Note, however, that although interest paid to creditors is fully taxable to them, dividends are taxable only to the extent of corporate earnings and profits and even then are entitled to a dividend exclusion of $100 on an individual return and $200 on a joint return. Id. §116. Furthermore, dividends paid to a corporation are entitled to a dividends-received credit of at least 85 percent and, in the case of "affiliates," 100 percent. Id. §243.
[69] Id. §1232. Note that, as regards bonds or other corporate indebtedness issued after May 27, 1969, Section 1232(a)(3) of the Code, added by the Tax Reform

is classified as stock, its "redemption" will at best be taxed at capital gains
rates but frequently it may be considered as a distribution "essentially
equivalent" to a dividend, and thus taxed at ordinary rates to the extent of
corporate earnings and profits at the time of redemption.[70] There is also the
possibility that where the corporation sets aside amounts necessary to redeem the stock, this accumulation will be considered unreasonable and will
be subjected to a penalty tax on unreasonably accumulated earnings,
whereas if the amounts are accumulated for the purpose of meeting debt
repayment requirements, there is less likelihood that the accumulation
would be found unreasonable.[71] If the security becomes worthless—although debt and stock are generally treated alike, their worthlessness giving rise to capital loss[72]—there are a few situations where an ordinary loss
deduction is available, as in the case of certain claims not fitting within the
classification of securities but held by a corporation rather than an individual and thus entitled to deduction as "business bad debts." [73]

There is no clear test as to when a corporate structure will be found to be
excessively thin. As one might expect, much depends upon the facts of each
individual case. At one time, when practitioners attempted to get the best of
both worlds by creating so-called hybrid securities, centaurlike instruments
having some of the characteristics of debt and some of stock, courts placed
considerable emphasis on the form of the security. Thus, if the security,
although in the form of debt, was subordinated to the claims of other creditors, was entitled to interest only out of corporate earnings, had an unduly
lengthy or indefinite period of maturity, or carried voting rights, it was
likely to be considered as stock.[74] Due to the uncertainties in this area,
practitioners eventually chose to draft their instruments in unambiguous
form and thus the cases came to emphasize not the form of the instrument
but the circumstances surrounding its issuance.[75] As a result of two Supreme Court cases, it was thought for a time that one of the crucial factors
would be the ratio of debt to equity. This led to the search for so-called safe
ratios and it was suggested that a ratio of debt to equity of no more than

---

Act of 1969, will require the inclusion of original issue discount in income ratably
over the life of the obligation. If the obligation is discharged for less than its face
value, the corporation may have cancellation of indebtedness income. Id. §61(a)(12).

[70] Id. §302.

[71] Id. §531. See Ch. V, text accompanying note 110.

[72] Int. Rev. Code of 1954, §165(g)(2)(C), covering indebtedness having interest
coupons or in registered form.

[73] Id. §166. Individuals will ordinarily receive a nonbusiness bad-debt deduction,
treated as a short-term capital loss. Only in the somewhat unusual case will they be
considered as being in the same trade or business as the corporate debtor. Whipple
v. Commissioner, 373 U.S. 193 (1963).

[74] See B. Bittker and J. Eustice, Federal Income Taxation of Corporations and
Shareholders 123 (1966).

[75] See D. Herwitz, Business Planning 134 (1966).

4:1[76] or, more conservatively, 3:1[77] was safe. Even here there were problems of how the ratio was to be computed. Thus, should assets be valued at market or at book value for the purpose of determining the pro rata portion of assets represented by debt?[78] Should only shareholder-held debt be included, or should outside debt be counted as well, particularly if guaranteed by shareholders?[79]

The way in which the case law has developed indicates that, although the ratio of debt to equity is of obvious importance, no one ratio is safe in the sense that other factors in the equation may not predominate, resulting in the debt's being classified as stock. Perhaps the three most important factors are whether debt and stock are held in the same proportion to one another, whether corporate assets attributable to the issuance of debt are essential for the needs of the business (i.e., the business could not be conducted without them) and what the parties "intended." Of these the last is undoubtedly the broadest and, except for its vagueness and subjectivity, the most important consideration. As in the contract area, what the parties intended can only meaningfully be found by the way in which they acted in a given situation. Thus, if there was no real intention that the loan be repaid, if interest payments were not met, if the loan was subordinated to the claims of others, and if the risk of the business was such that there was little likelihood that the amounts represented by the loan would ever be withdrawn from the business, then the intent of the parties may be to make a capital contribution notwithstanding their attempt to describe their behavior as creating a debt.[80] Also, in ascertaining intent the debt-equity ratio is obviously relevant, although not conclusive, particularly when considered against the background of the risks of the particular business.[81]

Where the debt is held pro rata with the stock, this may imply that the debt was a contribution to capital. Yet it is not conclusive if there are other features of the situation that point more clearly in the direction of debt, such as an intention to repay, meeting interest payments as they become

---

[76] Talbot Mills Co. v. Commissioner, 326 U.S. 521 (1946); John Kelley Co. v. Commissioner, 326 U.S. 521 (1946). See Caplin, The Caloric Count of a Thin Incorporation, N.Y.U. 17th Inst. on Fed. Tax. 771 (1959).

[77] See B. Bittker and J. Eustice, id. at 126.

[78] Id. at 125 (suggesting market value).

[79] Ibid. See S. Surrey and W. Warren, Federal Income Taxation—Cases and Materials 1195–1196 (1960) (containing a useful summary of many of the cases); Goldstein, Corporate Indebtedness to Shareholders: "Thin Capitalization" and Related Problems, 16 Tax L. Rev. 1 (1960).

[80] See Gooding Amusement Co., Inc., 23 T.C. 408 (1954), aff'd, 236 F.2d 159 (6th Cir. 1956), cert. denied, 352 U.S. 1031 (1957). See also Gilbert v. Commissioner, 248 F.2d 399 (2d Cir. 1957).

[81] Nassau Lens Co., Inc. v. Commissioner, 308 F.2d 39, 47 (2d Cir. 1962). See Stone, Debt-Equity Distinctions in the Tax Treatment of the Corporation and Its Shareholders, 42 Tul. L. Rev. 251, 257–258 (1968), pointing out that a factor equally as important as the risks of a business is the benefit of sharing in a corporation's success and growth which is represented by an equity interest.

due, lack of subordination to outside debt and so forth. Conversely, mere disproportion in holdings of debt relative to equity should not in itself mean that the debt is really debt if other factors point in the opposite direction. And where the debt is held by members of a family, "family solidarity" may be taken into account to lessen the significance of disproportionate holdings,[82] perhaps by analogy with the attribution or constructive ownership rules in various sections of the Code.[83]

Where a sole proprietor or partnership contributes assets which are essential to the running of the business in exchange for stock and a substantial proportion of debt, the latter may be held to have been a contribution to capital in view of the nature of the assets attributable to the debt.[84] Although the logic of this approach is not particularly convincing since, if the corporation borrowed from outside sources funds which it then used to purchase "essential" assets, the use of the funds would hardly be grounds for disallowing debt status to the claims of outsiders,[85] it may be that the nature of the assets represented by shareholder-held debt is relevant to the general question of what the parties intended. In short, it is but one of the factors which go into determining the net result.[86] Although there is no absolute rule preventing those who transfer a going business from characterizing some of their investment as debt,[87] the matter is obviously more sensitive than debt financing through outside sources. Thus, as one commentator has suggested, for a small enterprise which would rarely qualify for substantial amounts of long-term outside debt, it would be well for shareholder-creditors to limit their claims to short-term debt, preferably secured by a mortgage.[88] Obviously there should be a conscientious effort to comply with the terms of the debt, making interest payments as called for and paying off the notes at maturity. If the debt is of too short a term it may not, as we have seen, qualify as a security in a Section 351 transaction. Thus the transferor of a going business is caught between the Scylla of possible taxation of gain on the exchange to the extent of the boot (i.e., if the debt is not a security) and the Charybdis of having the debt treated as

[82] See B. Bittker and J. Eustice, Federal Taxation of Corporations and Shareholders 124 (1966). For a collection of cases relating to pro rata holding of stock and debt, see D. Herwitz, Business Planning 136–138 (1966).

[83] See, e.g., Int. Rev. Code of 1954, §§267(c), 318.

[84] Brake & Electric Sales Corp. v. United States, 185 F. Supp. 1 (D. Mass. 1960), aff'd, 287 F.2d 426 (1st Cir. 1961); Sam Schnitzer, 13 T.C. 43 (1949), aff'd per curiam, 183 F.2d 70 (9th Cir. 1950), cert. denied, 340 U.S. 911 (1951). For a general discussion of problems encountered in connection with changing from a partnership to a corporate form of business, see Note, Section 351 of the Internal Revenue Code and "Mid-Stream" Incorporations, 38 U. Cin. L. Rev. 96 (1969).

[85] See B. Bittker and J. Eustice, id. at 126.

[86] Charter Wire, Inc. v. United States, 309 F.2d 878 (7th Cir. 1962), cert. denied, 372 U.S. 965 (1963). For a good summary of the various factors to be considered see Tomlinson v. 1661 Corporation, 377 F.2d 291 (5th Cir. 1967).

[87] Daytona Marine Supply Co. v. United States, 61–2 U.S. Tax Cas. ¶9523 (S.D. Fla. 1961).

[88] See D. Herwitz, Business Planning 147 (1966).

stock. If the latter happens, although Section 351 will make the exchange tax free, deduction of interest payments on the debt will be disallowed, along with various other unpleasant consequences already described.[89] Thus a maturity date of greater than five and no more than ten years is probably called for in these situations. Furthermore, although the debt-equity ratio is not conclusive, a particularly conservative ratio may be in order here. Holdings in the nontax area have sustained debt classification under similar circumstances where the ratio was approximately 50–50.[90] Although this may seem overly cautious, equal portions of debt and equity may have the best chance of withstanding attack where the debt arises from a transfer of essential assets.[91] Further safety may be had, as already indicated, by keeping the term of the debt relatively short, having it secured and taking care that interest payments are met.

The Tax Reform Act of 1969, by adding Section 385 to the Code, gave the Internal Revenue Service further rule-making powers in this area. Thus Section 385(b) provides that the regulations shall set forth factors which are to be taken into account in determining whether a debtor-creditor relationship or a corporation-shareholder relationship exists. Several such factors are suggested, but it is clear that the Internal Revenue Service is free to include other factors or that it may omit various factors if it considers that this is necessary or appropriate:

(1) whether there is a written unconditional promise to pay on demand or on a specified date a sum certain in money in return for an adequate consideration in money or money's worth, and to pay a fixed rate of interest,

(2) whether there is subordination to or preference over any indebtedness of the corporation,

(3) the ratio of debt to equity of the corporation,

(4) whether there is convertibility into the stock of the corporation, and

(5) the relationship between holdings of stock in the corporation and holdings of the interest in question.

One hazard presented by the way in which courts have dealt with the problem of when debt should be considered equity is their so-called all or nothing at all approach. Suppose, for example, that a corporation were to have shareholder-held debt of $100,000 and common stock of only $10,000.

---

[89] See text accompanying note 70 *supra.*

[90] See Obre v. Alban Tractor Co., 228 Md. 291, 179 A.2d 861 (1962).

[91] In J. S. Biritz Construction Co. v. Commissioner, 387 F.2d 451 (8th Cir. 1967), the court observed that a debt-equity ratio of 2:1 was "not so inordinately high as to qualify this as a 'thin capitalization' case." Although the note amounting to $20,653 represented land valued at $27,310, which was the principal asset transferred (the total assets being only $30,765), the court found that the land was not essential to the operations of the corporation and was more in the nature of inventory, being held for subdivision and sale to customers. Although the note was a demand note and was not secured, interest was paid annually either in cash or by the issuance of a further promissory note which in turn was later paid.

If this ratio is considered too thin or if there are other factors, such as subordination of the debt to claims of other creditors, failure to meet interest payments and so forth, the entire $100,000 in debt is likely to be considered equity. Although the corporation might argue that it is entitled to have at least a reasonable portion of the debt recognized as such, since there is no prohibition on a shareholder's characterizing *some* of his investment as a claim against his corporation, this argument has been rejected in favor of a more categorical approach—either the entire amount is truly debt or it is not.[92] Although this might at times be justified if the test being used is that of ascertaining the intent of the parties, and where there appears to be no real reason for segregating only part of the debt and treating it as something else, an inflexible dogma that the entire amount of debt must always be treated in the same way hardly seems consistent with the fact-oriented approach which the courts have in other respects adopted. Suppose, for example, that shareholders make loans to their corporation at differing times, some of the loans being made when the corporation is formed and others being made later, perhaps to cover operating losses and keep the business from collapsing. This was the situation in *Arnold v. Phillips*,[93] where a mortgage had been taken out to cover both the initial loans and the subsequent advances. Although the court refused to recognize the first set of advances as claims in a bankruptcy proceeding because the corporation had been inadequately capitalized, the shareholder was given a status of a secured creditor with respect to the later advances. Although the weight of authority in the analogous tax area has not been in favor of making any distinction between advances made at differing times,[94] it seems appropriate to do so, not only in the interests of a more flexible and fact-oriented approach, but also to encourage shareholders to come to the aid of failing corporations. As has been pointed out, if all shareholder advances are treated alike, outside creditors may suffer should shareholders be reluctant to add further funds to strengthen a failing enterprise, and as a result the entire business collapses.[95]

[92] For a criticism of this approach, see Goldstein, Corporate Indebtedness to Shareholders: "Thin Capitalization" and Related Problems, 16 Tax L. Rev. 1 (1960). As pointed out in B. Bittker and J. Eustice, Federal Income Taxation of Corporations and Shareholders 122 (1966), the all or nothing at all approach may be more suitable as as a means of settling a case on the administrative level than as a guide in judicial determination of controversies.

[93] 117 F.2d 497 (5th Cir.), *cert. denied,* 313 U.S. 583 (1941).

[94] See D. Herwitz, Business Planning 145 (1966), citing Bijou-Pensacola Corp. v. United States, 172 F. Supp. 309 (N.D. Fla. 1959), as the only holding which has made a distinction between shareholder advances at differing times. Two other cases, Diamond Brothers Co. v. Commissioner, 322 F.2d 725 (3d Cir. 1963), and Schine Chain Theaters Inc., 22 CCH Tax Ct. Mem. 488 (1963), *aff'd per curiam,* 331 F.2d 849 (2d Cir. 1964), emphasized the fact that the shareholders continued to make advances where financial conditions were steadily deteriorating as a reason for refusing to classify the advances as bona fide debt.

[95] See D. Herwitz, id. at 144–145.

If shareholder-held debt is considered to be stock and is then transferred to a nonshareholder, does it still retain its status as stock? One case has assumed so without discussion of the point,[96] but here again it would seem advisable to avoid a categorical approach of "once stock then always stock," particularly if, at the time of transfer, outsiders would have made loans to the corporation. If loans from outsiders are guaranteed by shareholders, as is often the case in the closely held enterprise, it seems that a shareholder-guaranteed loan should be treated the same as a shareholder loan (although there is little authority on the point).[97]

If shareholder-held debt qualifies as debt and not as stock, it may serve as a useful means of withdrawing funds from a corporation either tax free or at a capital gains rate—funds which might otherwise be taxed at ordinary rates as dividends. Thus, if the debt is created at the inception of the corporation, payment of the debt will later be either tax free or, as already seen, taxed as a capital gain under Section 1232. As pointed out previously, if the debt is really stock, its redemption may be "essentially equivalent to a dividend" and hence taxed at ordinary rates to the extent of earnings and profits.[98] Also, if instead of being created when the corporation is formed, the debt is distributed later on, receipt of the debt will be taxed as a dividend to the extent of the fair market value of the debt (assuming there are earnings and profits to cover it).[99] In addition, although there is a split of authority here, there are some situations where the debt so distributed has been reclassified as stock, and interest deductions disallowed to the corporation.[100] If this happens, although the receipt of the stock should not give rise to tax,[101] the later redemption of the stock (or payment of the debt) might be subject to "essentially equivalent to a dividend" treatment under Section 302. There is also the further possibility that if the distribution is thought to be equivalent to preferred stock, as a tax-free stock dividend on common or preferred, the preferred so distributed would be Section 306 stock and so give rise to ordinary income upon its redemption or sale.[102] All

[96] Texoma Supply Co., 17 CCH Tax Ct. Mem. 147 (1958).

[97] See J. A. Maurer, Inc., 30 T.C. 1273 (1958), *acquiesced in,* 1959–1 Cum. Bull. 4, and Moore and Sorlien, Adventures in Subchapter S and Section 1244, 14 Tax L. Rev. 453, 493 n.108 (1959), citing Putnam v. Commissioner, 352 U.S. 82 (1956). See also B. Bittker and J. Eustice, Federal Income Taxation of Corporations and Shareholders 125 (1966), and S. Surrey and W. Warren, Federal Income Taxation—Cases and Materials 1195–1196 (1960).

[98] See text accompanying notes 69–70 *supra.*

[99] See B. Bittker and J. Eustice, id. at 195–196.

[100] *Compare* Kraft Foods Co. v. Commissioner, 232 F.2d 118 (2d Cir. 1956), *with* Wetterau Grocery Co. v. Commissioner, 179 F.2d 158 (8th Cir. 1950). And see other cases discussed and criticized in S. Surrey and W. Warren, id. at 1193–1194.

[101] Int. Rev. Code of 1954, §305. Although this section has been amended extensively by the Tax Reform Act of 1969, so as to broaden the number of situations in which a stock dividend may not be received free of tax, stock dividends of the conventional type are still tax free.

[102] See Ch. VI, text accompanying notes 101–131.

of this indicates that if debt is to be used as a means of withdrawing profits from a corporation free of tax, the debt should be created when the corporation is formed, instead of being distributed later on either as a dividend or in exchange for stock.

2.5 SMALL BUSINESS CORPORATION STOCK: SECTION 1244

We have seen that losses on stock or debt are usually given capital loss treatment.[103] In sharp contrast, partnership losses are passed through and deductible by the various partners to the extent of each partner's basis in the firm.[104] When Congress enacted Subchapter S in 1958 as part of a program to stimulate investment in small business and correct the imbalance in tax effect of doing business as a corporation and as a partnership, it also enacted another provision which gives individuals a limited right to deduct losses on stock as ordinary losses. This is of particular importance to those who embark in a venture which involves considerable risk. If the venture fails, they are entitled to the benefits of ordinary loss treatment to the extent provided by Section 1244. If the business is a success, any gain on sale of the stock is taxed at capital gains rates. In this regard the investor in a small business corporation may have the best of both possible worlds. In view of the importance of this provision, and the regrettable tendency of some attorneys and tax consultants to overlook it, as well as its fairly technical character, a reasonably extensive discussion of this area seems in order.

First, it should be observed that Section 1244 losses may be taken only by individuals and not by corporations, trusts or estates. If a partnership composed of individuals owns Section 1244 stock, then losses on the stock may be passed through to the various partners.[105] Furthermore, in order to qualify, an individual or partnership must have held the stock continuously from the date of issuance; the loss is thus not allowed if the stock was acquired by purchase, gift or legacy. Oddly enough, this rule also applies to disqualify losses on stock originally issued to a partnership and distributed by the firm to the various partners.[106] And where Section 1244 stock is sold to the public by means of a "firm" underwriting, whereby the underwriter takes title to the stock and then resells to his customers, the latter, being vendees, are not entitled to deduct losses under Section 1244.[107] Thus underwritings of Section 1244 stock should take the form of a "best efforts" or a "standby" arrangement whereby the underwriter either acts

[103] See text accompanying note 72 *supra*.
[104] See Ch. I, text accompanying note 16.
[105] Treas. Reg. §1.1244(a)–1(c), Ex. (1).
[106] Id. §1.1244(a)–1(c), Ex. (2). For a criticism, see B. Bittker and J. Eustice, Federal Income Taxation of Corporations and Shareholders 140 n.52 (1966).
[107] Treas. Reg. §1.1244(a)–1(b).

merely as selling agent for the issuer or agrees to purchase for its own account any stock left unsold by the issuer.[108]

The stock must be issued to the taxpayer for money or other property, and not for services or for stock or securities.[109] Since the regulations merely prohibit losses on stock if issued for services "rendered or to be rendered to, or for the benefit of, the issuing corporation," [110] there seems to be no reason why such stock may not be issued for property which in turn is earned through the performance of services.[111] Care should be taken, however, to insure that the future Section 1244 shareholder has in fact a property interest with which to pay for the stock and also that his services are rendered to someone other than the corporation, or that there is no understanding that the stock is being issued for future services.

The amount of Section 1244 loss which may be deducted in any one year is limited to $25,000 on an individual return and $50,000 on a joint return.[112] In the latter situation, however, it is not necessary that both spouses own the stock.[113] Where there is a partnership, the limitation is determined separately for each partner.[114] Any losses in excess of the allowable limit are deductible as capital losses. If, because of low taxable income, a taxpayer is able to use up only part of his Section 1244 loss, any unused amount is eligible for treatment as a net operating loss, which can be carried back for a three-year period and carried forward for a five-year period under Section 172.[115] Suppose that an individual sustains a loss of $85,000 on Section 1244 stock. If he files a joint return, he may use $50,000 of the loss as an ordinary deduction. If he should have only $20,000 of taxable income against which to deduct the loss, the $30,000 of unused Section 1244 loss may be carried back or (if carry-back treatment is not feasible because of little or no income in prior years) it may be carried over to future years. That part of the loss which was not deductible under Section 1244 because of the $50,000 limitation (i.e., $35,000) is treated as a

---

[108] For a description of the various forms of underwriting see 1 L. Loss, Securities Regulation 159–172 (2d ed. 1961 and 1969 Supp.). Standby underwriting is sometimes referred to as "strict" or "old fashioned" underwriting and is rarely used.

[109] Int. Rev. Code of 1954, §1244(c)(1)(D), and Treas. Reg. §1.1244(c)–1(f). Thus, if notes or advances, in fact, represent capital contributions rather than debt, they will not qualify as consideration for Section 1244 stock. Hollenbeck v. Commissioner, 422 F.2d 2 (9th Cir. 1970). An exception to the rule that Section 1244 stock may not be issued in exchange for stock or securities is Int. Rev. Code of 1954 §1244(d)(2), and Treas. Reg. §1.1244(d)–3, providing that stock dividends declared with respect to Section 1244 stock also qualify under Section 1244. A similar exception applies to stock issued in a recapitalization or reorganization which involves merely a change in identity, form or place of organization. See Int. Rev. Code of 1954, §368(E), (F).

[110] Treas. Reg. §1.1244(c)–1(f).

[111] See text accompanying note 16 *supra.*

[112] Int. Rev. Code of 1954, §1244(b).

[113] Treas. Reg. §1.1244(b)–1.

[114] Ibid.

[115] Int. Rev. Code of 1954, §1244(d)(3).

capital loss. If Section 1244 loss is carried over as a net operating loss, it is probably deductible as such without diminution by reason of further Section 1244 losses in years to which the unused loss is carried. Thus, in the illustration given, the $30,000 unused Section 1244 loss may be carried over as a net operating loss and fully deducted in another year even though in that year the taxpayer may be using the full amount of his allowable Section 1244 deduction from losses on other stock.[116]

Section 1244 losses may be taken only on common stock of a "small business corporation" which has been issued pursuant to a written plan. The term "common stock" is meant to exclude securities which are convertible into common or common which is convertible into some other security.[117] But the common may be nonvoting.[118] Unlike Subchapter S, there is no requirement that the small business corporation have but one class of stock. Yet, as already stated, Section 1244 losses can be taken only on the common.

A small business corporation is one which has met two tests at the date that the plan to issue the Section 1244 stock was adopted: First, the sum of the aggregate amount of common which may be offered under the plan, plus the aggregate amount of money and other property (valued at adjusted basis to the corporation reduced by any liabilities to which the property was subject or which were assumed) received by the corporation for stock, as a contribution to capital, or as paid in surplus does not exceed $500,000.[119] Secondly, the aggregate amount which may be offered under the plan plus the "equity capital" of the corporation on the date the plan is adopted may not exceed $1 million.[120] A corporation's equity capital is equal to the sum of its money and other property (taken at its adjusted basis to the corporation for determining gain) less its indebtedness (other than indebtedness to shareholders).

A few illustrations of how these tests are applied may be helpful. Suppose a corporation has two classes of stock, one of common, issued for $200,000 in cash, and one of preferred, issued for $200,000 worth of property having a basis to the corporation of $100,000. Since, in applying the limitation of $500,000 on the total amount which may be received by a small business corporation for stock, contributed to capital, or paid in surplus, the *basis* of the property contributed (reduced by any liabilities, of which there are none) is used, rather than its fair market value, this will allow the corporation to issue Section 1244 stock for $200,000 in money or for property having a basis no greater than $200,000.[121] The second test,

---

[116] See B. Bittker and J. Eustice, Federal Income Taxation of Corporations and Shareholders 143 (1966).

[117] Treas. Reg. §1.1244(c)–1(b).

[118] Ibid.

[119] Int. Rev. Code of 1954, §1244(c)(2)(A).

[120] Id. §1244(c)(2)(B).

[121] See Treas. Reg. §1.1244(c)–2(d), Ex. (2).

namely the limitation of $1 million on the equity capital of the corporation, will be met if the corporate assets minus all liabilities other than shareholder-held debt do not exceed $1 million. In applying the latter test, assets are valued at the adjusted basis to the corporation for the purpose of determining gain. It is apparent, then, that, although a corporation such as the one described might qualify initially as a small business corporation, if it should turn into a profitable venture and accumulate a sizable surplus, or if there were to be loans from shareholders, the $1 million test might not be met after the business has reached a certain size. If the Section 1244 plan is adopted *before* the $1 million equity capital limit is exceeded, then stock may be issued under the plan even though the $1 million limit has been exceeded when the stock is actually issued. This is because the date for applying the $1 million equity capital limitation is the date the plan is *adopted*.[122] But it should be noted that, in determining whether the $1 million limit has been exceeded, the total amount which may be offered under the Section 1244 plan must be included. Thus, if a corporation were to have equity capital of $800,000 on the date the plan is adopted, only $200,000 in Section 1244 stock could be issued under the plan. In addition, it should not be forgotten that there is a $500,000 limit on amounts received under the plan or otherwise in payment for stock, as a contribution to capital or as paid in surplus. If, in our illustration the company had already issued stock for $400,000 in money or property (taken at adjusted basis less liabilities), then only $100,000 in stock could be offered under the Section 1244 plan.

The two tests for a small business corporation might then be summarized as imposing a limit on the amount which can be received for stock, contributed to capital or paid in surplus (whether in Section 1244 stock or otherwise), and restricting the overall size of the corporation, as measured by its assets less liabilities other than shareholder-held debt. Both tests must be met when the Section 1244 plan is adopted.

There are several other requirements which must be met. Not only must the Section 1244 stock be common stock issued for money or property (other than services, stock or securities), but it must be issued by a domestic corporation pursuant to a written plan which specifies that the stock may be offered for a period lasting not more than two years after the plan is adopted.[123] At the date the plan is adopted, not only must the corporation qualify as a small business corporation under the tests already mentioned but there must be no portion of a prior offering of stock (whether or not qualified under Section 1244) outstanding.[124] If, while the stock is being offered under the Section 1244 plan, an offering of other stock is made, this automatically terminates the right to offer further Section 1244 stock under

[122] Id., Ex. (3).
[123] Int. Rev. Code of 1954, §1244(c)(1)(A).
[124] Id. §§1244(c)(1)(B) and 1244(c)(1)(C).

that plan. The subsequent offering does not, however, cause the stock which has already been issued under the plan to lose its Section 1244 status.[125] More Section 1244 stock might be issued at a later date when the offering of other stock has terminated, but only under a new plan, which means that the $500,000 and $1 million tests must be applied all over again.[126]

Often a taxpayer loses his right to a Section 1244 loss deduction because his attorney has given insufficient attention to the requirements of a valid Section 1244 plan. As previously stated, the plan must be in writing and must specify in terms of dollars the maximum amount to be received by the corporation for the Section 1244 stock. It must also be clear from the plan that the stock may be issued only within a two-year period running from the date the plan is adopted.[127] According to the regulations, the plan "must appear upon the records of the corporation." [128] Since minutes of a directors' meeting constitute a "plan," [129] it is customary to have a written plan approved by the directors on a particular date, and attached as part of or as an exhibit to the minutes of the directors' meeting. This not only formalizes the plan but fixes the date of its "adoption." [130] The regulations also state that the corporation must maintain records showing the persons to whom the stock was issued, the date of issuance and a description of the consideration received for the stock. If the stock is paid for in property, then the corporate records must show the basis of the property in the hands of the shareholder and its fair market value when received by the corporation. Other corporate records must indicate which certificates represent stock issued pursuant to the plan and also set forth evidence to support the fact that the $500,000 and $1 million tests have been met (i.e., the amount received by the corporation in payment for its stock, as a contribution to capital or as paid in surplus—with property being valued at adjusted basis less liabilities—and also the amount of the corporation's equity capital computed in the manner previously described). Finally, the corporation must record any tax-free stock dividend distributed on Section 1244 stock, or

[125] Treas. Reg. §1.1244(c)–1(h).
[126] Id. §1.1244(c)–1(h)(2).
[127] Id. §1.1244(c)–1(c).
[128] Id. §1.1244(e)–1(a).

[129] Rev. Rul. 66–67, 1966–1 Cum. Bull. 191. However, care must be taken that the directors' minutes are specific enough, clearly identifying the stock to be issued under the plan, stating the maximum amount which may be received in consideration for the stock, the maximum number of shares to be issued and the total period (not more than two years) during which the stock may be issued. See, e.g., Godart v. Commissioner, 425 F.2d 633 (2d Cir. 1970); Childs v. Commissioner, 408 F.2d 531 (3d Cir. 1969); Spillers v. Commissioner, 407 F.2d 530 (5th Cir. 1969); John H. Rickey, 54 T.C. 680 (1970); W. Siebert, 53 T.C. 1 (1970); W. O. Hayden, 52 T.C. 1112 (1969), *acquiesced in,* 1970 Int. Rev. Bull. No. 18, p. 5; Gerald Hoffman, 29 CCH Tax Ct. Mem. 44 (1970).

[130] For discussion of a similar problem regarding the date of "adoption" of a plan to sell corporate assets and liquidate under Code §337, see Ch. VII, text accompanying note 151.

stock issued in exchange for Section 1244 stock pursuant to a reorganization.[131] The shareholder is required to keep records showing the manner in which he acquired the stock, the nature and amount of his payment and, if he paid for it in a nontaxable transaction (e.g., under Section 351) with property, the type of property, its fair market value at the date it was transferred to the corporation and its adjusted basis to him as of that time.[132]

As we have seen, at the date the Section 1244 plan is adopted, there must be no portion of a prior offering outstanding. The regulations provide that stock rights, warrants, options or securities convertible into stock which are outstanding at the time that the plan is adopted are deemed to constitute prior offerings.[133] Hence they must be withdrawn by affirmative action before the Section 1244 plan can be adopted.[134] Similarly, the issuance of stock rights, warrants or options during the period when the Section 1244 stock is being offered constitutes a "subsequent offering" of other stock and so terminates the right to offer Section 1244 stock.[135] All this means simply that when a Section 1244 offering is being made, the issuer may offer no other type of stock. Also the regulations provide that a modification of an existing Section 1244 plan may constitute a "subsequent offering" if the plan is changed to include preferred stock or to increase the amount of stock which may be issued under the plan so that if the total amount, including the increase, had been offered initially, the plan would not have qualified when it was adopted (i.e., the $500,000 or $1 million tests would not have been met). A similar result follows if the plan is extended so as to run for a period of more than two years after the date it was initially adopted.[136] Rather than extend the period of the plan, the proper technique is to cancel the plan and adopt a new one, assuming that the tests for a small business corporation can be met when the second plan is adopted.

A final test must be met before a Section 1244 loss may be deducted. Unlike the other tests, which apply as of the date the plan is adopted, this one is imposed when the loss is sustained (i.e., when the taxpayer sells his stock at a loss or when it becomes worthless). The loss is not deductible unless, for the five most recent taxable years prior to the date the loss is sustained, the corporation derived more than 50 percent of its aggregate gross receipts from sources other than royalties, rents, dividends, interest, annuities and sales or exchanges of stock or securities.[137] If the corporation

---

[131] Treas. Reg. §1.1244(e)–1(a).

[132] Id. §1.1244(e)–1(b).

[133] Id. §1.1244(c)–1(e). For a discussion of analogous problems of when the offer of an option or convertible security constitutes an offer of the underlying security under the Securities Act of 1933, see 1 L. Loss, Securities Regulation 673–686 (2d ed. 1961 and 1969 Supp.).

[134] Treas. Reg. §1.1244(c)–1(e).

[135] Id. §1.1244(c)–1(h)(1).

[136] Id. §1.1244.

[137] Int. Rev. Code of 1954, §1244(c)(1)(E).

has not been in existence for five taxable years, then the gross receipts test must be met for whatever period it has been in existence. In the situation where the corporation has been operating at a loss (i.e., its deductions—other than for net operating loss carry-over, partially tax-exempt interest and dividends received—exceed its gross income), the gross receipts test does not apply.

Suppose a taxpayer has property which has a high adjusted basis relative to its fair market value. If he transfers the property to a corporation in exchange for Section 1244 stock, his basis in the property becomes his basis in the stock. Can he then immediately sell the stock at a loss and receive a deduction against ordinary income? As one might expect, the answer is no. Section 1244(d)(1) provides that the excess of the basis of the property over its fair market value must go to reduce the basis of the Section 1244 stock, *but only for the purpose of computing the amount of Section 1244* (i.e., ordinary) *loss.* Thus, suppose that property having a basis of $12,000 and a fair market value of $7000 is transferred to a corporation in exchange for Section 1244 stock. The stock is later sold for $6000. The basis of the stock for computing the amount of Section 1244 loss is the fair market value of the property previously transferred to the corporation, i.e., $7000, and the amount of Section 1244 loss is thus $1000. However, it should be noted that the *total* loss on the stock is the difference between its basis computed by the regular method under Section 358 ($12,000) and the amount realized on the sale ($6000). Thus $5000 of the loss is deductible as a capital loss and $1000 qualifies as a Section 1244 ordinary loss.

If more than one item of property is transferred to a corporation in exchange for Section 1244 stock, as is often the case, the regulations provide that the properties may be aggregated together for the purpose of computing whether an adjustment in the basis of the stock is necessary if some of the properties have a fair market value lower than basis. Thus, suppose that two properties are transferred, one with a basis of $1000 and a fair market value of $1500 and the other with a basis of $3000 and a fair market value of $2000. The two bases can be added together ($4000) and compared to the sum of the two market values ($3500). Hence, a downward adjustment of only $500 in the basis of the stock is necessary for the purpose of computing the amount of Section 1244 loss on a later sale or worthlessness.[138]

2.6 ADVANTAGES OF SENIOR SECURITIES

Some attention has already been given to the advantages of debt.[139] Mention should now be made of some advantages of other types of senior securities in setting up the capital structure of a closely held corporation. As

[138] Treas. Reg. §1.1244(d)–1(b).
[139] See text accompanying note 68 *supra.*

we have seen, there are limits on the amount of debt which can be prudently used in a given situation, not only from the standpoint of "thinness" in the tax sense but also because of the practical exigencies of preserving the corporation's credit rating. This suggests the use of a more junior security, typically preferred stock. Although preferred does not have any of the tax advantages of debt, aside from its priority to the common in its claim to earnings and in the event of liquidation, there is one advantage to preferred that is not characteristic of debt, namely the ability of one corporation to receive nearly tax-free dividends paid by another corporation. As already mentioned, there is a deduction of 85 percent in the case of dividends received from domestic corporations and, if the paying corporation is an "affiliate" of the recipient corporation, the dividends may be received free of tax if an election to do so is made under Section 243(b)(2) of the 1954 Code.[140] Thus, if one corporation holds stock in another, earnings may be received in large part free from tax, which is not so in the case of interest paid on debt.

There are further advantages to the use of preferred. Where several persons make unequal contributions to a corporation and yet wish to have approximately equal control of its affairs, allowance for the disparity in contributions can be made by providing for differing amounts of preferred stock and debt issued to those who contribute relatively greater amounts of capital. Suppose, for example, that X, Y and Z form a corporation, with X contributing a going business worth $50,000, Y contributing $25,000 in cash and Z contributing only $1000 plus his agreement to render services as a sales manager for five years. If X has sufficient need of Y's additional capital, and Z's future services are considered crucial to the prosperity of the business, then Y and Z may be able to persuade X to share control equally, with each man then being given one third of the common stock. If only one class of common stock is used, and no debt, there will be several unfortunate tax and corporate problems.

Considering the latter (i.e., the corporate problems) it is first clear that, with few exceptions,[141] a corporation may not issue stock for services which have not yet been performed. Many statutes either expressly prohibit the issuance of stock for future services[142] or speak in terms of "labor done" as being the only valid consideration for stock other than property or cash.[143] Thus, in our illustration Z may not be given the stock until the services have been performed, necessitating some arrangement whereby the stock

[140] See Ch. I, text accompanying note 28.
[141] See Petrishen v. Westmoreland Finance Corp., 394 Pa. 552, 147 A.2d 392 (1959) (reasoning that, where a person may be paid cash to leave another's employment and work for the corporation, the latter may require that the cash be invested in stock, in which case there seems little objection to issuing the stock as an inducement without the use of cash as a medium of exchange).
[142] See Model Bus. Corp. Act §19.
[143] E.g., Del. Gen. Corp. Law §152 (1967).

will be escrowed for the five-year period of his employment agreement or a scheme whereby he is paid periodically in stock. He cannot be given voting or dividend rights in the interim with respect to stock which has not been "earned," and this in turn will frustrate the desire of the parties to share control equally from the outset. On the other hand, if through the use of preferred stock and debt issued to X and Y to compensate them for their superior capital contributions, a "high leveraged" but low value common stock may be obtained, Z will be able to pay for all his common with his small contribution of $1000. To do this we might establish the following capital structure:

Assets		Liabilities and Capital	
Business assets (re-		Notes	$25,000
ceived from X)	$49,000	Preferred Stock	48,000
		Common Stock	
Cash	27,000	X	1,000
		Y	1,000
		Z	1,000
Total	$76,000	Total	$76,000

All of the notes could be issued to X, along with one half of the preferred and one third of the common, with the rest of the preferred and one third of the common going to Y. If X is a corporation, however, it may choose to have more preferred stock, because of the dividends-received deduction, already mentioned, or possibly Y may have sufficient bargaining power to receive some of his interest in the form of notes. Whatever result the bargaining between the parties produces, the important feature of the above scheme is that, through the use of senior securities, the value of the common stock has been reduced, enabling Z to purchase his one-third interest for cash and obviating the troublesome corporate problem of issuing stock for services which have not yet been performed.[144]

There are tax advantages as well. Z, in the example above, will receive "compensation income" to the extent that he receives stock for services, whether or not those services have been performed.[145] Thus, with an all common stock structure, and even assuming that stock could be issued to Z for services not yet rendered, Z would have to pay a tax on a one-third interest in the entire corporation ($25,333 or ⅓ of $76,000) in the year the stock is received. As mentioned, the tax will be imposed at ordinary rates. On the other hand, with senior securities providing leverage and lowering the value of the common, not only will the amount of compensation

---

[144] For further analysis see Herwitz, Allocation of Stock Between Services and Capital in the Organization of a Close Corporation, 75 Harv. L. Rev. 1098 (1962).
[145] See text accompanying note 12 *supra*.

income taxable to Z be lessened, but, to the extent that Z is able to pay for his stock in cash, he will receive no compensation income. From Z's standpoint this makes sense not only in terms of taxes but also it gives him essentially what he wants (i.e., one-third interest in future profits accruing to the corporation after payment of carrying charges on the notes and preferred issued to X and Y).

There is one further very important tax advantage to the above arrangement. We have seen that if a person receives more than 20 percent of the outstanding stock of a corporation for services, the transfer of properties by other persons may not be tax free because the transaction will not qualify under Section 351. The reason for this is that services are not property for Section 351 purposes.[146] Thus, unless Z is able to contribute more than a relatively small amount of cash in relation to the total value of the stock he receives,[147] his stock cannot be counted as having been received by a transferor of property. The result will be that X and Y, the only transferors of property in the Section 351 sense, will own only 66⅔ percent of the common, which is well short of control as defined in Section 368(c). If, on the other hand, senior securities are used, Z's stock may be paid for entirely in cash, qualifying him as a transferor of property and rendering the entire exchange tax free.[148] Since there is no requirement that each of the parties own any particular amount of the stock or securities (all three together must, however, own at least 80 percent of the common and 80 percent of each other class of stock), the preferred and notes can be distributed between X and Y in accordance with the particular bargain reached between them.

[146] See text accompanying note 13 *supra.*

[147] See text accompanying note 14 *supra,* and Treas. Reg. §1.351–1(a)(1)(ii).

[148] For further discussion see Herwitz, *supra* at 1098. As the author states, at 1135–1137, the question of whether Z will have compensation income from the receipt of the stock where he has purported to pay for it in cash depends upon a determination of the value of the stock. The Commissioner may argue that, despite the cash payment, the stock is in reality worth more, imposing a tax on the excess of the value over the purchase price (a so-called bargain-purchase theory). Because of the difficulty of valuing the stock of a closely held concern, the outcome is not always predictable. For cases dealing with the question of how much stock issued to promoters is worth when there is a subsequent sale to the public at a higher price, see Elsie L. Dees, 21 CCH Tax Ct. Mem. 833 (1962), and Bruce Berckmans, 20 CCH Tax Ct. Mem. 458 (1961). See also D. Herwitz, Business Planning 273–278 (1966). Essentially the matter turns upon whether, at the time the stock is issued to the promoters, uncertainties surrounding the future prospects of the corporation are such as to inject an element of risk into the situation which is not present when similar stock is later sold to the public, such risk supposedly justifying a lower sale price to the promoters. Considering the problems of proof in this regard, the taxpayer-promoters appear to have been surprisingly successful in persuading courts as to the greater risk. See the *Dees* and *Berckmans* cases, *supra.* If there is no later sale to the public, as is often the case in a closely held concern, this does not mean that there was not a bargain purchase initially. The essential question remains the same, i.e., how much was the stock worth when it was purchased?

2.7　ADVANTAGES OF LEASING

In some situations it may be disadvantageous for the owners of a business to transfer all of its assets to a newly formed corporation. For example, it has already been pointed out that transfer of depreciable properties by an individual to an 80-percent-owned corporation may result in ordinary income.[149] Ordinary income may also result from the depreciation recapture provisions of Sections 1245 and 1250. If for some reason the transfer cannot be made tax free under the provisions of Section 351, and if the transferor has no substantial losses from other sources to absorb the gain recognized on the transfer, it may be better to retain title to the properties and lease them to the corporation. If a substantial part of the properties might otherwise have been transferred in exchange for debt, this also avoids the thin incorporation problem previously discussed.

Although it might seem that if a taxpayer could sell property to his corporation, there should be no problem about leasing it, care should be taken that the lease is really a lease and not in substance a sale with a mortgage back, a conditional sale, or a contribution to capital followed by a series of dividend payments. The problem of how to tell the difference is the familiar one of substance versus form. If the lease really is a lease, then no gain or loss will be realized on transferring possession of the property to the corporation, the rental payments will be deductible by the latter and taxed as ordinary income to the lessor and the lessor will be entitled to deduct depreciation on the leased properties.[150] If the lease is in substance a sale with a mortgage back, gain or loss will be realized on the sale and recognized depending upon how the transaction may fit within the tax-free transfer provisions of Section 351 or, if it does not, whether Sections 1239, 1245, and 1250 (in the case of gain) and Section 267 (in the case of loss) apply. The payments made by the corporation on the lease will not be deductible if the lease is in substance a mortgage, except to the extent that the payments constitute interest on the unpaid balance of the "loan." Such interest is taxable to the shareholder-"mortgagee" at ordinary rates. Since he no longer owns the property, the corporation and not he will be entitled to deduct depreciation.[151] There is also the possibility that the payments by the corporation might be treated as installment payments of the purchase price rather than mortgage payments. If this happens, the situation is, as we have seen, somewhat unclear in view of the tendency of some courts to consider the installment payment agreement as boot (i.e., not a security) in what otherwise would be a Section 351 transfer, and other courts to take

---

[149] See text accompanying note 3 *supra*.
[150] See Rev. Rul. 55–540, 1955–2 Cum. Bull. 39.
[151] Ibid.

the view that an installment sale can never qualify, even as boot, as part of a Section 351 exchange.[152] This divergence in judicial approach, together with the problem of whether a particular installment sale is a separate and non-interdependent part of a prior Section 351 exchange,[153] makes it difficult to predict how the transferor will be taxed. In any event the transferor will lose his right to deduct depreciation on the properties and the corporation will be able to deduct not only depreciation but also any component of the installment payments which represents interest due on the unpaid balance of the purchase price.

The final possibility is that the transfer will be treated as a contribution to capital, rather than as a sale with a mortgage back or an installment purchase, and the subsequent payments by the corporation will be taxed as dividends to the transferor of the property. The transfer to the corporation will not result in tax if it was part of a Section 351 exchange and the corporation will be entitled to deduct depreciation, although it will not, of course, be entitled to deduct the dividend payments, which are taxed to the shareholder to the extent of corporate earnings and profits.

There are few real guidelines as to precisely when a lease will be recast into one of the above alternative business arrangements or as to which particular one will be chosen. Nevertheless, there are several things which should be avoided if at all possible. Neither the rental payments nor the period of the lease should correspond generally with the payments or the period which might prevail in an installment purchase or a sale financed by a mortgage.[154] Also the rental payments should not exceed the fair rental value of the property.[155] It goes without saying that no portion of the rent should be designated as "interest" or otherwise be identifiable as equivalent to interest and no portion of any payment should be applicable to an equity to be acquired by the lessee.[156] It is particularly hazardous to provide that, after a designated number of payments, the lessee may take title to the property or that it may do so on payment of an additional sum which is nominal in relation to the fair value of the property at the time the option to purchase is exercised.[157] In summary, as in the thin capital situation, the facts of each case are likely to be considered in the light of the real or presumed intent of the parties. If the facts support a finding of an arm's-length lease on terms which approximate those which would be found in a lease with an outsider, then the form of the transaction may be respected. If

[152] See text accompanying note 41 *supra*.
[153] See text accompanying note 42 *supra*.
[154] Rev. Rul. 55–540, 1955–2 Cum. Bull. 39.
[155] Ibid.
[156] Ibid.
[157] Ibid. See, in general, Kirby, Considerations in Business Lease Arrangements, 34 Taxes 34 (1956); Blumenthal and Harrison, The Tax Treatment of the Lease with an Option to Purchase, 32 Texas L. Rev. 839 (1954); Note, Tax Treatment of "Lessors" and "Lessees" Under Lease-Purchase Agreements, 62 Yale L.J. 273 (1953).

the terms of the deal resemble those which would characterize a purchase, then the form of the lease will be disregarded in favor of its substance, a purchase either by installments or financed through a mortgage. Finally, and particularly if the payments are excessive either as rentals (as they *purport* to be) or as payments of the purchase price (which they *might* be), either the excessive amount or possibly the entire amount of the payment may be considered as a disguised dividend with the initial transfer being considered as a contribution to capital.[158] As pointed out, this is particularly disadvantageous to the corporation since it loses its right to deduct that part of the payments which constitutes a dividend, being left with only a depreciation deduction, which, of course, the former owner of the property loses.

2.8 MULTIPLE CORPORATIONS

It will often be cumbersome and unwise for a closely held concern to form more than one corporation, but there may be some advantages of doing so in particular situations. Although each corporation may be entitled to a separate $25,000 surtax exemption, as well as an automatic credit of $100,000 in computing any tax on excess accumulations of earnings,[159] it is extremely hazardous to form several corporations if the principal purpose[160] or even a "major purpose"[161] of doing so is to get the benefit of additional surtax exemptions. On the whole it is necessary to show that the main reasons for setting up several corporations were not tax reasons. And even if the transaction qualifies in this sense, members of an "affiliated group" of corporations (e.g., subsidiaries which are 80 percent owned by a parent) will collectively be entitled to but one surtax exemption and one

---

[158] See, e.g., Stanwick's Inc., 15 T.C. 556 (1951), *aff'd per curiam,* 190 F.2d 84 (4th Cir. 1951); Iron City Industrial Cleaning Corp., 6 CCH Tax Ct. Mem. 1237 (1947). For a collection of further cases see B. Bittker and J. Eustice, Federal Income Taxation of Corporations and Shareholders 171 n.55 (1966), and S. Surrey and W. Warren, Federal Income Taxation—Cases and Materials 1205–1206 (1960).

[159] See Ch. I, text accompanying note 39.

[160] Int. Rev. Code of 1954, §269(a)(1). For cases using this provision to disallow surtax exemptions to newly created subsidiaries, see B. Bittker and J. Eustice, id. at 636 n.50.

[161] Int. Rev. Code of 1954, §1551. As D. Herwitz, Business Planning 179 (1966), points out, there may be a question whether this provision reaches the simultaneous organization of two or more corporations, as where several corporations are formed to take over a going business. However, if the major purpose of forming the subsidiaries is to gain surtax exemptions, the latter would probably be disallowed, if not under Section 1551, then under some other provision, e.g., Int. Rev. Code of 1954, §269(a)(1), or §482. The regulations specifically state that Section 269 is applicable where "A person or persons organize two or more corporations instead of a single corporation in order to secure the benefit of multiple surtax exemptions. . . ." Treas. Reg. §1.269–3(b)(2).

credit of $100,000 for the purpose of determining the penalty tax on excess accumulations of earnings.[162] Finally, Section 482, an extremely broad provision, permits the Internal Revenue Service to reallocate items of gross income, deductions, credits and other allowances among corporations which are owned or controlled directly or indirectly by the same interests, if this is necessary "to prevent evasion of taxes or clearly to reflect the income" of any of the corporations.[163] Similar "reallocation" has been achieved through the even broader Section 61, which merely taxes a person or corporation on all income "from whatever source derived." [164]

Although it is sometimes suggested [165] that where there are advantages in having some of the properties transferred in a taxable exchange and others transferred free of tax, it might be possible to set up two corporations, qualify the transfer to the first under Section 351 and have the second transfer fall outside Section 351 (e.g., through retention by the transferors of less than 80 percent control), this tactic is likely to be hazardous if motivated primarily by tax reasons, due to the Code provisions already mentioned, as well as the well-known judicial proclivity to regard two or more formally separate transactions as one in substance if the separation is dictated by tax exigencies rather than business or economic realities.[166] This does not mean, however, that, given a multi-corporate scheme which is independently justified by sound nontax purposes, one may not take advantage of it in terms of taxes. Thus it may be advisable to have each entity adopt a taxable year and accounting method best suited to its particular needs, and in certain situations[167] it may be easier to qualify a smaller separate entity for specialized tax treatment than the entire business operation. Furthermore, where parts of the business are expected to be sold at a later date, the creation of multiple entities at the outset may be a useful and more flexible

[162] Int. Rev. Code of 1954, §1561, as amended by the Tax Reform Act of 1969. Prior to the amendment, members of an affiliated group could elect multiple surtax exemptions by paying an additional tax at the rate of 6 percent on the first $25,000 of taxable income. This can still be done, to a limited extent, in accordance with a schedule of gradually decreasing exemptions and credits, until the taxable year ending December 31, 1974. See id. §1564.

[163] Id. §482.

[164] See Aldon Homes, Inc., 33 T.C. 582 (1959).

[165] See, e.g., 1 G. Hornstein, Corporation Law and Practice 47 (1959).

[166] See B. Bittker and J. Eustice, Federal Income Taxation of Corporations and Shareholders 672 (1966), suggesting that courts may disregard separate corporate entities or tax one corporation on another's income by application of assignment of income principles.

[167] E.g., the special tax treatment for Western Hemisphere Trade Corporations under Int. Rev. Code of 1954, §§921–922. Also it is sometimes suggested that one corporation might qualify for or wish a Subchapter S election whereas others might not qualify or wish it. However, if one of the corporations wishes to elect Subchapter S treatment, care should be taken that it is not part of an "affiliated group" (i.e., is not under 80 percent control with the other corporations), since the election is not available to members of an "affiliated group." See Ch. I, text accompanying note 86.

method of achieving capital gains treatment, rather than cope with the vagaries of Section 355 ("spin-offs," "split-ups," etc.), Section 346 (partial liquidations) or Section 341 (collapsible corporations).[168]

If more than one corporation is formed and it is necessary to do business in several states, since each corporation doing business in a state other than its state of domicile must qualify as a foreign corporation and pay franchise and other taxes, qualification of several entities may increase the overall cost of doing business. Conversely, it may be possible to avoid qualifying the entire business under the laws of a particular jurisdiction by operating through a subsidiary, which can be either formed under the laws of that state or qualified to do business therein. Whether the parent corporation must also qualify to do business in a particular state will depend upon the extent and nature of its activities within that state as well as the attitude of that state's courts and agencies.[169] However, if the parent's only activities within a state consist of the solicitation of orders for sales of tangible personal property and the orders are sent outside the state for approval or rejection and then filled by shipment or delivery from outside the state, federal law precludes the imposition of a state income tax on income derived from within the state.[170] Whether or not it will be less expensive to do business through several corporations can thus be determined only on the basis of a given fact situation.

A major purpose of forming more than one corporation may be to attain limited liability and prevent the entire business from being exposed to the risks of each particular phase of the business. If manufacture of the product involves considerable hazards, risks of manufacture may be confined to that part of the business by forming a separate corporation. If the corporation is not grossly undercapitalized or so conducted as to invite judicial scrutiny and classification as merely a "sham," [171] liability will be confined to one entity rather than threatening the entire business. Also the exigencies of dealing with particular unions and specialized needs of management and labor may make a separate corporation more convenient. Sometimes it is considered desirable to finance through a subsidiary rather than have all of the financing incurred by a single organization.[172] And separate organiza-

---

168 See B. Bittker and J. Eustice, id. at 671.

169 For a collection of cases see M. Caplin, Doing Business in Other States (1959).

170 See the Federal Interstate Income Act, 73 Stat. 555 (1959), 15 U.S.C. §381. For a good discussion see 3 Z. Cavitch, Business Organizations §61.03[2][b] (1968).

171 The classic article in this area is Douglas and Shanks, Insulation from Liability Through Subsidiary Corporations, 39 Yale L.J. 193 (1929). For other authorities see W. Cary, Cases and Materials on Corporations 134–143 (4th ed. unabr. 1969). Separate corporations have been used and no doubt abused in the transportation industry, particularly with the device of separately incorporated taxicabs. See, e.g., Walkovszky v. Carlton, 18 N.Y.2d 414, 223 N.E.2d 6, 276 N.Y.S.2d 585 (1966), and Note, "Piercing the Taxi Medallion," 19 N.Y.U. Intra. L. Rev. 1 (1963).

172 This technique has been used for years in connection with tanker financing and has been adapted to pipeline financing by the use of the so-called through-put

tions may be used to simplify marketing and other problems and increase operating efficiency, although sometimes this can be done through the use of a division rather than the formal creation of a separate subsidiary. Finally, it may be desirable to give certain individuals stock in a company which corresponds generally with their particular area of responsibility, e.g., give a sales manager stock in a corporation which acts as a selling agent for the manufacturing entity. Along with stock might go a title, such as President of Ajax Sales, Inc., which may sound more impressive than sales manager or Vice-President for Sales in the parent concern. However, it will often not be profitable to create new corporations solely for the purpose of allocating responsibility or creating separate patterns of ownership in different phases of the business in view of the increased complexities of dealing with several entities. Thus, although it may be desirable to give one person control of the selling end of the business, if he is given a controlling interest in the selling corporation, it is difficult (but not impossible) to prevent his receiving a major share of the profits. Since this is often undesirable, more complex control schemes, such as classification of shares, must be used. Along with increased expense and effort, and the necessity of keeping separate books, records, holding separate directors' and shareholders' meetings, and preparing separate state and federal returns (unless a consolidated tax return is filed), there are several tax disadvantages. Losses from one corporation may not be offset against profits of another (unless the returns are consolidated), and it may be difficult to transfer income from one of several controlled corporations to another without the transaction being taxed as an imputed dividend to the controlling shareholder or, if the transfer takes the form of a loan, being attacked as an unreasonable accumulation of surplus by the lending corporation.[173]

Rather than create several corporations, it may at times be beneficial to operate in hybrid fashion by using a corporation and one or more partnerships. A useful alternative to a shareholders' pooling agreement or a voting trust as a means of insuring that control will be kept within a small group of shareholders is to have the shares held by a partnership.[174] Also a combination of different entities with leases or other operating agreements may have special advantages, as where title to properties is held by a corporation and the properties are leased to a partnership for operational purposes. However, one should be wary of tax traps in such arrangements, such as the

---

agreement (the subsidiary borrows the money and the parent agrees to "put through" the subsidiary's pipeline a certain quantity of oil, gas, etc., so that the subsidiary will be put in funds to meet the sinking fund and carrying charges on the debt). For a good discussion see Everdell and Longstreth, Some Special Problems Raised by Debt Financing of Corporations Under Common Control, 17 Bus. Law. 500 (1962). See also Gant, Illusion in Lease Financing, 37 Harv. Bus. Rev. 121 (March-April 1959).

[173] See Treas. Reg. §1.537–2(c)(3).

[174] See Ch. III, text accompanying notes 83–155.

imposition of personal holding company surtax where rents constitute less than 50 percent of the corporation's adjusted ordinary gross income.[175] Also, as we have seen, the broad provisions of Section 482 permit reallocation of income, deductions, credits, etc., among various businesses, whether or not incorporated, "to prevent evasion of taxes or clearly to reflect the income of any of such organizations, trades, or businesses."

All of this suggests that it is unwise for a small, closely held enterprise to fragment itself into several entities unless there are pressing business reasons for doing so. And even if separate corporations are a wise choice, care should be taken that each is adequately capitalized for that particular activity in which it is engaged, that the formalities of separate corporate life are observed (separate directors' meetings, shareholders' meetings, books, bank and other accounts), that dealings between the corporations be as much as possible at arm's length (no contracts which are unduly advantageous to one corporation at another's expense) and that all dealings with the public are consistent with the concept that separate corporations are involved (avoid collective advertising or misleading letterheads). It is of paramount importance that each corporation be functionally justified, i.e., that the various corporations correspond with natural divisions of the business rather than artificial or obviously tax-motivated ones. Thus, for a real estate business it might be desirable to form separate corporations for long-term investment in land, for development (i.e., construction of new buildings) and for sales of houses to the public. Separate incorporation of each building or house is in most cases artificial and implies an exclusive tax motivation.[176] Similarly, separate corporations for separate retail stores, particularly if engaged in different lines of business (e.g., women's clothing, men's clothing) may be justified. Separate incorporation of each floor of a building will not.[177]

[175] See Int. Rev. Code of 1954, §543(a)(2).

[176] See Aldon Homes, Inc., 33 T.C. 582 (1959). Query on separately incorporated taxicabs. See note 171 *supra*.

[177] See generally 3 Z. Cavitch, Business Organizations §61.03(1)(a) (1968).

III   Maintaining Control of the Close Corporation

We must now consider problems which may be thought of as the core of close corporation law, the various ways in which those who form a close corporation may keep it "close," i.e., methods for maintaining the control which in most cases is a necessity. Along with the need for maintaining control is the need for retaining a meaningful interest in the enterprise, and this involves the problem of "squeeze-outs" by a majority shareholder of a minority shareholder. Since the problem of maintaining control and the problem of squeeze-outs are inextricably intertwined, both relating to the preservation of a shareholder's status in the firm, it is difficult to consider the one without the other. More often than not, a principal way in which to prevent a squeeze-out is through intelligent drafting of the various instruments involved in setting up the corporation, such as the articles of incorporation, bylaws, preincorporation agreement and shareholders' agreement. However, in the interests of simplicity we shall first consider the substantive problems raised by various control devices together with general points of draftsmanship, and then in the following chapter proceed with a detailed discussion of various squeeze-out devices and what may be done to forestall them.

3.1   STOCK TRANSFER RESTRICTIONS

A common wish of those who form a closely held concern is the desire to control who shall be their associates. As we know, members of a partnership exercise what amounts to a veto power over the taking in of new partners. Thus, although a partner may assign his right to profits or his right to whatever distribution may be made on dissolution of the firm,[1] no person may become a member of a partnership without the consent of all the other partners unless this is expressly provided in the partnership agreement.[2] Since a closely held corporation is in an analogous situation, and is sometimes referred to as a "chartered partnership," it is altogether understand-

[1] Uniform Partnership Act §27.
[2] Id. §18(g).

able that the shareholders, who may have been partners with one another formerly, may wish to retain veto powers similar to those permitted in the case of a partnership. Thus, at first blush there would seem to be no problem with the validity of these restrictions from the policy standpoint. As Holmes, when Chief Justice of the Supreme Judicial Court of Massachusetts put it, in a leading early decision: "there seems to be no greater objection to retaining the right of choosing one's associates in a corporation than in a firm." [3]

In view of this it is indeed odd that there has been so much furor in the American cases about the validity of stock transfer restrictions. When one considers that nearly all restrictions on transfer are upheld in England as matters of simple contract law,[4] either the courts in this country appear to have been curiously obstinate in refusing to recognize the importance of freedom of individuals to contract with one another, or there must have been some particularly pressing policy reason which was thought to justify the intense scrutiny which has at times been focused upon various restrictions.

The supposed policy which sets limits on freedom of contract is that of discouraging or prohibiting "unreasonable restraints on alienation of personal property." Most of the early cases dealing with the validity of restraints were impressed with the fact that since stock is, often by express statutory fiat, "personal property," [5] the latter should be freely transferable as a matter of public policy. In view of the doubtful marketability of much stock in closely held concerns, and the close, although not perfect analogy to a partnership, it is curious that American courts have been so preoccupied with preserving free transferability rather than freedom of contract. Yet we must keep in mind that, legally speaking, a partner is never "locked in" to a firm, since he can dissolve it at any time, although doing so may expose him to liability for breach of the partnership agreement.[6] Corporations are not normally subject to dissolution at the will of any shareholder. Under virtually all statutes, voluntary dissolution requires the vote of at least those holding a simple majority of the outstanding shares and involuntary dissolution requires a showing of oppression, fraud or some other reason sufficient to convince a court of the wisdom of bringing an end to the firm.[7] Hence, in view of the possible locked-in predicament of the shareholder in the closely held firm, one could rationalize a different policy as regards the transferability of shares than the transferability of partnership interests. On

---

[3] Barrett v. King, 181 Mass. 476, 479, 63 N.E. 934, 935 (1902).

[4] See Gower, Some Contrasts Between British and American Corporation Law, 69 Harv. L. Rev. 1369, 1377–1378 (1956).

[5] E.g., Del. Gen. Corp. Law §159 (1967). The 1967 amendments to the Delaware law made Delaware perhaps the most progressive state in encouraging freedom to enter into stock transfer restrictions. See id. §202 (1967).

[6] See Uniform Partnership Act §31.

[7] See Ch. VII, text accompanying note 68.

the other hand, as in the case of partnerships, shareholders in a closely held corporation are relatively free to agree on rights of dissolution; in other words they need not be locked in if they agree to the contrary. There seems to be no policy reason for permanence merely because a firm happens to be incorporated. Thus it may have been unwise for courts to have focused on the supposed value of free transferability of shares in contrast to the equally important freedom to agree not only as to how shares shall be transferred but also as to other matters, including when the corporation might be dissolved.

Nonetheless, perhaps partly through a quirk of history and an early declaration by the United States Supreme Court that, at least as regards national banks, restraints on the transfer of shares created "secret liens" which were against public policy and threatened the interests of depositors and other creditors,[8] many of the early decisions weighted the scales in favor of free transferability of shares, unless restrictions were expressly permitted by statute.[9]

---

[8] First Natl. Bank v. Lanier, 78 U.S. (11 Wall.) 369 (1871), interpreting the repeal by the Currency Act of 1864, ch. 106, §62, 13 Stat. 118 (1864), of an earlier provision in the Currency Act of 1863, ch. 58, §36, 12 Stat. 675 (1863), which permitted restrictions on stock in national banks, to be an implied Congressional declaration that such restraints must be against public policy. For further discussion see Painter, Stock Transfer Restrictions: Continuing Uncertainties and a Legislative Proposal, 6 Vill. L. Rev. 48, 51–52 (1960).

[9] See, e.g., Farmers' & Merchants' Bank v. Wasson, 48 Iowa 336, 340 (1878); Driscoll v. West Bradley & Cary Mfg. Co., 59 N.Y. 96, 105 (1874); Kretzer v. Cole Bros. Lightning Rod Co., 193 Mo. App. 99, 181 S.W. 1066 (1916); O'Brien v. Cummings, 13 Mo. App. 197 (1883). Later cases argued that restrictions are valid unless expressly prohibited by statute. See, e.g., Mason v. Mallard Telephone Co. 213 Iowa 1076, 1079, 240 N.W. 671, 672 (1932). Since the statutes only referred to restrictions in general terms, the legislative intent in this regard would be ambiguous. Thus, in the *Mason* case the statute merely gave the corporation power to "render the interests of the shareholders transferable" and in *Driscoll, supra,* it merely authorized bylaws for "the regulation of the company's affairs, and for the transfer of its stock." In Massachusetts a statute requiring the articles of incorporation to set forth the "restrictions, if any, imposed upon . . . transfer [of the shares]" was construed as an implied grant of authority to place an absolute restraint on alienation of stock. Longyear v. Hardman, 219 Mass. 405, 106 N.E. 1012 (1914). The *Longyear* decision drew an interesting but questionable analogy between restraining the alienation of stock and restraining the alienation of church pews; absolute restraints as to the latter have been traditionally valid in Massachusetts. See Crocker v. Old South Society, 106 Mass. 489 (1871); French v. Old South Society, 106 Mass. 479 (1871). Query whether Chief Justice Holmes' reasoning in Barrett v. King, 181 Mass. 476, 479, 63 N.E. 934, 935 (1902), concerning the right to choose one's associates was thought applicable on an *a fortiori* basis when it came to Sunday morning services. At any rate, due to the limited interest in marketability of pews, the reasoning of these cases is hardly persuasive when applied to stock. For a more recent case allowing what amounts to "callable common" stock on the basis of a statutory provision of a very general nature, see Lewis v. H. P. Hood & Sons, 331 Mass. 670, 121 N.E.2d 850 (1954), noted in 68 Harv. L. Rev. 1240 (1955); 54 Mich. 132 (1955), 103 U. Pa. L. Rev. 819 (1955). See also Note, 48 A.L.R.2d 392 (1956). Although callable common stock is not permitted in England, the attitude of the Massachusetts courts appears more English than American, stressing

The main factors which determine the validity of various types of restrictions are (1) the form of the restriction, (2) the location of the restriction, whether it is in the articles of incorporation, the bylaws or is imposed by a shareholders' agreement, (3) the overall objectives of the restriction, particularly as related to the type of business in which the corporation happens to be engaged, and (4) express or implied requirements of statutory law.

The first two of the foregoing have been of the greatest importance. Thus, although an absolute prohibition on transfer or a restriction which requires the consent of the directors or other shareholders before a transfer may be made has almost uniformly been held invalid,[10] so-called first option or first refusal type restrictions, giving an option to purchase the stock upon the happening of a specified condition, have been upheld if "reasonable." [11] A survey of the cases indicates that nearly all restrictions of the latter type have been held reasonable, even where there has been a wide

---

the importance of freedom of contract. See Gower, Some Contrasts Between British and American Corporation Law, 69 Harv. L. Rev. 1369, 1378 (1956). For a recent case exemplifying the Massachusetts approach and upholding a consent-type restriction, see Colbert v. Hennessey, 351 Mass. 131, 217 N.E.2d 914 (1966).

[10] People ex rel. Malcolm v. Lake Sand Corp., 251 Ill. App. 499 (1929); Farmers' & Merchants' Bank v. Wasson, 48 Iowa 336, 340 (1878); Steele v. Farmers' & Merchants' Mutual Telephone Assn., 95 Kan. 580, 148 Pac. 661 (1915); Rafe v. Hindin, 23 N.Y.2d 759, 244 N.E.2d 469, 296 N.Y.S.2d 955 (1968); Fisher v. Bush, 35 Hun 641 (N.Y. Sup. Ct. 1885); Miller v. Farmers' Milling & Elevator Co., 78 Neb. 441, 110 N.W. 995 (1907); Morris v. Hussong Dyeing Machine Co., 81 N.J. Eq. 256, 86 Atl. 1026 (Ch. 1913); State ex rel. Howland v. Olympia Veneer Co., 138 Wash. 144, 244 Pac. 261 (1926); In re Klaus, 67 Wis. 401, 29 N.W. 582 (1886). For useful discussions of the validity of particular restrictions, see 2 F. O'Neal, Close Corporations: Law and Practice §§7.01–7.29 (1958); Bradley, Stock Transfer Restrictions and Buy-Sell Agreements, [1969] Ill. L.F. 139; Cataldo, Stock Transfer Restrictions and the Closed Corporation, 37 Va. L. Rev. 229 (1951); Hayes, Corporation Cake with Partnership Frosting, 40 Iowa L. Rev. 157 (1954); Hornstein, Judicial Tolerance of the Incorporated Partnership, 18 Law & Contemp. Prob. 435 (1953); O'Neal, Restrictions on Transfer of Stock in Closely Held Corporations: Planning and Drafting, 65 Harv. L. Rev. 773 (1952); Painter, Stock Transfer Restrictions: Continuing Uncertainties and a Legislative Proposal, 6 Vill. L. Rev. 48, 51–52 (1960). For additional secondary materials see 2 F. O'Neal, Close Corporations: Law and Practice §7.01 n.1, (1958), and Hayes, *supra* at 157 n.3. See also Notes, 61 A.L.R.2d 1318 (1958); 2 A.L.R.2d 745 (1948); 138 A.L.R. 647 (1942); 65 A.L.R. 1159 (1930). A special group of cases confined largely to small telephone companies, cooperative apartment houses and farmers' cooperatives has upheld even consent-type restrictions. See, e.g., Mason v. Mallard Telephone Co., 213 Iowa 1076, 240 N.W. 671 (1932); 68 Beacon Street, Inc. v. Sohier, 289 Mass. 354, 194 N.E. 303 (1935); Penthouse Properties, Inc. v. 1158 Fifth Avenue, Inc., 256 App. Div. 685, 11 N.Y.S.2d 417 (1939); Chaffee v. Farmers' Co-operative Elevator Co., 39 N.D. 585, 168 N.W. 616 (1918). For other cases see Painter, *supra* at 55 n.20.

[11] See, e.g., Lawrence v. Sudman, 70 F. Supp. 387 (S.D.N.Y. 1945); Lawson v. Household Finance Corp., 17 Del. Ch. 343, 152 Atl. 723 (Sup. Ct. 1930); Douglas v. Aurora Daily News Co., 160 Ill. App. 506 (1911); New England Trust Co. v. Spaulding, 310 Mass. 424, 38 N.E.2d 672 (1941); Krauss v. Kuechler, 300 Mass. 346, 15 N.E.2d 207 (1938); Prindiville v. Johnson & Higgins, 92 N.J. Eq. 515, 113 Atl. 915 (Ch. 1921), *aff'd*, 93 N.J. Eq. 425, 116 Atl. 785 (Ct. Err. & App. 1922); Feldstein's Estate, 25 Pa. Dist. 602 (Orphan's Ct. 1915).

discrepancy between the option price and the fair value of the stock at the time the option to purchase was exercised [12] or, indeed, a considerable variance between the two at the time the restriction was entered into.[13] A useful rule might then be that if a restriction takes any form other than a first refusal or option, it should be regarded as of doubtful validity in the absence of an express statutory provision. In this regard, statutes containing only a general permission to impose stock transfer restrictions should not normally suffice. Thus only statutes such as that of Wyoming and the more recent Delaware provision which expressly permit consent-type restraints should be relied upon.[14] Similar reasoning might be extended to those provisions which are occasionally used to prohibit transfer of the stock to specified classes of persons (i.e., competitors or non-employees).[15] Although the restraint in these cases is obviously less than an absolute prohibition or consent-type restraint, and can more easily be justified on the grounds of a reasonable business purpose, it is still safer to cast the restriction in the form of a first refusal which can be made to apply to *any* transfer, regardless of the particular transferee. It is sometimes suggested that an absolute or consent-type restraint may be valid if limited to a relatively short period of time. Although these may be useful in specialized situations, such as to reinforce an exemption from registration requirements under the Securities Act of 1933,[16] there are surprisingly few cases which

[12] See Allen v. Biltmore Tissue Corp., 2 N.Y.2d 534, 141 N.E.2d 812, 161 N.Y.S.2d 418 (1957).

[13] See In re Estate of Mather, 410 Pa. 361, 189 A.2d 586 (1963) (purchase price was $1 per share notwithstanding the fact that when the agreement of repurchase was entered into, stock was worth at least $50 per share). For an argument that such wide disparity between price and value may amount, in effect, to an absolute restraint on transfer, see Osborn, Developments in Corporate Law, 19 Bus. Law. 577, 587 (1964); Notes, 72 Harv. L. Rev. 555 (1959); 48 Minn. L. Rev. 808 (1964); 59 Nw. L. Rev. 91 (1964); 16 Stan. L. Rev. 449 (1964). For other cases see 2 F. O'Neal, Close Corporations 9 n.22 (1958).

[14] Del. Gen. Corp. Law §202 (1967); Wyo. Bus. Corp. Act §32(d) (1965). For more general statutory provisions see Ark. Bus. Corp. Act §64–211 (1966); Conn. Stock Corp. Act §33–306(a) (1960); Tex. Bus. Corp. Act art. 2.22(B)(2) (1965).

[15] See, e.g., Kretzer v. Cole Bros. Lightning Rod Co., 193 Mo. App. 99, 181 S.W. 1066 (1916) (holding such a restriction invalid). Gray suggested that there may be a valid distinction between a restriction on transfer to designated individuals and a restriction on transfer to all persons other than a selected few. J. Gray, Restraints on the Alienation of Property 30 (2d ed. 1895). This merely points up the fact that the extent of the restraint may be a matter of degree. Query whether such a restraint should be held invalid if its purposes could have been achieved through a simple first refusal provision.

[16] See When Corporations Go Public 21–23 (C. Israels and G. Duff eds. 1962). As 2 F. O'Neal, id. at 4 n.4.11 points out, restrictions prohibiting transfer except in compliance with the Securities Act might possibly be considered invalid. Query, however, whether the classical prejudice against impairing transferability might be unjustified where transferring the shares might be in violation of federal or state law. A similar problem arises in connection with restraints imposed in order to protect a Subchapter S election, whether the restraint takes the form of a prohibition against transfer to a shareholder who refuses to consent to the Subchapter S election or the safer provision which merely gives the corporation or its shareholders a right

stress the limited duration of a consent restraint as a basis for its validity. Similarly, there appear to have been few modern cases discussing the validity of consent restraints imposed for particular purposes, such as Securities Act registration.[17]

Some of the early cases invalidated even first refusal restrictions if they were contained only in the bylaws and not in the articles of incorporation.[18] The reasoning of these early cases is often confused, and no doubt the result was influenced by the early hostility to all transfer restrictions regardless of form. Often those who contested the validity of the bylaw alleged that they had not agreed to it, and courts were inclined to hold that, unless the restriction was in the articles, it would not automatically bind all shareholders. This reasoning was also used to uphold restrictions when applied to those who *had* consented to the adoption of a bylaw, the cases stating that even if the bylaw were invalid as such, it could still bind those who had consented to its adoption as a simple contract.[19] From this it follows that a restriction is not required to be either in the articles or in the bylaws but may be in a shareholders' agreement, in which case it binds the parties to the agreement and their successors in interest (i.e., those who purchase stock held by parties to the agreement) if the restriction is noted on the stock certificate.[20] This latter requirement, that the restriction be noted on the stock certificate, is necessary under the Uniform Commercial Code and a predecessor provision in the Uniform Stock Transfer Act whenever the restriction has been "imposed by the issuer." [21] Since its function is to give purchasers of the stock notice of the restriction, failure to comply will result in a purchaser taking free of the restriction unless he has

of first refusal in the event of a proposed transfer. See Ch. I, text accompanying note 114. As we have seen, the Delaware statute now expressly authorizes restraints of this type. See Ch. I, note 115.

[17] Cf. Prudential Petroleum Corp. v. Rauscher, Pierce & Co., 281 S.W.2d 457, 460–461 (Tex. Civ. App. 1955) (dictum, restriction valid if placed on stock certificate). See also Israels, Some Commercial Overtones of Private Placement, 45 Va. L. Rev. 851 (1959).

[18] See, e.g., Brinkerhoff-Farris Trust & Savings Co. v. Home Lumber Co., 118 Mo. 447, 24 S.W. 129 (1893); Robertson v. L. Nicholes Co., 141 Misc. 660, 253 N.Y.S. 76 (Mun. Ct. 1931); Ireland v. Globe Milling & Reduction Co., 19 R.I. 180, 32 Atl. 921 (1895); Petre v. Bruce, 157 Tenn. 131, 7 S.W.2d 43 (1928).

[19] Searles v. Bar Harbor Banking & Trust Co., 128 Me. 34, 145 Atl. 391 (1929); First Natl. Bank v. Shanks, 34 Ohio Op. 359, 73 N.E.2d 93 (C.P. 1945). Nonconsenting shareholders whose shares were not originally subject to the restriction are probably not bound by it. *Compare* Sandor Petroleum Corp. v. Williams, 321 S.W.2d 614 (Tex. Civ. App. 1959), *with* Tu-Vu Drive-In Corp. v. Ashkins, 61 Cal. 2d 283, 391 P.2d 828, 38 Cal. Rptr. 348 (1964). See McNulty, Corporations and the Intertemporal Conflict of Laws, 55 Calif. L. Rev. 12 (1967).

[20] Weismann v. Lincoln Corp., 76 So.2d 478 (Fla. 1954); Arentson v. Sherman Towel Service Corp., 352 Ill. 327, 185 N.E. 822 (1933); Douglas v. Aurora Daily News Co., 160 Ill. App. 506 (1911); Jones v. Brown, 171 Mass. 318, 50 N.E. 648 (1898); Scruggs, Vandervoort & Barney Bank v. International Shoe Co., 227 Mo. App. 378, 52 S.W.2d 1027 (1932); Scruggs v. Cotterill, 67 App. Div. 583, 73 N.Y.S. 882 (1902); Fitzsimmons v. Lindsay, 205 Pa. 79, 54 Atl. 488 (1903); Coleman v. Kettering, 289 S.W.2d 953 (Tex. Civ. App. 1956).

[21] Uniform Commercial Code §8–204. See also Uniform Stock Transfer Act §15.

actual knowledge of it.[22] This would seem to be so also in the case of a restriction which was not "imposed by the issuer" but appears in a shareholders' agreement.

The foregoing suggests that the prudent draftsman had best include the stock transfer restriction in the articles of incorporation and also note the restriction conspicuously on the stock certificate. If the restriction is relatively brief, it can be set forth in full on the stock certificate. Otherwise its more important features should be summarized and a reference made to that part of the articles of incorporation where it may be found.[23] It has also been suggested that the restriction should be included not only in the articles but also in the bylaws in view of the fact that the latter are often used by directors and corporate officials as a guide for corporate activities.[24] If the restriction is at all unusual and there is doubt as to its validity as a clause in the articles or as a bylaw provision, it is wise to include it in a shareholders' agreement since, as we have seen, even though a restriction may be invalid as a bylaw, it may be enforced against those who have agreed to it.[25] However, it is unwise to rely solely on a shareholders' agreement to enforce a restriction; as already indicated, the restriction should be in the articles of incorporation and possibly in the bylaws as well.[26]

[22] At least this is the case where the Uniform Commercial Code provision is in effect. Under the predecessor provision in the Uniform Stock Transfer Act, although early decisions held that a transferee with knowledge of the restriction was bound by it even though the restriction did not appear on the stock certificate (Doss v. Yingling, 95 Ind. App. 494, 172 N.E. 801 (1930); Baumohl v. Goldstein, 95 N.J. Eq. 597, 124 Atl. 118 (Ch. 1924)), subsequent decisions interpreted the Act more strictly and invalidated the restriction even as applied to one with knowledge of it if it did not appear on the stock certificate. Security Life & Accident Ins. Co. v. Carlowitz, 251 Ala. 508, 38 So.2d 274 (1949); Age Publ. Co. v. Becker, 110 Colo. 319, 134 P.2d 205 (1943); Sorrick v. Consolidated Telephone Co., 340 Mich. 463, 65 N.W.2d 713 (1954); Costello v. Farrell, 234 Minn. 453, 48 N.W.2d 557 (1951); Hopwood v. Topsham Telephone Co., 120 Vt. 97, 132 A.2d 170 (1957). The Uniform Commercial Code reverted to the doctrine of the older cases and binds the transferee if he has actual knowledge of the restriction.

[23] For cases dealing with the question of what is an adequate summary of the restriction, or whether a summary rather than a full statement is even permissible, see 2 F. O'Neal, Close Corporations §7.16 (1958). The Comments to the Uniform Commercial Code provision observe that the requirement that the provision be "noted" on the stock certificate "removes an ambiguity under the former Act and makes clear that the restriction need not be set forth in full text." Uniform Commercial Code §8–204, Comment 1.

[24] See 2 F. O'Neal, id. at 24.

[25] Id. at 22–23. As the author points out, insertion of the restriction in a shareholders' agreement also guards against the possibility that a majority of the shareholders might later seek to remove the restriction from the articles of incorporation or bylaws by amending them. In most cases this can be prevented by the usual provision requiring a high or unanimous vote for amendments to the articles or bylaws which delete the restriction. Notwithstanding earlier cases casting doubt on the validity of such high vote requirements, such as Benintendi v. Kenton Hotel, Inc., 294 N.Y. 112, 60 N.E.2d 829 (1945), many modern statutes expressly permit high vote requirements. See text accompanying note 183 *infra*.

[26] Thus a shareholders' agreement might not be enforceable against a minor and a damage claim resulting from breach of the agreement might be an ineffective remedy even where it is possible to prove the extent of the harm. If the restriction

Mention has already been made of the fact that the validity of a restriction may depend upon its overall objectives, with particular reference to the type of business in which the corporation happens to be engaged.[27] Thus in *Lawson v. Household Finance Corporation*[28] the court in upholding a first refusal type restriction which permitted repurchase of shares at book value, excluding good will, as determined by appraisers, emphasized the fact that the restriction was conducive to the development of experienced and trustworthy management personnel by providing them with an interest in the business, which, since it involved the making of loans, the court considered to be "precarious" in nature. In a later case from the same jurisdiction[29] involving a much broader restraint (a provision which, in effect, gave the corporation an option to repurchase the shares at any time—if they were not owned by an employee—at "asset" value exclusive of going concern value or good will), the court, in invalidating the restriction, referred to the earlier *Lawson* case and somewhat ominously suggested, "Had it not been for the special circumstances involved in that case, we must infer that even the milder clause there involved would have been declared to constitute an unlawful restraint upon alienation." [30] This reasoning was criticized [31] on the ground that too much uncertainty as to the validity of the restriction is produced if the matter turns not only on the form of the restriction but also upon the particular business in which the issuer happens to be engaged. Although a special case might be made for banks and other financial institutions,[32] most other businesses should be treated uniformly, with the validity of the restriction thus depending not upon the particular business involved, but upon the form of the restriction, its purpose and possibly its location (i.e., whether it is in the articles of incorporation or merely in a shareholders' agreement). With the exception of the two cases

---

is inserted in the articles, there is a greater likelihood that the transfer of the shares may be prevented or invalidated. Finally, although transferees of shares which are subject to a restriction in a shareholders' agreement might be bound by the restriction if they have knowledge of it, the agreement might not bind those who purchase their shares directly from the corporation. See 2 F. O'Neal, id. at 23–24.

[27] See text accompanying note 9 *supra*.

[28] 17 Del. Ch. 343, 152 Atl. 723 (Sup. Ct. 1930).

[29] Greene v. E. H. Rollins & Sons, 22 Del. Ch. 394, 2 A.2d 249 (Ch. 1938).

[30] 22 Del. Ch. at 404, 2 A.2d at 254. This holding, along with another Delaware decision, Starring v. American Hair & Felt Co., 21 Del. Ch. 380, 191 Atl. 887 (Ch. 1937), aff'd per curiam, 21 Del. Ch. 431, 2 A.2d 249 (Sup. Ct. 1937), are generally cited for the proposition that callable common stock is invalid not only in Delaware but probably elsewhere, with the exception of Massachusetts. See Lewis v. H. P. Hood & Sons, 331 Mass. 670, 121 N.E.2d 850 (1954). These relatively old Delaware cases will be of little future influence in Delaware because of the broad provisions of Del. Gen. Corp. Law §202 (1967), which validates most types of restrictions, even those of the consent type, regardless of the type of business involved.

[31] See Painter, Stock Transfer Restrictions: Continuing Uncertainties and a Legislative Proposal, 6 Vill. L. Rev. 48, 58–62 (1960).

[32] It is ironic that whereas the *Lawson* case upheld a restriction on the ground that it was important to safeguard the "precarious" business of making loans, restrictions on bank stock were initially thought to prejudice the safety of depositor's claims. See First Natl. Bank v. Lanier, 78 U.S. (11 Wall.) 369 (1871).

referred to, the great majority of the remaining cases place no great emphasis upon the particular business which happens to be involved.

Agreements which not only restrict transfer of securities but also obligate the various parties to purchase or sell them are commonly entered into. These are generally valid and are not testamentary in character even though they purport to govern the disposition of shares on the death of a shareholder.[33] The agreement might specify that the shares will be offered back to the corporation on the shareholder's ceasing to be an employee, on his reaching a designated age, in the event of his incapacity or upon death. If the other shareholders are obligated to purchase the shares, such agreements are commonly referred to as "buy-and-sell" agreements, or, if they operate on death, "survivor purchase" agreements. A contract obligating the corporation to purchase is commonly referred to as a "stock purchase" or "stock retirement" agreement.[34]

A possible ground on which a stock purchase or stock retirement agreement might be invalid is if it obligates a corporation to purchase its shares when it does not have sufficient funds to do so legally. Most states restrict corporations in the purchase of their own shares to "surplus," either earned surplus or (with some further restrictions) capital surplus.[35] A contract which obligates a corporation to purchase its own shares may be enforced only if the corporation has sufficient funds. One New York case of doubtful validity gave this as a reason for setting aside a repurchase agreement on the ground that it lacked mutuality even though, when it came time for the shares to be repurchased, there were, in fact, sufficient funds to do so.[36] Subsequent New York cases had little difficulty in distinguishing the case, often on the ground that, where the agreement was funded by insurance, there was no lack of mutuality.[37] Ultimately the case was legislatively repealed and so is no longer the law in New York, although it may have some influence in a few states.[38] Thus, to be on the safe side, some provision should be made for the corporation to have sufficient funds to carry out the agreement. As will be seen, this is best done through insurance.[39]

Among the more important things to be considered in drafting a stock

[33] 2 F. O'Neal, Close Corporations 16 (1958).

[34] Id. at 15.

[35] E.g., Model Bus. Corp. Act §6.

[36] Topken, Loring & Schwartz, Inc. v. Schwartz, 249 N.Y. 206, 163 N.E. 735 (1928).

[37] E.g., In re Farah's Estate, 13 N.Y.2d 909, 193 N.E.2d 641, 243 N.Y.S.2d 858 (1963); Greater New York Carpet House, Inc. v. Herschmann, 258 App. Div. 649, 17 N.Y.S.2d 483 (1940). See Note, 11 W. Res. L. Rev. 278, 283 (1960).

[38] N.Y. Bus. Corp. Law §514(a) (1961). See also Cutter Labs, Inc. v. Twining, 221 Cal. App. 2d 302, 314, 34 Cal. Rptr. 317, 324 (1963) (refusing to follow the *Topken* holding).

[39] See Ch. VI, text accompanying note 140. Other techniques are to provide in the shareholders' agreement that the corporate capital will be reduced, if necessary, to provide for adequate surplus for share repurchases, or, to the extent permissible by law, assets will be revaluated upwards to create revaluation surplus. Or shareholders might agree to donate sufficient funds to finance the repurchase. See 2 F. O'Neal, Close Corporations 16 n.48.20 (1958).

transfer restriction are (1) the scope of the restriction, (2) the method of determining the purchase price of the shares subject to the restriction, (3) the parties who are entitled to purchase the shares and (4) how the restriction shall be enforced. As already stated, it is also important to consider where the restriction should be placed, e.g., in the articles of incorporation, bylaws or a shareholders' agreement. In most instances it is advisable to place the restriction at least in the articles of incorporation.

It is important to specify the various events which give rise to the option to purchase the shares. One of the most frequent oversights is failing to specify that the restriction covers any transfer of shares under a will, through specific legacy or residual bequest, through passage of title by intestacy or by any such operation of law.[40] Also inter vivos transfers of various types may present problems, such as inter vivos gifts, pledges, transfers to a voting trust, foreclosure and sale by a pledgee of shares or judicial sale pursuant to a decree in bankruptcy or otherwise.[41] Even where it is clearly apparent that the restriction applies to a sale or gift by a shareholder, it may not be clear that the restriction covers a sale or gift by one shareholder to another shareholder.[42] If the major purpose of the restriction is to prevent transfers to outsiders, transfers between shareholders might be permitted. Conversely, if the major purpose is to preserve a particular pattern of share ownership, transfers between shareholders should not be permitted without compliance with the restriction.

As already indicated, a restriction may arise on the happening of an event other than a proposed transfer of the shares. Thus a repurchase option may arise if the shareholder ceases to be an employee (the restriction should specifically state whether the restriction applies to involuntary termination of employment)[43] or if an employee becomes disabled and cannot work for a specified period of time. Less frequently encountered is a repurchase option if the employee ceases to reside in a particular locality.[44]

Once the event which gives rise to the option is identified, it should be

[40] E.g., Globe Slicing Machine Co. v. Hasner, 333 F.2d 413 (2d Cir. 1964), *cert. denied*, 379 U.S. 969 (1965).

[41] See Monotype Composition Co. v. Kiernan, 319 Mass. 456, 66 N.E.2d 565 (1946) (restriction inapplicable to pledge but applicable to foreclosure of pledge by pledgee); McDonald v. Farley & Loetscher Mfg. Co., 226 Iowa 53, 283 N.W. 261 (1939) (restriction inapplicable to judicial or bankruptcy sale). For other cases dealing with various situations see 2 F. O'Neal, id. at 28. See also H. Henn, Handbook of the Law of Corporations 557 (2d ed. 1970).

[42] E.g., Lank v. Steiner, 43 Del. Ch. 262, 224 A.2d 242 (Sup. Ct. 1966); Gibbon v. Lake Shore Drive Bldg. Corp., 310 Ill. App. 2d 385, 34 N.E.2d 109 (1941); Campbell v. Campbell, 198 Kan. 181, 422 P.2d 932 (1967). For other cases see 2 F. O'Neal, id. at 28, and W. Cary, Cases and Materials on Corporations 506 (4th ed. unabr. 1969).

[43] See Lawrence v. Sudman, 70 F. Supp. 387 (S.D.N.Y. 1945); Lawson v. Household Finance Co., 17 Del. Ch. 343, 152 Atl. 723 (Sup. Ct. 1930); Douglas v. Aurora Daily News Co., 160 Ill. App. 506 (1911); Prindiville v. Johnson & Higgins, 92 N.J. Eq. 515, 113 Atl. 915 (Ch. 1921).

[44] Cf. Adams v. Protective Union Co., 210 Mass. 172, 96 N.E. 74 (1911).

specified how long the option is to remain open. As one commentator has pointed out,[45] the period should be reasonable from the standpoint of both parties, that is, long enough to permit the corporation or other shareholders to determine whether to exercise the option, and not so long that the shareholder's ability to transfer the shares is unduly impaired. Thirty to ninety days would seem to be sufficient.[46]

Another important matter to be covered is whether the party entitled to purchase the shares may purchase less than the entire amount which the shareholder proposes to transfer. Thus, if a shareholder wishes to sell 1000 shares, may the corporation exercise its option with respect to only 500 of the shares? If the 1000 shares represent a majority interest, the other shareholders may seek to acquire only part of the block in order that the shares so acquired, along with their other shares, may constitute a majority, thus leaving the former majority shareholder in the awkward position of having a minority interest which is not readily marketable.[47] Also, occasionally a majority shareholder who wishes to sell to an outsider may seek to vote his shares against the decision to have them repurchased (assuming that the matter is put to a shareholders' vote) or may influence those directors which he controls to vote against the repurchase. Similarly, an executor or other representative of a deceased shareholder may attempt to vote the shares against exercise of a repurchase option which has arisen because of death. It is therefore important to specify whether the shares subject to the option may vote on the matter of exercising the option.[48]

A particularly troublesome point is determining the purchase price of the shares. Although sometimes a fixed dollar figure is provided in the agreement,[49] frequently the value is left for later determination. It is therefore crucial that there be agreement on the precise method to be used.

Often the parties agree that the shares may be purchased at "book value" and that "good will" and other intangibles may be excluded from the computation.[50] This may be inappropriate if much of the value of the business consists of good will, franchises and the like.

The death or departure of a major shareholder may result in the disappearance of much of the good will but this is not necessarily so. Good will is, of course, difficult to value, but some indication of its worth may be

[45] 2 F. O'Neal, Close Corporations 31 (1958).
[46] Ibid.
[47] Id. at 30 (also suggesting that a restriction could specify that, in the event of a sale of a majority interest, any person who held less than a majority might sell his shares at the same price per share as the majority block). See also Phillips v. Newland, 166 So.2d 357 (Ct. App. La. 1964), *writ refused*, 246 La. 872, 167 So.2d 679 (1964).
[48] 2 F. O'Neal, id. at 30.
[49] E.g., Allen v. Biltmore Tissue Corp., 2 N.Y.2d 534, 141 N.E.2d 812, 161 N.Y.S.2d 418 (1957) (shares subject to repurchase at original cost).
[50] E.g., Lawson v. Household Finance Corp., 17 Del. Ch. 343, 152 Atl. 723 (Sup. Ct. 1930).

found by comparing the value of the tangible assets to the earnings of the company as a whole.[51] Another problem with the book value test is determining the value to be given fixed assets. These are usually carried on the books at original cost less depreciation, which may be considerably less than their actual value or the cost of their replacement. This is particularly true in the early years of depreciating an asset where accelerated depreciation methods may be followed. If asset values have gone up, many accountants and regulatory agencies are reluctant to recognize the increased value of the asset on the corporate books until the gain has been "realized," i.e., until the asset has been sold.[52] Similarly, in the case of inventory the usual method is to set the value on particular items at cost or market, whichever is lower. Thus, in a period of rising prices the purchaser of stock priced at book value may have an advantage, and yet the seller receives less if the prices of inventory fall below original cost.

Another method for determining the value of shares is to capitalize earnings. This proceeds on the assumption that the value of an enterprise represents an investment that produces income at a characteristic rate of return. The rate of return will vary in accordance with the particular business and particularly will reflect the degree of risk which pertains to that type of business. One of the most frequently quoted commentators suggests that old, established businesses with little risk be valued at a capitalization which reflects a yield of 10 percent (or ten times net earnings).[53] Small industrial businesses of a highly competitive nature which require relatively small amounts of capital might be valued to yield 25 percent (or four times earnings), and if they depend upon the unusual skill of a relatively small number of people, the value would be even lower (two times net earnings, representing a yield of 50 percent).[54] Certain personal service businesses, which require almost no capital and depend almost exclusively upon the

[51] See, e.g., the procedure set forth in A.R.M. 34, 1920–2 Cum. Bull. 31. Under this method the earnings derived from good will are deduced by valuing tangible assets and computing the earnings produced by the tangibles at an assumed rate of return. The difference between the actual earnings of the enterprise and the earnings produced by the tangibles is considered to be equivalent to the earnings produced by the intangibles. These earnings are then "capitalized" at a set rate (e.g., 20 percent or a multiplier of five) to arrive at the value of the intangibles. In Rev. Rul. 65–192, 1965–2 Cum. Bull. 259, the Internal Revenue Service stated that A.R.M. 34 should be used only in situations where "no better basis [is] available." See also Rev. Rul. 68–609, 1968–2 Cum. Bull. 327.

[52] See Accounting Principles Board, Opinion no. 6 (1965). For the attitude of the SEC (discouraging write-ups) see L. Rappaport, SEC Accounting Practice and Procedure 3.9–3.16 (2d ed. 1963). Some taxing authorities have recognized write-ups where they appear on the company's books, for the purpose of franchise or other taxes. See Oxford v. Macon Telegraph Publishing Co., 104 Ga. App. 788, 123 S.E.2d 277 (1961); Scott Building Supply Corp. v. Mississippi State Tax Commission, 235 Miss. 22, 108 So.2d 557 (1959). New York is one of the few states which permits write-ups for the purpose of computing the fund available for dividend payments. See Randall v. Bailey, 288 N.Y. 280, 43 N.E.2d 43 (1942).

[53] See 1 A. Dewing, The Financial Policy of Corporations 281–391 (5th ed. 1953).

[54] Ibid.

talents of particular individuals, may have a value equivalent to one year's net earnings.[55] The foregoing values are very likely too conservative in view of the tendency of today's stocks to sell at much higher multiples.[56] It has been suggested that a multiplier of five or six times annual earnings is suitable for many small businesses but that even that may be on the conservative side.[57]

Even if it is possible to select some appropriate multiplier for earnings of a closely held concern, there is considerable uncertainty in any method of valuation which relies solely on capitalization of earnings. For one thing, earnings must be adjusted for nonrecurring income and cost items as well as for temporary market conditions. It is often well to compute earnings on an average basis over a period of three years or more, making a suitable adjustment for taxes.[58] Even so, it may very well be that earnings so computed do not fairly reflect the true value of a concern if the practice is to withdraw most of the earnings in the form of salaries.[59] Thus some adjustment might have to be made to increase earnings by a portion of the salaries which reflects the yield which might otherwise have been paid in the form of dividends. Further uncertainties are introduced if the value of the business suffers as a result of the death of a key man.[60]

In some situations, generally those involving computation of the value of shares in satisfaction of dissenters' appraisal rights in mergers and other corporate combinations, it has been possible to use a mixture of differing methods. Thus the worth of shares is computed both on an asset value or book value basis, and by a capitalization of earnings method. In addition, the market value of the shares is determined by prices at which the stock has traded over a set period of time. These differing values are then weighted and combined into an average which reflects all of these various factors in a manner appropriate to the particular company concerned. If a considerable part of the value of the company resides in its assets, and this is not reflected in earnings, a heavier weight can be given to asset value and less to earnings value.[61] Where the corporation is closely held, it will rarely be possible to compute market value by examining recent quotations for the stock, and yet in some instances it may be possible to compare the value per share with that of another company in a similar line of business (possibly a competitor) whose shares are publicly traded.

[55] Ibid.

[56] See D. Herwitz, Business Planning 18–19 (1966).

[57] See 2 F. O'Neal, Close Corporations 44 n.31 (1958). See Estate of Snyder v. United States, 285 F.2d 857 (4th Cir. 1961) (using a multiplier of 8.37 for a closely held concern where profits and sales were declining in the face of increased competition, costs, etc.).

[58] See D. Herwitz, id. at 27.

[59] See 2. F. O'Neal, id. at 44.

[60] Ibid. The author also points out that earnings are a poor test of the worth of an enterprise in its early years.

[61] See Swanton v. State Guaranty Corp., 42 Del. Ch. 477, 215 A.2d 242 (Ch. 1965). For a survey of the various Delaware cases involving appraisal rights, see Note, 79 Harv. L. Rev. 1453 (1966).

Because of the uncertainties involved, the parties to a buy-and-sell agreement may merely specify that the price is to be determined by an appraiser, generally a disinterested third party. Several appraisers can be used, as where the seller selects one appraiser, the buyer selects a second and the two appraisers so selected choose a third. If more than one purchaser of the stock is involved, this may result in several different sets of appraisers who are likely to arrive at differing values for the shares.[62] An alternative to this is to designate some person or persons in the agreement who are acceptable to all parties. In this case some provision must be made for appointing substitutes should those designated be unwilling or unable to serve.[63] A disadvantage to the appraisal method is its possible expense. However, it does have some flexibility which other methods, such as book value, do not have, although it may not avoid the real uncertainties which are inevitably entailed in valuing a closely held concern.

One method which avoids some of the uncertainties is to have the parties set a price in the agreement and agree to set a new value on the shares at designated intervals. Although this has the merit of comparative certainty, it is really little more than an agreement to agree. Thus if one party refuses to set a new price on the shares, or the two parties are not able to agree on their value,[64] some supplementary method, such as arbitration or appraisal, must be used to resolve the dispute.

Another technique is to agree that in the event of a proposed transfer of the shares the corporation or other shareholders may purchase them at the best bona fide price offered by a prospective purchaser. If third parties are reluctant to make offers which would determine the price under these circumstances, an alternative technique is to have the person who desires to sell the shares set a price on them and give the corporation or the other shareholders a right to purchase at that price. If the offer is declined, then the shareholder may sell the shares to anyone else at the same price or higher.[65]

Since no one of the various possible methods for setting the option price is completely satisfactory, it may be desirable to use two or more methods in conjunction with one another. The parties could agree on a base price and then provide for periodic reappraisal in accordance with a formula which would take into account earnings as well as asset value. It might also be provided that, if the value so determined should be less than a bona fide offer from a third party, then the price set by the offer should control. The price set by the book value method could be agreed on as a minimum price.[66]

---

[62] See 2 F. O'Neal, id. at 44–45.

[63] Ibid.

[64] See Helms v. Duckworth, 249 F.2d 482 (D.C. Cir. 1957).

[65] See 2 F. O'Neal, id. at 43 (suggesting also that it may be wise to provide that the shares may not be sold to third parties in lots smaller than those offered to the optionees).

[66] See 2 F. O'Neal, id. at 47–48.

Assuming that some suitable method is found for determining the option price, it is still necessary to specify the person or persons who are entitled to exercise the option. Here the alternatives are fairly clear. The first possibility is to have the corporation exercise the option; the second is to have the option run to those shareholders who are not disposing of their shares. A third possibility is to have successive options, one running to the corporation, and if the latter should refuse to exercise its option, then the shareholders should receive an option to purchase. Each method has its advantages and disadvantages. Although detailed discussion of the mechanics of buy-and-sell agreements, particularly from the taxation and insurance standpoint, is deferred to a later chapter,[67] it is well to summarize the possibilities and indicate briefly some of the problems.

As already stated, one of the difficulties with having the option run in favor of the corporation is the fact that there are legal inhibitions on the ability of a corporation to purchase its own shares if it has insufficient funds to do so. This generally means that a corporation must have some form of surplus, either earned surplus or capital surplus.[68] Although this factor has been seized upon as a reason for invalidating some stock purchase agreements,[69] it should be no serious obstacle, particularly if there is insurance. If the parties are not insurable or if the cost of insurance is too great, the corporation might fund the repurchase by establishing a reserve to which funds are added each year. Although the accumulation of funds in a reserve, and the payment of insurance premiums for that matter, may run afoul of the prohibition on "excess accumulations" and thus incur a penalty tax, this is by no means inevitable and it may very well be that the payment of reasonable premiums or the setting aside of reasonable amounts yearly in a reserve, although not tax deductible, will be regarded as meeting the reasonable needs test, particularly when that test is put in terms of reasonably anticipated needs.[70] Moreover, although a corporate purchase of shares differs from a shareholder purchase in that with the former there are legal prohibitions against the use of certain funds (i.e., stated capital) to finance the repurchase, the practical problem of raising the funds is just as severe in the case of a shareholder purchase. In certain ways it may be even more complex. Thus, aside from funding the purchase through insurance, there is no guarantee that all of the shareholders will be able to exercise the option. If some of the shareholders are financially able to purchase the shares when the option becomes exercisable and others are not, this raises the problem of whether the option is exercisable in part or whether the entire block of stock must be purchased by those who can afford to do so. If

---

[67] See Ch. VI.

[68] See note 35 *supra*.

[69] See Topken, Loring & Schwartz, Inc. v. Schwartz, 249 N.Y. 206, 163 N.E. 735 (1928).

[70] See generally B. Bittker and J. Eustice, Federal Income Taxation of Corporations and Shareholders 230–233 (1966), and Ch. V, text accompanying notes 101–117.

the entire block is purchased by some shareholders and not by others, then those who purchase acquire greater control relative to those who do not purchase. This may be undesirable if the intent of the parties is that control be equally divided or remain in some other preestablished pattern. On the other hand, if less than the entire block is purchased, then not only do those who purchase still acquire greater relative control as compared to those who fail to purchase, but the selling shareholder may be left with an undesirable minority interest which he cannot dispose of due to its doubtful marketability. All of this merely highlights the fact that funding the purchase is necessary regardless of whether the purchase is by the corporation or by the other shareholders, and the technical disability of a corporation to purchase its own shares except out of surplus is not the major problem. The real problem in both cases is insuring that there will be sufficient funds to finance the purchase.

Providing that the *corporation* is to have the option of repurchasing the shares is a simpler method. Where the option runs to the shareholders rather than to the corporation, there are the already mentioned complexities of deciding who is to purchase how much if less than all the shareholders wish to exercise the option. If the corporation repurchases, these problems will not exist. It is important in both situations to specify whether the option may be exercised as to only part of the shares in a block.[71]

If it is provided that the repurchased shares are to be retired and cancelled and thus not reoffered to the shareholders, the pattern of relative ownership will not be affected, although the percentage of the corporation which each shareholder has will change and some may find that they have a controlling interest where before they held only a minority interest. For example, suppose a corporation has 1000 shares outstanding, 500 of which are held by one shareholder, 300 by another and 200 by a third. The repurchase and cancellation of the 500 shares from the majority shareholder will result in there being only 500 shares outstanding, of which one shareholder holds 200, or 40 percent, and the other holds 300, or 60 percent. Although the percentage ownership of each has been increased by the same amount (i.e., doubled) one shareholder has received control, a factor which is of crucial importance in a closely held corporation. The same thing would have happened if the transaction had taken the form of a cross-purchase option among the various shareholders, the major difference being that the funds to finance the purchase would have come from the shareholders and not from the corporation.

If the corporation is given the option to purchase, then it is obviously important to specify what, if anything, is to be done with the shares. As just suggested, it may be desirable that the shares be retired and cancelled. This eliminates any possibility that they might be issued on a preferential basis to certain shareholders and not to others, or sold for too low a price. Although

[71] See text accompanying note 47 *supra.*

it might be thought that the shares should be retained by the corporation for possible issuance to others, such as those with the requisite skills and other qualifications to fill the vacuum left by the departure of the shareholder whose shares were purchased,[72] this can always be done by selling newly issued shares. In fact, the necessity of gaining shareholder approval for new issues of shares might act as a safeguard on the fairness of the transaction, in contrast to the situation that might prevail if the directors were able to resell reacquired shares on terms they deem satisfactory but which are unfair to a minority group. This does not, of course, prevent a majority of the shareholders from selling newly issued shares to themselves at an unfair price. However, the need for obtaining shareholder approval, coupled with the possible exercise of preemptive rights (which do not apply to sales of treasury shares unless the articles of incorporation expressly so provide,[73]) with the possibility of a shareholder derivative suit if the terms of the sale are unfair,[74] serves to lessen the probability of breach of fiduciary duty.

Some procedure should be provided in the restriction for its enforcement. As previously suggested,[75] there should be a period within which the shares must be tendered to the corporation or to the other shareholders for purchase and within which the option must be exercised. If the option is not exercised, then the shares may be transferred free of the restriction. This leaves unsettled the question of whether the restriction might still apply with regard to later transfers of the same shares. Thus, although X might have been able to transfer his shares to Y free of the restriction because the corporation was unable or unwilling to exercise its right of purchase, this does not necessarily mean that Y should be able to transfer the shares without first offering them to the corporation. In fact, the normal expectation of the parties might be that the corporation should have a right of first refusal on any shares, whether or not it may have failed to exercise its right of first refusal on the same shares on other occasions. This can

---

[72] See 2 F. O'Neal, Close Corporations 32 (1958).

[73] See, e.g., Borg v. International Silver Co., 11 F.2d 147 (2d Cir. 1925), and Note, Shareholders' Rights of Preemption in Treasury Shares, 36 Yale L.J. 1181 (1927). For other cases see H. Henn, Handbook of the Law of Corporations 321 n.4 (2d ed. 1970).

[74] Even in a close corporation the suit may be brought under SEC rule 10b–5, 17 C.F.R. §240.10b–5, promulgated under the Securities Exchange Act of 1934, §10, 48 Stat. 896 (1934), 15 U.S.C. §78p, if any means or instrumentality of interstate commerce (e.g., the telephone) or the mails are used. See Hooper v. Mountain States Securities Corp., 282 F.2d 195 (5th Cir. 1960), *cert. denied*, 365 U.S. 814 (1961); Ruckle v. Roto American Corp., 339 F.2d 24 (2d Cir. 1964). For the advantages of suing derivatively under the federal rule, see Lowenfels, Rule 10b–5 and the Stockholder's Derivative Action, 18 Vand. L. Rev. 893 (1965) (nationwide service of process, liberal venue requirements, immunity from state security-for-expense bonding provisions, possibility of a relatively long statute of limitations, more liberal attitude of federal courts in not requiring demand on shareholders as a prerequisite for bringing suit, broad discovery procedures, etc.).

[75] See text accompanying note 46 *supra*.

easily be spelled out, i.e., that the corporation's failure to exercise its right of first refusal on shares subject to a restriction shall not prevent it from later exercising the same right with respect to those shares or any other shares, and that all shares issued by the corporation shall accordingly be subject to first refusal in the event of any later transfer, death, etc. Recall, however, that it is crucial that the restriction be noted on the stock certificate in order that transferees be bound.[76]

Although a restriction should expressly bind the executor or administrator of a deceased shareholder, it is helpful that the shareholders, by will, specifically direct those who administer their estates to comply with the restriction and tender the shares to the corporation or to the other shareholders at death. Also the restriction might provide that, if the shares are not tendered within the designated period, or if the holder of the shares refuses to abide by the terms of the restriction, then no dividends shall be paid on the shares subject to the restriction and the shares shall not be voted.

In some states there are local regulations or traditions which limit the form of the restriction. Apparently, in Massachusetts the Commissioner of Corporations and Taxation has a special form for a first refusal restriction and, unless the restriction complies with the form, he has been known to refuse to file the incorporation papers.[77] Briefly, the form requires any shareholder who wishes to sell his shares to offer them first to the corporation through its board of directors and specify the price at which he is willing to sell along with the name of one arbitrator. The directors have a period of thirty days within which to accept the offer. Within the thirty days they may indicate to the shareholder the name of an arbitrator to act on behalf of the corporation, and the two arbitrators then name a third, all three to ascertain the value of the stock. After the arbitrators have set the value, the corporation has another thirty days within which to purchase the stock. If the stock is not purchased within that period it may be sold free of the restriction.

The Massachusetts form appears to be satisfactory, although it may be unduly brief and leaves open a number of important points, such as whether it applies to sales by one shareholder to another or by a transferee of shares which have been previously transferred free of the restriction because of the corporation's failure to exercise its right of first refusal. Also the form does not provide for successive options, i.e., an option to the shareholders to purchase the stock in the event that the corporation does not exercise its option. Finally, the arbitration method of determining the option price may not always be satisfactory, and there are no standards for guiding the arbitrators in fixing the value. If the shareholders of a Massachusetts corporation wish to adopt some other form of restriction, they may do so by a shareholders' agreement or bylaw. The Massachusetts cases are

[76] See text accompanying note 21 *supra*.
[77] See 2 F. O'Neal, Close Corporations 19 n.58 (1958).

perhaps the most liberal in permitting restraints of various sorts and in enforcing them on a contractual basis,[78] and such agreements and bylaws bind those who consent to them. It is ironic that the Massachusetts courts are so permissive with regard to stock transfer restrictions and yet the Commissioner of Corporations and Taxation is so inflexible when a restriction happens to be contained in the incorporation papers.

California, through its Department of Corporations, approves only certain restrictions. Briefly, these are restrictions which "are not of such a nature as to unfairly prejudice the opportunity of the holder to realize a reasonable price for his securities." [79] A first refusal provision which bases the option price upon the appraised value of the securities, on an offer received from a third party, or on book value ("except in the case of a type of business where book value is not a significant indication of the value of the securities") is presumptively reasonable. Conversely, restrictions which allow for repurchase at par value or original purchase price, absolute or consent-type restrictions or restrictions which give an option to the corporation or the other shareholders to purchase regardless of whether the holder of the shares wishes to sell them are permitted only in unusual circumstances. However, an option which arises for a limited time upon termination of employment or death of the shareholder is permitted.[80] In addition, there appears to be a practice of requiring the shares to be kept in escrow with the Corporations Commissioner if the terms of the restriction prevent the holder of the shares from recovering the full price for them for longer than thirty days.[81]

The foregoing discussion has been confined to general aspects of stock transfer restrictions. More specialized problems relating to buy-and-sell agreements, survivor purchase agreements, stock purchase and stock retirement agreements are deferred until a later chapter,[82] in which we shall consider the whole problem of planning for the death or retirement of a shareholder.

3.2 VOTING TRUSTS

A useful means of maintaining control of a corporation is a voting trust. Essentially this is no more than a trust of the stock whereby it is conveyed to a voting trustee into whose name the shares are transferred. Thus the trustee becomes the holder of record, has legal title to the shares, and votes them as directed by the voting trust agreement. Certificates of beneficial

[78] See note 9 *supra*.

[79] See regulations promulgated pursuant to the Corporate Securities Law of 1968, Reg. §260.140.8 in 1 Blue Sky L. Rep. ¶8617.

[80] Ibid.

[81] See 2 F. O'Neal, id. at 18 n.56.

[82] See Ch. VI.

ownership are issued to those who formerly held record title as evidence of their equitable interests. Dividends and other asset distributions are remitted by the voting trustee to the beneficial owners, who retain some (but not all) of the rights of shareholders other than voting rights.[83]

Voting trusts have been frequently used in corporate reorganizations to give control of a corporation to those who hold its senior securities, such as bondholders, debenture holders and so forth. They are also useful where those who invest in a corporation wish to assure themselves that the present management will continue.[84] Sometimes those who form a corporation wish to retain control with a relatively small capital investment. If their shares are held in a voting trust or if others who purchase an interest in the corporation are sold beneficial ownership interests in the trust rather than in the stock itself, control may be maintained. Or certain shareholders may wish to band together to gain minority representation on a board of directors or to resist attempts by others to take over control.[85]

[83] Thus a holder of a voting trust certificate may bring a derivative suit against the management of the corporation if the voting trustee refuses to do so on his behalf. See e.g., Neb. Bus. Corp. Act §21–2047 (1963); N.Y. Bus. Corp. Law §626 (1961); Pa. Bus. Corp. Law §516(A) (1968). For cases allowing an equitable owner of shares to sue derivatively, see W. Cary, Cases and Materials on Corporations 924 (4th ed. unabr. 1969), and R. Stevens, Handbook on the Law of Private Corporations 811 n.56 (1949). But see Matthies v. Seymour Mfg. Corp., 270 F.2d 365 (2d Cir. 1959), cert. denied, 361 U.S. 962 (1960). On the other hand, an equitable owner may not (in the absence of statutes such as the above) enforce a right to inspect corporate books and records if this is confined by statute to shareholders of record. See W. Cary, id. at 1028 (collecting cases). This seems unjust since inspection of books and records is often the preamble to a derivative suit and is an effective way of uncovering corporate wrongdoing. Among the statutory provisions permitting a voting trust certificate holder to inspect corporate books and records are Cal. Gen. Corp. Law §3003 (1947); Ill. Bus. Corp. Act §45 (1969); Ind. Gen. Corp. Act §25–263 (1967); Md. Gen. Corp. Law §51(c) (1967); Minn. Bus. Corp. Act §301.34 (1961); N.Y. Bus. Corp. Law §624(b) (1964); N.C. Bus. Corp. Act §§55–38(a), 55–72(b) (1955). For a criticism of voting trusts which deprive the shareholder of voting and other rights, such as to receive notice of important corporate activities and to vote on fundamental matters such as mergers and asset sales, see H. Ballantine, Corporations 431 (rev. ed. 1946).

For a discussion of other respects in which a holder of a voting trust certificate may be able to assert rights normally accorded only to shareholders of record, see 1 G. Hornstein, Corporation Law and Practice §217 (1959) (observing that holders of voting trust certificates have been given the right to review corporate elections and to bring a proceeding to wind up a corporation under an insolvency statute).

[84] See Massa v. Stone, 346 Mass. 67, 190 N.E.2d 217 (1963). See also A. Frey, C. Morris and J. Choper, Cases and Materials on Corporations 351–352 (1966), and H. Ballantine, id. at 429–430 (observing that a lender may not, however, exact as a condition of his loan that the shareholders create a voting trust requiring the directors of the borrower to abdicate their discretionary powers and management of the corporation, citing Marvin v. Solventol Chemical Products, Inc., 298 Mich. 296, 298 N.W. 782 (1941)). See also A. Dewing, Financial Policy of Corporations 109 (1953).

[85] See A. Frey, C. Morris and J. Choper, id. For discussions of voting trusts see J. Leavitt, The Voting Trust (1941); Ballantine, Voting Trusts, Their Abuses and Regulation, 21 Texas L. Rev. 139 (1942); Bergerman, Voting Trusts and Non-Voting Stock, 37 Yale L.J. 445 (1928); Burke, Voting Trusts Currently Observed,

Although voting trusts, in the latter part of the nineteenth and the early part of the twentieth century, were regarded with suspicion, if not with outright hostility,[86] and were frequently held to be invalid as an unlawful separation of voting rights from the beneficial ownership of the shares, to-day they are lawful if for a proper motive or bona fide business purpose. In a majority of states there are statutory provisions regulating voting trusts, the most popular being similar to Section 32 of the Model Business Corporation Act. This provides that a voting trust may be established for a period not in excess of ten years by entering into a written voting trust agreement, depositing a counterpart of the agreement with the corporation at its registered office in the state of incorporation and transferring the shares to the voting trustee. The counterpart of the voting trust agreement is subject to the same right of inspection as are the books and records of the corporation and may also be examined by any holder of a beneficial interest in the voting trust at any reasonable time for any proper purpose. Statutes in other states vary from a simple permission to establish voting trusts, with no restriction on the period of the trust or other safeguards (except presumably the common law requirement that the trust be for a bona fide business purpose),[87] to more elaborate provisions setting forth requirements similar to those of the Model Act and adding procedures whereby voting trusts may be extended for additional periods (frequently ten years)[88] and persons not members of the voting trust may be allowed to join.[89] Although it has been held that where a voting trust is, by its terms, capable of lasting for more

---

24 Minn. L. Rev. 347 (1941); Finkelstein, Voting Trust Agreements, 24 Mich. L. Rev. 344 (1926); Giles, Is the Voting Trust Agreement a Dangerous Instrumentality? 3 Catholic U.L. Rev. 81 (1953); Gose, Legal Characteristics and Consequences of Voting Trusts, 20 Wash. L. Rev. 129 (1945); Smith, Limitations on the Validity of Voting Trusts, 22 Colum. L. Rev. 627 (1922); Wormser, The Legality of Corporate Voting Trusts and Pooling Agreements, 18 Colum. L. Rev. 123 (1918); see also Note, The Voting Trust: Drafting Suggestions, 42 N.Y.U.L. Rev. 349 (1967); Note, The Voting Trust, 34 N.Y.U.L. Rev. 290 (1959); Note, 105 A.L.R. 123 (1936).

[86] One of the leading cases in this regard is Warren v. Pim, 66 N.J. Eq. 353, 59 Atl. 773, 781, 785 (Ct. Err. & App. 1904), describing a voting trust as a "masterpiece of professional ingenuity" and the voting trustee as "only a sham owner vested with a colorable and fictitious title for the sole purpose of permanently voting upon stock that [he] does not own." See also the observation of Mr. Justice Douglas, during his early years with the Securities and Exchange Commission, that voting trusts were "little more than a vehicle for corporate kidnapping." Democracy and Finance at 43, quoted in W. Cary, id. at 404.

[87] E.g., Mo. Gen. & Bus. Corp. Law §351.246 (1965).

[88] E.g., Conn. Stock Corp. Act §33–338(d) (1969); Del. Gen. Corp. Law §218(b) (1969); N.Y. Bus. Corp. Law §621(d) (1961) (allowing the trust to be extended for more than one ten-year period); N.C. Bus. Corp. Act §55–72(d) (1963); Wash. Bus. Corp. Act §23A.08.330 (1965).

[89] E.g., Idaho Bus. Corp. Act §30–135 (1929); La. Bus. Corp. Law §12:78 (1968) (unless trust provides otherwise); Md. Gen. Corp. Law §45 (1951); Tenn. Gen. Corp. Law §48–7.15 (1968) (restricting the right to join to those who hold shares which are the subject of the trust).

than the statutory maximum number of years it is void,[90] more modern statutes provide that the trust is valid for the statutory period, although it is ineffective thereafter unless renewed.[91] Similarly, it has been held that some shareholder agreements may, in substance, constitute a voting trust, in which case they are invalid unless they comply with the applicable statute (usually a ten-year duration and filing requirement),[92] the theory being that the statute preempts the field and thus outlaws common law voting trusts. Since this often presents a hazard to those who enter into shareholder pooling agreements with so-called irrevocable proxies built into the agreement to aid in its enforceability, Delaware recently amended its statute to provide that the voting trust provisions of the code will not invalidate any voting or other agreement among shareholders or any irrevocable proxy which is "not otherwise illegal." [93]

Although in most states those who create a voting trust may delegate all the voting powers to the voting trustee, in a few states voting power on certain matters must be reserved to those who own a beneficial interest in the trust. Thus in North Carolina, holders of voting trust certificates must have the same rights as shareholders of record with regard to voting on any amendment of the corporate charter, any amendment of the bylaws, reduction of stated capital, sale of the entire assets, merger, consolidation or dissolution.[94] Although a good argument can be made for preventing those who establish a voting trust from completely delegating their powers,[95] as in the case of stock transfer restrictions the fundamental point is the extent to which freedom of shareholders to contract with one another should be permitted. In view of equitable limitations on the ability of a voting trustee to vote the shares against the interest of the beneficial holders,[96] it seems better not to set statutory limits on the extent to which shareholders may delegate their voting powers and permit them to restrict, if they choose, the voting rights of the trustee on particular matters, with the assurance that they may receive equitable relief against actions which are oppressive or otherwise in breach of the trustee's fiduciary duty.

Although many states set limits on the duration of a voting trust, or the number of times the statutory period can be extended,[97] only a few provide for its termination by the vote of a majority in interest of those holding

[90] Perry v. Missouri-Kansas Pipe Line Co., 22 Del. Ch. 33, 37–42, 191 Atl. 823, 825–827 (Ch. 1937).

[91] E.g., Del. Gen. Corp. Law §218(a) (1969); S.C. Bus. Corp. Act §12–16.16(f) (1962).

[92] *Compare* Abercrombie v. Davies, 36 Del. Ch. 371, 130 A.2d 338 (Sup. Ct. 1957), *with* Lehrman v. Cohen, 43 Del. Ch. 222, 222 A.2d 800 (1966).

[93] Del. Gen. Corp. Law §218(d) (1969).

[94] N.C. Bus. Corp. Act §§55–72(c) (1963).

[95] See H. Ballantine, Corporations 431 (rev. ed. 1946).

[96] See, e.g., Brown v. McLanahan, 148 F.2d 703 (4th Cir. 1945); Jesser v. Mayfair Hotel, 316 S.W.2d 465 (Mo. 1958). For other cases see R. Baker & W. Cary, Cases and Materials on Corporations 357 n.1 (3d ed. unabr. 1959).

[97] See note 88 *supra*.

voting trust certificates.[98] Here again the basic problem is freedom of contract. If those who set up the trust are desirous of maintaining control of the corporation for the statutory period, then the purposes of the trust may be defeated if an automatic right of termination resides in those who hold beneficial title to the majority of shares. Since a control arrangement may be to protect a minority as well as a majority, it would seem better not to provide for a statutory right of termination but allow this to be included as a term of the voting trust if the parties so choose. Adequate safeguards against the shares being indefinitely locked into the trust are provided in most states by the requirement of a set period, plus the right to renew for additional periods, where those who do not wish to renew may have their shares released from the trust.[99]

As far as drafting a voting trust is concerned, from what has already been said it should be fairly obvious which principal provisions the draftsman should have in mind. Thus, in view of the fact that a voting trust may only be for a lawful business purpose, the trust agreement should state with some particularity the one or more purposes which motivate the creation of the trust, such as to preserve control among a designated group of shareholders, to safeguard the interests of those who lend money to the corporation in order to insure that capable management may be retained throughout the period of the loan, or to forestall the possibility that outsiders may seek to gain control of the corporation.

The term of the voting trust should be specified and, if there is a statutory provision which limits the allowable term of a trust in the corporation's domiciliary jurisdiction, the trust must not be capable of continuing beyond the statutory period, except that provision may be made, if allowed by statute, for extension of the trust period by the vote of those holding voting trust certificates representing a designated majority in interest of the shares in the trust. If this is done, then a procedure should be established for releasing the shares from the trust to those who do not consent to its extension.[100]

As already indicated, in some states a voting trust must be open to all those who wish to become parties.[101] Even if the statute does not so spe-

---

[98] See Cal. Gen. Corp. Law §2231 (1965); Minn. Bus. Corp. Act §301.27 (1961). For a criticism of the California statute see Note, The Voting Trust: California Erects a Barrier to a Rational Law of Corporate Control, 18 Stan. L. Rev. 1210 (1966).

[99] Where voting trusts are permitted to last indefinitely (e.g., Mo. Gen. & Bus. Corp. Law §351.246 (1965); Wis. Bus. Corp. Law §180.27 (1953)), or for a relatively long period (e.g., California, 21 years), a more convincing argument can be made for a statutory requirement that the trust may be terminated if those holding a majority in interest wish to do so.

[100] See notes 88 and 91 *supra*. Professor Hornstein believes that a provision for extension of the trust by majority vote and binding upon all members of the trust would probably be unenforceable. See 1 G. Hornstein, Corporation Law and Practice §215, at 297 (1959).

[101] See note 89 *supra*.

cify, it may be desirable in certain situations to allow nonmembers of the trust to join, possibly to avoid friction between the "insiders" and the "outsiders." This matter should, however, be approached with caution because, as already pointed out, if any shareholder is allowed to join, then there is a distinct possibility that those who are not members originally may take over the trust and the original purposes of retaining control within a designated group may be frustrated. Therefore, if it is thought desirable to open the trust to nonmembers, considerable care should be taken to determine the eligibility of those entitled to join. For example, if the corporation has two or more classes of shares and the common stock is placed in a voting trust, it should be specified whether those who own preferred stock may join. Even if the preferred is not entitled to vote except when dividends are in arrears, it is always possible that under the terms of the voting trust agreement members of the voting trust may be given voting rights as to certain extraordinary matters, such as a sale of assets, a merger or the issuance of new shares, in which case, if there are many shares of preferred outstanding, the preferred votes may outnumber the common shares.[102]

Along with a statement of the duties and powers of the voting trustee, there should be a clear indication of whether the trustee may vote the shares in the trust only on such matters as election of directors, approval of those who are to make annual audits of the company's books and other routine affairs which are normally handled at an annual meeting, or whether the trustee's voting rights go beyond this to include the power to vote the shares on more fundamental matters such as mergers, sales of assets, amending the articles of incorporation or bylaws, reducing the capital, increasing the authorized number of shares, creating new classes of stock or dissolving the corporation. As already stated, some jurisdictions require that the voting power on such matters be reserved to those who hold beneficial title to the shares.[103] Even if the applicable statute contains no such requirement, however, it may be wise to set some restrictions on the voting power of the trustee to forestall the possibility that the trustee will vote the shares in some manner which prejudices the interests of the minority shareholders. If residual voting rights are reserved to those who hold beneficial interests in the trust, then the trust agreement should set forth with some particularity the procedure for casting votes by holders of voting trust certificates, giving of proxies and so forth.

If the statute requires that a voting trust be subject to termination upon the vote of those holding a designated majority of shares in the trust, or if apart from statute such a termination provision is thought to be desirable, then there should be a procedure for terminating the trust and for returning and transferring record title to the shares to those who may be entitled to receive them upon surrender of their voting trust certificates.

---

[102] See W. Cary, Cases and Materials on Corporations 405 (4th ed. unabr. 1969).
[103] See text accompanying note 94 *supra.*

It is, of course, important that those who are to serve as voting trustees be designated in the trust agreement. If one or more trustees should be unwilling or unable to serve, there should be a procedure for filling the vacancy, perhaps by the vote of the remaining trustees[104] or by the majority in interest of those who hold trust certificates.

The duties, powers and qualifications of the trustee should be spelled out, as has already been indicated with regard to voting powers. Thus it may be provided that a trustee may not be a director of the corporation, although in many closely held concerns such a provision may be unworkable or undesirable. Similarly, it is important to consider whether the voting trustee should be selected from among the shareholders. One commentator has suggested that this is always desirable,[105] but it may very well be that in particular situations the voting trustee should be some neutral party, such as a bank.[106] It has also been suggested that there be a provision that "short-swing" profits made by a trustee in a purchase and sale, or sale and purchase, of shares of the same class as those held in the voting trust, or of any shares of the company for that matter, be recoverable by the corporation.[107] Since such short-swing recovery provisions may be easily evaded by holding for longer than the specified period (e.g., longer than six months), it might be better to provide that any profits made by the trustee in purchasing or selling the stock shall inure to either the corporation or the trust. This would be merely a codification of the common law rule that any profits made by a fiduciary belong to the *cestui que trust* whether or not such profits were made at the latter's expense.[108]

It might be well to spell out the standard of care expected of the voting trustee in carrying out his duties. Trustees, in general, are required to exercise such care and skill as a man of ordinary prudence would exercise in dealing with his own property.[109] A similar standard has been imposed

[104] See, e.g., Idaho Gen. Bus. Corp. Law §30–135 (1929).

[105] See Burke, Voting Trusts Currently Observed, 24 Minn. L. Rev. 347, 375 (1940).

[106] For example, see the situation in Ringling Bros.–Barnum & Bailey Combined Shows v. Ringling, 29 Del. Ch. 610, 53 A.2d 441 (Sup. Ct. 1947), discussed in text accompanying note 128 *infra*.

[107] See Burke, id. at 375.

[108] See 2 A. Scott, Trusts §203 (2d ed. 1956). For recent holdings see Diamond v. Oreamuno, 29 App. Div. 2d 285, 287 N.Y.S.2d 300 (1968), *aff'd*, 24 N.Y.2d 494, 248 N.E.2d 910, 301 N.Y.S.2d 78 (1969) (profits from insider trading recoverable by corporation); Ramacciotti v. Joe Simpkins, Inc., 427 S.W.2d 425 (Mo. 1968).

[109] See 2 A. Scott, id. at §174. Note that the standard of care expected of trustees is different from the standard of loyalty. As regards the latter, the classic expression is that of Chief Justice Cardozo in Meinhard v. Salmon, 249 N.Y. 458, 464, 164 N.E. 545, 546 (1929): "A trustee is held to something stricter than the morals of the market place. Not honesty alone, but the punctilio of an honor the most sensitive, is then the standard of behavior. As to this there has developed a tradition that is unbending and inveterate. Uncompromising rigidity has been the attitude of courts of equity when petitioned to undermine the rule of undivided loyalty by the 'disintegrating erosion' of particular exceptions."

on corporate directors, although some state statutes speak in terms of that degree of diligence and skill which ordinarily prudent men would exercise under similar circumstances.[110] The former version of the standard of care to be applied may be relatively strict, particularly if it is thought to take into account the professional or other skills of the person who happens to be a trustee. For example, a recent case construing similar language in the Securities Act of 1933 ("the standard of reasonableness . . . required of a prudent man in the management of his own property") has created considerable disquiet among members of the corporate bar as to whether, under such a high standard of care, it is worth being a director of a corporation in view of the potential liabilities.[111] A less stringent standard of care might be, as Professor Ballantine suggests, "that degree of care and diligence which an ordinarily prudent director could reasonably be expected to exercise in a like position under similar circumstances." [112] Any formulation of standard of care should, however, be taken with a grain of salt since courts are likely to formulate their own standards of what is or is not proper depending upon the circumstances of each individual case.[113]

Naturally a voting trust agreement should carefully adhere to the applicable statutory requirements regarding the manner in which the trust is to be created, i.e., the transfer of the stock into the name of the voting trustee and the appropriate method of indicating this on the transfer books of the corporation, as well as the issuance of the voting trust certificates to those entitled to receive them. The stock issued to the voting trustee should be stamped with a legend indicating that it is held by the trustee under the terms of a voting trust, with the date of the trust and where it is available for inspection. Each voting trust certificate should bear a similar legend. Unless it is considered wise to have the voting trust certificates freely transferable, each certificate should also bear a legend indicating the extent of the transfer restriction, in much the same manner as stock transfer restriction legends on ordinary stock certificates.

Frequently, by analogy to the first refusal options commonly given to corporations, a voting trustee may be given a right of first refusal as to any voting trust certificates which a member of a voting trust may wish to dispose of, pledge, etc., or which may descend to legatees and next of kin on such member's death. The funds for the repurchase of the voting trust certificates are furnished by the other members of the voting trust in the same proportion as their interests in the trust. Generally speaking, the problems of drafting such a first refusal option are similar to those which have already been enumerated in our earlier discussion of stock transfer restrictions.

[110] E.g., Pa. Bus. Corp. Law §408 (1968).
[111] See Escott v. Bar-Chris Constr. Corp., 283 F. Supp. 643 (S.D.N.Y. 1969), construing the meaning of the term "reasonable investigation" as regards those who have duties under Section 11 of the Securities Act of 1933.
[112] See H. Ballantine, Corporations 159 (rev. ed. 1946).
[113] Ibid.

If the applicable statute requires, the voting trust agreement must impose on the voting trustee the duty of filing the agreement, together with any amendments thereto, in the principal office of the corporation within the state, where the agreement shall be open to inspection to all interested parties in the manner required by law.

Reference has already been made to the wisdom of setting limits on the powers of the voting trustee,[114] and this is particularly so as regards his ability to amend the trust agreement. Although, as pointed out previously, there are equitable remedies against a trustee who acts so as to endanger the interests of the *cestui que trust,* or who places himself in a conflict of interest position vis-à-vis those to whom he bears a fiduciary duty,[115] it may be wise to avoid temptation, as well as the expense of litigation, by removing entirely any power to amend the voting trust agreement from the trustee except with the consent of a requisite percentage of those holding voting trust certificates.

3.3 SHAREHOLDERS' POOLING AGREEMENTS

A useful device for maintaining control of a closely held corporation is a so-called shareholders' pooling agreement. Such an agreement differs from a voting trust in that title to the shares remains in the individual shareholders. The agreement is, in effect, a covenant among the shareholders as to how they shall vote their shares. As in the case of voting trusts, the early court decisions relating to pooling agreements were hostile, regarding them as invalid attempts to separate voting rights from ownership of stock, or as violating a policy which encourages those who attend shareholders' meetings to enter into free discussion of corporate affairs and vote their shares without restriction.[116] Shortly after the beginning of the present century, however, pooling agreements of various sorts began to be upheld,[117] and the modern tendency is to consider them valid if for a reasonable business purpose, not fraudulent in character, nor oppressive to minority shareholders.[118] One caveat must be added, however. Due to the well-recognized prohibition against "vote selling" by shareholders,[119] any arrangement whereby a shareholder enters into an agreement to vote his shares in accordance with another's directions is invalid where the consideration for the agreement is some personal benefit to the shareholder. Thus, if one shareholder should be indebted to another and if, to induce the latter to forgive the debt, he should agree to vote his shares as directed by the lender, the

---

[114] See note 96 *supra.*

[115] See Brown v. McLanahan, 148 F.2d 703 (4th Cir. 1945), and W. Cary, Cases and Materials on Corporations 407–408 (4th ed. unabr. 1969).

[116] See 1 F. O'Neal, Close Corporations 228 (1958).

[117] Id. at 229–230.

[118] See H. Henn, Handbook of the Law of Corporations 527 (2d ed. 1970).

[119] See W. Cary, id. at 376–377 (collecting cases). For a thoughtful analysis and critique of the traditional prohibition against vote selling, see Manne, Some Theoretical Aspects of Share Voting, 64 Colum. L. Rev. 1427 (1964).

agreement would not be enforceable.[120] And "kickback" arrangements of various sorts have been struck down, as where a shareholder agrees to vote for a sale of assets in return for part of the proceeds of the sale.[121]

In some situations it may be difficult to distinguish between invalid shareholder agreements of the vote-selling variety and others which are promoted by more respectable motivations. Although the law prohibits a shareholder from selling his vote for a private benefit, any contract whereby he agrees to vote in accordance with the wishes of others is bound to be motivated by factors which, in a sense, involve a personal benefit. The reasons for pooling agreements are hardly ever solely altruistic or confined exclusively to the good of the corporation (if indeed it is even meaningful to regard the corporation as an entirely distinct entity apart from its shareholders except in a legalistic sense, where the shares are closely held). On the other hand, assuming that vote selling is wrong,[122] there is still a legitimate distinction between a shareholder agreeing to vote in some predetermined manner strictly for private gain and shareholders agreeing to vote their shares together to receive a benefit which inures collectively to the group. Even though this may be distasteful as a form of group selfishness, a rule which would prohibit shareholders from casting their votes except for the "good of the corporation" would be hopelessly unrealistic, as well as abhorrent, if shareholder votes could be invalidated unless in accordance with some preconceived concept of corporate well-being, possibly dictated by the views of those who might, at a particular moment, hold power. Perhaps this, or some similar policy, is behind the maxim that, at least within certain limits, a shareholder "may vote as he pleases." [123] Similarly, although a few cases have held shareholder pooling agreements invalid on the ground that parties to such an agreement should not be able to restrict their discretion to cast their votes in the best interests of the corporation,[124] this is a naive and unrealistic concept of how shareholders behave, particularly in a closely held corporation. Even if there be some analogy between a meeting of a board of directors and a meeting of a deliberative governmental body such as a legislature or legislative committee (and this itself is doubtful in a close corporation), the notion that a shareholders' meeting is a deliberative body exercising its dispassionate discretion for the corporate good is outdated, to put it mildly. Hence shareholders should be able to agree in advance as to how they shall vote their shares.

[120] See Palmbaum v. Magulsky, 217 Mass. 306, 104 N.E. 746 (1914); Stott v. Stott, 258 Mich. 547, 242 N.W. 747 (1932).

[121] Brady v. Bean, 221 Ill. App. 279 (1921).

[122] A proposition which has not been universally accepted by commentators. See Manne, id. at 1427.

[123] For a discussion of problems in this area see Sneed, Stockholder Votes Motivated by Adverse Interest, 58 Mich. L. Rev. 961 (1960). See also W. Cary, id. at 589–590.

[124] See H. Henn, Handbook of the Law of Corporations 528 n.6 (2d ed. 1970) (collecting cases).

It is important to distinguish between a simple agreement between share-holders as to how their shares shall be voted and an agreement which extends beyond this, covering such matters as how the parties to the agreement shall vote *as directors*—appointing officers, and setting salaries, corporate policies and any other matters on which directors are, at least in theory, committed to exercise their unimpeded discretion in the best interests of the corporation. As we shall see, such agreements have frequently been invalidated on public policy grounds, the courts using the admonition that the directors' hands may not be "tied in advance" or the less fortunate metaphor that the board of directors may not be "sterilized." Although even agreements of this type have been upheld if all of the shareholders join in the agreement and it constitutes only a reasonable impediment to directorial discretion,[125] they are nonetheless hazardous unless expressly permitted by statute.[126] Such agreements will be considered in greater detail in a later portion of this chapter.

Shareholder pooling agreements which contain a so-called deadlock-breaking provision have sometimes been held unenforceable for various reasons. Such agreements commonly provide that if the parties to the agreement cannot resolve their differences as to how the shares are to be voted, then one of the shareholders, or perhaps some designated person who is not a party to the agreement acting as arbitrator, will determine how the shares shall be voted and, in some cases, will actually cast the votes. The reasoning of these cases is often confused and bound up with the troublesome problem of the validity of irrevocable proxies coupled with an "interest," and the equally thorny matter of how the technical requirement of "consideration" for the agreement is to be satisfied.[127] Rather than enter into this thicket, let us postpone discussion of these technical requirements

---

[125] See Clark v. Dodge, 269 N.Y. 410, 199 N.E. 641 (1936). But see Long Park, Inc. v. Trenton-New Brunswick Theatres Co., 297 N.Y. 174, 77 N.E.2d 633 (1948), invalidating an agreement among all of the shareholders which delegated, for nineteen years, to one shareholder the power to select the manager of the corporation who would have full supervisory powers.

[126] See McQuade v. Stoneham & McGraw, 263 N.Y. 323, 189 N.E. 234 (1934); Manson v. Curtis, 223 N.Y. 313, 119 N.E. 559 (1918). These New York cases, as well as the *Long Park* case, 297 N.Y. 174, 77 N.E.2d 633 (1948), which for years have been considered leading authorities in this area, have been weakened somewhat, particularly in New York, where they have been legislatively repealed. See N.Y. Bus. Corp. Law §620(b) (1965). Similar and even broader provisions allowing shareholders to inhibit the discretion of directors may be found in Del. Gen. Corp. Law §§350, 351 and 354 (1967). For a discussion of statutory provisions see Ch. XI, text accompanying note 49.

[127] See State ex rel. Breger v. Rusche, 219 Ind. 559, 39 N.E.2d 433 (1942); Johnson v. Spartanburg County Fair Assn., 210 S.C. 56, 41 S.E.2d 599 (1947); Roberts v. Whitson, 188 S.W.2d 875 (Tex. Civ. App. 1945). *Contra:* Smith v. San Francisco & N. P. Ry. Co., 115 Cal. 584, 47 Pac. 582 (1897); Storer v. Ripley, 1 Misc. 2d 235, 125 N.Y.S.2d 831 (Sup. Ct. 1953), *aff'd,* 282 App. Div. 950, 125 N.Y.S.2d 339 (2d Dept. 1953); State ex rel. Everett Trust & Sav. Bank v. Pacific Waxed Paper Co., 22 Wash. 2d 844, 157 P.2d 707 (1945); see W. Cary, Cases and Materials on Corporations 377–380 (4th ed. unabr. 1969).

in the hope of clarifying the discussion somewhat by a detailed account of a classic and colorful leading Delaware case on pooling agreements, *Ringling v. Ringling Bros.–Barnum & Bailey Combined Shows, Inc.*[128]

In 1941 Edith Conway Ringling and Aubrey B. Haley (at that time Aubrey B. Ringling) entered into a "Memorandum of Agreement," the primary objective of which was to insure that, by voting their shares together (each owned 31½ percent of the outstanding shares of Ringling Bros.–Barnum & Bailey Combined Shows, Inc.), they could maintain control of the board of directors. The remaining 37 percent of the outstanding shares was held in a trust established by John Ringling, one of the five sons of August Ringling, founder of the circus; the trust was administered by John and Henry North, John Ringling's two nephews, the beneficiary being the state of Florida.[129] After providing that if either party to the

---

[128] 29 Del. Ch. 318, 49 A.2d 603 (Ch. 1946), *modified on appeal*, 29 Del. Ch. 610, 53 A.2d 441 (Sup. Ct. 1947).

[129] Some further background may be helpful to understand the full import of the agreement between the two ladies, the relationship between them and the underlying reasons for the litigation. The Ringling Circus was founded in Baraboo, Wisconsin, in the latter part of the nineteenth century by five sons of August Rüngeling, an immigrant German harness maker. The sons were Al, Charles, Alf T., Otto and John Ringling, each owning one fifth of the enterprise. As a result of its growing prosperity it was able to acquire, in 1907, its major competitor, Barnum & Bailey, founded by P. T. Barnum in 1870. Otto and Al died in 1911 and 1916, respectively, leaving their shares in the circus to the surviving three brothers. Alf T. Ringling died in 1919, leaving his share to his son, Richard Ringling, who, on his death, left his interest to his wife, Aubrey Ringling, the defendant in this litigation. Charles Ringling died in 1926 and left his share to his wife Edith, the plaintiff. Thus Aubrey and Edith each owned 31½ percent of the outstanding shares. The remaining 37 percent had been left in trust by John Ringling, who had managed the circus and who in large part was responsible for the success it achieved during the days preceding the Depression. As a result of the 1929 Crash, in which John suffered financial reverses, the circus found itself in financial difficulty. In part, this was also due to the emergence of several smaller competing circuses (the Al G. Barnes, Sparks, John Robinson, Hagenback-Wallace and Sells-Floto enterprises). Due to an oversight, Ringling's Madison Square Garden lease for the 1929 New York performance was not renewed and his competitors were able to secure the lease for themselves. Since it would have been disastrous for the circus not to open in New York in its usual fashion, Ringling was forced to buy out his competitors and borrowed $1.7 million from a New York loan company, Allied Owners, Inc., to finance the purchase. As a result of the collapse of several other business ventures in which John Ringling was involved, as well as the Depression of the early 1930s, the circus was unable to meet its payments on the loan from Allied Owners. The loan defaulted and Allied acquired control of the circus, putting in charge a former Coney Island entertainment man by the name of Samuel Gumpertz, with John continuing on as nominal president. This lasted until after John's death, when John Ringling North, John's nephew and co-executor of his estate, managed to regain control of the circus through a loan from Manufacturer's Trust Company. Under the terms of this loan, the shares of the circus were to be placed in a voting trust with John Ringling North, acting on behalf of the estate of his uncle, entitled to elect three of the seven directors, Manufacturer's Trust entitled to appoint one director, and the two other shareholders, Aubrey and Edith, entitled to elect the remaining three. In this manner control of the circus was maintained under John Ringling North, the business prospered and the loan was eventually repaid. When the voting

agreement wished to sell any shares in the corporation she would offer them for sale to the other party on the same terms as those at which she proposed to sell to the outsider, the memorandum set forth the following two provisions:

2. In exercising any voting rights to which either party may be entitled by virtue of ownership of stock or voting trust certificates held by them in either of said corporations each party will consult and confer with the other and the parties will act jointly in exercising such voting rights in accordance with such agreement as they may reach with respect to any matter calling for the exercise of such voting rights.

3. In the event the parties fail to agree with respect to any matter covered by paragraph 2 above, the question in disagreement shall be submitted for arbitration to Karl D. Loos, of Washington, D.C., as arbitrator and his decision thereon shall be binding upon the parties hereto. Such arbitration shall be exercised to the end of assuring for the respective cor-

---

trust expired, Edith and Aubrey, having resented John Ringling North's control of the circus (despite its obvious successes), entered into an arrangement whereby they might, by voting their shares collectively, regain control. North had offered to buy out the two ladies, but this only added fuel to the fire. In addition, Edith had ambitions that her son, Robert, might replace John Ringling North as president of the circus. John was eventually replaced by Robert in early 1943, and James A. Haley, a former Sarasota, Florida, accountant whom Aubrey had married, became first vice-president. John Ringling North thus lost control and the circus operated prosperously under the new management until misfortune struck on July 6, 1944, when a disastrous fire broke out at a matinee performance in Hartford, Connecticut. The Big Top burned, collapsing on spectators, performing artists and animals, and when the smoke had cleared it was found that 168 persons had died, two thirds of them children, and an additional 487 persons were injured. Although all the damage claims were eventually settled by arbitration, criminal proceedings were brought against several circus officials, including James A. Haley, who received a suspended sentence in order that the circus might, under his management, get back on its feet and thus start payments on the damage claims. Subsequently, James A. Haley served his sentence after hearings had been conducted as to whether his management was "indispensable" to the continued running of the circus. Robert Ringling, testifying at the hearings as to Haley's "indispensability," was lukewarm in his appraisal of Haley's services (for some reason, Robert, president of the circus at the time of the Hartford fire, was never indicted, having been out of the state at the time the fire took place). When Haley was subsequently required to serve his prison sentence, it is understandable that his feelings towards Robert Ringling, who never even visited him in prison, were not marked by cordiality. This hostility continued until his release, was shared by his wife, Aubrey Haley (formerly Aubrey Ringling), and in large part was responsible for the falling out between the two ladies, the breach of the agreement between them and the litigation which followed.

The foregoing account of the history of the circus and the background of the litigation is based on an article, "Ringling Wrangling" in 36 Fortune, July, 1947, at 114. See also Taylor, The Triumph of Hoopla, 30 New Yorker, April 10 & April 17, 1954, at 39.

After the litigation, and after John Ringling North regained control of the circus, the Haleys sold the bulk of their interest to North for $200,000. Control of the circus was resold in 1967 to a syndicate headed by Judge Roy Hofheinz, operator of the Houston, Texas, Astro-Dome Stadium, and the circus subsequently "went public" with an offering of 346,000 shares of common stock underwritten by a group headed by Sutro & Co. (with approximately 90 percent control being retained by the Texas syndicate).

porations good management and such participation therein by the members of the Ringling family as the experience, capacity and ability of each may warrant. The parties may at any time by written agreement designate any other individual to act as arbitrator in lieu of said Loos.[130]

The provisions of the voting agreement were carried out until the annual meeting of shareholders in 1946, at which time James A. Haley, husband of Aubrey Ringling Haley, holding a proxy for the shares owned by her, refused to vote the shares along with those held by Edith Ringling so as to be able to elect five out of the seven directors on the board and thus perpetuate control of the circus by the two ladies. The arbitrator, Mr. Loos, after unsuccessfully attempting to persuade Mr. Haley to vote his wife's shares to adjourn the meeting, then directed that the stock of the two parties be voted for five nominees (Edith Conway Ringling, Robert Ringling, William P. Dunn, Jr., Aubrey B. Haley and James A. Haley). James Haley refused to abide by Mr. Loos' ruling and voted his wife's shares for the election of his wife and himself. Edith Ringling voted her shares as directed by Mr. Loos. John Ringling North voted his shares as follows: 864 votes for a Mr. Woods, 863 for a Mr. Griffin and 863 for himself. The chairman then ruled that the five candidates proposed by Mr. Loos, together with Mr. Woods and Mr. North, were elected but this ruling was disputed by the Haley-North faction who argued that Mr. Griffin instead of Mr. Dunn had been elected.[131] In the directors' meeting which followed, Mrs. Ringling participated but stated that she was doing so "without prejudice to her position that the stockholders' meeting had been adjourned and that the directors' meeting was not properly held." Mr. Dunn and Mr. Griffin, each challenged by the opposing group, attempted to join in the voting for differing slates of officers. The result was an impasse and Edith Ringling shortly thereafter brought an action in the Delaware Chancery Court to contest the election of directors and officers.[132]

[130] Ringling v. Ringling Bros.–Barnum & Bailey Combined Shows, Inc. 29 Del. Ch. 318, 322, 49 A.2d 603, 605 (Ch. 1946).

[131] Each of the two ladies was entitled to cast 2205 votes (each owning 315 shares, cumulative voting being in effect and there being seven vacancies in the directorate). Thus the two, voting together, could have cast a total of 4410 votes, enough to allow 882 votes for each of five candidates. Mr. North, who held 370 shares, was entitled to cast 2590 votes, which could not be divided so as to give more than two candidates as many as 882 votes apiece. Thus, for the two ladies to be able to elect five directors (regardless of how North voted), they would have to act together, dividing their combined votes among five candidates, with at least one of the five being voted for by both Mrs. Ringling and Mrs. Haley. This was in fact the way in which Mr. Loos had directed that the shares be voted, i.e., that Mrs. Ringling cast 882 votes for herself, 882 for her son, Robert, and 441 for Mr. Dunn and that Mrs. Haley cast 882 for herself, 882 for her husband and 441 for Mr. Dunn. See the opinion on appeal, Ringling Bros.–Barnum & Bailey Combined Shows v. Ringling, 29 Del. Ch. 610, 615, 53 A.2d 441, 444 n.1 (Sup. Ct. 1947). See also W. Cary, id. at 367 n.1.

[132] See Ringling Bros.–Barnum & Bailey Combined Shows v. Ringling, 29 Del. Ch. 610, 615, 53 A.2d 441, 444–445 (Sup. Ct. 1947).

The lower court found that the Memorandum of Agreement was a valid pooling agreement and that the mutual promises of the parties were sufficient consideration to render it enforceable. It also rejected an argument posed by the defendants that the agreement amounted in substance to a voting trust and was therefore invalid due to its having failed to comply with the Delaware statutory provision regulating voting trusts.[133] Unlike a voting trust, the two ladies had retained the title to their shares and the right to vote them, though they had agreed to vote in accordance with the agreement. Having thus concluded that the agreement was not a voting trust, the court upheld it as not against public policy, having been for a legitimate business purpose. The most controversial aspect of the court's holding, however, related to how the agreement should be enforced. The court's view of what the parties intended was that in the event that they should disagree as to how their shares were to be voted, Mr. Loos was to resolve the dispute, and if one of the parties to the agreement refused to abide by Mr. Loos' decision, then the agreement implied that the other party, willing to abide by the decision, would have an irrevocable proxy to cast the votes represented by the shares held by the dissenting party in accordance with the manner directed by Mr. Loos. Thus the court concluded that it might, in effect, grant specific performance of the agreement. However, rather than attempt to reconstruct the contested meeting, the court decided that it would be appropriate to direct that a new shareholders' meeting be held before a court-appointed master, pointing out that it might also be possible for the two litigants to arrive at a resolution of their dispute before the meeting was held, thus rendering it unnecessary.

On appeal, although the Delaware Supreme Court did not quarrel with the Chancellor's views as to the validity of the pooling agreement and his finding that the agreement did not amount to a voting trust, it did differ as to how the agreement should be enforced. Although the agreement specifically stated that the decision of Mr. Loos as arbitrator "shall be binding upon the parties," [134] it contained no provision which gave either party an irrevocable proxy to vote the shares of the other, nor did it give Mr. Loos the power to vote the shares. This led to the somewhat incongruous situation that, although the agreement purported to make Loos' decision binding upon both parties, "no decision of the arbitrator could ever be enforced if both parties to the agreement were unwilling that it be enforced, for the obvious reason that there would be no one to enforce it." [135] If the Chancellor was therefore incorrect as to what the parties had intended, what *did* they intend? To put the matter differently, what remedy should be given to

---

[133] See text accompanying notes 90–92 *supra* and Perry v. Missouri-Kansas Pipe Line Co., 22 Del. Ch. 33, 37–42, 191 Atl. 823, 825–827 (Ch. 1937).

[134] See paragraph 3 of the agreement, quoted in text accompanying note 130 *supra*.

[135] See Ringling Bros.–Barnum & Bailey Combined Shows v. Ringling, 29 Del. Ch. 610, 615, 53 A.2d 441, 445 (Sup. Ct. 1947).

Mrs. Ringling, who abided by Mr. Loos' decision? The Supreme Court's answer was that, since the votes cast by the Haley group were in breach of the agreement, they should be given no effect. Thus the only effective votes were those cast by Edith Ringling and Mr. North. Since Mr. North's vote against the motion for adjournment of the meeting was sufficient to defeat it, the court then declared that those candidates for whom Mrs. Ringling and Mr. North voted should be declared elected. Since this resulted in the election of only six directors, there was thus one vacancy, but the court did not consider it advisable to pass on how the vacancy should be filled in view of the possibility that the matter might be resolved at the forthcoming 1947 shareholders' meeting.

The result of this rather extraordinary litigation is somewhat ironic. The two ladies had entered into the pooling agreement to insure that by voting their shares together they would be able to keep control of the circus away from John Ringling North. As a result of their dispute, and the manner in which it was resolved by the Delaware Supreme Court, Aubrey and James Haley were not reelected as directors. Since North held 370 shares compared to Edith Ringling's 315 shares, his superior voting power might eventually enable him to dictate how the vacancy should be filled if the deadlock between the two ladies persisted. At least he and Edith Ringling would meanwhile be in effective control of the circus, with the two Haleys playing a subservient role. In view of this it is not surprising that the Haleys subsequently sold their interest in the circus to Mr. North.[136]

Turning from the practical consequences of the *Ringling* case to the legal aspects, it is apparent that although pooling agreements entered into without fraud and for a reasonable business purpose are valid (assuming that they merely relate to the manner in which the parties to the agreement are to vote as *shareholders* and do not purport to bind them as to how they are to vote as *directors*), one is left in doubt as to how such agreements are to be enforced. If the Ringling agreement *had* provided for irrevocable proxies to the nondissenting shareholder, or to Mr. Loos, so that the shares of the dissenting shareholder might thereby be voted in accordance with Mr. Loos' decision, the lower court might have been proper in its view that specific performance of such a pooling agreement might be granted. Nonetheless, even if specific performance *had* been given, since Mrs. Ringling and Mrs. Haley were unwilling to cooperate as shareholders, the likelihood would have been that their dispute would continue on the director level.

---

[136] For a further analysis see Chayes, Madam Wagner and the Close Corporation, 73 Harv. L. Rev. 1532, 1540 (1960), where the author points out that no satisfactory explanation has ever been given as to why Mr. Haley refused to abide by Mr. Loos' ruling. If he had done so, then he and his wife would have been voted in as directors and they, along with the two directors representing Mr. North, would have been able to out-vote as directors Edith Ringling, Robert (her son), and Mr. Dunn. As a result of poor tactics and the Delaware Supreme Court's invalidation of the votes of the Haley faction, the two Haleys were not even elected as members of the board.

Thus, unless they, Robert Ringling and James Haley acted together as *directors,* they would be unable to maintain effective control of the circus. Either faction, by voting as directors along with the directors elected by Mr. North, would have been able to render the other faction effectively powerless. From this it seems to follow that although a pooling agreement is a lawful means of attempting to maintain control of a closely held corporation, it is likely to be an ineffective means of doing so unless the parties to the agreement are willing to cooperate with one another. Essentially the same point has been made by one commentator who drew an analogy between these problems of a closely held corporation and the well-known reluctance of equity courts to grant specific performance of agreements to render personal services because of the impracticality and difficulty of forcing someone to perform services of a personal nature.[137] Essentially the same problem has arisen in the partnership area, where courts have traditionally refused to grant specific performance of partnership agreements. In this regard the law is wise, since, if parties to a business venture cannot work together amicably, it is impractical to attempt to *force* them to work together. Considerations of this sort no doubt underlie the rule that a partnership may be dissolved at any time by any partner (at the risk of being held liable in damages for breach of the partnership agreement).[138] Although, as we shall see,[139] a corporation may not be dissolved as easily as a partnership even when deadlocked, the problems involved in both situations are remarkably similar and the predicament of the locked-in and unhappy shareholder is indeed a serious one if his shares are not readily marketable.

Since these problems of deadlock in the closely held corporation will be

[137] See id. at 1535–1545. But see Weil v. Beresth, 154 Conn. 12, 220 A.2d 456 (1966) (specific performance of shareholders agreement not to amend bylaws or increase number of directors).

[138] See Uniform Partnership Act §31(2). See also J. Crane & A. Bromberg, Partnership 428 (1968).

[139] See Ch. VII. See also Professor Chayes' discussion of the leading New York case in this area, In re Radom & Neidorff, Inc., 307 N.Y. 1, 119 N.E.2d 563 (1954), in Chayes, *supra* at 1536–1546. Chayes concludes that "A judicial treatment of the close corporation which is responsive to the underlying reality of a personal, intimate, ongoing association among the enterprisers will be somewhat readier to dissolve the corporate shell rather than leave the parties in an Ugoline embrace." Id. at 1546. The obscure reference to an "Ugoline embrace" is apparently based on an incident involving a Pisan nobleman and partisan leader of the thirteenth century who, after being defeated by Archbishop Ruggieri, the leader of the Ghibellines, was imprisoned by the Archbishop along with his two sons and nephews in the Tower of the Gualandi and left there to starve. The poet, Dante, alludes to the incident in the Inferno, Canto XXXIII, where he portrays Ugolino as voraciously devouring the Archbishop's head, the two enemies being forever frozen to one another in a lake of ice. Professor Chayes' reference, though obscure, effectively dramatizes the predicament of unfriendly associates locked into a close corporation due to judicial unwillingness to dissolve it. For another discussion see Israels, The Sacred Cow of Corporate Existence—Problems of Deadlock and Dissolution, 19 U. Chi. L. Rev. 778 (1952).

considered in detail in a later chapter,[140] it might be well to examine some other factors which may determine the validity of pooling agreements even though their efficacy as a control device may be in doubt.

As previously stated,[141] some of the early cases involving pooling agreements, as well as various other control devices such as voting trusts and irrevocable proxies, regarded them with suspicion and frequently invalidated them if they were thought to be against public policy, if they separated voting rights from either the legal or beneficial title to the shares, or if they otherwise departed from what was thought to be the proper relationship shareholders should bear toward one another. Today, however, the tendency is to uphold such agreements if they are reasonable and not oppressive toward the other shareholders. Several factors appear to be of particular importance:[142] the duration of the agreement, the consideration supporting it and its purpose.

As far as the length of the agreement is concerned, perhaps the only generalization which can safely be made is that the longer the term of the agreement the greater the risk that a court might invalidate it. Nonetheless, there are decisions which have sustained agreements lasting for as long as twenty years or even indefinitely.[143] Since there is, then, no clear test as to what constitutes a reasonable period, it might be wise, as a practical matter, to follow as a guide the permissible period for voting trusts in a particular jurisdiction. Thus, if a statute were to specify that a voting trust may not last longer than ten years, but may be renewed for an additional ten-year period,[144] it would be wise to limit the term of a shareholders' agreement to ten years and provide for its extension in similar fashion. However, if there are justifiable business reasons why the agreement should be for a longer term, then, if the purposes of the agreement are adequately spelled out, the term might safely be made longer than the period applicable to voting trusts. A voting trust is, in a sense, a more inflexible control device since it involves the transfer of title of shares to a voting trustee and thus, in effect, locks in beneficiaries of the trust for the duration of the trust. In a pooling agreement, title to the shares remains in the shareholders, who continue to have exclusive voting rights, except for whatever arrangement may be made for proxies to vote the shares of those who refuse to abide by the agreement in the event of a dispute.[145] Thus there is more overall freedom in a pooling agreement, less likelihood that voting rights will be divorced from share ownership and, although the shares may often be subject to stock transfer restrictions, the pooling agreement has less of a locked-in quality than a voting trust. Accordingly, even though there may be in some

[140] See Ch. VII.
[141] See text accompanying note 116 *supra*.
[142] For a more extensive list see 1 F. O'Neal, Close Corporations 240–242 (1958).
[143] Id. at 246.
[144] See note 88 *supra*.
[145] See the discussion of the *Ringling* case in text accompanying note 134 *supra*.

jurisdictions a statutory policy as to the allowable duration of voting trusts, that policy need not necessarily be decisive as to the reasonableness of a pooling agreement.

As far as the consideration for the agreement is concerned, the primary question appears to be whether mutual promises between shareholders constitute sufficient consideration in the technical sense to make the agreement enforceable as a contract. Although, as we have seen, the lower court in the *Ringling* case expressly found that mutual promises were sufficient consideration,[146] there are a few cases, representing what now might be characterized as a minority view, that mutual promises standing alone are not enough.[147] Some of this thinking is doubtless due to confusion from a related area, namely, that involving the enforceability of irrevocable proxies and the dogma that, for a proxy to be irrevocable, it must be "coupled with an interest." Although this question will be considered shortly in greater detail,[148] it may suffice to say that as far as shareholder pooling agreements are concerned (i.e., agreements which merely specify how the shareholders shall vote their shares), most jurisdictions would uphold an agreement founded solely upon mutual promises.[149] This seems to be an eminently sensible approach since it is in accord with the general rules of contract law that mutual promises are sufficient consideration to make a binding agreement. There seems to be little reason why pooling agreements should be governed by substantially different rules.

As to the purposes of a pooling agreement, the purpose must be to achieve a corporate benefit rather than one which is purely in the interests of those who are members of the pooling agreement. Although shareholders may lawfully agree to vote together so as to elect directors in order that the corporation may be run efficiently and well, if the purpose is to exploit or harm the business or to prejudice the minority shareholders, then it is invalid.[150] In essence this means that shareholders may agree to vote their shares in a specified manner to elect directors so long as the effect and intent of the agreement is not to act in breach of their fiduciary duty to the corporation and to the minority shareholders.

There may be some doubt as to the validity of certain pooling agreements which, in effect, give one shareholder voting power which is greater than that which he would normally have. Thus one court invalidated an agreement whereby three shareholders gave a fourth, who held 25 percent of the shares, voting power equal to 50 percent (in contrast to the 25 percent

[146] See text accompanying note 133 *supra*.

[147] For a discussion and collection of the decisions, see 1 F. O'Neal, id. at 249–250.

[148] See text accompanying note 156 *infra*.

[149] See 1 F. O'Neal, id. at 249–250.

[150] See 1 F. O'Neal, id. at 243, citing White v. Snell, 35 Utah 434, 100 Pac. 927, 929 (1909), where the court also observed that an agreement which has as its purpose the limiting of a corporation's products in restraint of trade would be invalid as against public policy.

which he would normally have had). The agreement was entered into in consideration of his lending the corporation $10,000 and was not mentioned in the corporate charter or bylaws. In invalidating the agreement the court expressed its fear that "any smaller proportion might be selected and a chosen individual (a favored creditor perhaps) given despotic authority, of which authority stockholders not parties to the agreement and others dealing with the corporation would be in complete ignorance." [151]

In view of the possible invalidity of pooling agreements which give one shareholder disproportionate voting power, a safer method of accomplishing the same result is through classifying the shares.[152] Thus, rather than have four shareholders, each owning 25 percent of the outstanding shares, agree to give one of the four voting power equal to 50 percent of the shares, two classes of stock could be issued, each class carrying the right to elect two out of the corporation's four directors. All the shares in one class could then be issued to one shareholder and the shares in the other class split equally among the other three shareholders. Share classification will be discussed in greater detail at a later point.[153]

In addition, as we shall see,[154] various states have statutory provisions which expressly permit shareholder pooling agreements of a wide variety of types[155] and thus, if there is doubt as to the validity of a particular pooling agreement under the laws of a given jurisdiction, it might be wise to consider the advantages of incorporating elsewhere.

3.4 IRREVOCABLE PROXIES

Although most shareholder pooling agreements are lawful, there are, as we have seen, problems concerning their effectiveness, particularly the manner in which they may be enforced.[156] Hence, to supplement or effectuate an agreement among shareholders as to how their shares should be voted, one or more shareholders may give another a proxy to vote their shares and stipulate that the proxy will be irrevocable for the period of the agreement.

Although, as in the case of pooling agreements, the early decisions frequently took a skeptical attitude toward any attempt to make a proxy irre-

---

[151] Nickolopoulos v. Sarantis, 102 N.J. Eq. 585, 587, 141 Atl. 792, 793, (Ct. Err. & App. 1928). A later New Jersey case distinguished the *Nickolopoulos* decision on the ground that the agreement's invalidity resulted from its secrecy, thus implying that such an agreement might be valid if disclosed to the other shareholders and to the corporate creditors. Katcher v. Ohsman, 26 N.J. Super. 28, 97 A.2d 180 (Ch. 1953). For a discussion of the *Nickolopoulos* case see 1 F. O'Neal, id. at 254–255, where the author collects the conflicting authorities in this area.

[152] See 1 F. O'Neal, id. at 254–255.

[153] See text accompanying note 213 *infra*.

[154] See Ch. XI, text accompanying notes 31–57.

[155] E.g., Del. Gen. Corp. Law §354 (1967).

[156] See text accompanying note 137 *supra*.

vocable, more recent cases generally uphold such arrangements if the proxy is coupled with an "interest" and if it does not run counter to some statutory provision.[157]

The requirement that a proxy, to be irrevocable, must be "coupled with an interest" proceeds from the assumption that a proxy is merely a form of agency. It is generally held that an agency relationship may be terminated by the principal at any time, unless the agency is "coupled with an interest,"[158] and this reasoning has been applied to proxies. Thus a proxy is generally revocable unless coupled with an interest or unless there is a specific statute which permits irrevocable proxies.[159]

The cases are unclear as to what constitutes an interest sufficient to make a proxy irrevocable. Essentially the controversy concerns whether the interest, to be legally effective, must be an interest in the shares themselves (such as the interest of a pledgee or of one who, by agreeing to purchase shares, has equitable title) or whether some other form of interest is sufficient. Under the more conservative view, the interest must be in the shares themselves,[160] but more liberal (and possibly more enlightened) decisions have found an interest where the shareholders make further loans to the corporation in reliance on the shareholders' agreement[161] or where, under the terms of the agreement, each party has a right of first refusal to purchase the other's shares in the event of a proposed sale.[162] In fact, in the case just cited, the court did not rely heavily upon the fact that the parties had cross-purchase options and merely stated that "[t]he power to vote the stock was necessary in order to make . . . control of the corporation secure."[163] If the interest concept is thus watered down, there seems to be little reason why it should not be eliminated entirely.[164]

---

[157] See 1 F. O'Neal, id. at 316–317. See also Comment, Irrevocable Proxies, 43 Texas L. Rev. 733 (1965).

[158] See Restatement of Agency Second §§118, 138–39 (1958). Note, however, that the principal may be liable in damages to the agent for terminating the relationship if the termination is in breach of an agreement between the two, such as an employment agreement. See Restatement of Agency Second §455 (1958).

[159] For a critique of the assumptions underlying the analogy between a proxy and an agency, and the doctrine that a proxy, to be irrevocable, must be coupled with an interest, see 1 F. O'Neal, id. at 323–324. See also Chayes, Madam Wagner and the Close Corporation, 73 Harv. L. Rev. 1532, 1542–1545 (1960). According to the late Professor Mechem, the decision which is generally believed to have given rise to the doctrine that only a power coupled with an interest is irrevocable is Hunt v. Rousmanier's Administrators, 21 U.S. (8 Wheat.) 174 (1823) (opinion by Chief Justice Marshall). See F. Mechem, Outlines of the Law of Agency §§267–269 (1952), criticizing the case. For a further analysis and criticism see Seavey, Termination by Death of Proprietary Powers of Attorney, 31 Yale L.J. 283 (1922).

[160] See 1 F. O'Neal, id. at 319.

[161] See Abercrombie v. Davies, 123 A.2d 893 (Del. Ch. 1956), *modified,* 125 A.2d 588 (Del. Ch. 1956), *rev'd as to another point,* 130 A.2d 338 (Del. Sup. Ct. 1957).

[162] State ex rel. Everett Trust & Savings Bank v. Pacific Waxed Paper Co., 22 Wash. 2d 844, 157 P.2d 707 (1945).

[163] 22 Wash. 2d at 852, 157 P.2d at 711.

[164] See 1 F. O'Neal, id. at 323.

However, as far as the practicalities are concerned, where shareholders wish to use irrevocable proxies in connection with a pooling agreement, it might be well to insert cross options running in favor of each shareholder to purchase the other's shares in the event of a proposed sale or death so that if the agreement is tested under the more technical view that there must be some interest in the shares themselves, it may be upheld. In addition, such a first refusal option might be wise for reasons other than mere fulfillment of the technical interest requirement.[165] If cross options are not used, however, and there is a risk that the agreement, if tested, might be invalidated by an unduly conservative court, alternative arrangements might be to form a voting trust or to incorporate under the laws of some jurisdiction which by statute expressly permits irrevocable proxies in connection with shareholders' agreements.[166]

3.5 SHAREHOLDER AGREEMENTS WHICH RESTRICT DISCRETION OF DIRECTORS

Although it may be proper for shareholders to agree as to how their shares are to be voted, it is generally held that it is improper for them to extend the agreement to matters which fall within the directors' discretion, such as the appointment of officers, setting of salaries and payment of dividends.[167] The policy behind this is that directors should be free to exercise their discretion for the benefit of the corporation and that they cannot properly do this if they are committed in advance to a predetermined course of action. Also a freezing of the status quo by agreement may result in positive harm to the corporation. One reason for having a board of directors and giving it discretion to run the business is to permit flexibility to meet changing conditions.

On the other hand, where a corporation is closely held and the same persons are likely to be principal shareholders, directors and officers, it seems somewhat unrealistic to bifurcate each person's role and allow him to agree to do certain things as a shareholder but not to do others as a director. To put the matter differently, although the theory behind all of this is that the directors are supposed to exercise their discretion for the corporate benefit, the reality is more likely to be that those who participate in a close corporation will generally not be able to differentiate between being shareholders, directors and officers and will act in all three capacities in a manner which more or less reflects their personal attitudes and wishes. Although in doing so they may not be acting in pure selfishness, and may in fact be

[165] See, in general, the discussion of the uses of first refusal options in text following note 11 *supra*.

[166] E.g., N.Y. Bus. Corp. Law §609(f)(5) (1965).

[167] See 1 F. O'Neal, id. at §5.16. See also Delaney, The Corporate Director: Can His Hands Be Tied in Advance, 50 Colum. L. Rev. 52 (1950).

seeking to do what is best for the corporation, the notion that they cannot agree to certain things as directors but may agree to other matters as shareholders may strike them as bizarre.

This becomes particularly apparent when a close corporation is formed to take over the affairs of a partnership. Under the rules of partnership law, partners may agree as to anything which falls within the scope of the business. This is the function of a partnership agreement. Hence they may agree on the manner in which partnership profits are to be distributed, on the roles of various partners in handling particular phases of the partnership business, or on supervision of the business by a managing partner. When the partnership becomes a close corporation, it may seem odd that such agreements are prohibited.

Although authorities in this area are in conflict,[168] several representative cases may illustrate what is permissible and the way in which the law may be developing.

Among the most frequently discussed decisions are those from New York. In *McQuade v. Stoneham & McGraw*[169] three shareholders entered into an agreement which provided that they were to continue as directors and also as officers: Charles A. Stoneham as president, John J. McGraw as vice-president and Francis X. McQuade as treasurer. Stoneham was to receive a salary of $45,000, with McGraw and McQuade each receiving salaries of $7500. The corporation involved in the dispute was the National Exhibition Company, owner of the New York Giants, of which McGraw was manager. When the contract was entered into, McQuade was a city magistrate. Stoneham owned a majority of the shares and sold seventy shares each to McQuade and McGraw. In addition to setting forth who were to be the directors and officers, and what their salaries would be, the agreement went on to provide that there was to be no change in the salaries, amount of capital, number of shares, bylaws, "or any matters regarding the policy of the business of the corporation or any matters which may in any wise affect, endanger or interfere with the rights of minority stockholders" except upon the unanimous consent of the three parties to the agreement.

Stoneham, through his ownership of a majority of the shares, controlled the board of directors by electing four directors in addition to himself. These, together with McQuade and McGraw, made up a board of seven. McQuade continued to serve as treasurer of the corporation (and his salary was even increased to $10,000) until May 2, 1928, when he was replaced by a Leo J. Bondy. At the next shareholders' meeting he was also dropped as director. He thereupon brought an action for specific performance of the agreement and to compel his reinstatement. Although the lower courts had refused to grant reinstatement, they had awarded McQuade damages. In

[168] Ibid.
[169] 263 N.Y. 323, 189 N.E. 234 (1934).

reversing, the New York Court of Appeals held that the contract was unlawful and unenforceable on two grounds, first because the Inferior Criminal Courts Act prohibited a city magistrate from engaging in any other business or profession, and second because "a contract is illegal and void so far as it precludes the board of directors, at the risk of incurring legal liability, from changing officers, salaries or policies or retaining individuals in office, except by consent of the contracting parties." [170] Interestingly enough, the trial court had found that the reason for McQuade's discharge was that he had disagreed with and had "antagonized" Stoneham, challenging his power over the corporate treasury. In doing so, McQuade was purporting to act for the benefit of the corporation and the minority shareholders and Stoneham had discharged him because of his wish to retain personal control over the way in which the business was run. The Court of Appeals brushed this aside with the observation that the minority shareholders were not complaining about his discharge and that it was impossible to see how the corporation had been injured by the substitution of Bondy in McQuade's place.

The *McQuade* holding, and an earlier New York case, *Manson v. Curtis,*[171] are fairly representative of the decisions following the general rule that shareholders may not agree as to matters which fall within their discretion as directors. Two years later, however, the same court upheld an agreement between two persons, who owned *all* the stock in two New Jersey corporations, which provided that one of them, the plaintiff Clark, should continue as a director and as general manager as long as he should be "faithful, efficient and competent." [172] In addition, he would, during his life, receive one fourth of the net income of the corporations by way of either salary or dividends and it was agreed that no unreasonable or incommensurate salaries should be paid to other officers or agents which would so reduce the net income as to affect Clark's profits materially. In return for Dodge's agreement to these provisions, Clark, who was the sole possessor of the formulae and methods of manufacture of various medicinal preparations made by the two companies, agreed to disclose the formulae to Dodge's son, to instruct him (the son) in the details and methods of manufacture and

---

[170] 263 N.Y. at 330, 189 N.E. at 237.

[171] 223 N.Y. 313, 119 N.E. 559 (1918). Here an agreement between the two largest shareholders in a corporation provided that neither the corporation's president nor its directors should interfere, for one year, with the plaintiff's operation of the business. The court held the agreement to be unlawful since it would have "sterilized" the board of directors, although it did point out that it was not illegal for those owning a majority of the stock "to unite upon a course of corporate policy or action, or upon the officers whom they will elect." In addition, the court suggested that *"all* the stockholders by their universal consent may do as they choose with the corporate concerns and assets, provided the interests of creditors are not affected, because they are the complete owners of the corporation. . . ." 223 N.Y. at 325, 119 N.E. at 562–563 (emphasis supplied).

[172] Clark v. Dodge, 269 N.Y. 410, 199 N.E. 641 (1936). Also see Galler v. Galler, 32 Ill. 2d 16, 203 N.E.2d 577 (1964).

finally, on his (Clark's) death, if he should have no surviving issue, to bequeath his stock to Dodge's wife and children.

In finding the agreement enforceable, the court pointed out that all of the shareholders were parties to the agreement and, unlike the earlier *Manson* case,[173] there had been no attempt to "sterilize" the board of directors. The prime test of validity, in the court's view, should be who might be harmed by the agreement and the extent of the possible harm. Since no rights of minority shareholders were involved, the only possible harm might be to outsiders, such as creditors. If the agreement posed no harm to the corporation, then creditors might not complain, and here the court found that "If there was any invasion of the powers of the directorate under that agreement, it is so slight as to be negligible; . . ."[174] The agreement had stipulated that Clark was to be retained as general manager only so long as he proved "faithful, efficient and competent." This, the court thought, could harm no one. Moreover, as regards the agreement to pay Clark one fourth of the net income of the corporations, the court assumed that the parties had intended this to refer to whatever was left for distribution after the directors had in good faith set aside whatever they deemed wise.

One might infer from the above three cases that for an agreement which restricts directorial discretion to be valid, at least three conditions must be fulfilled: (1) *all* the shareholders must be parties to the agreement; (2) the agreement must not take *all* discretionary powers away from the directors, even for a short period of time; and (3) it must not harm other interested persons, such as creditors. Thus, in a later case, the same court held that, even though all the shareholders were parties to an agreement, if it provided that for nineteen years one shareholder might select the manager of the corporation, who should have full power to supervise and direct its operation, this was more than the "slight invasion" of directorial powers that the court in the earlier *Clark* case had held to be "negligible."[175]

Since, even if all the shareholders are parties to the agreement, its validity will depend upon the extent to which the directors' discretion has been impeded, and the potential harm to others, such as creditors, the question of whether the agreement is enforceable can be resolved only on the facts of each case, unless a particular jurisdiction expressly permits shareholder agreements which interfere with the directors' powers.[176] Therefore, the

---

[173] 223 N.Y. 313, 119 N.E. 559 (1918).

[174] Clark v. Dodge, 269 N.Y. 410, 417, 199 N.E. 641, 643.

[175] Long Park, Inc. v. Trenton–New Brunswick Theatres Co., 297 N.Y. 174, 77 N.E.2d 633 (1948). Even if all the shareholders are not parties to the agreement, it may be upheld if the number of shareholders who are not parties to the agreement is relatively small and if the agreement is not unfair, fraudulent or otherwise prejudicial to the interests of others. See Glazer v. Glazer, 374 F.2d 390 (5th Cir. 1967), *cert. denied,* 389 U.S. 831 (1967).

[176] See Del. Gen. Corp. Law §§350, 351, 354 (1967); Fla. Gen. Corp. Law §608.0105 (1963); N.Y. Bus. Corp. Law §620(b) (1965); N.C. Bus. Corp. Act §55–73(b) (1955); S.C. Bus. Corp. Act §12–16.15 (1962).

wisest thing is to avoid, as much as possible, shareholder agreements of this type unless the degree of interference with the directors' powers is relatively slight, there is a clear benefit to the corporation and there is no harm to others.

From a practical standpoint the two matters which are particularly likely to be involved in such agreements are promises of long-term employment at a particular salary and covenants to pay out a specified percentage of the net profits of the corporation as dividends. Although some shareholder agreements have been invalidated even though they were restricted to these two areas, the tendency of the courts is to uphold them if they do not work a fraud or are not otherwise harmful to the corporation.[177] If the salaries specified in the agreement are fair and the directors are not deprived of their power to discharge an unfaithful or inefficient employee, the agreement is likely to be upheld even though not all the shareholders are parties to it,[178] although it is obviously better if all the shareholders join in or at least ratify the agreement.

Another way of assuring long-term employment is an employment agreement between the executive and the corporation. Although the difference here is mainly one of form, particularly where the corporation is closely held, it may be helpful if the employee has a contract with the corporation, approved by its directors and, again, ratified by the shareholders if possible. As in the case of shareholder agreements, not all employment agreements are valid, particularly if they guarantee lifetime employment, but the tendency is to uphold them if the compensation is reasonable, if the agreement is limited to a reasonable period of time, if there is no fraud or waste of corporate assets and, as before, if the directors have residual power to discharge the employee for disloyal or inefficient service.[179]

Much the same thing can be said of shareholder agreements relating to the percentage of net profits of a corporation which must be paid out as dividends. As before, the key factors are fairness, absence of fraud and overall benefit or lack of harm to the corporation.[180] If all the shareholders join in the agreement, it is more likely to be upheld.[181] Another technique of handling the matter is through a charter or bylaw provision. Although, as in the prior case of the employment contract, the difference here is mainly one of form where the corporation is closely held, the courts may be less likely to construe a charter or bylaw provision as a shareholder attempt to interfere with directorial discretion. In any event, such provisions have been

---

[177] For a detailed discussion and collection of cases see 1 F. O'Neal, Close Corporations §5.17 (1958).

[178] Ibid.

[179] Id. at §§6.01–6.14. This topic is also discussed in Ch. IV, text accompanying note 4.

[180] 1 F. O'Neal, id. at §5.21. See also Galler v. Galler, 32 Ill. 2d 16, 203 N.E.2d 577 (1964).

[181] 1 F. O'Neal, id. at §5.21.

upheld,[182] although one should take care that the provision is reasonable and not harmful to the corporation.

3.6 HIGH VOTING OR QUORUM REQUIREMENTS FOR SHAREHOLDER OR DIRECTOR ACTION

Another important control device for the closely held corporation is a charter or bylaw provision which requires that for any action taken by shareholders, a designated percentage of the outstanding shares must be present in order to constitute a quorum and, once a quorum is present, a further percentage of the shares must vote in favor of a particular matter in order to authorize it. The same technique can be used with regard to directors' meetings, and the two techniques may be used in combination with one another.

Sometimes such provisions are referred to as veto powers. Thus, where a person holding only 15 percent of the outstanding shares wishes to be protected in certain respects against those holding a majority, he may insist that as to various important matters, such as the issuance of new shares, mergers, sales of assets, dissolution, increases in director or officer salaries, reduction in dividend payments, reduction in the number of directors and so forth, 90 percent of the shares outstanding must be present at a meeting in order to form a quorum. If the matter involves director action, the shareholder, if he is sitting on a board of four directors, will be protected if all four directors are required for a quorum. As already indicated, the same result may be achieved through the slightly different technique of requiring a specified percentage of a quorum for effective action by either shareholders or directors.

The leading case in this area is *Benintendi v. Kenton Hotel.*[183] There, two persons owning unequal amounts of all the stock of a corporation entered into an agreement providing that (1) no action should be taken by the stockholders except by unanimous vote of all of them; (2) the directors of the corporation should be the three persons receiving, at the annual stockholders' meeting, the unanimous vote of all the stockholders; (3) no action should be taken by the directors except by unanimous vote of all of them; and (4) the bylaws should not be amended except by unanimous vote of all the stockholders. The New York Court of Appeals invalidated all but the fourth provision of the agreement. The overall reasoning of the majority opinion was that any agreement which required unanimity for all

---

[182] See F. O'Neal and J. Derwin, Expulsion or Oppression of Business Associates §7.06 (1961). For further discussion see Ch. IV, text accompanying note 10. In some states statutory provisions expressly authorize shareholder agreements respecting dividends. See Del. Gen. Corp. Law §354 (1967); Fla. Gen. Corp. Act §608.0105 (1) (1963). See also N.Y. Bus. Corp. Law §620 (1965).

[183] 294 N.Y. 112, 60 N.E.2d 829 (1945).

shareholder or director action was inconsistent with the statutory scheme, which, in the case of shareholder action, provided designated percentages of shareholder vote to pass various resolutions (such as changing the capitalization of the corporation, which required a two-thirds vote, and dissolving it, which required a majority vote or a vote of only half the stock if there was a deadlock on the question of dissolution). The court was of the view that any scheme which gave a minority shareholder a veto power over such matters was inconsistent with the statute. Interestingly enough, however, it inserted a caveat that "We do not hold that an arrangement would necessarily be invalid, which, for particular decisions, would require unanimous consent of all stockholders." [184] Thus it was only because unanimous consent was required for *every* shareholder action that the *Benintendi* agreement was held invalid.

An extensive analysis of the reasoning of the *Benintendi* case does not seem appropriate, in view of its having been legislatively repudiated three years later by a provision which permitted greater than majority quorum and voting requirements for shareholder or director action to be included in the certificate of incorporation.[185] Similar statutory provisions have become common in many states,[186] although a few states may continue to have statutory schemes which are unfavorable to high or unanimous vote requirements.[187] The primary problem today is not whether high or unanimous voting requirements are valid but how and when they should be used as control devices.

Although on rare occasions it may be necessary for persons who set up a close corporation to adopt an arrangement similar to that in *Benintendi*, since it gives *any* shareholder or director a veto power over *any* proposed course of action, it seems to be on the whole an unwise and dangerous scheme, for it paves the way for pressure plays and extortion and virtually invites deadlock at every opportunity.[188] This is easily seen by envisaging the same type of arrangement in a partnership context: if each partner were given a veto power over all partnership decisions, the partnership might not be able to function effectively and, as in the corporate situation, might become deadlocked. As a practical matter, majority rule on *routine* business decisions is wise and even necessary whether a firm is operating as a partnership or as a corporation. The problem, then, is to determine which matters are routine and which should be considered as possible subjects for high or unanimous shareholder or director requirements.

Perhaps the easiest way in which to approach this matter is to consider

[184] 294 N.Y. at 118–119, 60 N.E.2d at 831.

[185] N.Y. Stock Corp. Law §9 (1948). See N.Y. Bus. Corp. Law §§616, 709 (1961). See also Roland Park Shopping Center v. Hendler, 206 Md. 10, 109 A.2d 753 (1954).

[186] See, in general, Model Bus. Corp. Act §§32, 40.

[187] See 1 F. O'Neal, Close Corporations, §4.19 (1958).

[188] E.g., In re Radom & Neidorff, Inc., 307 N.Y. 1, 119 N.E.2d 563 (1954).

the predicament of particular minority shareholders in a given situation. Suppose, for example, a corporation with one hundred outstanding shares, of which A, B, and C own fifty-one, twenty-nine and twenty shares, respectively. A, by his ownership of a controlling interest, is in a position to effectuate certain corporate acts which might prejudice the interests of B and C, the two minority shareholders. In addition, A and C, or A and B, by voting together, may act adversely to B or C, as the case may be. What is needed, then, is a provision which will protect both B and C against A, or against any combination of shareholders. Although, as in the *Benintendi* situation, it might be possible, if permitted by statute, to require unanimous consent to certain fundamental acts which might prejudice the minority interests, it has been suggested [189] that, although the difference is largely one of form,[190] a high percentage vote, in situations where the validity of the clause is at all doubtful, may be more likely to receive a favorable judicial reception than a unanimity requirement. Assuming that this is so, then it is readily apparent that the requirement which best suits the interests of B and C is that of approval by those holding at least 81 percent of the outstanding shares.

The next step is to pinpoint the possible ways in which B or C might be adversely affected by the acts of the other two shareholders. Since this will be the subject of a separate chapter,[191] it may suffice merely to list some of the major areas which should be considered.

(a) Major organic changes, such as increase of authorized number of shares, reduction of capital, recapitalization, reclassification, merger, consolidation, sale of assets

(b) Issuance of new shares or sale of treasury shares

(c) Corporate repurchase of outstanding shares in any amount

(d) Change in amount of dividends paid on outstanding shares

(e) Change in salaries of officers or other major employees

(f) Involuntary termination of employment of any corporate officer

(g) Change in the number of directors constituting the board

(h) Classification of the directors, so that less than the total number of directors are elected each year

(i) Amendment of the articles of incorporation or bylaws

(j) Approval of contracts with any corporation, partnership or other business entity in which any shareholder has an interest or has a substantial interest (e.g., more than 20 percent)

(k) Dissolution of the corporation

(l) Filing or consent to a petition in bankruptcy or reorganization

---

[189] See 1 F. O'Neal, id. at §4.27.

[190] See Katcher v. Ohsman, 26 N.J. Super. 28, 97 A.2d 180 (Ch. 1953), pointing out that where the stock is equally divided, a 51 percent shareholder approval requirement is equivalent to unanimity.

[191] See Ch. IV.

The above list does not purport to be exhaustive, but it covers some of the main ways in which minority shareholders may be adversely affected or, as is sometimes said, squeezed or frozen out. For example, although a minority shareholder may have preemptive rights to purchase new issues of shares, he may not be able to afford to exercise them and the shares may thus be issued to others, diluting his interest.[192] If the shares are issued at an especially attractive price (e.g., at par when the book value or fair value is greater than par), then the dilution is even greater. Although the minority shareholder may have an equitable remedy against this type of maneuver, he will generally have to show fraud or at least unfairness,[193] which may not be easily done.

To take another example from the list, any shareholder or director action which threatens a person's status as a director or officer, or threatens his share of corporate profits paid either through compensation or through dividends, is potentially adverse in effect. One need only consider the plight of McQuade and Clark in the two cases previously discussed to appreciate the possibilities.[194] This may be the most frequent way in which minority shareholders are frozen out, i.e., their discharge as officers or directors, with the continued payment of substantial salaries to remaining officers and meager dividends to the shareholders.

After selecting the particular topics which should be covered by veto provisions,[195] there are several other matters which should be considered. Should the veto take the form of a high quorum requirement or a high vote requirement or possibly both? Should the veto be placed in the articles of incorporation, in the bylaws or possibly in both? Should there be safeguards against repeal of the veto provisions without the assent of the requisite majority? Should there be a reference to the veto arrangement on each stock certificate, as in the case of other important restrictions on shareholder rights?

One problem with casting the veto power solely as a high quorum requirement (either as to shareholders' meetings or as to directors' meetings) is that the New York Court of Appeals has held [196] that where a director absented herself from a board meeting with the express purpose of preventing a quorum, she could not thereafter contest the validity of action taken

---

[192] See, e.g., Hyman v. Velsicol Corp., 342 Ill. App. 489, 97 N.E.2d 122 (1951).

[193] *Compare* Bennett v. Breuil Petroleum Corp., 34 Del. Ch. 6, 99 A.2d 236 (Ch. 1953), *with* Maquire v. Osborne, 388 Pa. 121, 130 A.2d 157 (1957).

[194] See McQuade v. Stoneham & McGraw, 263 N.Y. 323, 189 N.E. 234 (1934), and Clark v. Dodge, 269 N.Y. 410, 199 N.E. 641 (1936).

[195] It should not be assumed that all of the topics in the foregoing list should always be subject to veto powers. The selection of particular topics will depend upon the fact situation as well as on the bargaining power of the parties.

[196] Matter of Gearing v. Kelly, 11 N.Y.2d 201, 182 N.E.2d 391, 227 N.Y.S.2d 897 (1962). For discussions of the case see 4 B.C. Ind. & Com. L. Rev. 195 (1962); 62 Colum. L. Rev. 1518 (1962); [1963] Duke L.J. 154.

at the meeting (in that case, the filling of a vacancy in the board caused by
a director's resignation). The reasoning of the opinion was that the director
should not be permitted to complain of an irregularity which she herself
caused. If this approach is taken in other jurisdictions, then there is little
utility in a high quorum requirement standing by itself. Thus the veto
power had best be put as a high vote requirement. A question might then
be raised as to whether this might be sufficient standing by itself. Although
there may in some jurisdictions be special reasons for wishing to employ
both high quorum and high vote requirements,[197] it is difficult to conceive
of a situation where a minority shareholder, such as C in the foregoing
illustration,[198] would not be protected if the veto were put simply as a high
vote requirement. This of course assumes that the requirement is high
enough so that, regardless of whether or not a quorum is present at the
meeting, the action cannot be taken without the assent of the shares held by
him. Care should be taken that the high vote requirement refers to a designated percentage of the shares *outstanding*, rather than merely to a percentage of the shares *represented at the meeting*. If the latter approach is used,
then a high quorum requirement would be necessary to assure full protection for the minority shareholder.

As to where the high vote requirements should be placed, in view of the
occasional judicial reluctance to enforce certain restrictions unless they appear in the articles of incorporation,[199] this would seem a wise precaution.
However, quorum and vote requirements for shareholder and director meetings also commonly appear in corporate bylaws. Care should be taken that
the clauses in the articles are consistent with the bylaws.

The high vote or quorum requirement is an illusory protection unless the
articles of incorporation and bylaws provide that they cannot be altered,
amended or repealed without the consent of the applicable percentage of
outstanding shares. Otherwise, a majority shareholder, having amendment
power, need only amend out the troublesome provisions and authorize various acts through a simple majority vote.

In order to bind transferees of shares, notice of the high vote or quorum
requirement should be placed on each stock certificate. This is expressly
required by some statutes.[200] Even in the absence of a statutory requirement, however, transferees can only be precluded from asserting that the
requirement, although applicable to others, does not apply to them since
they had no notice or knowledge of it, by noting the requirement on the
stock certificate and, if possible, setting it forth verbatim.[201]

[197] See 1 F. O'Neal, Close Corporations 209 (1958).
[198] See text accompanying note 190 *supra*.
[199] See 1 F. O'Neal, id. at §4.23.
[200] See N.Y. Bus. Corp. Law §§616(c), 709(c) (1961).
[201] See 1 F. O'Neal, id. at 217.

3.7   CUMULATIVE VOTING

The right to vote shares in cumulative fashion is an important feature of a closely held corporation, insofar as it enables a minority shareholder to elect himself or a representative as a director. Briefly, cumulative voting permits a shareholder to multiply the number of shares held by him by the number of directors to be elected and cast all his votes for one candidate or spread his votes among such candidates as he wishes. Since this permits him to concentrate all his voting power on a single candidate, he may thus be able to elect himself a director whereas, under a straight system of voting, anyone owning a majority interest would be able to elect the entire board.[202]

This is not the place to debate the merits and failings of cumulative voting, particularly when applied to large, publicly held corporations.[203] Suffice it to say that the arguments generally concern whether it is beneficial to have minority representation on a board of directors. With the closely held corporation it should seem rather obvious, even to most majority shareholders, that minority shareholders should have some representation. About half the states require cumulative voting either as a constitutional right or as a statutory right.[204] In the remainder, with the possible

[202] A minority shareholder may compute the number of shares he must hold in order to elect a given number of directors by using the following formula: Assume r as the number of shares to be voted by the shareholder, t as the total number of shares at the meeting (or the total outstanding if all the outstanding shares are voted at the meeting), R as the maximum number of directors the minority shareholder may be able to elect, and T as the total number of directors to be elected. Then to elect R directors, a shareholder must own r votes, as follows:

$$r = \frac{tR}{T+1} + 1$$

To illustrate, suppose that there are four directors to be elected and 100 shares outstanding. To elect one director a shareholder must have 21 shares because $t = 100$, $R = 1$, $T = 4$ and thus $r = 21$. See Cole, Legal and Mathematical Aspects of Cumulative Voting, 2 S.C.L.Q. 225 (1950). For more precise formulae applicable to specialized situations, such as where fractional shares are permitted to vote, see Mills, The Mathematics of Cumulative Voting, [1968] Duke L.J. 28.

[203] For a summary of the arguments see Williams, Cumulative Voting, 33 Harv. Bus. Rev. 108, 111 (1955). See also Sturdy, Mandatory Cumulative Voting: An Anachronism, 16 Bus. Law. 550 (1961); Sobieski, In Support of Cumulative Voting, 15 Bus. Law. 316 (1960). According to Sturdy, the movement to require cumulative voting as a constitutional right arose from the efforts of Joseph Medill, editor of the Chicago Tribune, in the Illinois constitutional reform program of 1870. Medill was an ardent advocate of John Stuart Mill's views regarding minority representation in legislative bodies. As Sturdy points out, even assuming the desirability of minority representation in state legislatures, the analogy between a legislative body and a board of directors, which may have executive functions, is not clear.

[204] See A. Frey, C. Morris and J. Choper, Cases and Materials on Corporations 315 (1966).

exception of two states which may not permit it,[205] cumulative voting is permissible—that is, the statute provides either that the shareholders shall have the right to vote cumulatively unless otherwise specified in the articles of incorporation or bylaws, or that straight voting shall prevail unless otherwise specified.[206]

Since cumulative voting protects the minority shareholder, he should take care that it is specified in the articles of incorporation and bylaws, particularly in those jurisdictions where this is necessary in order that the right be effective. Not only this, but to guard against the possibility that the applicable provisions in the articles of incorporation or bylaws might be repealed, he should, as in the case of veto powers,[207] require a sufficiently high percentage vote to alter, amend or repeal them. However, even this does not give him complete protection. If the number of directors on the board is reduced, or if the number to be elected each year is less than the full number on the board, as with a classified board of directors, then it should be fairly easy to see that the minority shareholder will need a greater number of shares in order to elect one director, or whatever number he wishes.[208] Although there is a conflict of authority as to whether classification of the board of directors may be used to dilute a cumulative voting right where the right is guaranteed by constitution or statute,[209] it is best to avoid uncertainty by providing that the board of directors may not be classified or reduced without the consent of a specified majority of the outstanding shares.[210] Similarly, although some statutes provide that a director may not be removed if the votes cast against his removal would be sufficient to elect him if then cumulatively voted at an election of the entire board,[211] it is best to provide that a director may not be removed with or without cause except with the consent of a specified majority of the shares outstanding.

[205] The two states are Massachusetts and Wisconsin. See 1 G. Hornstein, Corporation Law and Practice 151 (1959).

[206] Ibid.

[207] See text following note 199 *supra*.

[208] This is apparent from the formula, *supra* note 202. Since T, the total number of directors to be elected, will be reduced, more shares are required to elect one director. In the illustration given in the note, if only three directors are up for election, then 26 votes are necessary to elect one director instead of 21, as would be the case if four directors were to be elected.

[209] *Compare* Wolfson v. Avery, 6 Ill. 2d 78, 126 N.E.2d 701 (1955) (classification of directors invalid as interfering with constitutional right), *with* Humphrys v. Winous Co., 165 Ohio St. 45, 133 N.E.2d 780 (1956), and Janney v. Philadelphia Transportation Co., 387 Pa. 282, 128 A.2d 76 (1956). For criticism of the *Wolfson* holding see Sell and Fuge, Impact of Classified Corporate Directorates on the Constitutional Right of Cumulative Voting, 17 U. Pitt. L. Rev. 151 (1956). A recent Michigan holding is in accord with the *Humphrys* and *Janney* cases. McDonough v. Copeland Refrigeration Corp., 277 F. Supp. 6 (E.D. Mich. 1967). In Missouri there may be doubt as to whether classified boards are constitutional. See Comment, 32 Mo. L. Rev. 251 (1967).

[210] See text accompanying note 191 *supra*.

[211] Model Bus. Corp. Act §39. See N.Y. Bus. Corp. Law §706(c)(1) (1961).

In those few states that require a shareholder to give advance notice to the other shareholders of his intention to vote cumulatively,[212] a minority shareholder should be careful to comply with the statutory notice provisions or he may inadvertently be deprived of his right to cumulate votes and may thus lose his seat on the board, something of a disaster.

Although election to the board of directors assures some degree of representation, it may be rendered to some extent ineffective through the use of an executive committee, at which most major policy matters may be considered, with pro forma approval being given at directors' meetings held as infrequently as possible. Since there will be little need for an executive committee if the number of directors is relatively small, it may be better to provide against the establishment of such a committee or of any other committee of the board without unanimous consent of all the directors.

3.8   CLASSIFICATION OF SHARES

A useful method of allocating control between several groups of shareholders is by classifying shares. Thus, if one group wishes to elect three directors on a board of seven and each of two other groups wishes to elect two directors, three classes of stock may be issued, with each class entitled to elect the appropriate number of directors. This is also a useful technique where, because of unequal contributions of property by several shareholders or groups of shareholders, it is not possible to issue the requisite number of shares to each shareholder or group to reflect their respective contributions without distorting the pattern of voting rights. Suppose, for example, four persons form a corporation with two contributing equally to a total of 75 percent of the assets, a third contributing 15 percent and a fourth contributing 10 percent. Each wishes to elect one director on a board of four directors. If only one class of stock is used, the shares must be issued in sufficient numbers to reflect the contributions of each person. The first two shareholders will thus each receive 37½ percent of the shares issued, the third will receive 15 percent and the fourth will receive 10 percent.

However, even if there is cumulative voting, the third and fourth shareholders will not have enough shares to vote one director on the board.[213] We have already seen that one way out of this dilemma is through the use of senior securities, which are especially appropriate where one or more shareholders is to receive stock for services.[214] Another is through several

212 See Minn. Bus. Corp. Act §301.26 (1965); N.C. Bus. Corp. Act §55–67(c) (1969); Ohio Gen. Corp. Law §1701.55(c) (1955); S.C. Bus. Corp. Act §12–16.20(b) (1962).

213 As indicated in note 202 *supra,* at least 21 percent of the shares is necessary to elect one director on a board of four.

214 See Ch. II, text accompanying note 141.

classes of stock. In our illustration, four classes could be issued, each class to have the right to elect one director. Class A and Class B would each have 375 shares, Class C 150 shares and Class D 100 shares. In this way the requisite voting rights are obtained for each shareholder and yet each has the appropriate number of shares to reflect his capital contribution.

Rather than use share classification to achieve disproportionate voting power, it may be used to give disproportionate dividend or liquidation rights. Thus two classes of stock might be created with one class entitled to twice as many dividends or amounts on liquidation as the other. In all other respects, including voting rights, the two classes could be equal. Preferred stock is but a variant of this technique, where the right to dividends is preferential and possibly cumulative, with voting rights which are contingent on nonpayment of the dividend. With few exceptions,[215] state statutes permit classification of shares.

One disadvantage of share classification is its tendency to result in relatively complex capital structures. This in turn may lead to unanticipated problems. For example, many statutes provide that for certain transactions requiring shareholder authorization, a vote of each class of shares is necessary.[216] Another source of difficulty is with preemptive rights. The cases differ as to whether preferred shareholders have a preemptive right to subscribe to new issues of common and vice versa.[217] Although this is sometimes spelled out by statute,[218] the best approach is to deal with this expressly in the articles of incorporation.

In addition, as we have seen,[219] a corporation having several classes of stock may not elect special tax treatment under Subchapter S, except where each class of shares is identical with the other, aside from its right to elect members of the board of directors in a number proportionate to the number of shares in each class.[220]

As in the other situations we have considered,[221] the draftsman should guard against the possibility that, once the various classes have been established, the articles of incorporation might be amended to vary the rights and preferences or otherwise adversely affect particular classes. Although there

[215] Classification of shares has been considered unlawful in Missouri as conflicting with the constitutional right to vote cumulatively. Mo. Atty. Gen. Opinion no. 238 (1964). The opinion gives no authority for this position and efforts to obtain clarification of the legal basis for it from the Attorney General's office have thus far been unsuccessful. A contrary result has been reached in West Virginia. Diamond v. Parkersburg-Aetna Corp., 146 W. Va. 543, 122 S.E.2d 436 (1961).

[216] E.g., Ill. Bus. Corp. Act §54 (1965).

[217] See W. Cary, Cases and Materials on Corporations 1167–1168 (4th ed. unabr. 1969), and Frey, Shareholders' Pre-Emptive Rights, 38 Yale L.J. 563 (1929). See also R. Stevens, Private Corporations 507–508 (2d ed. 1949).

[218] See N.Y. Bus. Corp. Law §622 (1961).

[219] See Ch. I, text accompanying note 117.

[220] Treas. Reg. §1.1371–1(g).

[221] See notes 199 (veto powers) and 207 (cumulative voting) *supra*.

is sometimes statutory protection expressly requiring a class vote if the class is adversely affected,[222] it is better to provide for a class vote or veto power in the articles of incorporation.[223]

3.9 NONVOTING STOCK

An important way of maintaining control of a close corporation is through nonvoting stock. The latter may be an attractive investment vehicle to one who, although not interested in a role in management, wishes to share in corporate growth. As previously suggested, nonvoting shares may be preferred as to dividends and rights on liquidation.

Nonvoting shares are lawful in most states, although in some there are constitutional barriers which either prohibit them [224] or permit only nonvoting preferred.[225] Moreover, although the right to vote for directors may be taken away, in many states all shareholders must still be allowed to vote on mergers, consolidations, sales of assets, dissolution and amendments to the articles which alter the rights, preferences, etc., of a particular class of shares.[226] And even in those states where nonvoting shares are lawful under the applicable statutory or constitutional provisions, it may be unlawful to offer them under the state securities (Blue Sky) laws, unless some exemption is available.[227] The New York Stock Exchange will not list nonvoting shares and will not list shares of any company which has nonvoting shares outstanding.[228] Moreover, nonvoting stock is not allowed in situations which involve the Public Utility Holding Company Act of 1935,[229] the Investment Company Act of 1940 [230] and reorganizations under the Bankruptcy Act.[231]

Nonvoting shares may also be used to iron out discrepancies arising as a result of unequal capital contributions of different shareholders where equal control is desired. Thus, as in the prior illustration in the discussion of share classification,[232] if one or more shareholders contribute a substan-

---

[222] See N.Y. Bus. Corp. Law §§804(a), 903(a)(2) (1961).

[223] See 1 F. O'Neal, Close Corporations 108 (1958).

[224] Ill. Const. art. 11, §3. People ex rel. Watseka Telephone Co. v. Emmerson, 302 Ill. 300, 134 N.E. 707 (1922).

[225] Miss. Const. art. 7, §194, and Miss. Bus. Corp. Act §§14, 32 (1962); Neb. Const. art. XII, §5. In Missouri, nonvoting common and preferred have been held lawful despite the constitutional quarantee of cumulative voting. Shapiro v. Tropicana Lanes, Inc., 371 S.W.2d 237 (Mo. 1963); State ex rel. Frank v. Swanger, 190 Mo. 561, 89 S.W. 872 (1905).

[226] See Model Bus. Corp. Act §§60, 73, 79, 84.

[227] E.g., Mo. Sec. Commn. Rule VI (I). See Statement of Policy of Midwest Securities Commissioners Association, June 27, 1968. 1 Blue Sky L. Rep. ¶4781.

[228] N.Y.S.E. Company Manual §A. 15 (nonvoting preferred must be given contingent voting rights in the event dividends are in default).

[229] 49 Stat. 815 (1935), 15 U.S.C. §79(g)(c)(1).

[230] 54 Stat. 821 (1940), 15 U.S.C. §80a–18(i).

[231] 52 Stat. 897 (1938), 11 U.S.C. §616(12)(a).

[232] See text accompanying note 214 *supra*.

tial part of the assets and others contribute lesser amounts or receive stock for services, and yet all wish an equal voice in control, nonvoting shares may be issued to those who contribute relatively more, in amounts sufficient to reflect their greater investment. As we have seen,[233] such shares frequently take the form of senior securities, such as preferred stock, notes, debentures or bonds, or combinations of these.

Another use of nonvoting stock is to shift voting power among family members, as to transfer control from father to son. Later we shall examine the tax consequences of using preferred stock in this manner as an estate planning device and as a means of providing more income to certain family members and more control to others.[234] The arrangement may differ with the needs and objectives of the various parties. Thus, if the father wishes to retain control and pass on to other family members the right to receive dividends, he may issue nonvoting stock to the latter.[235] Conversely, he may, upon his retirement, wish to pass on control to his sons, to other members of the family or others who manage the business and increase his share of dividends. If this is his purpose, he should also consider debt securities, such as notes and bonds, since interest on these is deductible and, in addition, payment of the obligations will not risk being treated as essentially equivalent to a dividend, as with the redemption of stock. However, as we shall see in a later chapter,[236] if a person owns common stock and exchanges part or all of his interest for corporate obligations, the exchange will be taxable, albeit at capital gains rates, whereas, if the common is exchanged for preferred stock, no tax is imposed (although, if less than all of the common is exchanged for preferred, problems may arise under Section 306 of the Code). In some situations it may therefore be advisable to exchange common for a package of preferred stock and corporate obligations, minimizing the tax on the shareholder and retaining the advantage of deductibility of interest on the debt.

[233] See Ch. II, text accompanying note 141.
[234] See Ch. VI, text accompanying note 268.
[235] See 1 F. O'Neal, Close Corporations 102 (1958).
[236] See Ch. VI, text accompanying note 280.

IV Techniques of Squeeze-Out of Minority Shareholders and Planning to Prevent a Squeeze-Out

In the prior chapter we considered various devices for maintaining control of a closely held corporation, with particular reference to problems of legality and draftsmanship. In this chapter we shall deal specifically with various methods of adversely affecting the rights and interests of minority shareholders and ways to prevent overreaching by those who own a majority interest. Since the question of maintaining control, or at least of having a voice in how a corporation is run, and the question of preventing oneself from being "squeezed out" are but different aspects of the same problem, that of preserving a shareholder's status in the firm,[1] it is not surprising that the ways to prevent a squeeze-out often involve the control techniques already discussed.

4.1 DEPRIVING A SHAREHOLDER OF SALARY AND DIVIDENDS

Among the most powerful techniques for making life unpleasant for a minority shareholder is to deprive him of his corporate office, thus terminating his salary. The result is that his only income from the corporation is by way of dividends. However, since those who control the corporation almost invariably receive considerable income from salaries and also control the corporation's dividend policies, they may either not wish additional income in dividends or they may reduce the dividend as a method of persuading the minority shareholder to sell his interest, often at a sacrifice price.[2] If, as is

[1] See Ch. III, text preceding note 1. For an extensive discussion of squeeze-out techniques, see F. O'Neal and J. Derwin, Expulsion or Oppression of Business Associates (1961). See also Note, Freezing Out Minority Shareholders, 74 Harv. L. Rev. 1630 (1961). For contrast of American and English remedies see O'Neal, Oppugnancy and Oppression in Close Corporations: Remedies in America and Britain, 1 B.C. Ind. & Com. L. Rev. 1 (1959).

[2] Witness the predicament of McQuade in McQuade v. Stoneham & McGraw, Ch. III, note 169.

often the case, the minority interest is difficult to dispose of to outsiders, or is subject to stock transfer restrictions, the shareholder who receives little by way of dividends and nothing from salary is in an awkward position. Coupled with this is the possibility that the majority shareholders, if they wish a greater share of corporate earnings, may increase their own salaries, sometimes to exorbitant levels, rather than increase dividends. Since salaries are deductible on the corporate level *if reasonable,* they may seek to justify this by the tax benefit to the corporation as well as the purported value of their own services. Withholding of dividends may be justified by an alleged need to provide for future needs and to finance expansion plans, acquisitions and so forth. If a minority shareholder challenges the good faith of the majority in running the corporation in this fashion, as in an action to force the corporation to pay more dividends or to contest allegedly unreasonable salaries, he has the burden of proof. As we shall see in the next chapter, the "business judgment" rule will generally protect the directors except in cases of fraud or bad faith and the majority shareholders may thus be given the benefit of the doubt. Moreover, it may be extremely difficult to establish that salary levels are unreasonable due to the difficulty of setting a value on the services of particular individuals. Here again, although in some situations due to conflict of interest the burden of proof may shift to those receiving the salaries to show that they are fair, determination of fairness will often be influenced by the business judgment rule and judicial reluctance to question the propriety of corporate policies unless some clear abuses are shown. The upshot of all this is that, although a minority shareholder is always entitled to contest actions taken by majority shareholders, doing so may be both expensive and difficult, and the outcome uncertain. For that reason, it is far better for him to plan in advance to prevent these situations from arising. The various techniques will generally involve the use of some of the control devices already discussed to achieve at least two objectives: (1) the assurance of corporate employment of the minority shareholder at a minimum salary, and (2) prevention of increases in officers' salaries without the consent of the minority shareholder. In addition, the minority shareholder may wish to commit the corporation to paying a certain minimum dividend if there are earnings available to do so.

Corporate employment may be assured in several ways. We have seen that in some situations *all* of the shareholders may agree on certain corporate policies, provided that the agreement does not unduly impair the discretion of the board of directors. We have also seen, however, that such agreements are hazardous since the law is unclear, and that in the absence of a statutory provision expressly permitting such an agreement[3] it is often difficult to predict whether a court will enforce it.

Another method of achieving the same objective is through the use of veto powers. When the corporation is first established, the general tendency is for things to run fairly smoothly. Minority shareholders are represented

[3] E.g., Del. Gen. Corp. Law §354 (1967).

on the board of directors and also receive salaries. It is only at a later date, when friction develops, or when the minority shareholder's role in corporate affairs appears superfluous to the majority, that the possibility of a squeeze-out becomes a reality. Accordingly, it is important at the beginning to provide that certain basic changes may not be made without the consent of a specified minimum of the outstanding shares. This could include a decrease in the number of directors, an increase in the number of shares issued, a change of corporate officers or a change in officers' salaries.

An effective way in which to supplement the foregoing is through an employment agreement. As previously stated,[4] such agreements are valid if reasonable in duration (i.e., not for the lifetime of the employee), if there is no fraud or other unfairness and if the directors have the power to discharge the employee for disloyalty or incompetency. A disadvantage with an employment agreement is that since it involves personal services, courts may be reluctant to grant specific performance. The result is that an officer discharged in breach of the agreement may have only a right to damages.[5] Nonetheless, the very existence of the agreement, along with the potential damage liability for its violation, may serve as a deterrent, and lessen the likelihood of the employee's losing his position.

In preparing an employment agreement, several things should be kept in mind. The agreement should be specifically approved by the board of directors, preferably by a "disinterested" majority (i.e., the employee's presence should not be necessary for a quorum nor his vote required to pass the resolution). If this is not possible, or in any case as a valuable supplement, shareholder ratification is helpful. In seeking shareholder ratification, full disclosure of the terms of the agreement is necessary since mere approval of the action taken by the board of directors at a prior meeting may be ineffective. In addition, it is well for the articles of incorporation to include a provision expressly permitting the corporation to enter into long-term employment agreements.[6]

The employment agreement should, as we have seen, be reasonable in duration—fifteen to twenty years should suffice in many cases if there is a provision for renewal of the agreement. It should provide that the employee will be entitled to serve unless found to be disloyal or incompetent and that any determination of disloyalty or incompetency will, upon the employee's request, be reviewed by an independent arbitrator or board of arbitrators. Along with routine matters, such as specifying the employee's duties, the amount of time he should devote to his employment, and his compensation (including fringe benefits, if any), there are often provisions restricting his participation in outside activities, particularly, engaging in competing busi-

---

[4] See Ch. III, text accompanying note 179.

[5] Model Bus. Corp. Act §51. See Streett v. Laclede-Christy Co., 409 S.W.2d 691 (Mo. 1966).

[6] See 1 F. O'Neal, Close Corporations: Law and Practice 356 (1958).

nesses. Such covenants can be made to survive the term of the agreement, as where the employee retires or his employment terminates for some other reason, and are generally upheld if reasonable in character, i.e., reasonably limited in time, geographical area and other respects. Similarly, the employee may be expressly prohibited from divulging trade secrets and other confidential information during or after the term of his employment.[7] The agreement should also provide for mergers, consolidations, or sale of the employer's assets and bind successors in interest.[8] If there is any doubt concerning the agreement's validity due to its extending for a particularly long period of time, it may be wise to provide for some form of additional consideration coming from the employee. For example, it can be recited that, as part of the agreement, the employee has been induced to leave the employ of another or has agreed to acquire an interest in the employer.[9]

Suppose, however, that a minority shareholder is not an employee and thus cannot be protected by an employment agreement. In such situations it is well to commit the corporation to pay a certain percentage of its net profits as dividends, and also to limit the extent to which profits may be withdrawn by others in salaries. Salary increases may be subject to veto through a requirement of shareholder approval of all increases exceeding a designated dollar amount or a designated percentage of an officer's annual salary. If preferred stock is issued to the minority shareholder, it may require that dividends be paid on the preferred to the extent of available net earnings. If common is issued, the articles of incorporation may provide that a designated percentage of net profits must be paid out in the form of dividends. Such agreements are valid even in the absence of statutory provisions expressly authorizing them.[10] Although it may in some cases be wise to give the board of directors authority to reserve a reasonable amount of net profit for working capital and contingencies,[11] it is also wise to limit the extent to which such amounts may be withheld. Thus the directors might be permitted to reserve up to 50 percent of the net profits for contingencies, etc., and be required to pay out the remaining 50 percent as dividends.

[7] See 2 R. Callmann, Unfair Competition, Trademarks and Monopolies §33.4(d) (1968) (covenants not to compete), and 2 id. §51.2(c) (trade secrets). See also Restatement of Contracts §516(f) (1932). Such agreements may be coupled with covenants binding the employee to make himself available, after the termination of his employment, for consultation services if required by the employer. See Osborne v. Locke Steel Chain Co., 153 Conn. 527, 218 A.2d 526 (1966) (agreement not to compete and to render consulting services held valid even though it purported to last for plaintiff's lifetime, since the agreement did not contemplate that plaintiff would be assigned specific managerial duties, his obligation being merely to render consulting services on request).

[8] See 1 F. O'Neal, id. at 353.

[9] Id. at 342.

[10] See Ch. III, notes 180–182.

[11] See F. O'Neal and J. Derwin, Expulsion or Oppression of Business Associates §7.06 (1961).

4.2 ISSUANCE OF ADDITIONAL SHARES

A significant way in which a minority shareholder's interest may be adversely affected is through the issuance of additional shares of stock, thereby diluting his proportionate voting rights, rights to dividends and rights to distributions on liquidation. To safeguard against this at least two methods are particularly useful. First, the shareholder's preemptive right to subscribe to additional shares may be broadened, and secondly the issuance of new shares may be made subject to veto powers.

The shareholders' preemptive right to subscribe to additional issuances of shares is only a moderate protection against squeeze-outs of this type. In the first place, the right as it exists at common law is confined to *new* issuances of shares for *cash*. Thus, if a corporation has 500,000 shares authorized and issues only 100,000 of them, the subsequent issuance of up to 400,000 additional shares may not be subject to preemptive rights. In large part the question depends upon whether the eventual issuance of the entire 500,000 shares was contemplated at the time the corporation was formed and whether the subsequent issuance of the additional shares was part of the same plan of financing.[12] Although the determination of whether the subsequent issuance is part of the original issue is primarily factual, in some jurisdictions the matter has been resolved by statute.[13] Since the sale of treasury stock is not considered to be a new issue, preemptive rights do not ordinarily attach unless this is expressly provided in the articles of incorporation.[14] And in any event only issuances for *cash* are covered. Thus issuances of shares for property,[15] in repayment of a debt,[16] or in connection with a merger, consolidation or other corporate acquisition[17] are not subject to the preemptive right unless expressly specified in the corporate articles. Accordingly, it is of crucial importance to the minority shareholder that when the corporation is formed, the articles specify that preemptive rights are to apply in these situations. Although this might arguably hamper the corporation in acquiring properties, merging and so forth, this is not likely to be the case with the closely held concern, since the acquisition will al-

---

12 Yasik v. Wachtel, 25 Del. Ch. 247, 17 A.2d 309 (Ch. 1941).

13 N.Y. Bus. Corp. Law §622(e)(5) (1961).

14 E.g., Borg v. International Silver Co., 11 F.2d 147 (2d Cir. 1925).

15 E.g., Thom v. Baltimore Trust Co., 158 Md. 352, 148 Atl. 234 (1930) (shares of stock); Meredith v. New Jersey Zinc & Iron Co., 55 N.J. Eq. 211, 37 Atl. 539 (Ch. 1897), *aff'd,* 56 N.J. Eq. 454, 41 Atl. 1116 (Ct. Err. & App. 1897) (mining properties).

16 E.g., Musson v. New York & Queens Elec. Light & Power Co., 138 Misc. 881, 247 N.Y.S. 406 (1931).

17 E.g., Thom v. Baltimore Trust Co., 158 Md. 352, 148 Atl. 234 (1930); Bingham v. Savings Investment & Trust Co., 102 N.J. Eq. 302, 140 Atl. 321 (Ct. Err. & App. 1928). See generally Comment, Exceptions to Stockholder's Preemptive Right, 35 Colo. L. Rev. 482 (1963).

most always have to be authorized by the shareholders and, if this is done, the preemptive right can be waived as to that particular transaction.

In some jurisdictions there is a statutory provision to the effect that, unless otherwise provided in the articles of incorporation, shares may be issued to officers or employees of the corporation free of the preemptive right if there has been approval by the majority of the shareholders.[18] Although such a provision arguably increases the ability of a corporation to attract capable personnel, it is primarily designed for the publicly held corporation. In a close corporation the majority shareholders should not be permitted to issue shares to corporate officers without the approval of a designated percentage of the outstanding shares (i.e., a veto power), and in any case preemptive rights should be made expressly applicable to this situation. In drafting the broadened preemptive rights provision in the articles of incorporation, one should be careful lest, due to the maxim of *inclusio unius exclusio alterius*, a listing of the various situations in which preemptive rights expressly apply implies that in all other situations such rights do not apply. Thus a broad preemptive rights clause might provide that preemptive rights are to apply to all issuances or sales by the corporation of any shares of its stock, whether newly issued or otherwise, or treasury stock, *including but not limited to* the sale of stock for cash or any other consideration such as property, satisfaction of a debt, services, other stock of any class, bonds, debentures, notes, or in connection with mergers, consolidations, or any other form of corporate or other acquisition, and in connection with any plan involving the issuance of stock to officers or employees, through stock options, bonuses or any other means of compensation.

Merely broadening the preemptive right, however, is little protection standing by itself. Preemptive rights merely give a shareholder an opportunity to subscribe to additional shares and this presupposes that he has sufficient funds to purchase more stock and that he is willing to make the investment. If a minority shareholder is not as wealthy as the other shareholders in the corporation, they may be able to "out-invest" him and so dilute his interest to relative insignificance. Thus in *Hyman v. Velsicol Corp.*[19] the plaintiff, a research chemist, assigned two patent applications to a newly formed corporation in return for a minority interest in its stock. The majority interest was equally divided between two other corporations. The corporation prospered and sales rose from $1021 in 1932 to $4,096,356 in 1945. The plaintiff had served as managing vice-president of the corporation since its formation, but in 1946, after a dispute resulting from his refusal to assign certain insecticide patent applications to the corporation, he resigned as officer and also as director, thereafter organizing his own corporation to exploit the insecticide patents. The original company, Velsicol, eventually established its right to the insecticide patents and, shortly thereafter, its

[18] See Model Bus. Corp. Act §26A.
[19] 342 Ill. App. 489, 97 N.E.2d 122 (1951).

directors decided upon a plan of "recapitalization," whereby the par value of the Velsicol stock was decreased from $100 to $10 per share and the number of authorized shares increased from 200 to 2000. The charter was also amended to authorize an additional 100,000 shares of stock, 68,000 of which were authorized for issuance to the Velsicol shareholders, to be purchased either in cash or "by credit against sums owing by this corporation on outstanding notes." The two other corporations which held a majority of Velsicol's stock had each previously advanced $264,000 to Velsicol for building and operating purposes in return for demand notes. These were surrendered to the corporation, along with $8000 in cash by each corporation, in return for 27,200 shares each of additional stock. Although the plaintiff had a right to subscribe to 13,600 shares at $10 per share ($136,000) he failed to do so and subsequently brought an action to restrain the Velsicol directors from carrying out the plan of recapitalization. In reversing the determination of the Chancellor (who had found the recapitalization plan inequitable and motivated by a desire to oppress and defraud the plaintiff) and ordering the suit dismissed for want of equity, the Illinois appellate court concluded that the reorganization and the price at which the new stock was issued were not abuses of discretion on the part of the majority shareholders or directors and were not fraudulently oppressive, observing that the defendants were not to blame for the plaintiff's failure to obtain the money necessary to avail himself of his preemptive rights.[20] Although a plaintiff may obtain equitable relief against the issuance of shares at a grossly inadequate price[21] due to the difficulty of establishing the value of shares in a closely held corporation, along with the usual presumption in favor of the directors' judgment in setting a sale price, the plaintiff may have difficulty in showing either fraud or gross unfairness, which may be the same thing.[22] For example, in *Maguire v. Osborne*,[23] the plaintiff owned twelve of the forty outstanding shares of the defendant corporation, the remaining shares being held by two others who, along with the plaintiff, constituted the board of directors. The shares carried a par value of $50. After a shareholders' meeting at which the authorized capital of the corporation was increased to 2000 shares of $50 par value each, the directors authorized the issuance of 200 more shares at $50, with the plaintiff being given a right to purchase sixty shares, her proportionate allotment. In denying relief the court pointed out that, since the corporation was

[20] See also Bellows v. Porter, 201 F.2d 429 (8th Cir. 1953); Maguire v. Osborne, 388 Pa. 121, 130 A.2d 157 (1957). But if the sole or primary purpose is to eliminate or "dilute out" the minority shareholder's interest, the issuance of additional shares is invalid. Katzowitz v. Sidler, 24 N.Y.2d 512, 249 N.E.2d 359, 301 N.Y.S.2d 470 (1969) (wide disparity between issue price and value of shares, no reasonable business purpose for issuance); Browning v. C & C Plywood Corp., 248 Ore. 574, 434 P.2d 339 (1967).

[21] See Bennett v. Breuil Petroleum Corp., 34 Del. Ch. 6, 99 A.2d 236 (Ch. 1953).

[22] Maguire v. Osborne, 388 Pa. 121, 130 A.2d 157 (1957).

[23] Ibid.

closely held, book value, earnings or dividends alone did not establish the worth of its stock and observed, somewhat sardonically, that "The fact that plaintiff is financially unable to purchase the newly issued stock is unfortunate but it is to be observed that the fixing of the value of the newly issued shares at a higher price would be no solution to her predicament." [24]

It should be fairly clear from the foregoing that neither preemptive rights nor the possibility of equitable relief can guarantee a minority shareholder that he will not be "diluted out" through the issuance of new shares. Thus it is particularly important that any increase in the authorized capital or any issuance of additional shares be subject to the approval of a high enough percentage of the outstanding shares so that each minority shareholder is protected.

4.3 ORGANIC CHANGES—MERGERS, ASSET SALES, ETC.

Several particularly effective ways of squeezing out minority shareholders are suggested by the power of majority shareholders to effect certain organic changes. These include amendments to the articles of incorporation altering the rights and preferences of one or more classes of stock, mergers or consolidations, and sales of all or substantially all of a corporation's assets.

Aside from increases in the authorized number of shares and their issuance to majority shareholders or outsiders already discussed, alteration of the rights of those who hold common stock is infrequently used as a squeeze-out device since any alteration of the rights of shares held by the minority also affects the shares held by the majority.[25] This technique is primarily relevant, then, where there is more than one class of stock. This includes

[24] 388 Pa. at 124, 130 A.2d at 159.

[25] One possibility, that of making the common stock redeemable or "callable" by the board of directors at any time, exists only in Massachusetts. See Lewis v. H. P. Hood & Sons, Inc., 331 Mass. 670, 121 N.E.2d 850 (1954). In Delaware, and probably in other states, "callable common" is not permitted. Greene v. E. H. Rollins & Sons, Inc., 22 Del. Ch. 394, 2 A.2d 249 (Ch. 1938). See Starring v. American Hair & Felt Co., 21 Del. Ch. 380, 191 Atl. 887 (Ch. 1937), aff'd, 2 A.2d 249 (Sup. Ct. 1937). However, agreements between shareholders (as distinct from charter provisions) providing that a majority of the shareholders may repurchase shares have been upheld. Halsey v. Boomer, 236 Mich. 328, 210 N.W. 209 (1926); Boggs v. Boggs & Buhl, 217 Pa. 10, 66 Atl. 105 (1907). In any case, even in Massachusetts, it is highly doubtful whether the majority shareholders could render common shares callable by amending the articles of incorporation if such shares were previously not subject to call. Thus the callable common situation presupposes the express or implied consent of the shareholder whose shares are subject to call.

A second possibility involves the elimination of preemptive rights adhering to common stock. Where this is permissible under a statutory provision, it has been held constitutional if the state constitution reserves the power to amend corporate charters. Mobile Press Register, Inc. v. McGowan, 271 Ala. 414, 124 So.2d 812 (1960). However, a minority shareholder may protect himself against this tactic by requiring a high percentage shareholder vote to eliminate preemptive rights.

situations where the common stock has been classified so as to enable each class to elect a designated number of directors. Most of the cases, however, involve attempts by the holders of common stock to alter the rights and preferences of preferred shares, and particularly to eliminate "arrearages" which have accumulated on preferred shares due to dividends having been earned but not paid in prior years.

It has been held that the elimination of arrearages accrued on preferred stock cannot be accomplished merely through amending the articles of incorporation. The leading case is *Keller v. Wilson & Co.*[26] where a recapitalization involving such an amendment was held invalid. Although the case proceeded on a somewhat obsolete "vested rights" theory, it has been followed in other states.[27] Its significance, however, has been considerably diminished due to the availability of several alternate techniques to accomplish the same objective. These involve mergers, asset sales and the creation of a class of "prior" preferred which is then offered on a "voluntary" basis to those who hold the preferred on which the arrearages have accumulated.

In *Federal United Corp. v. Havender*,[28] a merger between a corporation and a wholly owned subsidiary which resulted in the elimination of preferred arrearages was upheld, the *Keller* case being distinguished in that it not only involved a different section of the statute and a different technique, direct amendment of the charter, but also on the ground that, in a merger, a dissenting shareholder is given the right to be paid the value of his shares, whereas under Delaware law this right was not available to those who dissented from an amendment to the corporate charter. This reasoning was carried to what might be its ultimate conclusion when it was held that a corporation might eliminate preferred arrearages by merging with a wholly owned subsidiary created expressly for the purpose of effecting the merger.[29] Thus, aside from the availability of dissenters' appraisal rights in a merger as distinct from a charter amendment under Delaware law, the line of authority following the *Keller* case seems to have lost much of its

[26] 21 Del. Ch. 391, 190 Atl. 115 (Sup. Ct. 1936). However, preferred shares may be "collapsed" into common through an amendment of the certificate of incorporation and compulsory exchange through recapitalization *if* dividends accrued up to the date of amendment and recapitalization are paid. See R. Baker and W. Cary, Cases and Materials on Corporations 1496 (1959), citing Bailey v. Tubize Rayon Corp. 56 F. Supp. 418 (D. Del. 1944); Dunn v. Wilson & Co., 53 F. Supp. 205 (D. Del. 1943).

[27] W. Cary, Cases and Materials on Corporations 1769 (4th ed. unabr. 1969) (collecting cases from New Jersey, North Carolina, Ohio and Pennsylvania). See, however, E. Dodd and D. Billyou, Cases and Materials on Corporate Reorganization 512 (1950), indicating that an opposite result might obtain in Illinois, Maryland, Minnesota, New Jersey, New York, Ohio and Virginia.

[28] 24 Del. Ch. 318, 11 A.2d 331 (Sup. Ct. 1940). See also Langfelder v. Universal Laboratories, Inc., 163 F.2d 804 (3d Cir. 1947).

[29] Bove v. Community Hotel Corp. of Newport, R.I., 249 A.2d 89 (R.I. Sup. Ct. 1969); Hottenstein v. York Ice Machinery Corp., 136 F.2d 944 (3d Cir. 1943), *cert. denied*, 325 U.S. 886 (1945).

vitality, particularly insofar as it is based on an outdated vested rights approach.[30]

Another possibility, somewhat along the lines of the merger cases just discussed, involves a sale of substantially all the assets of a corporation to another in exchange for a package of securities which carry no arrearages.[31] This technique may be broadened so as to effect a total elimination of minority shareholders, whether holding preferred or common. Thus those who hold a majority of the shares may organize a second corporation and sell the assets of the first to the second for *cash,* then distribute the cash to those who hold shares in the first corporation in dissolution of the latter.[32] The cash received by the majority shareholders in the first corporation (who are sole owners of the second corporation) can then be turned back to the newly created entity as a contribution to capital. The result is that those who held a minority interest in the first (now dissolved) corporation have been "bought out" for cash. Even though the terms of the transaction are fair (if unfair, the sale and dissolution could probably be enjoined [33]) and, as is frequently the case in asset sales, those who dissent from the sale are given appraisal rights,[34] the fact remains that a shareholder in this situation has a choice only between the cash offered to him under the terms of the sale and dissolution and the amount available to him by way of appraisal rights. He may not retain his proprietary interest in the old corporation or obtain an interest in the second corporation (as he would be able to do in the merger situation).

An alternate route to the same objective is through a so-called short-form merger. In some states, if a parent corporation owns 90 or 95 percent of the stock of a subsidiary, it may effect a merger with the latter without having the transaction approved by the shareholders of either corporation, assuming that the board of directors of the parent corporation authorizes the merger.[35] And where the statute permits the terms of the merger to specify that shares of the merging corporation are to be surrendered for cash, a

[30] See the observation by Circuit Justice Biggs in the *Hottenstein* case that "The *Keller* case remains a landmark in the law of Delaware only to signify that what cannot be done directly under Section 26 of the General Corporation Law may be done by subterfuge under Section 59." 136 F.2d 944, 953 (3d Cir. 1943).

[31] See W. Cary, id. at 1774.

[32] See F. O'Neal and J. Derwin, Expulsion or Oppression of Business Associates 79–80 (1961).

[33] Id. at 80. This is so at least in those jurisdictions where the shareholder's appraisal right is not held to be the exclusive remedy. See Vorenberg, Exclusiveness of the Dissenting Shareholder's Appraisal Right, 77 Harv. L. Rev. 1189 (1964); Manning, The Shareholder's Appraisal Remedy: An Essay for Frank Coker, 72 Yale L.J. 223 (1962).

[34] See Model Bus. Corp. Act §80 (providing for appraisal rights in mergers and sales of substantially all the assets except, in the latter situation, where the sale is for cash and the proceeds are distributed to the shareholders within one year of the sale).

[35] Model Bus. Corp. Act. §75 (90 percent); Del. Gen. Corp. Law §253 (1969) (90 percent). N.Y. Bus. Corp. Law §905 (1969) (95 percent).

minority shareholder cannot insist that he be given an interest in the surviving corporation.[36] Thus a minority shareholder may be "merged out," given cash and deprived of his proprietary interest. If the laws of the jurisdiction do not, however, permit a short-form merger, a squeeze-out is still possible through a merger whereby the shareholders of the merging corporation are given redeemable preferred stock. Thus in *Matteson v. Ziebarth*,[37] the majority shareholders organized another corporation, solely owned by them, and merged another corporation with it, the merger providing for the issuance of redeemable preferred stock. Since the minority shareholder could assert his dissenter's appraisal rights, the court thought that he was adequately protected.

Another technique might be termed "transplantation." If one corporation owns a sufficient number of shares of another to insure shareholder approval for a merger, it may organize a wholly owned subsidiary in a jurisdiction whose laws permit short-form mergers. The second step is to merge the first corporation into the subsidiary. If the minority shareholder dissents from the merger, he is paid off in cash pursuant to his appraisal rights. If he does not, he receives shares in the subsidiary, which is then merged into the parent under the short-form procedure in a transaction which provides that the minority shareholder is to receive cash for his shares.[38]

A more subtle technique involves what might be called a "carrot and stick" approach. This is the so-called voluntary exchange of preferred stock with arrearages for another class of "prior" preferred. The prior preferred is commonly entitled to dividends before any dividends are payable on the other class of (now subordinated) preferred and, to make the exchange even more attractive, it may be entitled to dividends at a higher rate of return. The holders of the old preferred are then offered shares of the prior preferred in exchange for their preferred shares with arrearages. Although the exchange is voluntary, those not exchanging their shares are left with shares which have been subordinated to another class of preferred, dividends on which must be paid before any dividends (including arrearages) may be paid on their shares. Attempts to enjoin such transactions have frequently been unsuccessful.[39]

[36] Coyne v. Park & Tilford Distillers Corp., 38 Del. Ch. 514, 154 A.2d 893 (Sup. Ct. 1959); Beloff v. Consolidated Edison Co. of New York, 300 N.Y. 11, 87 N.E.2d 561 (1949).

[37] 40 Wash. 2d 286, 242 P.2d 1025 (1952).

[38] Stauffer v. Standard Brands, Inc., 40 Del. Ch. 202, 178 A.2d 311 (Ch. 1962), *aff'd*, 41 Del. Ch. 7, 187 A.2d 78 (Sup. Ct. 1962). For an ineffective attempt to accomplish a similar result through a sale of assets for stock of a corporation which was then to be placed in a voting trust, the terms of which permitted the voting trustee to sell the shares in the trust for cash, see Eisenberg v. Central Zone Property Corp., 306 N.Y. 58, 115 N.E.2d 652 (1953).

[39] See, e.g., Barrett v. Denver Tramway Corp., 53 F. Supp. 198 (D. Del. 1943), *aff'd*, 146 F.2d 701 (3d Cir. 1944); Shanik v. White Sewing Machine Corp., 25 Del. Ch. 371, 19 A.2d 831 (Sup. Ct. 1941). For other cases see W. Cary, Cases and Materials on Corporations 1786–1787 (4th ed. unabr. 1969). The predicament of

Another technique is for the majority shareholders to cause the corporation to be dissolved and its assets transferred to another corporation which they own.[40] A variant of this approach is to cause the corporation to file a voluntary petition in bankruptcy in the hope that, at the bankruptcy sale, those holding a majority of the shares of the bankrupt will be able to outbid those who hold the minority interest.[41]

Both of these techniques basically involve an appropriation by the majority shareholders of the going concern value of the business, along with its operating assets. Although a minority shareholder in such a situation may have equitable relief [42] or damages[43] if he can establish that the motivation behind the dissolution was to exclude him from the business, bad faith may be difficult to show if the majority shareholders are able to establish a bona fide business reason for doing what they did. *Lebold v. Inland Steel Co.*[44] is a dramatic illustration of an attempt to use such a technique. There, Inland Steel Co. owned 80 percent of Inland Steamship Co., whose principal assets were three ships used to carry steel, coal and stone for the parent company. The subsidiary was a "captive" in the sense that its business depended almost entirely upon its dealings with Inland Steel Co. The latter paid carriage rates, based on competition, which resulted in the Inland Steamship shares being given a "going concern" value substantially in excess of the book value of its assets, the three ships. The Steel Company made a bid for the shares held by the minority, which was refused inasmuch as the bid did not take into account the earnings of the subsidiary. A representative of the Steel Company was reported to have stated that "in his opinion the Steel Company had been 'suckers' and had acted foolishly in permitting the minority to continue to participate in the profits." After the bid for the minority stock was turned down, Inland Steel called a special meeting of the shareholders of the Steamship Company to dissolve the business, planning to enter a bid for its assets at the same per share price that it had offered to the minority ($700 per share). Although a bill for equitable relief was dismissed as "premature," [45] the minority shareholders were ultimately successful in recovering damages equal to the difference

---

the preferred shareholder with arrearages has been set to poetry by Dean Latty. See 10 Duke Bar Assn. J. 19 (1941).

[40] See F. O'Neal and J. Derwin, Expulsion or Oppression of Business Associates §4.09 (1961), citing Lebold v. Inland Steel Co., 125 F.2d 369 (7th Cir. 1942), *modified,* 136 F.2d 876 (7th Cir. 1943), *cert. denied,* 316 U.S. 675 (1942); Kavanaugh v. Kavanaugh Knitting Co., 226 N.Y. 185, 123 N.E. 148 (1919), and Theis v. Spokane Falls Gaslight Co., 34 Wash. 23, 74 Pac. 1004 (1904).

[41] F. O'Neal and J. Derwin, id. at §4.13, citing Porterfield v. Gerstle, 222 F.2d 137 (5th Cir. 1955).

[42] See Kavanaugh v. Kavanaugh Knitting Co., 226 N.Y. 185, 123 N.E. 148 (1919), and Theis v. Spokane Falls Gaslight Co., 34 Wash. 23, 74 Pac. 1004 (1904).

[43] See Lebold v. Inland Steel Co., 125 F.2d 369 (7th Cir. 1942).

[44] Ibid.

[45] Lebold v. Inland Steamship Co., 82 F.2d 351 (7th Cir. 1936).

between the price which they had received for their shares and the going concern value (estimated at $1350 per share).[46]

As far as preventive measures to forestall the various squeeze-out devices involving organic changes, such as mergers, asset sales, dissolution and the like are concerned, as in other situations the most powerful weapon is a veto power or requirement of approval by a high enough majority of the outstanding shares so that the consent of the smallest minority shareholder is in effect required. Although this might in some situations hamper the corporation in undertaking changes which may be beneficial to it, the potential harm to minority shareholders from actions taken in bad faith, and the uncertainty, expense and delay of litigation would seem to justify a veto over various fundamental corporate acts, though this might result in less flexibility.

4.4   OTHER SQUEEZE-OUT TECHNIQUES

Although the foregoing discussion enumerates the major ways in which majority shareholders may deal unfairly with minority shareholders, there are various other abuses, roughly falling within the category of breach of fiduciary duty or misappropriation of corporate assets, which can be used to lessen the value of minority interests or discourage shareholders so that they are willing to sell their shares at a sacrifice price to those who hold a majority interest.

We have already considered the possibility that the majority shareholders may cause the corporation to pay exorbitant salaries or other compensation. Much the same thing can be done by other methods, such as leasing property to the corporation at an unduly high rental, leasing property from the corporation at a nominal rental, loaning money to the corporation at too high an interest rate or borrowing funds from it at little or no interest.[47] Or the majority shareholders may form a management company and cause it to enter into a management contract with the company in which they hold a majority interest, whereby they are to receive indirectly, through corporate payments to the management company, excessive compensation for the services performed, or possibly compensation covering services which they were obligated to render as officers and for which they were previously paid (i.e., double compensation for the same services).[48] Although such contracts may be set aside in a derivative suit by a minority shareholder upon a showing of unfairness to the corporation,[49] a better precaution is, as with

[46] Lebold v. Inland Steamship Co., 136 F.2d 876 (7th Cir. 1943), *cert. denied,* 320 U.S. 787 (1943).

[47] See F. O'Neal and J. Derwin, Expulsion or Oppression of Business Associates §5.02 (1961).

[48] E.g., Heit v. Bixby, 276 F. Supp. 217 (E.D. Mo. 1967); Cullen v. Governor Clinton Co., 279 App. Div. 483, 110 N.Y.S.2d 614 (1952).

[49] The classical and stricter view is that such contracts are either void *per se* or

the other squeeze-out devices, a high shareholder vote requirement or veto power as regards any contract between the corporation and one of its officers, with a shareholder or with any other corporation in which an officer or a shareholder may have an interest.

Other methods used to discourage minority shareholders include the failure to hold shareholders' or directors' meetings as required by law or under the bylaws[50] or the denial to the minority shareholder of inspection of corporate books and records.[51] Although shareholders usually have statutory rights of inspection of books and records, the tendency is to limit such rights to stock transfer books, books of account and minutes of shareholders' and directors' meetings.[52] A shareholder may also be prevented from inspecting the books if the corporation is able to establish that his purpose is improper, i.e., is not for the corporate benefit, such as to use the information in connection with a competing business.[53] In a closely held concern, however, all shareholders should be given much broader rights of inspection and access to corporate properties, analogous to the rights of partners to inspect partnership books.[54] This can be provided in the articles of incorporation and bylaws.[55]

Excellent opportunities for squeeze-outs are presented when a corporation is deadlocked, i.e., its shareholders are so evenly divided that they are unable to elect a board of directors, or the directors are similarly divided so that they cannot act effectively as a board. In such a standoff, one shareholder may seek to buy out the other at an unduly low price, possibly threatening to bring a proceeding to dissolve the corporation if his demands are not met.[56] Since this may amount to a type of extortion, it is not surprising that courts are sometimes unwilling to grant a petition for dissolution merely upon a showing that the shareholders and the board of directors are deadlocked.[57] As this topic will be considered in considerable detail in a later chapter,[58] it may suffice to say that various contractual arrangements can be entered into which are specifically designed to resolve deadlocks. For example, the dispute may be subject to arbitration or it may be agreed that

---

voidable unless authorized by a disinterested majority of the directors at a meeting at which the "interested" director's presence was not necessary for a quorum. For a comprehensive analysis of the trend of decisions in this area, see Marsh, Are Directors Trustees? 22 Bus. Law. 35 (1966). As the author indicates, the emphasis in the more recent cases appears to be on whether the contract is fair rather than on the formalities whereby it was authorized.

[50] See F. O'Neal and J. Derwin, id. at §5.07.

[51] Id. at §5.13.

[52] E.g., Donna v. Abbotts Dairies, Inc., 399 Pa. 497, 161 A.2d 13 (1960).

[53] See W. Cary, Cases and Materials on Corporations 1020–1027 (4th ed. unabr. 1969).

[54] See Uniform Partnership Act §19. See also J. Crane and A. Bromberg, Partnership §66 (1968).

[55] See 1 F. O'Neal, Close Corporations §3.63 (1958).

[56] E.g., In re Radom & Neidorff, Inc., 307 N.Y. 1, 119 N.E.2d 563 (1954).

[57] Ibid. See Chayes, Madam Wagner and the Close Corporation, 73 Harv. L. Rev. 1532, 1536 (1960).

[58] See Ch. VII.

an independent third party will be appointed to serve as a director to break the deadlock or even to manage the business while the impasse persists.[59] If the deadlock cannot be resolved, it can be provided that a majority shareholder will offer the minority a fair price for its shares; if there is a dispute over the price, this can be resolved by arbitration.[60] Another technique is to give any shareholder the right to dissolve the corporation if a deadlock persists for a given length of time, but to require that he must first offer his shares to the other shareholders at a specified price.[61] A variant of this arrangement is an agreement whereby, if the other shareholders are unwilling to purchase his shares at the price he wishes, then they must offer their shares to him at the same price and he must purchase them. The objective of such a scheme is to encourage an arm's-length bargaining situation whereby one or more shareholders will be bought out at a fair price rather than squeezed out at an unfair one. This highlights what may be a central consideration of the whole squeeze-out problem, that although a minority shareholder may not be able to retain indefinitely a proprietary interest in a corporation where there is a basic disagreement among the shareholders and directors, he is at least entitled to receive a fair price for his shares. Although the analogy between a close corporation and a partnership may be imperfect, it is still fairly clear that no corporation is likely to prosper if there is fundamental disagreement among those who own and run it. If basic differences between the various parties persist, then the minority shareholder would probably be wiser to invest his money elsewhere. Most courts are aware of the impracticalities of attempting to compel persons to continue a business association when they are unwilling to do so.[62] In view of this, a minority shareholder's paramount objective should be not to retain his proprietary interest but rather to receive a price for it which adequately reflects its going concern value and earnings prospects once the impasse has been resolved through the purchase of his shares.

[59] See F. O'Neal and J. Derwin, Expulsion or Oppression of Business Associates §7.04 (1961).

[60] See Note, Arbitration as a Means of Settling Disputes Within Close Corporations, 63 Colum. L. Rev. 267 (1963). For further discussion see Ch. VII, text accompanying note 20.

[61] Cf. Ch. III, text accompanying note 49, for a discussion of similar problems arising in connection with setting a price on shares subject to a first refusal type option. See also Hetherington, Special Characteristics, Problems, and Needs of the Close Corporation, [1969] U. Ill. L.F. 1. Professor Hetherington points out that minority shareholders frequently neglect to anticipate the problems which may later arise by virtue of their minority status and observes that, since the attorney who drafts the organization papers frequently represents the majority shareholder, he does not normally raise these problems on his own. The result is that the interests of minority shareholders often go unprotected. He suggests the need for some form of statutory protection whereby minority shareholders are given automatic liquidation rights if they are not bought out at a fair price.

[62] See Chayes, id. at 1536.

V Distribution and Accumulation of Corporate Earnings

In this chapter we shall consider various corporate and tax problems relating to corporate earnings, their distribution and accumulation.

5.1 COMPELLING DIVIDENDS FROM THE CLOSELY HELD CONCERN

As we saw in our discussion of squeeze-outs in the previous chapter, one of the paramount concerns of a minority shareholder is to insure that dividends in reasonable amounts will continue to be paid on his shares.[1] As previously indicated,[2] this may be done by a shareholders' agreement or a provision in the articles of incorporation obligating the company to pay out a certain percentage of its net profits in dividends. Although two states have had statutory provisions which required a set percentage of net profits to be paid out as dividends, it is perhaps significant that both statutes have now been repealed.[3]

Another way of forcing a corporation to disgorge profits is by a suit to compel payment of dividends. In such a suit the burden of proof is generally upon the minority shareholder to establish that the directors, in failing to pay a dividend or in paying an unreasonably low amount, are acting fraudulently or in bad faith, or are unreasonable or arbitrary.[4] Since the

[1] See Ch. IV, text accompanying notes 2–11.

[2] See Ch. IV, note 10. See also Comment, 56 Nw. U.L. Rev. 503 (1961).

[3] N.C. Bus. Corp. Act §55–50(i) (repealed October 1, 1969) (which required at least one third of the net profits to be paid out as dividends upon the written demand of holders of 20 percent or more of the shares). For a criticism see Robinson, North Carolina Corporation Law and Practice §§159–160 (1964). See also N.M. Gen. Corp. Law §51–3–16 (repealed January 1, 1968) (requiring a corporation to pay dividends equal to the whole of its accumulated profits after reserving over and above capital stock paid in a sum fixed by the shareholders as working capital).

[4] See 2 F. O'Neal, Close Corporations: Law and Practice 113–114 (1958). For other discussions see Scholder, Dividends and the Minority Stockholder in a Closely Held Corporation, 14 N.Y.U. Intra. L. Rev. 140 (1959); Comment, 56 Nw. U.L. Rev. 503 (1961); Note, 64 Harv. L. Rev. 299 (1950).

directors are generally permitted to select the appropriate accounting method for computing net profits and to reserve such amounts as they deem necessary for contingencies, expansion and the like,[5] a minority shareholder will have an uphill fight to convince a court that the situation warrants overturning the judgment of the directors. Where the corporation is closely held, and the minority is locked in due to limited marketability of the shares, one would think that the courts would be more likely to provide equitable relief and less inclined to apply the somewhat shopworn "business judgment" rule, but this does not seem to have been the case. The emphasis upon substantial capital gains which often characterizes large, publicly held, growth-oriented corporations is less appropriate to the smaller, closely held one, since the shareholder will usually be able to sell his shares only to the corporation or to other shareholders and the price may be fixed by a stock transfer restriction.[6] Moreover, unless there is an agreement obligating the corporation or other shareholders to purchase the stock, the holder of a minority interest may not be able to dispose of it at all, in which case capital gains have only a theoretical appeal. Finally, in the large, publicly held corporation, management will generally wish to maintain a good dividend record since this will increase the market value of the shares, which in turn will produce substantial capital gains to those who own large blocks of stock or stock options. Conversely, if the dividends are reduced, the market value of the shares will generally decrease, making the company more vulnerable to take-over through a cash tender offer or exchange of shares by an outsider.[7] Thus, where the shares are publicly traded, management is understandably sensitive to the dividend performance of the company. In sharp contrast, where the shares are closely held, the risk of a take-over is not as great, and is virtually nonexistent if a majority of the shares is held by management. In such a situation the "market value" of the shares is generally not dependent upon dividends but is more a function of earnings and asset value.[8] A good argument can therefore be made for different rules for the close corporation, particularly since an action to compel a dividend is less likely to be a "strike suit" than if the corporation were publicly held.[9]

All of this merely indicates that in the close corporation there is a far greater likelihood that in pursuing a niggardly dividend policy the directors will be motivated by personal reasons, such as to avoid substantial additional income tax liability or to acquire the interests of the minority shareholders as inexpensively as possible.[10] Sometimes, a minority shareholder is able to

[5] 2 F. O'Neal, id. at 113.

[6] See Ch. III, text accompanying note 49.

[7] See Manne, Our Two Corporation Systems: Law and Economics, 53 Va. L. Rev. 259, 280 (1967). See also Manne, Some Theoretical Aspects of Share Voting, 64 Colum. L. Rev. 1427, 1430 (1964).

[8] See Ch. III, text accompanying note 49.

[9] See 2 F. O'Neal, id. at 115.

[10] See Gottfried v. Gottfried, 73 N.Y.S.2d 692, 695 (Sup. Ct. 1947).

show that this is the motivation of the directors, thus establishing "bad faith" [11] or fraud, but unless it is a relatively clear-cut case, he will find it difficult and expensive to satisfy the burden of proof. It may be persuasive, if not compelling, proof that the dividend policy has been unreasonable if the company has been exposed to a penalty tax upon excess accumulations.[12] However, as we shall see, such a tax is imposed only if profits have been allowed to accumulate "beyond the reasonable needs of the business," including "reasonably anticipated needs." [13] Hence there is considerable leeway for the business judgment rule to operate before the tax will be imposed.

If a minority shareholder is not able to show that the directors are acting fraudulently or in bad faith but are only acting unreasonably or pursuing an unwise policy of devoting corporate profits to excessive expansion, maintenance of unneeded reserves and the like, the likelihood of his success in an action to compel dividends is considerably less. Although the cases are in conflict,[14] there are numerous decisions holding that a mere showing that a corporation has a large undistributed surplus is insufficient to justify a decree compelling a distribution.[15] The shareholder's task is made exceptionally difficult by the tendency of courts to give the directors the benefit of the doubt, except where there is a clear abuse of discretion, and also the fact that in most corporations there are numerous ways in which the retention of earnings may be justified.[16]

Where the alleged reason for retaining earnings is not solely to benefit the corporation (and indirectly its shareholders) but to pursue other social objectives, the minority shareholder's case may be slightly stronger. Essentially this involves the much disputed question of whether corporations should be run primarily or even exclusively for the benefit of the shareholders or whether, particularly with larger corporations, it may be proper to view them as quasi-sociopolitical entities having wider responsibilities.[17] According to the classical concept of the corporation, although the directors are not confined to short-range policies having an immediate economic re-

[11] Ibid.

[12] See Int. Rev. Code of 1954, §§531–537. See also Whittemore v. Continental Mills, 98 F. Supp. 387 (S.D. Maine 1951).

[13] See Int. Rev. Code of 1954, §§533, 537.

[14] For a collection of the cases see 2 F. O'Neal, id. at 114. Despite the conflict, the author concludes that "most courts will require reasonably sound business judgment from the directors and some consideration for minority shareholders."

[15] See W. Cary, Cases and Materials on Corporations 1587 (4th ed. 1969 unabr.), summarizing the authorities and concluding that "plaintiffs have won only a small minority of the cases."

[16] Ibid. (citing illustrative cases dealing with retention of earnings to provide internal financing for the corporation in times where outside credit is limited, increase working capital and inventories, pay indebtedness, repair and improve real properties, change methods of production, expand productive capacity and increase fixed assets).

[17] The classic articles illustrating the conflicting views on this point are Dodd, For Whom Are Corporate Managers Trustees? 45 Harv. L. Rev. 1145 (1932), and Berle, For Whom Corporate Managers Are Trustees, id. at 1365.

turn to the shareholders, nonetheless, expenditure of funds for long-range objectives, such as improving employee morale and bettering customer relationships, must have an ultimate justification in increasing profits. Thus, in a well-known English case the court observed that "The law does not say that there are to be no cakes and ale, but there are to be no cakes and ale except such as are required for the benefit of the company. . . ." [18]

A leading case following this reasoning is *Dodge v. Ford Motor Co.*[19] There, the Ford Motor Co., a highly profitable operation from its organization in 1903 until 1916 when an action to compel more dividends was brought, had accumulated surplus of $112 million, including cash and municipal bonds of nearly $54 million. On November 2, 1916, the directors decided to spend $11,325,000 for blast furnaces and other equipment for making iron and steel and $5,150,000 for expansion of the existing plant. Regular cash dividends had been declared at the rate of 60 percent on the invested capital of $2 million between December, 1911, and October, 1915, and so had special cash dividends which, during this period, amounted to $41 million. However, except for an additional special dividend of $2 million, declared on November 8, 1916, special dividends were sharply curtailed. The primary justification for this change in policy was the increased need for plant expansion motivated, in large part, by Henry Ford's hope that ultimately an annual production of one million cars would be achieved, along with a reduction in the price of the product. He considered that those who had invested in the company had already received copious returns and that thereafter they should be content with what he chose to distribute. The Ford Motor Company had, he thought, made too much money, if anything, and, although large profits might still be made, it would be well to share them with the public by reducing the price of the product. In affirming a decree ordering the distribution of $19,275,385.96, the court pointed out that

> A business corporation is organized and carried on primarily for the profit of the stockholders. The powers of the directors are to be employed for that end. The discretion of directors is to be exercised in the choice of means to attain that end, and does not extend to a change in the end itself, to the reduction of profits or to the nondistribution of profits among stockholders in order to devote them to other purposes.[20]

The court also drew a distinction between corporate expenditures having an "incidental humanitarian" objective, such as to benefit employees by building a hospital for their use, and broader schemes to benefit mankind generally at the expense of the shareholders. However, in view of the possible benefits which might result from plant expansion, the court did not inter-

[18] Hutton v. West Cork Ry. Co., 23 Ch. D. 654, 673 (Ct. App. 1883).
[19] 204 Mich. 459, 170 N.W. 668 (1919).
[20] 204 Mich. at 507, 170 N.W. at 684.

fere with this aspect of the company's plans. Nonetheless, it considered that funds for expansion were already available and, if the company's annual profit of $60 million were to continue, a large part of future needs could be financed out of current revenues. Even if the cost of the proposed expenditures for expansion and other uses were withdrawn in cash, there would still be a surplus (consisting in money and bonds) of nearly $30 million. Despite the need for a reasonable amount of liquid assets, this, the court thought, was an excessive amount. Hence it ordered a distribution.

If another *Ford* case were to arise in today's somewhat different judicial climate, the outcome would be more uncertain. For one thing, the common stock of Ford is now widely distributed and listed on the New York Stock Exchange as a result of a series of secondary offerings by the Ford Foundation commencing in January of 1956. But even assuming that the company were still closely held, there has been a considerable shift in perspective on the role of large corporations. Charitable giving,[21] corporate patronage of the arts[22] and corporate rehabilitation of distressed communities all point to the fact that the larger corporations may have broader duties than merely to increase profits for the shareholders or benefits to the employees. Thus it may well be that, in the *large* closely held concern, minority shareholders will have an increasingly difficult time in overcoming a broadened business judgment rule where funds are being devoted towards legitimate social ends. However, in the more usual case of the smaller close corporation, having fewer public responsibilities, minority shareholders may still rely on reasoning such as that of the *Ford* decision. As previously indicated, the likelihood of success is far greater if there is at least some showing of bad faith or fraud.[23]

Even assuming the right to recovery, there are some procedural obstacles which may have to be overcome. For one thing, there is a conflict of authority as to whether an action to compel dividends is derivative in nature or is a direct suit.[24] If derivative, then a minority shareholder must satisfy the traditional requirements of derivative actions, such as making a demand on the board of directors, and possibly on the shareholders, to bring the action and the requirement in some jurisdictions that the plaintiff post a bond as

[21] See R. Eells, Corporation Giving in Free Society (1956); Prunty, Love and the Business Corporation, 46 Va. L. Rev. 467 (1960).

[22] See R. Eells, The Corporation and the Arts (1967).

[23] See, however, Long v. Norwood Hills Corp., 380 S.W.2d 451 (Mo. App. 1964), an action to have a receiver appointed and the corporation dissolved on the ground that its profit-making purpose had been abandoned. The court dismissed the suit, finding that the directors had acted in good faith, even though there had been no distribution of dividends.

[24] *Compare* Gordon v. Elliman, 306 N.Y. 456, 119 N.E.2d 331 (1954) (derivative), *with* Knapp v. Bankers Securities Corp., 230 F.2d 717 (3d Cir. 1956) (direct, construing Pennsylvania law). The authority of the *Gordon* case, which may have been erroneous anyway, has been reduced by the enactment of N.Y. Bus. Corp. Law §626(a) (1961), changing the result.

security for expenses.[25] The better view is that an action to compel dividends is direct in nature, since recovery will go to the shareholders if the suit is successful and since failure to declare dividends, if unjustified, is a breach of fiduciary duty to the shareholders rather than to the corporation. Notwithstanding this, the corporation is a necessary party defendant in any action to compel payment of dividends, since the matter relates to corporate policies and the payment of corporate funds.[26] Although some cases have also required the plaintiff to join a majority of the directors as defendants, it seems better not to insist on this, particularly if he has previously requested the board to act on the matter and it has refused to do so, as is generally the case.[27] In such a situation the plaintiff and the directors are likely to be at an impasse and it would be fruitless to give the board a further opportunity to exercise its discretion.[28]

Even assuming that a minority shareholder is successful, there is no guarantee that a further suit will not be required if the directors persist in withholding funds. Thus he will have to satisfy the burden of proof again, often under changed circumstances. Although on occasion a minority shareholder has been able to obtain a decree ordering the payment of a set percentage of dividends in the future,[29] relief of this nature is rather unusual, no doubt because, with changing economic conditions and changes in the nature of a business, it may be unwise for courts to decide what portion of the future profits should be distributed and what portion may legitimately be withheld to meet corporate needs as they develop.

We have already considered the possibility that a minority shareholder may be able to obtain a veto power over any reduction in the amount of dividends being paid or any increase in salaries paid to officers and may even insist on a clause in the articles of incorporation or bylaws which compels the corporation to pay out a specified percentage of its net profits each year.[30] Although such a provision should be drafted with considerable care in order that the corporation will not be hampered by having insufficient operating funds to meet legitimate corporate needs, arrangements of this kind are a valuable way to insure that the minority shareholder will not be squeezed or starved out.

[25] E.g., Cal. Gen. Corp. Law §834 (1967); Colo. Corp. Act §45 (1958); Md. R. Proc. 328b; N.Y. Bus. Corp. Law §627 (1965); N.J. Bus. Corp. Act §14A:3–6 (1968); Pa. Bus. Corp. Law §516 (1968); Wis. Bus. Corp. Law §180–405(4) (1953).

[26] See N. Lattin, The Law of Corporations 461–462 (1959).

[27] Ibid.

[28] See Kroese v. General Steel Castings Corp., 179 F.2d 760 (3d Cir. 1950), *cert. denied*, 339 U.S. 983 (1950).

[29] See Patton v. Nicholas, 154 Tex. 385, 279 S.W.2d 848 (1955).

[30] See Ch. IV, text accompanying note 10.

5.2 NONDEDUCTIBILITY OF DIVIDENDS; LOANS AND OTHER DISTRIBUTIONS AS CONSTRUCTIVE DIVIDENDS

Since dividends are not deductible by a corporation for federal income tax purposes, the question frequently arises, particularly in closely held corporations, whether various distributions, including unreasonable salaries and "loans" to officers, directors and others, are in substance dividends. In the case of loans, the question is not one of deductibility to the corporation but rather one of taxability to the shareholder, since dividends are taxable at ordinary rates to the extent of either current or accumulated corporate earnings and profits,[31] whereas the receipt of a bona fide loan does not give rise to tax. Although dividends are entitled to a limited exclusion of $100 in the case of single individuals and $200 on a joint return,[32] generally it will only be advantageous to a corporate recipient to argue that a distribution is a dividend, in view of the 85 percent dividends received credit (or 100 percent credit in the case of an electing group of affiliated, i.e., 80 percent owned, corporations).[33]

Although statutes often prohibit a corporation from making loans to its officers and directors[34] and sometimes prohibit loans to shareholders,[35] all too often those who own a majority interest in a closely held corporation may wrongfully assume that they may use the corporate treasury as a means of short- or long-term financing. Sometimes such an attitude may carry over from an earlier period when a sole proprietor was in the habit of shifting funds between his business account and his personal account, or indeed commingling the two. Also, since there is no prohibition on loans to partners, unless this is forbidden by the partnership agreement,[36] it may be difficult for those who change from a partnership or sole proprietorship to a corporation to realize that there may be restrictions on their ability to borrow from "their" corporation. And there is also the possibility (one would not like to say probability) that officers and others may characterize certain withdrawals as loans when they would be better described as embezzlements. Since embezzled proceeds are clearly taxable,[37] albeit not as divi-

---

[31] Int. Rev. Code of 1954, §316.

[32] Id. §116.

[33] Id. §243.

[34] Model Bus. Corp. Act 47 (prohibiting loans to directors without specific authorization from shareholders and restricting loans to employees to those which have been authorized by the directors and which will benefit the corporation).

[35] E.g., Mo. Gen. & Bus. Corp. Law §351.165 (1963).

[36] The main problem here may be a technical one of whether a note given by a partner to his firm (or vice versa) is enforceable without an accounting. See J. Crane and A. Bromberg, Law of Partnership §70 (1968).

[37] James v. United States, 366 U.S. 213 (1961). For a discussion of the differing

dends but rather as gross income under Section 61(a) of the Code, the matter can become a tax question as well as a criminal one.

The criteria used to determine whether a loan from a corporation to an officer or shareholder is really a loan or something else are roughly the same as those used in determining whether purported loans by shareholders to a corporation are bona fide or are contributions to capital.[38] Thus, if the loan has no maturity date and interest payments are not provided for or, even if provided, are not in fact made, then it is likely that the distribution will be considered as a dividend [39] or, less fortunately, as an unauthorized misappropriation of corporate funds. Even if the loan were considered a bona fide one, if the interest charged to the shareholder is unduly low, there is a possibility that he may be deemed to have received a cash benefit (and hence a dividend) to the extent of the difference between the interest charged and what would be charged in an arm's-length transaction. However, normally any income realized would be offset by a deduction for interest paid.[40]

If a shareholder sells property to his corporation at an excessive price, not only may this be considered as a breach of fiduciary duty[41] but also the excess may be held a constructive dividend.[42] The same is true in the case of properties rented to the corporation for excessive amounts.[43] Conversely,

---

tax consequences of treating the withdrawal as a dividend as compared to a misappropriation, see Gardner, The Tax Consequences of Shareholder Diversions in Close Corporations, 21 Tax L. Rev. 223, 238 (1966). Briefly, the main difference is that a dividend will be taxable only to the extent of current or accumulated corporate earnings and profits, whereas a misappropriation will be taxed not as a dividend but as gross income under Section 61(a), which does not depend upon the presence of earnings and profits. In some situations a corporation may be able to claim a deduction for a loss by theft. See Int. Rev. Code of 1954, §165(c)(3). But see Gardner, *supra* at 258, for a discussion of the problems the corporation is likely to encounter in establishing its right to a deduction, e.g., majority shareholders will generally be unwilling to admit that the funds were misappropriated and the corporation may have a difficult time proving that there is no possibility that the funds will be recovered.

[38] See Ch. II, text accompanying note 88.

[39] See B. Bittker and J. Eustice, Federal Income Taxation of Corporations and Shareholders 167 n.44 (1966) (collecting the cases). See also Werner, Stockholder Withdrawals—Loans or Dividends? 10 Tax L. Rev. 569 (1955).

[40] See B. Bittker and J. Eustice, id. at 170.

[41] For a good summary of the cases see Marsh, Are Directors Trustees? 22 Bus. Law. 35 (1966). In addition, the shareholder's acquisition of property for purposes of sale to his corporation may be held a usurpation of a corporate opportunity. See Note, Corporate Opportunity, 74 Harv. L. Rev. 765 (1961).

[42] Goldstein v. Commissioner, 298 F.2d 562 (9th Cir. 1962). For other cases see B. Bittker and J. Eustice, id. at 171 n.55.

[43] Ibid. The properties being rented to the corporation may have been previously owned by it and distributed to the shareholder, who then leased it back. The objective is to secure a deduction for the corporation as to the rentals paid and depreciation deductions for the shareholder-lessor. As might be expected, there are numerous cases denying deductions where the sole motivation behind the transaction was a tax one. E.g., Armston Co., Inc. v. Commissioner, 188 F.2d 531 (5th Cir. 1951); Shaffer Terminals Inc., 16 T.C. 356 (1951), *aff'd per curiam*, 194 F.2d 539 (9th Cir.

if property is sold by the corporation to a shareholder for less than its fair value[44] or is rented to him at an excessively low rental,[45] dividend income may result in an amount equal to the difference between the sale price and the fair market value in the first situation, or, in the latter case, the difference between the rental charged and the property's fair rental value. *A fortiori*, if no rent is charged and the shareholder is permitted free use of corporate property for his personal benefit, he may be considered as having received an amount equal to the fair rental value of the property.[46] On a similar theory, payment by a corporation of personal expenses or debts of a shareholder is considered as the receipt of a taxable benefit.[47]

5.3 NONDEDUCTIBILITY OF EXCESSIVE COMPENSATION

One of the most troublesome tax problems encountered by the close corporation is that of establishing its right to deduct compensation paid to officers and other employees who are also shareholders. The Code restricts the deduction to "ordinary and necessary expenses . . . including . . . a reasonable allowance for salaries or other compensation for personal services actually rendered. . . ." [48] Thus compensation is deductible only if "reasonable." That portion of the compensation which is not reasonable is treated either as a constructive dividend (not deductible by the corporation and taxed to the shareholder-recipient to the extent of current or accumulated earnings and profits) or merely excessive compensation (not deductible by the corporation and taxed to the recipient regardless of whether he is a shareholder or whether there are corporate earnings and profits).[49] Where the excess amounts are paid to persons not owning stock, or are not

---

1952). For further discussion see S. Surrey and W. Warren, Cases and Materials on Federal Income Taxation 1205–1206 (1962); Oliver, Income Tax Aspects of Gifts and Lease-backs of Business Property in Trust, 51 Corn. L.Q. 21 (1965); Cary, Current Tax Problems in Sale, or Gift, and Leaseback Transactions, N.Y.U. 9th Inst. on Fed. Tax. 959–974 (1951).

[44] Treas. Reg. §1.301–1(j). See, e.g., Lacy v. Commissioner, 341 F.2d 54 (10th Cir. 1965); Timberlake v. Commissioner, 132 F.2d 259 (4th Cir. 1942).

[45] Rev. Rul. 58–1, 1958–1 Cum. Bull. 173; 58th St. Plaza Theatre, Inc. v. Commissioner, 195 F.2d 724 (2d Cir. 1952), *cert. denied*, 344 U.S. 820 (1952). An alternate approach is to tax as a dividend the excess of the corporate depreciation and maintenance expense on the property over the rent paid by the shareholder. See B. Bittker and J. Eustice, id. at 170 n.53.

[46] American Properties, Inc., 28 T.C. 1100 (1957), *aff'd per curiam*, 262 F.2d 150 (9th Cir. 1958); Greenspon v. Commissioner, 229 F.2d 947 (8th Cir. 1956); cf. International Trading Co. v. Commissioner, 275 F.2d 578 (7th Cir. 1960) (denying deduction to a corporation of expenditures for maintaining summer resort for shareholders).

[47] Old Colony Trust Co. v. Commissioner, 279 U.S. 716 (1929).

[48] Int. Rev. Code of 1954, §162(a).

[49] See B. Bittker and J. Eustice, id. at 171 n.57.

paid in proportion to the number of shares held, the latter approach (i.e., not a dividend but nonetheless fully taxable) may be particularly appropriate. Conversely, if the payments are measured by corporate profits or number of shares held, dividend treatment is more likely.[50]

As might be expected, the determination of what is reasonable is a question of fact. Generally it is said that the burden of proof to show reasonableness is on the taxpayer,[51] although perhaps more accurately the taxpayer has the burden of introducing reliable evidence in support of reasonableness, at which point any presumption in favor of the Commissioner's determination loses its effect and, if the taxpayer's evidence is not adequately rebutted, the deduction is allowed.[52]

As to the various factors which are relevant in determining reasonableness, the regulations provide that

> It is, in general, just to assume that reasonable and true compensation is only such amount as would ordinarily be paid for like services by like enterprises under like circumstances. The circumstances to be taken into consideration are those existing at the date when the contract for services was made, not those existing at the date when the contract is questioned.[53]

More specifically, a leading case summarized the principal factors as including

> the employee's qualifications; the nature, extent and scope of the employee's work; the size and complexities of the business; a comparison of salaries paid with the gross income and the net income; the prevailing general economic conditions; comparison of salaries with distributions to stockholders; the prevailing rates of compensation for comparable positions in comparable concerns; the salary policy of the taxpayer as to all employees; and in the case of small corporations with a limited number of officers the amount of compensation paid to the particular employee in previous years.[54]

---

[50] Ibid. See also Treas. Reg. §§1.162-7(b)(1), 1.162-8. The regulations point out that the payment may also be treated as payment for property received by the corporation, as where a partnership sells its business to a corporation and the former partners agree to continue as corporate officers. In such a situation, part of the compensation may in fact be payment for the purchase of the partnership assets, in which case the payment would not be deductible by the corporation but would, rather, be capitalized as the purchase price of a corporate asset.

[51] Botany Worsted Mills v. United States, 278 U.S. 282 (1929).

[52] Roth Office Equipment Co. v. Gallagher, 172 F.2d 452 (6th Cir. 1949). For other decisions see 1 CCH 1969 Stand. Fed. Tax Rep. ¶1372.012.

[53] Treas. Reg. §1.162-7(b)(3).

[54] Mayson Manufacturing Co. v. Commissioner, 178 F.2d 115, 119 (6th Cir. 1949). For other cases and discussion see Dixon, Planning Reasonable Compensation, N.Y.U. 19th Inst. on Fed. Tax. 181, 182–185 (1961). Even if the amount of compensation paid to a shareholder-employee may be reasonable if considered apart from a corporation's dividend policy, if the corporation has not paid dividends since its formation, a court may allocate a percentage of the compensation as amounting in substance to a distribution of profits. McCandless Tile Service Co. v. United States 422 F.2d 1336 (Ct. Cl. 1970).

Although the court went on to state that the action of a board of directors in voting salaries is entitled to a presumption that the salaries are reasonable and proper, it is generally held that if the board of directors is not independent, i.e., if members of the board are also officers, little or no weight will be given to the directors' determination.[55]

Although it is usually fatal to base compensation on the recipient's proportionate interest in the corporation, a salary which depends wholly or in part on corporate profits is deductible if reasonable and if it appears that the amounts were paid pursuant to a contract entered into at arm's length before the services are rendered. Thus the regulations provide

> While any form of contingent compensation invites scrutiny as a possible distribution of earnings of the enterprise, it does not follow that payments on a contingent basis are to be treated fundamentally on any basis different from that applying to compensation at a flat rate. Generally speaking, if contingent compensation is paid pursuant to a free bargain between the employer and the individual made before the services are rendered, not influenced by any consideration on the part of the employer other than that of securing on fair and advantageous terms the services of the individual, it should be allowed as a deduction even though in the actual working out of the contract it may prove to be greater than the amount which would ordinarily be paid.[56]

The fact that there is an arm's-length contractual arrangement worked out in advance will not always insure deductibility, as where the employee is entitled to a specified share of net profits and, although such share might have been reasonable at the time the contract was entered into, due to an inordinate growth of the business and a surge in profits which is not attributable to the employee's efforts, the amount of compensation computed on the original formula becomes grossly disproportionate to any credible estimate of the worth of the recipient's services. Although the regulations take the position that the circumstances to be taken into account are those existing at the time the contract is entered into and not when the contract is questioned,[57] they also state that contingent compensation is not to be treated "fundamentally on any basis different from that applying to compensation at a flat rate." [58] Thus the worth of the employee's services and the extent to which he is responsible for the increased profits are still important in determining deductibility.[59] And despite the language in the regulations, courts have looked to circumstances existing at the time the deduc-

---

[55] See Glenshaw Glass Co., 5 CCH Tax Ct. Mem. 864 (1946), *aff'd per curiam,* 175 F.2d 776 (3d Cir. 1947), *cert. denied,* 333 U.S. 842 (1948); Kerrigan Iron Works, Inc., 17 T.C. 566 (1951).

[56] Treas. Reg. §1.162–7(b)(2).

[57] Treas. Reg. §1.162–7(b)(3), *supra* note 53.

[58] Treas. Reg. §1.162–7(b)(2), *supra* note 56.

[59] See, e.g., Van's Chevrolet, Inc., 26 CCH Tax Ct. Mem. 809 (1967); Kenneth D. Smith, 24 CCH Tax Ct. Mem. 899 (1965). For discussion of these cases see 36 U. Mo. K.C.L. Rev. 163 (1968).

tion is sought as well as those prevailing when the contract was executed.[60] This is not necessarily inconsistent with the statement in the regulations that contingent compensation should be allowed as a deduction "even though in the actual working out of the contract it may prove to be greater than the amount which would ordinarily be paid." [61] The question here is mainly one of degree (i.e., the extent of the increase in compensation attributable to bonuses) and whether or not the employee's efforts were a material factor in producing the higher profits on which his compensation is based.

Where a corporation is closely held, officers who are also majority shareholders and thus in control of the board of directors will generally encounter considerable difficulty in establishing that their contract for contingent compensation was entered into at arm's length. Thus, as one court pointed out, those who control a corporation should not be given "the tactical and practical opportunity from the tax perspective of adhering to and relying upon the contract as long as it might be advantageous for them to do so, or causing the execution of a new contract or arrangement if and when it better served their purposes." [62] Nonetheless, two controlling shareholders may enter into an arm's-length agreement as to their compensation, particularly if their salaries are unequal or if they play different roles in connection with the business, as where one is more active than the other in managing it.[63] If an employee enters into an arm's-length agreement and subsequently acquires control of his employer, although there is some authority for respecting the continuing integrity of the agreement and allowing a deduction of contingent compensation, there is also a line of decisions following the view that where a person owns or controls his own business, the concept of contingent compensation as an incentive for him to exert his best efforts in managing what is substantially his is incongruous.[64]

In the case of family corporations, excessive compensation paid to a rela-

[60] See Brodsky, What Constitutes Reasonable Compensation: Contingent Compensation Plans; Factors In Proving Reasonableness of Compensation, N.Y.U. 19th Inst. on Fed. Tax. 169, 173 (1961). By analogy, see Rogers v. Hill, 289 U.S. 582 (1933), holding that, although bonuses paid in accordance with a percentage formula in a bylaw might have been reasonable when the bylaw was adopted, the percentage might become unreasonable and the bonuses invalid as a matter of corporate law if they had no relation to the value of the services rendered and were attributable largely to enormous increases in sales due to the success of the company's product (cigarettes) and vast growth of the entire industry, rather than the individual efforts of those who were entitled to receive the bonuses. On the other hand, a temporary rise in profits due to unexpected successes or economic conditions in a particular year will not generally invalidate a bonus computed on a percentage basis. See 1 CCH 1969 Stand. Fed. Tax Rep. ¶1372.0124.

[61] Treas. Reg. §1.162-7(b)(2), *supra* note 56.

[62] Adams Tooling, Inc., 33 T.C. 65, 74 (1959), *acquiesced in,* 1960-2 Cum. Bull. 3, *aff'd,* 289 F.2d 554 (7th Cir. 1961).

[63] See James J. McHale Co. v. United States, 151 F. Supp. 115 (N.D. Ohio 1957); Howard Sole, Inc. 12 CCH Tax Ct. Mem. 238 (1953).

[64] See Brodsky, *supra* at 172–173 (collecting the conflicting cases).

tive, such as a son who renders services of relatively low value, may be disallowed as a deduction and may, in addition, be taxed as a dividend to the father, on assignment of income principles.[65]

A useful planning device in situations where there is doubt as to the deductibility of compensation is an agreement between employer and employee that, in the event a deduction is disallowed to the employer for any part of the compensation paid to the employee, the latter will refund the same to the employer. Such an agreement, if legally binding, will probably entitle the employee to a deduction for the amount he is required to refund to his employer. Thus, although the employee must still include the amount of compensation in income in the year it is received, under the doctrine of "claim of right," [66] his tax liability will be roughly counterbalanced by the deduction if allowed in the year of refund.[67]

Finally, as pointed out in our discussion of Subchapter S, one of the primary benefits resulting from a Subchapter S election is the elimination of any need to show reasonableness in order to establish the right to a deduction on the corporate level.[68] This follows from the fact that all corporate profits are taxable to the shareholders of a Subchapter S corporation whether or not they are distributed as salaries or as dividends.

5.4 TAX ON IMPROPER AND EXCESSIVE ACCUMULATIONS OF EARNINGS

Although one of the main advantages of doing business in the corporate form is to insulate the earnings of an enterprise from taxation to those who own it,[69] there are limitations on the extent to which a corporation may accumulate and plough back earnings without being itself subject to an additional tax. The tax is imposed on the "accumulated taxable income" of a

[65] See Minnie F. Lasker, 11 CCH Tax Ct. Mem. 50 (1952); Charles Goodman, 5 CCH Tax Ct. Mem. 1126 (1946), *aff'd,* 176 F.2d 389 (2d Cir. 1949), *cert. denied,* 338 U.S. 904 (1949).

[66] North American Oil Consolidated v. Burnet, 286 U.S. 417 (1932).

[67] See United States v. Lewis, 340 U.S. 590 (1951). Some cases, however, have adopted a so called transactional approach and have excluded the excessive compensation from income in the year of receipt. Under this approach, the taxpayer receives no deduction in the year of refund. For a discussion see S. Surrey and W. Warren, Cases and Materials on Federal Income Taxation 509–510 (1962). In addition, Section 1341 of the Code adopts a transactional approach where the amount in question exceeds $3000. See Rev. Rul. 69–115, 1969–1 Cum. Bull. 50 (employee entitled to deduction in year of repayment and not entitled to transactional treatment under Section 1341). See also Harley, Dealings Between Closely Held Corporations and Their Stockholders, 25 Tax L. Rev. 403, 426–427 (1970), discussing Vincent E. Oswald, 49 T.C. 645 (1968), *acquiesced in,* 1968–2 Cum. Bull. 2, which permitted a deduction in the year of repayment.

[68] See Ch. I, text accompanying note 84.

[69] See Ch. I, text accompanying note 4.

corporation (other than certain exempted ones[70]) which has been "formed or availed of for the purpose of avoiding the income tax with respect to its shareholders or the shareholders of any other corporation, by permitting earnings and profits to accumulate instead of being divided or distributed." [71] Also it is provided that "the fact that the earnings and profits of a corporation are permitted to accumulate beyond the reasonable needs of the business shall be determinative of the purpose to avoid the income tax with respect to shareholders, unless the corporation by the preponderance of the evidence shall prove to the contrary." [72] In this regard, the "reasonable needs of the business" are defined as including "reasonably anticipated needs." [73]

From the foregoing it should be apparent that, although the key factor which determines whether or not the tax should be imposed is the presence of "purpose to avoid income tax . . . by permitting earnings and profits to accumulate instead of being divided or distributed," a central consideration (one might almost say *the* central one) is whether earnings and profits have been allowed to accumulate beyond the "reasonable needs of the business." However, a tax avoidance purpose must always be shown. Thus even though earnings have been permitted to accumulate beyond the reasonable needs of the business, if this was done through error, difference of opinion as to how the funds should be used,[74] poor judgment, stupidity, parsimony, spite or a freeze-out attempt on a minority shareholder,[75] the tax should not be imposed since the earnings were not retained to avoid taxes. But if there is a showing of a tax avoidance purpose, it need not be shown that tax avoidance was the dominant purpose; it need only be *one* of the purposes for accumulating the earnings (i.e., there may be other equally powerful motivating factors).[76]

Although whether or not a tax avoidance purpose is present depends on the facts of each case, the regulations provide that the following circumstances will be considered:

[70] Personal holding companies, foreign personal holding companies and corporations exempt from tax under Section 501 of the Code (e.g., charitable organizations) are exempt. Int. Rev. Code of 1954, §532(b).

[71] Id. §532(a).

[72] Id. §533(a). The Code also provides that the fact that any corporation is a "mere holding or investment company" shall be prima facie evidence of the purpose to avoid income tax. Id. §533(b).

[73] Id. §537.

[74] Duke Laboratories, Inc. v. United States, 337 F.2d 280 (2d Cir. 1964); Casey v. Commissioner, 267 F.2d 26 (2d Cir. 1959); T. C. Heyward & Co. v. United States, 66–2 CCH Tax Ct. ¶9667 (W.D.N.C. 1966).

[75] See B. Bittker and J. Eustice, Federal Income Taxation of Corporations and Shareholders 216 (1966) (citing one case to the contrary, which required a reasonable purpose for the retention of earnings in order to escape the tax: Smoot Sand & Gravel Corp. v. Commissioner, 274 F.2d 495 (4th Cir. 1960)).

[76] United States v. Donruss Co., 393 U.S. 297 (1969) (resolving a conflict in the prior cases).

(i) Dealings between the corporation and its shareholders, such as withdrawals by the shareholders as personal loans or the expenditure of funds by the corporation for the personal benefit of the shareholders,

(ii) The investment by the corporation of undistributed earnings in assets having no reasonable connection with the business of the corporation . . . and

(iii) The extent to which the corporation has distributed its earnings and profits.[77]

As we have already seen,[78] personal loans or the corporate expenditure of funds for the benefit of shareholders may, under appropriate circumstances, be taxed to the recipients as "constructive dividends." However, if such a tax is not imposed, the corporation may be held to have accumulated its earnings for the purpose of tax avoidance if the funds could have been distributed to the shareholders by way of a dividend. Similarly, a poor dividend record is evidence of a tax avoidance motivation as indicating an unwillingness to make distributions to shareholders, as is a good dividend record evidence to the contrary. The fact that a corporation invests its surplus funds in unrelated businesses implies that the funds are not really needed for its primary business and, but for its wish to avoid tax on its shareholders, such funds might have been distributed as dividends. All of these factors, however, are merely evidentiary and may be rebutted by a showing of good business (i.e., nontax) reasons for the failure to make distributions. Conversely, the fact that a company has a good dividend record does not necessarily insulate it from attack if a greater percentage of surplus might have been distributed had it not wished to avoid taxation on the shareholder level.[79] And where a stock dividend is distributed instead of a cash dividend, although earned surplus is capitalized, earnings and profits in the tax sense remain the same and thus the distribution does not lessen the likelihood that the tax on excess accumulations will be imposed.[80]

Due to the Code provision that the accumulation of earnings and profits beyond the reasonable needs of the business (including reasonably anticipated needs) shall be determinative of the purpose to avoid income tax unless the corporation proves to the contrary by a preponderance of the evidence,[81] the most frequently litigated question is what constitutes reasonable needs in particular fact situations. Here the regulations provide illustrative examples of various grounds on which earnings may be reasonably accumulated and also instances where the accumulation would be un-

[77] Treas. Reg. §1.533–1(a)(2).

[78] See text accompanying note 34 *supra.*

[79] See B. Bittker and J. Eustice, id. at 217–218.

[80] E-Z Sew Enterprises, Inc. v. United States, 260 F. Supp. 100 (E.D. Mich. 1966). An earlier case to the contrary, Harry A. Koch Co. v. Vinal, 228 F. Supp. 782 (D.C. Neb. 1964), has been discredited. See Rev. Rul. 65–68, 1965–1 Cum. Bull. 246.

[81] See text accompanying note 72 *supra.*

reasonable. As regards the latter, the regulations provide that accumulations for any of the following objectives may indicate that the accumulation is beyond the reasonable needs of the business:

(1) Loans to shareholders, or the expenditure of funds of the corporation for the personal benefit of the shareholders;

(2) Loans having no reasonable relation to the conduct of the business made to relatives or friends of shareholders, or to other persons;

(3) Loans to another corporation, the business of which is not that of the taxpayer corporation, if the capital stock of such other corporation is owned, directly or indirectly, by the shareholder or shareholders of the taxpayer corporation and such shareholder or shareholders are in control of both corporations;

(4) Investments in properties, or securities which are unrelated to the activities of the business of the taxpayer corporation; or

(5) Retention of earnings and profits to provide against unrealistic hazards.[82]

Furthermore, in determining whether earnings and profits of the current year have been retained for the reasonable needs of the business, accumulations of prior years are taken into consideration. If prior accumulations are sufficient to meet current and anticipated needs, then further accumulations out of current income may be unjustified.[83]

The regulations list five situations in which accumulations may be upheld as meeting the reasonable needs test:

(1) To provide for bona fide expansion of business or replacement of plant;

(2) To acquire a business enterprise through purchasing stock or assets;

(3) To provide for retirement of bona fide indebtedness created in connection with the trade or business, such as the establishment of a sinking fund for the purpose of retiring bonds issued by the corporation in accordance with contract obligations incurred on issue;

(4) To provide necessary working capital for the business, such as, for the procurement of inventories; or

(5) To provide for investments or loans to suppliers or customers if necessary in order to maintain the business of the corporation.[84]

The first two grounds suggest that a corporation may both expand and diversify its business and may accumulate funds for doing so. Thus it need not borrow the funds from outside sources but may generate the same through so-called internal financing.[85] An important question is whether

[82] Treas. Reg. §1.537–2(c).
[83] Id. §1.535–3(b)(ii).
[84] Id. §1.537–2(b).
[85] However, if a corporation has financed through borrowing, and the debt can be refinanced through further borrowing, there is authority to the effect that an accumulation of funds to pay off the debt may be unreasonable. Helvering v. Chicago Stock Yards Co., 318 U.S. 693 (1943). Note, however, that among the permissible grounds of accumulation of earnings listed in the regulations, Treas. Reg. §1.537–2(b), is the "retirement of bona fide indebtedness." For a discussion and collection of cases permitting financing of business needs through retained earnings, see B.

there are any limits to expansion or diversification. We have already seen that the regulations provide that investments in properties or securities "which are unrelated to the activities of the business of the taxpayer" may indicate that there has been an unreasonable accumulation.[86] May a steel company invest in a publishing house in the interests of diversification? A food processing company in a computer manufacturer? Can we differentiate between the use of accumulated funds for mere investment through the purchase of stock or other securities and the use of such funds for business expansion and diversification? What is meant by the reference to the taxpayer's "business"? The regulations attempt to do some line drawing here in the following way:

(a) The business of a corporation is not merely that which it has previously carried on but includes, in general, any line of business which it may undertake.

(b) If one corporation owns the stock of another corporation and, in effect, operates the other corporation, the business of the latter corporation may be considered in substance, although not in legal form, the business of the first corporation. However, investment by a corporation of its earnings and profits in stock and securities of another corporation is not, of itself, to be regarded as employment of the earnings and profits in its business. Earnings and profits of the first corporation put into the second corporation through the purchase of stock or securities or otherwise, may, if a subsidiary relationship is established, constitute employment of the earnings and profits in its own business. Thus, the business of one corporation may be regarded as including the business of another corporation if such other corporation is a mere instrumentality of the first corporation; that may be established by showing that the first corporation owns at least 80 percent of the voting stock of the second corporation. If the taxpayer's ownership of stock is less than 80 percent in the other corporation, the determination of whether the funds are employed in a business operated by the taxpayer will depend upon the particular circumstances of the case. Moreover, the business of one corporation does not include the business of another corporation if such other corporation is a personal holding company, an investment company, or a corporation not engaged in the active conduct of a trade or business.[87]

According to the above, the mere acquisition by one corporation of stock in another corporation is not of itself sufficient to constitute expansion or diversification of the business of the taxpayer. If enough stock is acquired to make the acquired corporation a "subsidiary" of the taxpayer, then the accumulation of funds for the acquisition may be justified. This would be so if the acquired corporation were either a mere instrumentality of the other corporation or if the latter were to own at least 80 percent of its voting

Bittker and J. Eustice, Federal Income Taxation of Corporations and Shareholders 226 (1966).

[86] See text accompanying note 82 *supra.* See also Treas. Reg. §1.533–1(a)(2) in text accompanying note 77 *supra* (reference to investment in assets "having no reasonable connection with" the business of the taxpayer).

[87] Id. §1.537–3.

stock. The reference to "mere instrumentality" is somewhat puzzling in view of its use in a radically different nontax sense to indicate a situation where, because of the relationship between two corporations, such as excessive domination by one corporation of the policies of another, intermingling of funds, failure to observe corporate formalities and the like, the corporate form is legally disregarded and one corporation is held liable for the obligations of the other.[88] Despite the reference to the possibility that through stock ownership one corporation might operate another, it is somewhat unlikely that the regulations, by the use of the mere instrumentality language, intend the somewhat extreme situation encountered in the cases which hold that the corporate entity may be disregarded entirely. Certainly the mere ownership of 80 percent of the voting stock would not be enough to justify disregard of the corporate entity, although the regulations indicate that this may be sufficient to justify an accumulation of funds. The overall intent of the regulations is obviously to differentiate between the passive use of funds for mere investment and their use in a more active sense in connection with related businesses.[89] The latter may retain their separate identities in the corporate sense and yet be part of the business of the taxpayer in the tax sense.

Although the regulations permit accumulation of earnings to provide for the retirement of "bona fide indebtedness created in connection with the trade or business," [90] where the debt is held by the shareholders, and especially if it is held pro rata, accumulation to pay off debt is subject to attack.[91] As we have seen in another context, shareholder advances may be characterized as capital contributions.[92] If this is so, then accumulations to pay off shareholder-held "debt" may be in substance equivalent to redemption of stock rather than debt. If such redemption is held to be "essentially equivalent to a dividend" and thus taxed at ordinary rates to the shareholders,[93] then the accumulation of funds to effect redemption is similar to an accumulation to pay dividends in later years rather than currently. Although there may be a question of whether the accumulation was for the purpose of tax avoidance, it would seem that if dividend treatment were assured, albeit at a later date, the risk of a penalty tax is less than where funds are accumulated without any plans to make a taxable distribution to

---

[88] For cases summarizing the various factors which will be taken into consideration, see Steven v. Roscoe Turner Aeronautical Corp., 324 F.2d 157, 161 (7th Cir. 1963); Natl. Bond Fin. Co. v. General Motors Corp., 238 F. Supp. 248, 256 (W.D. Mo. 1964), aff'd, 341 F.2d 1022 (8th Cir. 1965); Garrett v. Southern Ry. Co., 173 F. Supp. 915 (E.D. Tenn. 1959), aff'd, 278 F.2d 424 (6th Cir. 1960), cert. denied, 364 U.S. 833 (1960).

[89] See B. Bittker and J. Eustice, id. at 228.

[90] See Treas. Reg. §1.537-2(b)(3), in text accompanying note 84 supra.

[91] See B. Bittker and J. Eustice, id. at 222, 226.

[92] See Ch. II, text accompanying note 67.

[93] See Int. Rev. Code of 1954, §302(b). For further discussion see Ch. VI, text accompanying note 13.

the shareholders.[94] However, if the redemption is not essentially equivalent to a dividend, then the advance accumulation is more likely to be held unreasonable.

The regulations expressly permit the retention of earnings to provide necessary working capital, inventories, etc.[95] Obviously the amount of working capital will vary with the particular business and also with fluctuations in economic conditions both in a particular industry and in general. Although the cases have suggested various rule-of-thumb tests as to sufficiency of working capital, such as a ratio of $2\frac{1}{2}$ to 1 of current assets to current liabilities,[96] or the accumulation of funds to meet one year's operating expenses,[97] the matter must ultimately be resolved under the circumstances of each particular case, as each situation has its own unique requirements as to what is reasonable. In addition, it should not be forgotten that even though the judgment of the board of directors or company officers as to necessary working capital is erroneous or their financial calculations ill-founded, if they are made in good faith, then the tax avoidance motive requisite for the penalty tax may be absent.[98]

In addition to the various grounds for justifiable retention of earnings already enumerated, various others have been held reasonable. The regulations expressly provide that investments or loans to suppliers or customers are permitted "if necessary in order to maintain the business of the corporation." [99] Accumulation has also been justified for financing pension and profit-sharing plans, self-insurance against casualties, threatened litigation, strikes, loss of important customers, and other common business contingencies.[100]

Among the more controversial grounds for accumulating earnings is funding redemptions of stock. As we shall see in the following chapter, an important aspect of planning for the death, retirement or possible disability of shareholders in a close corporation is a so-called buy-and-sell agreement whereby the corporation is obligated to purchase, and the shareholder obligated to sell, shares upon the happening of a specified event. In order to insure that the corporation will have funds legally available to purchase the stock[101] it may either accumulate part of its earnings in a reserve or pur-

---

[94] See text accompanying note 102 *infra*.

[95] See Treas. Reg. §1.537–2(b)(4), in text accompanying note 84 *supra*.

[96] See B. Bittker and J. Eustice, id. at 222.

[97] See Bremerton Sun Publishing Co., 44 T.C. 566 (1965); F. E. Watkins Motor Co. 31 T.C. 288 (1958), *acquiesced in*, 1959–1 Cum. Bull. 5; but see Dixie, Inc. v. Commissioner, 277 F.2d 526 (2d Cir. 1960), *cert. denied*, 364 U.S. 827 (1960). For discussion see Horwitz, Operating Cycle Test Provides Needed Guidelines for Measuring 531 Accumulation, 24 J. Tax. 326 (1966); Luria, The Accumulated Earnings Tax, 76 Yale L.J. 793 (1967); Ziegler, The "New" Accumulated Earnings Tax: A Survey of Recent Developments, 22 Tax L. Rev. 77, 91 (1966).

[98] See text accompanying note 74 *supra*.

[99] See Treas. Reg. §1.537–2(b)(5), in text accompanying note 84 *supra*.

[100] See B. Bittker and J. Eustice, id. at 223 (collecting the cases).

[101] See Ch. III, text accompanying note 35.

chase insurance. Both the maintenance of such reserves and the periodic payment of insurance premiums raise the possibility that this will be held to be unreasonable accumulation.

If the stock redemption is pro rata, and is held to be essentially equivalent to a dividend, although there is a residual possibility that an accumulation to fund the redemption might be motivated by tax avoidance (e.g., to postpone the tax on the shareholders until the year of redemption when their tax bracket might be lower),[102] the eventual imposition of tax at the shareholder level lessens the likelihood of a penalty tax. The probability of a penalty tax is far greater if the redemption is not pro rata, as where a minority or majority shareholder's interest is repurchased by the corporation. In such a case it is arguable that the redemption does not serve a *corporate* purpose but rather is to accommodate the wishes of one or more individual shareholders. Accumulation of funds for a noncorporate purpose is not a "reasonable need of the business." Moreover, entirely apart from the reasonable needs test, it might be argued that an accumulation which lessens or eliminates the ability of the corporation to pay dividends to its shareholders and which is primarily for the accommodation of a controlling shareholder may be actuated, at least in part, by a tax avoidance motive.[103] On the other hand, some stock redemptions rather clearly do serve a corporate purpose and may be necessary to assure that the corporation functions smoothly or even continues to exist. Where a shareholder dissents from policies currently being observed by the directors and his objections pose a threat to the efficient running of the business, it is clearly in the corporate interest to buy him out.[104] Similarly, where two shareholders or shareholder groups are equally divided and deadlocked on corporate policies, making it difficult for the corporation to function normally, the redemption of the shares of one group may be highly beneficial and even necessary for the corporation.[105] A more difficult case is presented by a majority shareholder who wishes to retire or wishes to receive more income from the corporation and so exchanges his stock for notes. If the redemption is motivated largely by such personal reasons, as well as the wish to shift control

---

[102] See text accompanying note 94 *supra.*

[103] See Pelton Steel Casting Co. v. Commissioner, 251 F.2d 278 (7th Cir. 1958), *cert. denied,* 356 U.S. 958 (1958). For a good discussion of the *Pelton Steel* case, as well as the other aspects of this area, see Herwitz, Stock Redemptions and the Accumulated Earnings Tax, 74 Harv. L. Rev. 866, 881–886 (1961).

[104] See, e.g., Gazette Publishing Co. v. Self, 103 F. Supp. 779 (E.D. Ark. 1952); Dill Mfg. Co., 39 B.T.A. 1023 (1939), *nonacquiesced in,* 1939–2 Cum. Bull. 47. In both of these cases, however, the accumulation was justified by additional business needs other than the redemption. Herwitz, *supra* at 909, seems to imply that the potential nuisance of a minority shareholder group is not generally sufficiently deleterious to the corporation to justify redemption for the corporate good.

[105] Mountain State Steel Foundries, Inc. v. Commissioner, 284 F.2d 737 (4th Cir. 1960); see also Penn Needle Art Co., 17 CCH Tax Ct. Mem. 504 (1958) (accumulation also justified by other business reasons). But see Hedberg-Friedheim Contracting Co. v. Commissioner, 251 F.2d 839 (8th Cir. 1958).

into the hands of younger members of the family, the accumulation of funds to carry out the plan does not appear to serve a corporate purpose.[106] On the other hand, if the shareholder is a key employee, it may be that an arrangement which insures a smooth transition of management into the hands of others on his retirement is beneficial to the corporation and so may qualify as a reasonable ground for accumulating corporate funds.[107] And if the majority shareholder proposes to sell his interest to an outsider who might make detrimental changes in the policies of the corporation, or if as an alternative he should threaten to liquidate the enterprise, redemption of his stock might be justified as meeting a pressing corporate need.[108] However, where a majority shareholder's interest is concerned, it is often difficult to differentiate between the reasonable needs of the corporation and the personal interests of the one who controls it. If the two are coequivalent and if the redemption is in fact motivated by the personal desire of those in control to get out, then it cannot be so easily justified either under a reasonable needs test or as lacking a tax avoidance motive.[109] Clearly there can be no hard and fast rule here and any accumulation for the purpose of redemption, whether it be of the interest of a minority shareholder or of someone in control, must be judged on its own peculiar facts.

If funds have not been accumulated in advance of redemption but are accumulated in order to pay off a corporate note issued to redeem the shares, then the accumulation is more readily justified. We have already seen that the regulations expressly state that an accumulation to "provide for retirement of bona fide indebtedness created in connection with the trade or business . . ."[110] meets the reasonable needs test. It is possible, of course, to argue that if the redemption itself was not for a corporate purpose but was rather to accomodate the personal interests of the shareholder, the giving of a note for the redemption price would not be "indebtedness created in connection with the trade or business." However, regardless of how the indebtedness was created, if it is a legally enforceable obligation of the corporation, it is clearly in the corporate interest that it be paid at maturity. Otherwise the credit rating of the corporation will suffer and the en-

[106] See B. Bittker and J. Eustice, Federal Income Taxation of Corporations and Stockholders 231 (1966).

[107] Ibid. The author advises caution in relying on those decisions which favor the taxpayer in this situation, especially if the redemption is not likely to occur in the near future. He also observes that the redemption of shares on retirement of an employee is not always a corporate necessity. Thus only in particular situations is the corporation threatened with possible adverse effects as a result of diverging interests among those who play a passive role and those who manage. Id. at 231–232. In the *Mountain State* case, 284 F.2d 737 (4th Cir. 1960), the court observed that the resolution of such a conflict was clearly in the interests of the corporation and its employees, especially where the situation results in demands that the corporation be sold or liquidated.

[108] See Herwitz, *supra* at 910.

[109] Ibid.

[110] See Treas. Reg. §1.537–2(b)(3), in text accompanying note 84 *supra*.

terprise itself may be jeopardized. Accordingly the accumulation of funds to meet the debt may satisfy the reasonable needs test without too much inquiry into the circumstances of the redemption, provided, of course, that the indebtedness is bona fide and is not a masquerade for something else.[111] One argument against this analysis is that if a different status is given to accumulations to meet a note than is given to accumulations for the redemption itself, a corporation which contemplated redemption could avoid the risk of preredemption accumulations being subjected to a penalty tax by adopting a "redeem first, pay later" policy.[112] Although the matter is troublesome, it would appear that if the note itself is bona fide, i.e., is legally enforceable and was given in good faith, the corporation should be permitted to accumulate funds to "clean up" its balance sheet by discharging liabilities if this is in its best interests. For example, if the corporation were not to give a note but were to redeem the shares with cash or assets and were then to accumulate future earnings in order to "expand back" into its previous balance sheet position, this might find support in the regulations, which permit accumulation to "provide for bona fide expansion or replacement of plant." [113] Assuming that this would be proper,[114] should the situation be any different if, rather than deplete assets, the corporation gives a note? Or would the substance of the transaction be the same if cash or assets were first distributed and then loaned back to the corporation? Finally, suppose the corporation were to borrow funds from an outside source, such as a bank, to fund the repurchase? In all of these cases, it seems exceedingly difficult to draw hard and fast lines. In view of the essentially subjective underpinnings of the tax requiring a showing of tax avoidance motivation, and the difficulty of ascertaining reasonable needs except on the basis of each particular fact situation, any distinctions such as "accumulation before" versus "accumulation after," accumulation to repay a note or to replenish assets dispersed in a redemption, and even distinctions between redemptions of minority interests and majority interests, are likely to have only a limited utility. At best they can point towards possible trouble spots where the corporate planner should exercise caution. Nonetheless it is pos-

[111] See Mountain State Steel Foundries, Inc. v. Commissioner, 284 F.2d 737 (4th Cir. 1960). See also Herwitz, *supra* at 900–904.

[112] See B. Bittker and J. Eustice, Federal Income Taxation of Corporations and Shareholders 233 (1966).

[113] See Treas. Reg. §1.537–2(b)(1), in text accompanying note 84 *supra*.

[114] The assumption should not go unquestioned in all cases, however. Thus if it were clear that, but for a corporate willingness to satisfy the personal desire of the shareholder to have his stock redeemed, the corporation would not have acquired the stock, that such acquisition would have resulted in no corporate benefit but would, rather, have amounted to a decided detriment, then the dispersal of assets would be unjustified from a business standpoint and a subsequent accumulation might be less easily defended if the whole matter could have been avoided and took place only because of pressure from the shareholder. However, it should be remembered that honest miscalculations by the board of directors, abuse of discretion or even stupidity are still consistent with the absence of a tax avoidance motive. See text accompanying note 75 *supra*. Thus even though the reasonable needs test might not be met, tax avoidance motivation might still be absent and a penalty tax unjustified.

sible to generalize that accumulations of earnings expressly for the purpose of redeeming the shares of one who holds a majority interest and thus exerts a controlling influence over the board of directors is by far the most sensitive of the areas which have been discussed. Accumulations to redeem a minority interest, to repay a note or to replenish assets used to redeem shares, and the use of funds which were previously accumulated for other purposes to finance a redemption[115] are less likely to incur difficulty.

Whatever the status of corporate accumulations to fund a redemption of stock, the cases appear to be relatively favorable to the diversion of earnings toward payment of premiums on insurance for stock redemptions at death or retirement of an employee.[116] Although there seems to be little reason for distinguishing between insurance and self-insurance, the frequent use of key man insurance by closely held concerns may lend some support to the idea that the payment of reasonable premiums can be justified as a need of the business. Theoretically a distinction could be made between different types of insurance, depending upon the cost to the company and the extent to which the premium covers only pure insurance (as in term insurance) or is devoted to an additional savings component (as in so-called ordinary life insurance, where higher premium payments can build up sizable cash reserves). Also a single premium payment for a policy covering a senior executive might be more sensitive to attack if the premium were relatively high because of the employee's age or health. Fundamentally, the same considerations should apply as in the case of accumulations of corporate reserves, namely, is the funding (and the contemplated stock redemption) likely to produce a corporate benefit or is it merely to accommodate the personal wishes of the shareholder? Also, if insurance is used not to redeem stock but to offset losses and expense likely to result from the retirement of an employee, the possibility of a penalty tax is even more remote.[117]

[115] See Treas. Reg. §1.537–1(b)(2), stating that "subsequent events shall not be used for the purpose of showing that the retention of earnings or profits was unreasonable at the close of the taxable year if all the elements of reasonable anticipation are present at the close of such taxable year." Thus the reasonableness of the accumulation is determined on an annual basis. "Each taxable year stands on its own footing. . . ." Herwitz, *supra* at 905. If the funds are properly accumulated, then they may be used for other purposes, such as redemptions, if it subsequently appears that fulfillment of the original purposes of the accumulation is unnecessary, undesirable or not feasible. See Penn Needle Art Co., 17 CCH Tax Ct. Mem. 504 (1958). The regulations, §1.537–1(b)(2), do qualify this by the observation that "subsequent events may be considered to determine whether the taxpayer actually intended to consummate or has actually consummated the plans for which the earnings and profits were accumulated. . . . If a corporation has justified an accumulation for future needs by plans never consummated, the amount of such an accumulation shall be taken into account in determining the reasonableness of subsequent accumulations."

[116] Cf. Emeloid Co., Inc. v. Commissioner, 189 F.2d 230 (3d Cir. 1951); see also Bradford-Robinson Printing Co. v. United States, 58–1 CCH Tax Ct. Rep. ¶9262 (D. Colo. 1957).

[117] See B. Bittker and J. Eustice, id. at 232 n.44a. See also Goldstein, Tax Aspects of Corporate Business Use of Life Insurance, 18 Tax L. Rev. 133, 207 (1963); Note, 71 Harv. L. Rev. 687 (1958).

The Tax Reform Act of 1969 added an important provision to Section 537(a) of the Code which permits accumulation of amounts needed, or "reasonably anticipated to be needed," to make a redemption of stock included in the gross estate of the decedent, but not in excess of the maximum amount of stock to which Section 303(a) may apply. Section 303, to be discussed in greater detail in the following chapter, permits capital gain or loss treatment for the redemption of shares which are included in a decedent's gross estate (within certain minimum percentage limits) in an amount not exceeding the death taxes and funeral and other administrative expenses imposed on the estate. The new provision also states that the discharge of an obligation incurred to make a redemption under Section 303 shall, for the purpose of the tax on excess accumulations, be treated as the making of such a redemption. In other words, a corporation may now accumulate, free of risk of excess accumulations tax, an amount equal to the maximum permitted to fund a Section 303 redemption or to discharge an obligation entered into in order to make such a redemption.[118]

Turning now to the more mechanical aspects of the accumulated earnings tax, we have yet to consider some additional points relating to the burden of proof and the manner of computing the tax.

It has already been pointed out that the corporation must prove "by the preponderance of the evidence" the lack of tax avoidance motivation if earnings and profits are permitted to accumulate beyond the reasonable needs of the business. This burden is in addition to the usual burden on the taxpayer resulting from the presumption that the Commissioner's determination of a deficiency is correct unless proven otherwise. Once earnings and profits are shown to have been accumulated beyond the reasonable needs of the business, the taxpayer is then doubly disadvantaged by a "presumption on a presumption." It is therefore not surprising that the battleground on which most of the cases have been fought is whether the business needs for the accumulation have been reasonable. If the taxpayer is unsuccessful in this respect, it is unlikely that he will prevail in his last-ditch defense of showing lack of a tax avoidance motive.[119] There is a mechanism, however, whereby the burden of proof (in Tax Court cases *only*) may be shifted to the Commissioner. This is where the taxpayer, in response to a notification by the Commissioner informing him of a proposed deficiency relating to the imposition of an accumulated earnings tax, files a statement of the grounds ("together with facts sufficient to show the basis thereof") on which he relies to establish that all or any part of the earnings and profits have not been permitted to accumulate beyond the reasonable needs of the business. If such a statement has been filed within the prescribed thirty-day period following the Commissioner's notification, then

---

[118] See Int. Rev. Code of 1954, §§537(a)(2), 537(b)(1), (3). See Ch. VI, text accompanying note 79. The new provision covers only accumulations in the year of the shareholder's death or subsequent years—i.e., not advance accumulations.

[119] See B. Bittker and J. Eustice, id. at 219 n.22, 233.

the latter has the burden of establishing that the earnings and profits have been permitted to accumulate beyond the reasonable needs of the business.[120] The burden is shifted, however, only with respect to the grounds set forth in the statement filed by the taxpayer. In effect, this provision amounts to a statutory endorsement of a form of "horse trading"; if the taxpayer will disclose, in advance, the grounds and specific facts with which it proposes to prove its case, then the burden of proof or persuasion as to those grounds is shifted from the taxpayer to the Commissioner. However, the regulations provide that the burden is shifted only if the grounds asserted by the taxpayer "are supported by facts (contained in the statement) sufficient to show the basis thereof." [121] Thus, if the grounds on which the taxpayer relies are not relevant to the Commissioner's allegation of deficiency or if the taxpayer's statement does not contain sufficient facts to show the basis of his case, then the burden remains with the taxpayer.[122] This provision, then, although helpful in some situations, is relatively narrow. Moreover, since the Tax Court has generally refused to rule on the adequacy of the taxpayer's statement prior to trial, and there is thus no assurance that the burden of proof has shifted until the time comes for submitting evidence on the question of reasonable needs of the business, most attorneys contemplate introducing all the available evidence in their favor regardless of where the burden lies.[123] Accordingly, although it would be misleading to characterize the Code provision as useless, it does not give the taxpayer all the tactical advantages that it may seem to promise at first blush.

As to the manner in which the tax is computed, the amount of the tax is set at $27\frac{1}{2}$ percent of the "accumulated taxable income" not in excess of $100,000, plus $38\frac{1}{2}$ percent of the accumulated taxable income in excess of that amount.[124] The accumulated taxable income is computed on a yearly basis and thus each year's accumulation must be separately justified.[125] Accumulations in prior years are only relevant insofar as they may have a bearing on whether current accumulations are reasonable (as where the contemplated purpose for prior accumulations was never achieved and thus such amounts may be put to other uses, so that current accumulations may not be needed).[126]

Accumulated taxable income is equal to the corporation's taxable income with certain adjustments. Taxable income is reduced by corporate income

---

[120] Int. Rev. Code of 1954, §534. The burden also shifts if the Commissioner fails to notify the taxpayer, in advance of mailing a deficiency notice, that the proposed deficiency includes an amount assessed with respect to the accumulated earnings tax. Id. §534(a)(1).

[121] Treas. Reg. §1.534–2(a)(2).

[122] Id. §1.534–2(b)(2).

[123] See B. Bittker and J. Eustice, id. at 234.

[124] Int. Rev. Code of 1954, §531.

[125] See note 115 *supra*.

[126] See Treas. Reg. §1.537–1(b)(2).

taxes, charitable contributions in excess of the amount allowable by the usual limiation of 5 percent, and capital losses which may have been disallowed due to the limitation in Section 1211(a) (which permits a deduction of capital losses only to the extent of capital gains).[127] Upward adjustments are required for such items as the dividends-received deduction, net operating loss deduction and capital loss carry-over.[128] Thus these items, previously deducted to arrive at taxable income, are, along with the excess of net long-term capital gains over net short-term capital loss, in effect added back in to arrive at accumulated taxable income.

Two further adjustments are required, namely a deduction for dividends paid during the taxable year, together with so-called consent dividends, and the accumulated earnings credit. The consent dividend involves a procedure whereby the shareholders agree to treat earnings as having been distributed and consequently taxed even though such earnings are in fact retained by the corporation, thus obviating the need for an actual distribution to lessen the likelihood of a penalty tax.[129] As regards the further deduction for dividends actually paid, there is a provision which allows dividends paid within two and one-half months following the close of the taxable year to be considered as having been paid during the taxable year.[130] This is because of the difficulty of precisely estimating the amount of earnings and profits at the year's end without an audit after the year has closed. As might be expected, only dividends which are in fact taxable to the shareholders are allowed as deductions (although it is not necessary that the shareholder's actual tax be increased by the dividend, i.e., he may have no tax at all due to other losses, deductions, etc.).

The "accumulated earnings credit" is the last adjustment which must be made in the process of computing accumulated taxable income. In effect, this permits a corporation to accumulate a total of $100,000 during its lifetime without any possibility of a penalty tax. Technically the credit is equivalent to that part of the earnings and profits as is retained for the reasonable needs of the business, adjusted downwards by any excess of net long-term capital gains over net short-term capital losses, but in no event less than the amount by which $100,000 exceeds the accumulated earnings and profits at the close of the preceding taxable year.[131] This means that the $100,000 amount is adjusted for accumulations carried over from prior years, since, as previously indicated, this is the total that a corporation may accumulate during its lifetime without any question of a penalty tax. Amounts accumulated in excess of this figure must be justified under the

---

[127] Int. Rev. Code of 1954, §535.
[128] Ibid.
[129] Id. §565.
[130] Id. §563(a).
[131] Id. §535(c). If the corporation is a mere holding or investment company, the credit is simply equivalent to the amount by which $100,000 exceeds the accumulated earnings and profits at the close of the preceding taxable year.

reasonable needs test. In the case of corporations formed for the purpose of avoiding income tax, and also certain affiliated corporations, the accumulated earnings credit is either limited or denied entirely.[132]

5.5 PERSONAL HOLDING COMPANY TAX

Aside from the tax on excess accumulations just discussed, another danger area for the closely held corporation is the penalty tax on "undistributed personal holding company income." Since the tax rate is set at 70 percent,[133] the imposition of a tax can be a major disaster. Fortunately there is a "deficiency dividend" procedure whereby, if a distribution is made after it has been determined that a tax is due, the amount of the tax can be lessened or eliminated.[134]

The function of the personal holding company provisions is to prevent or discourage the use of the corporation as a "tax shelter" for income which might otherwise be taxed at a relatively high rate to those who earn or are otherwise entitled to receive it. If a person is in a relatively high tax bracket, it might occur to him that, by "incorporating himself," he might have his dividend and other investment income taxed at corporate rates rather than individual rates. This will be advantageous only if his tax bracket is higher than the corporate tax rate. A similar technique has been used where a person, such as a motion picture or television performer, taxed at high rates on the income he receives for his services, sets up a corporation which then contracts with the motion picture or television producer for the services of its "employee." All payments for the "employee's" services are then made by the producer to the employer company, which is taxed at corporate rates. The employee receives a "salary" which, he hopes, is tax deductible to the corporation. But for the personal holding company provisions, the performer thus might insulate himself from tax on income which he does not presently need. The retained income could then be invested by the corporation in other income sources, creating more income and capital gains.

A personal holding company may also be used to offset investment income by other deductions, such as charges for depreciation, maintenance and the like. Thus a yacht may be transferred to a corporation along with other investment property in the hope that the corporation might deduct depreciation and other expenses on the yacht against its other investment income. Another technique might be to argue that the yacht could not be rented to an outsider for an amount equivalent to the expense, including

---

[132] See id. §1551. See Ch. II, text accompanying note 161.

[133] Int. Rev. Code of 1954, §541. Personal holding companies are not subject to the tax on excess accumulation of earnings. Id. §532(b)(1).

[134] Id. §547(d). Liability for interest due on the tax, or penalties, is not avoided even though the amount of the tax is itself reduced.

depreciation, necessary for its maintenance. If the yacht is then "chartered" to the shareholder (who, of course, was its former owner), the latter might transfer enough income-producing property to the corporation to make up the difference between the charter payments made by him and the corporation's expenses in maintaining the yacht. In any case, the effect is much the same, i.e., depreciation expense, etc., on the yacht is offset against income from other sources.[135]

Although the personal holding company provisions are designed to discourage intentional tax avoidance schemes such as those just described, their primary significance for most closely held concerns is that they constitute a potential trap for those who might inadvertently fall within their scope. A "personal holding company" is defined as any corporation (with certain exceptions)[136] that has at least 60 percent of its "adjusted ordinary gross income" in the form of "personal holding company income" and, at any time during the last half of its taxable year, more than 50 percent in value of its outstanding stock is owned, directly or indirectly, by or for not more than five individuals.[137] "Personal holding company income" is, briefly, income from certain "passive" or investment sources, as well as certain types of personal service income. Thus dividends, rents, mineral, oil and gas royalties, copyright royalties, produced film rents, amounts received as compensation for the use of certain properties of the corporation, income from personal service contracts and, finally, income from an estate or trust where the corporation is a beneficiary, are all considered as personal holding company income. Some of these categories will be discussed later in greater detail.[138]

From the foregoing it is apparent that, for the tax to apply, a corporation must have 60 percent of its adjusted ordinary gross income from any of the enumerated sources and also must meet the 50 percent ownership test. In regard to the latter, a very important consideration, and a potential tax trap, is the fact that constructive ownership rules apply. Thus stock owned by a corporation, partnership estate or trust is considered as owned proportionately by its shareholders, partners or beneficiaries.[139] An individual is considered as owning stock owned by his partner, his spouse, brothers, sisters, ancestors or lineal descendants.[140] If a person has an option to acquire

[135] See B. Bittker and J. Eustice, Federal Income Taxation of Corporations and Shareholders 238–239 (1966).

[136] The exceptions are certain tax-exempt corporations (e.g., charities and educational foundations), banks, building and loan associations, life insurance companies, surety companies, foreign personal holding companies (which are subject to special provisions—Int. Rev. Code of 1954, §§551–558), lending or finance companies, small business investment companies and, finally, any foreign corporation if, in the latter case, its gross income from sources within the United States is less than 50 percent of its total gross income from all sources and if, in addition, all of its stock is owned by nonresident alien individuals. Id. §542(c).

[137] Id. §542(a).

[138] Id. §543. See text accompanying note 149 *infra*.

[139] Id. §544(a)(1).

[140] Id. §544(a)(2).

stock, he is considered as owning the stock.[141] If securities (such as convertible bonds) are convertible into stock, then such securities are considered as part of the outstanding stock.[142] Also certain of the constructive ownership rules can be combined: Stock constructively owned by virtue of the first and third of the above rules (attribution from a corporation, partnership, estate, or trust to various individuals and also the option situation) is treated as being "actually owned" for the purpose of applying the first and second rules (attribution from a corporation, partnership, estate or trust, etc., and also attribution between partners and family members).[143] This may lead to some unexpected situations. Suppose, for example, that a person has a 20 percent beneficial ownership interest in a trust or estate. The latter owns 60 percent of the outstanding shares in a corporation. Under the first of the above rules, the person is considered as owning 12 percent of the outstanding shares in the corporation (20 percent of 60 percent). This 12 percent interest is then considered as actual ownership for the purpose of attribution to a wife or family member, such as brother, sister, father or son, as well as to a partner. However, if the 12 percent ownership is attributed to the wife, it cannot be "reattributed" to the wife's father, since the family attribution rule (which also applies between partners) cannot be used "over again." [144] The first of the above rules can, however, be used over again. Thus, if the A corporation owns all the stock in the B corporation which in turn owns all the stock in the C corporation, and the latter owns a 50 percent interest in the D corporation, the B corporation is considered as owning 50 percent of the D corporation and this 50 percent ownership interest may then be attributed to the A corporation.[145] Suppose, then, that a person owns 20 percent of the outstanding stock of the A corporation. Since the latter owns 50 percent of the D stock, the A shareholder is the constructive owner of 10 percent of the D stock (i.e., 20 percent of the 50 percent interest). This 10 percent ownership can then be reattributed to the person's wife, sister, son, father, partner, etc., but cannot be reattributed from the wife to his mother, etc. Suffice it to say that, due to the complexity of the foregoing rules, and the probability that they may not be understood or even known to many, if not most people, it is altogether probable that many shareholders may find themselves unawares in a personal holding company situation.

The danger is heightened by the possibility that shareholders in a closely held corporation may die, retire or wish to dispose of their shares to other shareholders. Even though more than 50 percent of the stock is owned by more than five individuals (applying, of course, the constructive ownership rules just discussed), if a shareholder acquires more stock, or if some stock is repurchased by the corporation (pursuant to a first refusal stock

141 Id. §544(a)(3).
142 Id. §544(b).
143 Id. §544(a)(5).
144 Ibid.
145 See Treas. Reg. §1.544–6(b), Ex. (1).

transfer restriction, for example) then five individuals may end up owning more than 50 percent. If all of a corporation's stock is held by less than ten persons, then of necessity five or fewer persons will own more than 50 percent.[146] Thus, if the additional requirement of 60 percent of adjusted ordinary gross income being personal holding company income is met, such a corporation will automatically be a personal holding company.

Aside from the transfer or redemption of shares, which we have seen may result in a corporation's inadvertently falling within the personal holding company provisions, "accidental" application of the provisions may also result from a company's having, in one particular year, an unusual amount of personal holding company income. For example, a corporation may sell a substantial amount of its assets on credit and, if its operating receipts are low (as might be the case if the corporation were in the process of winding up its affairs), more than 60 percent of its income might be attributed to interest on the sale price of its assets. If this were so and if the corporation were closely held, it would be a personal holding company.[147] This might also be the case if a manufacturing company were to experience a drop in its profit margin so that the cost of goods sold rises and thus sharply curtails the amount of operating income. If the company is closely held and has other income from dividends, rents, royalties, etc., it may fall within the personal holding company provisions even though there may not have been any attempt to avoid taxation.[148]

The term "adjusted ordinary gross income" is defined as the gross income of the corporation less certain adjustments. Thus capital gains and gains from the disposition of Section 1231 property are subtracted, as well as depreciation, property taxes, interest and rent incurred in connection with rental income and mineral royalties.[149]

As already pointed out, the term "personal holding company income" includes income from certain designated passive sources—e.g., dividends, interest (including "imputed interest" under Section 483 of the Code), rents, and royalties—as well as income from personal service contracts and amounts paid a corporation for use of its property. There are some fairly complicated provisions relating specifically to the latter four items.

The provision relating to rental income is particularly troublesome. The problem here is to include rents as personal holding company income and yet exempt a bona fide real estate corporation from the tax if a certain percentage of its income consists in rents. Although the law prior to 1964 provided that rents were not treated as personal holding company income if they amounted to 50 percent or more of a corporation's gross income, this provided a type of tax shelter in that it permitted a corporation to have up

[146] See B. Bittker and J. Eustice, Federal Income Taxation of Corporations and Shareholders 252 (1966).

[147] See O'Sullivan Rubber Co. v. Commissioner, 120 F.2d 845 (2d Cir. 1941).

[148] See B. Bittker and J. Eustice, id. at 244.

[149] Int. Rev. Code of 1954, §543(b)(2).

to 50 percent of its gross income from other passive sources (e.g., dividends, interest, etc.) without falling within the personal holding company provisions. Under the 1964 revisions, the 50 percent test is applied to "adjusted income from rents" (i.e., rental income less depreciation, property taxes, interest and other expenses incurred in connection with the rental property). Thus adjusted income from rents must constitute 50 percent or more of the corporation's adjusted ordinary gross income (i.e., gross income less similar and other deductions as previously discussed). In addition the corporation must have distributed a minimum percentage of its personal holding company income from nonrental sources. Hence dividends for the taxable year must equal or exceed the amount by which the nonrental personal holding company income exceeds 10 percent of ordinary gross income.[150]

Suppose, for example, that a corporation has gross income of $200,000 and that $110,000 of this consists in income from rents. Under the law prior to 1964, the 50 percent test (which applied to gross income rather than adjusted gross income) would have been met. Suppose, however, that the corporation has $30,000 in adjustments due to expenses incurred in connection with the rental property (e.g., depreciation, taxes, etc.). In such a situation adjusted income from rents would be $80,000 and adjusted ordinary gross income would be $170,000. The 50 percent test would not therefore be met. If the adjustments were only $20,000, then the test would be met since adjusted income from rents would equal $90,000 and adjusted ordinary gross income would equal $180,000. However, the further test of a minimum distribution of nonrental personal holding company income would have to be met. Assuming that $90,000 of the $200,000 gross income came from dividends, at least $70,000 of the $90,000 would have to be distributed in order to avoid the personal holding company provisions. Thus dividends for the taxable year must equal or exceed the amount by which nonrental personal holding company income ($90,000) exceeds 10 percent of ordinary gross income ($20,000 or 10 percent of $200,000).

Mineral, oil and gas royalties are personal holding company income unless they amount to 50 percent of adjusted ordinary gross income. The royalties must be adjusted for amortization or depletion, property taxes, etc., and such "adjusted royalty income" must meet the 50 percent test. Furthermore, other personal holding company income may not exceed 10 percent of the ordinary gross income. In addition, the corporation's business expenses which are deductible under Section 162 of the Code (other than deductions for personal services rendered by the shareholders and other business deductions specifically allowable under sections other than Section 162) must equal or exceed 15 percent of the corporation's adjusted ordinary gross income.[151] The 10 percent test is designed to prevent mineral, oil and gas royalties from acting as a tax shelter for other types of investment in-

[150] Id. §§543(a)(2), 543(b)(3).
[151] §543(a)(3).

come; the 15 percent test is intended as a method of distinguishing between operating companies and mere holding companies. Copyright royalties are treated in an analogous fashion. Thus, if a company, such as a publisher, has copyright royalties (except for works created by shareholders) equal to 50 percent or more of ordinary gross income, if its other personal holding company income does not exceed 10 percent of ordinary gross income and if a minimum level of Section 162 deductions allocable to copyright royalties is maintained, such royalties do not constitute personal holding company income.[152]

Produced film rents are personal holding company income unless they amount to 50 percent or more of the corporation's ordinary gross income. The term "produced film rents" means payments received with respect to an interest in a film for the use of the film but only if such interest was acquired before substantial completion of production of the film.[153]

As regards amounts received by a corporation as compensation for the use of its property by a shareholder, such amounts are includible in personal holding company income if the shareholder owns 25 percent or more in value of the outstanding stock of the corporation at any time during the taxable year. This is so only as regards a corporation which has personal holding company income (other than income for the use of corporate property by a shareholder and income from rents), including copyright royalties and adjusted income from mineral, oil and gas royalties, in excess of 10 percent of its ordinary gross income.[154] The latter provision is designed to permit certain situations, primarily those involving real estate, to fall outside the personal holding company concept. Thus, if a corporation receives rent from a shareholder for the use of a hotel which he operates as a bona fide business, such rent, but for the 10 percent proviso, would be personal holding company income.[155] This would not seem proper in view of the frequent use of a real estate corporation to avoid personal liability on a mortgage or other liabilities in connection with financing properties.

In order to complete the statutory scheme and prevent the use of incorporated yachts, etc., as a means of offsetting operating losses against other investment income, Section 545(b)(8) provides that for the purpose of computing undistributed personal holding company income, the corporation is allowed a deduction for trade or business expenses or depreciation allocable to corporate property only to the extent of the rent received for the use of the property.[156] This is unless the corporation is able to establish

[152] Id. §543(a)(4).
[153] Id. §543(a)(5).
[154] Id. §543(a)(6).
[155] See Hatfried, Inc. v. Commissioner, 162 F.2d 628 (3d Cir. 1947).
[156] See text accompanying note 135 *supra*. Thus any excess or "loss" created by receiving less by way of rent than the expenses attributable to the property cannot be set off against other personal holding company income, such as dividends, interest, etc. For a discussion see B. Bittker and J. Eustice, Federal Income Taxation of Corporations and Shareholders 249 (1966).

that the rent was the highest obtainable, that the property was held in the course of a business carried on bona fide for profit and that there was a reasonable expectation that the operation of the property would result in a profit or the property was necessary to the conduct of the business.

Income from personal service contracts is includible as personal holding company income if some person other than the corporation has the right to designate the individual who is to perform the services, or if such individual is designated in the contract, and if the individual performing the services owns, at any time during the taxable year, directly or constructively, 25 percent or more of the corporation's stock.[157] Although the individual's services do not have to be "unique" in order to fall within this provision, the contract must designate that the individual (who is also owner of at least 25 percent of the stock) must perform the services. Thus a mere expectation that he will perform is not enough, although it is not required that the contract be in writing, i.e., there can be a binding oral agreement.[158] Also, if the contract requires that persons other than the 25 percent shareholder are to perform services, compensation received for such services is not included as personal holding company income if the services of such other persons are "important and essential." [159] If, however, the services are merely "incidental" to the services performed by the shareholder, then compensation for such services is included, along with the compensation for the shareholder's services, in personal holding company income.

As far as the actual computation of the tax is concerned, we have already seen that the tax is levied at a 70 percent rate on undistributed personal holding company income.[160] This is arrived at by taking the corporation's taxable income and adjusting it downwards for such items as federal income taxes, charitable contributions—to the extent that such contributions exceed the amount deductible by the corporation for its regular tax purposes (5 percent) but not in excess of the amount deductible by an individual (20 to 50 percent)—and the excess of the net long-term capital gain over the net short-term capital loss, minus the taxes attributable to such excess.[161] An upwards adjustment is also made for such items as the dividends-received deduction normally allowed to corporations and a portion of the corporation's net operating loss.[162] There are also other adjustments, such as the one previously mentioned which limits the deduction for trade or business expenses or depreciation allocable to corporate property only to the extent of the rent received for the use of the property.[163] The final

[157] Int. Rev. Code of 1954, §543(a)(7).

[158] See S. O. Claggett, 44 T.C. 503 (1965). See also B. Bittker and J. Eustice, id. at 251 n.77. Query, however, as to the effect of the statute of frauds provision regarding contracts not to be performed within a year.

[159] Treas. Reg. §1.543–1(b)(8)(ii).

[160] See Int. Rev. Code of 1954, §541, text accompanying note 133 *supra*.

[161] Id. §545(b).

[162] Id. §545(b)(3)(4).

[163] Id. §545(b)(8), discussed in text accompanying note 156 *supra*.

adjustment is to subtract the dividends-paid deduction. This consists of the dividends paid during the taxable year together with any amounts which have been treated as "consent" dividends (i.e., amounts which, although not distributed, are, with the consent of the shareholders, treated as having been distributed and thus subject to tax[164]). The corporation is also permitted to deduct a "dividend carryover," which consists of the excess of the dividends paid in the two preceding taxable years over the corporation's taxable income, adjusted in the manner already described.[165]

If a corporation should have any undistributed personal holding company income, it may, as previously indicated, avoid the tax by distributing a deficiency dividend, i.e., a distribution of personal holding company income made after a determination that a personal holding tax is due.[166] Although interest and penalties due on the tax are not avoided, the tax may be reduced or eliminated entirely. Since the shareholders are taxed on any amounts distributed by way of a deficiency dividend, the overall purpose of the statute, i.e., preventing tax avoidance at the shareholder level, is achieved.

5.6 COLLAPSIBLE CORPORATIONS

We have seen how the Code imposes penalty taxes upon corporations which constitute personal holding companies or which accumulate earnings for improper purposes. A brief word is necessary regarding a similar provision, directed towards so-called collapsible corporations, which imposes a tax at ordinary rates on gain which, but for the collapsible corporation rules, would be taxed at capital gain rates. Since the collapsible corporation provisions are exceedingly complex, it would be hazardous to do little more than outline their primary features, with the hope that those who sense that they might have a collapsible corporation problem will make a more exhaustive investigation before proceeding with any transaction which may fall within the scope of the statute.[167]

The overall intent of the collapsible provisions is to prevent certain tax avoidance schemes which have as their object the taxation, at capital gain rates, of income which would normally be taxed at ordinary income rates. A convenient example of this might be a real estate developer who purchases tracts of land, subdivides them, builds houses and sells the latter at a profit.

---

[164] Id. §565, discussed in text accompanying note 129 *supra*.

[165] Id. §564.

[166] Id. §547(d), discussed in text accompanying note 134 *supra*.

[167] See, e.g., B. Bittker and J. Eustice, Federal Income Taxation of Corporations and Shareholders §§10.01–10.09 (1966); D. Kahn, Basic Corporate Taxation 37–44 (1970); Bittker and Eustice, Collapsible Corporations in a Nutshell, 22 Tax L. Rev. 127 (1967); Hall, The Consenting Collapsible Corporation—Section 341(f) of the Internal Revenue Code of 1954, 12 U.C.L.A.L. Rev. 1365 (1965).

If he does this himself or through a corporation or partnership, the sale of the houses would result in ordinary income since the houses would be treated as inventory, being held for sale to customers in the ordinary course of business. Suppose, however, that the taxpayer causes a corporation owned by him to purchase land and construct houses but that, before the houses are sold, the corporation is liquidated and its assets are distributed to the taxpayer. If it were not for the collapsible corporation provisions, the liquidation might give rise to tax at capital gain rates.[168] The taxpayer would take a basis in the assets received by him equal to their fair value at the date of liquidation and, upon subsequent resale, little if any gain would result since the sales price would very likely be equal to the fair value. Another variant of the same approach would be for the taxpayer to sell the stock of the corporation before the latter sold the houses. Gain on the sale of the shares would normally be taxed at capital gain rates. The purchaser would receive a basis in the shares equal to the purchase price. Other illustrations of the collapsible corporation situation might be taken from the motion picture or television industries, where a producer might set up a corporation for the creation of a film and liquidate the corporation shortly before the film is licensed for use in theaters, distributing its assets, which would then receive a basis equivalent to fair market value on the date of liquidation. As in the redevelopment situation, the stock of the corporation could also be sold.

To combat these and other such devices, the Code taxes, at ordinary rates, gain from (1) the sale or exchange of stock of a collapsible corporation, (2) a distribution in partial or complete liquidation of a collapsible corporation, and (3) a nondividend distribution by a collapsible corporation (i.e., a distribution which would not result in taxation at ordinary rates inasmuch as Section 301(c)(3)(A) of the Code would treat the excess of the value of the distribution over the adjusted basis of the stock as capital gain). These three forms of gain from a collapsible corporation are subject to tax at ordinary rates only to the extent that they would be taxed at long-term capital gain rates if it were not for the application of the collapsible corporation rules. The provision does not, therefore, cover short-term capital gain situations or cases where an exchange would be free of tax altogether.

Most of the central issues in this area revolve around the definition of the term "collapsible corporation." The Code defines this as follows:

> a corporation formed or availed of principally for the manufacture, construction, or production of property, for the purchase of property which (in the hands of the corporation) is property described in paragraph (3),

---

[168] See B. Bittker and J. Eustice, id. at §10.02 (indicating that the transaction might be attacked on several different theories, such as the assignment of income doctrine and the "sham" transaction, although the Internal Revenue Service has not had appreciable success along these lines).

or for the holding of stock in a corporation so formed or availed of, with a view to—

(A) the sale or exchange of stock by its shareholders (whether in liquidation or otherwise), or a distribution to its shareholders, before the realization by the corporation manufacturing, constructing, producing, or purchasing the property of a substantial part of the taxable income to be derived from such property, and

(B) the realization by such shareholders of gain attributable to such property.[169]

The above definition comprises corporations "formed or availed of" principally for the manufacture, construction or production of property or for the purchase of certain properties which are defined as "Section 341 Assets," or for the holding of stock in a corporation "formed or availed of" for either of these two purposes. Since most business corporations (except for some personal service enterprises) may be thought of as being "formed or availed of" principally for the manufacture, construction or production of property (the Code providing that the definition will be complied with if a corporation engages in these activities "to any extent"), the more important part of the definition relates to the language following the phrase "with a view to. . . ." However, to plug up a loophole in the statutory scheme which would otherwise permit a taxpayer to form a corporation for the purchase of certain properties, such as inventory, and sell the stock of the corporation to a person who subsequently liquidates it (a common example being inventories of whiskey),[170] the definition includes corporations "formed or availed of" for the purchase of "Section 341 Assets." The latter term embraces not only inventory[171] but accounts receivable and Section 1231(b) property (i.e., depreciable property used in a trade or business which is held for more than six months and which is not used in connection with the manufacture, construction, production or sale of inventory or other property held primarily for sale to customers in the ordinary course of business). If assets are held for more than three years, they cease to be "Section 341 Assets."

As previously suggested, the primary problems encountered with the collapsible corporation definition are those of determining when such a corporation has been "formed or availed of . . . with a view to" certain prescribed activities, which may be broadly described as "acts of collapse." The "formed or availed of" language makes it clear that existing and not merely newly formed corporations may fall within the statutory web (e.g., a taxpayer may utilize a hitherto dormant corporate entity for his "collapsing" activities).

---

[169] Int. Rev. Code of 1954, §341(b)(1).

[170] See H.R. Rep. No. 586, 82d Cong., 1st Sess., reprinted in 1951–2 Cum. Bull. 357, 375, and quoted in B. Bittker and J. Eustice, id. at 424.

[171] The regulations exclude from the definition those corporations which have a normal amount of inventory if they have a substantial prior business history involving the use of such property. See Treas. Reg. §1.341–5(c)(1).

The phrase "with a view to" is troublesome, being largely subjective in content. The regulations clarify the matter somewhat by pointing out that the requirement is satisfied in any case in which the "acts of collapse" were contemplated

> by those persons in a position to determine the policies of the corporation, whether by reason of their owning a majority of the voting stock of the corporation or otherwise. The requirement is satisfied whether such action was contemplated, unconditionally, conditionally, or as a recognized possibility. If the corporation was so formed or availed of, it is immaterial that a particular shareholder was not a shareholder at the time of the manufacture, construction, production, or purchase of the property, or if a shareholder at such time, did not share in such view.[172]

The sweeping character of the regulation appears to embrace nearly every state of mind, even of the average investor in an enterprise which would not ordinarily be thought of as "collapsible" (i.e., it includes an intent to sell shares conditioned upon a satisfactory rise in price or even a recognition that a sale of the shares is a "possibility"). Note, however, that the regulations do provide some relief for a "change of circumstances" (to use a phrase from an analogous area of federal securities regulation,[173]), e.g., an illness, dissension or deadlock among shareholders, unexpected fluctuations in property values, or a shareholder's unforeseen need for funds to enter another business. Nonetheless, such events must arise *after* the manufacture, construction, production or purchase of the collapsible properties and thus the regulations leave open the possibility that an intent to sell might have existed at some earlier date, in which case the collapsible corporation provisions might apply notwithstanding the supervening change of circumstances.[174] The requisite state of mind must exist during the process

---

[172] Treas. Reg. §1.341–2(a)(2). Note, however, an escape hatch in Section 341(d) of the Code, rendering the collapsible corporation provisions inapplicable to a shareholder who at no time after the commencement of the manufacture, construction, or production of the property (or at the time of purchase of the Section 341 Assets) owned actually or constructively more than 5 percent in value of the corporation's outstanding stock, or owned stock which was considered as owned at such time by another shareholder who then owned more than 5 percent of the stock. Ownership, here, is determined by applying the attribution of ownership rules of Section 544(a) (relating to personal holding companies), except that an individual's "family" also includes spouses of that individual's brothers and sisters and spouses of that individual's lineal descendants. The escape hatch, at the risk of considerable complexity, insulates some minority shareholders from the impact of the collapsible corporation rules. Note, however, that the attribution of ownership rules will normally deprive minority shareholders in family corporations of the benefits of this provision. Note, also, the other exclusions provided in Section 341(d)—i.e., the tax does not apply unless more than 70 percent of a corporation's gains during a taxable year are attributable to properties of a collapsible nature, nor does it apply to gains realized after three years following the completion of manufacture, construction, production or purchase of the property. The latter exclusion is particularly elusive in view of the difficulties of determining when the process of manufacture, construction, production, etc., has been fully completed. See B. Bittker and J. Eustice, id. at 435.

[173] See Ch. IX, text accompanying note 72.

[174] Treas. Reg. §1.341–2(a)(3) and B. Bittker and J. Eustice, id. at 428.

of manufacture, production, construction or purchase[175] although there are some holdings to the effect that all that need be shown is that the state of mind existed when the corporation was "availed of" for the collapsible activity.[176]

The regulations provide that a corporation will ordinarily be considered to be collapsible (1) if a shareholder sells or exchanges his stock, or receives a liquidating distribution or a distribution which would otherwise be taxable at capital gain rates under Section 301(c)(3)(A) of the Code, (2) if the shareholder realizes gain attributable to properties of a collapsible nature (i.e., properties manufactured, produced, constructed or purchased), (3) if at the time of manufacture, production, construction or purchase of the properties, such activities were "substantial in relation to the other activities of the corporation . . . ," and (4) if the corporation has not realized a substantial part of the taxable income to be derived from the properties.[177] The Code contains a somewhat more specific presumption of collapsibility. Section 341(c) provides that a corporation shall, unless shown to the contrary, be deemed to be collapsible if, at the time a shareholder's stock is sold or exchanged or at the time the shareholder receives a distribution, the fair market value of the corporation's Section 341 Assets (except for cash, obligations which are capital assets in the hands of the corporation, including certain short-term federal and state obligations, and stock in any other corporation) is "(A) 50 percent or more of the fair market value of its total assets, and (B) 120 percent or more of the adjusted basis of such section 341 assets."

Finally, even though a corporation fails to rebut the presumption of collapsibility, it must be shown that the shareholder sold or exchanged his shares or received a distribution "before the realization by the corporation manufacturing, constructing, producing, or purchasing the property of a substantial part of the taxable income to be derived from such property." [178] Although the statute expressly refers to the "realization . . . of a substantial part of the taxable income to be derived from such property," the regulations state the test in terms of whether a substantial part of the income has *not* been realized (i.e., we must determine substantiality by looking to the percentage of unrealized income rather than to the percentage of realized potential income).[179] Thus, if 25 percent were considered to be "substantial," a corporation which had realized 75 percent of its potential income would still fail the test under the Treasury Department's interpretation, whereas, under the statutory language, the realization of only 25 percent of the potential income would be sufficient.[180] The

175 Treas. Reg. §1.341–2(a)(3).
176 See B. Bittker and J. Eustice, id. at 427 (collecting the conflicting cases).
177 Treas. Reg. §1.341–5(b).
178 Int. Rev. Code of 1954, §341(b)(1)(A).
179 Treas. Reg. §§1.341–2(a)(4) and 1.341–5(c)(2).
180 See B. Bittker and J. Eustice, id. at 429–430, citing Commissioner v. Kelley,

various courts are split accordingly, the Fifth and Tenth Circuits, as well as the Tax Court, looking to the percentage of income "realized" and the Third Circuit looking to the percentage of unrealized income.[181]

Section 341(e) of the Code was enacted in 1958 to alleviate certain "overkill" aspects of Section 341 insofar as it caught within its sweep transactions (largely corporations formed to purchase rental properties) which would have given rise to taxation at capital gain rates even if the taxpayer had not conducted his business through a corporate intermediary. In other words, the collapsible corporation provision went considerably beyond its original function of preventing the conversion of ordinary income items into items of capital gain. Although the structure of Section 341(e) is highly complex, it can be thought of as applying to four situations: (1) sales or exchanges of stock (other than to the issuer or to a related shareholder), (2) certain distributions in complete liquidation of a corporation pursuant to Section 337 of the Code,[182] (3) sales or exchanges by a corporation pursuant to Section 337 and (4) complete liquidations pursuant to Section 333 of the Code.[183] In general, Section 341(e) provides a scheme whereby the collapsible corporation provisions will not be applicable if the net unrealized appreciation in property of the corporation which would produce ordinary income if sold by it or by any shareholder holding more than 20 percent of its stock is less than 15 percent of the corporation's net worth.

A further relief provision is Section 341(f), which sets forth a procedure whereby a corporation may file a consent to have gain recognized on the sale or exchange of its "Section 341(f) Assets" (principally real estate and noncapital assets), even if such sale or exchange would otherwise be entitled to nonrecognition of gain. Once such a consent has been filed, sales of stock by any shareholder within a period of six months may be made without fear of the collapsible corporation provisions, and once such a sale has been made, the consent cannot be revoked. After the six-month period has elapsed, a new consent may be filed. If a shareholder takes advantage of this

---

293 F.2d 904 (5th Cir. 1961), holding that the realization of approximately one third of the potential income would be sufficient to meet the "substantiality" test. The Internal Revenue Service has indicated, however, that it would not follow the *Kelley* case. Rev. Rul. 62–12, 1962–1 Cum. Bull. 321. According to B. Bittker and J. Eustice, id. at 430 n.27, it is possible to obtain a favorable ruling on collapsibility if 85 percent of the potential income has been realized. See Ryan, What Is a Substantial Part of the Taxable Income? 16 J. Tax. 246 (1961).

[181] See D. Kahn, Basic Corporate Taxation 37–44 (1970), citing Commissioner v. Kelley, 293 F.2d 904 (5th Cir. 1961) (a Fifth Circuit decision affirming the Tax Court), Commissioner v. Zongker, 334 F.2d 44 (10th Cir. 1964) (realization of 34 percent sufficient), and Abbott v. Commissioner, 258 F.2d 537 (3d Cir. 1958) (adopting the Treasury Department's approach of looking to the percentage of *unrealized* income).

[182] See Ch. VII, text accompanying note 144.

[183] See Ch. VII, text accompanying note 108.

procedure, neither he nor any person related to him may take advantage of it again for five years as regards any other corporation.

In summary, the collapsible corporation provisions have a relatively broad sweep, but they are subject to several relief provisions, such as the exception for 5 percent shareholders,[184] the 70 percent rule,[185] and the three-year waiting period,[186] as well as the complex provisions of Section 341(e) and the consent procedures of Section 341(f). Even if these escape hatches should not be available, a corporation may avoid collapsible treatment by the realization of a substantial part of its potential income from collapsible properties.[187] Further techniques might be to take advantage of Section 337 of the Code[188] or the provisions of Subchapter S.[189]

[184] See note 172 *supra.*

[185] Ibid.

[186] Ibid.

[187] See text accompanying note 178 *supra.*

[188] See Ch. VII, text accompanying note 144, and B. Bittker and J. Eustice, Federal Income Taxation of Corporations and Shareholders 447 (1966). If the corporation is not collapsible, the gain on the corporate sale of assets will not be recognized due to the provisions of Section 337. If the corporation is collapsible, although Section 337 will not apply to provide nonrecognition of gain, the collapsible corporation provisions will not apply if the corporation realizes a substantial part of its potential income from disposal of its collapsible properties.

[189] See Ch. I, text accompanying note 152, pointing out, however, that the special rule on so-called one-shot elections imposed by Section 1378 of the Code may greatly restrict the advantages of this technique. For further suggestions on avoiding the collapsible corporation provisions, see B. Bittker and J. Eustice, id. at 447–448 (i.e., use of multiple corporations, spreading out income through the use of the installment method of reporting under Section 453 of the Code). Although the authors also suggest that the stock of a collapsible corporation might be advantageously donated to a charitable institution, this tactic appears to have been foreclosed by Section 170(e)(1)(A) of the Code, added by the Tax Reform Act of 1969.

VI   Buying Out a Shareholder

One of the most important aspects of planning a close corporation is arranging a means whereby majority or minority interests may be reacquired by the corporation or by other shareholders. This is particularly significant for at least two reasons: First, there is generally little or no market for the shares of a closely held concern, and this may be so even if they represent a controlling interest. Secondly, it is often vital for those who wish to continue in the business to have some control over those who may wish to become shareholders. This, we saw, is generally done through a first-refusal stock transfer restriction.[1] As previously pointed out, the most likely events which trigger the disposal of shares are a shareholder's death, retirement, termination of employment or disability. In such situations the shareholder may wish to dispose of his entire interest, part with only some of it or alter the character of his interest, as where he exchanges all or part of his common stock for preferred stock, or a package of preferred and notes or bonds. In addition, he may wish to sell his shares to other shareholders, sell them back to the corporation or have them redeemed.

Since the tax consequences will often differ with the form which the transaction takes, as well as the circumstances of the particular case, we should examine the various possibilities in detail both from tax and from other perspectives, including matters of state and federal corporation law, problems of accounting and overall business considerations.

6.1   INCOME TAX CONSEQUENCES OF STOCK REDEMPTIONS

Although a corporation may merely have an option to repurchase the shares of a deceased, retired, discharged or disabled shareholder, this offers little protection to the shareholder (unless he owns a majority interest, controls the board of directors and thus may effectively force the corporation to exercise the option), and thus a common arrangement is a stock purchase or retirement agreement between the shareholder and the corporation, obligat-

[1] See Ch. III, text following note 11.

ing the one to sell and the other to purchase all or part of the shares at a specified price or at a price to be determined by formula.[2] Various methods of setting the price have already been discussed in relation to first-refusal stock transfer restrictions,[3] and essentially the same alternatives are available for the stock purchase or retirement agreement. Since, as we have seen, there are state-imposed limitations on the ability of a corporation to acquire its own shares unless it has funds available to do so, generally referred to as "surplus" (which may be "earned surplus" or "capital surplus"), this has led many corporations to use insurance to provide the necessary funds.[4] Although insurance is not the only method of solving this problem (we shall discuss some other possibilities, such as revaluing assets to reflect unrealized appreciation, or, as an alternative, reducing capital), it is certainly one of the most popular ways of funding share reacquisitions. It is appropriate, then, that we consider the tax effect on the shareholder whose shares are purchased or redeemed, the tax effect on the other shareholders, the tax effect on the corporation and the various ways in which differing insurance arrangements may affect the situation from both a tax and a general business standpoint.

For the corporation, there is generally no tax effect on the redemption of its stock. This, at least, is the situation where the redemption is for cash or for a corporate note. Where the redemption is for property, the corporation may realize gain if the distributed property takes the form of installment obligations, inventory which has been carried on a "last-in-first-out" method, property which is subject to a liability in excess of its basis, Section 1245 or 1250 property and, under certain conditions, property which has appreciated in value.[5]

As far as the shareholder is concerned, his primary objective is to dispose of his shares either in a nontaxable exchange or to have any gain taxed at capital gain rates rather than at ordinary income rates. Where he is in a "loss" position, in that his basis for the shares exceeds their fair value, he

---

[2] Id. note 34.

[3] Id. notes 49–66.

[4] Id. note 68.

[5] Int. Rev. Code of 1954, §§311, 453(d), 1245(a), 1250(a). The legislative history of Section 311 of the Code indicates that it was not intended to be exclusive and that there may be other situations where a corporate distribution may result in gain. See B. Bittker and J. Eustice, Federal Income Taxation of Corporations and Shareholders §5.21 (1966). The Tax Reform Act of 1969 added Section 311(d), which taxes gain on distributions of appreciated property (other than corporate obligations) in redemption of stock. The new provision has a number of exceptions, the most important of which for our purposes are (1) a distribution in complete redemption of all the stock of the distributee (as determined by Section 302(b)(3) of the Code, but without the application of Section 302(c)(2)(A)(ii), where the distributee, at all times within a twelve-month period ending on the date of the distribution, owned at least 10 percent of the outstanding stock of the distributing corporation, and (2) distributions pursuant to Section 303 of the Code. See text accompanying note 79 *infra.*

will naturally wish to have the loss recognized and, if possible, deductible to him at ordinary rates.

Taking the loss situation first, we have seen that losses on stock are generally deductible only at capital loss rates, except for the important advantages of Section 1244 stock, already discussed in detail, which allows for an ordinary loss deduction within certain limits ($25,000 for any taxable year on an individual return and $50,000 on a joint return) if the relatively strict requirements of Section 1244 have been met.[6] We have also seen, however, that if shares are resold to a corporation in which an individual has a greater than 50 percent interest, or are sold to another member of the individual's family (i.e., brothers, sisters, spouse, ancestors, lineal descendants), the loss will be disallowed. Even if an individual should own less than 50 percent in value of the outstanding stock, he should take care that his ownership is not greater due to the constructive ownership rules, which, as we have seen, often raise complex and unexpected problems.[7]

In many share repurchase or redemption situations, however, the shareholder is not likely to be in a loss position, i.e., the value of his shares is likely to exceed his tax basis. Thus his primary objective is to insure that his gain will either not be recognized or will be taxed at capital gain rates rather than at ordinary rates. As we shall see in a later discussion, the only way in which a shareholder may prevent the recognition of gain on an exchange is through use of the "reorganization" provisions, which permit a tax-free exchange of common stock for preferred stock or a package of preferred and common.[8] If the common is repurchased or redeemed for cash or for corporate obligations, such as notes or bonds, gain will be taxable and then the problem is to insure that such gain is taxed at capital gain rates rather than ordinary rates.

The overall approach of the Code is to treat any corporate distribution as taxable at ordinary rates if it amounts to a dividend (i.e., if it is out of either current or accumulated earnings and profits).[9] The two primary methods of avoiding dividend treatment are (1) to show that the distribution was either a "substantially disproportionate" redemption or a complete termination of the shareholder's interest in the corporation[10] or (2) to show that it was a distribution in partial or complete liquidation.[11] A third method is also available, in that within certain permissible limitations a shareholder's interest may be redeemed to the extent of estate, inheritance, legacy and succession taxes, as well as funeral and administration expenses.[12] Before considering this more specialized provision, as well as

[6] See Ch. II, text following note 103.
[7] See Int. Rev. Code of 1954, §267, discussed in Ch. II, text accompanying note 4.
[8] See text accompanying note 269 *infra*.
[9] Int. Rev. Code of 1954, §§301, 316.
[10] Id. §302.
[11] Id. §§331, 346.
[12] Id. §303.

the partial liquidation situation, it is well to consider Section 302, which generally governs stock redemptions, as well as the complex constructive ownership rules of Section 318.

The general approach of Section 302 is to treat stock redemptions as qualifying for capital gain or loss treatment if they fall within one of four reclassifications. The first of these is the broadest and most difficult to define, namely that the redemption must not be "essentially equivalent to a dividend." [13] The second consists of a mathematical test of determining when a distribution is "substantially disproportionate with respect to the shareholder." [14] If the redemption is substantially disproportionate, then it qualifies for capital gain or loss treatment. The third situation in which a capital gain or loss is available is where the redemption "is in complete redemption of all of the stock of the corporation owned by the shareholder." [15] The fourth and last is a specialized case covering the redemption of railroad stock pursuant to a plan of reorganization under Section 77 of the Bankruptcy Act. [16]

Aside from the last situation, the overall objective of Section 302 is to differentiate between those transactions which truly merit capital gain or loss treatment, in that they have a close analogy with a sale by a shareholder of his interest in the corporation, and other transactions where, because the shareholder's interest in the concern remains substantially unchanged, the distribution of cash or property in redemption of stock has the net effect of a distribution of earnings and profits to him which normally would be paid out in dividends and taxed at ordinary rates.

Section 302 resembles a spectrum. At one end of the spectrum are situations which are akin to a sale, i.e., a complete termination of a shareholder's interest in his corporation. At the opposite extreme are pro rata redemptions, where all shareholders are treated alike, as where five shareholders, each owning a 20 percent interest in a corporation, have one half of their shares redeemed. After such a redemption each shareholder is in precisely the same position as he was before, i.e., he owns 20 percent of the outstanding stock; he merely has half as many shares as he had before, but that is of little consequence since, if the requisite shareholder majority vote is obtained to authorize a stock split or stock dividend, the situation can be restored to the *status quo ante* through the issuance of as many additional shares as have been redeemed. If such redemptions were not taxable as dividends, then tax policy would have fallen victim to tax magic. It is thus not surprising that pro rata redemptions have always involved the highest degree of risk that the transaction may be considered as "essentially equivalent to a dividend." [17] It should not, however, be assumed that all pro rata redemptions are taxable as dividends, since certain distributions, namely

13 Id. §302(b)(1).
14 Id. §302(b)(2).
15 Id. §302(b)(3).
16 Id. §302(b)(4).
17 See Treas. Reg. §1.302–2(b).

those made in partial or complete liquidation, are given capital gain or loss treatment. In the interest of simplicity, discussion of this area will be deferred [18] until we examine the workings of Section 302 in greater detail.

With complete terminations at one end of the spectrum and pro rata redemptions at the other end, the middle ground is composed of situations where stock is redeemed from various shareholders in differing percentage amounts. Thus one shareholder may have half his shares redeemed, another may have only 20 percent of his shares redeemed, a third 10 percent and a fourth none at all. Should we look at the transaction as a whole and consider whether it falls closer to one end of the spectrum than the other, i.e., whether it is akin to a partial sale or termination of the shareholder's interest or whether it is essentially equivalent to a dividend? Should we look at the "business purpose" of the transaction and whether there are overtones of tax avoidance? Should we consider the possibility that one or more shareholders, in high tax brackets, who are in control of the corporation may be using the redemption to "bail out" earnings and profits, hopefully at capital gain rates, which might otherwise be taxed as dividends at ordinary rates? Or that the corporation has paid meager dividends in the past and yet has accumulated substantial earnings and profits? Such facts as these may be helpful in determining whether, in a doubtful case, a redemption should be held essentially equivalent to a dividend.[19] Another approach is suggested by the mathematical test set forth in Subsection 302(b)(2).

The test is composed of two parts. The first requires that immediately after the redemption the shareholder must own "less than 50 percent of the total combined voting power of all classes of stock entitled to vote." [20] Assuming this part of the test is met, we must consider the percentage diminution of the shareholder's proportionate voting power which has resulted from the redemption. Thus his voting power before the redemption is compared to his voting power afterwards. If his voting power has been reduced by more than 20 percent, then the redemption, as to *him*, is viewed as having been substantially disproportionate and thus entitled to capital gain or loss treatment. More technically, the test is put in terms of whether

 (i) the ratio which the voting stock of the corporation owned by the shareholder immediately after the redemption bears to all of the voting stock of the corporation at such time,
  is less than 80 percent of—

[18] See Ch. VII, text accompanying notes 77–195.

[19] See Treusch, Corporate Distributions and Adjustments: Recent Case Reminders of Some Old Problems Under the New Code, 32 Taxes 1023, 1037 (1954). For further discussion see B. Bittker and J. Eustice, Federal Income Taxation of Corporations and Shareholders 276 n.5 (1966). However, such factors, along with the concept of business purpose, have been considered less relevant in the more recent cases, particularly United States v. Davis, discussed in text accompanying note 29 *infra*, which takes the view that unless there is a meaningful reduction in a shareholder's proportionate interest, lack of tax avoidance motivation, etc., is irrelevant to the proper tax result.

[20] Int. Rev. Code of 1954, §302(b)(2)(B).

(ii) the ratio which the voting stock of the corporation owned by the shareholder immediately before the redemption bears to all of the voting stock of the corporation at such time.[21]

Needless to say, the test is applied to each shareholder separately. Thus where shares are redeemed from several shareholders in differing amounts, the redemption may be substantially disproportionate as to some shareholders and not as to others. In the case of a series of redemptions, the series is viewed as a whole if it is "pursuant to a plan." Then the net effect of the series of redemptions is determinative rather than each step in the series being considered independently.[22]

Perhaps the best method of comprehending this scheme is to examine an illustration from the regulations.[23] Suppose that a corporation has outstanding four hundred shares of common stock owned in equal proportions by four shareholders, A, B, C and D. No stock owned by any of the shareholders is constructively owned by any of the others (a complication which will be considered shortly). Suppose that fifty-five shares are redeemed from A, twenty-five shares from B and twenty shares from C. The corporation has thus redeemed a total of one hundred shares and now has only three hundred shares outstanding. Before the redemption each shareholder held 25 percent of the voting stock. After the redemption the voting power is distributed as follows:

A. owns forty-five shares and hence 15 percent (45 out of 300)

---

[21] Id. §302(b)(2)(C).

[22] Id. §302(b)(2)(D). See Otis P. Leleux, 54 T.C. 408 (1970) (piecemeal redemptions of stock held not pursuant to an alleged plan to terminate distributee's interest and not justified by business purpose—hence essentially equivalent to a dividend). Plans for the periodic redemption of stock may now result in dividend treatment due to the broadening of Section 305 of the Code by the Tax Reform Act of 1969. If the effect of a plan is to give the shareholders an option to receive cash or to have their proportionate share in the assets or earnings and profits of a corporation increased, then a redemption of shares will result in a tax not only on the person whose shares are redeemed but *also* on the person whose proportionate equity ownership is increased. Thus, if a corporation were to agree that a designated percentage of any shareholder's interest might be redeemed annually at his option, with the result that some shareholders redeemed part of their interests and the interests of others were proportionately increased, the redemption and proportionate increase would result in a tax on *all* the shareholders. See S. Rep. No. 91–552 on H.R. 13270, 91st Cong., 1st Sess. 153 (1969). Hence all the shareholders are, in effect, treated as if they had an election to receive a distribution of either money or additional shares, a situation which would have given rise to a taxable distribution even prior to the broadening of Section 305 by the Tax Reform Act of 1969. Notwithstanding this, the Senate Finance Committee Report, *supra* at 153–154, emphasizes that "isolated" redemptions of stock would not be taxable merely because the proportionate interest of some other shareholder is increased. Thus a holder of 30 percent of a corporation's shares "would not be treated as receiving a constructive dividend because a 70 percent stockholder causes a corporation to redeem 15 percent of its stock from him." In such a situation the tax treatment of the person whose shares are redeemed would be governed by Section 302. For a discussion of the tax effect on the other shareholders, see text accompanying note 132 *infra*.

[23] Treas. Reg. §1.302–3(b).

    B. owns seventy-five shares and hence 25 percent (75 out of 300)

    C. owns eighty shares and hence $26\frac{2}{3}$ percent (80 out of 300)

    D. owns one hundred shares and hence $33\frac{1}{3}$ percent (100 out of 300)

In order for the distribution to be "substantially disproportionate" with respect to any shareholder, his percentage ownership of the voting shares after the redemption must be less than 80 percent of his percentage ownership before the redemption and he must also own less than 50 percent of the voting power after the redemption. Although all four shareholders meet the latter 50 percent test, only A qualifies under the other "percent-shrinkage" test. Thus, for qualification each shareholder must hold less than 20 percent of the outstanding shares after the redemption (i.e., less than 80 percent of the 25 percent held before the redemption). Only A, with his 15 percent equity, qualifies under this test.

    Consider, however, the possibility that, pursuant to the same plan, there might be a series of redemptions and, subsequently, seventy-five of D's shares might be redeemed. In such a situation the corporation would have outstanding only 225 shares. A would own forty-five of these (20 percent), B would own seventy-five (33.33 percent), C would own eighty (35.56 percent) and D would own twenty-five (11.11 percent).[24] Since, to qualify under the substantially disproportionate redemption test, a shareholder's voting strength must be reduced from 25 percent to less than 20 percent (i.e., less than 80 percent of 25 per cent), only D will qualify. Interestingly enough, A, who is left with precisely 20 percent, will not qualify, although, if it were not for the redemption of D's stock, A, as we have seen, would have qualified.

    It should be noted that the mathematical test just described applies only to the redemption of voting stock. If nonvoting stock is redeemed, then the question is whether the redemption was essentially equivalent to a dividend or whether it falls within the provisions of Section 306, to be discussed later in Section 6.2. Assuming that nonvoting preferred stock is not Section 306 stock, then, according to the regulations, its redemption will receive capital gain or loss treatment if voting stock is redeemed at the same time and the latter redemption qualifies under the substantially disproportionate test.[25] If, however, the redemption of the voting stock is not substantially disproportionate with respect to the person whose shares are being redeemed, then the failure to meet the mathematical test does not automatically mean that the redemption is essentially equivalent to a dividend.[26] Thus the facts of the particular case are always pertinent to resolving the issue if the more specific statutory tests are not met. Notwithstanding this, however, failure to meet the statutory tests will not augur well for the

24 The example is taken from B. Bittker and J. Eustice, id. at 286.

25 Treas. Reg. §1.302–3(a)(3).

26 Int. Rev. Code of 1954, §302(b)(5). See also Treas. Reg. §1.302–2(a).

taxpayer's case in proving lack of dividend equivalence. The statutory history of Section 302(b)(1) indicates that it was probably intended to provide capital gain or loss treatment in the relatively narrow area of redemptions of preferred shares from minority shareholders. The regulations pursue this theme in citing, as the only example of nondividend equivalence, a redemption, from one who holds no voting shares, of half his interest in nonvoting stock which is limited and preferred as to dividends and liquidation (and also does not constitute Section 306 stock).[27] Despite this, there are doubtless other situations where nondividend equivalence is a possibility. Thus, if a redemption of shares from a minority shareholder is treated as pro rata only because of the application of the constructive ownership rules which attribute ownership of shares from one person to another who is in fact independent and perhaps hostile,[28] or if the redemption is justified by legitimate corporate purposes, such as to acquire shares for issuance to other executives, to fund stock option plans or to "capitalize" shareholder claims against the corporation, nondividend equivalence might be a persuasive argument. However, a recent decision of the United States Supreme Court, *United States v. Davis*,[29] rejected business purpose justification and treated a redemption of shares from a person who was constructive owner of all the shares of a corporation (by virtue of the "family" attribution rule, to be discussed shortly) as essentially equivalent to a dividend even though the transaction appeared to have a clear business purpose, i.e., to repay interim financing which had been insisted upon as a condition of obtaining a loan from the Reconstruction Finance Corporation. If this case means what it says, a redemption which does not have the effect of reducing a shareholder's proportionate ownership in a corporation (computed in accordance with the attribution of ownership rules) will *always* be essentially equivalent to a dividend even though the redemption itself may not have been motivated by tax avoidance reasons and might have been independently justified by a business purpose. Thus the rules governing attribution of ownership or constructive ownership of shares are given a new and vital importance as a result of the *Davis* decision.

Section 318 contains a virtual spiderweb of rules for constructive ownership. Although we have dealt with similar provisions in other contexts,[30] the constructive ownership rules which apply to stock redemptions are particularly complex and likely to trap the unwary.[31]

27 Ibid. See B. Bittker and J. Eustice, id. at 291–292.

28 Id. at 292. See Estate of Arthur H. Squier, 35 T.C. 950 (1961), *acquiesced in*, 1961–2 Cum. Bull. 5.

29 397 U.S. 301 (1970).

30 E.g., Int. Rev. Code of 1954, §267(c), discussed in Ch. II, text accompanying note 4 (disallowance of losses in transfers between related persons); id. §544, discussed in Ch. V, text accompanying note 139 (personal holding companies).

31 For a good discussion see Ringel, Surrey and Warren, Attribution of Stock Ownership in the Internal Revenue Code, 72 Harv. L. Rev. 209 (1958). See also Goldstein, Bringing the Attribution Rules into Sharper Focus: How and Where They

This is an area where the only reliable guide is a close reading of the statute. Four types of attribution are provided, along with four so-called operating rules, which specify how and when the various attribution rules may be used in combination with one another. The first form of attribution relates to members of a family (defined as the spouse, other than one legally separated or divorced; children, including those legally adopted; grandchildren; and parents).[32] The second rule deals with attribution *from* partnerships, estates, trusts and corporations *to* those owning an interest in such entities (sometimes referred to as "vertical" or "direct" attribution),[33] and the third rule applies to the converse situation, attribution *to* partnerships, estates, trusts and corporations *from* those holding an interest in such entities (sometimes referred to as "back" attribution).[34] The fourth and final rule merely specifies that a person who has an option to acquire stock is considered as owning the stock under option.[35]

Unlike the family attribution rules of other areas which we have discussed,[36] Section 318(a)(1) does not attribute ownership between brothers and sisters. And due to the second of the so-called operating rules, the family attribution rule may not be used "over again" so as to effect a reattribution.[37] Thus if F, a father, has two sons, A and B, and each owns one-third of the stock of a corporation, A is considered to own stock owned by his father, F, but is not constructively the owner of the stock held by his brother, B. Even though F is the constructive owner of B's stock, such constructive ownership is not reattributed to A (i.e., A is the constructive owner only of that stock actually held by F and not of F's constructively held stock).[38]

The second and third attribution rules, dealing with attribution from and to partnerships, estates, trusts and corporations, are the most complex. In addition, the operating rules permit, in certain cases, the use of the rules in combination with one another so as to create what has been called "chain" or "double" attribution. Before discussing what is and what is not permissible by way of combinations, it is best to focus on what might, with some irony, be termed the "simpler" applications of the two rules.

As has been mentioned, the second rule deals with attribution from partnerships, estates, trusts and corporations to those who own an interest in such entities. Stock owned, directly or indirectly, by or for a partnership or estate is considered as owned *proportionately* by its partners or beneficiaries,

---

Apply, 26 J. Tax. 280 (1967); Goldstein, Attribution Rules: Undue Multiplicity, Complexity Can Create Liabilities, 15 Tul. Tax Inst. 384 (1966).

[32] Int. Rev. Code of 1954, §318(a)(1).

[33] Id. §318(a)(2).

[34] Id. §318(a)(3).

[35] Id. §318(a)(4).

[36] See note 30 *supra*.

[37] Int. Rev. Code of 1954, §318(a)(5)(B).

[38] See Treas. Reg. §1.318–4(b).

as the case may be.[39] For example, if A, an individual, owns a 50 percent interest in a partnership and the partnership owns 50 percent of the outstanding shares in a corporation, then A is the constructive owner of 25 percent of the shares, (i.e., 50 percent of the partnership's 50 percent interest).[40] In the case of trusts (other than an employees' trust under Section 401(a)), stock owned directly or indirectly by or for the trust is considered as owned by the trust's beneficiaries in proportion to the actuarial interest of each beneficiary.[41] If the trust is one of those where, pursuant to the rules of Sections 671–678 of the Code, the grantor of the trust or some other person is taxable on the income of the trust, then stock held by the trust is constructively owned by the person who is taxable on the trust's income.[42] Finally, as to corporations, if anyone is, directly or indirectly, the owner of 50 percent or more in value of the outstanding stock of the corporation, then he is considered to constructively own the stock owned, directly or indirectly, by or for the corporation, but only in that proportion which the value of the stock he owns bears to the value of all the outstanding stock.[43] Thus if A owns 70 percent of the stock (in value) of Corporation M and the latter owns fifty shares in Corporation O, then A is the constructive owner of thirty-five shares of Corporation O (70 percent of fifty).[44] However, it should be observed that if B, an unrelated individual, owns the other 30 percent of the Corporation M stock, then he is not the constructive owner of the Corporation O shares held by Corporation M since his interest in the latter did not amount to 50 percent or more, which is a prerequisite for constructive ownership in this situation.[45] According to the regulations, when determining whether an individual owns 50 percent or more in value of a corporation's stock, shares which he constructively owns (such as shares held by his father or son) are aggregated with shares which he actually owns.[46] Notwithstanding this, when determining the percentage of the shares held by the corporation which should be attributed *to* the shareholder, only the latter's actual (and not constructive) interest in the corporation is taken into account.[47] Thus, in the above illustration, if B were A's father, then, although A would constructively own *all* of the stock in Corporation M, only his actual 70 percent ownership would be taken into account in computing his constructive ownership of the Corporation O stock (i.e., he would still constructively own only thirty-five shares of Corporation O). However, since B (A's father) would *also* constructively own 100

[39] Int. Rev. Code of 1954, §318(a)(2)(A).
[40] Treas. Reg. §1.318–2(c), Ex. (1).
[41] Int. Rev. Code of 1954, §318(a)(2)(B)(i).
[42] Id. §318(a)(2)(B)(ii).
[43] Id. §318(a)(2)(C).
[44] Treas. Reg. §1.318–2(c), Ex. (4).
[45] Id. §1.318–2(c), Ex. (5).
[46] Id. §1.318–1(b)(3).
[47] See B. Bittker and J. Eustice, Federal Income Taxation of Corporations and Shareholders 282 n.15 (1966).

percent of the stock of Corporation M, 30 percent of the O stock (fifteen shares) held by Corporation M would be attributed to B, since B constructively owns more than 50 percent of the stock of Corporation M.

When we come to consider the third rule, which, as has been said, attributes stock held by partners, beneficiaries of estates and trusts, and shareholders in corporations *to* such entities (the converse of the second rule), we find a somewhat similar approach but with several important differences.

In the partnership or estate situation, *all* of the stock held by a partner or beneficiary is attributed to the partnership or estate (not just an amount proportionate to his interest). Thus if A owns a 50 percent interest in a partnership and also owns fifty shares in a corporation, the partnership constructively owns the fifty shares owned by A.[48]

The rule is similar on attribution to a trust of stock held by a beneficiary except that there is no attribution if the beneficiary's interest is a "remote contingent interest" (nor if the trust is an employees' trust, as in the earlier situation dealt with in the second rule). A contingent interest is remote if, "under the maximum exercise of discretion by the trustee in favor of . . . [the] beneficiary, the value of such interest, computed actuarially, is 5 percent or less of the value of the trust property." [49]

As in the situation previously discussed with regard to the second rule,[50] if the trust is one where, pursuant to the rules of Sections 671–678 of the Code, the grantor of the trust or some other person is taxable on the income of the trust, then *all* stock held by him is attributed to the trust.[51] Similarly, *all* stock held by a shareholder is attributed to a corporation if he owns (actually or constructively) 50 percent or more in value of the corporation's stock.[52]

Since stock held by an individual may be attributed to an entity, such as a trust or corporation, and since stock held by an entity may be attributed to an individual, the question naturally arises whether, by a combination of the second and third attribution rules, stock held by an individual can be attributed to an entity and then again to another individual. This form of double attribution is now prohibited by the third operating rule enacted in 1964.[53] For example, if two unrelated individuals are beneficiaries of the same trust, stock held by one individual which is attributed to the trust may not be "reattributed" to the other individual.[54] However, another form of double attribution through a combination of the second and third rules is possible. Thus stock constructively owned by a person by application of the

---

[48] Treas. Reg. §1.318–2(c), Ex. (1).
[49] Int. Rev. Code of 1954, §318(a)(3)(B)(i).
[50] See text accompanying note 42 *supra.*
[51] Int. Rev. Code of 1954, §318(a)(3)(B)(ii).
[52] Id. §318(a)(3)(C). See also Treas. Reg. §1.318–1(b)(3).
[53] Int. Rev. Code of 1954, §318(a)(5)(C).
[54] Treas. Reg. §1.318–4(c).

second rule may be reattributed and thus constructively owned by an entity by application of the third rule. For example, if A were the owner of all of the stock in two corporations, X and Y, and if Corporation X were to own stock in a third corporation, Z, then the Z stock could be attributed to A (under the second rule) and then to Corporation Y (under the third rule).[55] To put the matter differently, although the third operating rule forbids double attribution through the technique of first using the third attribution rule and then using the second attribution rule (i.e., from an individual to an entity and then to an individual), it does not prohibit double attribution through the use of the two rules in the converse order (i.e., from an entity to an individual and then back to an entity). Finally, another form of double attribution is possible through a combination of the second and first attribution rules. Thus, to use a previous illustration,[56] if A owns 70 percent of the stock (in value) of Corporation M and the latter owns fifty shares in Corporation O, then A's constructive ownership of thirty-five shares in Corporation O may be reattributed to A's spouse, children, grandchildren or parents. However, as we have seen,[57] the ownership of the thirty-five shares cannot be reattributed to A's spouse's ancestors through further use of the first attribution rule (i.e., the family rule) since that rule may be used only once.

Needless to say, the attribution rules are complex. One might almost surmise that they were cunningly devised with diabolical intent to trap shareholders in closely held corporations who might wander unwittingly into the web so intricately woven. Suppose, for example, that two persons, A and B, who are unrelated, own equally all the shares of Corporation X. A wishes to make a bequest to B in his will and to leave his residuary estate to his wife, AW. If A dies, then B, the legatee, will be a beneficiary of A's estate. Since B's interest is neither contingent nor remote, his ownership of X shares will be attributed to the estate of A. Thus A's estate will be deemed to own all the outstanding shares of Corporation X and the redemption by Corporation X of those shares formerly held by A will not completely terminate the estate's interest in the corporation. In fact the estate would continue as constructive owner of *all* the X stock by virtue of the attribution from the beneficiary, B.[58] One way out of the tangle might be through Section 303 of the Code, yet to be discussed.[59] Another might be through the use of an inter vivos revocable trust whereby the interest proposed for transfer to B on the death of A might be conveyed without mention of B in A's will, or A's stock could be placed in such a trust and thus, if B were not a trust beneficiary, then B's ownership of X stock would

[55] Ibid.

[56] See text accompanying note 44 *supra*.

[57] See id. note 37 *supra*.

[58] The illustration is based on a hypothetical in D. Kahn, Basic Corporate Taxation 227 (1970).

[59] See text accompanying note 79 *infra*.

not be attributed to the trust.[60] If there be a moral to all of this, it is to use extreme caution and foresight, planning in advance wherever possible.

As might be expected, there are some Code provisions which afford relief in particular situations. For example, strict application of the family attribution rules would prevent the complete termination of the interest of any family member through redemption or corporate repurchase of his stock. An important escape from this dilemma is provided by Subsection 302-(c)(2) of the Code. This, in effect, waives the application of the family attribution rules (but *not* the other attribution rules previously discussed). However, the waiver is subject to several conditions and has two exceptions which, in turn, are qualified by an "exception to the exceptions." The provision is a useful one but it rivals in complexity the very attribution rules from which it seeks to afford relief.[61]

The fundamental requirement for waiver of the family attribution rules through Subsection 302(c)(2) is that, immediately after a distribution in redemption of a person's stock, the distributee must have no "interest" in the corporation (including an interest as officer, director or employee) other than an interest as a creditor. Further, he must acquire no such interest (other than stock acquired by bequest or inheritance) within ten years from the date of the distribution in redemption of his stock. Finally, he must, at the time of distribution, file an agreement to notify the Internal Revenue Service of his acquiring such an interest within the ten-year period and retain such records (including tax returns) as will indicate fully the amount of tax which would have been payable had the distribution been taxable under Section 301.[62]

Before exploring what is meant by the term "interest" in Subsection 302(c)(2) (i.e., when might a person be considered to have acquired a forbidden interest so as to fail to qualify for waiver of the family attribution rules), it is well to mention the exceptions to the waiver rule. In general they are intended to catch a tax avoidance maneuver which might otherwise be possible through gifts of stock between family members followed by redemptions. Thus, if a father wishes to make a cash gift to his son, rather than using funds withdrawn from the corporation and taxable to him as dividends, or funds obtained through the redemption of his own stock (which would also in all likelihood be taxed as dividends if the father continued to own stock[63]), he might transfer stock to the son and then have

---

[60] See D. Kahn, id. at 227.

[61] See B. Bittker and J. Eustice, Federal Income Taxation of Corporations and Shareholders 290 (1966), describing the provision as being "as intricate as a minuet."

[62] Int. Rev. Code of 1954, §302(c)(2)(A). See Treas. Reg. §1.302–4(b).

[63] The father's interest would not be completely terminated and thus Section 302(b)(3) of the Code would not apply. Section 302(b)(2), regarding substantially disproportionate redemptions, would not apply if the father retained 50 percent or more of the voting power of the stock outstanding. See text accompanying note 20 *supra*. Section 302(b)(1) (the "essentially equivalent" language) might also apply.

the corporation redeem the stock for cash. If the son could take advantage of the waiver of the family attribution rules then, since the stock retained by the father would not be attributed to him, the redemption would be in complete termination of his interest in the corporation and the cash distribution would thus qualify for capital gains treatment. Although such a maneuver might well be considered as a "sham" or anticipatory assignment of dividend income,[64] Subsection 302(c)(2)(B) renders the "waiver" of attribution inapplicable if any portion of the redeemed stock was, within a ten-year period prior to the date of the distribution in redemption, acquired from a person whose ownership would be attributable to the distributee under the Section 318(a) family attribution rule (i.e., the father-son situation as well as spouse and grandchildren). Also, to forestall the possibility that the father might give *all* the stock to the son and then the latter might give part of it to a related person and redeem the rest, the waiver is made inapplicable where any person owns stock acquired from the distributee within the ten-year period prior to the distribution and such person is one of those enumerated in the family attribution rule (e.g., the distributee's spouse).[65] But a further exception to the exceptions provides that if the various transfers just described did not have a principal purpose of avoiding federal income tax, then, assuming the other conditions of Section 302(c)(2)[66] are met, the family attribution rules may be waived. According to the regulations, the fact that the person from whom the stock is subsequently redeemed is in a lower tax bracket than the person who transferred the stock to him is not sufficient in and of itself to indicate a tax avoidance purpose.[67] However, if the purpose of the transfer and redemption is to reduce the total tax burden on the entire family, then this might be sufficient to establish tax avoidance and prevent the waiver of family attribution.[68]

Aside from the structural complexities of Section 302, a primary problem with applying it to specific fact situations is determining what is meant by the term "interest." Although the Code specifies that the distributee may not, within the ten-year period following a distribution in redemption of his shares, serve as officer, director or employee, would this prohibit the rendering of any services to the corporation, such as serving as a consultant or dealing with the corporation as an independent contractor? Even if such roles were covered if compensation was given for performing the services, would the prohibition extend to serving as an unpaid consultant? Although the regulations do not provide much elucidation on this point, the Internal

---

Finally, the whole transaction might be treated either as a "sham," or as an anticipatory assignment of a dividend. See B. Bittker and J. Eustice, id. at 289 nn.28–29.
    [64] Ibid.
    [65] Int. Rev. Code of 1954, §302(c)(2)(B)(ii).
    [66] See text accompanying note 62 *supra*.
    [67] Treas. Reg. §1.302–4(g)(2).
    [68] See B. Bittker and J. Eustice, id. at 290.

Revenue Service apparently considers any service arrangement, whether or not for compensation, to be an interest in the corporation.[69] Query whether this would also extend to other contractual arrangements, such as acting as a supplier, distributor or customer of the business. Thus suppose that, due to a disagreement as to how a corporation should be run, one of the principal shareholders decides to leave the company and his shares are redeemed for cash. He organizes another business, and within a year or so, his former company becomes a customer of the new enterprise. It could be persuasively argued that the former shareholder had effectively terminated his financial interest in his former corporation[70] and that he should be able to enter into an arm's-length agreement for the sale of goods if the agreement is bona fide and no different from one which he would enter into with any other customer. However, the problem is still somewhat unsettled and much will depend upon the facts of the particular situation. What should be avoided at all costs is any inference that the former shareholder-employee is leaving the business only in form and not in substance, i.e., that despite redemption of his shares he retains a continuing relationship with the company whereby he shares in benefits and possibly exerts some of the control which he possessed in his former capacity.

Similar problems are likely to arise if a shareholder's interest is redeemed or repurchased for a note or other corporate obligation. Here the regulations are fairly specific. The statute expressly permits the former shareholder to retain an interest merely as a creditor and the regulations articulate the creditor concept as follows:

> For the purpose of section 302(c)(2)(A)(i), a person will be considered to be a creditor only if the rights of such person with respect to the corporation are not greater or broader in scope than necessary for the enforcement of his claim. Such claim must not in any sense be proprietary and must not be subordinate to the claims of general creditors. An obligation in the form of a debt may thus constitute a proprietary interest. For example, if under the terms of the instrument the corporation may discharge the principal amount of its obligation to a person by payments, the amount or certainty of which are dependent upon the earnings of the corporation, such a person is not a creditor of the corporation. Furthermore, if under the terms of the instrument the rate of purported interest is dependent upon earnings, the holder of such instrument may not, in some cases, be a creditor.[71]

The foregoing obviously indicates that, to be safe, a shareholder who has his interest repurchased for a corporate note should take care that the note is not subordinate to the claims of general creditors and that interest and prin-

---

[69] Rev. Rul. 70–104, 1970–10 I.R.B. 9; Rev. Rul. 59–119, 1959–1 Cum. Bull. 68; Rev. Rul. 56–556, 1956–2 Cum. Bull. 177, modified by Rev. Rul. 57–387, 1957–2 Cum. Bull. 225.

[70] See B. Bittker and J. Eustice, id. at 289.

[71] Treas. Reg. §1.302–4(d).

cipal payments on the note are fixed and not in any manner contingent upon corporate earnings.

There is a particularly troublesome problem, however, arising from a line of authority to the effect that, where a corporation gives its note in payment for shares purchased or redeemed, its obligation to make payments on the note, or on a series of notes, is conditional upon the availability of sufficient surplus at the time the payment becomes due. Thus in *Mountain State Steel Foundries, Inc. v. Commissioner*[72] the court rather ominously referred to a note given under such circumstances as an "executory agreement" and characterized the corporation's promise to pay as "conditional" upon the availability of sufficient surplus at the time of payment so that its capital would not be impaired through the disbursement of funds.[73] Although the case did not involve the question of whether such a note would be an interest in the corporation for the purpose of Subsection 302(c)(2), the language of the opinion is hardly reassuring when set alongside the strict approach taken by the regulations. In short, is a note which is conditional upon the availability of funds or corporate surplus really a note? Would the holder of such a note qualify as a "creditor" within the meaning of that term as described in the regulations? It is difficult to justify anything but a negative answer if the regulations are taken literally. Under the *Mountain State* holding, the "amount or certainty" of the payments on the note are clearly "dependent upon the earnings of the corporation" and such a note, although it might not by its express terms be subordinated to the claims of general creditors, would still not be a note in the usual sense—that is, the obligation would be conditional and, as the *Mountain State* court expressed it, the arrangement might even be termed a mere "executory agreement." The disquieting implications of all of this are increased by the refusal of the Internal Revenue Service to issue advance rulings as to "The tax effect of the redemption of stock for notes, where the payments on the notes are to be made over a period in excess of 15 years from the date of the issuance of such notes." [74] The same procedural ruling also raises another warning flag, namely, the danger of securing the notes by a pledge of the stock which has been repurchased or redeemed. Thus the Service will not rule as to

> Whether Section 302(b) applies where the consideration given in redemption by the corporation consists entirely or partly of its notes payable, and the shareholder's stock is held in escrow or as security for payment of the

[72] 284 F.2d 737 (4th Cir. 1960). Also see In re Trimble Co., 339 F.2d 838 (3d Cir. 1964); Kleinberg v. Schwartz, 87 N.J. Super. 216, 208 A.2d 803 (App. Div. 1965), *aff'd on opinion below*, 46 N.J. 2, 214 A.2d 313 (1965); Burk v. Cooperative Finance Corp., 62 Wash. 2d 740, 384 P.2d 618 (1963). For an extensive discussion of the problem see Herwitz, Installment Repurchase of Stock: Surplus Limitations, 79 Harv. L. Rev. 303 (1965).

[73] Mountain State Steel Foundries, Inc. v. Commissioner, 284 F.2d 737, 742 (4th Cir. 1960).

[74] Rev. Proc. 69–6, 1969–1 Cum. Bull. 396; but see Rev. Rul. 57–295, 1957–2 Cum. Bull. 227 (involving a redemption for cash plus ten-year notes).

notes with the possibility that the stock may or will be returned to him in the future, upon the happening of specified defaults by the corporation.[75]

As far as Subsection 302(c)(2) is concerned, although the regulations expressly permit the use of notes secured by corporate assets, and provide that the acquisition of such assets on default of the note would not be an acquisition of an interest in the corporation, they contain a proviso strongly implying that this would not be so if stock of the corporation, or of its parent or subsidiary, were acquired.[76] The upshot of all of this, then, is that the use of stock as a pledge to secure the payment of a corporate note given in repurchase or redemption of stock is hazardous, particularly if there is any need for a waiver of the family attribution rules under Subsection 302(c)(2). The better approach, both from a tax standpoint and from a practical business posture,[77] is to employ a chattel mortgage or, if feasible, a corporate bond secured by real property.[78]

At this point in our discussion it would be altogether reasonable for the reader to have reached the limit of his endurance in his efforts to unravel the intricacies of the stock redemption area with its attribution rules, waivers, exceptions to waivers and exceptions to exceptions. By way of some respite, we might shift the discussion to another useful provision which in a very real sense offers an "escape hatch" from all of these complexities, namely Section 303 of the Code, which provides for capital gain or loss treatment for stock redeemed to pay death taxes and funeral and other administrative expenses.

A redemption which qualifies under Section 303 of the Code automatically becomes entitled to capital gain or loss treatment even though, apart from that provision, it might be taxed as essentially equivalent to a dividend. For example, we saw that, due to the attribution rules, difficulties might arise if a testator wished to leave a bequest to a person already owning shares in the same corporation.[79] Although such difficulties might be alleviated by proper planning in advance of death, another alternative would be to take advantage of Section 303 of the Code.

---

[75] Rev. Proc. 69–6, *supra* note 74.

[76] Treas. Reg. §1.302–4(e).

[77] For example, if a 50 percent shareholder sells his shares to the corporation for a note and note is partly paid but thereafter the corporation defaults in making payments, should the shareholder be entitled to foreclose on all the shares pledged to secure the note, thus regaining his 50 percent interest, despite the fact that some of the shares have been paid for? If only some of the shares are returned to him (representing the unpaid balance on the purchase price), his minority interest would be of little value from a practical standpoint and would offer him little tactical advantage in persuading the corporation to continue making payments. For a discussion of the problem see Herwitz, *supra* at 315 (suggesting various solutions to the dilemma, such as to give contingent voting rights to the note holder without restoring to him the full equity in the shares. In those states where note holders may not be given voting rights, a voting trust might be a workable alternative).

[78] See Tracy v. Perkins-Tracy Printing Co., 278 Minn. 159, 153 N.W.2d 241 (1967).

[79] See text accompanying note 58 *supra*.

In order to qualify a redemption under Section 303, the stock of the corporation which is being redeemed must be included in the decedent's gross estate.[80] Although the usual situation is where stock is being redeemed from the executor or administrator of an estate, Section 303 will also apply if the stock which is being redeemed has been included in the gross estate due to its having been transferred to another in contemplation of death, bequeathed to a legatee, or redeemed from a surviving spouse where the stock was included in her husband's gross estate due to his having furnished all of the consideration for the stock.[81] Also, if the stock is redeemed from someone who acquired it due to the decedent's failure to exercise a general power of appointment or from a trust created by the decedent, it qualifies under Section 303.[82] However, if the stock is redeemed from someone who acquired it by gift or purchase from another who in turn acquired it from the decedent, Section 303 will not apply, nor will it apply if the stock is redeemed from someone who acquired it from the decedent's executor in satisfaction of a specific monetary bequest.[83] Thus, if the stock which is redeemed was transferred to the decedent's widow to satisfy a marital deduction pecuniary formula clause, its redemption will not qualify under Section 303. In such cases it would be preferable to redeem the stock directly from the estate and remit the proceeds to the widow either directly or in trust.[84] Similarly, in the case previously discussed (where a decedent wished to leave a legacy to another who already owned stock in the corporation), Section 303 would not apply to any stock acquired by the legatee from the executor in satisfaction of a monetary bequest. It would, however, apply to stock which passed to a legatee under the decedent's will (i.e., stock specifically left for him under the terms of the will and not transferred to him in satisfaction of a cash legacy). Obviously, Section 303 would also apply, in the illustrative case, to a redemption of stock from the estate itself, provided the other conditions of Section 303 are met.

Section 303 specifies not only that the stock which is subject to redemption must be included in the decedent's gross estate but also that the value of *all* the stock of the corporation (whether or not redeemed) which is included in his gross estate must be either (a) more than 35 percent of the value of the gross estate or (b) more than 50 percent of the taxable estate.[85] If the decedent owned stock in two or more corporations, then, for the purpose of qualifying under the 35 or 50 percent rule, the corporations may be treated as a single corporation if more than 75 percent of the value of the outstanding stock of each corporation is included in the decedent's gross estate.[86]

[80] Int. Rev. Code of 1954, §303(a).
[81] Treas. Reg. §1.303–2(f).
[82] Ibid.
[83] Ibid.
[84] See D. Kahn, Basic Corporate Taxation 34 (1970).
[85] Int. Rev. Code of 1954, §303(b)(2)(A).
[86] Id. §303(b)(2)(B). For an illustration see Treas. Reg. §1.303–2(c)(2).

A further qualification for Section 303 treatment is that the distribution in redemption of the stock must be made within a prescribed period after the decedent's death. The distribution must be made before the expiration of the three-year statute of limitations for the assessment of the estate tax under Section 6501(a) of the Code, or within ninety days after the expiration of that period.[87] If a petition for a redetermination of a deficiency in the estate tax has been filed with the Tax Court within the period prescribed in Section 6213, then the redemption will qualify if the distribution is made within sixty days after the decision of the Tax Court becomes final.[88]

There may be situations where the corporation does not have sufficient funds to redeem the stock within the prescribed period. In such a case it may wish to redeem the stock for notes. If the notes are given within the statutory period, then the redemption will qualify even though the notes are not paid until the period has expired.[89] This is, of course, on the assumption that the notes are bona fide and not, in substance, an equity interest in the corporation, since, if the notes are really stock, then the payment of the notes may be considered as equivalent to the redemption of stock, and if the payment takes place after the statutory period has expired, then Section 303 will not be available.[90]

Although, as previously stated, the amount of the distribution which will qualify for Section 303 treatment must not exceed the sum of the estate, inheritance, legacy and succession taxes, along with the deductible funeral and administration expenses of the decedent, it is not necessary that the reason for the redemption was to raise money to pay these expenses. For example, an estate could have ample cash to pay taxes and funeral and administration expenses and yet it may wish to take advantage of Section 303 for redemption purposes because of difficulties encountered with the attribution of ownership rules. Also Section 303 may be employed as to redemptions of stock held by someone other than the estate, where the stock was includible in the estate.[91]

If the stock which is being redeemed was acquired in exchange for other stock which was included in the decedent's gross estate, and the basis of the redeemed stock is determined in accordance with the basis of the other stock (as in a reorganization or other tax-free exchange), then the redemp-

---

[87] Int. Rev. Code of 1954, §303(b)(1)(A).

[88] Id. §303(b)(1)(B). This applies only to bona fide contests over the amount of the tax and not to petitions filed solely for the purpose of extending the statutory period. Treas. Reg. §1.303–2(e).

[89] Rev. Rul. 67–425, 1967–2 Cum. Bull. 134; Rev. Rul. 65–289, 1965–2 Cum. Bull. 86.

[90] See D. Kahn, id. at 35. For a discussion of analogous problems arising under Section 302(c)(2) and the puzzling question of whether, in view of such cases as Mountain State Steel Foundries, Inc. v. Commissioner, 284 F.2d 737 (4th Cir. 1960), and In re Trimble Co., 339 F.2d 838 (3rd Cir. 1964), a corporate note given under such circumstances is really a note or merely an executory agreement, see text accompanying note 71 *supra*.

[91] See id. note 81 *supra*.

tion qualifies under Section 303.[92] This is so even though the stock redeemed is so-called Section 306 stock (discussed later in this chapter). Thus, even though the redemption of such Section 306 stock might otherwise give rise to ordinary income treatment, if Section 303 applies, then the latter will produce capital gain or loss if its conditions are met.[93]

Although the importance of Section 303 in providing an otherwise "cash-poor" estate with means to meet its tax and other obligations should not be overemphasized since in certain situations the federal estate tax may be paid in installments over a ten-year period,[94] it is still true that Section 303 provides, within its limited scope, an escape hatch for stock redemptions which might otherwise run into difficulty because of the attribution of ownership rules. Hence it is a useful means of withdrawing funds from a closely held corporation at capital gains rates even though there is no immediate need of such funds to pay taxes and other expenses.

Where one or more persons are in control of two corporations, Section 304 of the Code plugs a possible loophole that might result if, instead of having stock redeemed by the corporation which issued it, a shareholder were to sell the stock to the other corporation and claim capital gains treatment, whereas, if the transaction were treated as a sale to the issuing corporation, it might be subject to tax at ordinary rates as being essentially equivalent to a dividend. In such a control situation,[95] Section 304 treats the stock as if it were redeemed in a transaction falling within Section 302. For the purpose of determining whether the redemption qualifies for capital gains treatment under Section 302, the transaction is treated as if it were a redemption of the stock by the *issuing* corporation. [96] If the transaction does not qualify for capital gains treatment under the Section 302 test (i.e., "dividend equivalence," or a redemption which is not substantially disproportionate or in complete termination of the shareholder's interest), then, for the purpose of determining the *extent* of the tax which is to be imposed at ordinary rates, the transaction is treated as a redemption by the *acquiring* corporation[97] (i.e., if a shareholder, in control of Corporations X and Y, sells his stock in Corporation X to Corporation Y, then, although for the purpose of ascertaining dividend equivalence, etc., the transaction is treated as if it were a redemption by Corporation X, if it is determined that capital gains treatment should not be given, then the extent of the tax at ordinary rates is determined by looking at the earnings and profits of Corporation Y, which acquired the stock, rather than Corporation X, which issued it).

[92] Int. Rev. Code of 1954, §303(c).

[93] Treas. Reg. §1.303–2(d).

[94] Int. Rev. Code of 1954, §6166.

[95] The term "control" is defined as ownership of stock possessing at least 50 percent of the total combined voting power of all classes of stock entitled to vote, or at least 50 percent of the total value of all classes of stock. Id. §304(c).

[96] Id. §304(b)(1). See also Rev. Rul. 70–496, 1970–39 I.R.B. 6.

[97] Id. §§304(a)(1), 304(b)(2)(A). The stock is treated as if it were a contribution to capital to the corporation acquiring it. Id. §304(a)(1).

If, instead of the "brother-sister" corporation situation, there is a parent-subsidiary relationship and stock of the parent is sold to the subsidiary, then the transaction is considered as if the stock issued by the parent had been redeemed by it. In this case the earnings and profits of the parent determine the extent of any tax imposed at ordinary rates.[98]

6.2 SECTION 306 STOCK; THE BAIL-OUT PROBLEM

One danger to be avoided is the so-called preferred stock bail-out problem presented in connection with certain redemptions of preferred or, in rather unusual cases, of common shares. Perhaps the best way in which to approach the problem is to examine a leading case decided before the enactment of Section 306 of the Code. In *Chamberlin v. Commissioner*[99] a corporation with substantial earnings and profits declared a stock dividend of preferred stock. The receipt of the preferred stock as a dividend would not normally be a taxable event.[100] However, shortly after the distribution of the preferred, nearly all of the recipient shareholders, as a result of prior negotiations, entered into a "purchase agreement" whereby two life insurance companies agreed to purchase the preferred at par plus accrued dividends. The preferred was subject to redemption on any quarterly dividend date in whole or in part at par plus specified premiums and dividends accrued to the date of redemption, and it was also subject to mandatory redemption requirements so that all of the shares would be redeemed within seven and one-half years. The question presented was whether the receipt of the purported tax-free stock dividend, followed by the sale of stock to outsiders pursuant to a preexisting plan, constituted in substance a taxable dividend. Although the Tax Court held that this was so, the holding was reversed by the Sixth Circuit Court of Appeals on the ground that the transaction was bona fide (i.e., not a sham), that by its form it amounted to a tax-free stock dividend followed by a sale and that there had been no distribution of funds *by the corporation* (as the statute defined a dividend) but rather a payment for the stock by an outsider. Thus the court considered that the form of the transaction should, at least in this situation, control and held that the sale of the preferred was not taxable as a bail out of earnings which otherwise would have been distributed as a dividend.

Any satisfaction tax practitioners may have been able to derive from the Circuit Court opinion was short-lived, for the tax avoidance possibilities suggested by the case became a matter of Congressional concern and re-

---

98 Id. §§304(a)(2), 304(b)(2).

99 207 F.2d 462 (6th Cir. 1953), *cert. denied,* 347 U.S. 918 (1954).

100 This would have been the law under Strassburger v. Commissioner, 318 U.S. 604 (1943). The determination of whether a distribution of stock was tax free depended upon the facts of each case, since the matter arose prior to the enactment of Int. Rev. Code of 1954, §305.

sulted in the enactment of Section 306 of the Code, which is essentially a loophole closing provision.

Section 306 defines stock such as that distributed as a stock dividend in the *Chamberlin* case as "Section 306 Stock" and provides for taxation at ordinary rates where such stock is subsequently sold or where it is redeemed from the recipient shareholder. More accurately, Section 306 stock is stock which has been distributed as a tax-free stock dividend, except that a dividend of common stock issued with respect to common stock is not included within the definition.[101] Also, if a corporation has no earnings and profits (either current or accumulated), then even the distribution of preferred shares would not entail a Section 306 problem.[102] The reasoning behind this is that the bail-out device would not be employed except where a corporation has earnings and profits which would be taxed if distributed as dividends and also that holders of common are not likely to use dividends of additional common shares as a bail-out mechanism since the sale of the common would result in dilution of their voting and dividend rights.[103] It should be noted, however, that a dividend of common shares distributed to holders of preferred results in the common stock's falling within the Section 306 stock category. Also the presence of *any* earnings and profits (even one dollar) causes the entire distribution of stock to qualify as Section 306 stock.[104]

Stock need not be received as a stock dividend in order to be Section 306 stock. Thus, if preferred stock is received tax free in a reorganization, it will generally be Section 306 stock if there are earnings and profits and if the effect of the transaction is "substantially the same as the receipt of a stock dividend." [105] For example, if those who hold common stock exchange their shares for a package of common and preferred stock pursuant to a tax-free "recapitalization," then the preferred stock is Section 306 stock if there are earnings and profits. The same would be true if shareholders having a package of common shares and preferred shares which were Section 306 stock were to exchange them for other common and preferred shares. In the latter

---

[101] Id. §306(c)(1)(A).

[102] Id. §306(c)(2).

[103] Although this would be so in a sale, obviously a redemption of common shares previously distributed as a stock dividend would not have the same result. However, such a redemption, unless substantially disproportionate, would in all likelihood be considered as essentially equivalent to a dividend. See Section 302(b) of the Code and also text accompanying note 13 *supra*.

[104] Treas. Reg. §1.306–3(a). Where the earnings and profits are relatively modest, it has been suggested that, although the entire distribution of stock qualifies as Section 306 Stock, a disposition or redemption might not be taxed at ordinary rates if it were shown that there was no intent to avoid taxes (i.e., no intent to bail-out earnings and profits—which by hypothesis are nominal—at capital gains rates). See Section 306(b)(4) of the Code and B. Bittker and J. Eustice, Federal Income Taxation of Corporations and Shareholders 329 n.8 (1966).

[105] Int. Rev. Code of 1954, §306(c)(1)(B).

situation the new preferred would be Section 306 stock because it had been received in exchange for Section 306 stock.[106] Similar rules are also applicable to stock received in a so-called divisive reorganization (i.e., "spin-offs," "split-offs" and "split-ups"). As to the question of when the receipt of stock pursuant to a reorganization is substantially the same as the receipt of a stock dividend, the regulations take the view that the test is whether cash received in lieu of the stock would have been taxable as a dividend.[107]

Another situation in which Section 306 stock can be created is where a shareholder receives stock the basis of which is computed by reference to the basis of Section 306 stock which he has surrendered.[108] Although this might apply in the recapitalization case already discussed, it could also apply in other situations, as where a person has received Section 306 stock as a gift, or transfers it to a corporation, formed under the tax-free provisions of Section 351, in exchange for common stock. In the latter situation, since the basis of the common shares would be determined by reference to the basis of the Section 306 stock surrendered,[109] the common stock would be Section 306 stock. This is somewhat unusual since, as previously indicated, Section 306 stock is generally preferred stock or something other than common stock. However, if the result were otherwise, a two-step bailout loophole would exist, in that a shareholder would be able to transfer his Section 306 stock to a wholly owned corporation in exchange for common shares which he might then dispose of at capital gains rates. Although the Code closes the loophole, it also creates two issues of Section 306 stock where only one issue previously existed. Not only is the common stock received in exchange for the Section 306 stock treated as Section 306 stock, but also the Section 306 stock received by the corporation retains its character as Section 306 stock, since the basis of the stock for the corporation is determined by reference to the basis which the stock had in the hands of the transferor.[110] Thus, if the shareholder and the corporation both dispose of their stock, a double tax at ordinary rates might be imposed.

As already indicated, a sale or redemption of Section 306 stock may result in taxation at ordinary rates. However, the tax treatment is slightly different, depending upon whether the shares are sold or redeemed. If the shares are sold, then that part of the sale price which equals the amount which would have been taxed as a dividend to the shareholder at the time he received his Section 306 stock—if cash had been distributed to him in lieu of the stock—is treated as ordinary income (i.e., taxable at ordinary rates to the seller, although not technically a dividend to him, and thus, for

106 Id. §306(c)(1)(B)(ii). See also Treas. Reg. §1.306–3(d), Ex. (2).

107 Id. §1.306–3(d). For further discussion see text accompanying note 282 *infra* and Ch. VIII, text accompanying note 66.

108 Int. Rev. Code of 1954, §306(c)(1)(C).

109 Id. §358.

110 Id. §362(b).

example, not eligible for the $100 dividends-received exclusion).[111] No loss is recognized.[112] Thus, in any sale of Section 306 stock, the critical factor in determining the amount of ordinary income is the earnings and profits of the corporation at the time the Section 306 stock was *distributed*. In sharp contrast, if a redemption is involved, the amount realized is treated as a distribution of property under Section 301 of the Code.[113] The result is that the distribution will be taxable as a *dividend* (and thus eligible for the $100 dividends-received exclusion, etc.), depending upon the earnings and profits of the corporation at the time of the *redemption* (in contrast to a sale, where the critical point for computing earnings and profits is the time of the initial *distribution* of the shares). In both the sale and redemption situations, that part of the amount realized which is not subject to tax at ordinary rates is applied against the basis of the shares, being treated as a return of capital. If there is any excess over basis, the excess is taxed at capital gains rates. Any "left over" basis (i.e., the basis of the Section 306 stock reduced in the fashion already described) is added to the basis of the shares which are retained by the shareholder.[114]

Suppose, for example, that Section 306 stock with a basis of $2000 is sold for $5000 and that, at the time the stock was initially received by the shareholder, the corporate earnings and profits were $3500. In such case $3500 of the amount realized on the sale would be taxed at ordinary rates and the $1500 remaining of the $5000 sale price would be applied to reduce the $2000 basis to $500. This $500 would then be added to the basis of any other shares which the seller continued to hold in the corporation.[115] If, on the other hand, the shares were redeemed and if, at the time of redemption, corporate earnings and profits were $5000, the entire amount received for the shares (i.e., $5000) would be taxed as a dividend and the $2000 basis remaining would be added to the basis of any other shares the shareholder continued to hold in the corporation.[116]

Even though there is a sale or redemption of Section 306 stock, several statutory exceptions provide for tax relief in particular situations. Thus if a person sells Section 306 stock to someone other than a member of his own family and the sale terminates his interest in the corporation (determining such interest in accordance with the family attribution rules of Section 318(a) already discussed),[117] then the sale will not give rise to taxation

---

[111] See id. §116. Also the earnings and profits of the corporation are not reduced by the amount which was taxed at ordinary rates to the shareholder since such amount was not technically a "dividend."

[112] Id. §306(a)(1)(C).

[113] Id. §306(a)(2).

[114] Treas. Reg. §1.302–2(c).

[115] The illustration is based on that in B. Bittker and J. Eustice, Federal Income Taxation of Corporations and Shareholders 331–332 (1966).

[116] Ibid.

[117] See text accompanying note 36 *supra*.

at ordinary income rates.[118] A similar result follows if the shares are re-deemed and if the redemption terminates the shareholder's entire interest in the corporation. Here, as previously seen,[119] the family attribution rules of Section 318(a) may, under some circumstances, be waived if the condi-tions of Section 302(c)(2) are met (principally if the person from whom the shares are redeemed does not have any interest in the corporation, in-cluding one as an officer, director or employee, other than an interest as a creditor, and does not acquire any such interest within ten years from the date of redemption). The reasoning for relaxing Section 306 in these areas is fairly obvious, namely, that a bail out of earnings and profits is unlikely to occur where the shareholder severs his relationship with the corporation.

Similar reasoning justifies another exception to Section 306. If a share-holder, before or at the time the Section 306 stock is sold or redeemed, disposes of the stock with respect to which the Section 306 stock was issued (i.e., the common stock where there has been a stock dividend of preferred on common), then ordinary tax treatment will not be given if the Internal Revenue Service is satisfied that the transaction was not in pursuance of a plan having as one of its principal purposes the avoidance of federal income tax.[120] The precise outlines of tax avoidance motivation are unclear in this area. The regulations refer to "isolated dispositions of Section 306 stock by minority shareholders" as being within the exception.[121] It would also seem that a shareholder need not dispose of all his common stock but only that part of it "with respect to which the Section 306 stock disposed of (or redeemed) was issued." [122] Thus, if a person holds one thousand shares of common stock and receives a dividend of five hundred shares of preferred stock, he might be able to sell one hundred (i.e., one fifth) shares of pre-ferred if he previously or simultaneously sells two hundred (i.e., one fifth) shares of common.[123] On the other hand, if a publicly held corporation were regularly to declare stock dividends and the shareholders were regu-larly to sell portions of common and preferred, then tax avoidance would be a clear possibility since the common could easily be repurchased on the open market and the shareholder could thus recoup and maintain his un-derlying equity position.[124] Finally, it should be noted that the exception for nontax avoidance motivated transactions extends beyond the situation where underlying common is previously or simultaneously sold. The regula-tions give little indication of the circumstances under which the exception

[118] Int. Rev. Code of 1954, §306(b)(1)(A).

[119] See text accompanying note 61 *supra.*

[120] Int. Rev. Code of 1954, §306(b)(4).

[121] Treas. Reg. §1.306–2(b)(3).

[122] Int. Rev. Code of 1954, §306(b)(4)(B).

[123] See B. Bittker and J. Eustice, Federal Income Taxation of Corporations and Shareholders 335 (1966).

[124] Ibid. See also the Tax Reform Act amendments to Section 305, discussed in note 22 *supra.*

might apply other than to mention, as already indicated, "isolated dispositions of Section 306 stock by minority shareholders."

As in the above situation where the shareholder terminates his interest in the corporation, if the corporation is liquidated, or even if there is a "partial" liquidation, then Section 306 does not apply.[125] Finally, if an exchange is completely free of tax, as where there is a corporate reorganization or a corporation is formed tax free under Section 351 of the Code, then Section 306 does not apply, unless some consideration other than stock or securities is received (i.e., boot).[126] Also, as previously pointed out, the basis of stock "carries over" in these tax-free exchanges and thus, although ordinary income might not result from the exchange itself, the Section 306 problem persists in that the stock held by the transferor and transferee continues to be Section 306 stock.[127]

Despite the possibility of taxation at ordinary rates under Section 306, preferred stock has some very real uses in a closely held concern. Primarily these relate to estate planning and the reallocation of income within the corporation. Shareholders who are senior in years and who anticipate estate tax problems in the event of their death may wish to convert all or part of their interest into preferred stock in order that such stock may be more readily valued (common stock in a closely held concern being notoriously difficult to value) and also in order to derive a greater yield than is possible through the retention of common. If all of a shareholder's common stock is surrendered for preferred, the risk of Section 306 liability is virtually nil due to the previously discussed exception relating to a prior disposition of the underlying equity. Even if only some of the common is exchanged for preferred, if the latter is held until death and if it receives a "new" basis in the hands of the estate, then it no longer falls within Section 306 and thus may be redeemed without risk of taxation at ordinary rates. Finally, it has been held that a gift of preferred stock to a charity is not a disposition for the purpose of Section 306, permitting a tax deduction to be claimed for the gift without the risk of taxation at ordinary rates.[128] This apparently is so even though the charitable recipient subsequently surrenders the stock for redemption by the corporation.[129] There is, of course, a distinct possibility of real abuse in this device, and it might be argued that a charitable contribution followed by quick redemption should result in taxation to the donor under general principles of Section 302 and the "assignment of income" doctrine.[130] In fact, entirely apart from the charitable contribution

[125] Int. Rev. Code of 1954, §306(b)(2).

[126] Id. §306(b)(3). See also id. §§351(b), 356.

[127] See text accompanying note 108 *supra*.

[128] Rev. Rul. 57–328, 1957–2 Cum. Bull. 229.

[129] See Robert L. Fox, 27 CCH Tax Ct. Mem. 1001 (1968); cf. Richard P. Makoff, 26 CCH Tax Ct. Mem. 83 (1967).

[130] See B. Bittker and J. Eustice, Federal Income Taxation of Corporations and Shareholders 336 (1966).

area, it might be asked whether Section 306 was intended to preempt the field of "anti-bail-out" regulation or whether courts should be free to disregard form in favor of substance where there is a transparent attempt to withdraw corporate earnings and profits without paying a tax at ordinary rates. In any event, this loophole has now been effectively foreclosed by an amendment to Section 170 of the Code by the Tax Reform Act of 1969, which provides that any deduction for a charitable contribution of property must be reduced by the amount of gain, other than long-term capital gain, which would have been realized had the contributor-taxpayer sold the property at its fair market value and contributed the proceeds.[131] Since a sale of Section 306 stock would usually give rise to ordinary income, any charitable contribution deduction for Section 306 stock is correspondingly reduced, so that there is no longer any tax advantage in the use of Section 306 stock for charitable contributions.

6.3 TAX EFFECT OF REDEMPTION ON REMAINING SHAREHOLDERS

In the foregoing we have discussed the tax treatment of one whose shares are redeemed by a corporation. It is now time to consider the tax effect on one whose shares are not redeemed but who benefits substantially from a redemption of the shares of others. Suppose, for example, that a corporation has $1 million in assets and is owned by five individuals, each having 20 percent of the outstanding shares. If the shares of one of these individuals are redeemed for $200,000, each of the remaining four shareholders would have a 25 percent interest in a corporation with assets of only $800,000. The percentage of each one's equity interest has increased although the actual value of such interest has remained the same (i.e., $200,000). However, if the shares of one of the five original shareholders were to be redeemed or repurchased for less than $200,000, then the interests of the other shareholders would be correspondingly benefited. Should such a benefit result in a tax on those receiving it? If the transaction had been set up not as a corporate repurchase or redemption but rather as a buy-out arrangement between shareholders, and if the $200,000 had originally been equally distributed to the five shareholders to enable four of them to purchase the interest of the fifth, then $40,000 would be taxable as a dividend to each shareholder (including the one whose shares were being purchased). Should the matter be differently treated if the $200,000 is never distributed by the corporation but is paid directly to the person whose shares are being redeemed?

In this area the crucial distinction appears to be whether one shareholder has *obligated* himself to purchase the shares of another and if the corpora-

---

[131] Int. Rev. Code of 1954, §170(e)(1)(A).

tion has discharged the obligation. If such is the case, then a court is likely to view the corporate payment of the shareholder's personal obligation as, in substance, a dividend to the shareholder, following the familiar principle that the discharge of a personal liability is equivalent to the payment of the amount in question to the person receiving the benefit.[132] However, if one shareholder merely has an *option* to purchase the shares of another and assigns the option to the corporation, which then exercises the option and acquires the shares, since the shareholder is not personally obligated in any way, he is not taxable even though he may receive some benefit. Thus, in *Holsey v. Commissioner*[133] a corporation repurchased shares for less than their book value and the taxpayer became sole owner of all the outstanding shares, yet he received no taxable income. The court took the position that, although the taxpayer may have received a benefit, he could not be constitutionally taxed under the Sixteenth Amendment in that he neither received any distribution from the corporation nor had he realized upon his gains by disposing of his shares.[134] Whether this approach is constitutionally compelled is questionable.[135] Moreover, the stress which the cases have placed upon whether the shareholder has personally obligated himself

[132] The classic case in this regard is Old Colony Trust Co. v. Commissioner, 279 U.S. 716 (1929), involving an employer's payment of an employee's taxes. For cases applying this principle to the stock repurchase area, see Sullivan v. United States, 363 F.2d 724 (8th Cir. 1966), *cert. denied*, 387 U.S. 905 (1967); Zipp v. Commissioner, 259 F.2d 119 (6th Cir. 1958), *cert. denied*, 359 U.S. 934 (1959); Wall v. United States, 164 F.2d 462 (4th Cir. 1947). In some situations the shareholder has been successful in establishing that, despite his personal obligation to pay for the shares, he was acting as agent for the corporation. If so, the corporation, by purchasing the shares, is in reality discharging its own obligation. See John A. Decker, 32 T.C. 326 (1959), *aff'd*, 286 F.2d 427 (6th Cir. 1960); Fox v. Harrison, 145 F.2d 521 (7th Cir. 1944).

[133] 258 F.2d 865 (3d Cir. 1958). The Internal Revenue Service indicated that it would follow the holding in the *Holsey* case, reserving its rights to question the transaction regardless of its particular form "if the stock is in reality purchased by a remaining shareholder and paid for by the corporation. . . ." Rev. Rul. 58–614, 1958–2 Cum. Bull. 920. A valuable guide to the position which the Internal Revenue Service will take on particular agreements is set forth in Rev. Rul. 69–608, 1969–2 Cum. Bull. 42. There it is stated that the fact that a corporation may satisfy a shareholder's executory contractual obligation to purchase the shares of another will not result in constructive dividend treatment if the continuing shareholder is not subject to an existing "primary and unconditional obligation to perform the contract" and the corporation pays no more than fair market value for the stock. The shareholder's obligation does not become primary and unconditional until his duty to perform becomes unconditional, and therefore a duty to purchase the shares at some time in the future upon the happening of an event, such as death or retirement, is not primary and unconditional.

[134] In this regard the court relied upon Eisner v. Macomber, 252 U.S. 189 (1920), which involved a stock dividend.

[135] B. Bittker and J. Eustice, id. at 199, indicate that the constitutional theory of the *Eisner* case has "few defenders today." Also, see note 22 *supra*, discussing the broadening of Section 305 of the Code by the Tax Reform Act of 1969 to impose a tax on a basis of dividend equivalence on *all* shareholders, whether or not their shares are redeemed, if they are given a periodic election between redemption or a proportionate increase in their equity interest.

or whether he has merely assigned an option may be an exaltation of form over substance. Often the parties are unaware or indifferent to the legal consequences of the precise arrangement. Thus, in a corporation where all the shares are owned by two individuals, the seller is not normally concerned with whether he disposes of his shares to the corporation or to the other shareholder. In his naivete he may even confuse the two. And the purchaser may not be fully aware of the tax consequences which may follow from his agreeing to purchase the stock in contrast to a corporate repurchase agreement. Once the shares are purchased, the surviving shareholder is likely to regard himself as equivalent to the corporation, for he owns it. It is odd, then, that so much should depend upon what, to the parties involved, may seem so slight a difference—and a difference which may be easily overlooked. In view of this it is not surprising that some courts have relaxed the rigors of the rule, primarily in situations where a shareholder has obligated himself to purchase shares of another and, finding it difficult or impossible to discharge the obligation, has arranged for a third party to purchase the shares. If the shares are then purchased by the third party and shortly thereafter redeemed or repurchased by the corporation at a profit to the third party, there are no unfavorable tax effects on the shareholder whose liability has been discharged not by the corporation but by someone else.[136] Again, it is hard to see any difference here other than a purely formal one. Finally, if the corporation should agree to purchase some of the shares and the other shareholder should agree to purchase the balance, there is no dividend equivalence as long as the corporation does not purchase more than the stock allotted to it.[137] This is so even though the shareholder may have pledged his shares to assure that the corporation would perform its obligation.[138] Even if the shareholder were personally to guarantee the corporation's performance of the contract, this would apparently make no difference provided that the corporation did not purchase stock which the shareholder was required to purchase as primary obligor rather than as guarantor.[139]

[136] See Milton F. Priester, 38 T.C. 316 (1962); Henry C. Goss, 22 CCH Tax Ct. Mem. 1219 (1963).

[137] See Ray Edenfield, 19 T.C. 13 (1952), *acquiesced in,* 1953–1 Cum. Bull. 4.

[138] Ibid.

[139] See Milton F. Priester, 38 T.C. 316 (1962). See generally Sexton, Sarner and Cannon, Maintaining Control and Continuity in the Close Corporation: Buy-Sell Agreements, N.Y.U. 24th Inst. on Fed. Tax. 555–631 (1966). Note, Estate Planning for the Disposition of Control of a Family Corporation, 52 Minn. L. Rev. 1019 (1968).

6.4　STOCK REDEMPTION OR REPURCHASE AGREEMENTS; CROSS-PURCHASE AGREEMENTS

We are now in a position to examine the various aspects of stock redemption and repurchase agreements in contrast to "cross-purchase" agreements entered into between shareholders. In doing so we shall also consider the tax and business features of funding such agreements through the use of life insurance.

A major advantage of a corporate stock repurchase agreement is its simplicity. Each shareholder has but one agreement, entered into with his corporation, in contrast to several agreements, each with a different shareholder. This is particularly helpful if life insurance is used as a funding device, in that only one policy is required with respect to each shareholder and there is but one beneficiary—the corporation. Although the corporation may not deduct premiums paid by it on any policy of which it is the beneficiary,[140] this is no disadvantage when the arrangement is compared with a cross-purchase agreement, for in the latter situation the shareholders are not entitled to deduct the premiums paid by them on the policies insuring their fellow shareholders.[141] When the corporation pays premiums on the policy, such payment is not a constructive dividend to any of the shareholders, provided the corporation retains the incidents of ownership of the policy and is itself the beneficiary.[142] Similarly, when the policy matures due to

[140] Int. Rev. Code of 1954, §264(a)(1). Among the helpful discussions of stock repurchase and cross purchase agreements are D. Kahn, Basic Corporate Taxation 179–248 (1970); Abrams, Tax Planning for Agreements Disposing of a Shareholder's Closely Held Stock at Death, 57 Geo. L.J. 1211 (1969); Sexton, Sarner and Cannon, supra 555–631; Polasky, Planning for the Disposition of a Substantial Interest in a Closely Held Business, 46 Iowa L. Rev. 516 (1961); Note, The Use of Life Insurance to Fund Agreements Providing for Disposition of a Business Interest at Death, 71 Harv. L. Rev. 687 (1958). Note, Estate Planning for the Disposition of Control of a Family Corporation, 52 Minn. L. Rev. 1019 (1968).

[141] Such expenditures are probably in the nature of personal expenses and not incurred in connection with the business of the taxpayer-shareholder. Merely because a corporation is closely held, a shareholder is not considered to be in the same business as the corporation in which he invests. Cf. Whipple v. Commissioner, 373 U.S. 193 (1963). Even if payment of the premiums is considered to be incidental to the taxpayer's business, a deduction of the premium would be disallowed under Section 264(a)(1) of the Code, if the taxpayer is a beneficiary of the policy, which is usually the case.

[142] Sanders v. Fox, 253 F.2d 855 (10th Cir. 1958); Prunier v. Commissioner, 248 F.2d 818 (1st Cir. 1957); Casale v. Commissioner, 247 F.2d 440 (2d Cir. 1957). See also Rev. Rul. 59–184, 1959–1 Cum. Bull. 65. As these cases indicate, if the corporation pays the premiums on a policy of which a shareholder is beneficiary or with regard to which the shareholder retains incidents of ownership (such as the right to change the beneficiary), then such payment is a constructive dividend to the shareholder. If a trustee is the beneficiary of the policy, as in the case of a so-called life insurance trust, then the payment of the premiums by the corporation is not a constructive dividend to the shareholder if the policy proceeds are payable to him only upon the surrender of his shares for redemption or repurchase by the corporation.

the death of the insured, the proceeds are not included in corporate income for tax purposes[143] nor are they taxable to anyone else.[144] Finally, if the corporation pays the premiums and retains the incidents of ownership of the policy, the proceeds are not included in the estate of the deceased shareholder for estate tax purposes.[145]

Despite these advantages there are some tax and other problems entailed in the corporate repurchase approach. Some of these have already been suggested in our consideration of the possibility that a corporate repurchase or redemption might be held to be essentially equivalent to a dividend, resulting in ordinary income to the extent of corporate earnings and profits.[146] As we have seen, some of the risk in this area may be lessened or eliminated through the use of the waiver of the family attribution rules of Section 318 of the Code through compliance with Section 302(c)(2).[147] Another possibility is through the use of Section 303, also discussed earlier in this chapter.[148]

Even though the essentially equivalent problem is solved, if the corporation accumulates funds to satisfy anticipated obligations under a repurchase agreement, this may constitute an unreasonable accumulation of earnings and profits, thus exposing the corporation to a penalty tax.[149] As previously

---

[143] Int. Rev. Code of 1954, §101(a).

[144] If the proceeds are payable to the corporation but, pursuant to its direction, are paid by the insurance company directly to one or more shareholders, the tax consequences depend upon whether the payment is considered as having been made to redeem shares held by the estate of the deceased (perhaps the most common situation), in which case capital gain or loss will probably result under either Section 302(b)(3) or Section 303 of the Code, or whether the payment is in the nature of a dividend (as where it is made to all the shareholders). See Golden v. Commissioner, 113 F.2d 590 (3d Cir. 1940). But see Ducros v. Commissioner, 272 F.2d 49 (6th Cir. 1959), holding, possibly erroneously, that such a payment was exempt under Section 101 of the Code as having been made "by reason of the death of the insured." Despite the *Ducros* case, even though the payment is made directly to the shareholder by the insurance company, if the corporation was the real beneficiary and retained the incidents of ownership of the policy, the payment should be considered as having been made on its behalf, in which case it should be taxed either as a sale or exchange or as a dividend, depending upon the nature of the transaction (i.e., whether the payment is for redemption of shares). Thus, although the form of the transaction might be a direct payment by the insurance company to one or more shareholders, the substance should be considered as a payment by the insurance company to the corporation (exempt from income taxation under Section 101 of the Code) and a payment by the corporation to the shareholder, which, as previously stated, is taxed according to the nature of the payment.

[145] Int. Rev. Code of 1954, §2042. The term "incidents of ownership" includes a reversionary interest only if the value of such interest exceeds 5 percent of the value of the policy immediately before the decedent's death. Another situation in which the policy proceeds are includible in a decedent's estate for estate tax purposes is where the proceeds are payable to his executor. Id. §2042(1). For this reason the policy proceeds should be payable to the corporation.

[146] See text accompanying notes 13–29 *supra*.

[147] See id. note 61 *supra*.

[148] See id. note 80 *supra*.

[149] See Ch. V, text accompanying notes 101–118. As pointed out in id. note 118, the Tax Reform Act of 1969 added a provision which permits accumulations up to

pointed out, the problem is especially acute as to the repurchase of shares of a majority shareholder. There, because of the latter's control of the corporation, an accumulation might be attacked as motivated largely by a personal and not a business purpose, to accommodate the needs of the majority shareholder. However, if the majority shareholder is also a key employee, which is likely to be the case, his death may pose severe business problems for the corporation and it would not be unreasonable for the latter to make some provision in advance for a smooth transition, whereby control is shifted into the hands of others.[150] Similarly, if failure to redeem stock held by a majority shareholder might result in a sale of the stock to an outsider by the estate of the deceased, or in the dissolution of the corporation, then a corporate accumulation might be more easily justified.[151]

Problems of unreasonable accumulation are more likely to arise if a major shareholder is uninsurable or if premiums on a policy insuring life are so high as to be unfeasible from a business standpoint. If insurance is possible and its cost is within reach economically, it is highly doubtful that corporate payment of premiums could be attacked as an unreasonable accumulation of earnings and profits, particularly if low-cost term insurance is used.[152]

The overall cost of funding a buy-out plan through insurance is generally less where a corporate repurchase or redemption plan is used than with a cross-purchase arrangement between the various shareholders. This is particularly so where the shareholders are in relatively high tax brackets. In such a situation, funds to pay the premiums must be withdrawn from the corporation in the form of taxable dividends, and thus taxed twice—once to the corporation and a second time to the shareholders—or they must be withdrawn in the form of increased compensation. If the latter is done, then, although the corporation may be entitled to a deduction *if* the total compensation paid is reasonable, such amounts are still taxed to the shareholder-employee at his relatively high individual tax rate. If all the shareholders are not employees, then this lessens the ability of the corporation to convey funds to them in the form of tax deductible compensation. All of this suggests that the cross-purchase arrangement is comparable in cost to the corporate repurchase scheme only where the amounts required to pay premiums may be paid to the shareholders through tax-deductible compensation and then only where the shareholders are in relatively low tax brackets. Even then, the overall cost may be greater due to the multiplicity of policies involved with the cross purchase, entailing greater overhead expense in issuing and servicing the policies, particularly where large numbers of shareholders are involved.

---

the amount which may be used to fund a redemption of shares pursuant to Section 303 of the Code.

[150] See Ch. V, text accompanying note 107.

[151] See id. note 108.

[152] See id. notes 116–118.

Although the cost of paying premiums may be less with a corporate repurchase or redemption plan, the overall amount of insurance required to fund the buy-out may have to be greater. This, in turn, increases the cost. The reason for this cost increase is that when insurance proceeds are paid to the corporation on the death of the insured, this increases the corporate assets and, correspondingly, the book value of the shares to be repurchased.[153] Suppose, for example, that five shareholders each own 20 percent of the shares of a corporation with net assets amounting to $100,000. The book value of the shares of each shareholder is $20,000. If the corporation purchases $20,000 worth of insurance to fund a repurchase of the shares of any shareholder, then on his death the net assets of the corporation increase to $120,000 and the value of each shareholder's interest increases to $24,000. Accordingly, at least $24,000 of insurance will be needed to fund a repurchase of the interest of any shareholder. Obviously, however, the death of any shareholder will then increase the net assets of the corporation to $124,000 and increase the value of each shareholder's interest to $24,800. This will entail the need to purchase at least $24,800 in insurance. To fund the repurchase fully, approximately $25,000 in insurance will be required instead of the $20,000 originally contemplated. If the cross-purchase approach is used, on the other hand, the policy proceeds will not go to increase the corporate assets or the book value of the shares subject to the purchase.

One answer to this may be to specify that the book value of the shares will be computed without regard to the receipt by the corporation of the insurance proceeds. This will be unfair to the person who is unlucky enough to die first and whose shares are repurchased at a figure which fails to reflect their true value. The unfairness is particularly apparent if so-called ordinary life insurance is used, rather than term insurance, because the policy will then have a cash value which, in a very real sense, constitutes a corporate asset even in advance of the death of the insured. Even if term insurance is used, if the policy has been in effect for a number of years and the corporation has thus paid premiums out of amounts which otherwise could have been used for dividends, it seems unfair not to take the policy proceeds into account in estimating the value of the shares, for the proceeds have, in a sense, been "purchased" by the corporation from its earnings.

If an ordinary life policy is chosen, then the repurchase agreement might specify that only the cash surrender value of the policy at the date of death shall be included as a corporate asset for the purpose of determining the book value of the shares. This lessens, but does not eliminate, the problem of "pyramiding" of coverage where it is planned that the repurchase be fully funded. Even with this approach, surviving shareholders receive a

[153] See Land & Simmons Co. v. Arconti, 223 Md. 204, 162 A.2d 478, 163 A.2d 455 (1960) (two dissents).

windfall, particularly if the insured dies shortly after the policy is taken out. Since it is unknown who will die first, the shareholders are, in a sense, gambling on their longevity. This may be unfair and unacceptable to older shareholders. Although this disparity may be alleviated somewhat by setting a particularly favorable price on their shares, the uncertainties involved may lead to friction and possible misunderstanding. Obviously all the shareholders should be adequately informed of the problem and the various risks prior to any decision to fund a repurchase program through insurance.

The disparity between the interests of senior shareholders and those of younger age may be further alleviated by not fully funding the repurchase through insurance, thereby avoiding pyramiding of coverage and lessening the windfall problem. This is particularly appropriate where the corporation is able, through periodic diversion of earnings to a reserve, to self-insure. A disadvantage with this approach might be the risk that, if the reserve should become unduly large, the scheme might be subject to attack as an unreasonable accumulation of corporate earnings.[154] The likelihood of such an attack is correspondingly lessened if more insurance is used, but this, of course, aggravates the problem of resolving inequities between differing shareholder groups. The solution thus becomes a matter of finding a suitable balance between funding through insurance and funding through corporate reserves.

Another technique might be to use term insurance, which carries no cash surrender value and which is lower in overall cost than ordinary life insurance. If a relatively inexpensive declining term policy is used, then, since the coverage shrinks with the passage of time, it is obviously important to supplement the policy through corporate reserves in order to fund the repurchase adequately. Although this increases the risk that the reserves might be attacked as an unreasonable accumulation of earnings, the comparatively low cost of term insurance may make this approach desirable. However, since the policy has no cash surrender value, the windfall problem already alluded to is perpetuated throughout the life of the policy. This is in contrast to an ordinary life policy, where the amount of windfall to surviving shareholders lessens with the passage of time, due to increased cash surrender values which may be taken into account in determining the book value of shares to be repurchased. The inequity of the arrangement may be particularly great if a term policy has been in effect for a number of years and the cost of maintaining it represents a diversion of a relatively large aggregate amount of corporate earnings. For this reason it might be desirable, in the term insurance situation, to provide that the *total* policy proceeds shall be included in corporate assets in determining the book value of the repurchased shares. Although this will entail pyramiding of coverage, and increased cost if the parties wish the repurchase to be fully funded, the expense may be justified in that relatively low-cost term insurance is being

[154] See Ch. V, text accompanying notes 101–118.

used instead of an ordinary life policy. Finally, with declining term insurance, the shareholders could agree not to fully fund the repurchase program through insurance, thus eliminating the pyramiding problem and reducing the cost, and yet agree that the full amount of the policy will be taken into account in computing book value of shares for repurchase.[155] The arrangement could then be supplemented by additional funding through corporate reserves, subject, of course, to the risk of a penalty tax on excess accumulation of earnings.

As one commentator has pointed out,[156] the choice between an ordinary life policy, term insurance or the use of reserves may, in the final analysis, resolve itself into whether or not the company considers itself able to obtain a better yield on invested funds by supervising its own investment program than by having such funds invested by an insurance company. If those in charge of investing corporate reserves are particularly astute, they may well be able to do better, even with conservative investments, than through an insurance scheme which necessarily involves the payment of overhead and other expenses to an outsider. In addition, if the company is fortunate to have a relatively good return on its own investment capital (i.e., a relatively high profit on assets employed in the business), the best investment of all may be to plow back reserves into the business itself rather than to invest them in outside sources. However, if the business involves a substantial degree of risk, and if profits are volatile and uncertain, although the potential profit of such an arrangement may be relatively great, the speculative element involved may render it inappropriate for funding a repurchase scheme, particularly if the shareholders are interested in security rather than gain. This may, in turn, suggest the funding of the program through at least a minimum amount of insurance. In addition, unlike the investment of reserves in outside sources or in the company itself, the yield of insurance, insofar as it is represented by increased cash surrender values, is not subject to income tax, although dividends paid by an insurer which are left with the company for further investment may give rise to taxable income in the form of interest paid on such invested amounts.[157] This makes insurance relatively attractive, especially for those companies which are unable to obtain reliable yields from invested funds in an amount sufficiently greater than that possible through insurance to compensate for the fact that such investment income is fully taxable.

It should be pointed out that the windfall problem arises also in connection with a cross-purchase arrangement between shareholders. Thus if two persons, each owning 50 percent of the shares of a corporation, were to take

[155] Another possibility is to include an amount equal to the aggregate premiums paid on the policy in corporate assets for the purpose of determining the book value of the shares.

[156] See D. Kahn, Basic Corporate Taxation 221 (1970).

[157] Theodore H. Cohen, 39 T.C. 1055 (1963), *acquiesced in*, 1964–1 Cum. Bull. (Part 1) 4; cf. Abram Nesbitt 2d, 43 T.C. 629 (1965).

out policies on the lives of one another and one were to die shortly thereafter, the surviving shareholder would receive the face amount of the policy and be able to acquire sole ownership of the corporation at a nominal cost (i.e., the premiums paid on the policy). The possible inequities in such an arrangement are even more apparent where shareholders own differing amounts of stock. Thus if one shareholder owns 80 percent of the shares and another 20 percent, the latter is required to maintain a policy four times the size of the former's policy, since he must fund a cross purchase of four times as much stock. If, after paying high premiums for a number of years, the person owning 20 percent of the shares were to die first, then his estate would receive only the book value of the 20 percent interest and nothing to reflect the cost of maintaining insurance on the other shareholder. Thus a minority shareholder who is relatively elderly and, perhaps, in poor health would be ill-advised to enter into an arrangement of this sort unless specific provisions are made to equalize the burden of paying premiums. In the case supposed, the two shareholders could agree that each would pay that percentage of the total premiums required to service the two policies that corresponds to his percentage interest in the company (i.e., the shareholder holding the 80 percent interest would pay 80 percent of the premiums on the two policies with the other shareholder paying the remainder). Another way of alleviating inequities between the two shareholders is through the use of ordinary life insurance, which would have a cash value on the date of death. Such a scheme is costly, however, particularly where one shareholder is elderly and owns large amounts of stock. One source of consolation in this situation might be the possibility that the majority shareholder might die first, perhaps shortly after the policies are taken out. In the latter case the minority shareholder would acquire sole ownership of the company at nominal cost. In any event, it is apparent that, as in the corporate repurchase arrangement, all the shareholders should be apprised of the fact that they are taking a gamble on their own longevity. To put the matter in its worst light, such insurance schemes may cause each shareholder to feel that he has, in a sense, a vested interest in having others predecease him. This is, at the very least, an unhealthy psychological perspective and it may have even more unfortunate repercussions in individual cases.

The corporate repurchase scheme may involve less of a gamble, or at least may be fairer in that where differing amounts of stock are held by various shareholders, those owning larger amounts indirectly bear a larger share of the burden of maintaining the insurance coverage. Thus, suppose that one shareholder owns 75 percent of the shares and another owns 25 percent and that the corporation takes out a policy on the life of each shareholder and pays the premiums. The indirect burden of maintaining such an arrangement (i.e., the amount of dividend income lost through diversion of corporate funds into the payment of premiums) will be three times as great on the person owning the larger percentage interest than it will be on the person owning only 25 percent interest (e.g., for every $100 the corporation spends in premium payments on the two policies, the 75 percent shareholder foregoes $75 in possible dividends whereas the other foregoes but $25).

Enough has probably been said to indicate the values and weaknesses of various types of insurance arrangements. All of them involve, to some extent, the element of risk or a gamble on who is to survive. All of them involve, to greater or lesser extent, cost through use of funds for premium payments which otherwise could be distributed in dividends or reinvested in the corporation. Such costs may be lessened through term insurance or corporate self-insurance through reserves, although, as already indicated, the latter alternative may increase the possibility of a penalty tax on excess accumulations. This, in turn, may be avoided through the use of corporate notes to pay part of the purchase price of the shares. As previously seen, it is relatively unlikely that a penalty tax would be imposed upon accumulations *subsequent* to the repurchase which were earmarked for the payment of principal and interest due on the notes.[158] However, it has also been seen that the use of notes involves some uncertainties for the note holder in that it has been held that payment on the notes may not be made when the corporation has insufficient surplus.[159] Thus the claimant can never be sure that he will receive the total amount due, since his note is but a conditional obligation. Although a pledge of shares to secure payment of the purchase price is unwise from a tax and business standpoint, the note holder may take a chattel mortgage or lien on real property to protect his interest more adequately.[160]

Where insurance is used, some consideration should be given to a life insurance trust. The trustee may either act on behalf of the corporation (receiving the policy proceeds and handling repurchases of shares) or on behalf of the shareholders (paying premiums, having custody of the policies, receiving the proceeds and handling the mechanics of cross purchases.) Needless to say, the trust instrument should clearly specify on whose behalf the trustee is acting, for otherwise the tax consequences of premium payments, receipt of proceeds, etc., become unclear. Use of the trust device in the cross-purchase situation will reduce the overall cost of the insurance through reducing the number of policies required. Thus, if there are three shareholders, instead of each shareholder taking out a policy on the lives of the other two shareholders (resulting in six policies), the trustee need take out only one policy on each shareholder in an amount necessary to

---

[158] See Ch. V, text accompanying notes 110–115.
[159] See text accompanying note 72 *supra.*
[160] See id. note 77 *supra.*

fund the repurchase of his shares. The advantages of this approach obviously increase with the number of shareholders involved and the number of policies which otherwise would be required.

Another significant advantage of a life insurance trust is to enable the shareholders to select various settlement options available under the policy (in contrast to where the corporation is the beneficiary and the shareholders have no such right of selection). The various settlement options will differ with the type of policy and the particular insurer. Common options include schemes whereby the proceeds are paid out in equal installments over a fixed period of time (the amount of each installment depending upon the earning capacity of the principal balance retained by the insurer), fixed amounts over a period of time which depends upon the earnings of the principal balance retained (the period of payment and the total number of payments increasing if the principal amount invested by the insurer earns more), and annuities of various types, such as simple annuities, joint and survivor annuities and annuities with refund arrangements (i.e., payments for the life of an individual, or for his life and the life of the survivor, with a fixed sum guaranteed regardless of the longevity of either or both annuitants).[161] Whether or not a trustee is used, it is important that the arrangement specify in some way that the policy proceeds are not to be paid over until the shareholder, or his estate, surrenders the stock for repurchase. This can easily be done by suitable terms in the instrument creating the trust, requiring the trustee to hold the proceeds until the shares have been surrendered. If no trustee is used, then the clause in the policy which designates the manner in which the proceeds are to be paid by the insurer can specify that the latter will distribute the proceeds only upon receiving notice from the company that the shares have been surrendered and that, in default of receiving such a notice, that the proceeds will be paid to the company.[162] Even if the less cumbersome method of using a trustee is employed, care should be taken that the arrangement meets with the approval of the insurer, since many policies prohibit a trustee from making an election among various optional types of settlements.[163] In addition, if a Subchapter S election is in effect, one should avoid having the trustee hold shares in the company, for that may result in a termination of the election on the ground that a trust may not hold shares in a Subchapter S corporation.[164] Thus the shares should be surrendered directly to the company for cancellation or for resale or reissuance to other shareholders.

Cross-purchase plans, although used less frequently than corporate repurchase plans, have several advantages. First, the repurchase of the shares by other shareholders will not entail the tax problems encountered in con-

---

[161] For a more detailed description of various settlement options, see D. Kahn, id. at 210–216.

[162] Id. at 212 (setting forth suitable language for such a clause).

[163] Ibid.

[164] See Ch. I, text accompanying notes 118–121.

nection with corporate repurchases or redemptions, namely, that the corporate repurchase might be essentially equivalent to a dividend and thus give rise to taxation at ordinary rates. Secondly, there is no problem as regards excessive accumulation of earnings and the consequent risk of a penalty tax. Thirdly, the shareholders who acquire shares under a cross-purchase plan receive a basis of "cost" in the shares so acquired. Often this will be a higher basis than the basis which they carry on their original shares (which, of course, retain that lower basis so that the shareholders thereafter have at least two blocks of stock, each with a separate basis). With a corporate repurchase, the surviving shareholders continue to retain their own shares, probably at a relatively low basis. The basis of the reacquired shares in the hands of the corporation is a purely theoretical consideration, since no gain is recognized to the corporation on the resale of the stock.[165] Although the surviving shareholders would receive a new cost basis if the corporation were to resell the shares to them for cash or property, they receive no new basis if the shares are distributed as a stock dividend.[166] Thus, unless the shareholders make further capital contributions to the corporation, they retain their original basis in their investment. Compared with the cross-purchase scheme, where the survivors end up with at least two blocks of stock, one of which may carry a higher cost basis, the corporate repurchase or redemption scheme is less advantageous. The tax difference is only important if the surviving shareholders intend to dispose of their shares, either by sale to each other or to an outsider, or by sale or redemption to the corporation, before death. If the shares are held until death, they receive a new basis, either the value at the date of death or on the alternate valuation date one year after death.[167] Obviously this new basis resulting from death is advantageous to any shareholder, including the one whose shares were originally subject to either a corporate repurchase or a shareholder cross purchase, in that it is unlikely that there will be a significant difference between the new basis, i.e., the fair market value at the date of death, and the price at which the shares are sold to the corporation or to the other shareholders. The result is that the amount of gain is likely to be negligible.

A disadvantage with the cross-purchase arrangement arises from the unfavorable tax consequences which flow from the surviving shareholders' acquiring life insurance policies held by the estate of the decedent. Thus, in a corporation consisting of three shareholders, A, B and C, if A should die and his shares should be acquired equally by B and C, the latter would require more insurance to fund a further cross purchase between themselves since their interests would be worth more. Since A had previously taken out policies on the lives of B and C, an obvious possibility would be for B to purchase from A's estate the policy A held on C's life and for C to purchase

---

[165] Int. Rev. Code of 1954, §1032.
[166] Id. §307(a).
[167] Id. §1014.

the policy A held on B's life. Although such policies would probably require lower premium payments than new policies taken out on the lives of either of the survivors, the tax disadvantage with this approach would become apparent if either B or C should die. Thus if B should die the proceeds of the policy on B's life that C acquired from A's estate would not be fully exempt from taxation under Section 101 of the Code. Rather, the so-called "transfer for value" rule would require C to include the proceeds of the policy as ordinary income, except that amount which represented what he paid A's estate to acquire the policy, plus any premium payments he made after the policy was acquired.[168] In sharp contrast, the "transfer for value" rule does not apply if the policies are acquired by the corporation.[169] Accordingly, on A's death the corporation could acquire his policies and, if B and C were to agree that, thereafter, the scheme would be converted into a corporate repurchase or redemption arrangement, the program could be funded with the least expense and with few adverse tax consequences. In this manner, B and C, having purchased A's shares, would receive a new cost basis, but the corporation, having purchased from A's estate the policies on the lives of B and C, would not be subject to the "transfer for value" rule as regards its subsequent receipt of the insurance proceeds. If the plan is to make a transition to a corporate repurchase arrangement, then the policies that B and C hold on the lives of each other can be assigned to the corporation, which then continues payment of premiums, being the sole beneficiary and retaining the incidents of ownership, in order that its payment of the premiums may not be taxed as a constructive dividend to B and C.[170]

Further disadvantages with the cross-purchase scheme have already been mentioned, namely, the increased cost of the programs where there are numerous shareholders and each shareholder must take out a separate policy on each of the other shareholders, and also the unfavorable tax consequences of having funds distributed by the corporation to enable shareholders to pay premiums on the policies, where the shareholders are in relatively high tax brackets.[171] And if the shareholders are in differing tax brackets, the tax impact is unequal. Added to this are further disparities, arising where younger minority shareholders, who receive less by way of compensation, must take out insurance in relatively large amounts on older shareholders, who hold large blocks of stock, paying high premiums because of the advanced age of the insured or his poor health, such that the whole arrangement becomes unfeasible. This is particularly so if some shareholders die and others receive a windfall when they have paid relatively little in premiums.[172]

[168] Id. §101(a)(2).
[169] Id. §101(a)(2)(B).
[170] See text accompanying note 142 *supra*.
[171] See id. note 152 *supra*.
[172] See id. note 157 *supra*. D. Kahn, Basic Corporate Taxation 242 (1970), points

Although the choice between a corporate repurchase or a shareholder cross-purchase program must inevitably depend upon the facts of each particular situation, it seems safe to say that the cross-purchase technique will be advisable only where there are relatively few shareholders, where all shareholders are of approximately the same age, and where they have modest income and thus are in relatively low tax brackets. Even here the arrangement will result in favorable tax treatment only if the corporation can distribute sufficient amounts of additional compensation in tax deductible form to enable shareholders to pay the premiums on the various insurance policies.

In view of what has been said, it would appear that the usefulness of the cross-purchase approach is confined to a relatively specialized fact situation. If the cross-purchase approach is chosen, the utmost care should be taken that the corporation must not repurchase the shares and thus satisfy the personal obligations of the shareholders. As we have seen, except where each shareholder holds merely an *option* on the shares of the others, such a corporate repurchase will result in a constructive dividend to the shareholder whose obligation is discharged.[173] Thus, in the situation previously described, where the shareholders initially enter into a cross-purchase agreement and then, in order to avoid the "transfer for value" rule, the policies are transferred to the corporation and the scheme is converted into a corporate repurchase arrangement, care should be taken that the obsolete cross-purchase agreement is cancelled, i.e., that there is a complete novation and the personal obligation of each shareholder is effectively replaced by a corporate obligation. Unless this is done, a later repurchase of shares by the corporation may be attacked as a constructive dividend. In addition, as already pointed out, a constructive dividend will result from the corporate payment of the premiums unless the corporation is given full incidents of ownership and becomes the sole beneficiary of the policies.[174] Corporate ownership of the policies will also insure that the policy proceeds are not subject to estate tax if any shareholder should die.[175]

Where a corporate stock repurchase or redemption approach is used, var-

---

out that, although the younger shareholder, who also may own a minority interest, is required to pay larger premiums to insure the life of an older shareholder, he may be compensated for this by the likelihood that the older shareholder will probably predecease him. If this happens at a relatively early date, then the survivor receives a windfall. Even if the older shareholder lives for some period of time, the younger shareholder is likely eventually to receive an ample *quid pro quo* for the high insurance premiums which he must pay. The real financial loss will come only if the younger shareholder dies first. And all of this assumes that the younger man either can afford the higher premiums or that increased compensation can be paid to him in tax deductible form so as to enable him to make the payments. Whether or not this can be done obviously depends upon the situation—i.e., the age of the other shareholder, his health and the amount of stock he owns.

173 See text accompanying note 133 *supra.*
174 See id. note 142 *supra.*
175 See id. note 145 *supra.*

ious problems arise in connection with the effect of the corporate payment of premiums on the policies, and the receipt of the policy proceeds, on the earnings and profits of the company. Since the taxability of dividend distributions depends upon the extent of corporate earnings and profits,[176] it will obviously be advantageous for shareholders to argue that earnings and profits are reduced or at least are not increased by events such as the foregoing. The earnings and profits are reduced to the extent that the premiums paid exceed the increase in the cash surrender value of the various policies (i.e., the extent to which the payment does not reflect a purchase or growth of a capital asset represented by increased cash surrender values).[177] According to the Internal Revenue Service, the receipt by the corporation of the policy proceeds, although not taxable to the corporation,[178] increases its earnings and profits to the extent that the amount received exceeds the aggregate premiums paid on the policy.[179] Seemingly, that amount of the premiums paid which was previously deducted from earnings and profits[180] should also be included in earnings and profits when the policy proceeds are received, but it is uncertain whether the Internal Revenue Service requires this.[181] Where the stock is repurchased or redeemed (whether or not through the use of the policy proceeds), the effect on earnings and profits depends upon how the redemption is characterized. To the extent that the redemption is essentially equivalent to a dividend and thus taxable under Section 301 of the Code, the amount distributed reduces earnings and profits in the same manner as any other dividend.[182] If the redemption is not given dividend treatment, then the Code provides that "the part of such distribution which is properly chargeable to capital account shall not be treated as a distribution of earnings and profits." [183] The regulations, rulings and case law are unclear as to the proper method of determining the amount which should be properly chargeable to capital account in specific instances. Thus, where stock was originally paid for with property or services, it is unclear whether, on the repurchase of the stock, the capital account should be reduced by the fair market value of the property or services (presumably on the date the property was contributed or the services rendered) or whether the capital account should be reduced by the basis of the property to the corporation (which, in a tax-free exchange under Section 351 of the Code, will correspond to the adjusted basis of the transferor,

176 Int. Rev. Code of 1954, §316.
177 See D. Kahn, id. at 201–202. See also B. Bittker and J. Eustice, Federal Income Taxation of Corporations and Shareholders 160 n.25 (1966).
178 Int. Rev. Code of 1954, §101, and text accompanying note 143 *supra*.
179 Rev. Rul. 54–230, 1954–1 Cum. Bull. 114.
180 See text accompanying note 177 *supra*.
181 See D. Kahn, id. at 207–208. See also B. Bittker and J. Eustice, id. at 157 n.16, 160 n.25.
182 Int. Rev. Code of 1954, §312(a) (providing that, where property is distributed, the earnings and profits are reduced by an amount equal to the adjusted basis of the property).
183 Id. §312(e).

increased by any gain recognized to him).[184] And if the distribution reduces earnings and profits, is the amount of the reduction limited to the distributee's ratable share of earnings and profits at the time of the distribution?[185] Even more perplexing are problems arising where there are several classes of stock, each carrying different par values (or some with no par) and different liquidation preferences. Pending further clarification from the case law or rulings, the proper result must depend upon the facts of each situation.[186]

Both with the corporate stock repurchase and with the shareholder cross-purchase situations, it will be important for the shareholder whose shares are repurchased to avoid having the policy proceeds subjected to estate tax and also to see that the price at which the shares are repurchased also sets their value for estate tax purposes. As previously pointed out,[187] the policy proceeds will not be included in the decedent's gross estate if, under the terms of the policy, they are not payable to his executor and if he possessed no incidents of ownership in the policy at the date of his death. The price at which the shares are repurchased will normally be the value at which the shares are taxed for estate tax purposes *if* (a) the estate of the decedent is obligated to sell the shares, (b) the agreement prevented the decedent from disposing of the shares during his lifetime without first offering them to the corporation or to the other shareholders at the stipulated price and (c) the agreement was entered into at arm's length with the corporation and does not represent a self-serving attempt by those in control to lessen their estate tax by disposing of their shares for an amount which is unreasonably low, in the light of the conditions prevailing at the time the agreement was entered into.[188] In addition, the agreement itself must be valid from the corporate

---

[184] Id. §362(b).

[185] *Compare* Helvering v. Jarvis, 123 F.2d 742 (4th Cir. 1941) *with* Woodward Investment Co., 46 B.T.A. 648 (1942) *acquiesced in,* 1942–2 Cum. Bull. 20 (pro rata distribution in partial liquidation held chargeable to earnings and profits in the proportion that the latter bears to the corporation's net worth). See Rev. Rul. 70–531, 1970–42 I.R.B. 7, withdrawing a prior acquiescence in the *Jarvis* case and acquiescing in the result of the *Woodward* case.

[186] For further discussion and some illustrative problems, see B. Bittker and J. Eustice, id. at 323–325.

[187] See text accompanying note 145 *supra.*

[188] Treas. Reg. §20.2031–2(h) and Rev. Rul. 59–60, 1959–1 Cum. Bull. 237, 243–244. See May v. McGowan, 194 F.2d 396 (2d Cir. 1952); Slocum v. United States, 256 F. Supp. 753 (S.D.N.Y. 1966); Estate of Orville B. Littick, 31 T.C. 181 (1958), *acquiesced in,* 1959–2 Cum. Bull. 5. The reasonableness of the agreement is determined by facts existing at the time it was entered into. Thus a disparity between the price as set by the agreement and the apparent fair value of the shares at the date of death does not prevent the sale price (rather than the fair value) from being determinative for estate tax purposes. However, a wide disparity might well lead to a contest on the point with the Internal Revenue Service and thus, to avoid litigation, it is best, especially in family corporations, to adopt a flexible price such as book value which more nearly reflects the actual worth of the shares. See Note, The Use of Life Insurance to Fund Agreements Providing for Disposition of a Business Interest at Death, 71 Harv. L. Rev. 687, 693 (1958). For a discussion of various methods of setting a purchase price on shares, see Ch. III, text accompanying notes 49–66.

law standpoint, for otherwise it does not bind the shareholder to sell.[189] What must be avoided, then, is an agreement which merely gives the decedent or his estate an *option* to sell the shares, i.e., the agreement must provide that he or his estate is bound to offer them to the corporation or the other shareholders at the stipulated price. If the prospective purchasers are not themselves bound to purchase, i.e., if, although the seller is *bound* to sell, the corporation or its shareholders merely have *options* to purchase, then the price stipulated in the agreement is controlling for estate tax purposes *if* the other requirements, previously mentioned, are also met (i.e., if the agreement bound the decedent during his lifetime and if it represented a bona fide business bargain) and if the shares are not sold to a third party for a greater amount.[190] To be on the safe side, however, the agreement should bind both parties to buy and sell and this arrangement is of course far more satisfactory from the standpoint of the decedent and his estate. In fact, due to the limited marketability of shares in a closely held corporation, the decedent can be assured liquidity of his investment only through a guarantee that either the corporation or the other shareholders will purchase them.

If, for some reason, the policy proceeds are included in the decedent's estate, as where the decedent possessed incidents of ownership in the policy, then it is only fair that the value of his shares for estate tax purposes be reduced by the policy proceeds.[191] Otherwise he is taxed twice.

As already indicated, one problem with having a corporate repurchase agreement is that of taking suitable precautions that the corporation will have sufficient funds to lawfully perform its part of the agreement. Under most state statutes this is expressed in terms of sufficiency of surplus —either earned surplus which results from accumulated corporate profits, or capital surplus, which results from an excess of amounts paid into the capital account over the par value or stated consideration for shares issued.[192] Although most repurchases are funded through the use of insur-

---

[189] Thus an absolute prohibition against selling the shares or requiring the consent of directors or shareholders would probably be invalid under most state laws. See id. note 10. However, for a recent statute validating such restrictions, see Del. Gen. Corp. Law §202(c) (1967). See also Ch. XI, text accompanying note 87. Although agreements requiring a corporation to purchase shares have sometimes been held invalid if they lack "mutuality of obligation" due to the uncertainty that the corporation will have sufficient surplus to perform the agreement, such agreements are generally valid if entered into for a reasonable business purpose, if their terms are fair and if some provision has been made for enabling the corporation to perform its part of the agreement, such as by funding through insurance. See Ch. III, text accompanying note 33.

[190] Commissioner v. Bensel, 100 F.2d 639 (3d Cir. 1938).

[191] Estate of John T. H. Mitchell, 37 B.T.A. 1 (1938), *acquiesced in,* 1938–1 Cum. Bull. 20; cf. Estate of Ray E. Tompkins, 13 T.C. 1054 (1949), *acquiesced in,* 1950–1 Cum. Bull. 5.

[192] See Ch. III, text accompanying note 35. For a good discussion of the general problems in this area, see Herwitz, Installment Repurchase of Stock: Surplus Limitations, 79 Harv. L. Rev. 303 (1965). As Herwitz points out, many states also prohibit

ance or by the maintenance of adequate reserves, there are other ways. Principally these consist of writing up assets to create "revaluation surplus" or reducing capital to create "reduction surplus." Of these two methods, writing up assets is by far the more controversial. The leading case permitting such write-ups is *Randall v. Bailey*.[193] Although the question presented there was whether a corporation could revalue assets for the purpose of determining surplus available for cash dividends, the considerations are basically the same where the repurchase of shares is restricted to surplus. The decision has not generally been followed in other states.[194] Although it has been argued that the Model Business Corporation Act permits the revaluation of assets for the purpose of determining the availability of surplus either for dividend payments or for the repurchase of shares,[195] this procedure is controversial and, except in those situations where repurchases may be made out of stated capital [196] (in which case a revaluation of assets would not be necessary), revaluation is permissible only in a minority of states.[197] Even where permitted, assets should be revalued only if their appreciation is likely to be more or less permanent. Thus land might be revalued to reflect increases in value over a relatively long period of time. In sharp contrast, temporary fluctuations in the values of more volatile assets, such as investments in a portfolio or inventory, should not be reflected in write-ups to surplus. In fact, one of the main reasons for not permitting asset values to be written up is the unreliability of surplus accounts which are based on gains which may or may not be realized on sale of the assets. Where asset values fluctuate widely and often, the unreliability is obviously at its greatest.

If there has been depreciation or unrealized diminution in the value of assets, this generally must be taken into account in determining net assets in excess of stated capital, even in those states which do not permit unrealized appreciation to be used for a similar purpose. Although, here again, much will depend upon the character of the asset involved (e.g., inventory items

---

a corporation from purchasing its own shares when it is insolvent or when the effect of the purchase would make it insolvent. See Model Bus. Corp. Act §6. The Model Act §2(n) defines "insolvent" as meaning inability to pay debts in the usual course of business.

[193] 299 N.Y. 280, 43 N.E.2d 43 (1942).

[194] See 7 Z. Cavitch, Business Organizations 381 (1969).

[195] *Compare* Seward, Earned Surplus—Its Meaning and Use in the Model Business Corporation Act, 38 Va. L. Rev. 433, 440 (1952), *with* Hackney, The Financial Provisions of the Model Business Corporation Act, 70 Harv. L. Rev. 1357, 1377 (1957). See also Gibson, Surplus, So What?—The Model Act Modernized, 17 Bus. Law. 476 (1962).

[196] Thus the Model Act permits use of stated capital for acquisition of shares in eliminating fractional shares, collecting or compromising indebtedness to the corporation, paying dissenting shareholders the value of their shares (as in a merger) or effecting the redemption or repurchase of redeemable shares (i.e., preferred) for retirement. Model Bus. Corp. Act §6. See 7 Z. Cavitch, id. at 823.

[197] See 7 Z. Cavitch, id. at 381.

must be carried at the lower of cost or market, investment securities should be treated like inventory items if held for trading purposes and, if held for long-term investment, should be written down only if a loss appears to be more or less permanent in nature[198]), the decisions appear to be stricter in imposing write-downs than they are liberal in allowing write-ups.[199] There is one exception, namely, where write-downs are required because of losses, etc., which threaten to bring about a capital impairment, then write-ups are permitted to the extent required to offset the write-downs, provided that the write-ups represent more than a transitory appreciation in value.[200] In one state this procedure is expressly permitted by statute.[201]

Since writing up assets is permitted only in a few states,[202] a much better technique for generating surplus in share repurchase is through a reduction of capital. This is permitted, with various statutory safeguards, in most states.[203] The most common requirements are a shareholder vote and a prohibition against reducing capital to an amount which is less than the involuntary liquidation preference of any preferred shares.[204] However, in some states distributions of assets to shareholders in connection with a capital reduction are prohibited unless the corporate assets remaining after the reduction of capital (and presumably the assets remaining after the proposed distribution) are sufficient to pay any debts of the corporation, "the payment of which shall not have been otherwise provided for." [205] There may also be a requirement that notice of the reduction be published in a newspaper where the registered office of the corporation is located.[206]

Where there are several classes of stock, the question arises whether the capital of one class may be reduced with the capital of the other left intact, and also whether the capital of senior securities (such as preferred shares) may be reduced when the capital of shares having subordinate rights has not been exhausted. Although one state requires the exhaustion of the capi-

---

[198] For a good discussion of the whole area see W. Cary, Cases and Materials on Corporations 1506–1509 (4th ed. unabr. 1969). The classic exposition of the many ramifications of the problem is E. Dodd and R. Baker, Cases and Materials on Corporations 1054–1103 (2d ed. 1951).

[199] Ibid.

[200] See Titus v. Piggly Wiggly Corp., 2 Tenn. App. 184, 194–197 (1925).

[201] Mich. Gen. Corp. Act §21.22 (1948).

[202] E.g., New York and possibly Missouri, where the statutory provision, although patterned after a similar provision in the Illinois statutes, omitted Illinois' express prohibition against write-ups. Compare Ill. Bus. Corp. Act §41 (1933), with Mo. Gen. & Bus. Corp. Law §§351.220, 351.390 (1963). This has led some commentators to conclude by negative implication that the Missouri legislature intended to permit unrealized appreciation to be taken into account. See Lyons, Relationship of Officers, Directors and Shareholders to the Corporation (Missouri Business Enterprises 351, 361 (Mo. Bar Cont. Leg. Ed. 1962)).

[203] See Model Bus. Corp. Act §69.

[204] Ibid.

[205] E.g., Mo. Gen. & Bus. Corp. Law §351.195 (1965). See also Del. Gen. Corp. Law §244(a) (1967).

[206] E.g., Del. Gen. Corp. Law §244(e) (1967).

tal of common shares before the capital of preferred may be reduced,[207] most states have no such requirement, although in a number of states capital of the preferred may not be reduced without a class vote.[208] A number of statutes permit the reduction of capital through a repurchase of shares followed by their cancellation. The mere act of repurchase does not itself amount to a capital reduction if the shares are held as treasury shares. In this situation the Model Act requires that earned surplus, if used for the repurchase, must be "restricted" as long as the shares are held as treasury shares.[209] In effect this makes the earned surplus unavailable for further distributions, by dividends or otherwise, unless the shares are resold and the restriction is lifted.[210] If the shares are cancelled, this results in the reduction of capital and the creation of capital surplus.[211] In contrast to other methods of capital reduction, no shareholder vote is required.[212] Where the cancelled shares were previously acquired out of earned surplus and the latter has been restricted, the Model Act is unclear as to the effect of the cancellation on the earned surplus account. Some commentators have assumed that the restriction is lifted on cancellation, just as it would have been lifted if the shares had been sold.[213] However, another and possibly better approach would be to view the earned surplus account as having been permanently reduced and any surviving surplus account would be in the nature of capital surplus.[214] In effect this would mean that earned surplus could not be used "over again" to effect a seriatim or "creeping" reduction of capital, i.e., earned surplus could be used for share repurchases but not in an amount greater than the total earned surplus available and could be used only once. If the shares are cancelled, then any surplus arising from cancellation would be capital surplus. Cash distributions and share repurchases out of capital surplus are generally subject to greater restrictions than those made out of earned surplus.[215]

Although some statutes have required that a purchase of shares for retirement be made pro rata among the holders of the shares in order to assure

[207] Page v. Whittenton Mfg. Co., 211 Mass. 424, 428, 97 N.E. 1006, 1007 (1912).

[208] See W. Cary, Cases and Materials on Corporations 1560–1561 (4th ed. unabr. 1969). See also, e.g., N.Y. Bus. Corp. Law §§802, 804 (1961).

[209] Model Bus. Corp. Act §6. In the case of a repurchase or redemption of redeemable shares, the Model Act provides that the repurchase or redemption "effects" a cancellation. Yet a statement of cancellation must still be filed under Section 67 of the Act.

[210] For further discussion as to the effect of resale on earned surplus which has been previously restricted, see Hackney, The Financial Provisions of the Model Business Corporation Act, 70 Harv. L. Rev. 1357, 1392–1396 (1957).

[211] Model Bus. Corp. Act §§68, 70.

[212] Ibid.

[213] See Hackney, *supra.* See also Rudolph, Accounting for Treasury Shares Under the Model Business Corporation Act, 73 Harv. L. Rev. 323, 328 (1959).

[214] See D. Herwitz, Business Planning 426 (1966).

[215] Model Bus. Corp. Act §§6, 46. For further discussion see Comment, The Current Law Regarding Reduction of Capital: Its Methodology, Purposes and Dangers, 110 U. Pa. L. Rev. 723, 727 (1962).

that one or a small number of shareholders are not unduly favored,[216] a number of statutes now provide that the purchase may be made "at private sale" or pro rata as the directors deem advisable unless the articles of incorporation specifically require that reacquisitions be pro rata.[217]

6.5 FIDUCIARY DUTIES IN SHARE REPURCHASES

Where shares are repurchased, officers and directors have a fiduciary duty to disclose to those from whom the shares are acquired information known to them which has a material bearing on the value of the shares where there are "special facts" which give rise to the duty. This, at least, is the rule under the laws of most states.[218] The classical view that the officers and directors owe no duty to shareholders other than to refrain from fraud has now been completely discredited.[219] In fact, some states go further than the so-called special facts rule and impose on officers and directors fiduciary duties akin to those imposed on a trustee.[220] This requires disclosure even in the absence of special facts. The difference between this and the special facts rule is largely one of degree, since a court, by broadening its concept of what is meant by special facts, can tighten the duty of disclosure to a strict fiduciary standard.[221] If the corporation, its officers and directors have a duty of disclosure, then a similar duty is imposed on those who hold a majority of the shares, in purchasing shares from others who hold a minority interest. At least this is so where the majority shareholders have "access" to information which is not available to the minority.[222] However, if a minor-

---

[216] E.g., General Inv. Co. v. American Hide & Leather Co., 98 N.J. Eq. 326, 331, 129 Atl. 244, 246 (Ct. Err. & App. 1925). The *American Leather* case has now been superseded by a statutory permission to purchase other than by pro rata. See R. Baker & W. Cary, Cases and Materials on Corporations 1412 n.2 (3d ed. unabr. 1959).

[217] See e.g., Martin v. American Potash & Chemical Corp., 33 Del. Ch. 234, 92 A.2d 295 (Sup. Ct. 1952). See also H. Ballantine, Corporations 632–633 (1946).

[218] The leading case is Strong v. Repide, 213 U.S. 419 (1909). There the defendant, a director and owner of three fourths of the shares of a Philippine corporation, was also its administrator general and, in this capacity, was in charge of negotiations leading to the sale of company lands to the United States Government. While the negotiations were approaching a climax, he acquired the plaintiff's shares through a third party, without disclosing his identity as purchaser nor disclosing the state of the negotiations. In finding that these "special facts" gave rise to a duty of disclosure, the Supreme Court was applying civil law, since the case came up from the Philippines, yet it indicated that the common law rule was the same. See 3 L. Loss, Securities Regulation 1447 (1961).

[219] See 3 id. at 1446–1448.

[220] E.g., Oliver v. Oliver, 118 Ga. 362, 45 S.E. 232 (1903); Hotchkiss v. Fischer, 136 Kan. 530, 31 P.2d 37 (1934); Stewart v. Harris, 69 Kan. 498, 77 Pac. 277 (1904).

[221] 3 Loss, id. at 1447, indicates that "In actual results the old 'majority' rule has substantially merged into the 'special circumstances' doctrine, which in turn is scarcely distinguishable from the so-called 'minority' rule."

[222] E.g., Zahn v. Transamerica Corp., 162 F.2d 36 (3d Cir. 1947).

ity shareholder is also an officer or director, as is often the case in a closely held concern, then he is likely to be familiar with the operations of the company. In this situation majority shareholders are not required to disclose facts which are known to him or which he could quickly ascertain by making an appropriate investigation.[223]

In the case of a redemption or repurchase of redeemable shares, disclosure is not required unless the person from whom the shares are acquired has some alternative other than to surrender them for redemption. Thus, if the shares are convertible into common stock, a repurchase or redemption is unlawful unless the corporation or those in control disclose material facts, unknown to the shareholders, which are pertinent to the decision whether to surrender the shares or convert them.[224]

Although, as we have seen, the disclosure duties under state law have evolved from the classical view (and former so-called majority rule), that only misrepresentation or active concealment is prohibited, to the special facts rule which, in turn, is coalescing with the stricter minority rule imposing even broader duties, state law itself is rapidly being displaced by a veritable flood of litigation under rule 10b-5 promulgated by the Securities and Exchange Commission under Section 10(b) of the Securities Exchange Act of 1934.[225]

A common error of those who are unacquainted with the federal securities laws is to assume that they are inapplicable to dealings in shares of closely held corporations. To some extent the error is understandable since the Securities Act of 1933 [226] covers only a public offering of shares and many provisions of the Securities Exchange Act of 1934 formerly covered only those companies whose shares were listed on a national securities exchange.[227] Although the latter statute has now been broadened to include companies whose shares are traded over the counter if they have assets in excess of $1 million and a class of equity security held of record by at least five hundred persons,[228] it goes without saying that such companies are not closely held within any sensible definition of the term. However, at least one section of the Securities Exchange Act of 1934 goes well beyond the other provisions of the statute and includes purchases or sales of securities in *any* company, regardless of its size and regardless of whether its shares are held publicly, actively traded or held only by a few individuals. This is

---

[223] See Kohler v. Kohler Co., 319 F.2d 634 (7th Cir. 1963). There the plaintiff-seller held 11 percent of the shares in a closely held family corporation and was a former officer-director.

[224] See Zahn v. Transamerica Corp., 162 F.2d 36 (3rd Cir. 1947). See also Speed v. Transamerica Corp., 99 F. Supp. 808 (D. Del. 1951).

[225] 48 Stat. 881, 891 (1934), 15 U.S.C. §78j. SEC rule 10b–5 is at 17 C.F.R. §240. 10b–5 (1942).

[226] 48 Stat. 74 (1933), 15 U.S.C. §§77a–77bbbb.

[227] See Securities Exchange Act of 1934, §12, 15 U.S.C. §78-1, before its amendment on August 20, 1964, by Pub. L. 88–467, 78 Stat. 565.

[228] Securities Exchange Act of 1934, §12(g), 15 U.S.C. §78-1(g).

Section 10(b), which makes it unlawful for *any person*, by the use of any means or instrumentality of interstate commerce or the mails, or of any facility of a national securities exchange, to use or employ any "manipulative or deceptive device or contrivance" in connection with the purchase or sale of *any* security in contravention of SEC rules. In 1942 the SEC promulgated its rule 10b-5, which reads as follows:

> It shall be unlawful for any person, directly or indirectly, by the use of any means or instrumentality of interstate commerce, or of the mails, or of any facility of any national securities exchange,
>
> (1) to employ any device, scheme, or artifice to defraud,
>
> (2) to make any untrue statement of a material fact or to omit to state a material fact necessary in order to make the statements made, in the light of the circumstances under which they were made, not misleading, or
>
> (3) to engage in any act, practice, or course of business which operates or would operate as a fraud or deceit upon any person, in connection with the purchase or sale of any security.

This is not the place to engage in an extensive analysis of the above rule and the extraordinary way in which it has developed, through case law and administrative interpretation, into a pervasive structure of federal regulation not only of so-called insider trading but also of breaches of fiduciary duty when they arise "in connection with the purchase or sale of any security." Treatises have been written on the subject and the law remains unclear.[229] It may suffice to say that since it has now been firmly established that violations of the rule give rise to civil liability,[230] a person from whom shares are purchased or redeemed may have a federal cause of action if he can show the necessary jurisdictional facts (i.e., a purchase "by the use of . . . interstate commerce, or . . . the mails," etc.) and a breach of the duty created by the rule, namely, to refrain from untrue statements or half-truths and, in certain situations, to make affirmative disclosure of material facts known to the purchaser which might influence the seller's decision as to whether to part with his shares and as to the price he is willing to receive for them.[231]

As far as the jurisdictional basis for the rule is concerned, the courts have not required that the fraud itself be done through the mails. Thus a misrepresentation in a face-to-face conversation is sufficient if the mails are used to complete the purchase, as where the purchase is confirmed by a letter or the stock certificate is delivered by mail.[232]

---

[229] For a comprehensive treatment of rule 10b–5, see A. Bromberg, Securities Law: Fraud—SEC Rule 10b–5 (1967). See also 3 L. Loss, Securities Regulation 1445–1528 (1961); W. Painter, Federal Regulation of Insider Trading (1968).

[230] See A. Bromberg, id. at §2.4. The first case imposing civil liability, Kardon v. National Gypsum Co., 69 F. Supp. 512 (E.D. Pa. 1946), involved the purchase by two officer-directors from two other officer-directors of stock in two closely held corporations.

[231] See List v. Fashion Park, Inc., 340 F.2d 457 (2d Cir. 1965), *cert. denied sub nom.* List v. Lerner, 382 U.S. 811 (1965).

[232] See 3 L. Loss, id. at 1519–1528; A. Bromberg, id. at §11.2.

One of the most difficult aspects of the rule is to determine when it requires affirmative disclosure of material facts—i.e., when pure nondisclosure unrelated to a half-truth gives rise to liability. Much depends upon the particular circumstances and who is doing the purchasing. Severe difficulties arise where a purchase is carried out on a national securities exchange. There the transaction is effected through brokers acting as agents for the real parties in interest and to require disclosure seems incongruous in the flurry and roar of trading. Yet, since the rule expressly applies to transactions on a national securities exchange, the courts have found a duty to disclose.[233] Since personal disclosure by the purchaser to the seller is unfeasible in this context (the two being unknown to one another as a general rule), what this means is that the purchaser may not buy until there has been public disclosure. The ramifications of this approach, particularly the baffling problem of who is liable to whom and for how much,[234] need not be considered here, for it is axiomatic that shares in a closely held corporation are not traded on a stock exchange and are infrequently traded at all. Most of the transactions will thus involve face-to-face dealings. The main problems arise in determining what is a "material" fact which must be disclosed and when the duty to disclose arises.

As already indicated, "materiality" relates to those facts which would influence a reasonable investor in his decision to part with the security at the price agreed upon, as well as facts which, "in reasonable and objective contemplation might affect the value of the corporation's stock or securities." [235] The test is really two pronged, i.e., it refers to what may be relevant to a reasonable investor and also to what might have a "substantial effect" on the value of the stock. The two are closely related and it is arguable that the tests are, in reality, one and the same. However, since at least one court has construed the term "reasonable investor" to include not only prudent investors but also others of a more speculative bent,[236] it is possible that the reasonable investor concept may embrace certain facts which would not necessarily have a substantial effect on the market price if disclosed. Thus developments in the research department of a pharmaceutical corporation might be material under a speculative investor test even though they are still in the exploratory stage and there is no assurance that they would result in a new product.[237]

Fortunately the problem of determining materiality is lessened where the

---

233 SEC v. Texas Gulf Sulphur Co., 401 F.2d 833 (2d Cir. 1968) (*en banc,* two dissents), *cert. denied,* 394 U.S. 976 (1969).

234 See W. Painter, id. at 107–122.

235 Kohler v. Kohler Co., 319 F.2d 634, 642 (7th Cir. 1963). This language was later endorsed by the Second Circuit Court of Appeals in List v. Fashion Park, Inc., 340 F.2d 457, 462 (2d Cir. 1965), and SEC v. Texas Gulf Sulphur Co., 401 F.2d 833, 849 (2d Cir. 1968), *cert. denied,* 394 U.S. 976 (1969).

236 Ibid.

237 401 F.2d at 876 (dissenting opinion of Moore, J.).

corporation is closely held because of the greater likelihood that all of the parties to the transaction will be sufficiently familiar with the company's activities that they can make their own evaluation of the facts.[238] The purchaser of the securities is not required to convey his estimate of the significance of the facts, much less to predict whether success will be attained along particular lines. He is only required to disclose the "basic" facts if they are unknown to the person with whom he deals.[239] And in the closely held concern, it is less likely that the basic facts will be unknown if all the shareholders are involved in corporate activities. Thus the liability will most frequently arise where an officer, director or major shareholder purchases from a minority shareholder who is not an employee, or at least does not hold a corporate office which makes him privy to confidential information.[240]

As far as the close corporation is concerned, the primary problem will be that of determining whether a given item of information is material and must therefore be disclosed before the shares may be repurchased. Although the substantial market effect and reasonable investor tests provide a general guide, only specific cases give an indication of how these tests are applied in practice and the cases themselves are only illustrative; each case must, of necessity, stand on its own facts. Several of the cases involved sales of assets, mergers and the like, and the question presented is whether negotiations have progressed to the point that a sale is sufficiently probable so as to be material. The cases present a spectrum of situations ranging from those where the sale was "assured" [241] to those where the sale, although not assured, was for all practical purposes certain,[242] to those where negotiations were taking place and the question of materiality was held to be one of fact,

---

[238] But see Kardon v. National Gypsum Co., 69 F. Supp. 512 (E.D. Pa. 1946), where the plaintiffs prevailed even though they were officers and directors.

[239] SEC v. Texas Gulf Sulphur Co., 401 F.2d 833, 864 (2d Cir. 1968), *cert. denied*, 394 U.S. 976 (1969). See also 401 F.2d at 852, where the court states that the intent of the legislation is merely to subject all investors to identical market risks, which include "the risk that one's evaluative capacity . . . may exceed another's capacity. . . ." All that is required is that the "basic" (i.e., material) facts be known to those on both sides of the transaction.

[240] It should not be assumed, however, that the duty of disclosure is restricted to those who are officers, directors or holders of large blocks of stock. As the court in the *Texas Gulf* case, 401 F.2d at 848, indicated, the duty is imposed on those who have "access, directly or indirectly, to information intended to be available only for a corporate purpose and not for the personal benefit of anyone" (quoting from Matter of Cady, Roberts & Co., 40 S.E.C. 907, 912 (1961)). This access test was broadened still further by the court to include anyone who *possesses* confidential information, regardless of his relationship with the company. Since the liability of so-called tippees was not passed upon in *Texas Gulf*, the precise scope of the rule was left unclear. For an argument in favor of the broad possession test, see Sandler and Conwill, Texas Gulf Sulphur; Reform in the Securities Marketplace, 30 Ohio St. L.J. 225, 239 (1969). For an argument in favor of a more conservative access-oriented approach, see Bromberg, Corporate Information: Texas Gulf Sulphur and Its Implications, 22 Sw. L.J. 731, 747–749 (1968).

[241] Kardon v. National Gypsum Co., 69 F. Supp. 512 (E.D. Pa. 1946).

[242] Schine v. Schine, 250 F. Supp. 822 (S.D.N.Y. 1966).

to be determined by the particular stage which the negotiations had reached at the time of the transaction,[243] to those where the negotiations had either not been begun or had not progressed sufficiently to require disclosure.[244] Professor Bromberg has suggested that materiality in most cases develops at least by the time the terms of a merger or asset sale are fixed and that it may develop at an earlier date where a closely held company is concerned or where the dealings between the seller and purchaser are "direct and personal" (in contrast to impersonal purchases on a stock exchange). Thus he observes that the "absence of market indicators of value" as well as the "greater feasibility of communication, the absence of a general market which might overreact to the disclosure, and the probable dependence relation of the parties"[245] all point in the direction of requiring disclosure at a comparatively early point, probably sometime during negotiation[246] and perhaps even earlier, such as when the board of directors of one or both companies authorizes that the possibility of merging be explored.[247]

Aside from mergers and the like, other corporate developments which are likely to be considered material are increases or decreases in earnings, increases or reduction in dividends[248] and significant discoveries or developments which ultimately would have an impact on earnings, such as the results of an exceptionally rich drill hole in the *Texas Gulf* case.[249] Other corporate developments of a relatively minor nature, such as the fact that employee morale is high, that orders seem to be as strong as in previous years or that "next year's models appear to be especially attractive" are probably

---

[243] Rogen v. Ilikon Corp., 361 F.2d 260 (1st Cir. 1966); Quirk v. Norfolk & Western, CCH Fed. Sec. L. Rep. ¶91,645 (1964–1966 transfer binder) (S.D.N.Y. 1966).

[244] List v. Fashion Park, Inc., 340 F.2d 457 (2d Cir. 1965); James Blackstone Memorial Library Assn. v. Gulf, Mobile & Ohio R.R., 264 F.2d 445 (7th Cir.), *cert. denied*, 361 U.S. 815 (1959).

[245] A. Bromberg, Securities Law: Fraud—SEC Rule 10b–5 at §7.4(4)(b) (1967).

[246] See cases collected in note 243 *supra*.

[247] In List v. Fashion Park, Inc., 340 F.2d 457 (2d Cir. 1965), the shares were repurchased before negotiations for a merger commenced but after the company's board of directors had adopted a resolution proposing that the company should seek to negotiate, and the court held that the pending sale or merger was not sufficiently developed so as to be material. The shares were traded over the counter. Thus, as Professor Bromberg suggests, id. at §7.4(4)(b), the result might have been otherwise if the shares were not publicly traded and if the dealings between the parties had been direct and personal.

[248] E.g., Matter of Cady, Roberts & Co., 40 S.E.C. 907, 912 (1961). See also Van Alstyne, Noel & Co., SEC Securities Act Release No. 8511, CCH Fed. Sec. L. Rep. ¶77,656 (1969); In the Matters of Merrill Lynch, Pierce, Fenner & Smith, Inc., SEC Securities Act Release No. 8459, CCH Fed. Sec. L. Rep. ¶77,629 (1968). A 4 percent stock dividend has been held not to be material. Hafner v. Forest Laboratories, 345 F.2d 167 (2d Cir. 1965). The determination of materiality here probably depends upon the size of the stock dividend and the degree of investor enthusiasm it is likely to generate. See A. Bromberg, id. at §7.4(4)(a). If the corporation is closely held, it is unlikely that even a relatively large stock dividend would be material in most situations, since the shares have no ready market.

[249] SEC v. Texas Gulf Sulphur Co., 401 F.2d 833 (2d Cir. 1968), *cert. denied*, 394 U.S. 976 (1969).

not material in the usual situation.[250] However, the fact that an officer or employee is purchasing relatively large amounts of stock or that the purchaser is an officer, is a director or is the company itself [251] may very well be material if it would influence a reasonable investor in his decision as to whether to part with his shares at the price offered to him.

Once liability for violation of rule 10b-5 has been established, the procedural problems of recovery are less than in an action under state law. Thus service of process can be had on any defendant in any district of which he is an inhabitant or in which he may be found (i.e., nationwide service of process), and the action itself can be brought in any district where the act or transaction constituting the violation occurred or where the defendant is found, is an inhabitant or transacts business (i.e., broad venue).[252] Needless to say, since the action is based on the violation of a federal statute, there need be no diversity of citizenship between the parties nor compliance with the minimum amount required for diversity actions. The substantive law which will be applied is the federal case law which has developed under rule 10b-5 rather than state law concepts of fiduciary duty, which may in some jurisdictions be somewhat more restrictive from the plaintiff's standpoint. The procedural rules will be those prevailing in the federal courts, which may be more liberal, from the plaintiff's perspective, than those in some state courts (e.g., in such areas as pretrial practice, discovery, etc.). The jurisdiction of the federal courts is exclusive as to violations of the Exchange Act (unlike violations of the Securities Act of 1933, where there is concurrent jurisdiction in state and federal courts) so that all rule 10b-5 actions must be brought on the federal level.[253] However, if the complaint alleges a separate *ground* of recovery based on a violation of state law (in contrast to a separate *cause of action*) then the claim based on state law may be coupled with the federal claim and the two adjudicated together in

---

[250] See Ferber, Duties of Disclosure of Corporate Insiders, 34 U. Mo. K.C.L. Rev. 222, 225 (1966).

[251] Ibid. Professor Loss has observed that all that can be safely concluded from the existing cases is that "an insider cannot be certain that failure to disclose his identity will *not* be considered a violation," particularly when such failure is taken into account with other aspects of the transaction. See 3 L. Loss, Securities Regulation 1465 (1961). In List v. Fashion Park, 340 F.2d 457 (2d Cir. 1965), although the lower court had found that the purchaser's identity was not material under the circumstances, the Court of Appeals expressly declined to pass upon the point. 340 F.2d at 464 n.4. For another case involving a closely held concern where the identity of the purchaser was held not to be material, see Ross v. Licht, 263 F. Supp. 395, 409 (S.D.N.Y. 1967). Notwithstanding these cases, where the defendant deliberately attempts to mislead the plaintiff by purchasing through an intermediary, liability for failure to disclose his identity is likely to follow. See Strong v. Repide, 213 U.S. 419 (1909), and Beggy v. Deike, 413 Pa. 74, 196 A.2d 179 (1963) (where the plaintiff assumed he was selling to the corporation whereas he was, in fact, selling to the chairman of the board). Although the *Strong* and *Beggy* cases were not decided under rule 10b–5, liability under the rule is, if anything, more likely since the duty of disclosure is at least as broad and probably broader than that required at common law.

[252] Securities Exchange Act of 1934, §27, 15 U.S.C. §78aa.

[253] Ibid. Cf. Securities Act of 1933, §22, 15 U.S.C. §77v.

the federal court, provided that the federal claim is not plainly wanting in substance. This is the doctrine of "pendent jurisdiction." [254] Although the authorities are split, the better view is to permit nationwide service of process even as to the state law-related claim if the federal claim is not dismissed for insufficiency.[255]

There are several other advantages to an action based on rule 10b-5, such as the possibility of choosing a forum with a relatively long statute of limitations. Since rule 10b-5 has no statute of limitations, the statute of limitations to be applied will be that of the forum state,[256] unless the suit is equitable in character, as in an action for an injunction, in which case the court may apply the doctrine of "laches." [257] And if the action is derivative in nature (as where the plaintiff asserts that his corporation was deceived into purchasing shares for an excessive price or selling them for less than fair value[258]), the plaintiff need not comply with a security for expenses statute which would apply to actions based on state law, since the right being enforced is a federal one.[259] The federal courts may dispense with a requirement that the plaintiff make a demand on the shareholders as a prerequisite to a derivative suit, whereas the state law requirements may be more restrictive.[260] Finally, the overall attitude of the federal courts toward investor protection is likely to be more liberal than that prevailing in many state courts. Thus recovery may sometimes be had on the federal level in situations where it might not be available under state law.[261]

[254] The leading case is Hurn v. Oursler, 289 U.S. 238 (1933). See also United Mine Workers of America v. Gibbs, 383 U.S. 715, 725–726 (1966).

[255] Sprayregen v. Livingston Oil Co., CCH Fed. Sec. L. Rep. ¶92,272 (S.D.N.Y. 1968), and other authorities collected in A. Bromberg, Securities Law: Fraud—SEC Rule 10b–5 §2.7(3) (1967). For an argument against permitting nationwide service of process as regards the state-related claim, see Note, 18 Stan. L. Rev. 1339, 1352 (1966).

[256] See A. Bromberg, id. at §2.5(1); 3 L. Loss, id. at 1771–1778.

[257] See Lowenfels, Rule 10b–5 and the Stockholder's Derivative Action, 18 Vand. L. Rev. 893, 904–905 (1965). See also 3 L. Loss, id. at 1777.

[258] E.g., Dasho v. Susquehanna Corp., 380 F.2d 262 (7th Cir. 1967), *cert. denied sub nom.* Bard v. Dasho, 389 U.S. 977 (1967); Ruckle v. Roto American Corp., 339 F.2d 24 (2d Cir. 1964); Hooper v. Mountain States Securities Corp., 282 F.2d 195 (5th Cir. 1960), *cert. denied*, 365 U.S. 814 (1961).

[259] McClure v. Borne Chemical Co., 292 F.2d 824 (3d Cir. 1961) *cert. denied*, 368 U.S. 939 (1961). See also Borak v. J. I. Case Co., 317 F.2d 838 (7th Cir. 1963), *aff'd*, 377 U.S. 426 (1964). In pendent jurisdiction situations, as regards that part of the plaintiff's case which depends on a violation of state law, a bond may be required. See A. Bromberg, id. at §2.5(3). However, due to the fact that the federal and state claims often "overlap," the amount of the bond may be less than if the plaintiff were suing only in the state court. See R. Jennings and H. Marsh, Cases and Materials on Securities Regulation 959 (2d ed. 1968). And as the latter points out, the state law-related claim can always be dismissed on the plaintiff's motion if he chooses not to post a bond.

[260] E.g., Levitt v. Johnson 334 F.2d 815 (1st Cir. 1964), *cert. denied*, 379 U.S. 961 (1965).

[261] *Compare* Goodwin v. Agassiz, 283 Mass. 358, 186 N.E. 659 (1933), *with* SEC v. Texas Gulf Sulphur Co., 401 F.2d 833 (2d Cir. 1968), *cert. denied*, 394 U.S. 976 (1969).

The measure of damages to be applied in a rule 10b-5 action will probably be the so-called out-of-pocket rule prevailing in the federal courts.[262] In effect this permits the plaintiff to recoup any actual losses he has suffered but does not give him the "benefit of his bargain." Suppose, for example, that the defendant sells shares, representing to the plaintiff that they are worth $75 but that he is being allowed to purchase them at a "discount" for $60. The shares are, in fact, worth only $50 since the defendant has concealed material facts which, if disclosed, would cause the plaintiff to pay only that amount. The actual loss or out-of-pocket recovery here is $10 (the plaintiff paid $60 and received only $50 worth of stock). The benefit of the bargain, however, is the difference between what was received and what was promised (i.e., $25). Although the federal courts do not generally allow damages except on an out-of-pocket theory,[263] some cases, principally those dealing with wrongful purchases of shares, have allowed the plaintiff to recoup not only his own losses but also any profits which the defendant has made as a result of the purchase. Suppose, for example, that the defendant purchased shares at $60 failing to disclose information which, if disclosed, would have made the shares worth $75. At the time the plaintiff brings an action to recover damages, the shares are worth $90. Since the shares were wrongfully acquired, a court might require the defendant to disgorge all of his profits (i.e., the difference between what he paid ($60) and what the shares were worth at the time the action was brought ($90)).[264] An alternate approach, expressly authorized by the statute, is to permit rescission. Thus the plaintiff would tender his $60 and the shares (now worth $90) would be returned to him.[265] Note that the plaintiff is here receiving more than his out-of-pocket loss, which in this case was the difference between what he received ($60) and what the shares were worth at the time they were sold ($75).

---

[262] See 3 L. Loss, id. at 1792–1794; A. Bromberg, id. at §9.1. See also Comment, 10 B.C. Ind. & Com. L. Rev. 337 (1969); Notes, 22 Rutgers L. Rev. 554 (1968); [1968] Wash. U.L.Q. 165.

[263] But see Esplin v. Hirschi, 402 F.2d 94 (10th Cir. 1968), cert. denied, 394 U.S. 928 (1969) (permitting recovery of the difference between what was paid for the shares and their worth at the time the fraud was discovered, or at the time it could have been discovered with reasonable diligence, whichever is earlier, instead of the difference between the cost and the worth of the shares at the time of purchase). As pointed out below, the plaintiff may also rescind the sale and his recovery amounts to much the same thing—i.e., refund of the purchase price in return for the shares.

[264] E.g., Baumel v. Rosen, 412 F.2d 571 (4th Cir. 1969); Myzel v. Fields, 386 F.2d 718 (8th Cir. 1967), cert. denied, 390 U.S. 951 (1968); Janigan v. Taylor, 344 F.2d 781 (1st Cir. 1965), cert. denied, 382 U.S. 879 (1965).

[265] See Securities Exchange Act of 1934, §29(b), 15 U.S.C. §78cc.

6.6 ALTERNATIVES TO SHARE REPURCHASES

Although repurchase of shares is the primary method of planning for the death or retirement of a shareholder, there are other alternatives. One of the most popular involves the issuance of preferred shares for all or part of a person's common stock. This is particularly appropriate where older shareholders retire and, since they no longer receive a salary from the company, wish to supplement their income by receiving more in dividends than is currently being paid on the common shares. This can easily be done by what amounts to a reshuffling of their interests so as to lessen or eliminate the amount of common stock and increase the amount of preferred they own. The preferred shares will characteristically carry a relatively high yield, the right to dividends will be cumulative and payment of dividends will perhaps be mandatory in years when there are earnings available. The shares may also be made subject to redemption, perhaps on a regular basis (sinking fund), so that the shareholder may, in effect, be bought out over a period of time. Obviously, in surrendering his common stock he surrenders his voting rights, unless the preferred is voting stock, which is somewhat unusual (except for contingent voting rights which arise when dividend payments are in arrears).

A primary disadvantage with preferred stock is that dividends on the preferred are not deductible as far as the corporation is concerned. This is in contrast to interest paid on notes or bonds, which is, of course, deductible except where the indebtedness is not bona fide because the corporation is excessively thin or the notes are, in reality, another form of stock.[266] Since, as we shall see,[267] the receipt of notes or any other corporate obligation for shares is a taxable event, whereas the receipt of preferred shares for common is not taxable if the exchange is pursuant to a plan of "recapitalization," it will be better from the shareholder's standpoint to receive preferred stock rather than notes. Often a compromise can be worked out between the shareholder and the corporation whereby he is to receive a package of notes and preferred shares. If the preferred shares are redeemable over several years, the shareholder's gain on the preferred will be taxable as the preferred is gradually redeemed, spreading out the tax impact instead of "bunching" the tax into one year, as might be so if the common shares were to be surrendered for notes exclusively.[268]

---

[266] See Ch. II, text accompanying notes 67–102.

[267] See text accompanying note 280 *infra*.

[268] In some situations the shares may be resold back to the corporation on an installment method. If the transaction qualifies under Section 453 of the Code (the primary requisite is that the payments in the year of sale do not exceed 30 percent of the selling price (Int. Rev. Code §453(b)(2)), then the gain may be spread out over the years when the payments are being received.

An exchange of common shares for preferred will not be taxable if made pursuant to a recapitalization, which is one form of tax-free reorganization. Although the Code does not define the term "recapitalization" it seems clear from the regulations that an exchange of this type falls within the recapitalization concept.[269]

A troublesome problem arises in arranging the desired "reshuffling" of interests by use of the "recapitalization" technique. If all the shareholders exchange part of their common shares for preferred, or all of their common for a package of preferred and common, the proportionate interests of everyone remain the same. Thus either some of the preferred must be sold to those shareholders who wish more preferred and less common or some other arrangement must be made.

If the preferred is sold from one shareholder group to another, the sale would probably be a taxable event, in which case the tax would be imposed on both shareholder groups. Those surrendering common would recognize gain equal to the difference between the basis of the shares surrendered and the fair value of the shares received, and the same would be true with those surrendering preferred for common. Moreover, since the preferred stock might well be Section 306 stock,[270] its disposition by one group in exchange for common might give rise to taxation at ordinary income rates.

As an alternative, a transaction of the so-called Hartzel-Dean type could be explored. Essentially this involves a "disproportionate" recapitalization whereby each group of shareholders is offered a package of common and preferred in exchange for its common shares. Each group accepts only part of the offer. Thus one group accepts the preferred shares in exchange for its

[269] Id. §§254, 368(a)(1)(E). Treas. Reg. §1.368–2(e). Some doubts and planning problems may arise in this area due to the broadening of Section 305 of the Code by the Tax Reform Act of 1969 so as to impose a tax on certain distributions and other transactions whereby the proportionate interest of certain shareholders in the earnings and profits or assets of a corporation is increased. See discussion in note 22 *supra*. Section 305(c) provides that the Treasury Department shall prescribe regulations further determining the extent to which certain transactions, including recapitalizations, shall be treated as taxable distributions because a shareholder's proportionate interest in a corporation has been increased. In discussing the applicability of the newly amended Section 305 to recapitalizations and the possible scope of any new regulations which will be issued thereunder, D. Kahn, Basic Corporate Taxation 15 (Supp. 1970), refers to a statement made on the Senate floor by Senator Long to the effect that the amendments to Section 305 would have no effect on the "classic type of reorganization" whereby older shareholders exchange some or all of their common shares for preferred in connection with their retirement from the business, and younger shareholders exchange preferred shares for more common. See 115 Cong. Rec. 204 (1969) p. S. 16221. Thus it is likely that recapitalizations of the so-called Hartzel-Dean variety, discussed in text accompanying notes 271–278 *infra*, will continue to be tax free under the new regulations when they are promulgated. If the new regulations should, however, delimit the tax-free nature of Hartzel-Dean recapitalizations, the effect, according to D. Kahn, id. at 15, will be "to place a premium on planning the original incorporation," presumably to issue preferred shares or other classes of common shares to certain shareholders who might later find such shares desirable for estate planning or in connection with their retirement.

[270] See text accompanying notes 101–131 *supra*.

common. The other group accepts the common shares. The net effect is that one shareholder group ends up with all of the preferred and the other shareholder group holds all of the common, precisely the result desired. The primary question is whether a disproportionate exchange of this type qualifies as a recapitalization or whether all the shares must be issued in accordance with the plan, with no shareholders waiving their rights to any part of the package.

The courts have with some consistency held that a recapitalization need not involve a pro rata exchange. Thus in *H. E. Muchnic*,[271] a corporation offered shares of 7 percent cumulative redeemable preferred for common stock. Seven out of sixteen shareholders exchanged their shares. Later, after all of the preferred had been redeemed, the corporation made another offer and this time only the taxpayer and his wife (who had not exchanged their stock in the prior offer) exchanged their stock for preferred. The court held that the exchange was a recapitalization in that "New priorities as to the company's assets and earnings were assumed upon the issue of the preferred stock, which, together with the reduction in the common stock outstanding, effected a revision of the existing interests of the common stockholders." [272] In *Elmer W. Hartzel* [273] the question presented was slightly different. There the transaction took the form of a pro rata exchange of common for new preferred and common shares in which all shareholders technically participated, followed by an exchange between different shareholder groups so that one group ended up with the preferred stock and the other group ended up with the common, in a manner similar to that which has already been discussed. As might be expected, the Commissioner, although conceding that the initial distribution was a tax-free recapitalization, argued that the subsequent exchange was a taxable transaction. The taxpayer argued that the "exchange" was merely a formality or "detour" which counsel had advised was necessary to comply with Ohio law and that in fact the shares were issued directly by the corporation to the various shareholder groups (i.e., all the preferred shares to one group and all the common to the other). Thus, the taxpayer urged, although the form of the transaction might have been technically different from that in *Muchnic*, the substance was the same, a recapitalization. In upholding the taxpayer's contention that the exchange was pursuant to a plan of reorganization (recapitalization), the court pointed out that

> The plan was initiated by written agreement of all the individual stockholders with the definite object in view of finally placing in the ownership of the old stockholders all the preferred stock and in the ownership of the younger stockholders all the common stock for the sole purpose of giving the younger stockholders a greater voice in the control of the company because of certain contingencies which might arise in the future, i.e., that

[271] 29 B.T.A. 163 (1933), *acquiesced in,* XIII–1 Cum. Bull. 11 (1934).
[272] 29 B.T.A. at 166–167.
[273] 40 B.T.A. 492 (1939), *acquiesced in,* 1939–2 Cum. Bull. 16.

some of the older stockholders might die, their stock go to their children, and voting control of the company thus pass into the hands of people totally unfamiliar with its affairs, who might displace the younger stockholders from the positions they held with the company.[274]

The court thus accepted the taxpayer's contention that the exchange between shareholders should be given no significance in that it was a mere detour, required by Ohio law, and did not affect the substance of the transaction so as to alter the tax effect. Finally, when the Commissioner contended that, because of the way in which the interests of the various parties were reshuffled, the exchange lacked "continuity of proprietary interest," the court dismissed the argument with the observation that those who received greater voting rights and more common stock as well as those who received the preferred received a "definite, substantial, and continuing interest in the reorganized company." [275] The *Hartzel* holding was subsequently followed in *Marjorie N. Dean*,[276] which involved a similar problem of tax planning, although there was no problem of the form of the transaction being that of a pro rata distribution followed by an exchange between the shareholders. The purpose of the plan was to induce certain inactive female shareholders to surrender their common shares for preferred in order that control might not, on the death of the other shareholders, fall into their inexperienced hands. The Commissioner attacked the transaction as an attempt to bail out earnings and profits of the corporation at capital gains rates, citing several prior cases where it had been held that the issuance of debentures was equivalent to cash and hence should give rise to tax.[277] The court held that the purpose of the transaction was not to bail out earnings but was to shift potential control away from the female shareholders into the hands of others who were more experienced, enabling the corporation to attract new managerial talent. The Internal Revenue Service acquiesced in the *Dean* case and in several instances since then has ruled that similar exchanges, even though not pro rata, are tax-free recapitalizations.[278]

If common or preferred stock is surrendered in exchange for stock and bonds, debentures or notes, although the transaction qualifies as a recapitalization, unless there is a clear absence of business purpose or the exchange is an attempt to withdraw corporate earnings which normally would be distributed as dividends,[279] the securities received (i.e., the bonds, debentures, etc.) are considered as boot or other property, with the result that gain on

[274] 40 B.T.A. at 500.

[275] 40 B.T.A. at 502.

[276] 10 T.C. 19 (1948), *acquiesced in,* 1949–1 Cum. Bull. 1.

[277] E.g., Bazley v. Commissioner, 331 U.S. 737 (1947).

[278] E.g., Rev. Rul. 59–84, 1959–1 Cum. Bull. 71; Rev. Rul. 55–112, 1955–1 Cum. Bull. 344.

[279] *Compare* Bazley v. Commissioner, 331 U.S. 737 (1947) (dividend treatment to distribution of callable debentures), *with* Alan O. Hickok, 32 T.C. 80 (1959), *nonacquiesced in,* 1959–2 Cum. Bull. 8; Daisy Seide, 18 T.C. 502 (1952); Wolf Envelope Co., 17 T.C. 471 (1951), *nonacquiesced in,* 1952–1 Cum. Bull. 6.

the exchange is taxed to the extent of the fair market value of the securities.[280] If securities (corporate obligations) are surrendered in the same exchange, then the boot is the fair market value of the excess of the principal amount of the securities received over the principal amount of the securities surrendered.[281] It should be noted that the receipt of securities will give rise to tax under Section 356(d) of the Code only if there is *gain* on the exchange. However, if it is found that the exchange has the "effect of the distribution of a dividend," then that amount of the gain recognized which is not in excess of the taxpayer's ratable share of earnings and profits is taxed as a dividend (i.e., at ordinary rates).[282] Just when this situation exists (i.e., when the exchange "has the effect of . . . a dividend") is not entirely clear, but it would seem that a pro rata distribution to those who hold common stock of securities which are either readily marketable or which are immediately callable by the corporation may have a "dividend effect," particularly where those receiving the securities, because of their control of the corporation, have it within their power to determine whether the securities will be called.[283] On the other hand, if the securities are issued to holders of preferred or are not readily marketable or callable, there is correspondingly less chance of a tax at dividend rates, although gain will, of course, be recognized (at capital gains rates) to the extent of the fair value of the securities received.[284] Interestingly, the so-called continuity of proprietary interest requirement, which has been applied to invalidate other types of corporate reorganizations where a shareholder relinquishes his equity status to assume the role of a creditor, has not generally been applied in the recapitalization area. Thus if some preferred shareholders surrender their stock for common stock and others exchange preferred for cash or bonds, this will qualify as a recapitalization despite the arguable loss of proprietary interest on the part of some of the parties.[285] However, despite its recapitalization status, the transaction still gives rise to the recognition of gain, as previously described. Hence it is advantageous only where there is relatively little gain on the transfer because of a high basis in the stock or securities surrendered.

Finally, it should be pointed out that recapitalization treatment will not be given if stock is surrendered exclusively for securities. Thus if all the preferred shares are exchanged for bonds or notes, the transaction falls outside the reorganization provisions and is taxed as a distribution, or a redemption or liquidation under Sections 301, 302, 331 or 346.[286]

---

280 Int. Rev. Code of 1954, §§354(a)(2), 356(a), 356(d).

281 Id. §356(d)(2)(B).

282 Id. §356(a)(2).

283 See, e.g., Bazley v. Commissioner, 331 U.S. 737 (1947). For further discussion see Ch. VIII, text accompanying note 66.

284 See, e.g., Daisy Seide, 18 T.C. 502 (1952).

285 See Rev. Rul. 56–179, 1956–1 Cum. Bull. 187. See also B. Bittker and J. Eustice, Federal Income Taxation of Corporations and Shareholders 546–547 (1966).

286 See Treas. Reg. §1.354–1(d), Ex. (3).

As already indicated,[287] where shares are sold back to a corporation in exchange for notes, the gain on the sale can be spread out if the shares are sold on the installment method, permitted by Section 453 of the Code. In order to qualify under this provision the sale price must exceed $1000 and the payments in the year of sale may not exceed 30 percent of the "selling price." The selling price includes the total consideration agreed upon for the transfer of the property, including the amount of any liabilities to which the property is subject. Thus if property worth $50,000 and subject to a mortgage of $20,000 is sold and the purchaser agrees to pay $30,000 in installments, the selling price is $50,000.[288] A possible problem is whether the buyer's assumption of liability on a mortgage constitutes a payment in the year of sale, in which case the total payment would, of course, exceed 30 percent of the selling price in the situation supposed. In the case of sales of real property, the regulations specify that a mortgage will be considered as a payment in the year of sale only to the extent that the mortgage exceeds the basis of the property.[289] Thus if, in the above illustration, the basis of the property were $17,000, the excess of the $20,000 mortgage over that amount (i.e., $3000) would be considered as a payment in the year of sale. If other payments during the year of sale did not exceed $12,000 (so that the total payments did not exceed $15,000—30 percent of the $50,000 selling price) the transaction would qualify for installment method reporting. Although the regulations do not specifically deal with sales of personal property, it would seem that the same rule would be applied as in the mortgage situation.[290] Additional problems are presented where the purchaser of the property discharges some of the liabilities by making payments (e.g., on the mortgage) during the year of the sale. Although assumption of the mortgage may not itself be a payment (except to the extent that it exceeds basis), are payments on the mortgage in the year of sale included in calculating the amount of payment during that year for the purpose of applying the 30 percent test? Although the Tax Court answered this question in the affirmative, it was reversed and two circuit courts of appeals have thus arrived at the opposite conclusion.[291]

One hazard which is sometimes overlooked by those seeking to take advantage of the installment method of reporting is that if installment obligations are sold or otherwise disposed of (except for transmissions resulting from death and certain other dispositions of a tax-free nature), the recognition of gain is "accelerated." In other words, instead of the gain being spread out over the period during which the payments are made, the entire

---

[287] See note 268 *supra*.
[288] Treas. Reg. §1.453–4(c).
[289] Ibid.
[290] United States v. Marshall, 357 F.2d 294 (9th Cir. 1966).
[291] Irwin v. Commissioner, 390 F.2d 91 (5th Cir. 1968); United States v. Marshall, 357 F.2d 294 (9th Cir. 1966). See D. Herwitz, Business Planning 520–521 (1966).

gain is recognized in the year of sale to the extent that the amount realized on disposition of the installment obligation exceeds the basis of the obligation.[292] The basis of the obligation is the excess of its face value over an amount equal to the income which would be recognized if the obligation were satisfied in full.[293] If the installment obligation is disposed of by gift, then gain will be recognized to the extent that the fair market value of the obligation exceeds its basis.[294] For example, if a father were to sell his shares to a corporation on the installment method and were subsequently to make a gift of the installment obligation to his son, not only would this be an ineffective attempt at assignment of income but, unlike some other situations where the father might avoid being taxed until the payments were actually made,[295] he would recognize the entire amount of gain in the year of the gift. This is a hazard which those entering into arrangements of this type should keep clearly in mind.

In view of what has been said about the ambiguous status of one who has sold his shares to a corporation in return for a corporate note,[296] it might be well to consider the possibility of spreading out the gain on the sale not by means of the installment method of reporting but by a plan whereby only a portion of the shares are sold each year. For example, a shareholder holding common stock might exchange his common for preferred in a transaction of the Hartzel-Dean type already described. The next step would be to enter into an agreement with the corporation whereby the latter would purchase a set amount of preferred stock each year at a designated price. The same result could be achieved through the use of sinking fund preferred. An advantage of this approach would be that some arrangement could be made for protecting the shareholder if the corporation were unable or unwilling to perform its part of the bargain. Thus it could be provided that in the event that the corporation failed to retire the preferred in accordance with the sinking fund provisions, the shares of preferred then outstanding might be given voting rights.

The net result of a surrender of common stock for a senior security is to increase the "leverage" of the underlying common stock. For example, suppose that a corporation has a net worth of $1 million and 10,000 shares of common stock outstanding. If 5000 shares of common are exchanged for 5000 shares of preferred, and assuming that the preferred shares are worth the same amount as the common, then the 5000 shares of common stock still held by the other shareholders will have a book value of $500,000, or $100 per share. If the 5000 shares of common repurchased by the corporation were then distributed on a share-for-share basis to those who hold common, the book value of the common would be reduced to $50 per share,

[292] Int. Rev. Code of 1954, §453(d)(1).
[293] Id. §453(d)(2).
[294] Id. §453(d)(1)(B).
[295] Cf. Helvering v. Horst, 311 U.S. 112 (1940).
[296] See text accompanying note 72 *supra*. See in particular note 77 *supra*.

since 10,000 shares would be outstanding. The reduced book value of the common stock is attributable to the presence of the senior preferred or debt, whichever the case may be. Obviously no one who holds common stock has suffered an economic loss since he holds twice as many shares, each share being worth half as much as before.

This leverage may be advantageous in several ways. First, it lowers the worth per share of the common stock, which makes it easier for younger and less wealthy participants in the business to acquire an interest. Secondly, if the earnings of the company show a substantial increase in future years, stock in a high leverage situation will increase in value more rapidly than shares which do not have leverage. This is due to the fact that the common shares represent a residual claim on all net profits remaining after payment of fixed charges on the senior securities. If a corporation is able to get a higher return on the invested capital represented by its senior securities than the fixed charges (i.e., dividends on preferred or interest on debt) which it must pay for the privilege of using the capital, then the excess represents additional earnings for those who hold common. Thus if a corporation were to earn 10 percent on its invested capital and if the fixed charges on senior securities were only 8 percent, the 2 percent difference would inure to the benefit of the common stock. Obviously the same thing works in reverse, i.e., if the corporation is not able to earn an amount at least equal to the fixed charges on its senior securities, the difference must be made up by a reduction in earnings per share on the common stock. For this reason, high-leverage common stock represents a relatively more speculative investment, prospering in good times and suffering in years when earnings are low. If the senior securities take the form of corporate obligations, the speculative advantage to the common stock is increased, since interest on the debt will be deductible for corporate tax purposes, thus making more earnings available for payment on the common stock.

As far as those who hold preferred shares are concerned, their priority on earnings and other distributions will give greater stability to the value of their investment. Since the investment is in a sense the reverse of leverage, a poor earnings performance by the corporation is less likely to have an adverse effect on its worth than where a corporation has only one class of stock. This makes the preferred shares much easier to value for estate or gift tax purposes and, of course, makes them particularly attractive for persons wishing a comparatively dependable and relatively high income from invested capital.

VII Deadlock and Dissolution of the Closely Held Corporation

A significant risk assumed by those who do business as a closely held corporation is that the shareholders or board of directors may at some time in the future become deadlocked, i.e., evenly divided in opinion as to important policy matters. If the deadlock is not resolved, then a form of corporate paralysis will set in with consequent adverse effects on corporate profits and possibly on the very future of the corporation. Important customer accounts may not be properly serviced and much business lost because of friction within the management structure. Obviously it is best to anticipate the possibility of deadlock well in advance, taking suitable precautions to lessen its likelihood as well as setting up some means whereby a deadlock may be resolved if it arises.

7.1 HOW DEADLOCKS MAY ARISE; PREVENTION

Since a deadlock exists where those who are entitled to vote on particular matters are evenly divided, they are more likely to occur where the shares are evenly distributed among an even number of shareholders or where there is an even number of directors. Obviously, then, if it can be arranged to have the shares held in some other manner and if the number of directors is an odd number, deadlocks are less likely.

However, deadlocks are still possible if the articles of incorporation or by-laws require, for particular actions to be taken by shareholders or directors, a relatively high quorum or vote. These high quorum and vote requirements, already discussed in some detail,[1] are obviously useful in preventing oppression or squeeze-outs of minority shareholders, but they also increase the risk of a deadlock due to a difference of opinion between the person who holds what in effect is a veto power and others who, but for the veto, would have authority to proceed. In extreme situations the veto power may be used to extort concessions from other shareholders which might not

[1] See Ch. III, text accompanying notes 183–201.

otherwise be forthcoming. This in turn leads to resentment and more friction, increasing the chances of a deadlock at a later date.

Since the problems will vary with the particular business, the way in which the shares are distributed and other factors, one can only stress the importance of restricting veto powers to those areas where they are of particular value.[2] The broader the veto power, the greater the possibility that it may be used in a "power play" rather than for legitimate purposes.

Since deadlocks frequently arise from conflicting interests of differing shareholder groups, it is well to forestall the development of situations which lead to opposing points of view. The most frequent situation of this type is the retirement or death of a shareholder. If a shareholder is no longer in the corporate employ, he ceases to draw a salary and is dependent upon dividends for income which may not be forthcoming. The remaining shareholders may wish to minimize taxes by withdrawing corporate earnings in the form of salaries, rather than dividends, which are not deductible on the corporate level. A shareholder's death may produce further complications if his shares descend to members of his family who have no familiarity with the business and yet may have views as to how the business should be run, or who even actively interfere with day-to-day operations. Even if such nonemployee relatives hold only a minority interest in the company, they may be able to enlist the support of other disgruntled minority shareholders and thus wield greater power, particularly if there is cumulative voting or a higher than majority quorum or voting requirement.

Conflicting interests such as these can often be prevented by judicious use of buy-out agreements of various types. As already described in the preceding chapter, a shareholder who retires or dies may have his shares repurchased by the corporation or by the other shareholders. Other alternatives are first-refusal stock transfer restrictions[3] which take effect on a shareholder's ceasing to be an employee of the company or on his death, and various arrangements whereby an employee's common stock, with attendant voting rights, may be exchanged for preferred stock, carrying only contingent voting rights when dividends are in default.[4] The choice between these alternatives is largely a matter of seeking the best accommodation of both the interests of the corporation and those of the shareholder. A first-refusal stock transfer restriction serves only to protect the corporation against transfer of the shares into unfriendly hands, and it offers the shareholder no guarantee that his shares will be purchased, as in the case of a stock repurchase agreement. A stock transfer restriction may avoid some of the difficult problems of funding the repurchase, since the corporation need not exercise its option if it has insufficient funds to do so. However, as a practical matter it must exercise the option or permit the transfer of the

[2] See id. note 191.
[3] See id. note 11.
[4] See Ch. VI, text accompanying note 271.

shares into the hands of others, such as uncooperative relatives or hostile outsiders. Thus the repurchase, although not legally compulsory, is a practical necessity and the problem of funding it continues to be a significant one.

Preferred stock can be a compromise between the continued holding of common stock and a "clean" buy-out. This may be advantageous both for the corporation and for the shareholder. From the corporate standpoint the use of preferred will eliminate or lessen the need to fund a repurchase immediately upon a shareholder's death or retirement. If the yield on the preferred shares is sufficiently generous, the shareholder may find that continued investment in the corporation is preferable to other sources of income. The advantages of the arrangement from the shareholder's standpoint are further increased if the preferred shares are retired over a period of time, thus spreading out the gain which, in a clean buy-out, would all be taxable in one year. This tax advantage disappears when the shareholder dies, for his shares then receive a new basis equal to their value at the date of death or the alternate valuation date one year later, greatly diminishing the gain when the shares are repurchased. In addition, the shareholder's estate will no doubt be more interested in obtaining funds for paying taxes, expenses of administration, legacies and so forth. We have already seen how the shares may be redeemed or repurchased with few adverse tax consequences under Section 303 of the Code.[5]

In a larger sense any arrangement which lessens the tension between differing shareholder groups also lessens the risk of a deadlock. In a prior chapter[6] we considered at some length various ways of preventing squeeze-outs of minority shareholders. It is not necessary to recapitulate that discussion other than to note that many of the prophylactic devices suggested there, such as employment agreements, judiciously used "veto" powers, and broad preemptive rights provisions, lessen the likelihood of friction. The important thing to keep in mind is that, in the friendly atmosphere in which most corporations are formed, it is all too easy to fail to anticipate the possibility of trouble developing at a later date. The sunny relationships between the parties may mislead counsel into assuming that the weather will always be fair.

If the weather worsens and a deadlock develops, then it is well to have some means of resolving the deadlock amicably without the need to bring a judicial proceeding to dissolve the corporation. More often than not a corporation is worth more as a going concern than if it is liquidated. This is particularly so where much of a corporation's value is in its good will, as where it is primarily a service corporation. In the latter case the assets may be minimal and the worth of the enterprise may consist largely in customer relationships and a reputation for reliable service built up over the years. If

[5] See id. notes 80–94.
[6] See Ch. IV.

the business is discontinued there may be little to distribute but pleasant memories of better days and bitter regrets that the parties have fallen out with one another. Thus the emphasis should be upon keeping the patient alive if at all possible. This may be done in several ways.

7.2   RESOLVING DEADLOCKS WITHOUT DISSOLVING THE CORPORATION

(a)   BUYING OUT ONE OR MORE SHAREHOLDERS

If there are two or more shareholder groups in conflict with one another, some arrangement may be made for the shares of one group to be acquired by the corporation or by the other shareholders. There are, of course, several problems, among which the most important are who is going to buy out whom and at what price? If one shareholder group holds a majority of the shares, then that group is the logical party to buy out the other. This may be done by a provision in the articles of incorporation or bylaws that, if the corporation becomes deadlocked in its affairs for a designated period of time (e.g., inability to elect directors at an annual shareholders' meeting and the "holding over" of directors previously elected for longer than six months, or inability of the directors to take affirmative action for a period of six months), then the majority shareholder will have (1) the option or (2) an obligation to purchase the shares of the minority group at a designated figure, such as book value, fair value computed by capitalizing net earnings at an agreed-upon multiple, etc.[7] An option obviously gives the majority shareholders a choice between perpetuating the deadlock (which may be to their advantage) or purchasing the shares. And it may be used as a device for pressuring the minority shareholders to surrender their shares for less than their true worth. A fairer arrangement would *require* the majority shareholders to repurchase the shares at the price agreed upon. This avoids the possibility that a minority group might be kept locked into a dead-locked concern until it acquiesces to the terms imposed by the majority.[8]

Much greater difficulties arise where the shares are evenly divided among two or more shareholder groups. Since there is no logical reason why one group should necessarily be the purchaser and the other group the seller, some way must be devised to determine who buys and who sells. If one shareholder group is composed of persons who are identified with management while the other consists of "passive" investors who, although directors, are not officers of the company, then the management group might be

[7] See Ch. III, text accompanying notes 49–66.

[8] For an illustration of such a lock-in, although it involved two 50 percent shareholders, see In re Radom & Neidorff, Inc., 307 N.Y. 1, 119 N.E.2d 563 (1954). See also Chayes, Madam Wagner and the Close Corporation, 73 Harv. L. Rev. 1532, 1536 (1960).

better suited to acquire the shares of the passive investor group than vice versa. However, more often than not both groups are represented in management and thus a choice must be made on some other basis. One group may consist of persons who are relatively old and are approaching retirement age, in contrast to the other group which may be composed of younger persons who, eager to advance in the company, are urging changes in its policies which the older group resists. In this situation the older group may be persuaded that the policy differences, although real enough, should not interfere with the long-term perspective of what will eventually become of the corporation when they retire. Thus, if there is a stock repurchase agreement with the corporation or a cross-purchase arrangement with other shareholders, even though the time may not yet have arrived for the repurchase, it may be well, in view of the deadlock, that the repurchase be in effect "accelerated." Since control of the corporation will eventually go to the younger shareholders, they may be the more appropriate ones to resolve the deadlock by purchasing the shares of the older faction.

It may be, however, that obstinacy or a wish to have their views recognized as the only "correct" policy for the corporation may lead shareholders to refuse to dispose of their shares when it would be prudent to do so. Although there is no foolproof solution to this predicament, several other approaches are possible. One approach is a requirement that if one shareholder group states a price which it would be willing to pay for the shares of the other group and if the other group refuses to *sell* at such a price, then the latter group must *purchase* the shares of the former group at the price stated. In other words where Group A makes an offer to Group B to purchase its shares at $50 per share, and Group B refuses to sell at that figure, then Group B *must* purchase the shares of Group A for $50 per share.[9] Under this approach, each group would be entitled to make the first offer to purchase. In doing so it would have to take into account the possibility that its offer might be refused, in which case it would be compelled to sell its shares at the price stated and the other group would be compelled to purchase them. Obviously this will not resolve the dispute unless one group makes an offer. However, as the deadlock continues, pressure is likely to mount and the likelihood increases that one of the groups will come forth with an offer. The offer is likely to be a relatively fair one in that the offeror, although free to set the price, must be prepared to *buy* as well as *sell* at that price. If the price is too low, the other side will refuse to sell and the offeror must part with his shares on the same terms. In such a situation the offeror is likely, if anything, to set a relatively high price in that he may be willing to pay a premium to obtain control and to resolve a dispute which, while it lasts, cannot help but affect his investment adversely. If the price is high enough, the other group may find it attractive to sell its shares, particularly if the alternative is purchasing the shares of the other faction at

[9] See 2 F. O'Neal, Close Corporations: Law and Practice 172 (1958).

the high price. Thus an atmosphere of "horse-trading" may be encouraged which will lead one group or the other to sell out.

A clause in the articles of incorporation or bylaws establishing such a scheme is not too difficult to draft. Thus it could be specified that if a deadlock (defined in terms such as those previously suggested) persists for a specified period of time, any shareholder or group of shareholders may make an offer to purchase shares held by any other shareholder or group of shareholders. If such offer is not accepted within ten days (or some other suitable period of time), then the shareholder or shareholders who made the offer to buy must sell their shares and the offerees must purchase them at the price stated in the offer.

It has been pointed out [10] that a possible disadvantage of a scheme such as the above is that it might encourage one shareholder or group of shareholders who are relatively prosperous to create a deadlock expressly for the purpose of buying out the shares of others who are not so favorably situated financially. This, of course, is true, and yet it should be kept in mind that the price paid for the shares is likely to be relatively fair for the reasons previously mentioned, since, if the offer is refused, the shoe is placed on the other foot and the offeror must sell. Although a relatively wealthy offeror may assume that his offer to purchase will be accepted when the offeree does not have access to abundant capital, still he cannot be certain that this will be so since the offeree, if able to acquire complete control of the corporation, may be able to finance the purchase through outside sources or through what has been called a "bootstrap" purchase.[11] Essentially such a scheme involves financing the purchase through use of corporate funds. For example, a bank or other financial institution may be willing to make a short-term loan to the corporation to enable it to repurchase the shares of those who wish to sell. When one shareholder group acquires complete control it then arranges for the corporation to repay the loan. A variant of this approach would be a loan from an outside source to the shareholders, or to a new corporation formed by them for the purpose of taking over the old corporation, with the understanding that, once control is obtained, the acquired corporation will assume liability for the obligation and repay it in accordance with its terms. Although technically this might be attacked as a misuse of corporate funds to finance a purchase of control by one or more shareholders, there will be no one to object if those who acquire control end up owning all the shares. Thus only a minority faction whose shares are not repurchased could object to the bootstrap technique. As a practical matter, such a minority could probably be persuaded to go along with those seeking

[10] Ibid. (Supp. 1969).

[11] See Polasky, Planning for the Disposition of a Substantial Interest in a Closely Held Business, 46 Iowa L. Rev. 516 (1961); Lange, Bootstrap Financing: The Redemption Technique, 18 Tax L. Rev. 323 (1963). See also B. Bittker and J. Eustice Federal Income Taxation of Corporations and Shareholders §7.25 (1966).

control or could be bought out if offered a sufficiently attractive price for their shares. After all, if the purchase did not go through, their alternative would be to continue to hold a minority interest in a corporation which is either deadlocked or dominated by a majority shareholder group which would not be responsive to their wishes. Their best course might be to sell out to either of the two opposing factions on the best terms they can get.

A variant of the above approach would be a provision in the articles of incorporation or bylaws which in effect permits a shareholder to force a repurchase of his shares by giving him the right to dissolve the corporation if his offer is not accepted. The main disadvantage with this is that the alternative remedy (dissolution) is likely to be harmful to all concerned. Thus it is useful mainly as a threat and negotiations conducted under duress may be neither friendly nor fruitful. It is particularly important in such a context that the price set for the repurchase be a fair one.[12] On the other hand, if the analogy between a close corporation and a partnership (i.e., the concept of a close corporation as a "chartered partnership") has any validity, it may make sense, particularly for minority shareholders who are most likely to take advantage of such a provision, to allow shareholders to withdraw from the business at any time, either through repurchase of their shares or by dissolving the corporation.

The partnership analogy is only approximate, however, and is particularly inaccurate if the tax aspects of dissolution are taken into account. Dissolution of a partnership does not necessarily result in taxation of the partners,[13] whereas, aside from the elective provisions of Section 333 of the Code discussed later in this chapter (which are useful only in specialized cases),[14] liquidation of a corporation is likely to give rise to tax at the shareholder level.[15] This factor adds to the pressure and force of the threat and makes the weapon of potential dissolution a powerful one. This is particularly so in that the tax impact on a minority shareholder is likely to be the same whether he resells his shares to the corporation or surrenders them in liquidation. From his standpoint, then, it may not be particularly important whether the corporation accepts his offer or liquidates. In sharp contrast, since a corporate repurchase or shareholder cross purchase will not result in a tax to the surviving shareholders[16] whereas liquidation of the corporation is likely to produce a tax, those who hold a majority interest will in most situations be vitally interested in keeping the corporation alive. However,

---

[12] See 2 F. O'Neal, id. at §10.28 (price set at 20 percent above book value of the shares, determined in accordance with appraisal proceedings).

[13] See Int. Rev. Code of 1954, §§731, 736, 741, 751.

[14] See text accompanying note 108 *infra*.

[15] The liquidation distribution will result in capital gain or loss. Int. Rev. Code of 1954, §331. Aside from Section 333 of the Code, the other exception is a complete liquidation of an 80 percent owned subsidiary. Id. §332.

[16] See Ch. VI, text accompanying notes 132–139.

since, as already pointed out, liquidation may result in loss of good will and of going concern value of the business,[17] it may be advantageous for the minority shareholders to have their shares repurchased rather than to adopt the liquidation alternative.

As with the other technique previously discussed,[18] it is possible that a majority shareholder might use dissolution in order to appropriate the operating assets of the company and squeeze out a minority shareholder. Thus the majority shareholder might intentionally bring about a deadlock and offer his shares to the minority shareholders knowing full well that the latter would not be able to finance a purchase. When the offer is turned down, then the corporation might be dissolved in accordance with the articles of incorporation or bylaws. Although it is likely that a minority shareholder would be able to obtain equitable relief in this situation, preserving the status quo may be of little value in that it would often be wiser to recognize the difficulties of continuing to do business with hostile or rapacious associates and be content with receiving a fair price for one's shares. And unless the majority shareholder made a fair offer for the shares of the minority, equitable relief could be granted.

Although the threat of dissolution is, as we have seen, a potent weapon, the problems which it may entail, particularly from the tax standpoint, may suggest another approach. Thus it could be provided that a shareholder might offer his shares to the corporation or to the other shareholders at a designated price and that if the offer were not accepted, then the parties would be required to submit their dispute to arbitration.[19] The decision of the arbitrator would be binding on all the parties. Here a minority shareholder would be assured either that his shares would be purchased or that the deadlock would be resolved in some fashion, which, one would hope, would enable the corporation to resume normal operations. The arbitrator's powers should be broad enough to include a determination that shares held by one or more persons should be purchased by the corporation or by the other shareholders at a figure determined by him to be a fair one. This would enable an arbitrator to assess the likelihood that, even if the present deadlock were resolved, another impasse might arise in the future, in which case a more realistic and permanent solution to the inability of the parties to agree on basic policy matters is that one or more shareholders should be bought out by the others.

---

[17] This is not necessarily so, however, as where the majority shareholders choose to continue the business and cause the operating assets to be transferred to a new corporation. In such a situation it is obviously important that the minority shareholders receive the going concern value of their shares (i.e., that good will is taken into account in determining the amount they are entitled to receive in liquidation). See the discussion of Lebold v. Inland Steel Co., 125 F.2d 369 (7th Cir. 1942), *cert. denied*, 316 U.S. 675 (1942), in Ch. IV, text accompanying notes 44–46.

[18] See text accompanying note 10 *supra*.

[19] See 2 F. O'Neal, Close Corporations 172 n.18 (Supp. 1969).

(b) ARBITRATION AS A REMEDY IN DEADLOCK SITUATIONS

The foregoing suggestion cannot be evaluated without inquiring whether arbitration is an effective way of resolving deadlocks. This in turn depends upon the extent to which state laws permit arbitration of existing disputes or agreements to arbitrate future disputes.

The history of arbitration as a means of settling disputes cannot be understood apart from the attitude of the courts which, at least traditionally, have viewed arbitration as a "usurpation" of their authority. Today, with the proliferation of federal, state and municipal agencies which set policies and resolve disputes, the classical emphasis upon the courthouse as *the* way in which disputes must be settled is generally recognized as an anachronism.[20]

The most sensitive area historically has been an agreement to arbitrate a future dispute (i.e., some disagreement which has not yet arisen). Agreements of this type generally were not enforceable at common law. Thus, despite his having entered into an agreement, a shareholder could not be bound to arbitrate. Indeed, even if he submitted to arbitration, he could withdraw and not be bound if he did so before the arbitrator came down with his award.[21] *A fortiori*, a person could not be prevented from litigating a question merely by his having previously agreed to submit it to arbitration.[22] Statutes in some states continue to take this approach.[23] On the other hand, many states have by statute provided that agreements to arbitrate future disputes may be specifically enforced.[24] In the absence of such statutes, however, courts have sometimes taken the view that an agreement to arbitrate not only ousts the courts of jurisdiction but also deprives a company's board of directors of its "discretion" to manage corporate affairs and constitutes an unlawful delegation of the power to make policy decisions to

[20] See Note, Arbitration as a Means of Settling Disputes Within Close Corporations, 63 Colum. L. Rev. 267, 268 (1963). The author indicates that the judicial concern over preserving the jurisdiction of the courts may have been influenced by the fact that, at one time, "English judges were dependent on court revenues for their livelihood." Id. at n.7.

[21] Id. at 269. See also 2 F. O'Neal, id. at 188–189.

[22] Ibid.

[23] See, e.g., Mo. Stats. Ann. §435.010 (Vernon 1939): "Any contract or agreement hereafter entered into containing any clause or provision providing for an adjustment by arbitration shall not preclude any party or beneficiary under such contract or agreement from instituting suit or other legal action on such contract at any time, and the compliance with such clause or provision shall not be a condition precedent to the right to bring or recover in such action."

[24] E.g., Cal. Civ. Proc. Code §1281 (1970 Supp.); Conn. Gen. Stats. Ann. §52–408 (1960); Mass. Ann. Laws ch. 251, §1 (1970 Supp.); Mich. Stats. Ann. §§27A.5001–27A.5035 (1962); N.J. Stats. Ann. §2A:24–1 (1952); N.Y. Civ. Prac. Law §§7501–14 (1963); Ohio Rev. Code Ann. §2711.01 (1969 Supp.); Pa. Stats. Ann. tit. 5, §161 (1963). For a complete listing see 2 F. O'Neal, id. at 190 n.74.

an outsider.[25] Such concern for preserving the discretion of a board of directors of a deadlocked closely held corporation by invalidating agreements made between shareholder-directors is incongruous, for the very fact of deadlock means that the directors cannot exercise discretion in any meaningful way. What is really being said in such decisions is that shareholders cannot lawfully agree to a method of settling intra-corporate disputes other than by resort to the courts. Aside from the traditional concern for preserving the jurisdiction of the judiciary, the policy reasons for this attitude are unclear. Thus it is difficult to see how persons other than shareholders (e.g., creditors, employees and others) are harmed by having deadlocks resolved by arbitration.[26] If it be thought that a corporation might be harmed by unwise policy decisions made by an "outsider," the fear would seem unjustified in any but the most unusual situation. This is particularly so if an arbitrator is selected for his expertise and experience in resolving problems in particular business situations. To deprive the shareholders of the power to select this method of resolving disputes is in a very real sense a judicial usurpation of *shareholder* discretion, thinly justified by a tenuous concern over preserving a discretion which the same persons supposedly have as directors when in fact they are deadlocked. If the only redress in such situations is resort to the courts or dissolution, it is difficult to see how the rights of shareholders, creditors, employees and others receive any better protec-

[25] See 2 id. at §9.15. See, e.g., In re Allied Fruit & Extract Co., 243 App. Div. 52, 276 N.Y.S. 153 (1st Dept. 1934). As 2 F. O'Neal, at 199, indicates, the *Allied Fruit* case may have been considerably weakened in authority by subsequent New York decisions, particularly Martocci v. Martocci, 2 Misc. 2d 330, 42 N.Y.S.2d 222 (Sup. Ct.), aff'd mem., 266 App. Div. 840, 43 N.Y.S.2d 516 (1st Dept. 1943). Other New York decisions have refused to submit disputes to arbitration on the ground that the disputes could not be "the subject of an action" under Section 1448 of the N.Y. Civ. Prac. Act. For example, in Application of Burkin, 1 N.Y.2d 570, 136 N.E.2d 862, 154 N.Y.S.2d 898 (1956), the New York Court of Appeals held that the question of *whether* a director should be removed was not arbitrable since, because of a provision in the certificate of incorporation and a shareholders' agreement requiring unanimity for removal of directors, a director-shareholder could not be removed without his consent. The N.Y. Civ. Prac. Law was subsequently changed so as to permit arbitration "without regard to the justiciable character of the controversy." N.Y. Civ. Prac. Law §7501 (1963). Even under the former law, if a director *had* in fact been removed, the question of whether his removal was proper was held to be arbitrable. See Staklinski v. Pyramid Elec. Co., 10 Misc. 2d 706, 172 N.Y.S.2d 224 (Sup. Ct. 1958), aff'd, 6 N.Y.2d 159, 160 N.E.2d 78, 188 N.Y.S.2d 541 (1959); Martocci v. Martocci, *supra;* Application of Landersman, 280 App. Div. 963, 116 N.Y.S.2d 495 (1st Dept. 1952). Thus, as 2 F. O'Neal, id. at 202, summarizes the New York cases, the question of *whether* a director *should* be removed could not be submitted to arbitration in the face of a shareholders' unanimity agreement, although in other situations, if a director *had* been removed, the propriety of his removal was considered arbitrable. For a relatively recent New York case which may exemplify a liberalizing trend, see Application of Vogel, 25 A.D.2d 212, 268 N.Y.S.2d 237 (1st Dept. 1965), aff'd mem., 19 N.Y.2d 589, 224 N.E.2d 738, 278 N.Y.S.2d 236 (1967).

[26] See Kronstein, Business Arbitration—Instrument of Private Government, 54 Yale L.J. 36, 61 (1944), for an argument to the contrary.

tion. In fact, crowded dockets, delay and, at times, judicial unfamiliarity with the problems of particular businesses may result in positive harm.

Another situation where the courts have occasionally invalidated arbitration agreements is where the agreement specifies that if shareholders are unable to agree as to how their shares should be voted, then the arbitrator shall decide, and if the shareholders refuse to vote in accordance with the arbitrator's decision, then he may vote the shares. Agreements of this sort have occasionally been struck down on the ground that they confer a proxy on one who has no "interest" in the shares and thus effect a separation of voting rights from beneficial ownership which contravenes the policy of the statute.[27] This approach seems as tenuous as the cases striking down arbitration agreements because they interfere with the discretion of the directors. In a closely held corporation, where the shareholders have agreed that another shall vote their shares if they are unable to agree on how to vote, the only harm might be to the shareholders (aside from a remote possibility that creditors, employees and others might be affected by an unwise decision by the arbitrator).[28] But the very function of the arbitrator and the sole reason for having one is to protect the shareholders. Accordingly, it seems farfetched to dwell on the possibility that the arbitrator might vote the shares in a manner which would not be in the shareholders' best interests. The policy against divorce of voting rights from beneficial ownership, exemplified by the traditional ban against vote-selling[29] should have no application here if that policy is intended to protect the interests of the shareholders, the corporation and other persons who might be adversely affected. If the shareholders are deadlocked and one shareholder refuses to vote in accordance with the arbitrator's decision, it is difficult to see how the interests of anyone are better protected by perpetuating the deadlock rather than by having the arbitrator vote the shares of the dissenting party.

In a case which has been previously discussed in considerable detail,[30] the parties agreed to vote their shares together so as to maintain control of a corporation and that, in the event of a disagreement, the manner in which the shares should be voted should be determined by arbitration, the arbitrator's decision to bind both parties. When a disagreement arose, the arbitrator directed that the shares be voted in a certain manner. The Delaware Chancery Court held that the agreement could be specifically enforced in that where one party to the agreement refuses to abide by the arbitrator's decision the other party is given an implied proxy to vote his shares, a proxy which is irrevocable since it is "coupled with an interest." On appeal the Delaware Supreme Court upheld the arbitration agreement, agreeing that

[27] E.g., Roberts v. Whitson, 188 S.W.2d 875 (Tex. Civ. App. 1945).
[28] See note 26 *supra*.
[29] See Ch. III, text accompanying note 119.
[30] See Ringling v. Ringling Bros.–Barnum & Bailey Combined Shows, Inc., 29 Del. Ch. 318, 49 A.2d 603 (Ch. 1946), *modified on appeal*, 29 Del. Ch. 610, 53 A.2d 441 (Sup. Ct. 1947), discussed in Ch. III, text accompanying notes 128–139.

it was enforceable, but disagreed as to the manner in which the agreement should be construed and the way in which it should be enforced. Since the agreement did not expressly provide for the enforcement machinery read into it by the lower court (i.e., the implied proxy agreement) the Supreme Court considered that it could do little more than invalidate the votes cast by the dissenting party to the agreement (i.e., those votes which were not cast in the manner directed by the arbitrator). This was required because the parties had failed to specify for cross proxies in the event that one party refused to vote as the arbitrator directed. There is nothing in the Supreme Court opinion that indicates that the arbitration agreement would have been invalid if it *had* provided for cross proxies or even if it had conferred a proxy on the arbitrator to vote the shares directly.

In a subsequent case[31] a shareholders' agreement which *did* provide for cross-proxy enforcement was upheld by the Chancery Court but was invalidated by the Supreme Court not because the arbitration agreement was invalid as such but because it constituted in substance a voting trust which, not having been created in accordance with a statutory provision regulating voting trusts, was invalid.[32] As we have seen, the latter decision has now been overruled by new legislation. Thus it would appear that an arbitration agreement which contains cross-proxy enforcement machinery would be valid under Delaware law. Whether such an agreement would be valid if the arbitrator were empowered to vote the shares himself is uncertain.[33] It has been argued that the judicial distaste for such arrangements is ill-founded and that the courts are confused and overly technical in invalidating proxies given to those whose only function is to protect the interests of the shareholders.[34] Whatever validity the rule prohibiting irrevocable proxies unless coupled with an interest may have, it should not be applied in this situation, for the interest being protected is a very real one, namely the interest the parties to the agreement have in its being enforced according to its terms. Nonetheless, pending further clarification of the area, cautious corporate counsel would be well-advised to adopt the cross-proxy method of enforcement rather than to confer voting powers on an arbitrator.

An interesting question is the effect of an agreement to arbitrate on a shareholder's right to dissolve a corporation. As we shall see, many statutes

[31] Abercrombie v. Davies, 36 Del. Ch. 371, 130 A.2d 338 (Sup. Ct. 1957).

[32] See Ch. III, text accompanying note 92.

[33] Id. note 93. Although cross proxies would be authorized by Section 212 of the Delaware law, stating that "an interest in the corporation generally" is sufficient to support an irrevocable proxy, and cross proxies are implicitly authorized as enforcement machinery in a shareholders' agreement under Section 218(c) of the law (authorizing the shares to be "voted as provided by the agreement, or as the parties may agree, or as determined in accordance with a procedure agreed upon by them"), it is not clear whether the "procedure agreed upon" may confer a proxy on an arbitrator who, technically, may not have an "interest in the corporation."

[34] See Ch. III, text accompanying notes 149 and 164.

provide for dissolution on the petition of an aggrieved shareholder if the corporation is deadlocked and if it appears that irreparable harm is being suffered by the corporation. Generally dissolution will be granted only where it appears that the corporation is no longer able to function effectively.[35] When a deadlock develops a shareholder might seek to avoid an agreement binding him to arbitrate the dispute by bringing an action to dissolve the corporation. The question is, then, whether a shareholder may be precluded from bringing such an action if he has entered into an arbitration agreement. As to this, the courts are divided, although the more recent decisions appear to take a relatively liberal attitude towards granting a stay of proceedings for dissolution where the shareholders have agreed to arbitrate their differences and where it appears that arbitration might lead to a settlement which would permit the corporation to continue as a viable enterprise.[36] From a practical standpoint, perhaps the best approach might be for the agreement to specify that arbitration shall be a condition precedent to a shareholder's petitioning to dissolve the corporation except where a court of equity shall determine that arbitration would be ineffective and that dissolution is the only practicable means of resolving the dispute. Conversely, it might also be provided that if one party refuses to arbitrate in the manner agreed upon, then the other party may either obtain a decree compelling arbitration or dissolve the corporation, and that the costs of either proceeding shall be paid by the recalcitrant shareholder.

An analogous problem is whether an agreement to arbitrate may be used to obtain a stay of litigation other than an action to dissolve the corporation. The question is particularly troublesome where a derivative suit is involved. Thus if an agreement to arbitrate merely refers to the rights of the shareholders *inter se,* it is possible to argue that the corporation, if not a party to the agreement, should not be precluded from enforcing whatever rights it may have. Accordingly, the argument goes, a shareholder should not be precluded from enforcing the corporate cause of action on a derivative basis *even though he might be a party to the arbitration agreement.*[37] Although

---

[35] See text accompanying note 73 *infra.*

[36] See 2 F. O'Neal, Close Corporations §9.18 (1958). For cases granting a stay of dissolution see Moskowitz v. Surrey Sleep Products, Inc., 30 A.D.2d 820, 292 N.Y.S.2d 748 (1968); In the Matter of Myers, 279 App. Div. 984, 112 N.Y.S.2d 489 (1st Dept. 1952), *aff'd,* 304 N.Y. 656, 107 N.E.2d 512 (1952); Zybert v. Dab, 276 App. Div. 1070, 96 N.Y.S.2d 374 (1st Dept. 1950), *aff'd mem.,* 301 N.Y. 632, 93 N.E.2d 917 (1950). The earlier cases are discussed in 2 F. O'Neal, id.

[37] The cases are collected in 2 F. O'Neal, id. at §9.19, and in Note, Arbitration as a Means of Settling Disputes Within Close Corporations, 63 Colum. L. Rev. 267, 281–283 (1963). In Siegel v. Ribak, 43 Misc. 2d 7, 249 N.Y.S.2d 903 (Sup. Ct. 1964), the earlier New York cases denying a stay of derivative actions were distinguished as either dictum or involving publicly held corporations. In addition, as the court observed, "many, if not most disputes can be framed in the form of a derivative action and a general rule that a stockholders' derivative suit forecloses arbitration would be too rigid since it may permit the parties to evade the agreement at will." 43 Misc. 2d at 13, 249 N.Y.S.2d at 909.

this argument may have a certain theoretical appeal, it is, as one commentator has suggested, overly conceptual, at least in a closely held corporation where all of those having any interest in the firm are parties to the agreement.[38] It makes too much of the fact that a corporation is a separate entity and ignores the reality, namely that a shareholder should not be permitted to litigate disputes which he has agreed to arbitrate merely by characterizing his action as derivative. However, because of the attitude which the courts have taken and the uncertainty of the case authority, it would seem advisable that even though all the shareholders in a closely held corporation are parties to an arbitration agreement, the corporation itself should be made a party. Even though a court might be persuaded to accept the separate identity concept, it might be more reluctant to permit a derivative suit where the corporation has agreed to arbitrate and where an arbitration proceeding is expressly made a condition precedent to the litigation of a corporate right. Needless to say, even though the corporation is a party to the agreement, *all* the shareholders should, if possible, be made parties. If the agreement does not bind a minority shareholder, and even though he might not be in a position to deadlock the corporation, there is no guarantee that this will always be so. Where other shareholders die or cease to be employees, they may sell their shares with the result that a surviving minority shareholder may become more powerful and be able to deadlock the corporation at a later date.

It has also been suggested [39] that it may be unwise to rely solely on an arbitration agreement between the shareholders and the corporation. The arbitration provisions should also be inserted in the articles of incorporation if this is legally permissible. There are at least two reasons for this. First, although the agreement may expressly bind successors and assigns of the original parties, it is always possible that a person subsequently acquiring shares may assert that he is not bound by the agreement because he was not a party to it and did not have notice of its provisions. If the arbitration provisions are in the articles of incorporation, then they bind all shareholders *if* some suitable notice of the provision is provided on each stock certificate. In this respect the problem is similar to that involving stock transfer restrictions.[40] A second reason for including arbitration provisions in the articles of incorporation is that in some jurisdictions the right of shareholders to petition for judicial dissolution in the case of deadlock may be restricted by the articles of incorporation.[41] If the articles of incorporation

---

[38] See Note, 63 Colum. L. Rev. 267, 282 (1963). See also Note, Mandatory Arbitration for Intra–Close Corporation Disputes, 56 Va. L. Rev. 271, 281–282 (1970), for a useful discussion of the entire arbitration area.

[39] See 2 F. O'Neal, id. at §9.21.

[40] See Ch. III, text accompanying note 20.

[41] E.g., N.Y. Bus. Corp. Law §1104 (1961). Note, however, that any shareholder entitled to vote at an election of directors may petition to dissolve a corporation if the shareholders because of deadlock have failed to elect directors for at

make arbitration a prerequisite for any action for dissolution, then it is less likely that dissolution may be used to avoid arbitration.

Difficult problems sometimes arise in connection with selecting an arbitrator. It has already been pointed out in another context (determining the purchase price of shares in a buy-and-sell agreement) [42] that a useful method is to permit each party to the dispute to select an arbitrator and then have the arbitrators so selected choose a third arbitrator. This approach will generally be satisfactory in disputes between only two shareholders but difficulties arise in more complex situations. Thus if four shareholders hold 50 percent of the shares and two other shareholders hold the remaining 50 percent, who selects the arbitrators? Each shareholder group may deadlock over the question, producing a "deadlock within a deadlock." It has been suggested that "the company" might designate an arbitrator, that "the shareholder who otherwise would be outvoted by his co-shareholders" might name the other arbitrator and that the two arbitrators so designated should choose a third.[43] The problem with this is that if there is a real deadlock, it may not be possible for the company to make a choice. This would be so where there is an even number of directors who are divided on policy matters or where the shareholders have been unable to elect directors. An even more unsatisfactory arrangement would be to permit each shareholder to select an arbitrator.[44] This merely carries the deadlock to a higher level, for there is no guarantee that the dispute may be resolved any more effectively by representatives of the shareholders than by the shareholders themselves. A far better solution is for the parties to agree upon a single individual who is as independent and impartial as possible. Obviously such an agreement is not likely to be reached once the dispute has arisen, but this is by no means so when the agreement is entered into, for then the parties are likely to be in a friendly and cooperative frame of mind. Other alternatives might be to agree that the arbitrator shall be selected from a panel presented by the American Arbitration Association or that the arbitrator shall be designated by a court.[45] The former (American Arbitration Association) seems a better method, for the very process of obtaining court approval for an arbitrator may involve litigation, expense and delay, particularly if the judge's decision is appealed to a higher court. Also it may invite the filing of a petition for dissolution of the corporation and thus raise the troublesome question of whether arbitration is the exclusive remedy.

---

least two consecutive annual meeting dates. No provision in the certificate of incorporation may qualify this right. N.Y. Bus. Corp. Law §1104(c) (1961). Query, however, as to the effect of a shareholders' agreement in this situation—i.e., whether arbitration can be made a condition precedent to an action for dissolution. See Moskowitz v. Surrey Sleep Products, Inc., 30 A.D.2d 820, 292 N.Y.S.2d 748 (1968).

[42] See Ch. III, text accompanying note 62.
[43] See 2 F. O'Neal, id. at 215.
[44] Ibid.
[45] Id. at 215–216.

The scope of the arbitrator's powers should also be considered with some care. Thus do the parties wish to submit only disputes as to particular matters to arbitration, such as the purchase price for shares in a buy-and-sell agreement or the question of whether a shareholder should be ousted from being a director or holding any other corporate office? Because of the tendency of courts to construe arbitration agreements relatively narrowly, it is preferable to define the scope of the arbitrator's powers as broadly as possible, and even to provide that any dispute as to this matter (i.e., a dispute as to what is arbitrable) shall itself be submitted to arbitration.[46] Thus the arbitrator may be given power to pass upon his own jurisdiction, as it were, instead of having this matter referred to the courts, which might adopt a more restrictive view. The precise language for an arbitration clause to accomplish this effect is a matter on which each lawyer is likely to have his particular preference. However, something akin to the following might be helpful:

> Any dispute among the parties hereto concerning the meaning of this agreement, or its application to any matter relating to the corporation, or arising between the parties hereto, shall be submitted to arbitration in the matter set forth herein, and the arbitrator shall resolve all such disputes, including any disputes as to whether or not a particular matter shall be submitted to arbitration. The decision of such arbitrator shall be binding upon the parties hereto, including the corporation, who, pending a decision by the arbitrator, shall be precluded from bringing any suit or other proceeding before any judicial, administrative or other body on any matter which has been submitted to arbitration or which could be so submitted under the terms of this agreement.

Although it is common to incorporate an arbitration agreement as part of a shareholders' agreement or preincorporation agreement, an argument for not doing so is that a shareholder who resists arbitration may be able to convince a court that the shareholders' agreement is itself invalid for some reason (as where it unlawfully purports to bind the directors in exercising their discretion or contains an unlawful stock transfer restriction). In such situations, unless the shareholders' agreement contains a "severability" clause (stating in effect that notwithstanding the invalidity of any particular provision of the agreement, the agreement shall continue to be enforceable in all other respects), the arbitration clause may be unenforceable if the shareholders' agreement is held invalid.[47]

Once an arbitrator has arrived at a decision, there is still little practical utility unless there is some means whereby the decision can be implemented. As previously suggested, if the matter relates to how the shares are to be voted, then those shareholders who are willing to abide by the arbitra-

[46] Id. at 220 n.83 (collecting the cases permitting this approach).
[47] Id. at §9.24.

tor's decision may be given irrevocable proxies to vote shares held by any parties to the agreement who are not willing to vote as directed.[48] This avoids the troublesome problems entailed in giving the arbitrator power to vote the shares and the possibility of such a scheme being invalidated on the technicality that the arbitrator does not have an interest in the shares. Since the subject of the arbitration will frequently extend beyond the way in which shares are to be voted, the agreement should specify that the arbitrator's decision shall be binding upon the parties and that any party to the agreement shall be entitled to have it specifically enforced by an appropriate judicial decree along with such other relief as may be required to effectuate fully the arbitrator's decision.

(c) OTHER METHODS OF RESOLVING DEADLOCKS WITHOUT
     DISSOLUTION

If we proceed further on the assumption that it is unwise to dissolve a profitable business if there are alternative ways to resolve deadlocks, we can consider two other methods to achieve this result, namely the possibility in some states of having a so-called provisional director appointed and also the possibility in a greater number of states of having a receiver appointed to manage the corporation until the parties are able to reach an agreement.

The provisional director technique is authorized by statute in at least six states.[49] Since three of the states (California, Missouri and Tennessee) have substantially the same statute, their general approach can be briefly described. A corporation with an even number of directors who are equally divided and cannot agree as to the management of the corporate affairs may have a provisional director appointed if "its business cannot longer be conducted to advantage or . . . there is danger that its property and business will be impaired and lost." A petition for the appointment of a provisional director may be filed by one half of the directors or by those who hold not less than one third of the outstanding shares. The provisional director must be impartial; he may not be either a shareholder or a creditor nor related "by consanguinity or affinity within the third degree" to any director[50] or any judge of the court by which he is appointed. When appointed he has all the rights and powers of a director, including the right to receive notice of directors' meetings and to vote, until the deadlock is broken or until he is removed by the court or by the vote or written consent of those who hold a

---

[48] See text accompanying notes 27–34 *supra*.

[49] Cal. Gen. Corp. Law §§819, 4655 (1947); Del. Gen. Corp. Law §353 (1967); Ga. Code Ann. §22–703 (1969); Mo. Gen. & Bus. Corp. Law §351.323 (1959); Pa. Bus. Corp. Law §384 (1968); Tenn. Gen. Corp. Law §48–8.09 (1968).

[50] In Missouri, the provisional director may not also be related to any corporate officer, although in California and Tennessee the prohibition extends only to a relationship with a director.

majority of the shares. He is entitled to such compensation as may be agreed upon between him and the corporation or, in default of such agreement, to compensation as decreed by the court.

One obvious limitation with the foregoing statutes is that they apply only to corporations with an even number of directors who are equally divided. Deadlocks may arise in other ways. Suppose, for example, that a corporation has a board consisting of five directors and that the articles of incorporation provide that the vote of two thirds of the directors is necessary in order to pass a resolution. This means, in effect, that four out of the five directors must vote in favor of the resolution in order to pass it. If the board deadlocks, three directors to two, a provisional director could not be appointed.[51] Even if the statutes made this possible, the provisional director could break the deadlock only if he voted along with the three directors and against the two others. Nonetheless, it might be worth a try, particularly since the provisional director may request the court to discharge him if he believes that he cannot effectively break the deadlock.[52] Also there are uncertainties as to whether there is an "even number of directors" where there are vacancies on the board or where one or more directors refuses to attend meetings. The California courts apparently look only to the number of directors in office and disregard vacancies.[53] On the other hand, it has been suggested that if the vacancy can be filled, a provisional director should not be appointed even though there may be an even number of directors pending the filling of a vacancy.[54] Similar problems of interpretation arise with regard to when a "business cannot longer be conducted to advantage or . . . there is danger that its property and business will be impaired and lost." In California a relatively broad interpretation has been given to this clause so as to authorize the appointment of a provisional director for a solvent and profitable concern where, because of a disagreement as to whether existing policies should be perpetuated, the board was deadlocked and unable to declare dividends, thus risking the imposition of a penalty tax on excess accumulations.[55] In addition there was a dispute concerning allegedly excessive salaries and payments to one of the shareholders for leased property. Thus the court stressed that the corporation was not

[51] See Comment, 48 Calif. L. Rev. 272, 278 n.27 (1960).

[52] See In re O'Brien Machinery, Inc., 224 Cal. App. 2d 563, 36 Cal. Rptr. 782 (1964).

[53] See Comment, 31 Mo. L. Rev. 536, 539 (1966), citing Desert Club v. Superior Court, 99 Cal. App. 2d 346, 221 P.2d 766 (1950). See also Comment, 48 Calif. L. Rev. 272, 278 (1960).

[54] In re Friedlieb, 184 N.Y.S. 753 (Sup. Ct. 1920). These problems are avoided by the new Delaware, Georgia and Pennsylvania statutes, none of which provide that a corporation must have an even number of directors to qualify for the appointment of a provisional director. See Del. Gen. Corp. Law §353 (1967); Ga. Code Ann. §22–703 (1969); Pa. Bus. Corp. Law §384 (1968).

[55] In re Jamison Steel Corp., 158 Cal. App. 2d 27, 322 P.2d 246 (1958).

able to manage its affairs *effectively* and that this was sufficient ground for the appointment of a provisional director.

Although the provisional director technique has some resemblance to arbitration in that the director presumably hears both sides of the dispute and then resolves it by voting as he thinks best, it also resembles to some extent a receivership, in that the procedure is carried out by a court appointment of a *deus ex machina* as it were. However, subject to its own limitations, a provisional director may have distinct advantages over a receivership in that receivership may, in the minds of creditors and others, indicate financial disability, if not insolvency. Thus a provisional director may be less likely than a receivership to have an adverse effect on a corporation's credit rating.[56]

(d)   JUDICIAL APPOINTMENT OF A RECEIVER

The technique of having a court appoint a receiver for a deadlocked corporation can be used for two purposes. First, the receiver may be appointed merely to take charge of the business, assume custody of the corporate assets and supervise the running of the corporation pending a resolution of the deadlock.[57] This approach resembles that of the provisional director except that the receiver in effect temporarily replaces the entire board of directors and acts as its surrogate on the ground that the board is incapable of functioning. Despite the traditional reluctance of courts to assume supervisory roles over the running of businesses, whether conducted as corporations or partnerships,[58] receivership seems to be a feasible approach to deadlocks in many cases, especially if the only other alternative is to dissolve the corporation. In fact, the very threat of receivership may impress the parties with the seriousness of the situation and the need to resolve their differences.

Receivership has, however, been used more frequently in connection with the actual winding up of the affairs of a corporation than as an interim or stopgap management technique. Here, although the classical attitude of the judiciary has been that, in the absence of an enabling statute, equity has

---

[56] See Comment, 48 Calif. L. Rev. 272, 280 (1960).

[57] See, e.g., Thisted v. Tower Management Corp., 147 Mont. 1, 409 P.2d 813 (1967); cf. Farrar v. Pesterfield, 216 Ga. 311, 116 S.E.2d 229 (1960). The Delaware, Pennsylvania and Virginia statutes expressly permit the appointment of a "custodian" in deadlock situations who has powers similar to those of a receiver, except that he is directed to continue the business and not liquidate its affairs other than as otherwise ordered by the court. Del. Gen. Corp. Law §226 (1967); Pa. Bus. Corp. Law §§383, 513.1 (1968); Va. Stock Corp. Act §13.1–94 (1968).

[58] See J. Crane and A. Bromberg, Partnership §72 (1968) (classical rule that courts will not interfere with partnership activities and will withhold relief until an accounting incident to a dissolution—modified by Uniform Partnership Act, §22). See also 2 F. O'Neal, Close Corporations §9.27 (1958).

no power to appoint a receiver to wind up the affairs of a solvent going concern solely on the ground of a deadlock,[59] the "rule" has come to have so many exceptions that, as one commentator has remarked, the question no longer appears to be whether equity has the *power*, but whether and when a court will exercise its *discretion* to appoint a receiver.[60] The many cases on this offer no clear indication of any general rule, but merely illustrate the myriad possibilities. Most cases seem to recognize that mere deadlock may not be enough to justify receivership. There must be "dissension plus" [61] other factors, such as fraud or oppression by the majority shareholders,[62] waste or dissipation of the corporate assets[63] or such serious dissension between shareholders that it is no longer possible to operate the corporation profitably and, unless the corporation is dissolved, its value will be lost.[64] The general impression one receives from a survey of the cases indicates that whether or not a receiver will be appointed in a particular situation depends largely upon a court's prognosis of whether the corporation is what in medicine would be called a "terminal case" or whether there is reasonable hope that it may be able to recover or at least continue as a viable entity despite the deadlock. The equity receivership approach has in most jurisdictions been supplemented or even replaced by statutory provisions expressly permitting judicial dissolution of a corporation if certain conditions are shown to exist. Such statutes offer a general guide in determining when dissolution will be granted, either through an equity receivership or by means of a statutory dissolution procedure.

7.3 STATUTORY DISSOLUTION

Most states have statutes which permit a specified percentage of the shareholders to file a petition for dissolution upon the occurrence of particular events, such as deadlock. These provisions should not be confused with so-called voluntary dissolution provisions which permit dissolution with the consent of all the shareholders,[65] by the incorporators where the corporation has not commenced business[66] or by a resolution of the board of directors which is subsequently approved by a designated percentage of the share-

---

[59] For a collection of the authorities see ibid.

[60] Id. at 228.

[61] See Note, 56 Mich. L. Rev. 1019 (1958).

[62] See, e.g., Drob v. National Memorial Park, Inc., 28 Del. Ch. 254, 41 A.2d 589 (Ch. 1945); Gidwitz v. Lanzit Corrugated Box Co., 20 Ill. 2d 208, 170 N.E.2d 131 (1960); Patton v. Nicholas, 154 Tex. 385, 279 S.W.2d 848 (1955).

[63] E.g., Leibert v. Clapp, 13 N.Y.2d 313, 196 N.E.2d 540, 247 N.Y.S.2d 102 (1964); In re Victorian Sales Corp., 32 Misc. 2d 275, 223 N.Y.S.2d 119 (Sup. Ct. 1960).

[64] See 2 F. O'Neal, id. at 227 nn.4, 5 (Supp. 1969) (collecting several cases).

[65] See Model Bus. Corp. Act §83.

[66] See id. §82.

holders.[67] Such provisions give an automatic right of dissolution if their requirements are met, and no judicial approval is therefore necessary.

In contrast to this is a proceeding for dissolution by judicial decree. The common pattern of such statutes is to permit any shareholder[68] or one or more shareholders who hold a designated percentage of the outstanding stock[69] to file a petition alleging facts such as the following:

(1) That the directors are deadlocked in the management of the corporate affairs and the shareholders are unable to break the deadlock, and that irreparable injury to the corporation is being suffered or is threatened by reason thereof; or

(2) That the acts of the directors or those in control of the corporation are illegal, oppressive or fraudulent; or

(3) That the shareholders are deadlocked in voting power, and have failed, for a period which includes at least two consecutive annual meeting dates, to elect successors to directors whose terms have expired or would have expired upon the election of their successors; or

(4) That the corporate assets are being misapplied or wasted.[70]

Even though one or more of the above conditions is shown to exist, some courts hold that the right to dissolution is not automatic and that a court may exercise its discretion to refuse dissolution if some other technique of resolving an impasse appears more attractive.[71] This approach appears to be a wise one, since dissolution is not only the most drastic remedy for deadlock but may on the whole be harmful to the shareholders if there is some viable alternative which permits the corporation to continue as a going entity. Thus in some states the majority shareholders may avoid having a corporation dissolved if they are willing to purchase the shares of the minority shareholder at a price determined by appraisal.[72] In effect this gives the minority shareholder what he wants—i.e., escape from the corporate deadlock and his pro rata share of the value of the corporation—and yet permits

[67] See id. §84 (a majority of the voting shares are required for approval unless the articles of incorporation require a class vote, in which case the approval of a majority of each class is required, in addition to the basic requirement of a majority of the voting shares).

[68] See id. §97(a). The Act also permits a creditor to file a petition for dissolution where the corporation is insolvent and the creditor has obtained an unsatisfied judgment or the corporation has admitted in writing that his claim is due and owing. See also Fla. Gen. Corp. Law §608.0107 (1963); N.J. Bus. Corp. Act §14A:12–7 (1968); Tenn. Gen. Corp. Law §48–12.08 (1968).

[69] E.g., Md. Gen. Corp. Law §79A(a)(1), (2) (1967). Holders of 25 percent of the voting shares are entitled to petition for dissolution if the directors are deadlocked or the shareholders cannot elect directors. If the shareholders have failed to elect directors for two successive annual meetings, then any voting shareholder may file a petition for dissolution. Id. §79A(b) (1967). See also id. §109 (1967).

[70] Model Bus. Corp. Act §97. For general discussion of this area see Tingle, The Stockholder's Remedy of Corporate Dissolution (1959).

[71] See, e.g., Jackson v. Nicolai-Neppach Co., 219 Ore. 560, 348 P.2d 9 (1959).

[72] Cal. Gen. Corp. Law §§4658–4659 (1947); Conn. Stock Corp. Act §33–384 (1959); Md. Gen. Corp. Law §109(c) (1967); W. Va. Gen. Corp. Law §31–1–81 (1943).

the corporation to continue, which is obviously an advantage not only to the remaining shareholders but also to customers, employees and others. Such a procedure is unfair, however, unless the minority shareholder is assured a price for his shares which is at least equivalent to the amount he would receive if the company were dissolved. And if the majority shareholders are permitted to retain the operating assets, it is arguable that the "dissolution price" should not be determinative but that the minority shareholder should receive the going concern value of his shares, namely, an amount which reflects corporate good will.

In some states courts have refused to dissolve a corporation even though it is hopelessly deadlocked if it continues to be a profitable enterprise. The leading case is *In re Radom & Neidorff, Inc.,*[73] a most unfortunate situation involving a deadlock between a brother and sister, equal owners of a corporation engaged in printing musical compositions. The deadlock was brought about by the death of one of the founders of the enterprise and his bequeathing his shares to his wife. Five months after the husband died the corporation was deadlocked and the brother filed a petition under the New York statutory provision which at that time permitted dissolution at the behest of the holders of one half of the voting stock. The court refused to grant dissolution even though it was alleged that the shareholders (two in number) were deadlocked and were unable to elect directors, and that one of them (the sister) had refused to sign the other's salary checks, had refused an offer of $75,000 for her shares and, finally, had brought a derivative suit against the petitioner charging him with enriching himself at the corporate expense. Although the statute did not make dissolution mandatory upon a showing that a deadlock existed, one wonders whether any solution other than deadlock would be realistic in this situation. It has been suggested that the underlying reason for the decision may be that the court may have sensed that the dissolution proceeding was being used as a device for compelling the sister to sell out to the brother at an unfair price.[74] Thus the court may have withheld dissolution as a way of encouraging the petitioner to make a fairer offer for the shares of his sister. In any event, the New York statute was subsequently amended to provide that dissolution is not to be denied "merely because it is found that the corporate business has been or could be conducted at a profit." [75] The basic test, in New York[76] as well as in other jurisdictions having similar statutes, is whether dissolution will, on the whole, be a benefit to the shareholders.

[73] 307 N.Y. 1, 119 N.E.2d 563 (1954).

[74] See Chayes, Madam Wagner and the Close Corporation, 73 Harv. L. Rev. 1532, 1536 (1960). See also Ch. III, note 139.

[75] See N.Y. Bus. Corp. Law §1111(b)(3) (1961). *Compare* Kruger v. Gerth, 16 N.Y.2d 802, 210 N.E.2d 355, 263 N.Y.S.2d 1 (1965), *with* Application of Surchin, 55 Misc. 2d 888, 286 N.Y.S.2d 580 (Sup. Ct. N.Y. Co. 1967).

[76] See N.Y. Bus. Corp. Law §1111(b)(2) (1961).

7.4 TAX ASPECTS OF DISSOLUTION

Although it has been suggested that "dissolution" of a corporation is one of the remedies for a deadlock, the proper tax parlance is to refer to a "liquidation." Distributions either in partial or complete liquidation are taxed as sales or exchanges (i.e., the surrender of the stock for cash or other property gives rise to capital gain or loss).[77] Although the Code does not define the term "liquidation," the regulations state that

> A status of liquidation exists when a corporation ceases to be a going concern and its activities are merely for the purpose of winding up its affairs, paying its debts and distributing any remaining balance to its shareholders. A liquidation may be completed prior to the actual dissolution of the liquidating corporation. However, legal dissolution of the liquidating corporation is not required.[78]

Despite the regulation, which permits liquidation without dissolution of a corporation as a matter of state law, it is hazardous to liquidate and then, by distributing assets to majority shareholders, cause the enterprise to be reactivated. In such situations the Internal Revenue Service may succeed in convincing a court that the liquidation was a sham and should be disregarded. This would result in the disallowance of losses purportedly realized on the liquidation and also the preservation of the basis of the assets in the hands of the corporation at their original book values for depreciation purposes, instead of the stepped-up values and increased depreciation basis which might result if the liquidation were bona fide and the new corporation were not considered to be merely an extension of the old one.[79]

Although, except for certain elective provisions of the Code,[80] it is not necessary that there be any "plan" of liquidation—i.e., formal action by the directors or shareholders prior to a distribution in liquidation—it is hazardous to distribute assets before such a plan has been adopted. Thus the Internal Revenue Service might succeed in showing that a distribution of cash was in reality a dividend and should be taxed at ordinary rates to the extent of available earnings and profits, instead of its being taxed at capital gains rates as part of a liquidating distribution.[81] The safest method of proceeding, then, is a directors' resolution to liquidate, ratified or confirmed by a shareholder vote, the liquidating distribution taking place after the plan has

---

[77] Int. Rev. Code of 1954, §§331, 346.

[78] Treas. Reg. §1.332–2(c).

[79] Cf. Rev. Ruls. 60–50 and 60–51, 1960–1 Cum. Bull. 150 and 169. For a comprehensive discussion of the "liquidation-reincorporation" problem, see B. Bittker and J. Eustice, Federal Income Taxation of Corporations and Shareholders §9.05 (1966).

[80] E.g., Int. Rev. Code of 1954, §§333, 337.

[81] See B. Bittker and J. Eustice, id. at 341.

been adopted, with the shares being surrendered for cancellation. If the shares are not surrendered, then the liquidation may be characterized as merely a guise to distribute cash or other property at capital gains rates, especially if, as previously suggested, the corporation is not dissolved as a legal entity.[82]

With some exceptions, gain or loss is not recognized to a corporation in distributing its properties in liquidation.[83] The primary exceptions relate to the disposition of installment obligations,[84] the distribution of property subject to the depreciation recapture rules of Section 1245 and 1250 [85] and certain decisions based on doctrines such as assignment of income, which have taxed corporations on such items as unrealized receivables or other income items which, prior to liquidation, had not been taken into account for tax purposes.[86]

As far as the shareholder is concerned, his gain or loss is computed on the basis of the shares surrendered. If his shares have differing bases or have been held for differing periods of time, then gain or loss is computed on each share separately. For example, suppose that a shareholder owned twenty shares, ten of which he acquired more than six months prior to liquidation at $150 per share and ten of which he acquired less than six months prior to liquidation at $290 per share. If he receives a distribution in complete liquidation of $250 per share, then he has a long-term capital gain of $100 per share on those shares acquired more than six months prior to liquidation and a short-term capital loss of $40 per share on the shares acquired less than six months prior to liquidation.[87] This same approach is followed where there is a series of distributions in complete or partial liquidation, except that in such a situation the taxpayer is allowed to recover the basis of each share tax free before any gain is realized. Where more than one block of stock is held, each liquidating distribution is pro rated among the differing blocks of stock in the same proportion as the number of shares in each block bears to the total number of shares outstanding. This may be illustrated by the following example adapted from a recent revenue ruling.[88]

Suppose that in October of 1969 a corporation adopted a plan of

---

[82] Id. at 342.

[83] Int. Rev. Code of 1954, §336.

[84] Ibid. See also id. §453(d), and Ch. VI, text accompanying note 292.

[85] See Gardner, The Impact of Sections 1245 and 1250 on Corporate Liquidations, 17 U. Fla. L. Rev. 58 (1964).

[86] See generally B. Bittker and J. Eustice, id. at §9.62. Similar problems arise as to whether a corporation should be required to "take down" certain reserve items into its income account which it has previously deducted where, because of liquidation, such reserves are no longer needed (e.g., bad-debt reserves, reserves for customer deposits, etc.). Although the Internal Revenue Service has urged that such items be included in corporate income on liquidation, it has not been generally successful in the courts. See id. at 385–386. Cf. United States v. Nash, 398 U.S. 1 (1970).

[87] Treas. Reg. §1.331–1(e).

[88] Rev. Rul. 68–348, 1968–2 Cum. Bull. 141.

complete liquidation whereby all of its assets, other than those required to meet claims, would be distributed to its sole shareholder, A. The shareholder had acquired 40 percent of the two hundred outstanding shares at a cost of $80,000 on January 1, 1960, and had acquired the remaining 60 percent of the stock at a cost of $360,000 on February 10, 1963. On November 1, 1969, the corporation sold all its assets for $1 million, consisting of $500,000 in cash and $500,000 in notes. On December 1, 1969, it distributed $500,000 to A. The remaining $500,000 was distributed to A in the following taxable year on January 2, 1970, and all the shares were surrendered for cancellation.

Forty percent of each distribution must be allocated to the first block of stock (which carried a basis of $80,000) and 60 percent of each distribution is allocated to the second block of stock (which carried a basis of $360,000). Thus $200,000 of the first $500,000 distribution (made in 1969) is allocated to the first block of stock, producing a gain of $120,000. No gain is recognized as to the $300,000 remaining of the first distribution allocated to the second block of stock since that block of stock carried a basis of $360,-000 and the taxpayer is allowed to recover his basis tax free before gain is realized. As to the second distribution in the succeeding taxable year (1970), the same method of allocation is used. Thus $200,000 is allocated to the first block and the entire $200,000 is taxable gain since the basis of that block of stock was recovered tax free in the prior year's distribution. The $300,000 remaining is allocated to the second block of stock and, after the $60,000 in "unrecovered basis" is deducted, the balance of $240,000 is taxed as capital gain.

Interestingly, the courts have not always followed this approach but have, instead, used an "aggregate basis" technique. In the above example, the aggregate basis of the shares would be $440,000 (the sum of the cost to A of the two blocks). This basis could be recovered free of tax before gain is realized, according to the case law, with the result that only $60,000 in gain is recognized as to the $500,000 distribution in 1969. Since the basis is thereby recouped in its entirety, the entire $500,000 in the second distribution would be taxed as gain in the subsequent taxable year, 1970.[89]

If a shareholder receives a liquidation distribution of properties subject to liabilities, the net amount (i.e., the value of the property less the liabilities to which it is subject) is taken into account for the purpose of computing gain or loss. Thus property worth $100,000 but subject to a liability of $20,000 would result in a gain of $30,000 when matched with a basis of $50,000 in stock surrendered (i.e., $80,000 in property received less the basis of $50,000).[90] If the liability is so uncertain or contingent that it cannot be taken into account (thus increasing the gain or reducing the loss which might otherwise be realized), then a later satisfaction of the liability

[89] See B. Bittker and J. Eustice, id. at 308 n.60 (collecting the cases).
[90] Ford v. United States, 311 F.2d 951 (Ct. Cl. 1963).

by the shareholder will probably give rise to capital loss in the year the liability is discharged on the theory that it is related to a "capital" transaction (i.e., a liquidating distribution) in a prior year.[91]

In certain "rare and extraordinary cases" [92] the properties received by the taxpayer in a liquidating distribution cannot be given an ascertainable value, as where the taxpayer receives a contract right or royalty payment contract pursuant to which the payments may be uncertain.[93] In such situations the taxpayer is permitted to adopt the so-called open transaction method of reporting. The payments received on the contract are not reported as gain until the basis in the stock surrendered for the contract right is recouped. Once the basis had been recouped tax free, then subsequent payments are taxed at capital gains rates.[94] An alternative approach would be to attempt an estimate of the value of the contract right and to report capital gain or loss on the difference between the value so determined and the basis of the stock. If the total amount paid pursuant to the contract should subsequently exceed the value as previously determined, the excess would be taxed at *ordinary* rates. The reasoning of this approach is that taxation at capital gains rates requires a "sale or exchange." [95] Unless the open transaction method of reporting is used, the sale or exchange takes place when the contract right is distributed in liquidation. Subsequent payments of amounts in excess of the estimated value of the contract are not considered to have been part of a sale or exchange and so are taxable at ordinary rates.[96] Similarly, if the amounts received on the contract turn out to be less than the estimated value as previously reported, the difference is deductible as an *ordinary* loss.[97] This creates an interesting dilemma for the taxpayer. If he attempts to estimate the value of the contract right and reports its receipt on a "closed" basis, then, if his estimate should later prove to have been too low he must pay a tax on the difference at ordinary rates in

---

[91] Arrowsmith v. Commissioner, 344 U.S. 6 (1952). See Note, Tax Treatment of Stockholder—Transferees' Payments in Satisfaction of Dissolved Corporations' Unpaid Debts, 61 Yale L.J. 1081 (1952).

[92] Rev. Rul. 58–402, 1958–2 Cum. Bull. 15. See also Treas. Reg. §1.1001–1(a).

[93] The classic case is Burnet v. Logan, 283 U.S. 404 (1931), where the taxpayer sold her shares for cash plus an agreement whereby the purchaser agreed to pay the taxpayer sixty cents per ton of ore it obtained from a certain mine. Since the obligation to pay royalties was only conditional, i.e., it depended upon whether and how much ore was mined, which could not be determined in advance, it was held that its value could not be readily ascertained and thus the taxpayer did not have to report gain until her basis had been recovered. See also Commissioner v. Carter, 170 F.2d 911 (2d Cir. 1948); Stephen H. Dorsey, 49 T.C. 606 (1968) (reviewed, three dissents).

[94] See, e.g., Commissioner v. Carter, 170 F.2d 911 (2d Cir. 1948).

[95] Int. Rev. Code of 1954, §1222 (defining capital gains as gains from a "sale or exchange of a capital asset").

[96] Cf. Osenbach v. Commissioner, 198 F.2d 235 (4th Cir. 1952); Hale v. Helvering, 85 F.2d 819 (D.C. Cir. 1936).

[97] See S. Surrey and W. Warren, Cases and Materials on Federal Income Taxation 674 (1962). Contrast this approach with that of Arrowsmith v. United States, 344 U.S. 6 (1952), in which the liquidation was reported on a "closed" basis and subsequent losses were treated as capital losses.

later years. If, on the other hand, he leaves the transaction "open" and reports gain only if the payments he receives exceed his basis, his receipt of *less* than his basis would be deductible only as a *capital* loss.[98] In most cases, however, the dilemma is resolved in favor of reporting transactions on a closed basis, for, as previously indicated, the Internal Revenue Service takes the view that the open method is appropriate only in rare and extraordinary cases.[99]

When a shareholder receives property in a liquidating distribution and recognizes gain or loss at capital rates, his basis in the property is equivalent to its fair market value at the time of distribution.[100] Subsequent gain or loss on the sale of the property depends upon whether the sale proceeds exceed the basis. If the property is sold shortly after liquidation, there will generally be no further gain. The nature of the gain on later resale depends upon the character of the asset in the hands of the taxpayer. Thus if the asset is held by him for sale to customers in the ordinary course of business (i.e., it is inventory), its sale will give rise to ordinary income. But even though the asset may have been inventory to the corporation, it does not necessarily follow that it continues to be inventory to the distributee shareholder. For example, on liquidation of a real estate corporation a shareholder might receive land which he might thereafter hold for personal use. If the shareholder is not in the business of selling land, his later sale of the land will not give rise to gain at ordinary rates since the land is not inventory to him, although it was inventory to the liquidating corporation. However, since capital gain treatment presupposes a sale or exchange, the collection of accounts receivable distributed in liquidation, since it does not involve a sale, will give rise to tax at ordinary rates if the amount collected exceeds the basis of the accounts receivable in the hands of the shareholder.[101] And even if the accounts receivable are sold to another, since they would not qualify as a capital asset,[102] gain would be ordinary gain and not capital gain.

The foregoing is a general description of the usual consequences of liquidating a corporation. There are numerous exceptions. Thus gain on liquidation of a so-called collapsible corporation will be taxed at ordinary rates.[103] And if one corporation holds at least 80 percent of each class of shares in another corporation (except for nonvoting preferred stock), it may liquidate the subsidiary without gain or loss.[104] In such case the assets of the subsidiary carry the same basis in the hands of the parent that they had in

---

[98] For a numerical illustration of the differing tax treatment, see B. Bittker and J. Eustice, Federal Income Taxation of Corporations and Shareholders 344–345 (1966).

[99] See note 92 *supra*.

[100] Int. Rev. Code of 1954, §334(a).

[101] See B. Bittker and J. Eustice, id. at 344–345.

[102] Int. Rev. Code of 1954, §1221(4).

[103] Id. §341(a)(2). See also Ch. I, text accompanying note 40 and Ch. V, Section 5.6.

[104] Int. Rev. Code of 1954, §332.

the subsidiary.[105] If stock in a corporation was acquired solely in order to obtain the corporate assets though a subsequent liquidation, then the courts have disregarded the form of the transaction and have treated it as, in substance, a purchase of assets. No gain or loss is therefore recognized,[106] although it has been held that any income derived by the corporation during the period between the stock purchase and the liquidation is taxable to it and not to the shareholder.[107]

Another very important exception to the general rules is contained in an elective provision of the Code, Section 333. In effect this permits relatively tax-free liquidations of corporations having comparatively little in the way of earnings and profits, cash, stock or securities. A prime example might be a real estate corporation whose assets consist largely in land, the value of which has appreciated substantially over a period of time. If the corporation were liquidated under the conventional method, then the excess of the value of the land over the basis of the shares surrendered in liquidation would be taxed at capital gains rates. If an election under Section 333 of the Code is made, then the land can be distributed with no tax effect other than that it receives, as its basis in the hands of the distributee, the relatively low basis "carried over" from the basis of the stock surrendered[108] instead of receiving a basis equal to its fair market value, as would be the case if an election were not made under Section 333.[109]

The Section 333 election applies only to *gains*. It has no effect on losses. If the Section 333 election is in effect, losses are deductible as capital losses, as in other cases, and gains are taxed, if at all, under the special provisions of Section 333. As with other liquidation situations, gain or loss is com-

---

[105] Id. §334(b)(1). Section 334(b)(2) provides for an exception to this where a parent purchases 80 percent control of a subsidiary and then liquidates it pursuant to a plan of liquidation adopted not more than two years after the stock was purchased. In effect this transaction, under what has come to be called the Kimbell-Diamond rule, is treated as, in substance, an asset purchase. Thus the purchase price of the stock determines the basis of the assets received by the parent, rather than have the latter receive the "carried-over" basis which those assets had in the hands of the subsidiary. The rule is justified by the assumption that the tax effect of the transaction should not in this situation depend upon its particular form. If the parent could have purchased the assets for $X, then that amount should determine the basis of the assets in its hands even though they were acquired through liquidating a corporation whose shares were purchased within a period of two years or less. See Kimbell-Diamond Milling Co. v. Commissioner, 14 T.C. 74, *aff'd per curiam*, 187 F.2d 718 (5th Cir. 1951), *cert. denied*, 342 U.S. 827 (1951). See generally Mansfield, The Kimbell-Diamond Situation: Basis to the Purchaser in Connection with Liquidation, N.Y.U. 13th Inst. on Fed. Tax. 623 (1955). For other discussions see authorities cited in B. Bittker and J. Eustice, id. at 376 n.49.

[106] Ruth M. Cullen, 14 T.C. 368 (1950), *acquiesced in*, 1950–2 Cum. Bull. 1; cf. H. B. Snively, 19 T.C. 850 (1953), *aff'd*, 219 F.2d 266 (5th Cir. 1955). The approach here is similar to that of the Kimbell-Diamond doctrine, used in connection with a parent's liquidation of a subsidiary. See note 105 *supra*.

[107] H. B. Snively, 19 T.C. 850, 858 (1953), *aff'd* 219 F.2d 266 (5th Cir. 1955).

[108] Int. Rev. Code of 1954, §334(c).

[109] See text accompanying note 100 *supra*.

puted on a per share basis.[110] The election is available only to "qualified electing shareholders." [111] In the case of a noncorporate shareholder, this means that written elections for Section 333 treatment (Form 964) must be filed within thirty days after the plan of liquidation is adopted by persons (other than corporations) who, at the date the plan is adopted, owned at least 80 percent of the total combined voting power of all classes of stock entitled to vote on the plan. The 80 percent requirement refers to all stock which was *not* held by a corporation. A similar requirement applies to the latter situation (corporate-owned stock). Thus for a corporation to be a qualified electing shareholder, written elections must be filed within the thirty-day limit by all corporate shareholders (other than so-called excluded corporations[112]) who, at the time the plan of liquidation is adopted, owned stock possessing at least 80 percent of the total combined voting power of all classes of stock entitled to vote on the liquidation. Here the 80 percent test is applied only to stock held by corporations (other than excluded corporations). In effect, then, shares entitled to vote are split into two groups: shares which are held by individuals and shares which are held by corporations (other than excluded corporations). For an individual to be a qualified electing shareholder, he must own stock at the time the liquidation plan is adopted and his written election as well as the written election of those holding at least 80 percent of the shares in his group (noncorporate), must be filed within thirty days. With corporations (other than excluded corporations) the same test applies except that the 80 percent requirement refers to shares owned by corporations (other than excluded corporations). Only the actual or beneficial owners of stock are entitled to file elections; thus, if stock is held by a nominee or broker, the election must be filed by the actual owner.[113] And where a shareholder is not entitled to vote on a plan of dissolution (as where he holds nonvoting preferred shares, for example), he may still receive the benefits of Section 333 treatment if he files his election to do so and if elections have been filed by at least 80 percent of the voting shares of the group (i.e., noncorporate or corporate) to which he belongs.[114] Since the regulations expressly state that "under no circumstances" will a shareholder be entitled to Section 333 treatment unless his written election is filed within the thirty-day limit,[115] it is crucial for the taxpayer to have some record of the filing, such as a stamped receipt for a certified or registered letter. The filing is timely if the postmark indicates

---

[110] See id. note 88 *supra*. See also Treas. Reg. §1.333–4(a).

[111] Int. Rev. Code of 1954, §333(c).

[112] An "excluded corporation" is one which, at any time between January 1, 1954, and the date the liquidation plan is adopted, owned 50 percent of more of the total combined voting power of all classes of stock entitled to vote on the plan. Id. §333(b).

[113] Treas. Reg. §1.333–2(d).

[114] Id. §1.333–2(b).

[115] Id. §1.333–3.

that the form was placed in the mail on or before midnight of the thirtieth day after the adoption of the plan of liquidation.[116]

Section 333 has other requirements which must be met. Thus, as already indicated, there must be a plan of liquidation. Normally a simple directors' resolution should suffice, although under most state laws a shareholder vote is required for a so-called voluntary dissolution,[117] in which case the date of adoption of the plan would be the date when the shareholders approved it.[118] Needless to say, the plan and procedure for dissolution should also comply with applicable state law.[119] After the plan has been adopted there must be a distribution of all the property of the corporation in complete cancellation or redemption of all its stock and a "transfer" of the property to the shareholders "within some one calendar month." [120] Neither the statute nor the regulations require that the distribution be made in the month following the adoption of the plan of liquidation. All that is required is that no part of the distribution take place before adoption of the plan[121] and that the entire distribution be made within some one calendar month, which can be any month following adoption of the plan, even though it may not fall within the same taxable year or calendar year in which the plan of liquidation was adopted.[122] The regulations also permit the corporation to retain a reasonable amount of cash to pay unascertained or contingent liabilities and expenses if this is done in good faith.[123] Finally, it is not necessary that the corporation dissolve as a matter of state law, although when the distribution of assets is made a "state of liquidation" must exist, i.e., the corporation must cease to be a going concern and its activities must be confined to winding up its affairs, paying its debts and distributing its assets to its shareholders.[124]

Assuming that the above requirements are met, gain is taxed to a qualified electing shareholder in the following manner. First, if the shareholder is an individual, that amount of the gain which does not exceed his ratable share of earnings and profits, accumulated by the corporation since February 28, 1913, until the close of the month in which the transfer in liquida-

---

[116] Ibid.

[117] See, e.g., Model Bus. Corp. Act §84. See note 67 *supra.*

[118] Cf. Treas. Reg. §1.337–2(b).

[119] See, e.g., Model Bus. Corp. Act §84, requiring a directors' resolution, written notice to each shareholder entitled to vote, approval by a majority of the shares entitled to vote, unless a class vote is required, and the filing of a "statement of intent to dissolve," executed in duplicate by the president or vice-president and by the secretary or an assistant secretary of the corporation, verified by one of the signing officers and filed in the office of the Secretary of State. See also Section 87 of the Act, requiring a notice of dissolution to be mailed to each known creditor of the corporation.

[120] Int. Rev. Code of 1954, §333(a)(2).

[121] Treas. Reg. §1.333–1(b)(1).

[122] Ibid.

[123] Ibid.

[124] Treas. Reg. §1.333–1(b)(1), (2).

tion occurred, is taxed as a dividend. The remainder of the gain is recognized and treated as long- or short-term capital gain (depending upon the holding period of the shareholder's stock) only to the extent that the value of the distribution he receives which is in excess of his ratable share of earnings and profits consists of money or of stock or securities acquired by the corporation after December 31, 1953.[125] Although the language of the Code provision may be difficult to follow, its theory is relatively simple: The shareholder's gain is taxed at dividend rates to the extent of his ratable share of accumulated corporate earnings and profits. Further gain is recognized to him at capital gains rates to the extent that he receives any money. And, finally, to forestall the possibility that a corporation might seek to postpone the recognition of gain to a shareholder by distributing securities in lieu of money, gain is recognized to the extent that the distribution consists in stock or securities acquired by the corporation after December 31, 1953. If the qualified electing shareholder is a corporation, then gain is recognized in the manner described above, except that the entire gain is taxed at capital gains rates and not as a dividend.[126]

An illustration of this may be helpful. Suppose that a corporation is owned by three shareholders in equal amounts, and that one shareholder is an individual and the other shareholders are corporations. All are qualified electing shareholders (since neither of the two corporations owns more than 50 percent of the voting stock and assuming that all the shareholdes have filed an election for Section 333 treatment). The basis of the stock held by each shareholder is $5000. The assets of the liquidating corporation consist in

Cash	$7,500
Stock and securities	9,000
Other property	24,000
Total	$40,500

Assume that the corporation has accumulated earnings and profits of $6000 and that it has no debts. It distributes its assets equally to the three shareholders. Each shareholder therefore receives

Cash	$2,500
Stock and securities	3,000
Other property	8,000
Total	$13,500

[125] Int. Rev. Code of 1954, §333(e).

[126] Id. §333(f). More precisely the gain is recognized to the extent of the greater of (1) the portion of assets received by the corporation which consists of money, stock or securities acquired by the liquidating corporation after December 31, 1953, or (2) the distributee corporation's ratable share of earnings and profits.

The gain on the transaction is computed as follows:

Amount realized	$13,500
Basis of stock	5,000
Gain	$8,500

The amount of gain *recognized* is computed as follows: In the case of the individual shareholder, one third of the accumulated earnings and profits of the corporation (the individual's pro rata share) is $2000 and therefore $2000 of the gain is taxed to him as a dividend. The remainder of the gain which is recognized (i.e., the sum of the cash and the stock and securities less the amount treated as a dividend: $2500 plus $3000 less $2000 or a net of $3500) is taxed as a capital gain. Thus $5500 of the $8500 gain is recognized and the $3000 of gain is not recognized. In the case of the corporate shareholders, the $5500 gain recognized to each is taxed as a capital gain and, as in the case of the individual shareholder, $3000 of gain is not recognized. If the basis of the shares had been $10,000 instead of $5000 then the gain on the transaction would have been only $3500. In this case, although $2000 of this would be recognized as a dividend to the individual shareholder, only $1500 would be recognized as capital gain, with the corporate shareholder being taxed at capital gains rates on the entire $3500 gain. Thus the total amount taxed cannot exceed the gain on the transaction.[127]

It is apparent from the foregoing that an election under Section 333 will be advantageous primarily where a corporation has relatively little in the way of earnings and profits, and relatively little cash or stock or securities. However, even though it may have relatively substantial amounts of cash or stock or securities, the tax is imposed only if these are distributed and then only to the extent of the gain on the transaction. Thus, if the cash, stock or securities are used to pay corporate debts or these assets are converted into other forms of property and then distributed, the statute does not expressly require a tax. However, if the transaction smacks of tax avoidance, the Internal Revenue Service might be expected to litigate the question of whether its form should control rather than its substance. Thus, if the corporation were to use cash to pay off a mortgage on property which, after being distributed to the shareholders, was immediately remortgaged, the transaction could be viewed as an indirect distribution of cash to the shareholders through the mortgagee as an intermediary.[128] A similar result might follow if the corporation used cash or securities to purchase property which, after distribution, was immediately sold for cash by the shareholders, or if the property purchased by the corporation was property that the shareholders had intended to acquire for themselves.[129]

---

[127] The illustration appears in modified form in Treas. Reg. §1.333–4(c)(2).

[128] This is suggested by B. Bittker and J. Eustice, Federal Income Taxation of Corporations and Shareholders 359 (1966).

[129] Ibid. The authors also suggest that the Internal Revenue Service might attack

Since *any* distribution is taxed (whether or not in the form of cash or stock or securities) to the extent of a shareholder's ratable share of earnings and profits, it is obvious that extreme care should be taken to ascertain correctly the amount in the earnings and profits account. Disastrous consequences can follow from elections under Section 333 where the earnings and profits are underestimated.[130] As we have seen, the result in such cases is to impose a tax at ordinary rates to noncorporate shareholders. If the Section 333 election were not in effect, earnings and profits could be withdrawn as part of a conventional liquidating distribution at capital gains rates. Although occasionally the courts have permitted shareholders to withdraw a Section 333 election under such circumstances, the Treasury Department and many courts have taken the view that the election, once made, is irrevocable.[131]

There is another potential trap in Section 333 elections. This is where the shareholders receiving a distribution which is to them tax free subsequently realize gain which is taxed at ordinary rates. A typical instance would be the collection of accounts receivable or the sale of inventory. Suppose, for example, that a corporation has assets consisting in inventory worth $80,000 and other properties worth $160,000 and that the shareholders have a basis in their shares of $60,000. In a Section 333 liquidation (assuming that the corporation has no earnings and profits, and no stock, securities or cash) [132] these assets could be distributed without tax effect. However, the shareholder's basis in the assets would be the basis in the shares they surrendered ($60,000) decreased by any money received and increased by the amount of any gain recognized (zero in both cases).[133] The $60,000 basis would be allocated between the inventory and the other properties in accordance with their fair market values.[134] Thus

a distribution of cash and securities to shareholders having a high basis for their shares (with little gain or even a loss on the transaction) or to tax-exempt shareholders, accompanied by a distribution of other properties such as land to shareholders having a relatively low basis. This might be "reconstructed" as a distribution of all the various properties to the shareholders pro rata with an exchange of differing properties then taking place between the shareholders.

[130] E.g., Meyer's Estate v. Commissioner, 200 F.2d 592 (5th Cir. 1952). For discussion of this and other similar cases see B. Bittker and J. Eustice, id. at 363–364.

[131] Ibid. See Treas. Reg. §1.333–2(b)(1) (election cannot be revoked except in one specialized situation). See Int. Rev. Code of 1954, §333(g)(4).

[132] An assumption which is obviously somewhat artificial. Thus most corporations would have at least some cash and a small amount of earnings and profits. The assumption is made merely for the purpose of simplicity.

[133] Id. §334(c).

[134] Treas. Reg. §1.334–2. Note that where shareholders assume unsecured liabilities on distributed property, the regulations permit an upward adjustment of basis. Thus the basis of the property is equal to the basis of the stock surrendered less any money received and increased in the amount of any gain recognized and the amount of any unsecured liabilities assumed by the shareholders. Where several properties are received, this basis is then allocated among the various properties in accordance with their *net* fair market values (i.e., the fair market value less any specific mortgage or pledge to which the properties are subject).

$20,000 would be allocated as basis to the inventory and $40,000 would be allocated to the other properties (worth twice as much as the inventory). Assuming that the inventory still remains inventory to the shareholders (i.e., the goods are held for sale to customers in the ordinary course of business), a subsequent sale of the inventory will result in $60,000 of ordinary income (i.e., the $80,000 worth of the inventory less its basis of $20,000). Similarly a sale of the other property (assuming it to be capital in nature) will result in capital gain of $120,000 (i.e., the $160,000 worth of the property less its basis of $40,000). Accordingly a total gain of $180,000 will be taxed, of which $60,000 will be taxed at ordinary rates. If an election had not been made under Section 333, the total gain would have been the same (i.e., the fair market value of the property, a total of $240,000, less the basis of the stock, $60,000, or $180,-000) but all of it would have been taxable at capital gains rates.[135] And since a non-Section 333 liquidation would be fully taxable, the distributee shareholders' basis in the assets would be their fair market value at the date of distribution, rather than a lower basis carried over from the basis of the shares they surrendered. Hence the subsequent sale of the inventory and property would give rise to little, if any, gain.

The upshot of all of this is that one must proceed cautiously before making a Section 333 election. Since the election cannot be revoked, not only must the earnings and profits be calculated with extreme care but attention should be directed to the tax impact of a later sale or disposition of the properties received, since, even though a tax might temporarily be postponed, the overall tax impact of a Section 333 election might be greater than a conventional liquidation if the assets are to be resold.

Turning now from Section 333 to another problem, namely, the "double tax" possibility presented by a corporate sale of assets followed by a liquidation, some attention should be given to the provisions of Section 337 of the Code. In order to appreciate the significance of Section 337, the following situation should be considered: Suppose that the shareholders of a closely held concern wish to "sell the corporation." The sale can take different forms. They may choose to merge the corporation with another corporation

---

[135] B. Bittker and J. Eustice, id. at 361–362, have a similar illustration. See Osenbach v. Commissioner, 198 F.2d 235 (4th Cir. 1952), where the taxpayer recognized ordinary income on the collection of claims which, in a taxable liquidation, would have been taxed to him at capital gains rates. Note, however, that regardless of whether the liquidation is a conventional one or an elective liquidation under Section 333, the *corporation* may have to pay a tax on such items as unrealized receivables due to the assignment of income concept, etc. See note 86 *supra*. See also note 85, regarding Section 1245 or Section 1250 properties. This does not avoid the shareholder's being taxed when the assets (i.e., the accounts receivable) are distributed to him (assuming that he has gain resulting from a low basis in his shares). However, if an election has been made under Section 333 and the corporation was previously taxed on the item, then the collection of the accounts receivable should not result in the shareholder's having to pay a *second* tax.

in which they receive shares in exchange for the shares they currently hold. They may sell the shares they currently hold to another person or corporation. The sale may be for cash or for shares in another corporation. Finally, they may sell the corporate assets, again either for cash or for shares in another corporation. If an asset sale is employed, two other alternatives are possible. First, the corporation might sell its assets and then distribute the proceeds of the sale to its shareholders in liquidation. Secondly, the assets could be distributed first to the shareholders who, in turn, would sell them to the purchaser. The tax consequences of all these various alternatives may differ. In the following chapter we shall consider the first-mentioned alternatives such as merger and exchange of shares, particularly from the standpoint of qualifying the exchange as a tax-free reorganization. The present discussion shall be confined to those asset sales which do not fall within the reorganization provisions of the Code.

The most significant point to consider is the tax effect, apart from Section 337 of the Code, of an asset sale by the corporation followed by a liquidation distribution, in contrast to a liquidation distribution followed by an asset sale by the shareholders. If a corporation sells its assets, gain on the sale is taxed to it if the basis of the assets is less than the sale proceeds. When the proceeds are distributed to the shareholders a second tax may be imposed, depending upon whether the proceeds (along with any other assets distributed in liquidation) exceed each individual's basis in the shares he surrenders. In this sense there may be a "double tax." In sharp contrast, where the assets are distributed first to the shareholders and then sold by them, there is, in all probability, but one tax, namely, that which is imposed on the liquidating distribution (i.e., amount received in liquidation less the basis of the shares surrendered). If the liquidation was taxable (was not a Section 333 liquidation, for example), then the assets receive a basis of fair market value in the hands of the distributee shareholders.[136] As a result, little gain is likely to be realized if the assets are sold shortly after the liquidation distribution, for the sale proceeds will approximate the basis of the assets disposed of.

This discrepancy in tax treatment is highlighted by two cases decided prior to the passage of Section 337. In *Commissioner v. Court Holding Co.*[137] a corporation, all of whose outstanding stock was held by a husband and wife, entered into negotiations for the sale of its only asset, an apartment building, to the lessees and to a sister and brother-in-law. After an oral agreement for the sale was reached, the parties met to reduce the agreement to writing, at which time the purchaser was advised by the corporation's attorney that the sale could not be consummated in that it would impose a large income tax upon the corporation. The following day the corporation declared a "liquidating dividend" and deeded the building to its sharehold-

[136] Int. Rev. Code of 1954, §334(a). See text accompanying note 100 *supra*.
[137] 324 U.S. 331 (1945).

ers in exchange for their stock. Shortly thereafter a sale contract was drawn up between the husband and wife and the purchasers on substantially the same terms and conditions as the previously proposed contract between the corporation and the purchasers. One thousand dollars, which previously had been paid to the corporation by the lessees, was applied towards the payment of the purchase price and three days later the property was conveyed to the lessees' sister. The Tax Court adopted the view that the corporation had not abandoned the sales negotiations and that the sale was in substance by it, characterizing the liquidating dividend and conveyance by the shareholders as mere formalities designed "to make the transaction appear to be other than what it was" in order to avoid tax liability. The Circuit Court disagreed and concluded that the corporation had "called off" the sale, thus giving effect to the form of the transaction, despite the prior negotiations. The Supreme Court reversed and held that there was evidence to support the findings of the Tax Court, observing that

> The incidence of taxation depends upon the substance of a transaction. The tax consequences which arise from gains from a sale of property are not finally to be determined solely by the means employed to transfer legal title. Rather, the transaction must be viewed as a whole, and each step, from the commencement of negotiations to the consummation of the sale, is relevant. A sale by one person cannot be transformed for tax purposes into a sale by another by using the latter as a conduit through which to pass title. To permit the true nature of a transaction to be disguised by mere formalisms, which exist solely to alter tax liabilities, would seriously impair the effective administration of the tax policies of Congress.[138]

The court's reference to "mere formalisms" is not without some unintended irony, for despite the stress on the importance of looking to the "substance" of the transaction to perceive its "true nature," this is an area of taxation where the form controls par excellence—i.e., everything depends upon whether the asset sale is by the corporation or by the shareholders, although the net effect of the two alternatives is, aside from the tax impact, precisely the same. In fact one might surmise that many nonlawyers would have difficulty in understanding the difference between a wholly owned corporation selling assets and a sale by the sole shareholder. Even if he could comprehend the difference, he might well be shocked to learn that the tax effects may differ depending upon which route is followed.

Five years later the Supreme Court was called upon to decide a similar case, *United States v. Cumberland Public Service Co.*[139] Again the situation involved a closely held concern, engaged in generating and distributing electric power in three Kentucky counties. Finding itself unable to compete with a newly formed cooperative facility which was distributing Tennessee Valley Authority power, it decided to sell its facilities to the cooperative.

[138] Id. at 334.
[139] 338 U.S. 451 (1950).

The first proposal was to sell the stock, but the cooperative refused this and countered with an offer to purchase from the corporation its transmission and distribution equipment. The offer was rejected by the corporation because of the heavy capital gains tax that could be imposed on such a sale. Instead, the shareholders offered to acquire the transmission and distribution facilities and then sell them to the cooperative. Accordingly the facilities were distributed to the shareholders in partial liquidation, the corporation sold its remaining assets and dissolved, and the shareholders conveyed the transmission and distribution facilities to the cooperative. The Court of Claims (one judge dissenting) found that at no time had the corporation planned to make the sale itself and that, although the method by which the shareholders disposed of the properties had been chosen in order to reduce taxes, the transaction should be viewed as a sale by them and not by the corporation. The Supreme Court affirmed, distinguishing its prior decision in the *Court Holding Co.* case as having rested on findings of fact by the Tax Court that a sale had been made by the corporation, which had entered into negotiations which were subsequently called off merely because of the unfavorable tax effect. There, one thousand dollars had already been paid to the corporation as part of the purchase price and the Tax Court also had found that it never really abandoned its sales negotiations nor did it dissolve. Referring to its earlier discussion of the importance of ascertaining the "substance" of a transaction rather than being governed by "mere formalisms," [140] the Court stated that

> This language does not mean that a corporation can be taxed even when the sale has been made by its stockholders following a genuine liquidation and dissolution. While the distinction between sales by a corporation as compared with distribution in kind followed by shareholder sales may be particularly shadowy and artificial when the corporation is closely held, Congress has chosen to recognize such a distinction for tax purposes. . . .
>
> The oddities in tax consequences that emerge from the tax provisions here controlling appear to be inherent in the present tax pattern. . . .
>
> Congress having determined that different tax consequences shall flow from different methods by which the shareholders of a closely held corporation may dispose of corporate property, we accept its mandate. It is for the trial court, upon consideration of an entire transaction, to determine the factual category in which a particular transaction belongs. Here as in the *Court Holding Co.* case we accept the ultimate findings of fact of the trial tribunal. Accordingly the judgment of the Court of Claims is affirmed.[141]

From a tax-planning perspective, the *Court Holding Co.* and *Cumberland Public Service Co.* cases placed tax practitioners in an awkward situation. Whether the overall approach of the two cases is best described as emphasizing the substance of a transaction over its form, or vice versa, the

[140] See quoted passage in text accompanying note 138 *supra*.
[141] 338 U.S. 451, 454–456 (1950).

practical implications were that if there were *any* negotiations with a prospective purchaser of corporate properties prior to liquidation of a corporation, it should be crystal-clear that such negotiations were not being conducted on behalf of the corporation but were being carried out on behalf of its shareholders. However, if a purchaser were not found, or if negotiations proved unfruitful, then it would usually not be in the best interests of the shareholders to liquidate, since liquidation would probably result in a tax, albeit at capital gains rates, and the shareholder distributees, absent a sale of the properties, might well not have the cash with which to pay the tax. Added to this is the possibility that the Internal Revenue Service might succeed in placing a higher value on the properties than might be so if the properties were sold, where the sale price would be presumptive and possibly conclusive as to their value when distributed.[142]

Fortunately Congress perceived the troublesome problems in this area and, perhaps recognizing what the Supreme Court in the *Cumberland Public Service* case referred to as the "oddities in tax consequences . . . inherent in the present tax pattern" [143] (whereby differing tax results follow from transactions which have identical net effects), determined that, at least under specified conditions, it should make no tax difference whether the asset sale preceded or followed corporate liquidation. This, essentially, is the approach of Section 337 of the Code.

The basic requirements of Section 337 are that a corporation must "adopt" a "plan of complete liquidation" and, within a twelve-month period beginning on the date the plan is adopted, all of the corporate assets must be distributed in complete liquidation, except for those assets which are retained to meet claims against the corporation. If the conditions are met, then no gain or loss is recognized to the corporation on a sale or exchange by it of property within the twelve-month period. This, in effect, eliminates the double taxation inherent in a situation such as *Court Holding Co.*

The exceptions to the rule are as important, perhaps, as the rule itself. Thus Section 337 does not apply to a sale of inventory.[144] Similarly, a sale of installment obligations resulting from a prior sale of inventory (whether the inventory was sold before or after the liquidation plan was adopted) or resulting from a sale of property other than inventory (if the sale took place before adoption of the liquidation plan) is not covered (i.e., the corporation may realize taxable gain).[145] However, if substantially all the inventory is sold or exchanged to one person in one transaction, then Section 337 applies (gain or loss is not recognized) both to the sale of the inventory and to

---

[142] See B. Bittker and J. Eustice, Federal Income Taxation of Corporations and Shareholders 389 (1966). See also Note, Tax-Free Sales in Liquidation Under Section 337, 76 Harv. L. Rev. 780, 781 (1963).

[143] See quote in text accompanying note 141 *supra*.

[144] Int. Rev. Code of 1954, §337(b)(1)(A).

[145] Id. §§337(b)(1)(B) and 337(b)(1)(C).

a sale of installment obligations acquired as a result of the inventory sale.[146] Other exceptions are that Section 337 does not apply to a sale or exchange by a collapsible corporation or where the elective provisions of Section 333, already discussed, apply.[147] Similarly, where the liquidation is tax free not because of the Section 333 election but because a parent corporation is liquidating an 80 percent owned subsidiary, then Section 337 does not apply.[148] Section 337 treatment is not available as regards the sale or disposition of properties subject to the depreciation recapture rules of Sections 1245 and 1250. As we have already seen, the depreciation recapture rules apply regardless of whether the transaction is tax free at the shareholder level.[149] Finally, Section 337 does not apply to insolvent corporations. Thus where a corporation distributes its assets entirely to its creditors, gain or loss on any sale by it of assets is recognized.[150] This is on the theory that Section 337 was intended to eliminate double taxation and that if there is no distribution to shareholders, the possibility of double taxation simply does not exist. Apparently, however, a barely solvent corporation may qualify for Section 337 treatment. In other words, a minimal distribu-

[146] Id. §337(b)(2). The "substantially all" requirement is determined as of the time of the bulk sale of inventory. See Treas. Reg. §1.337-3(b)(2). Thus a corporation might make taxable sales of inventory during the twelve-month period and make a nontaxable bulk sale of the remaining inventory at the end of the period to one purchaser. See B. Bittker and J. Eustice, id. at 399.

[147] Int. Rev. Code of 1954, §337(c)(1). Note that a Section 333 election by any shareholder group (such as individuals and noncorporate shareholders) will prevent the use of Section 337 by a corporation even though Section 333 has not been elected by all the shareholders (e.g., has not been elected by corporate shareholders). Since an asset sale by the corporation will increase its earnings and profits, this will increase the possibility of tax recognition at the shareholder level. See text accompanying note 125 *supra*. A possible solution is for the corporation to distribute the assets and have them sold by the shareholders, in reliance upon the *Cumberland Public Service* case, 338 U.S. 451 (1950). See B. Bittker and J. Eustice, id. at 407.

[148] Int. Rev. Code of 1954, §337(c)(2)(A). A special rule applies to a parent's liquidation of a subsidiary in the so-called Kimbell-Diamond situation covered by Section 334(b)(2) of the Code. See note 105 *supra* and Section 337(c)(2)(B) of the Code, providing, in general, that Section 337 applies only to gain attributable to appreciation in assets of the subsidiary prior to the parent's purchase of its stock. See Treas. Reg. §1.337-4. Also a special rule provides tax relief to minority shareholders in a tax-free liquidation, under Section 332 of the Code, of an 80 percent owned subsidiary. Since Section 337(c)(2) provides, in effect, that a sale of assets by the subsidiary prior to liquidation is not covered by Section 337, then minority shareholders are exposed to a form of double taxation if gain is recognized to them when the subsidiary's assets are distributed. Section 337(d) provides, in effect, that the minority shareholder is considered to have received an additional amount in liquidation of the subsidiary equivalent to his pro rata share of the additional tax imposed on the subsidiary which resulted from the nonapplicability of Section 337 (thus increasing his gain) and that such amount was paid by the minority shareholder as a tax (i.e., the amount is considered to be a down payment on his individual tax return). The net effect, for all practical purposes, is as if Section 337 had applied as far as the minority shareholder is concerned.

[149] See text accompanying note 85 *supra*. See also note 135 *supra*.

[150] See Rev. Rul. 56-387, 1956-2 Cum. Bull. 189.

tion to shareholders will avoid the recognition of gain or loss at the corporate level if the other requirements of the provision are met.

Since Section 337 requires that all the corporate assets be distributed within a twelve-month period beginning on the date of the adoption of the plan of complete liquidation, troublesome problems have arisen regarding the fixing of the precise date when a plan was adopted. This is important for at least two reasons. First, any sale of assets prior to the date the plan is adopted will not fall within Section 337 and thus gain or loss will be recognized to the corporation. If the sale is at a loss this will be to the advantage of the corporate taxpayer for otherwise no deduction would be available. Secondly, if all the assets are not distributed within twelve months following the date of the adoption of the plan, then Section 337 does not apply to *any* sales by the corporation and no gain or loss goes unrecognized.

The regulations take the view that ordinarily the date of adoption of a plan is the date when the shareholders adopt a resolution authorizing distribution of the assets in redemption of their stock.[151] This at least is so either where a corporation sells substantially all its property prior to the date the shareholders vote on the plan or where substantially all the property is not sold after that date.[152] The difficult cases relate to situations where only part of the properties (i.e., not substantially all) is sold prior to the date the shareholders vote on the plan. This might be so, for example, where a corporation holds certain properties which carry a high basis and a relatively low value and these properties are sold at a loss prior to the date the shareholders adopt the plan, with the other properties being sold at a gain after that date. In such situations the corporation will attempt to "straddle" the provisions of Section 337 and obtain the best of both possible worlds (i.e., recognition of the loss and nonrecognition of the gain). Interestingly enough, such tactics have been surprisingly successful.[153] The regulations provide that unless substantially all the assets are sold prior or subsequent to the date the shareholders vote on the plan, the date the plan was adopted "shall be determined from all the facts and circumstances."[154] If the Internal Revenue Service is successful in persuading a court to hold that a plan of liquidation was informally adopted at a date earlier than the shareholders' resolution, then there are two possible consequences: Section 337 will apply and losses on sales prior to the shareholders' vote will not be recognized, or Section 337 will not apply because all the assets of the corporation were not distributed within twelve months following the informal adoption of the plan. In the latter situation both gains and losses on sales by the corporation would be recognized.

The possibility of a court's finding an informal (and yet effective) adop-

[151] Treas. Reg. §1.337–2(b).

[152] Ibid.

[153] See City Bank of Washington, 38 T.C. 713 (1962), *nonacquiesced in,* 1964–2 Cum. Bull. 8; Virginia Ice & Freezing Corp., 30 T.C. 1251 (1958).

[154] Treas. Reg. §1.337–2(b).

tion of a plan highlights the hazards of attempting a straddle technique, despite taxpayers' success in those straddle cases which have thus far been litigated. Unless a corporation is willing to incur the risk and expense of litigation, the wisest course of action seems to be to adhere strictly to the Section 337 format—i.e., to abstain from sales prior to formal adoption of the plan of liquidation by the shareholders and to consummate all sales and complete the distribution of assets within the following twelve-month period. However, this does not eliminate all uncertainties. In some situations it may not be possible to determine whether a purchaser for the assets will be found within the twelve-month period following the plan's adoption. Where the sale is delayed for unexpected reasons, several alternatives are available. First, formal adoption of the plan by the shareholders might be deferred until the sale is reasonably assured. If the prospects of a sale appear to be reasonably favorable, then the plan might be adopted, and if it subsequently appears that the sale will be delayed, the plan could be cancelled by a shareholders' resolution to that effect and then, when the sale is assured, the plan could be "readopted." This latter technique seems to be relatively safe except in those situations where it appears that the corporation, by calling off the plan and then reinstating it, is in effect attempting to prolong the twelve-month period for asset distribution required under Section 337.[155] Thus if the plan is called off and subsequently reinstated, the corporation should refrain from asset sales or making distributions to its shareholders other than routine dividend distributions until the plan has been definitively reinstated. Perhaps this merely indicates the wisdom of not adopting the plan at all until the asset sale is reasonably assured. The other alternative is to adopt a plan which is contingent upon the asset sale. Thus the date of adoption will depend upon when the assets are sold. Although it has been suggested that such a technique might be effective for Section 337 purposes[156] the uncertainties inherent in such a scheme may indicate that it should be used only where the first alternative (i.e., deferring formal adoption of the plan until the sale is reasonably assured) is for some reason not feasible. It may be unwise to postpone formal shareholder authorization where the shareholders have been deadlocked as to whether the corporation should be dissolved and the deadlock has been resolved through arbitration or some other means.[157] If a shareholder vote were postponed, the deadlock might reoccur and further arbitration and delay might ensue. But in situations other than these specialized ones it would seem best that the plan not

[155] See B. Bittker and J. Eustice, Federal Income Taxation of Corporations and Shareholders 396 (1966). Where there is a valid reason for revoking a previously adopted plan and subsequently adopting another plan, as where a taking of property in condemnation proceedings is unforeseeably delayed, the subsequent adoption will be given legal effect. West Street–Erie Boulevard Corp. v. United States, 411 F.2d 738 (2d Cir. 1969).

[156] B. Bittker and J. Eustice, id.

[157] See text accompanying notes 20–48 *supra*.

be made contingent on an asset sale. In the usual case, then, the shareholders should defer acting upon the plan until the asset sale is fairly well assured, and unless the corporation is willing to litigate the tax issues, it should not attempt to straddle Section 337 through premature sales of some of its assets at a loss.

Somewhat related to the foregoing question is the problem of determining when all the assets have been "distributed" for the purpose of meeting the twelve-month requirement. The regulations specifically authorize a corporation to retain

> cash equal to its known liabilities and liquidating expenses plus an amount of cash set aside under arrangements for the payment after the close of the 12-month period of unascertained or contingent liabilities and contingent expenses. Such arrangements for payment must be made in good faith, the amount set aside must be reasonable, and no amount may be set aside to meet claims of shareholders with respect to their stock. If it is established to the satisfaction of the Commissioner that there are shareholders who cannot be located, a distribution in liquidation includes a transfer to a State official, trustee, or other person authorized by law to receive distributions for the benefit of such shareholders.[158]

From the above, it appears that, although the corporation is permitted to set aside in good faith reasonable amounts necessary to meet the claims of creditors, it cannot set aside amounts to meet claims of shareholders. In other words, it must distribute all amounts to which shareholders are or may be entitled either to the shareholders or to someone else, such as a trustee or escrow agent, acting on the shareholders' behalf. Where shareholders hold claims against their own corporation, and thus occupy a dual role as creditor-shareholders, it may be hazardous to set aside amounts required to meet their claims as creditors if, because the corporation is found to be excessively thin or for some other reason, it turns out that their claims are in reality but another form of stock.[159] In any such situation it is obviously wise to pay off shareholder-held debt within the twelve-month period permitted for distribution of assets to shareholders. In that way it will only be of theoretical interest whether the shareholder-held claims are debt or stock, since Section 337 will have been complied with in any case.

Where amounts are distributed to a trustee, escrow agent or other representative of the shareholders, it is vitally important to establish that the

---

[158] Treas. Reg. §1.337–2(b). See O.B.M., Inc. v. Commissioner, 427 F.2d 661 (2d Cir. 1970).

[159] See John Town, Inc., 46 T.C. 107 (1966), *acquiesced in,* 1966–2 Cum. Bull. 5, *aff'd,* 67–1 U.S. Tax Cas. ¶9462 (7th Cir. 1967). If the amounts involved are relatively small, it may be possible for the corporate taxpayer to rely on Mountain Water Co., 35 T.C. 418 (1960), indicating that a good faith retention by the directors of small amounts due shareholders will not necessarily disqualify the corporation from the benefits of Section 337. However, the *Mountain Water* case may be doubtful authority and the safer procedure is to pay off the claim. This should pose no serious problem if the claim is relatively small.

distributee is truly the agent of the shareholders and not merely an agent of the corporation. Although it used to be thought that the trustee or agent must be appointed by *all* the shareholders in order to qualify as their representative for Section 337 purposes, the Internal Revenue Service has, through its rulings and the above regulation, made it clear that a trustee or agent appointed pursuant to a plan validly adopted under local law will qualify even though local law permits a liquidation to be authorized by a vote of two thirds, three fourths or some other percentage of the shareholders.[160] The important consideration is that the trustee or other representative is, as a matter of local law, authorized to act on behalf of the shareholders and that no part of any amounts received by him can be returned to the corporation or used otherwise than for the shareholders' benefit. The trustee or escrow agent device is also useful where there is a dispute between shareholders as to the ownership of stock[161] or where, because of the nature of the property being distributed, it is not possible to break it up into component parts (as where shareholders have an undivided interest in real or tangible property, such as oil or mineral rights).

Occasionally shareholders may endeavor to avoid distributing property to themselves by organizing another corporation, having the first corporation sell its assets to it for notes or cash and then have the latter distributed in redemption of their shares. The net effect is that they hold claims against or stock in a new corporation which holds the assets of the former corporation which were purportedly sold under the provisions of Section 337. It may suffice to say that this device is risky, to say the least, unless the shareholders hold merely a "nominal" interest in the new corporation.[162] Otherwise, a court is likely to find that the entire transaction was lacking in business reality, that it was a sham and that the first corporation did not liquidate, making Section 337 inapplicable, raising numerous troublesome problems as to how the transaction should be treated for other purposes. Thus the second corporation might be regarded as merely the alter ego of the first corporation and the asset sale disregarded, or the transaction could be considered as falling within the tax-free reorganization provisions.[163]

[160] Rev. Rul. 63–245, 1963–2 Cum. Bull. 144. See also Rev. Rul. 65–257, 1965–2 Cum. Bull. 89 (indicating that an escrow agent appointed by corporate officers pursuant to a plan of liquidation authorized by shareholders would qualify).

[161] Cf. Henry Yeckes, 25 CCH Tax Ct. Mem. 924 (1966). See Comment, The Use of Liquidating Trusts to Obtain the Benefits of Section 337 of the Internal Revenue Code of 1954, 34 U. Chi. L. Rev. 563 (1967).

[162] See Rev. Proc. 69–6, 1969–1 Cum. Bull. 396. An interest of 20 percent or less of the common stock of the new corporation will generally qualify as "nominal." See Rev. Proc. 66–34, 1966–2 Cum. Bull. 1232.

[163] See B. Bittker and J. Eustice, Federal Income Taxation of Corporations and Shareholders §§9.67, 12.22 (1966).

7.5 PARTIAL LIQUIDATIONS

It has already been pointed out that one method of resolving a deadlock between shareholder groups is to have one group or the corporation purchase the interests of one or more shareholders. Where the corporation purchases the shares, the tax effects will normally depend upon the considerations discussed in the prior chapter dealing with stock redemptions.[164] However, very similar tax treatment is also available through the "partial liquidation" device, dealt with in Section 346 of the Code. Nonetheless, because of the somewhat specialized situations in which the partial liquidation technique is available, it is more likely that Section 302 of the Code, governing repurchases and redemptions, will be more appropriate to a deadlock-resolving corporate repurchase than the partial liquidation provisions of Section 346.

Briefly Section 346 provides that a partial liquidation is either a distribution which is (1) "one of a series of distributions in redemption of all of the stock of the corporation pursuant to a plan" or (2) a distribution which "is not essentially equivalent to a dividend, is in redemption of a part of the stock of the corporation pursuant to a plan, and occurs within the taxable year in which the plan is adopted or within the succeeding taxable year. . . ."[165] The concept of a distribution not being essentially equivalent to a dividend in order to qualify for capital gain or loss treatment has already been discussed in connection with Section 302(b)(1), relating to stock repurchases and redemptions.[166] In the context of partial liquidations, the not essentially equivalent requirement is satisfied either if there is a "genuine contraction" of the corporate business or if a mechanical test, set forth in Section 346(b) of the Code, is met. If a transaction qualifies as a partial liquidation, then it is treated as a sale or exchange and thus results in recognition of capital gain or loss. The overall approach, as far as the distributee shareholder is concerned, is similar to that taken in a complete liquidation.[167]

The most troublesome aspect of the partial liquidation area relates to what is a genuine contraction of a corporate business. A familiar example is

[164] See Ch. VI, text accompanying notes 13–29.
[165] Int. Rev. Code of 1954, §346(a).
[166] See Ch. VI, text accompanying note 26.
[167] Int. Rev. Code of 1954, §331(a)(2). As previously noted in the discussion of complete liquidations, the Internal Revenue Service takes the position that the taxpayer should compute gain or loss on each share or block of stock surrendered. See Rev. Rul. 68-348, 1968–2 Cum. Bull. 141, discussed in text accompanying note 88 *supra.* The courts have not always followed this approach and have permitted the basis of the shares to be aggregated and recovered free of tax before gain is recognized. See text accompanying note 89 *supra.* See also B. Bittker and J. Eustice, id. at 308–309.

the destruction of part of a business by fire, causing a cessation of that part of a company's activities, and a distribution of the insurance proceeds to shareholders in redemption of part of their stock.[168] Similarly, closing up an unprofitable department or division of a business would normally qualify as a genuine contraction.[169] And, although the question is more troublesome, a distribution because of a decline in the need for working capital may be a contraction of the business although no specific portion of the business has been discontinued.[170] The distribution of various reserves, such as a reserve for expansion, is even more difficult to justify under a corporate contraction concept. Thus, although some cases have held otherwise,[171] the regulations flatly state that "the distribution of funds attributable to a reserve for an expansion program which has been abandoned does not qualify as a partial liquidation." [172] Even if a part of the business should be discontinued, if it represented only a temporary investment of earnings, it may not qualify as a genuine contraction.[173] Otherwise a corporation could invest its earnings in business assets which it might intend to sell within a few years and attempt to qualify the resultant distribution as a contraction of its business when in substance it would be an earnings distribution. Capital gains treatment should not be permitted merely because the earnings have been temporarily invested in business assets. Similarly, where working capital has been increased with the intention of its subsequent distribution as part of a contraction of working capital, the transaction will not qualify as a partial liquidation.[174]

Although there may be a contraction in the business, if the amount of capital which it requires or which is committed to it is not reduced accordingly, partial liquidation treatment may be denied. Thus, in *Estate of Chandler*,[175] due to illness of one of its shareholders and the desire of another to resign as manager, it was decided that a department store should be sold. In lieu of the department store it was decided that the corporation should open a ladies' ready-to-wear store to be managed by the former manager of the ladies' ready-to-wear department of the discontinued department store. A men's store was also contemplated, and it was thought that approximately half of the assets of the company would be required for each of the

[168] See Joseph W. Imler, 11 T.C. 836 (1948), *acquiesced in,* 1949–1 Cum. Bull. 2. See also Treas. Reg. §1.346–1(a).

[169] See e.g., Commissioner v. Babson, 70 F.2d 304 (7th Cir. 1934), *cert. denied,* 293 U.S. 571 (1934). But see Estate of Chandler, discussed in text accompanying note 175 *infra.*

[170] See B. Bittker and J. Eustice, id. at 310 n.63 (collecting the conflicting cases).

[171] E.g., Commissioner v. Champion, 78 F.2d 513 (6th Cir. 1935); Samuel A. Upham, 4 T.C. 1120 (1945), *acquiesced in,* 1945 Cum. Bull. 7. *Contra:* McGuire v. Commissioner, 84 F.2d 431 (7th Cir. 1936), *cert. denied,* 299 U.S. 591 (1936).

[172] Treas. Reg. §1.346–1(a).

[173] See B. Bittker and J. Eustice, id. at 311 n.66.

[174] See Rev. Rul. 60–322, 1960–2 Cum. Bull. 118; cf. Rev. Rul. 60-232, 1960–2 Cum. Bull. 115.

[175] 22 T.C. 1158 (1954), *aff'd per curiam,* 228 F.2d 909 (6th Cir. 1955).

two stores. Notwithstanding this, however, the company adopted a plan of partial liquidation and one half of the shares held by each shareholder was redeemed at book value. The court found that the distribution did not qualify as a partial liquidation since, although the ladies' ready-to-wear business was smaller, the amount of capital actually committed to the business was not reduced in that approximately the same amount was allocated to fixed assets and inventories as had been required for the larger department store. Although the court acknowledged that the department store required larger reserves, the excess cash in the company account had arisen largely from a substantial increase in retained earnings and exceeded the amount required for the current operation of the business. Also the company had previously paid out only about one fourth of its earnings in dividends.

The case illustrates, if anything, the subtle problems involved in this area and the difficulty of determining the outcome other than on the basis of the various factors present in each case. Accumulation of cash beyond the needs of the business (even though not unreasonable to the extent of justifying a penalty tax on excess accumulations),[176] a meager dividend record and a continuation of even a smaller business with the same capital requirements will be of obvious relevance, as they were in the *Chandler* case. The absence of a business reason for the distribution or that it is motivated exclusively by tax factors would generally be fatal. Conversely, if there are non-tax motivations, they may justify partial liquidation treatment even though they might be questionable in other respects, as where a corporation distributes property in order to protect it from the claims of its creditors.[177]

The genuine contraction test, as well as the mechanical test in Section 346(b) of the Code, described below, stress the effect on the corporation rather than the effect on the person whose shares are redeemed. In this respect the partial liquidation concept differs from the problem of determining when a distribution is not essentially equivalent to a dividend for the purpose of the stock repurchase or redemption provisions of Section 302(b) of the Code. The latter emphasizes the effect on the shareholder (as where it is determined that a distribution was substantially disproportionate as to him or that his entire interest in the corporation has been terminated).[178] Despite the difference in approach, however, the cases in the two areas have a similarity in that the fundamental problem is the same, i.e., when a distribution should be taxed at ordinary income rates because it is in substance an attempt to withdraw corporate earnings in the guise of a stock redemption to avoid their taxation at ordinary rates. Hence the factors which are likely to influence the outcome of cases in the two areas are often the same, e.g., lack of a nontax or business purpose for the transaction,

---

[176] See Ch. V, text accompanying notes 69–132.
[177] See Commissioner v. Sullivan, 210 F.2d 607 (5th Cir. 1954).
[178] See Ch. VI, text accompanying notes 13–29.

accumulation of earnings, a relatively meager dividend payments history and so forth.

The mechanical test of Section 346(b) of the Code is merely intended to delineate an area within which a taxpayer can be assured that a distribution qualifies as a partial liquidation. Thus it does not in any sense preempt the field, and failure to meet its requirements does not even raise a presumption that a transaction is not a partial liquidation. The mechanical test requires that a corporation must have been engaged in the active conduct of at least two trades or businesses for a period of at least five years, that neither of the trades or businesses was acquired by the corporation in a transaction in which gain or loss was recognized in whole or in part, and that the distribution in partial liquidation must be attributable to the corporation's ceasing to conduct, or must consist of the assets of, one of the two trades or businesses. In a sense this is a statutory attempt to describe a type of contraction of an enterprise, although, as previously stated, failure to meet the test has no bearing on whether a transaction might be a genuine contraction for the purpose of the "not essentially equivalent to a dividend" test of Section 346(a)(2), already discussed.

The intent behind the requirements that at least two trades or businesses must have been actively conducted for at least five years, and that neither of them may have been acquired in connection with a taxable purchase, is to prevent corporations from investing surplus funds, which otherwise might be distributed as dividends, in the purchase of a business which is subsequently discontinued and its assets distributed to shareholders who might have purchased the business had the funds been made available to them in the first place. A similar approach is taken in the Code provision regulating so-called spin-offs.[179]

A troublesome question is the precise meaning of the phrase "trade or business." In this regard the regulations under Section 346(b) refer to the regulations governing the somewhat similar spin-off provisions of Section 355.[180] There the phrase "trade or business" is described as referring to

> a specific existing group of activities being carried on for the purpose of earning income or profit from only such group of activities, and the activities included in such group must include every operation which forms a part of, or a step in, the process of earning income or profit from such group. Such group of activities ordinarily must include the collection of income and the payment of expenses. It does not include—
> (1) The holding for investment purposes of stock, securities, land or other property, including casual sales thereof (whether or not the proceeds of such sales are reinvested),
> (2) The ownership and operation of land or buildings all or substan-

---

[179] See Int. Rev. Code of 1954, §355(b). Briefly, a spin-off is a distribution by a corporation to its shareholders of stock which it owns in another corporation which it controls.

[180] Treas. Reg. §1.346–1(c).

tially all of which are used and occupied by the owner in the operation of a trade or business, or

(3) A group of activities which, while a part of a business operated for profit, are not themselves independently producing income even though such activities would produce income with the addition of other activities or with large increases in activities previously incidental or insubstantial.[181]

For example, where a company is engaged in the manufacture and sale of hats in its own factory building and it proposes to transfer the factory building to a new corporation, the new corporation is not engaged in a trade or business. As the regulations point out, although the activities in connection with manufacturing hats constitute a trade or business, the operation of the factory building does not.[182] Moreover, where the manufacturing and selling operations constitute only one integrated business, they may not be separated into two trades or businesses by transferring the physical assets pertaining to the sales end of the enterprise to a new corporation.[183] Along the same lines, the activities of a research department cannot be made into a separate trade or business by transferring them to another corporation formed for research purposes.[184]

On the other hand, where a corporation maintains manufacturing facilities in differing states, such facilities, along with related sales organizations, may constitute separate trades or businesses.[185] The same is true for two different retail stores which are separately managed and which do not share common warehouse facilities.[186] Activities which are merely incidental to a primary activity cannot be a separate trade or business. Thus, where a bank owns and occupies a two-story building and leases approximately one half of the second floor of the building to a neighborhood retail merchant as storage space, the activity of leasing is merely incidental to the primary activity of banking and is not a trade or business.[187] But if the bank owns a larger building, occupies the ground floor and leases the ten remaining floors to outsiders, then the leasing activities might be a separate trade or business.[188] Finally, as the regulations indicate, holding for investment purposes cannot be a trade or business nor can the holding of non-income-producing property.[189] And even if the operation of a facility is profitable, it must produce income independently in order to qualify as a trade or business. For example, where a corporation is engaged in the manufacture of steel and steel products and owns and operates a coal mine for the sole purpose of supplying its requirements in the manufacture of steel, the operations of

181 Id. §1.355–1(c).
182 Id., Ex. (2).
183 Id., Ex. (11).
184 Id., Ex. (5).
185 Id., Exs. (8), (13), (14).
186 Id., Ex. (10).
187 Id., Ex. (4).
188 Id., Ex. (3).
189 Id., Exs. (1), (6).

the coal mine, although profitable, are not a trade or business since they do not produce income except as part of the primary business of making steel.[190]

It should be noted that the mechanical test will be satisfied either if the corporation has actively conducted two or more separate trades or businesses for five years or if a trade or business was acquired in a transaction in which gain or loss was not recognized in whole or in part. If the trade or business has been actively conducted for at least five years, there is no requirement that it also be actively conducted by the distributing corporation for a similar period. This would permit a corporation to acquire a number of trades or businesses in a tax-free exchange, such as a merger, and discontinue those which it considered unprofitable. If *any* gain is recognized in the acquisition by the transferor, however, the mechanical test is not satisfied. For example, if in a reorganization, such as a merger, which otherwise would be tax free, cash or some property other than stock or securities is received (so-called boot), then the mechanical test would not be met if gain or loss were recognized to the transferor because of the receipt of boot.[191] And even if the transferor had no gain on the transaction (as where the value of what he receives is equal to the basis of the shares or property he surrenders), it is probable that the mechanical test would not be met despite the statutory reference to a situation where "gain or loss *was* recognized." [192] The intent of the legislation was apparently to disallow partial liquidation treatment to businesses if they were acquired by purchase or in a reorganization where boot was present, and there is little evidence that it was intended that the tax treatment should differ merely because, in a particular situation, the transferor *had* no gain or loss (if gain or loss would otherwise have been recognized). Any other view would permit an illogical tax windfall to an acquiring corporation merely because it happened to find a seller who, from a gain or loss standpoint, was in a neutral position, a somewhat unlikely occurrence in any event. It has also been suggested that similar reasoning should extend to purchases from corporations which have disposed of their assets under the provisions of Section 337.[193] Although gain may be recognized with regard to certain types of assets in a Section 337 transaction,[194] even if no gain were recognized as far as the selling corporation is concerned, gain or loss would probably be recognized when the proceeds of the sale were distributed in complete liquidation of the transferor (depending upon the basis of the shareholders and the value of the property distributed to them). Thus, if the entire transaction is viewed as a whole, it might be said that gain or loss was recognized, although perhaps not to the selling

[190] Id., Ex. (12).

[191] Int. Rev. Code of 1954, §356.

[192] See B. Bittker and J. Eustice, Federal Income Taxation of Corporations and Shareholders 315 n.73 (1966).

[193] Ibid.

[194] See text accompanying notes 144–149 *supra*.

corporation.[195] The statute merely refers to the recognition of gain or loss and does not specify that such gain or loss must have been recognized to the immediate transferor.

7.6 SPIN-OFFS, SPLIT-OFFS AND SPLIT-UPS

As we have seen, a complete or partial liquidation will generally result in the recognition of capital gain or loss to the distributee. There is another method of resolving a deadlock between shareholders which has many of the advantages of dissolution without requiring that either or both share-holder groups pay a tax on realized gains. A liquidation, either partial or complete, necessarily involves taking assets out of corporate solution and distributing them to one or more shareholders. What is needed, then, is a method whereby a corporation may be separated into two or more parts without a distribution of assets, i.e., the assets remain in corporate solution and the interests of the shareholders are reshuffled so that one shareholder group holds shares in one corporation and another shareholder group holds shares in another corporation. This may be done through use of a "spin-off," "split-off" or "split-up." These terms may be defined roughly as follows:

A "spin-off" involves the distribution by one corporation to one or more of its shareholders of shares which it owns in another corporation which it controls. A "split-off" resembles a "spin-off" except that the distributees ex-change shares of the parent corporation for the shares in the controlled corporation (i.e., unlike the "spin-off," they surrender shares of the par-ent). A "split-up" also involves the surrender by the distributees of their shares in the parent, but unlike the "split-off," the "split-up" involves the dissolution of the parent corporation. In other words, the latter transaction entails the distribution of shares in two or more subsidiaries to the parent corporation's shareholders in exchange for all its shares and the dissolution of the parent corporation. Transactions such as these may be effected with-out recognition of gain or loss if they comply with the provisions of Section 355 of the Code.

The key aspect of Section 355 is that it permits tax-free treatment of divisive reorganizations such as those just described and yet prevents the misuse of these techniques to effect a bail-out of corporate earnings and profits which, if distributed, would normally be taxed as dividends at ordi-nary rates. Suppose, for example, that Corporation A has $25,000 in earn-ings and profits. If this is distributed to the A shareholders the result would be a taxable dividend. If the $25,000 were invested in shares of another corporation, B, and the B shares were spun off or distributed to the A share-holders, the result should be no different. Thus the central problem with which Section 355 contends is that of distinguishing between a divisive

195 See B. Bittker and J. Eustice, id.

reshuffling of interests in an existing business and a covert distribution of earnings and profits in the form of stock.

The main features of Section 355 may be briefly summarized. One corporation (the "distributing" corporation) must be in control of another corporation (the "controlled" corporation) immediately before the distribution. "Control" is defined as ownership of at least 80 percent of the combined voting power of the controlled corporation's voting shares and at least 80 percent of each other class of stock.[196] The stock held by the distributing corporation in the controlled corporation is, then, either distributed to the former's shareholders (a spin-off) or is exchanged for stock in the distributing corporation (a split-off or a split-up).

The second requirement is that

the transaction was not used principally as a device for the distribution of the earnings and profits of the distributing corporation or the controlled corporation or both (but the mere fact that subsequent to the distribution stock or securities in one or more of such corporations are sold or exchanged by all or some of the distributees (other than pursuant to an arrangement negotiated or agreed upon prior to such distribution) shall not be construed to mean that the transaction was used principally as such a device).[197]

The above suggests, by negative inference, that a prearranged sale of the shares of the controlled corporation will result in failure to comply with Section 355. This is justified if the tax-free character of the transaction is thought to be based on the assumption that the shareholders continue to own a proprietary interest in a business and that such interest has been merely reshuffled or redescribed. If the distributees emerge from the transaction with cash instead of shares, to that extent they have lessened their proprietary interest and this in turn might suggest that they have in reality bailed out corporate earnings and profits. A difficulty with this line of reasoning is that a sale of common stock correspondingly reduces a shareholder's voting power and right to participate in profits; hence, as we have already seen in another context,[198] common stock is not generally suitable as a device for effecting a bail out of earnings and profits.[199] Nonetheless, the statute is apparently based on the assumption that a prearranged sale even of common stock may suggest that there has been a bail-out. The regulations carry out this theme and even take the position that a post-distribu-

[196] Int. Rev. Code of 1954, §368(c). See also Rev. Rul. 59–259, 1959–2 Cum. Bull. 115, and Ch. II, text accompanying note 30.

[197] Int. Rev. Code of 1954, §355(a)(1)(B). See generally Jacobs, The Anatomy of a Spin-Off, [1967] Duke L.J. 1; Whitman, Draining the Serbonian Bog: A New Approach to Corporate Separations Under the 1954 Code, 81 Harv. L. Rev. 1194 (1968).

[198] See Ch. VI, text accompanying note 103 (discussing Section 306 of the Code).

[199] See B. Bittker and J. Eustice, Federal Income Taxation of Corporations and Shareholders 475 (1966).

tion sale which is not prearranged will be "evidence" that the transaction was used principally as a device for the distribution of earnings and profits.[200] This means, then, that not only a prearranged sale but *any* sale of substantial amounts of stock will endanger the tax-free character of the transaction. The tax result cannot be predicted with any certainty since it will necessarily depend upon the facts of each situation, i.e., how long the shares were held prior to sale, the number of shares sold, the earnings and profits of the distributing corporation, etc.[201] Finally, even in the absence of a sale of shares of the controlled corporation, an entire transaction may amount to a "device" for the distribution of earnings and profits. The regulations, at least, leave this possibility open.[202] If a transaction clearly lacks "business purpose"[203] or its facts suggest a bail-out opportunity (as where excessive amounts of liquid assets are retained in corporate solution),[204] then an actual sale of the spun-off shares may not be necessary to impose a tax liability.

Two further requirements of a tax-free spin-off, split-off or split-up are that the "active business" requirements of Section 355(b) of the Code be satisfied and that

> *as part of the distribution,* the distributing corporation distributes—
> (i) all of the stock and securities in the controlled corporation held by it immediately before the distribution, or
> (ii) an amount of stock in the controlled corporation constituting control within the meaning of section 368(c), and it is established to the satisfaction of the . . . [Internal Revenue Service] that the retention by the distributing corporation of stock (or stock and securities) in the controlled corporation was not in pursuance of a plan having as one of its principal purposes the avoidance of Federal income tax.[205]

Before discussing the "active business" requirement, a matter which has already been dealt with in some detail in connection with the analogous problem encountered in partial liquidations,[206] it should be noted that the statutory mandate is that either all the stock or securities of the controlled corporation or at least such an amount as constitutes "control" be received by the shareholders of the distributing corporation "as part of the distribution." Although this does not necessarily mean that there must be only one distribution, if there is more than one, they must be closely associated in time[207] and the distributions must be interdependent parts of the same scheme, i.e., there must be a binding commitment to make the later distri-

---

[200] Treas. Reg. §1.355–2(b)(1).

[201] See id. §1.355–2(b)(3).

[202] Ibid.

[203] Id. §1.355–2(c). See Ch. VIII, text accompanying note 70, discussing a leading case, Gregory v. Helvering, 293 U.S. 465 (1935).

[204] See B. Bittker and J. Eustice, id. at 478.

[205] Int. Rev. Code of 1954, §355(a)(1)(D) (emphasis supplied).

[206] See text accompanying note 180 *supra*.

[207] Commissioner v. Baan, 382 F.2d 485 (9th Cir. 1967), *aff'd sub. nom.* Commissioner v. Gordon, 391 U.S. 83 (1968).

bution.[208] Clearly, then, tax-free spin-off treatment is not available for a series of relatively small distributions of stock occurring over a period of several years.

Turning to the active business requirement, Section 355(b) of the Code requires that the distributing corporation and the controlled corporation be engaged immediately after the distribution in the "active conduct of a trade or business." [209] An additional requirement is that each trade or business must have been actively conducted throughout the five-year period ending on the date of the distribution and that neither trade nor business must have been acquired within the five-year period in a transaction in which gain or loss was recognized in whole or in part.[210] The overall approach and intent of these requirements is similar to those which have already been discussed in connection with partial liquidations,[211] namely, to prevent a corporation with substantial earnings and profits from investing its surplus funds (which otherwise might have been distributed as dividends) in a trade or business which is then owned for only a temporary period before being conveyed to the shareholders in the form of stock. The same reasoning applies to the division of an existing business into component parts. As previously indicated,[212] the regulations preclude separating out one or more phases of a trade or business which themselves do not produce income independently, such as a sales or research department.[213] The same is true for activities which are merely incidental to the main business, such as rental of small amounts of property not needed in the business[214] or the ownership of buildings or land used in the business[215] as well as the holding of other properties, such as stock, securities and land for investment purposes.[216] However, if an enterprise consists of separable units, such as the operation of a retail store in a downtown area and a suburban retail store,[217] or the operation of plants in separate states,[218] the regulations permit one or more units to be separately incorporated and spun-off if there is a

[208] Commissioner v. Gordon, 391 U.S. 83 (1968).

[209] An alternative requirement is that immediately before the distribution the distributing corporation have no assets other than stock or securities in the controlled corporations and that each of the controlled corporations be engaged immediately after the distribution in the active conduct of a trade or business. Int. Rev. Code of 1954, §355(b)(1)(B).

[210] Id. §355(b)(2)(B), (C). Also, Section 355(b)(2)(D) prohibits the acquisition of control of a corporation (other than in a tax-free transaction) during the five-year period. This prevents a corporation from purchasing stock in a corporation conducting a trade or business and then spinning off the stock to its shareholders, or acquiring the trade or business in a tax-free liquidation and then effecting a spin-off. See Treas. Reg. §1.355–4(b)(2).

[211] See text accompanying notes 179–195.

[212] See notes 182–190 *supra*.

[213] See Treas. Reg. §1.355–1(d), Exs. (5) and (11).

[214] Id., Ex. (4). Cf. Ex. (3) (rental activities a separate trade or business if relatively substantial in comparison to the primary business).

[215] Id., Ex. (2).

[216] Id., Exs. (1), (6), and (7).

[217] Id., Ex. (10).

[218] Id., Exs. (8) and (13).

reasonable business purpose for doing so.[219] The resolution of a deadlock among shareholders clearly qualifies as a legitimate purpose. Therefore, if there is such a deadlock and the business can be divided equitably among two or more shareholder groups so that each retains ownership of a trade or business which itself has been actively conducted for the minimum five-year period, the deadlock can be resolved through a spin-off, split-off or split-up without the parties incurring the tax liabilities which might follow from a complete or partial liquidation.

Suppose, however, that the business consists of a single profit-making activity, such as the rental or sale of real estate, and that it has been conducted for at least five years. Can a single trade or business be split "up the middle," separated into two businesses and divided between two shareholder groups? Although the regulations do not appear to permit this, to allow tax-free treatment in this situation does not seem inconsistent with the overall policy of Section 355, namely, to permit tax-free readjustment of proprietary interests in an existing enterprise where there is no attempt to bail out earnings and profits which otherwise might be distributed as dividends. Accordingly the courts have held that a single business may be divided into two operating halves, a result in which the Internal Revenue Service has acquiesced.[220] This makes Section 355 a useful device to resolve deadlocks.

Another aspect of Section 355 which lends itself to the resolution of deadlocks is that there is no requirement that the shares be distributed pro rata among the shareholders. Prior to 1954 it was unclear whether a distribution which was not pro rata would qualify for tax-free treatment. Section 355(a)(2) of the Code was then enacted to provide that a distribution need not be pro rata and that a shareholder need not surrender stock in the distributing corporation.[221] Accordingly, a business may be divided into two parts, one part transferred to a newly created corporation and the shares of that corporation distributed to one or more shareholders in exchange for their shares in the distributing corporation (i.e., a split-off). The distributees own all the shares of the new corporation and those who do not participate in the distribution own all the shares in the distributing corporation, which is thus freed from deadlock. If the transaction qualifies under Sec-

[219] Treas. Reg. §1.355–2(c).

[220] United States v. Marett, 325 F.2d 28 (5th Cir. 1963); Edmond P. Coady, 33 T.C. 771 (1960), *acquiesced in*, 1965–2 Cum. Bull. 4, *aff'd per curiam*, Coady v. Commissioner, 289 F.2d 490 (6th Cir. 1961); Rev. Rul. 64–147, 1964–1 (Part I) Cum. Bull. 136. See generally Jacobs, Spin-offs: The Pre-Distribution Two Business Rule—Edmond P. Coady and Beyond, 19 Tax L. Rev. 155 (1964).

[221] This provision also states that tax-free treatment may be had whether or not the distribution is in pursuance of a plan of reorganization within the meaning of that term in Section 368(a)(1)(D) of the Code. The latter provides for tax-free treatment for the transfer of assets to a controlled corporation if stock or securities of the latter are distributed to the shareholders of the transferor in a transaction which qualifies under Section 354 (corporate reorganization), Section 355 (spin-offs, split-offs, and split-ups) or Section 356 (distribution of boot or other property in connection with any of the foregoing).

tion 355, no shareholders recognize any gain or loss, except that gain (but no loss) is recognized to the extent that distributees receive property other than stock or securities (i.e., boot).[222]

The precise manner in which a business is to be divided must of necessity depend upon the wishes and needs of the individual shareholders and the negotiating situation. Indeed, some shareholders may wish to be bought out rather than to continue as owners of a business. In this event their shares can either be purchased by other shareholders or redeemed by the corporation, a transaction which in either case will result in capital gain or loss to them.[223]

In some situations it may not always be possible to divide a business into two equal parts, particularly if the active business requirement of Section 355 is kept in mind. In other words, Section 355 presupposes that both corporations (the distributing and the controlled corporation) be engaged in the active conduct of a trade or business. Both enterprises must thus consist in operational assets; one may not consist primarily in investment properties or inactive assets, such as vacant land. It might well be argued that a split-off which resolves a deadlock between shareholder groups does not present a significant threat of a bail out of corporate earnings and thus the strictures of the active business requirement should be relaxed if possible.[224] However, the fact remains that the statute does refer expressly to the *active conduct* of a *trade or business* and therefore, despite the lack of any intent to bail out corporate earnings, tax-free treatment should not be available where a substantial part of the corporate assets is nonoperational or passive in form. The upshot of all of this is that a shareholder in a deadlock situation must choose between retaining an investment in a business and not paying a tax, and receiving some other type of asset whereby any gain or loss on his original investment is recognized. If the shareholder is in a loss position (i.e., if the basis of his shares in the deadlocked corporation is relatively high when compared with their fair value), he will probably prefer to have the transaction fall outside Section 355. This can readily be done through a straight redemption of shares which terminates his interest in the corporation. If, on the other hand, he chooses tax-free treatment, some means must be found to subdivide the business so as to give him an

---

[222] Section 356(a) of the Code determines the tax effect of boot received in an exchange pursuant to Section 355 (i.e., a split-off or split-up); Section 356(b) governs the tax effect of boot in distributions (or spin-offs). Part of a Section 356(a) distribution may be taxed at ordinary rates if it "has the effect of the distribution of a dividend." For further discussion of this provision see Ch. VIII, text accompanying note 65.

[223] A sale of shares to another shareholder will normally result in capital gain or loss. A redemption of shares by the corporation will be treated the same way if it is not essentially equivalent to a dividend, if it constitutes a substantially disproportionate redemption or if it effects a complete termination of the shareholder's interest. For further discussion see Ch. VI, text accompanying notes 10–78.

[224] See D. Herwitz, Business Planning 931–932 (1966).

interest in its operational activities. Where the business is already, in a sense, subdivided, as where it maintains stores or factories in separate locations,[225] this may be done with relative ease. Even if the business is not so subdivided, it may in some cases be split into two integral parts.[226] For example, real estate corporations which engage in substantial rental activities may be subdivided, with the rental properties being allocated more or less evenly between two or more companies.[227] Other candidates for such treatment are construction businesses and service businesses of various types. On the other hand, where a business consists in a single plant with a sales office, it may not lend itself to subdivision into active operating components which themselves qualify as a trade or business, since, as we have seen, a single phase of an integrated profit-making enterprise, such as a sales organization, cannot be split off free of tax even if it were practical to do so.[228] In such a situation there may be little alternative to a taxable dissolution or redemption of shares unless the deadlock can be resolved in some fashion. If the potential tax impact of a taxable distribution is sufficiently severe, this might be a powerful incentive to the parties to resolve their differences.

[225] See notes 217–218 *supra.*

[226] See note 220 *supra.*

[227] See Cohen, Partial Liquidations and Spin-Offs of Real Estate Corporations, N.Y.U. 21st Inst. on Fed. Tax. 685 (1963).

[228] See note 213 *supra.* The practical difficulties are rather obvious. If two shareholder groups are hostile to one another, it is doubtful that one group would consent to have the other in charge of some phase of operations which is vital to the business owned by the other (e.g., to have one shareholder own the sales organization and the other the manufacturing end of the business).

VIII Selling the Corporation

If a closely held corporation prospers, there may come a time when the shareholders, for various reasons, decide to sell it to some other investor group or to a larger corporation. For example, some of those who founded the corporation and were responsible for its success may have retired or passed away, control of the corporation may have passed into younger and less-experienced hands and some shareholders may find it inconvenient to hold minority interests which are not readily saleable except to the corporation or to the other shareholders. Despite whatever arrangements may have been made for purchasing a shareholder's interest upon his retirement or death, as the worth of his shares grows he may find it unwise from an economic standpoint to have so much of his capital committed to stock which has relatively little liquidity. For example, he may require funds for payment of expenses, as in the case of illness, or to make gifts to others for estate planning purposes. Although it is always possible to use stock in a close corporation, particularly preferred shares, in connection with estate planning, setting up inter vivos trusts and so forth, it may be desirable to have a more diversified portfolio to protect the interests of the beneficiaries in the event that the business runs into financial difficulty.

Liquidity of investment may be achieved in at least two ways. First, the business can be sold to another corporation whose shares are publicly held and more or less widely traded. Secondly, the close corporation can "go public," or make a public offering of its stock. The second of these two alternatives will be discussed in the following chapter. In the present chapter we shall examine the various tax and corporate aspects involved in selling the business.

8.1 METHODS OF SELLING THE BUSINESS

A closely held concern may be disposed of in several ways:

A. Merger or consolidation
B. Sale of stock for either

    (1) stock or

    (2) other property, such as cash, notes, etc.

  C. Sale of assets for either

    (1) stock or

    (2) other property, such as cash, notes, etc.

Each of the above methods also raises the question of whether the transaction may be cast into a form whereby it is tax-free to the seller. Generally this will be so only if the transaction qualifies as a reorganization. Before discussing in detail the various ways in which a transaction may be made tax free, as well as various situations in which it may be desirable to make the transaction taxable, some of the corporate aspects involved in each of the methods outlined above will be examined.

8.2 MERGER OR CONSOLIDATION—CORPORATE ASPECTS

A merger or consolidation is a statutory device whereby corporations are amalgamated with one another. In a merger, one corporation is absorbed into another. The former is referred to as the "merging" corporation and, from a legal standpoint, it passes out of existence when it is merged into the second, or "surviving" corporation. A "consolation" involves the creation of a new entity, a third corporation into which the two corporations are absorbed. In both situations it is vitally important to follow precisely the prescribed statutory method, which generally involves approval of a plan of merger (or consolidation, if that be the case) by the board of directors of each corporation[1] followed by shareholder approval of the plan,[2] whereupon the articles of merger are signed by the appropriate corporate officers and filed with the proper state official, such as the Secretary of State of that jurisdiction in which the merging corporations have their domicile.[3] If the articles of merger are in proper form, then the merger becomes effective either on the filing date or on the effective date for the merger as set forth in the plan. When the merger becomes effective, the surviving corporation is automatically vested with title to the merging company's assets, along with its other rights, franchises, etc.,[4] and also becomes subject to all the merging company's liabilities, including those which are unknown and con-

---

  [1] E.g., Model Bus. Corp. Act §71. For a good checklist of business, corporate, tax and labor relations aspects of corporate combinations, see Sebring, Statutory Mergers and Asset Acquisitions, 21 Bus. Law. 799 (1966).

  [2] Model Bus. Corp. Act §73.

  [3] Id. §74.

  [4] This is so unless there is some reason why such rights are not assignable by operation of law, as where a leasehold is assignable only with the consent of the lessor.

tingent.[5] Shareholders who vote against the merger or consolidation and who file a written objection to it with either corporation have what is known as "dissenters' appraisal rights." This permits the shareholder to receive the value of his shares in accordance with a procedure whereby the shares are appraised under judicial supervision.[6]

A merger or consolidation has several advantages and disadvantages. First, as shall be indicated in greater detail in the discussion of tax aspects, the merger may be the most flexible method of achieving a tax-free transfer from one corporation to another.[7] Secondly, the transfer is by operation of law and there is no need for the preparation of numerous instruments of transfer, such as deeds, assignments and other conveyances. Thirdly, since the transaction is not technically a sale, local taxes frequently imposed on the transfer of real property and the sale of tangible property are often avoided.

There are disadvantages with the merger technique, however. As previously noted, those who dissent from a merger (including shareholders of the surviving corporation) are generally entitled to the value of their shares by way of appraisal rights. Although appraisal rights are also available in some states where substantially all the corporate assets are sold or otherwise disposed of outside of the usual and regular course of business,[8] they do not apply to a sale of a controlling block of stock. Hence the stock sale is in this respect superior to both the merger and the asset sale. If enough shareholders assert their appraisal rights, it may be difficult or impossible to effectuate the merger or asset sale, since the merging or selling corporation may have insufficient liquid assets to pay off the dissenting shareholders and the acquiring corporation may not wish to go through with the deal if the acquired corporation is substantially reduced in size. For that reason it is common to insert in a merger plan a clause which permits the board of directors to call off the merger if more than a designated percentage of the shareholders object to it.

Another disadvantage with a merger, as opposed to a stock sale or asset sale, is that the surviving corporation automatically succeeds to all the liabilities of the merging corporation. Thus hidden or unknown liabilities, such

[5] E.g., id. §76.

[6] Id. §§80–81. Recently enacted statutory provisions in Delaware dispense with the need for obtaining approval of the merger by the shareholders of the surviving (i.e., the acquiring) corporation if the net effect of the merger will not be to increase the surviving corporation's outstanding shares by more than 15 percent. In such cases the surviving corporation's shareholders have no appraisal rights. Del. Gen. Corp. Law §251(f) (1967). Also such appraisal rights are not available for shareholders of either corporation (to the extent Delaware law is applicable to either) where one or more corporation's shares are listed on a national securities exchange, or where such shares are held of record by not less than 2000 shareholders, whether or not such shares are listed on an exchange. Del. Gen. Corp. Law §262(k)(2) (1967).

[7] See text accompanying note 113 *infra*.

[8] Model Bus. Corp. Act §80(b).

as tax and tort claims, may be imposed upon the successor corporation. Unless some provision is made for this in the terms of the merger, the assumption of liabilities may cause the merger to be more expensive than had been anticipated. To guard against such liabilities, acquiring corporations sometimes require that a designated percentage of the shares to be issued in the merger to the shareholders of the acquired corporation be placed in escrow. If the liabilities turn out to be greater than as represented by the acquired corporation at the time of the merger, then fewer shares are issued and some of the escrowed shares are returned to the acquiring corporation, thereby adjusting the purchase price downwards. Similar techniques are used to adjust the purchase price where the latter is set by a formula which depends upon the earnings performance of the business which has been acquired. If the acquired business earns less than an expected amount during the escrow period, fewer shares are issued.

Sometimes mergers will run into difficulty when they cross state lines. If Company A, organized under the laws of State X, merges with Company B, organized under the laws of State Y, then each company must comply with the laws of its respective domicile, States X and Y.[9] If the laws of State X do not permit a merger with a corporation organized under the laws of another state, then the transaction must take some other form, such as an asset sale or sale of stock.

Occasionally the merging corporation will possess franchises or other rights which cannot be assigned by operation of law. For example, a lease may prohibit merger of the lessee without the consent of the lessor, and the same may be true in a franchise situation. One solution to this is to have the acquiring corporation, or one of its subsidiaries, merge into the acquired corporation, if this is feasible in other respects. Another approach is to have the acquiring corporation purchase the stock of the acquired corporation and continue it in existence as a subsidiary.

A disadvantage of a merger, in contrast to a stock acquisition, is the expense and trouble of complying with the various formalities which are required. As previously indicated, shareholder approval is necessary. If either corporation is subject to the proxy rules of the Securities Exchange Act of 1934, then it must file proxy materials with the Securities and Exchange Commission before seeking shareholder approval.[10] This is time-consuming and frequently expensive. In addition, there are civil and criminal liabilities for false or misleading proxy materials in violation of the SEC rules.[11]

---

[9] Id. §77.

[10] See Securities Exchange Act of 1934, §14, 15 U.S.C. §78n. Corporations covered by the filing requirements are those having a class of equity securities listed on a national securities exchange or those having total assets in excess of $1 million and a class of equity securities held of record by five hundred or more persons. Securities Exchange Act of 1934, §12, 15 U.S.C. §78(1).

[11] E.g., SEC rule 10b–5, 17 C.F.R. §240.10b–5, and SEC rule 14a–9, 17 C.F.R. §240.14a–9. See also Securities Exchange Act of 1934, §32, 15 U.S.C. §§78ff.

Although shareholder approval is also required in some jurisdictions for asset sales,[12] it is seldom, if ever, required for sales of stock. Stock sales also have the advantage of avoiding, in some situations, the need for the acquiring corporation to go through the procedure of formal qualification to do business in the various states where the acquired corporation does business, as might be required if the transaction took the form of a merger or asset purchase and the acquired corporation were not to be operated as a subsidiary.[13]

Finally, some mergers may require registration of the securities issued by the acquiring corporation to the shareholders of the acquired corporation with the SEC, under the Securities Act of 1933. This is a separate procedure and should not be confused with the filing of proxy materials with the SEC under the Securities Exchange Act of 1934. Although the so-called no-sale rule (SEC rule 133)[14] has thus far exempted many mergers from filing requirements under the 1933 Act, the rule is difficult to apply in some situations and may not always provide for an exemption, as where those in control of the merging corporation dispose of their shares in the open market shortly after the merger has become effective.[15] Although a detailed discussion of this area lies beyond the scope of our present study, suffice it to say that, particularly with the possibility of change in the rules proposed in the so-called Wheat Report of the SEC issued in March of 1969, it should not be assumed that mergers will never involve SEC registration of securities under the 1933 Act.

8.3 SALE OF STOCK—CORPORATE ASPECTS

From what has already been said it is apparent that the sale of stock avoids many of the problems encountered in connection with mergers and asset sales. Thus no shareholder vote is needed, unless required by the rules of a stock exchange[16] or unless the acquiring corporation needs additional authorized shares or the articles of incorporation or bylaws expressly provide for shareholder approval. A majority shareholder is free to dispose of his

[12] E.g., Model Bus. Corp. Act §79(c) (a majority of the voting shares unless a class vote is required).

[13] E.g., id. §77(b). Whether or not a parent corporation doing business through a subsidiary is required to qualify itself as a foreign corporation depends upon the factual situation and the idiosyncrasies of state law. See M. Caplin, Doing Business in Other States (1959).

[14] 17 C.F.R. §230.133.

[15] For a general discussion see Sommer, Mergers, Consolidations, Sales of Assets—Rule 133, 16 W. Res. L. Rev. 11 (1964).

[16] See N.Y. Stock Exch. Company Manual A–284 (shareholder approval required if the acquisition could result in an increase of 20 percent or more in the outstanding common shares, or where the fair value of common stock and any other consideration for the acquisition equals or exceeds 20 percent of the market value of the outstanding common shares).

stock on whatever terms he wishes unless the shares are subject to a stock transfer restriction, except that he may not sell control to someone whom he knows or has reason to believe is likely to mismanage the corporation or loot it.[17] Furthermore, in some situations courts have held a majority shareholder liable to the corporation or to the minority shareholders for any premium which he receives because of his ownership of a controlling block of stock.[18] Aside from these qualifications, however, the shares may be freely sold with little or no formality, except requirements imposed by the acquiring corporation, such as the furnishing of an opinion of counsel as to the legality of the transaction and validity of the shares, and certified financial statements. The acquiring corporation does not risk exposure to hidden liabilities, although such liabilities obviously are relevant to the price paid for the shares. Thus, as in the merger and asset sale situations, part of the shares issued for control may be placed in escrow.

There are no appraisal rights, unless these are provided for in the articles of incorporation or bylaws, and, as in the merger situation, there are no problems of preparing complicated instruments of transfer, such as deeds and assignments. Similarly, there are no problems of determining whether certain contract rights, franchises and the like are assignable, or of ascertaining what, if any, sales or transfer taxes should be paid. As previously pointed out, it may not be necessary to qualify the acquiring corporation to do business in those states in which the acquired corporation does business if the latter is maintained as a separate subsidiary.

Aside from the troublesome tax aspects of qualifying a stock-for-stock transaction as a tax-free reorganization, discussed later in this chapter, there are relatively few disadvantages with a stock acquisition as compared to a merger or asset sale. If the acquiring corporation is operated as a subsidiary, there is likely to be a minority shareholder group, which may prove to be troublesome, especially where cumulative voting is required. Such a minority interest may be eliminated through purchase of their shares or, if the

---

[17] E.g., Insuranshares Corp. v. Northern Fiscal Corp., 35 F. Supp. 22 (E.D. Pa. 1940).

[18] E.g., Perlman v. Feldmann, 219 F.2d 173 (2d Cir. 1955), *cert. denied,* 349 U.S. 952 (1955). Despite general approval of the *Perlman* case by the commentators, it remains a minority view. Thus it is by no means the law that he who sells a control block of stock at a premium is always liable to the corporation or its shareholders. For general discussions see Andrews, The Stockholder's Right to Equal Opportunity in the Sale of Shares, 78 Harv. L. Rev. 505 (1965); Bayne, A Philosophy of Corporate Control, 112 U. Pa. L. Rev. 22 (1963); Hill, The Sale of Controlling Shares, 70 Harv. L. Rev. 986 (1957); Javares, Equal Opportunity in the Sale of Controlling Shares: A Reply to Professor Andrews, 32 U. Chi. L. Rev. 420 (1965); Jennings, Trading in Corporate Control, 44 Calif. L. Rev. 1 (1956); Leech, Transactions in Corporate Control, 104 U. Pa. L. Rev. 725 (1956). For discussion of the problem as it arises in the context of rule 10b–5 under the Securities Exchange Act of 1934, see Schwartz, The Sale of Control and the 1934 Act: New Directions for Federal Corporation Law, 15 N.Y.L.F. 674 (1969).

applicable statutes permit, they may be squeezed out in a so-called short-form merger.[19]

A disadvantage of a stock acquisition is that SEC registration problems may be encountered if shares are issued by the acquiring corporation. In such a situation it must be assured that those who receive the shares intend to hold them indefinitely for investment and not for resale or that registration of the shares is not otherwise required. Since the whole topic of registration of stock will be discussed more extensively in the following chapter, it is best to defer further consideration of this point.

8.4 SALE OF ASSETS—CORPORATE ASPECTS

Although as already indicated a sale of assets may require shareholder approval and the payment of dissenters' appraisal rights, as well as the preparation of complicated instruments of transfer and the necessity of paying sales and transfer taxes, there are several advantages that this transaction has when compared with a merger or stock sale.

Unlike a merger, only the shareholders in the *acquired* corporation are generally entitled to vote on the transaction or to assert appraisal rights.[20] If the asset sale is approved, minority shareholders will be paid off or their claims otherwise satisfied. Unlike the stock acquisition, they will not continue to hold an interest in a subsidiary, although, if they receive shares of the acquiring corporation, they will, of course, become minority shareholders in that respect.

One of the primary advantages of an asset acquisition is that the acquiring corporation does not, by operation of law, succeed to all the liabilities of the acquired corporation. Thus, if there is any doubt as to contingent liabilities or hidden claims, the acquiring corporation may insulate itself from liability for all practical purposes by agreeing to acquire only certain designated assets and by not assuming any liabilities, except, perhaps, liens on the assets acquired, such as mortgages and the like. There are some exceptions to this, as where the transferor conveys its assets in fraud of creditors and this is known or should be known to the transferee[21] or where there has been a failure to comply with a bulk sales act, requiring notice to creditors. However, as a general rule the asset acquisition is safer than the

---

[19] See Ch. IV, text accompanying notes 35–38.

[20] Except where a national securities exchange requires approval by shareholders of the acquiring corporation or where additional shares must be authorized in order to finance the acquisition. See note 16 *supra*.

[21] See H. Ballantine, Corporations §287 (rev. ed. 1946). As Professor Ballantine points out, liability may be imposed on the transferee even apart from a fraudulent conveyance, as where the assets are sold for shares which are transferred directly to the shareholders of the acquired corporation. See id. at 679.

merger and shares some of the advantages of the stock acquisition insofar as it tends to insulate the acquiring corporation from liabilities except those which have been expressly assumed.

The disadvantages of asset acquisitions have already been mentioned. In brief summary they consist of the requirement of shareholder authorization and possible appraisal rights insofar as the acquired corporation is concerned, the preparation of instruments of transfer, the payment of sales and transfer taxes, and the possible difficulties with the transferability of certain rights, such as leasehold interests and franchises. As we shall see, the asset acquisition, from a tax standpoint, is somewhat more flexible than a stock acquisition, although less flexible than a merger or consolidation.

8.5 SHOULD THE TRANSACTION BE TAXABLE?

Although it will generally be to the overall advantage of the parties that the transfer be qualified as a reorganization and thus give rise to no recognition of gain or loss, this is not invariably so. It is well to examine some of the situations where the parties may wish to cast the transaction as a taxable "sale."

Viewing the matter from the standpoint of the "seller," it will generally be to his advantage not to qualify the transfer as a tax-free reorganization if he has a relatively high basis in low-value assets and wishes to recognize a loss. In doing so, however, he must take care that the loss is not disallowed under Section 267 of the Code. The most common cause of disallowance would be if the seller of the assets owns more than 50 percent in value of the outstanding stock of the corporation which purchases them. The 50 percent ownership figure is computed by taking into account not only shares owned by the seller but also shares owned by members of his family, such as brothers, sisters, spouse, ancestor and lineal descendants.[22] If the assets are sold for stock, the 50 percent requirement should be determined on the basis of the percentage ownership of the purchaser after the shares have been issued. Thus, if a corporation were to transfer assets to another in exchange for 51 percent of its shares, Section 267 would disallow deductibility of the loss.[23]

There may be other reasons why the seller may wish to avoid the tax-free reorganization provisions. If the amount of potential gain in the transaction

[22] Int. Rev. Code of 1954, §267(c)(4). For discussion see Ch. II, text accompanying notes 4–6. For useful checklists of the tax aspects of corporate combinations, see Bartolini, Taxable Sale and Purchase of a Corporate Business, 21 Bus. Law. 809 (1966); Lefevre, Tax Checklist for Acquisitions and Mergers, 25 Bus. Law. 355 (1969). See also Appendix B at the end of this volume.

[23] Consider also the possible application of Section 1239 of the Code, which may result in ordinary income treatment for the transfer of depreciable properties where the transferor or his family owns more than 80 percent in value of the outstanding stock of the transferee. See Ch. II, text accompanying note 3.

is not high and if the seller prefers to receive a substantial part of the purchase price in the form of cash or property, rather than stock or securities, then he will wish to have the transfer characterized as a sale rather than as a reorganization. As we shall see, all types of tax-free reorganizations require the transferor to receive at least a substantial amount of stock or securities in exchange for the property, and if anything other than stock or securities is received, then gain is taxable to the extent of the fair market value of the other property (or boot).[24]

From the purchaser's standpoint, it may be preferable to have the transfer cast in the form of a sale rather than a reorganization if the purchaser does not wish to issue substantial amounts of securities or stock (thereby diluting its equity). This would be so only if it were in a position to pay cash or transfer some type of property other than stock or securities, a somewhat unusual situation.

Perhaps the most common reason for wishing a taxable transfer, from the viewpoint of the purchaser, is the desire to receive a stepped-up basis for the assets it acquires. This permits increased depreciation deductions and lessens the gain on a later transfer wherever the fair market value of the assets is higher than the seller's adjusted basis. If the transaction is a tax-free reorganization, then the basis of the acquiring corporation is the same as that of the transferor, increased by the amount of gain, if any, recognized to the transferor.[25] Even though the purchaser may wish a stepped-up basis, the tax cost of achieving this is likely to be prohibitive as far as the seller is concerned. Where a business is sold, whether it be a corporation or a partnership, the gain or loss on each asset is computed separately.[26] If some of the assets fall within the scope of Section 1245 or Section 1250, then gain on their transfer is likely to be ordinary income rather than capital gain, thereby increasing the tax "cost" to the seller of stepping up the purchaser's basis. In a tax-free reorganization, Section 1245 or Section 1250 does not apply except to the extent that property other than stock or securities is received on the transfer.[27]

If the transaction takes the form of a sale of stock for cash or property other than stock or securities (and hence does not qualify as a tax-free reorganization), then, although the seller will have to recognize any gain on the stock, Sections 1245 and 1250 will not apply to tax any part of the gain at ordinary rates, nor would ordinary income result for any other reason (as where inventory, accounts receivable or installment obligations are sold). And if the purchaser acquires a controlling interest (i.e., 80 percent of the voting shares and 80 percent of all other classes of stock) and liquidates the subsidiary within two years, then the basis of the assets it receives is the

24 Int. Rev. Code of 1954, §356. See text accompanying note 48 *infra*.
25 Int. Rev. Code of 1954, §362(b).
26 Williams v. McGowan, 152 F.2d 570 (2d Cir. 1945). Cf. Rev. Rul. 68–55, 1968–1 Cum. Bull. 140, discussed in Ch. II, text accompanying note 64.
27 Int. Rev. Code of 1954, §§1245(b)(3), 1250(d)(3).

price it paid for the shares, rather than a carried-over basis which the assets had when owned by the subsidiary (this exception to the general rule, known as the Kimbell-Diamond rule has already been discussed).[28] Thus the purchaser may achieve a stepped-up basis and the seller's gain would be recognized only at capital gains rates.[29] In sharp contrast, if the shares were purchased solely for voting stock, then the transaction would probably qualify as a tax-free reorganization, in which case the transferee's basis in the assets received on liquidation of the subsidiary would be the basis carried over from the subsidiary, for the Kimbell-Diamond exception to the general rule would not apply.[30] Although the purchaser may attain a stepped-up basis by a taxable stock purchase followed by a liquidation within two years, this will not avoid the application of Sections 1245 and 1250 to the subsidiary when it is liquidated. As we have seen, those provisions take priority over the liquidation provisions even if the liquidation is itself tax free.[31] The end result is that liability under Sections 1245 and 1250 becomes a matter of concern for the purchaser and not for the seller.

If the purchaser should not have sufficient cash or other property to finance the purchase, then the sale may be made on the installment method. This, too, has been previously discussed.[32] Briefly, the principal requirement is that the payments in the year of sale (exclusive of evidences of indebtedness of the purchaser) do not exceed 30 percent of the selling price.[33] This requirement will be somewhat easier to meet in the case of a sale of shares than with an asset sale. For example, a sale of inventory cannot qualify for the installment method of reporting, whereas shares in a corporation having a substantial part of its assets in the form of inventory may so qualify. This is yet another reason why it may be to the seller's advantage to have the transaction take the form of a sale of shares.

If assets are sold instead of stock, then the seller may maximize his capital gain by attempting to allocate as much of the purchase price as possible to capital assets, including good will, rather than to ordinary income items, such as inventory, accounts receivable and Sections 1245 and 1250 property. In addition, any portion of the sales price allocated to a covenant not to

---

[28] Id. §334(b)(2), discussed in Ch. VII, note 105.

[29] Care should be taken, however, that the transaction does not lend itself to being restructured into an asset purchase due to a judicial determination that this was the substance of the parties' intention. See H. B. Snively, 19 T.C. 850 (1953), *aff'd*, 219 F.2d 266 (5th Cir. 1955); Ruth M. Cullen, 14 T.C. 368 (1950), *acquiesced in*, 1950–2 Cum. Bull. 1. This is most likely to occur where the shares are purchased with an immediate intent to dissolve the corporation in order to acquire its assets. See B. Bittker and J. Eustice, Federal Income Taxation of Corporations and Shareholders 347, 378 (1966).

[30] Int. Rev. Code of 1954, §§334(b)(3)(A), 362(b).

[31] See Ch. VI, text accompanying notes 85, 135 and 149.

[32] See id. notes 287–295.

[33] Int. Rev. Code of 1954, §453(b)(2).

compete entered into by the seller gives rise to taxation at ordinary income rates.[34] Conversely, the purchaser will attempt to have as much of the purchase price as possible allocated to depreciable property, including Sections 1245 and 1250 assets, in order to achieve a stepped-up basis. This is also true as regards ordinary income items, such as inventory and accounts receivable. In addition, since good will is not a depreciable item, whereas a covenant not to compete may be amortized over its life expectancy, the purchaser will seek to allocate as much of the sale price to such intangibles as the covenant not to compete and as little as possible to the good will. It can be readily seen that the interests of the purchaser and seller are opposed when it comes to allocating the purchase price. If there is arm's-length bargaining in good faith, the agreement is likely to be a fair reflection of the realities of the situation and thus will generally be respected by the Internal Revenue Service.[35]

If a corporation sells its assets, it need not necessarily dissolve or liquidate, although this is likely to be the usual outcome. As has been seen,[36] gain on the sale of assets will not be recognized if the corporation has adopted a plan of liquidation under Section 337 of the Code and distributes the proceeds of the sale within twelve months following the date the plan is adopted. Where the sale was for shares of stock of the purchaser, as well as for cash or other property, Section 337 treatment may not be available if the seller's shareholders end up owning 20 percent or more of the common stock of the purchasing corporation.[37] Moreover, as has been pointed out, Section 337 will not prevent the recognition of Sections 1245 and 1250 gain (ordinary income). And if the sale was made on the installment method, distribution of the installment obligation will result in gain to the corporation unless the installment obligation was acquired on a sale of non-inventory property (other than Section 1245 or Section 1250 property) or a sale of substantially all the inventory of the seller to one person within twelve months after the adoption of the Section 337 plan of liquidation.[38]

If the corporation is kept alive, then care should be taken that it does not fall within the scope of the personal holding company provisions.[39] For example, where a manufacturing corporation sold its assets on credit and more than 80 percent of its annual income consisted of interest on the sale price, the personal holding company provisions were held to apply.[40]

[34] See Ch. II, notes 7–8.
[35] Ibid.
[36] See Ch. VII, text accompanying notes 143–163.
[37] See id. note 162.
[38] Int. Rev. Code of 1954, §§337(b), 453(d)(1), 453(d)(4)(B). See generally B. Bittker and J. Eustice, Federal Income Taxation of Corporations and Shareholders 400 (1966). See also Ch. VII, text accompanying note 144.
[39] See generally Ch. V, text accompanying notes 133–166.
[40] O'Sullivan Rubber Co. v. Commissioner, 120 F.2d 845 (2d Cir. 1941).

8.6 TAX-FREE REORGANIZATIONS

Despite the foregoing advantages of a taxable exchange in some specialized situations, the technique more frequently used is that of the tax-free reorganization. This has several obvious advantages and a few which may not be so obvious.

From the seller's point of view, any transfer pursuant to a reorganization will not give rise to the recognition of gain or loss except to the extent that property other than stock or securities is received on the exchange.[41] The advantages of this type of treatment are particularly apparent not only where the assets are of relatively high value and carry a low basis but also where they consist of substantial amounts of inventory, accounts receivable and other ordinary income producing properties, including Sections 1245 and 1250 assets. Although the gain goes unrecognized, this does not mean that it might not ultimately be taxed. The stock and securities received for the properties transferred to the acquiring corporation are given a basis equivalent to the basis of the properties so surrendered, adjusted upward or downward to reflect any gain on the transfer or the receipt of any money or property other than stock or securities.[42] Thus the transfer of low basis properties will generally result in the receipt of low basis stock or securities. If these are held to the date of death, then they receive a "new" basis as of that date or the alternate valuation date one year later and the gain which was previously unrecognized is never taxed. If the stock or securities are sold, then the gain is taxed at capital gains rates. The advantages to the seller are, then, clearly apparent, particularly if the transaction is compared with a taxable sale of substantial amounts of ordinary income-producing properties.

From the acquiring corporation's perspective the advantages may not be as apparent, particularly inasmuch as it does not receive a stepped-up basis for the properties as it would in a taxable purchase of assets or a purchase of shares followed by a liquidation of the acquired corporation within two years.[43] However, in a tax-free reorganization the acquiring corporation may receive the benefit of a number of favorable tax attributes of the acquired corporation, such as loss carry-overs,[44] and some not so favorable, such as the earnings and profits account.[45]

---

[41] Int. Rev. Code of 1954, §§356, 361(b).

[42] Id. §358. See Ch. II, text accompanying notes 56–65.

[43] See Ch. VII, note 105.

[44] Int. Rev. Code of 1954, §381(c)(1). For limitations on use of the carry-over, see id. §382. See also id. §269. For an extensive discussion see B. Bittker and J. Eustice, Federal Income Taxation of Corporations and Shareholders §13.20 (1966).

[45] Int. Rev. Code of 1954, §381(c)(2). Since the availability of earnings and profits determines the extent to which a distribution is taxable as a dividend under

A nontax advantage of a tax-free reorganization may be the ability of the acquiring corporation to finance the acquisition through the use of voting shares and, at least to a limited extent in so-called A and C reorganizations (mergers and asset sales), through the use of other types of securities, such as bonds, notes or convertible debentures. There is no necessary reason why an acquisition which is financed in such a manner must be a tax-free reorganization. In fact, as we shall see, the issuance of too much by way of debt or nonvoting stock may sometimes disqualify the transaction from treatment as a reorganization and thus result in tax liability or the recognition of losses. All that is meant here is that where an acquiring corporation does not have or does not wish to expend large amounts of cash or other properties to finance a purchase, the transaction can be financed in a method which is tax free to the seller through the use of the purchaser's stock or securities.

It is now appropriate to examine in greater detail the three types of tax-free reorganization which are likely to be of greatest utility with regard to a corporate acquisition. These three forms of reorganization have already been discussed in some detail from a nontax perspective. In tax parlance, they are as follows:

Type A: a statutory merger or consolidation;

Type B: the acquisition by one corporation, in exchange *solely* for all or a part of its *voting* stock (or in exchange solely for all or a part of the *voting* stock of a corporation which is in control of the acquiring corporation) of stock of another corporation if, immediately after the acquisition, the acquiring corporation has *control* of such other corporation (whether or not such acquiring corporation had control immediately before the acquisition);

Type C: the acquisition by one corporation, in exchange *solely* for all or a part of its voting stock (or in exchange *solely* for all or a part of the *voting* stock of a corporation which is in control of the acquiring corporation), of *substantially all* of the properties of another corporation, but in determining whether the exchange is solely for stock the assumption by the acquiring corporation of a liability of the other, or the fact that property is acquired subject to a liability, shall be disregarded.[46]

The statutory scheme provides for nonrecognition of gain or loss where stock or securities in a corporation which is a "party to a reorganization" are, in pursuance of the plan or reorganization, "exchanged solely for stock or securities in . . . another corporation a party to the reorganization." [47] As

---

Section 316 of the Code, a relatively low earnings and profits account may permit certain distributions to be treated as a tax-free recovery of capital.

[46] Id. §368(a)(1) (emphasis supplied). Three other types of reorganization are also provided for, but they are not directly pertinent to the problem of corporate acquisitions: asset transfers by a corporation to another controlled corporation in exchange for stock which is distributed to the shareholders of the controlling corporation (i.e., a spin-off) (Type D); a recapitalization (Type E) and a "mere change in identity, form, or place of organization, however effected" (Type F).

[47] Id. §354(a)(1). To similar effect, Section 361(a) of the Code provides for

has already been pointed out, if property other than stock or securities is received, then gain is recognized to the extent of the fair market value of the other property (including cash).[48] No loss is recognized, however.

The statutory scheme must be rigidly adhered to. Thus care should be taken that the stock or securities received pertain to a corporation which is a "party to a reorganization" and that stock or securities of the same or another "party to a reorganization" are surrendered, all "in pursuance of the plan."[49] In this hypertechnical area, defined terms are of crucial importance and the phrase "party to a reorganization" is somewhat elaborately defined in Section 368(b) to include, among other things, the corporation resulting from a reorganization (as in a merger or consolidation—Type A) or both corporations, in the case of a reorganization resulting from the acquisition by one corporation of stock or properties of another (as in a stock or assets acquisition—Types B and C). Also, the definitions of the terms "reorganization" and "party to a reorganization" permit the issuance of stock of a controlling corporation—i.e., a parent corporation.[50] Thus Corporation X can convey substantially all of its properties to Corporation Y for voting stock of Corporation Z, which controls Y. And essentially the same result may be achieved through a merger (Type A) or exchange of stock (Type B).

The general scheme of computing the extent of gain where properties other than stock or securities (so-called boot) are received and the method of computing the basis to the transferor and transferee are similar to the rules applicable to other types of tax-free transfers, such as corporate formations under Section 351, already discussed to a considerable extent.[51] Thus the assumption by the transferee of liabilities of the transferor is not characterized as boot except where there is a tax avoidance purpose[52] or (in the case of a Type D reorganization) where the total liabilities exceed the total basis of the properties transferred.[53] As we shall see, however, an assump-

---

nonrecognition if a corporation which is a party to a plan of reorganization exchanges property in pursuance of the plan of reorganization solely for stock or securities in another corporation which is also a party to the reorganization.

[48] See note 41 *supra*. In a Type C reorganization, if the corporation receiving property other than stock or securities from the transferee distributes it to its shareholders in pursuance of the plan, then no gain is recognized. Int. Rev. Code of 1954, §361(b)(1)(A). Conversely, if the other property is retained, then gain is recognized to the corporation to the extent of the value of the other property. Id. §361-(b)(1)(B).

[49] For the meaning of the phrase "plan of reorganization," see Treas. Reg. §§1.368–2(g) and 1.368–3(a). See also Manning, "In Pursuance of the Plan of Reorganization": The Scope of the Reorganization Provisions of the Internal Revenue Code, 72 Harv. L. Rev. 881 (1959).

[50] Int. Rev. Code of 1954, §§368(a)(1), 368(a)(2)(D) and 368(b).

[51] See Ch. II, text accompanying notes 45–50.

[52] Int. Rev. Code of 1954, §357(b). See Ch. II, text accompanying notes 45–48.

[53] Int. Rev. Code of 1954, §357(c)(1)(B). See Ch. II, text accompanying notes 49–50.

tion of liabilities is also pertinent to the question of whether there is, in fact, a reorganization.[54] Without anticipating the discussion too much, it may be briefly stated that liabilities may be more or less freely assumed in a merger (Type A) or, with some reservations, in a transfer of substantially all the assets (Type C). In sharp contrast, an assumption of liabilities will generally disqualify the transaction for tax-free treatment if it takes the form of an exchange of stock (Type B).

As previously pointed out,[55] if a corporation receives money or boot in a Type C reorganization, then gain is recognized to the extent of the money or boot unless it is distributed to the shareholders. If money or boot is retained, then gain is recognized to the extent of the amount retained.[56]

The basis computations in tax-free reorganizations are governed by the same provisions and are similar to the basis computations of tax-free corporate formations, already discussed extensively. Thus the basis of the stock or securities of the acquiring corporation (or its parent) held by the transferor, or distributed to the latter's shareholders, is determined under Section 358 of the Code (basis of property transferred decreased by the fair market value of any boot or money received and increased by the amount of gain recognized to the transferor, including any amount which may have been treated as a dividend).[57] Similarly, the basis of the properties acquired is carried over to become the basis in the hands of the acquiring corporation,

[54] See text accompanying notes 135 and 140.

[55] Int. Rev. Code of 1954, §361(b)(1)(A). See note 48 *supra.*

[56] Int. Rev. Code of 1954, §361(b)(1)(B). If the gain is recognized as a result of an assumption of liabilities by the transferee corporation, then the transferor corporation may not avoid recognition of the gain by a distribution since an assumption of liabilities cannot be "distributed." See text accompanying note 51 *supra* and B. Bittker and J. Eustice, Federal Income Taxation of Corporations and Shareholders 583 (1966).

[57] See Ch. II, text accompanying notes 56–66. Where the taxpayer surrenders stock and securities for other stock and securities, the regulations require that a determination be made "upon the basis of all the facts" as to which stock or securities were received with respect to stock and securities of each class held. Thus suppose that an individual owns stock of Corporation Y with a basis of $5000 and a security of Corporation Y with a similar basis and with a principal amount of $5000. If, in a reorganization, he exchanges the stock for stock of Corporation Z with a value of $6000 and exchanges the security for stock of Corporation Z with a value of $1500 and a security of Corporation Z with a value and principal amount of $4500, then the basis of the stock received for the stock surrendered is $5000 (the carried-over basis) and the basis of the other stock and security is that of the security surrendered ($5000), allocated between the two in accordance with their fair market values, i.e., $1250 and $3750, respectively. See Treas. Reg. §1.358–2(c), Ex. (3).

If various shares within a single class of stock or various securities of the same type are acquired at different dates and at different prices and are subsequently surrendered for other stock or securities, the basis of the latter may be determined with reference to the average cost basis of the stock or securities surrendered, if particular shares or securities surrendered cannot be matched with particular shares or securities received. The average cost approach applies only to the determination of basis and does not permit the "netting" of gains against losses for the purpose of determining gain realized. Thus any gain must be determined separately on each identifiable block of stock or securities transferred. See B. Bittker and J. Eustice, id. at 594–595.

increased by the amount of any gain recognized to the transferor.[58] In a Type C reorganization, the transferee's basis in the property it receives will be stepped up only to the extent of the gain recognized to the transferor corporation and not to the extent of gain recognized to the transferor's shareholders. As has been said, the extent of the gain recognized to the transferor will generally depend upon the extent to which money or boot is received and is distributed to its shareholders. Whether or not the shareholders themselves recognize gain will depend upon the difference between the basis of the shares they surrender and the value of what they receive. In any case the amount of gain recognized to the shareholders of the transferor will not affect the amount by which the basis of the assets in the transferee's hands is stepped up.[59]

The acquiring corporation will not recognize gain in the reorganization due to the issuance of its shares, even though the shares used to finance the acquisition are treasury shares.[60] Although the Code does not provide that no gain is recognized to a subsidiary when it acquires property or shares in exchange for stock of a parent corporation in a tax-free reorganization, there is at least one ruling to that effect.[61]

Section 356 of the Code, which governs the taxability of exchanges involving the receipt of money or boot, has some specialized provisions which relate to the receipt of securities (i.e., obligations) and certain distributions which are said to have "the effect of the distribution of a dividend."

As pointed out in an earlier chapter, certain short-term obligations may not qualify as securities (primarily those having a maturity of less than five years).[62] Assuming, however, that an obligation is a security, although the receipt of securities, as well as of stock, is consistent with at least two forms of reorganization (Type A and, to a limited extent, Type C),[63] the provisions of Sections 354(a)(2) and 356(d) will result in boot treatment for the fair market value of any excess in principal amount of securities received over principal amount of securities surrendered. If no securities are surrendered, then the fair market of the securities received is treated as boot. Suppose, for example, that a shareholder surrenders an obligation with a principal amount of $1000 and receives another with a principal amount of $1500. The fair market value of the $500 excess is treated as boot. And if no $1000 obligation had been surrendered, the fair market value of the $1500 obligation would be treated as boot. The fair market value of an obligation will depend upon several factors, such as call and sinking fund provisions, interest rate, credit rating of the issuer and so

---

[58] Int. Rev. Code of 1954, §362(b).
[59] See B. Bittker and J. Eustice, id. at 586.
[60] Int. Rev. Code of 1954, §1032.
[61] Rev. Rul. 57–278, 1957–1 Cum. Bull. 124.
[62] See Ch. II, text accompanying notes 37–44.
[63] See discussion of the continuity of "proprietary interest" doctrine, in text accompanying note 86. See also the discussion of Type C reorganizations in text accompanying note 156.

forth. In any event, the fair market value of the excess of principal amount received over principal amount surrendered is boot and gives rise to tax, but only if there is gain on the exchange. Whether there is gain on the exchange will obviously depend upon the difference between the basis of what is given up and the fair market value of what is received (i.e., stock, securities, money and boot). Where several securities are received, then the boot is allocated to each in a proportion which corresponds to the ratio between the "excess" of total principal amount received over that surrendered and the total principal amount received. Suppose, for example, that a shareholder surrenders an obligation with a $1000 principal amount for two obligations, each having a principal amount of $750, with one having a fair market value of $750 and the other having a fair market value of $600. The excess of total principal amount received ($1500) over that surrendered ($1000) is $500, and this is one third of the total principal amount received. Thus one third of the fair market value of each obligation will be boot, i.e., $250 and $200, respectively.[64]

Section 356(a)(2) of the Code provides for "dividend equivalent" treatment of certain distributions in connection with a reorganization which have the effect of the distribution of a dividend. As in the foregoing situation involving securities, the tax is imposed only if there is an overall gain on the exchange. Unlike the test generally applied to dividends under Section 316 of the Code, where taxability depends upon either earnings and profits of the taxable year or earnings and profits accumulated since February 28, 1913, taxability under Section 356(a)(2) depends exclusively upon the taxpayer's "ratable share of the undistributed earnings and profits . . . accumulated after February 28, 1913." For these and other reasons the Internal Revenue Service apparently does not consider that a Section 356(a)(2) distribution is a "true" dividend and hence, despite the statutory mandate that the distribution "shall be treated as a dividend," it regards such distributions as ineligible for the dividends-received exclusion or the intercorporate dividends-received credit under Sections 116 and 243, respectively, of the Code.[65]

Although there has been some uncertainty as to the proper test for determining dividend equivalence for the purpose of Section 356(a)(2) of the Code, particularly as a result of the so-called automatic dividend concept of *Commissioner v. Estate of Bedford*,[66] the more recent cases have adopted a factual approach, like that taken with respect to other similar provisions of

---

[64] The example is taken from Treas. Reg. §1.356–3(b), Ex. (6). If *no* securities are surrendered and *only* securities are received (e.g., if the taxpayer exchanges his stock solely for bonds), then the transaction is not treated as a reorganization but is subject to the rules relating to redemptions under Section 302 of the Code. See Treas. Reg. §1.354–1(d), Ex. (3), and Ch. VI, text accompanying notes 13–78.

[65] See B. Bittker and J. Eustice, Federal Income Taxation of Corporations and Shareholders 592 (1966); Kanter, The Changing Complexion of the "B" Reorganization, 45 A.B.A.J. 1317, 1319 (1959).

[66] 325 U.S. 283 (1945). For a recent discussion see Shoulson, Boot Taxation: The Blunt Toe of the Automatic Rule, 20 Tax L. Rev. 573 (1965).

the Code, particularly Sections 302 and 346, already discussed in considerable detail.[67] As in these other areas, the main consideration is whether the distribution is merely a guise for conveying earnings and profits to the recipient under the tax-free umbrella of the reorganization provisions, with the hope that the distribution will, at worst, be treated as boot and give rise to taxation only at capital gains rates, thereby avoiding the taxation at ordinary rates which would result if the distribution were a conventional dividend.

Special treatment is provided for money or boot distributed in a reorganization in exchange for Section 306 stock.[68] Such a distribution is taxed under the general rules of Section 301 rather than under the dividend equivalence rule of Section 356(a)(2).[69] Ironically, this results in the distribution being taxed as a conventional dividend under Section 316, i.e., the tax impact depends upon the presence of earnings and profits for the taxable year or earnings and profits accumulated since February 28, 1913. Accordingly, there seems to be no reason why the distribution should not qualify for the dividends-received exclusion or the intercorporate dividends-received credit, even though Section 356(a)(2) distributions do not so qualify.

Having considered the general outlines of the tax treatment of corporate reorganizations it is now appropriate to consider in greater detail the three types of reorganization which shareholders in a closely held concern are likely to encounter in connection with a sale of their company to another concern. As already mentioned, these are a merger or consolidation (Type A), an acquisition of shares (Type B) and an acquisition of assets (Type C).

Before analyzing the statutory requirements for each of the three types of reorganization, it is well to consider various judicially developed doctrines which are applicable to reorganizations in general. These are the business purpose requirement, continuity of business enterprise, continuity of proprietary interest and the step transaction doctrine.

The business purpose requirement may be best understood against the background of a leading early case, *Gregory v. Helvering*.[70] There the taxpayer, Mrs. Gregory, owned all the stock of United Mortgage Corporation

---

[67] E.g., Hawkinson v. Commissioner, 235 F.2d 747 (2d Cir. 1956); Idaho Power Co. v. United States, 142 Ct. Cl. 534, 161 F. Supp. 807 (1958), *cert. denied*, 358 U.S. 832 (1958). See Ch. VI, text accompanying note 26, and Ch. VII, text accompanying note 165. Despite the judicial rejection of the automatic approach of the *Bedford* case, the Internal Revenue Service is inclined to favor it. See Treas. Reg. §1.356–1(c), Ex. (1).

[68] For a discussion of Section 306, see Ch. VI, text accompanying notes 101–127. As previously noted, Section 306 stock is not only stock which has been distributed in a tax-free stock dividend but may also be stock received in a reorganization if the effect of the transaction "was substantially the same as the receipt of a stock dividend." See Int. Rev. Code of 1954, §306(c)(1)(B), and Ch. VI, text accompanying notes 105–107.

[69] Int. Rev. Code of 1954, §356(e).

[70] 293 U.S. 465 (1935).

which in turn owned 1000 shares of Monitor Securities Corporation, the value of which exceeded their basis. Mrs. Gregory was interested in having the Monitor shares sold and in having the proceeds distributed to her. If this were done in the normal way, the distribution would have been taxable at ordinary rates as a dividend. In lieu of this she resolved upon a purported reorganization pursuant to Section 112(g) of the Revenue Act of 1928, which provided that no gain would be recognized on a distribution by a corporation, a party to a reorganization, of stock or securities of another corporation which was a party to a reorganization, and did not require a shareholder to surrender his shares to obtain the distribution.[71] Accordingly she caused another corporation to be organized, the Averill Corporation, to which the United Mortgage Corporation transferred its shares of Monitor Securities Corporation in exchange for Averill stock, which was then distributed to Mrs. Gregory. A few days later the Averill Corporation, having served its purpose, was dissolved and the Monitor shares distributed to Mrs. Gregory in exchange for her Averill shares. She thus paid a tax at capital gains rates on the liquidation and subsequently sold the Monitor shares for $133,333.33, thereby realizing her objective of avoiding taxation at ordinary rates. The Commissioner argued that the transaction was a sham and that the $133,333.33 should be viewed as a distribution of a dividend by United Mortgage. Since the taxpayer followed all the statutory steps and literally met the requirements of a reorganization, the Board of Tax Appeals held in her favor, only to be reversed by the Court of Appeals for the Second Circuit. In an opinion written by Judge Learned Hand, the court held that the value of the Averill shares should have been taxed as a dividend rather than the distribution of the Monitor shares, but that this made no practical difference since the value of the Averill shares was the same as that of the Monitor shares, which were Averill's only asset. Judge Hand's opinion skillfully and eloquently dealt with one of the most pervasive problems in tax law, namely, when the substance of a transaction should control the tax effect[72] rather than its form:

> We agree with the Board and the taxpayer that a transaction, otherwise within an exception of the tax law, does not lose its immunity, because it is actuated by a desire to avoid, or, if one choose, to evade, taxation. Anyone may so arrange his affairs that his taxes shall be as low as possible; he is not bound to choose that pattern which will best pay the Treasury; there is not even a patriotic duty to increase one's taxes. . . . Therefore, if what was done here, was what was intended by . . . [the statute,] it is of no consequence that it was all an elaborate scheme to get rid of income taxes, as it certainly was. Nevertheless, it does not follow that Congress meant to cover such a transaction, not even though the facts answer the dictionary definitions of each term used in the statutory definition. It is quite true,

---

[71] Cf. the present provisions of Int. Rev. Code of 1954, §§355, 368(a)(1)(D).
[72] For another illustration of the Supreme Court's grappling with the substance vs. form problem see Ch. VII, text accompanying notes 137–141.

as the Board has very well said, that as the articulation of the statute increases, the room for interpretation must contract; but the meaning of a
sentence may be more than that of the separate words, as a melody is more
than the notes, and no degree of particularity can ever obviate recourse to
the setting in which all appear, and which all collectively create. The purpose of the section is plain enough; men engaged in enterprises—industrial, commercial, financial, or any other—might wish to consolidate, or
divide, to add to, or subtract from, their holdings. Such transactions were
not to be considered as "realizing" any profit, because the collective interests still remained in solution. But the underlying presupposition is plain
that the readjustment shall be undertaken for reasons germane to the conduct of the venture in hand, not as an ephemeral incident, egregious to its
prosecution. To dodge the shareholders' taxes is not one of the transactions
contemplated as corporate "reorganizations." [73]

The United States Supreme Court affirmed, generally agreeing with the
above reasoning and adding that

an operation having no business or corporate purpose—a mere device
which put on the form of a corporate reorganization as a disguise for con-
cealing its real character, and the sole object and accomplishment of which
was the consummation of a preconceived plan, not to reorganize a business
or any part of a business, but to transfer a parcel of corporate shares to the
petitioner . . . [does not qualify for treatment as a corporate reorganization despite literal compliance with the statutory provisions].[74]

In a subsequent case Judge Hand found occasion to explicate further what
he thought the Supreme Court meant by its decision in the *Gregory* case:

It [the Supreme Court] was solicitous to reaffirm the doctrine that a man's
motive to avoid taxation will not establish his liability if the transaction
does not do so without it. . . . *The question always is whether the transaction under scrutiny is in fact what it appears to be in form;* a marriage
may be a joke; a contract may be intended only to deceive others; an agreement may have a collateral defeasance. In such cases the transaction as a
whole is different from its appearance. True, it is always the intent that
controls; and we need not for this occasion press the difference between
intent and purpose. We may assume that purpose may be the touchstone,
but *the purpose which counts is one which defeats or contradicts the apparent transaction, not the purpose to escape taxation which the apparent,
but not the whole, transaction would realize.* In Gregory v. Helvering . . .
the incorporators adopted the usual form for creating business corporations;
but their intent, or purpose, was merely to draught the papers, in fact not
to create corporations as the court understood that word. That was the
purpose which defeated their exemption, not the accompanying purpose to
escape taxation; that purpose was legally neutral. Had they really meant to
conduct a business by means of the two reorganized companies, they would
have escaped whatever other aim they might have had, whether to avoid
taxes, or to regenerate the world.[75]

[73] Helvering v. Gregory, 69 F.2d 809, 810–811 (2d Cir. 1934).
[74] Gregory v. Helvering, 293 U.S. 465, 469–470 (1935).
[75] Chisholm v. Commissioner, 79 F.2d 14, 15 (2d Cir. 1935), *cert. denied,* 296
U.S. 461 (1935) (emphasis supplied).

Any attempt to struggle with such basic concepts as appearance and reality or form and substance is bound to involve a considerable amount of uncertainty, whether it be in tax law or in the broader reaches of philosophy. Despite Learned Hand's illuminating suggestion that the "touchstone" should be the "purpose" of the transaction (as opposed to a motive to avoid taxation), there are no clear guidelines as to when a purpose is a business purpose or, to put the matter differently, how much by way of business purpose is required before the form of the transaction will withstand judicial scrutiny. If, for example, Mrs. Gregory had caused United Mortgage Corporation to convey other assets in addition to Monitor stock to Averill Corporation and if the latter had continued in existence for some period of time before liquidating, would the case have been more difficult? All that one can be reasonably certain about is that if a transaction has no business justification apart from its tax effects, then reliance upon its form is likely to be ill-advised from a tax-planning point of view. In other words the transaction should have a nontax purpose and, having that, it may then be cast in any form which the tax laws permit to minimize its tax effects.

Where a corporation is closely held, the question may arise whether a particular purpose is a business purpose or whether it relates only to the personal purpose of individual shareholders. Unlike other areas, such as the penalty tax on excess accumulations and the problem of determining the reasonable needs of the business,[76] the courts have not been inclined to draw sharp distinctions between a business purpose on the one hand and a shareholder purpose on the other. Although the Tax Court apparently attempted to differentiate between the two at one time, it abandoned this view.[77] This seems eminently realistic since, as one court put it:

> The separate legal identity of these [closely held] corporations should not obscure the fact that they are operated by their shareholders in a manner thought best calculated to serve the latter's interests. What is deemed best for the shareholders is deemed best for the corporation, and vice versa.[78]

This reasoning is particularly persuasive when applied to a one-man or wholly owned corporation.[79] Thus it should not be decisive that the purpose of the transaction may in large part be inseparable from a legitimate

[76] See Ch. V, text accompanying notes 81–117, particularly text accompanying notes 101–117.

[77] See Lewis v. Commissioner, 176 F.2d 646, 649–650 (1st Cir. 1949) (collecting the Tax Court cases).

[78] 176 F.2d at 650.

[79] See Estate of Parshelsky v. Commissioner, 303 F.2d 14 (2d Cir. 1962). The *Parshelsky* case, after an extensive review of the case authorities and the legislative background of the reorganization provisions, arrived at conclusions similar to those of Lewis v. Commissioner, 176 F.2d 646 (1st Cir. 1949), namely, that where corporations are closely held, "The separate legal entity . . . cannot obscure the fact that they are operated by their shareholders in the manner most likely to benefit themselves. . . . The benefits to the corporation and to the shareholders are virtually indistinguishable." (303 F.2d at 19.)

nontax purpose of one or more shareholders. Even the concept of business purpose should not "become a substitute for independent analysis." [80] The primary consideration appears to be whether the transaction as a whole has a purpose other than to achieve a given tax result. If it does, then it should not be decisive that the purpose may be inextricably intertwined with the personal objectives of various shareholders, provided that these are not grounded exclusively in considerations of the possible tax effect.[81]

In addition to the requirement of a reasonable business purpose, there are two other requirements which relate to continuity, one a requirement that there be a continuity of "business enterprise" and the other that there be a continuity of "proprietary interest."

Continuity of business enterprise may, at least in some respects, be of more historical than practical interest. For some time the Internal Revenue Service attempted to require that the identical business of the acquired corporation be carried on by the acquiring corporation in order to qualify for reorganization treatment. Under this reasoning a shoe manufacturer could not be acquired tax free by a food concern if its shoe business were discontinued. After meeting with little success in the courts, this construction of the statute was abandoned.[82] Yet the regulations still require that there be a continuity of business enterprise, although not necessarily the identical business which was carried on before the reorganization.[83] This requirement has met with a more favorable judicial reception and reorganization treatment has been denied where the acquiring corporation conducted little or no meaningful activity and was little more than a device for discontinuing the business and eventually selling its assets to others.[84] And the same is true if the business is "suspended"; resumption of business activity after a year or so has passed will not retroactively satisfy the continuity requirement and reorganization treatment is not available.[85]

---

[80] Lewis v. Commissioner, 176 F.2d 646, 650 (1st Cir. 1949).

[81] The regulations continue to emphasize the importance of reasonable business purpose as implicitly distinct from shareholder purpose. See Treas Reg. §§1.368–1(b), 1.368–1(c) and 1.368–2(g). For further discussion of the business purpose requirement, see B. Bittker and J. Eustice, Federal Income Taxation of Corporations and Shareholders §12.19 (1966); Bittker, What is "Business Purpose" in Reorganizations? N.Y.U. 8th Inst. on Fed. Tax. 134 (1950); Michaelson, "Business Purpose" and Tax Free Reorganization, 61 Yale L.J. 14 (1952); Rice, Judicial Techniques in Combating Tax Avoidance, 51 Mich. L. Rev. 1021 (1953); Spear, "Corporate Business Purpose" in Reorganization, 3 Tax. L. Rev. 225 (1947).

[82] Rev. Rul. 63–29, 1963–1 Cum. Bull. 77, revoking Rev. Rul. 56–330, 1956–2 Cum. Bull. 204. For the earlier case authorities see B. Bittker and J. Eustice, id. at 557 n.111. See Tarleau, "Continuity of the Business Enterprise" in Corporate Reorganization and Other Corporate Readjustments, 60 Colum. L. Rev. 792 (1960).

[83] Treas. Reg. §1.368–1(b).

[84] Standard Realization Co., 10 T.C. 708 (1948), *acquiesced in,* 1948–2 Cum. Bull. 3.

[85] Pridemark, Inc. v. Commissioner, 345 F.2d 35 (4th Cir. 1965). But a suspension of business may not destroy continuity if it is merely temporary. United States v. Adkins-Phelps, Inc., 400 F.2d 737 (8th Cir. 1968).

The continuity of proprietary interest requirement has a more extensive judicial endorsement and a firmer grounding in both the statute and the regulations. In effect it relates to the very concept of a reorganization and the reason for granting tax-free treatment. Thus, as the regulations express it:

> The purpose of the reorganization provisions of the Code is to except from the general rule certain specifically described exchanges incident to such readjustments of corporate structures made in one of the particular ways specified in the Code, as are required by business exigencies and which effect only a readjustment of continuing interest in property under modified corporate forms.[86]

In many ways the underlying rationale is similar to that justifying tax-free treatment for corporate formations under Section 351. As discussed in an earlier chapter, the critical distinction is between a transaction which in essence is a sale and one which merely redescribes an ownership interest.[87]

As far as the case law is concerned, a relatively early circuit court decision held that an acquisition of substantially all the properties of a corporation for cash and short-term promissory notes did not qualify as a reorganization.[88] This view was endorsed by the Supreme Court one year later in *Pinellas Ice & Cold Storage Co. v. Commissioner.*[89] Thus it seemed apparent that the receipt of at least *some* stock was necessary in order to meet the continuity of proprietary interest requirement but it was uncertain how much stock was necessary. In *Helvering v. Minnesota Tea Co.,*[90] the Court found that a corporation's transfer of substantially all its assets for voting trust certificates representing common stock in the amount of approximately $540,000, together with $426,842 in cash, qualified as a reorganization, the Court stating that ". . . [the interest in the transferee] must be definite and material; it must represent a substantial part of the value of the thing transferred." [91] Although the Court held that redeemable nonvoting preferred stock qualified under this test,[92] it also held that a transfer of

---

[86] Treas. Reg. §1.368–1(b).

[87] See Ch. II, text accompanying note 9.

[88] Cortland Specialty Co. v. Commissioner, 60 F.2d 937 (2d Cir. 1932), *cert. denied*, 288 U.S. 599 (1933).

[89] 287 U.S. 462 (1933).

[90] 296 U.S. 378 (1935).

[91] 296 U.S. at 385. An equity interest of 56 percent was held to be sufficiently definite, material and substantial, i.e., 56 percent of the consideration received for the transferred assets was in the form of equity. Obviously the standard does not require that the transferor must also receive an equally substantial percentage of the total equity of the acquiring corporation. Thus a small corporation could be absorbed into a relatively large one within the scheme of a tax-free reorganization even though the shareholders of the acquired corporation received only a small percentage of the outstanding equity of the large one. See also Southwest Natural Gas Co. v. Commissioner, 189 F.2d 332 (5th Cir.), *cert. denied*, 342 U.S. 860 (1951), adopting a similar standard of "substantiality" and finding an equity interest of less than 1 percent of the total consideration for the transfer to be sufficient.

[92] John A. Nelson Co. v. Helvering, 296 U.S. 374 (1935).

assets for cash and bonds did not qualify, since the transferor's status was changed from owner to creditor.[93] Thus at least some stock must be received, although it is not necessary that each of the former owners or shareholders receive stock.[94] For example, in a merger where some shareholders dissent from the merger and are paid off in cash, this will not disqualify the transaction as a reorganization. Since, as a practical matter, most mergers require authorization by at least a majority and frequently two thirds of the voting shares,[95] the continuity of proprietary interest requirement would pose a problem from a practical standpoint not as regards cash paid to dissenters but as regards the amount of securities (in contrast to stock) given to those who approve and the way in which the securities are distributed (i.e., whether only a minority of those who approved of the merger received stock and a substantial part of the financing of the acquisition took the form of obligations of the transferee). Here a rough guide, set forth in a revenue ruling,[96] is that a 50 percent continuity of proprietary interest is sufficient to qualify a transaction as a reorganization. Thus stock (whether voting or nonvoting) should be issued to the extent of at least 50 percent of the value of the assets transferred. If this is done, it does not appear to be necessary that the shares be distributed pro rata to all the former shareholders or that all of them receive at least some shares.

A separate but not unrelated problem, also involved in several of the cases already mentioned, is whether the receipt of certain obligations (often ones of only a few years in maturity) qualifies as the receipt of "securities." As already indicated, the reorganization provisions permit stock or securities to be received free of tax.[97] If property other than stock or securities is received, then the transaction will not *necessarily* be disqualified as a reorganization. Thus, if the continuity of proprietary interest requirement, as well as other judicially imposed or statutory requirements are met, the "other property" will give rise to recognition of gain under Section 356 of the Code and will generally be taxed at capital gains rates unless, perchance, the distribution is held to have the effect of the distribution of a dividend.[98] Notwithstanding this, however, the receipt of too little by way of stock (i.e., too much by way of other property, such as cash, for example) may result in the transaction's failing to meet the continuity of proprietary interest requirement. If this happens, then the transaction fails to qualify as a reorganization and the entire amount of gain *or loss* is recog-

---

[93] LeTulle v. Scofield, 308 U.S. 415 (1940).

[94] See Reef Corp. v. Commissioner, 368 F.2d 125 (5th Cir. 1966), *cert. denied*, 386 U.S. 1018 (1967) (simultaneous redemption of 48 percent of the shares of the transferor); Miller v. Commissioner, 84 F.2d 415 (6th Cir. 1936) (payment of cash to dissenting shareholders).

[95] See note 2 *supra*.

[96] Rev. Rul. 66–224, 1966–2, Cum. Bull. 114; Rev. Proc. 66–34, 1966–2 Cum. Bull. 1232.

[97] See text accompanying note 47 *supra*.

[98] See id. note 65 *supra*.

nized (in contrast to the recognition of *gain only* where the transaction qualifies as a reorganization, with the amount of recognized gain being limited by the fair market value of the boot or property other than stock or securities, including money, when the overall transaction qualifies for reorganization treatment).

The test for determining whether an obligation is a "security" is no different than that described in the other context in which we have encountered this problem, namely tax-free formation of a corporation. Thus short-term notes are generally not securities,[99] whereas bonds (long term) qualify as securities,[100] although the receipt of too much in bonds may disqualify the entire transaction for reorganization treatment if it fails to meet the continuity of proprietary interest requirement.[101] As previously indicated, no clear guidelines can be set. Although the term of the obligation (i.e., its maturity) is not necessarily decisive, and a number of other factors may be relevant,[102] it seems fairly clear that any obligation having a maturity of less than five years is likely to fail to qualify as a security, whereas obligations of longer maturity, particularly those having a maturity in excess of ten years, are likely to be securities.[103]

Ever since 1934 the statute has contained provisions that serve to crystallize the continuity of proprietary interest requirement developed prior to that time in the case law. Thus, as already indicated, the definition of a Type B or Type C reorganization expressly requires that stock or assets, respectively, be transferred "solely" for all or a part of the voting stock of the acquiring corporation or of its parent.[104] As we shall see, the Type B reorganization exhibits the most unremitting application of the continuity of proprietary interest principle in that it does not permit the receipt of *any* other consideration in addition to voting stock. The Type C reorganization is more flexible in permitting other forms of consideration to be received, provided that they amount to no more than 20 percent of the fair market value of the assets acquired by the transferee.[105] Finally, although there is no express requirement of continuity of proprietary interest in the Type A reorganization (merger or consolidation), and that form is therefore the most flexible of the three types in permitting the receipt of properties other

[99] E.g., Cortland Specialty Co. v. Commissioner, 60 F.2d 937 (2d Cir. 1932), *cert. denied*, 288 U.S. 599 (1933); Pinellas Ice & Cold Storage Co. v. Commissioner, 287 U.S. 462 (1933); Turner Construction Co. v. United States, 364 F.2d 525 (2d Cir. 1966).

[100] E.g., Helvering v. Watts, 296 U.S. 387 (1935).

[101] E.g., LeTulle v. Scofield, 308 U.S. 415 (1940).

[102] See Ch. II, text accompanying note 40. See Prentis v. United States, 273 F. Supp. 460 (S.D.N.Y. 1967), an unusual decision holding a six-month equipment note to be a security because it was intended that it should ultimately be surrendered for preferred stock.

[103] See Ch. II, text accompanying note 39.

[104] See text accompanying note 46 *supra*.

[105] See Int. Rev. Code of 1954, §368(a)(2)(B)(iii). See also text accompanying note 156 *infra*.

than voting stock (including, of course, securities), the general concepts of continuity of proprietary interest developed in the case law apply. Thus no merger which involves the issuance of less than 50 percent in value of the acquired assets in the form of stock (whether voting or nonvoting) is likely to have sufficient continuity of proprietary interest to qualify as a reorganization, although, as in any area governed by case law, much may depend upon the facts of each particular situation.[106]

Finally, some mention should be made of the step transaction doctrine. Although the step transaction concept is commonly associated with reorganizations, it pervades many other areas of tax law in that it is but a description of the form and substance dichotomy with which we have seen the courts struggle in determining whether, in a given factual situation, the statute should be followed literally or whether some other result might be appropriate in view of the net effect of the transaction.[107] In the reorganization area the problem generally arises in determining whether separate steps in a corporate reshuffling of interests should be considered in isolation from one another or whether they should be "compressed" or considered as part of an integrated whole. One way in which the problem may arise in the reorganization context is in determining the extent and manner in which a transferor of assets may dispose of unwanted assets prior to its being acquired by another corporation. To put the matter differently, suppose that one corporation (A) wishes to acquire another (B) and yet does not wish to acquire certain of B's assets. If B has substantial earnings and profits, it will have difficulty distributing the assets to its shareholders without the distribution being considered a taxable dividend or at least a partial liquidation (taxable at capital gains rates). If the acquisition takes the form of a Type C reorganization and A does not acquire the unwanted assets of B, then the transaction will probably not qualify as a transfer of substantially all of B's assets and thereby will fail to meet the requirements of Section 368(a)(1)(C) of the Code. One possible solution to the problem is to effect a tax-free spin-off of stock followed by a reorganization whereby the acquiring corporation receives the assets remaining in the acquired corporation after completion of the spin-off. Thus Corporation B could form a

---

[106] See id. note 96 *supra.*

[107] For illustrations see Ch. II, text accompanying notes 23–29 (determination of whether transferors of property have control immediately after the exchange for Section 351 purposes); id. note 42 (whether a purported sale of assets under the installment method should be integrated with a prior Section 351 exchange); Ch. VII, text accompanying notes 105–106 (whether a purchase of shares followed shortly thereafter by a liquidation of the acquired corporation should be treated as a purchase of assets). Note the relationship between the step transaction concept and the reasonable business purpose requirement, as illustrated by the Gregory v. Helvering case, 293 U.S. 465 (1935), already discussed in some detail. Although every step in Mrs. Gregory's plan was separately defensible from a literal statutory standpoint, the transaction *as a whole* lacked business reality.

third corporation, C, to which the assets unwanted by A could be transferred in exchange for stock which would then be distributed to B's shareholders, hopefully tax free if the requirements of Sections 355 and
368(a)(1)(D) of the Code were met. The next step would be an acquisition by A of Corporation B under one of the taxfree forms of reorganization. If the subsequent acquisition took the form of a Type C reorganization (asset acquisition), there might be difficulty with meeting the
requirement of a transfer of substantially all of B's assets, at least if the two
steps are considered as so interdependent that they are, in substance, parts
of a single transaction.[108] Greater success might be possible through a
merger of B into A since, at least as far as the statute is concerned, there is
no requirement (as in a Type C reorganization) of a transfer of substantially all the properties of the acquired corporation. Even here, however, the
transaction may run into difficulty, particularly if the acquired corporation
(B) were to be absorbed into the acquiring corporation (A) immediately
after the prior spin-off.[109] Another possibility is for Corporation A to merge
into B instead of the reverse, which would be the more usual method. Although this would avoid problems raised where B goes out of existence
shortly after the spin-off, it seems excessively technical to reach a different
result merely because A merges into B rather than vice versa.[110] Another
technique might be to spin off either (1) the unwanted assets or (2) the
assets wanted by A to a newly created corporation, C, to be followed by an
acquisition by A of the *stock* of either B or C in a purportedly tax-free Type
B reorganization, (i.e., if the *unwanted* assets had been spun off to C, then
A would acquire the B shares; if the *wanted* assets had been spun off, then
A would acquire the C shares). Although the consequences of this technique are also uncertain, particularly if C should be liquidated shortly after
the reorganization, tax-free treatment may be available, especially if the
unwanted assets are spun off and this is followed by A's acquiring the B
shares solely for A voting stock, with the B corporation being continued in

---

[108] E.g., Helvering v. Elkhorn Coal Co., 95 F.2d 732 (4th Cir. 1937), *cert.
denied*, 305 U.S. 605 (1938). See B. Bittker and J. Eustice, Federal Income Taxa-
ation of Corporations and Shareholders 560 (1966). The authors point out, however, that if the Type C reorganization were preceded by a *taxable* distribution of
the unwanted assets to Corporation B's shareholders (as in a partial liquidation or
redemption of stock under Section 302 of the Code), then it is at least arguable
that, since the assets have passed out of corporate solution in a taxable transaction, as
opposed to remaining *in* solution by way of a tax-free spin-off of stock, the step
transaction doctrine should not, as a matter of policy, apply so as to deny reorganization treatment because of a supposed failure to meet the substantially all test. See
J. Eustice and B. Bittker, id. at 559.

[109] *Compare* Curtis v. United States, 336 F.2d 714 (6th Cir. 1964), *with* Mary
Archer Morris Trust, 42 T.C. 779 (1964), *aff'd*, 367 F.2d 794 (4th Cir. 1966).
See also Rev. Rul. 68–603, 1968–2 Cum. Bull. 148, and B. Bittker and J. Eustice,
id. at 561–562.

[110] See B. Bittker and J. Eustice, id.

existence for an appreciable period of time as a subsidiary of A. Care also should be taken not to liquidate Corporation C immediately after the transaction but to keep it in existence as long as is feasible.[111]

Having considered the principal judicial doctrines governing the validity of various forms of reorganizations, it is now appropriate to examine in greater detail the statutory and regulatory requirements of the three types of "acquisitive" reorganizations: merger or consolidation, exchange of shares and transfer of assets.

8.7 TAX ASPECTS OF MERGERS OR CONSOLIDATIONS

The phrase "merger or consolidation" is not defined in the Code. The regulations merely refer to a merger or consolidation as being "effected pursuant to the corporation laws of the United States or a State or Territory or the District of Columbia." [112]

The merger or consolidation is the most flexible of the three types of corporate reorganization in that there is no requirement that the exchange be solely for voting stock. Thus bonds or notes may be issued by the acquiring corporation, except that if too much of the consideration takes the form of obligations, then, regardless of whether or not the obligations qualify as "securities," the continuity of proprietary interest test may not be met.[113] As previously indicated, a rough guide to whether continuity of proprietary interest has been maintained is to insure that at least 50 percent of the consideration for the transfer is in the form of stock.[114] If this test is met, there is no requirement that the shares be voting stock. Thus they can be nonvoting common shares or preferred shares. This adds further flexibility to the transaction in that an acquiring corporation need not dilute the "control" factor of a preexisting block of its shares by issuing more voting stock, as would be necessary in a Type B reorganization.

Another flexible feature of the A reorganization is the ability of the acquiring corporation to pay various expenses of the acquired corporation, or discharge its liabilities, without impairing the reorganization status of the exchange. Although payment of such expenses and the discharge of liabili-

---

[111] Id. at 562–563. See Cohen, Tax Free Acquisition of Part of a Corporation's Assets by Combining a Spin-Off With a Unifying Reorganization, N.Y.U. 26th Inst. on Fed. Tax. 849 (1968); Massee, Section 355; Disposal of Unwanted Assets in Connection with a Reorganization, 22 Tax L. Rev. 439 (1967).

[112] Treas. Reg. §1.368–2(b).

[113] E.g., Roebling v. Commissioner, 143 F.2d 810 (3d Cir. 1944), *cert. denied,* 323 U.S. 773 (1944). See text accompanying notes 88–96 *supra.*

[114] See note 96 *supra.*

ties may be held to be equivalent to the receipt of boot and thus give rise to the recognition of gain to the extent of the value of the boot, the transaction as a whole will still qualify as a reorganization. As we shall see, this is not so with regard to the Type B reorganization, where the acquiring corporation must be careful not to pay expenses or discharge liabilities of the acquired corporation. Although the Code provides that with a Type C asset acquisition the assumption of liabilities does not ipso facto count as boot, it may have to be taken into account in determining whether the transfer was solely for voting stock.[115]

One problem which should be closely watched not only in a merger or consolidation but in the other forms of reorganization is the possibility that the continuity of proprietary interest requirement might not be met if those who receive stock dispose of it shortly after the reorganization. If the resale of the stock is considered to have been an interdependent feature of the entire transaction, then the step transaction doctrine previously discussed may require that the reorganization be viewed in the light of its net result *after* the resale, thus ignoring a temporary ownership of shares immediately after the reorganization has taken place. This problem has a very close relationship with the uncertainties already explored in the Section 351 area as to what is necessary to meet the requirement of control immediately after the exchange.[116] As suggested in that connection, although the facts of each situation must necessarily determine the particular result, the general test applied by the cases is whether the subsequent resale was an interdependent part of the transaction whereby the properties were transferred to another entity in exchange for shares. Perhaps the greatest risk of having the transfer of properties and the resale of shares compressed and treated as parts of the same transaction is where the resale is to discharge a preexisting obligation. Although this does not mean that a shareholder may not use shares received in a reorganization to discharge a personal debt, if the obligation arises out of the financing itself, and is an interdependent feature of it, then this is another matter.[117] If the shares are held for a relatively lengthy period of time, such as five years,[118] then there is little doubt that the continuity of proprietary interest requirement would be met. If the holding period is less than that, as it often will be, then, as already indicated, every effort should be made to establish that the resale was not premeditated or planned prior to the merger.

Occasionally a corporation may wish to acquire another concern and operate it as a subsidiary. Doing so will segregate its assets and operations,

---

[115] See Int. Rev. Code of 1954, §368(c)(2)(B), and text accompanying note 156 *infra*.

[116] See Ch. II, text accompanying notes 23–29. See Note, Step Transactions in "A" Reorganizations: A Proposal for a Binding Commitment Test, 56 Va. L. Rev. 255 (1970).

[117] See Ch. II, text accompanying note 28.

[118] Cf. Rev. Rul. 66–23, 1966–1 Cum. Bull. 67.

which may be desirable for business and other reasons, as well as insulate the parent corporation from liabilities incurred by the subsidiary. Although the subsidiary relationship may be directly achieved through an exchange of shares in a Type B reorganization, this can also be done in the context of a Type A merger or consolidation or a Type C transfer of assets. As far as the merger or consolidation route is concerned, several techniques are possible. The acquired corporation can first be merged into the acquiring corporation and its assets then transferred to a wholly owned subsidiary under the tax-free provisions of Section 351 of the Code.[119] A second technique is for the acquired corporation to transfer, prior to the merger, all its assets to a newly organized subsidiary in exchange for its shares (tax-free under Section 351 of the Code). The transferor thus becomes a holding company with all its operating assets in one subsidiary. The holding company is then merged into the acquiring corporation.[120] A third technique is for the acquiring corporation to set up a subsidiary into which the acquired corporation merges.[121] A fourth technique, previously unavailable within the context of a merger or consolidation, but now permitted by a recent amendment of the Code, is for a subsidiary of the acquiring corporation to finance a merger between itself and the acquired corporation through the use of stock of the parent. Under prior law, such a merger would not have qualified for tax-free treatment because technically the parent corporation was not a "party to a reorganization." Under the amended provision,[122] the transaction qualifies if the subsidiary finances the transfer only through the use of its parent's shares (does not finance the merger by using both its own shares and shares of the parent). Also the subsidiary must receive substantially all the properties of the acquired corporation and it must be under the control of the parent (i.e., the parent corporation must own at least 80 percent of the subsidiary's voting shares and at least 80 percent of each other class of the subsidiary's stock). Finally, the transaction will qualify for tax-free treatment only if it *would* have qualified as a Type A reorganization if the acquired corporation had merged into the *parent* corporation instead of into its subsidiary.

Due to the fact that the acquiring corporation assumes the liabilities of the merging corporation, whether known or unknown, and also various other uncertainties relating to the value of the properties which have been acquired, a frequently used technique, already mentioned, is for the acquiring corporation to place some of the shares to be issued in the merger in escrow so as to be able to defer determination of the precise number of shares until the situation has clarified and the earnings and liabilities of the acquired business are more readily apparent. During the interim period it is

[119] See Int. Rev. Code of 1954, §368(a)(2)(C).
[120] Rev. Rul. 58–93, 1958–1 Cum. Bull. 188.
[121] See Rev. Rul. 68–261, 1968–1 Cum. Bull. 147.
[122] Int. Rev. Code of 1954, §§368(a)(2)(D), 368(b).

customary to issue certificates of "contingent interest" to those who may be entitled ultimately to receive shares from the escrow agent or depositary. The question thus arises whether such certificates of contingent interest qualify as stock or securities, permitted to be received without recognition of gain, or whether they constitute other property or boot. The Internal Revenue Service has clarified its position on this in a Revenue Ruling.[123] The general requirements for qualification of contingent stock as "nonrecognition property" (i.e., not boot) are that (1) all of the underlying stock to which the contingent certificates relate must be issued within five years from the date of the transaction claiming reorganization treatment; (2) the contingent stock must be justified by a valid business reason; (3) the maximum number of shares to be issued must be set forth; (4) at least 50 percent of the maximum number of shares of each class of stock to be issued must be issued in the initial distribution; (5) the certificate evidencing the contingent interest must be nonassignable except by operation of law, or the right to receive the contingent stock must not be evidenced by negotiable certificates or be readily marketable; and (6) the right to receive the contingent stock must give rise to the receipt of stock of the acquiring corporation or a corporation in control of the acquiring corporation.

Similar problems arise in connection with other aspects of the transaction. Thus, although the payment of cash in lieu of fractional shares is not boot,[124] and although boot treatment does not result from the acquiring corporation's payment of any cost of registering its shares with the SEC,[125] the payment by the acquiring corporation of brokerage fees and legal and accounting expenses of the acquired corporation or its shareholders would be considered as boot.[126] The determination of what is or is not

[123] See Rev. Proc. 67–13, 1967–1 Cum. Bull. 590; Rev. Proc. 66–34, 1966–2 Cum. Bull. 1232, 1233–1234; Rev. Rul. 66–112, 1966–1 Cum. Bull. 68.

[124] Rev. Rul. 66–365, 1966–2 Cum. Bull. 116.

[125] Rev. Rul. 67–275, 1967–2 Cum. Bull. 142.

[126] See B. Bittker and J. Eustice, Federal Income Taxation of Corporations and Shareholders 523 (1966) (indicating, however, that the payment by the acquiring corporation of any stock transfer taxes will not be treated as boot). Care should also be taken that payments under employment contracts with former officer-shareholders of the acquired corporation, if made by the acquiring corporation, are not subject to attack as additional consideration for their shares. Thus the Internal Revenue Service may be expected to scrutinize the employment contract, as well as any other payments, such as a payment for a covenant not to compete, to determine whether the payment is for services rendered, etc., or is a disguised distribution of boot with respect to the shares. The problem is especially acute where the acquired corporation is closely held and it is difficult to determine not only the value of its shares but also the value of the services rendered by officer-shareholders. If the payment is justified by the extent and nature of the services performed, increased responsibilities, etc., and if the officer-shareholder receives the same for his shares as other shareholders who are not parties to employment contracts, then a persuasive case can be made for characterizing the payments as what they purport to be, i.e., payments for services, etc. In any situation where there is doubt about whether the payment can be sustained as being for services, the payment can take the form of additional voting shares of the acquiring corporation. This will forestall attack by the Internal

boot is even more pertinent to the other forms of reorganization, i.e., Types B and C, for as we shall see, the presence of boot may entirely disqualify those transactions from reorganization treatment. This is particularly so with regard to a Type B reorganization.

8.8 STOCK ACQUISITIONS—TYPE B REORGANIZATIONS

As previously indicated, although a Type B reorganization has various advantages from a nontax standpoint, such as simplicity, avoidance of the assumption of unknown liabilities and avoidance of transfer or sales taxes (other than state taxes imposed on the transfer of stock), it is, from a tax standpoint, the most inflexible of the various reorganization forms. The transaction will not qualify as a reorganization unless the acquiring corporation finances the take-over solely for all or a part of its *voting* stock, or for *voting* stock of another corporation in control of the acquiring corporation. There must, then, inevitably be dilution of voting power. However, there is no requirement that the issued voting shares have the same voting *power* per share as the other outstanding shares of the acquiring corporation. For example, prior to the reorganization, an acquiring corporation with 500,000 shares of common stock outstanding, each entitled to one vote, might reclassify its common stock as "Class A" voting stock and authorize the issuance of 1 million shares of an additional "Class B" voting stock which, as a class, would be entitled to vote for the same number of directors as the Class A shares were entitled to vote for as a class. It can be easily seen that the Class B shares, although voting shares, have only half the voting strength of the Class A shares. Although there is no theoretical limit to the extent to which this technique can be used to attenuate the voting rights of the shareholders of the acquired corporation, a practical limit would be imposed by the bargaining situation and also by the Internal Revenue Service, which requires that those who receive shares in the acquiring corporation obtain the right to "significant participation in the management of the affairs of the corporation." [127] Much the same effect could be achieved through a separate class

---

Revenue Service in that, if the consideration is voting stock, it should make no difference whether it was for services or for other shares.

[127] See Rev. Rul. 63–234, 1963–2 Cum. Bull. 148. Further possibilities are available through the use of a voting trust or, where case law and statute permit, irrevocable proxies running to the acquiring corporation or its shareholders to vote the shares distributed to the former shareholders of the acquired corporation. As already pointed out in a previous discussion, such proxies are often enforceable only if coupled with an interest and reasonably limited in duration. See Ch. III, text accompanying notes 156–166. For a discussion of voting trusts see id. notes 83–115. The voting trust device may be preferable in jurisdictions where the law on irrevocable proxies is uncertain.

of shares with the same voting power per share as the other shares of the acquiring corporation but worth twice as much per share, thus requiring the issuance of only one half as many shares as would be required if the shares were of equal value.

Needless to say, the shares must not only have voting rights but must qualify as "stock." Thus warrants, options or convertible debentures will not qualify as stock even though they represent a right to acquire voting stock.[128] But preferred shares which have voting rights because dividend payments are in arrears have been held to be voting stock, as well as common shares which at the time of the reorganization were without voting power because dividend arrearages had conferred temporary voting control to the preferred shares.[129]

Another important requirement is that the acquiring corporation, immediately after the acquisition, must have control of the acquired corporation. As already indicated, "control" means ownership of at least 80 percent of the voting shares and 80 percent of each other class of stock.[130]

The requirement that at least 80 percent control be obtained solely through the issuance of voting stock raises an interesting problem of so-called creeping control and the possible application of the step transaction doctrine. Suppose that Corporation A acquires 10 percent of the shares of Corporation B for cash and, one year later, acquires 70 percent of the B shares solely for voting stock. If the two transactions are considered as part of the same transaction, then the 80 percent control has not been acquired "solely" for voting stock. Suppose another extreme example—that 79 percent of the B shares were acquired for cash and, one year later, an additional 1 percent of the shares were acquired solely for voting stock. Would the two transactions be entitled to separate tax treatment or would the step transaction doctrine apply? Although the statute does not require that 80 percent of the shares of the acquired corporation be obtained solely for voting stock and thus permits a Type B reorganization between one company and another where the former already owns a significant percentage of the shares, it does not permit the acquisition of control to be for other than voting stock. The regulations, while indicating that one corporation may purchase shares for cash and then subsequently engage in a Type B reorganization whereby control is acquired solely for voting stock, give as an illustration a situation where the time interval between the two transactions (i.e., the cash purchase and the reorganization) was over fifteen years. And by a reference to an acquisition of control "in a single transaction or in a series of transactions taking place over a relatively short period of time such as 12 months" there may be a negative implication that where two transac-

---

[128] Cf. Rev. Rul. 66–339, 1966–2 Cum. Bull. 274.
[129] Forrest Hotel Corp. v. Fly, 112 F. Supp. 782, 789 (S.D. Miss. 1953).
[130] See Ch. II, text accompanying note 30.

tions occur within a time span of longer than one year they would probably not be integrated with one another, although one cannot be sure.[131] In any event, if shares have been acquired solely for voting stock and further purchases are made for cash, with the ultimate acquisition of control being solely for voting stock, reorganization treatment would be denied either if all of the share acquisitions were integrated with one another (because of the intervening cash purchases) or if the final acquisition were integrated with the earlier acquisitions for cash. This merely points up the sensitivity of the Type B reorganization to attack and the fact that it appears to be the least flexible of the three forms of reorganization under consideration.

Another possible application of the step transaction doctrine might be where a substantial number of shareholders of the acquired corporation refuse to accept voting shares of the acquiring corporation and insist on receiving cash for their shares. Several solutions are possible here. First, those who wish to receive cash can sell their shares to those who are willing to receive stock and the shares can then be surrendered to the acquiring corporation in a tax-free reorganization. Those who sell for cash will recognize gain or loss on the transaction whereas those who later participate in the reorganization will not recognize gain or loss. This is not an unfair disparity in tax treatment since the receipt of cash for shares always gives rise to the recognition of gain whether or not in connection with a reorganization. To preserve tax-free treatment for the remaining shareholders, however, the key requirement is to make sure that the cash payment does not come from the acquiring corporation (since the consideration coming from it can take no form other than voting stock). A second alternative is for the acquired corporation to repurchase or redeem the shares prior to the reorganization. This, too, will not interfere with subsequent reorganization treatment for the remaining shareholders as long as the cash payment does not come from the acquiring corporation or the latter does not assume liabilities of the acquired corporation.[132] A third alternative would be for the acquiring corporation to issue its voting shares to all those holding shares in the acquired corporation and later to purchase or redeem the shares of those who "dissented" from the transaction. If the later purchase or redemption is separable and not integrated with the reorganization, then the latter will qualify for tax-free treatment.[133] However, this technique seems dangerous and

---

[131] Treas. Reg. §1.368–2(c). See American Potash & Chemical Corp. v. United States, 185 Ct. Cl. 161, 399 F.2d 194 (Ct. Cl. 1968), where the court held that a creeping acquisition of shares for voting stock and cash for fractional shares was not a Type B reorganization because the acquisition took place over a period of longer than twelve months. For discussion of the *American Potash* and other related cases, see Henderson, Voting Stock in a Two-Step Asset Acquisition: The Kimbell-Diamond Reorganization, 25 Tax L. Rev. 375 (1970).

[132] See Howard v. Commissioner, 238 F.2d 943 (7th Cir. 1956); Hoboken Land & Improvement Co. v. Commissioner, 138 F.2d 104 (3d Cir. 1943).

[133] See B. Bittker and J. Eustice, Federal Income Taxation of Corporations and Shareholders 522 n.35 (1966).

should not be used except where the acquired corporation cannot make arrangements to repurchase or redeem the shares beforehand. If the acquired corporation should borrow funds to redeem the shares and the indebtedness were later assumed by the acquiring corporation, although it could be argued that the assumption of the acquired corporation's indebtedness should not be treated as boot to its shareholders, this approach seems especially vulnerable to being recast as an indirect payment of cash by the acquiring corporation to the shareholders of the acquired corporation.[134]

Although there is no express prohibition against the acquiring corporation's discharging liabilities of the acquired corporation, this should be avoided, particularly in situations involving shareholder-held debt and where there is a possibility that the debt is, in substance, another form of equity.[135] And even if the debt is held by outsiders, it is always possible to argue, particularly with a closely held corporation, that the acquiring corporation's discharge of the debt is, in substance, part of the consideration for the transfer of the shares, in which case the transaction would, of course, fail to qualify for tax-free treatment.[136] Another possibility might be for the parent corporation, after acquiring the subsidiary in a tax-free Type B reorganization, to make open-account advances to it or, better still, subscribe for additional stock. The funds transferred from the parent could then be used to discharge the subsidiary's indebtedness to others. As in the other situations previously discussed, care should be taken that the transfer of funds by the parent corporation is not considered to be an integral part of the prior reorganization.

Another way in which the acquiring corporation might possibly be able to pay expenses or other liabilities of the acquired corporation or its shareholders without disqualifying the tax-free character of the exchange would be through the issuance of more voting stock than it would otherwise issue for the shares alone. It could be argued that a subsequent sale of the voting

---

[134] Id. at 522–523. See also id. at 522 regarding the treatment of cash payments for fractional shares. The Internal Revenue Service apparently does not contest the payment of cash for fractional shares and permits reorganization treatment, except, of course, that gain is recognized to the extent that the payment represents the sale proceeds of the fractional share. Rev. Rul. 66–365, 1966–2 Cum. Bull. 116; cf. Rev. Rul. 55–59, 1955–1 Cum. Bull. 35. Another arrangement is to have a bank "make a market" in the fractional shares, selling on behalf of those who wish to dispose of their fractions and purchasing on behalf of others who wish to purchase enough fractions to make up a whole share. This, too, does not prevent qualification as a reorganization if properly handled.

[135] See Ch. II, text accompanying notes 67–102. If the "debt" is another form of equity, then the likelihood is that it is a second class of stock, in which case not only would a cash payment for the debt disqualify the reorganization but the acquiring corporation would have to acquire at least 80 percent of the debt solely for voting stock in order to satisfy the control requirement (since 80 percent of *each* class of stock is required for "control"). See note 130 *supra.*

[136] See the discussion of this point in B. Bittker and J. Eustice, id. at 523. See also Rev. Rul. 69–91, 1969–1 Cum. Bull. 106 (cash purchase of convertible debentures).

shares for cash which was then used to discharge the liabilities was not an integral part of the reorganization and thus should not disqualify its tax-free character. Again, much depends upon the timing of the various transactions and their interrelationship as bearing upon whether the step transaction doctrine will be applied to compress them into a single integrated scheme. Needless to say, it is far better not to attempt to cut corners in this fashion, for the Type B reorganization represents a classic situation in which square corners are the norm and the slightest deviation is suspect.

Troublesome problems have arisen with regard to the relationship between a Type B reorganization, followed by a liquidation of the subsidiary, and a Type C reorganization. If the Type B reorganization and the subsequent liquidation are interdependent parts of a single scheme, then the net effect is substantially the same as a Type C asset acquisition.[137] The difficulties arise from the fact that somewhat different rules apply to a Type C reorganization than to a transaction of Type B. Thus, with a Type C asset acquisition no significant difficulties arise from an assumption by the acquiring corporation of liabilities of the acquired corporation (except where boot or other property is transferred as part of the consideration and the total boot and the liabilities assumed exceed 20 percent of the fair market value of the acquired properties).[138] On the other hand, unlike a Type B reorganization, the technique of acquiring so-called creeping control is not permitted with a Type C reorganization.[139]

8.9 ASSET ACQUISITIONS—TYPE C REORGANIZATIONS

The key requirements here are an acquisition of "substantially all" the properties of another corporation "solely" in exchange for voting stock of either the acquiring corporation or a corporation in control of the acquiring corporation. As in the merger situation, the transferor is permitted to receive either voting stock of the transferee or of its parent, but is not permitted to receive both.

What has already been said regarding the "solely for voting stock" requirement as it applies to exchanges of shares (Type B) applies as well to asset acquisitions except that here the statute expressly states that "in deter-

---

[137] See Commissioner v. Dana, 103 F.2d 359 (3d Cir. 1939), and Treas. Reg. §1.382(b)–1(a)(6). As B. Bittker and J. Eustice, id. at 524 n.44, point out, this approach is similar to that of the Kimbell-Diamond doctrine, discussed in Ch. VII, note 105. See Henderson, Voting Stock in a Two-Step Asset Acquisition: The Kimbell-Diamond Reorganization, 25 Tax L. Rev. 375 (1970).

[138] See Int. Rev. Code of 1954, §368(a)(2)(B), and text accompanying note 156 *infra*.

[139] See B. Bittker and J. Eustice, id. at 524, 532. See also Bausch & Lomb Optical Co. v. Commissioner, 267 F.2d 75 (2d Cir. 1959), *cert. denied*, 361 U.S. 835 (1959), and MacLean, "Creeping Acquisitions," 21 Tax L. Rev. 345 (1966). For further discussion see text accompanying note 159 *infra*.

mining whether the exchange is solely for stock the assumption by the acquiring corporation of a liability of the other, or the fact that property acquired is subject to a liability, shall be disregarded." [140]

Despite the above language, as a result of a Supreme Court holding that a liability whose "nature and amount were determined and fixed in the reorganization" was not a liability of the transferor within the meaning of the statutory provision and thus its assumption might prevent qualification as a reorganization,[141] the Internal Revenue Service customarily refuses to issue favorable rulings as to asset acquisitions where the expenses of reorganization have been assumed by the acquiring corporation.[142]

Additional problems may be encountered in determining whether there has been an "assumption" in a particular situation, as where the acquiring corporation issues to the creditors of the acquired corporation obligations having substantially different terms than the obligations of the acquired corporation. Although the cases have permitted relatively substantial modifications of the old obligations, if it is clear that the latter has been effectively replaced by an entirely different obligation, then there has been no "assumption." [143] The difference between a "modification" and the creation of a "new" obligation can be resolved only factually on the basis of the degree of difference between the two. Also there may be situations where what purports in form to be an assumption of an obligation is, in substance, the payment of cash, as where the transferor mortgages its properties immediately before the transfer and the mortgage is discharged by the acquiring corporation immediately afterwards.[144] As we saw in connection with tax-free formation of corporations under Section 351, this situation is one in which the "tax avoidance" exception to Section 357 of the Code would require that the total liabilities assumed be treated as money received by the transferor. If this happens, then, depending upon whether or not the 20

---

[140] Int. Rev. Code of 1954, §368(a)(1)(C), effectively repudiating a leading case, United States v. Hendler, 303 U.S. 564 (1938).

[141] Helvering v. Southwest Consolidated Corp., 315 U.S. 194 (1942).

[142] See B. Bittker and J. Eustice, id. at 551. Despite this the authors cite several cases holding that expenses of the reorganization can be assumed without disqualification from tax-free treatment. See also note 126 *supra,* relating to payments under employment contracts.

[143] *Compare* Helvering v. Taylor, 128 F.2d 885 (2d Cir. 1942), *with* Stoddard v. Commissioner, 141 F.2d 76 (2d Cir. 1944).

[144] See the discussion of this possibility in B. Bittker and J. Eustice, id. at 553. See Ch. II, text accompanying notes 45–48. As the authors indicate, problems also arise where, even though there has been no tax-avoidance motivation, the liabilities of the acquired corporation are satisfied by the acquiring corporation as part of the reorganization itself. For example, suppose that the acquired corporation owes money to the acquiring corporation and that this debt is discharged as part of the plan of reorganization. Although some cases have held that this is the same as if the liabilities were owed to a third party, had been assumed and then paid off after the reorganization (e.g., Arthur L. Kniffen, 39 T.C. 553 (1962)), it is difficult to distinguish this from the payment by the acquiring corporation of boot to the acquired corporation, which then discharged its own debt.

percent boot limitation for Type C reorganizations is exceeded,[145] the transaction may be disqualified as a reorganization. In any case the assumption of liability, if treated as the receipt of money, would give rise to the recognition of gain under Section 356.

The regulations also state that although the assumption of liabilities in a Type C reorganization will not ordinarily be taken into account in determining whether the assets have been transferred solely for voting stock, such assumption "may in some cases . . . so alter the character of the transaction as to place the transaction outside the purposes and assumptions of the reorganization provisions." [146] Although the regulations do not provide an illustration of when this might occur, one might surmise that if a thinly capitalized corporation, or one which has substantial amounts of debt and a relatively low net worth, is acquired, then most of the real consideration for the transfer of assets might be the willingness of the transferee to assume the liabilities, in which case the relatively small value of the voting stock also given in purported satisfaction of the technical requirements of the statute might not be enough to comply with the overriding doctrine of continuity of proprietary interest.[147]

Aside from the problem of assumption of liabilities, one of the most troublesome aspects of a Type C reorganization is determining whether the acquired corporation has transferred substantially all of its properties, as required by the statute. This language was evidently placed in Section 368(a)(1)(C) of the Code in order to afford tax-free treatment only to those asset acquisitions which have essentially the same net effect as a merger. In such "merger equivalent" [148] acquisitions the transferee acquires substantially all the transferor's properties in exchange solely for its voting stock. Although true merger equivalence would result only if the transferor corporation were liquidated and its assets (the voting stock of the transferee) distributed to its shareholders, the statute does not require that this be done. Thus the transferor can be kept in existence, although care should be taken that it does not then fall within the personal holding company provisions or, if it does, that all of its personal holding company income (e.g., dividends on the transferee's stock) is distributed to the shareholders.[149] Normally, however, the transferor corporation will liqui-

---

[145] See Int. Rev. Code of 1954, §368(a)(2)(B), and text accompanying note 156 *infra*.

[146] Treas. Reg. §1.368–2(d)(1).

[147] See B. Bittker and J. Eustice, id. at 527, 530.

[148] Id. at 526.

[149] Normally the transferor would liquidate after the transfer of substantially all its properties. If this is done, then the liquidation should be expressly required under the plan of reorganization in order that it not be taxed to the shareholders as a conventional liquidation under Section 331 of the Code. In other words, if the liquidation is pursuant to the plan of reorganization, the receipt by a shareholder of the acquired corporation of stock in the acquiring corporation in the liquidation will be tax free under Section 354 of the Code. For discussion of the status of the transferor corporation after a *taxable* asset sale, see text accompanying notes 36–40 *supra*.

date pursuant to the reorganization plan, in which case the net effect of the transaction is akin to a merger. In sharp contrast a transfer of only part of the properties (i.e., not substantially all) would have the effect of a so-called divisive reorganization and, although these are permitted to some extent, they are subject to the more elaborate safeguards of Sections 368(a)(1)(D) and 355, which deal with spin-offs and the like. Since some discussion has already been given to this topic in connection with the application of the step transaction doctrine to spin-offs of unwanted (or wanted) assets prior to a reorganization,[150] it may suffice to say that the substantially all requirement is to assure that only transactions having a nondivisive or merger equivalent effect receive tax-free treatment as Type C reorganizations and that all others comply with the more restrictive requirements of Sections 368(a)(1)(D) and 355.

The substantially all requirement may be considered from two aspects, i.e., the way in which this provision is viewed by the Internal Revenue Service and the way in which it is viewed by the courts. As far as the former is concerned, a procedural statement of policy[151] indicates that, for the purpose of issuing a favorable ruling, substantially all means a transfer of assets representing at least 90 percent of the fair market value of the *net* assets *and* at least 70 percent of the fair market value of the *gross* assets of the transferor immediately before the transfer. To illustrate this, suppose that a corporation has gross assets of $1 million which are subject to liabilities of $500,000. To comply with the substantially all test as formulated by the Internal Revenue Service, at least 90 percent of the net assets or 90 percent of $500,000 (i.e., $450,000) must be transferred. But the test also requires a transfer of at least 70 percent of the gross assets (i.e., $700,000). Suppose that shareholders holding 25 percent of the outstanding shares object to the asset sale and assert dissenters' appraisal rights. If such rights are satisfied, then the corporation must pay out 25 percent of its equity to its shareholders, or $125,000 (25 percent of $500,000). This leaves only $375,000 in net assets to be transferred, well below the $450,000 minimum required by the Internal Revenue Service. If, on the other hand, the acquiring corporation refused to assume the $500,000 in liabilities, even though there might be no dissenting shareholders, and the corporation were thus able to satisfy the net assets part of the test, the other requirement of 70 percent of the gross assets would not be met, since the corporation would have to reserve $500,000, or one half of its gross assets, to pay its creditors.[152]

As far as the courts are concerned, although the percentage of net or gross assets transferred is of obvious importance,[153] it is not the sole determining

---

[150] See id. note 107 *supra*. See also Ch. VII §7.6.

[151] Rev. Proc. 66–34, 1966–2 Cum. Bull. 1232, 1233.

[152] This illustration is taken from a speech by Newman T. Halvorson, Jr., at the U. Mo. K.C. Inst. on Corporate Combinations, Oct. 28, 1967.

[153] Assets amounting to 86 percent of the net assets have been held to be sub-

factor. A more lenient attitude might thus be taken to a failure by the transferor to convey significant amounts of cash if the transferor were liquidated as part of the plan of reorganization and the cash distributed to its shareholders.[154] On the other hand, if the transferor retains operating assets and does not liquidate, then it is highly likely that the substantially all requirement would not be met even if the other assets were transferred free and clear of liabilities and the amount transferred corresponded to the total net assets of the corporation (i.e., the transferor would continue in existence as a thin corporation holding a significant amount of operating assets).[155] Application of anything but a rigorous rule in such circumstances would undermine the very purpose of the substantially all requirement, namely, to prevent reorganizations which are essentially devisive in nature from being accomplished without compliance with the provisions of Sections 368(a)(1)(D) and 355 of the Code.

The Code provides for what might be termed a 20 percent "leeway" test in determining the amount of consideration other than voting stock which may be received in a Type C reorganization. If the substantially all test has been met, then the transferor may receive cash or boot equal to no more than 20 percent of the fair market value of the properties transferred.[156] Although liabilities assumed by the transferee are not ordinarily considered as boot, they count as boot for determining whether the 20 percent test has been met. Thus, if a corporation has assets of $1 million and liabilities of $100,000, it may receive only $100,000 in cash or other property in a reorganization whereby the properties are transferred subject to the liabilities or the latter are assumed by the transferee. If the 20 percent test has been met, then the boot (other than the liabilities) gives rise to the recognition of gain under Section 356 of the Code.[157] Gain is recognized only to the extent of

---

stantially all, Commissioner v. First Natl. Bank, 104 F.2d 865 (3d Cir. 1939), whereas 68 percent has been held insufficient. Arctic Ice Machine Co., 23 B.T.A. 1223 (1931).

[154] See James Armour, Inc., 43 T.C. 295 (1964).

[155] Cf. Rev. Rul. 57–518, 1957–2 Cum. Bull. 253, and other authorities cited in B. Bittker and J. Eustice, Federal Income Taxation of Corporations and Shareholders 526 (1966). It is also of importance that, where the corporation is liquidated, and liquid assets transferred to its shareholders, such assets would be boot and give rise to the recognition of gain, whereas if operating assets are retained in corporate solution, the effect is similar to a divisive spin-off. See text accompanying note 107 *supra*. Bittker and Eustice, ibid., also point out that even though the *percentage* of assets retained as compared with net or gross assets might be small, some attention should be given to the *value* of the retained assets. Thus the retention of $5 million out of $500 million in assets would still permit an evasion of the spirit of the statute, especially if the $5 million consisted in operating assets or investment properties and the corporation were kept in existence.

[156] Int. Rev. Code of 1954, §368(a)(2)(B). The statute expresses the test as requiring that the acquiring corporation must receive solely for its voting stock (or voting stock of another corporation in control of the acquiring corporation) property of the transferor having a fair market value of at least 80 percent of the fair market value of all the property of the transferor.

[157] See, however, Treas. Reg. §1.361–1, which permits the transferor or its share-

the fair market value of the boot, but the transferor corporation may be relieved of the recognition of gain to the extent that the boot is distributed to its shareholders, in which case gain may be recognized to the latter to that extent. If the 20 percent test is not met (e.g., if more than $100,000 in cash or other property was received in the previous illustration) then the entire transaction fails to qualify as a reorganization and gain or loss is recognized in full.

It should be noted that the test applies to the fair market value of all the properties of the transferor corporation, whether or not they are transferred. Thus where a corporation worth $50,000 reserves $5000 to pay its debts and transfers the remaining $45,000, it must receive at least $40,000 in voting stock and therefore can receive only $5000 in cash or other property (including liabilities assumed, etc.). Needless to say, extreme care should be taken in computing the fair market value of the assets, especially where there are intangibles, such as franchises, good will, etc., whether or not the latter will be transferred as part of the reorganization. This will generally mean that few corporations will be sufficiently sure of their value to risk receiving the full 20 percent in boot. As a matter of practice, the 20 percent escape hatch appears to be merely a safeguard to prevent accidental disqualification resulting from the receipt of small amounts of boot.

Although, as we have seen,[158] the concept of so-called creeping control is not inconsistent with a Type B reorganization, due to the requirement in a Type C reorganization of an acquisition of substantially all the properties of the transferor in exchange solely for voting stock, difficulties arise where one corporation which already owns shares in another seeks to acquire its assets in a Type C reorganization. In a classic case, *Bausch & Lomb Optical Co. v. Commissioner*,[159] one corporation had previously acquired 79 percent of the shares of another for cash and then, in a purported Type C reorganization, it issued more voting stock for the acquired corporation's assets and subsequently liquidated it, receiving back its own shares. Reorganization treatment was denied on the theory that only 21 percent of the assets was acquired for the voting stock in the Type C reorganization and that the remaining 79 percent of the assets had been acquired in respect of the liquidation rights of the 79 percent interest previously purchased for cash.[160] Note that this holding does not rely on a step transaction integration of the prior cash purchase with the subsequent Type C reorganization. Rather, it is based on the theory that substantially all the assets were not exchanged solely for voting stock pursuant to a reorganization, since 79 percent of the acquired corporation's assets were

---

holders to receive nonvoting stock or securities under Section 368(a)(2)(B) of the Code without boot treatment, but only of course up to the 20 percent limit.

[158] See text accompanying note 130 *supra.*
[159] Note 139 *supra.*
[160] See Rev. Rul. 54–396, 1954–2 Cum. Bull. 147.

received by way of a liquidation and not by way of a Type C reorganization. A subsequent Revenue Ruling[161] would permit a Type C reorganization between one corporation and another which owns shares in it in the following manner. Suppose that Corporation Y owns shares in Corporation X. If Corporation Y forms a new subsidiary, Z, by exchanging new Y stock for stock of Z, Z acquires the assets of X with the Y stock and X then liquidates, then the net effect is that the minority shareholders of X become shareholders of Y and the X assets are held in the newly formed subsidiary Z. The ruling permitted reorganization treatment on the theory that Corporation Y could have acquired the minority shares in X in a Type B reorganization and the foregoing transaction had the same net effect.[162] Also, if Corporation Y owns more than an 80 percent interest in Corporation X to begin with, then X can be liquidated under the tax-free provisions of Section 332 and there is no need for a reorganization. Finally, if Corporation Y owns less than 20 percent of Corporation X, then a Type C reorganization would be possible notwithstanding the *Bausch & Lomb* holding, in that Section 368(a)(2)(B) of the Code (the 20 percent leeway provision) would permit the 20 percent interest in X to be received by liquidation without risking failure to comply with the strict requirements of Section 368(a)(1)(C).[163]

The foregoing discussion of tax and nontax aspects of various methods of corporate acquisition is summarized in tabular form as Appendix B, "Selling the Business—Tax and Nontax Aspects," at the end of this volume.

[161] Rev. Rul. 57–278, 1957–1 Cum. Bull. 124.

[162] But see Rev. Rul. 69–48, 1969–1 Cum. Bull. 106, denying reorganization treatment where a parent corporation's purchase of an interest in the acquired corporation for cash was held to be an integral part of the plan whereby the corporation's assets were subsequently transferred to the parent's subsidiary for stock of the parent. Thus the step transaction doctrine was used to treat the prior cash purchase as part of the reorganization and the asset transfer was therefore not solely for voting stock. See S. Surrey and W. Warren, Cases and Materials on Federal Income Taxation 1534 (1962). As the authors point out, if it is desired to eliminate Corporation Z as a subsidiary, then this can be done by the formation of still another corporation, Corporation W, to which the assets of both Y and Z are transferred in exchange for W voting stock, with Y and Z then being liquidated. Note, however, that this presupposes the liquidation of Y, which may not be acceptable. See William Holton George, 26 T.C. 396 (1956). See also Fager, The Acquisition of Partly-Held Corporations, N.Y.U. 18th Inst. on Fed. Tax. 799 (1960); MacLean, "Creeping Acquisitions," 21 Tax L. Rev. 345 (1966); Seplow, Acquisition of Assets of a Subsidiary: Liquidation or Reorganization, 73 Harv. L. Rev. 484 (1960).

[163] See B. Bittker and J. Eustice, Federal Income Taxation of Corporations and Shareholders 532 (1966).

IX The First Public Financing of a Closely Held Corporation

In the previous chapter we examined various ways in which those who hold an interest in a closely held corporation may achieve liquidity of investment by selling the corporation, either for cash or, more likely, for shares in another corporation whose stock is publicly traded. In this chapter we shall explore an alternative method of gaining liquidity, namely, through "going public." If the public offering is successful, and an active over-the-counter market in the securities is established, then the liquidity problem is, if not solved, then at least greatly alleviated. Shareholders may thus dispose of their interests which previously may have been unmarketable and diversify their portfolios, thereby spreading their investment risks. Even if they should choose to hold on to their shares, since the latter are publicly held and traded, the problem of determining their value for estate tax purposes in the event of death is greatly simplified.[1]

9.1 ADVANTAGES OF GOING PUBLIC

There may be several other advantages both to the corporation and to its shareholders from "going public." As far as the corporation is concerned, its working capital and general financial position are likely to benefit by a broadened equity base and by the new funds it obtains from the public financing. In times where credit is "tight" and debt financing difficult, especially for close corporations, a public offering of equity securities is an attractive financing alternative, particularly if lenders insist not only that their loans be evidenced by notes, bonds or debentures, but that the debt be convertible into common stock or that they receive warrants or options to purchase common. If the common shares are publicly held, then the convertibility privilege or warrants become more attractive, rendering debt financing more feasible through this method. Thus, if funds must be borrowed in the future, the loans may be on better terms and perhaps at a

[1] See Ch. VI, text accompanying note 188.

more favorable rate of interest than would be so if the company were closely held. And if its shares are publicly held, a company may choose to forego the high fixed charges involved in debt financing (despite the tax deductibility of interest payments) and raise further funds through sales of additional common or preferred stock.

An additional advantage for the company that may result from a public offering is the increased prestige often coming with public ownership, which may lead to enhanced sales of its products. Also the company is likely to benefit from the fact that the price of its shares will generally be higher after a public offering than either their book value or their prior value when the corporation was closely held. This, at least, is so if the public offering is successful and properly handled.

The increase in the price of shares which commonly results from a public offering will generally produce a substantial benefit to the shareholders. A recent case study[2] of how this may happen cited, as an example, a company with a book value of only $55,000 for its shares before a public offering. One hundred thousand shares were offered at $3 per share[3] and the original shareholders retained two hundred thousand shares, a two-thirds controlling interest. Legal and underwriting costs of the offering were $60,000 so that the company received $240,000 in net proceeds, increasing the company's total book value from $55,000 to $295,000. After the financing those who retained the two-thirds controlling interest owned 200,000 shares valued at $3 per share, or an investment of $600,000. Thus prior to the financing the shareholders had complete control of a company worth only $55,000 with shares of little or no marketability. After the financing these same shareholders still held control and the market value of their investment had increased to $600,000, the book value being $196,667.

Even more dramatic examples than the foregoing can readily be found. If there is an enthusiastic public response to the offering and an active "after market," the price of the shares may increase substantially above the price at which the shares were initially offered to the public, particularly if the offering is a so-called hot issue.[4] Of course the long-term results of a speculative upswing in the market price of the issue may not be favorable, particularly if the speculative "bubble" bursts and the price later falls substantially, perhaps even below the initial offering price. However, if the price of the stock holds up and public confidence in the company's prospects remains unimpaired, those who control it may easily make a fortune.

[2] See R. Weaver, Public Financing of Small and Medium Sized Business 19 (Washington: Investment Bankers Association 1969). See also N.Y. Times, Nov. 22, 1969, at 54, cols. 7, 8.

[3] Such an offering would be exempt from the regular registration requirements under SEC Reg. A. See text accompanying notes 108–127 *infra.*

[4] For a discussion of the hot-issue problem see When Corporations Go Public 88–91, 165–167 (Israels and Duff eds. 1962).

The net result of all of this is that if all goes well, the company, its controlling shareholders and the investing public prosper. Hence it becomes critically important to insure that all does go well. This is the topic of the present chapter.

9.2 STEPS TO BE TAKEN PRIOR TO AN OFFERING OF SECURITIES

When a public offering of securities is being considered it is important that attention be immediately focused on several matters, some of a general business nature and others of a legal nature.

One of the most important business problems is the selection of an "underwriter" to handle the sale and the manner in which the company goes about looking for an underwriter. At the outset it is useful to distinguish between several alternative forms of underwriting. "Strict" or "old fashioned" underwriting, no longer in frequent use, involves an arrangement whereby one or more investment houses undertake to sell securities to the public and agree to purchase for their own account or for resale at their own risk only that portion of the offering which they are unable to sell publicly on the issuer's behalf. Thus their agreement is to solicit subscriptions on behalf of the issuer and to "stand by" to purchase any amount of the issue which remains unsubscribed.[5] As previously stated, this method is infrequently used, except in connection with an offering of warrants or "rights" to existing shareholders.

The two underwriting methods which are in general use today are the so-called best efforts underwriting and the firm commitment underwriting. Under the best efforts arrangement the underwriter merely agrees to use its best efforts to market the shares or securities, acting as agent for the issuer. In no sense does the underwriter insure the success of the offering or guarantee to purchase any unsold portion of it. A best efforts underwriting is frequently necessary for small companies which are not well established and where the underwriter is not willing to enter into a commitment which would obligate it to do anything more than make a sincere attempt to dispose of the shares. However, some large, well-established companies whose shares are easily sold may wish to save on underwriting costs by entering into a best efforts arrangement.[6] Since the underwriter is incurring no risk and is acting merely as agent for the issuer, his fees will be lower than if he were to undertake a firm commitment. The latter arrangement is basically a wholesaling method of marketing securities whereby the wholesaler (the underwriter or the underwriting syndicate) purchases the securities from

[5] See 1 L. Loss, Securities Regulation 159–163 (1961).
[6] Id. at 171. Firm commitment and best efforts underwriting are extensively discussed by Professor Loss at 163–172.

the issuer at a designated "firm" price (the firm commitment) and resells the securities by what amounts to a retailing process carried out through securities dealers, commonly known as the "selling group" (to distinguish them from the underwriting syndicate who, acting as wholesalers, purchase directly from the issuer). Since a firm commitment obligates the underwriter to purchase the securities at a designated price and in that respect shifts to him the risk that the offering may not be successful, the underwriting costs or "spread" (including options, warrants and other inducements to the underwriter to carry out the arrangement) are likely to be greater than in a best efforts underwriting. Of course much will depend upon the issuer, the type of securities being offered and market conditions. Thus some highly speculative offerings may be possible only on a best efforts arrangement, and even then the underwriting costs may be as high as 20 percent or more of the issue price due to the substantial amount of marketing effort which may be entailed in selling the securities, even though the underwriter itself takes no financial risk.[7]

Although occasionally a company or its shareholders may wish to sell securities directly to the public without using an underwriter (as in an offering to employees or existing shareholders), a closely held company which goes public for the first time almost always requires the services of an underwriter, either on a best efforts or on a firm commitment basis. The problem thus becomes one of locating an underwriting firm which is best suited and willing to market the securities.

In the securities business it is generally said that, unlike the used car market, it is highly unwise to attempt to "shop the deal" (i.e., for an issuer to go from one underwriting house to another to try to get the best terms for itself).[8] Although it may be inappropriate to draw an analogy between an underwriting and a marriage contract, the fact remains that underwriters may be sensitive when they hear that other firms have been approached and that the issuer is "shopping around." If the issuer is rebuffed by several underwriting houses, word is likely to circulate that others have found the prospective issue unattractive and the impression may be created that there is something wrong with the deal. As a result few underwriting houses may be interested in what appears to them to be a corporate reject, and the issuer will be forced to utilize the services of one of the less reputable and more expensive underwriting houses or, at worst, it may find that it is unable to find anyone who will underwrite the issue.[9]

From a practical standpoint the issuer's problem thus becomes one of locating a suitable underwriter. Frequently this will require the services of some intermediary, such as a bank, investment or management consultant or

[7] See When Corporations Go Public 65 (Israels and Duff eds. 1962).

[8] Id. at 42.

[9] Ibid. See also Wheat and Blackstone, Guideposts for a First Public Offering, 15 Bus. Law. 539, 544 (1960), reprinted in ABA, Selected Articles on Federal Securities Law 1, 6 (Wander and Grienenberger eds. 1968).

a professional "finder." In a sense such persons act as corporate match-makers, locating underwriters for companies wishing to sell securities and locating purchasers where the company itself is being sold, as with a merger, sale of stock or sale of assets. Although the finder's fee is normally paid by the underwriter,[10] this cost is, in effect, passed on to the issuer since the underwriter takes his overall expenses into account in computing the spread or underwriting discount.

Another important question to be considered is the amount of stock which should be sold to the public. In this regard there is no pat answer. The problem can only be resolved in terms of the total capital needs of the issuer, the anticipated expenses of the issue and the amount of "dilution" which those in control of the issuer are willing to tolerate with regard to their proportionate equity ownership. It has already been indicated that substantial amounts of capital can be raised without loss of control by the majority shareholders and that even greater amounts of capital may be obtained if the principal shareholders are willing to be content with less than 51 percent of the shares outstanding after completion of the public offering. If the shares sold to the public are distributed widely enough, "working" control may be retained without ownership of 51 percent of the shares; depending upon the facts of the particular situation, 20 or 30 percent of the common stock or even less may be enough for working control. In fact, even apart from technical working control of the shares, a type of de facto control is likely to exist solely because certain individuals occupy powerful management positions and thus are in control of the proxy solicitation machinery.[11] The amount of stock which should be issued will therefore depend upon a number of factors which will vary with each case, but the most important of these are likely to be: How much additional funds does the issuer require, and how much dilution of their interests are those currently in control willing to tolerate in order to raise sufficient funds? Also, how much financing will the public market absorb under prevailing economic conditions?

Another problem concerns the manner in which the financing should take place. Should the financing be through a sale by the issuer of newly authorized shares or should at least some of the shares which are sold be those which are currently held by controlling shareholders or others? If the transaction takes the form of a sale by the issuer of its shares, then it is referred to as a "primary" distribution. If the sale is by those in control of the issuer of their own shares, then the transaction is known as a "second-

[10] See When Corporations Go Public 37 (Israels and Duff eds. 1962).

[11] This is a topic on which numerous articles have been written. For a sampling of some of the authorities see Ch. VIII, note 18. See also Perlman v. Feldmann, 219 F.2d 173 (2d Cir. 1955), *cert. denied*, 349 U.S. 952 (1955); Essex Universal Corp. v. Yates, 305 F.2d 572 (2d Cir. 1962); Matter of Caplan v. Lionel Corp., 151 N.Y.L.J. No. 24, at 14 (Sup. Ct. 1964); cf. Honigman v. Green Giant Co., 309 F.2d 667 (8th Cir. 1962), *cert. denied*, 372 U.S. 941 (1963).

ary" distribution.[12] The financing can take one form or the other or can partake of both, i.e., some shares may be sold by the issuer and some shares may be sold by controlling shareholders. In either case, as we shall see, the issuer must file a registration statement covering the securities offered in either the primary or secondary distribution with the Commission under the Securities Act of 1933.

If the transaction takes the form of a secondary distribution, various capital changes may be necessary before the shares may be sold to the public. Suppose, for example, that three shareholders hold all of the 1000 outstanding shares of a corporation which has a net worth of $1 million. Each share will be worth $1000. If they wish to sell a little less than half of their interest to the public then the shares can be split on a one-hundred-for-one basis, making each share worth ten dollars. Forty-nine thousand shares can then be sold publicly, leaving the former owners with 51 percent control.

Aside from selecting an underwriter, an equally important business problem is that of selecting a suitable accountant. Although a company may already have its own accountant, he may not qualify as sufficiently "independent" for the purposes of meeting Commission requirements. Thus, in a full-fledged registration of securities (i.e., not an offering under one of the exemptions, such as Regulation A), the Commission requires the financial statements to be certified by an independent certified public accountant, and an accountant who serves as an officer or director or who holds stock in the issuing company would not qualify under the Commission's standards of independence.[13] This will generally mean that the issuer must enlist the services of an outside accounting firm and one which is sufficiently conversant with the problems of Commission registration. If an audit of the issuer's financial affairs is required, as is almost invariably the case, then the accountants should be given sufficient advance warning of the proposed time schedule and the date on which the securities are to be offered publicly. Frequently the matter may be simplified if the offering is so timed that it is possible to use the issuer's year-end financial statements, thus avoiding an additional audit of its affairs during the middle of its fiscal period and minimizing the need for unaudited figures for quarterly or half-year periods subsequent to the close of the issuer's fiscal year. In any event, those who are to be in charge of the accounting work should be chosen well in advance and alerted to the proposed time schedule in order that there may be maximum coordination between the issuer, the accountants and other parties who will be involved, such as the underwriter, the underwriter's counsel and the issuer's counsel or special counsel.

[12] See generally 1 L. Loss, Securities Regulation 182–184 (1961).

[13] Id. at 341–348. See also SEC Reg. S–X, rule 2–01, and SEC Securities Act Release No. 4002 (1958). A very recent Commission release indicates that counsel for the issuer should disclose any interest which it may have in the issuer exceeding $30,000 in the case of investments held by the firm and $10,000 for any firm associate or other employee. See SEC Securities Act Release No. 33–5094 (1970).

Finally, it should not be forgotten that stock certificates must be ordered and sufficient time must be given for their preparation. Although many state statutes permit certificates to be printed or lithographed,[14] the rules of the New York Stock Exchange (if listing is desired) require the certificates to be engraved.[15] If this is contemplated, sufficient advance notice must be given to the banknote company to prepare the engraved plates. Furthermore, if a large number of certificates will be required, as is usually the case, the issuer will normally wish to have the certificates signed with facsimile signatures and sealed with a facsimile seal, thereby avoiding the burdensome need for manual signing and sealing of each certificate. Although facsimile signatures and seals are permitted under most state laws, it is common to require the manual countersignature of a transfer agent or a registrar, who must be a person or institution (commonly a bank) other than the issuing corporation.[16] The issuer may therefore have to appoint a separate transfer agent or registrar or both, and this will generally require making the appropriate arrangements with one or more banks. Finally, the transfer agent and the underwriter should be consulted as to the number of stock certificates which will be required and the various denominations in which they are likely to be issued. Although this may not be precisely known before the issue has been sold, a shortage of stock certificates could be a troublesome problem and might even hinder the efficiency of the hoped-for active "after market" in trading of the issuer's securities once they have been sold.

Once the underwriter and accountants have been selected, and preliminary arrangements have been made for an audit of the issuer's books and for preparing the stock certificates, the next order of business is generally the preparation of a detailed time schedule and scheme for allocating and coordinating the considerable work which will be involved in preparing the registration statement, qualifying the securities for sale under the various state Blue Sky or securities laws and arranging for listing of the securities on one or more national securities exchanges if that is required. This is usually done through a meeting of the issuer's principal officers, as many of its directors as possible, representatives of the underwriter, the accountants, and the counsel for the issuer and the underwriter. Depending upon the circumstances of the situation, the meeting may be supervised by counsel for the issuer, often special counsel retained expressly for the purpose of supervising the registration work because of its expertise in this area. In addition to the preparation of the time schedule and the allocation of responsibilities to various members of the group,[17] it is well to stress the

---

[14] E.g., Mo. Gen. & Bus. Corp. Law §351.295 (1963).

[15] N.Y. Stock Exchange Company Manual A–224.

[16] E.g., Model Bus. Corp. Act §23. See also N.Y. Stock Exchange Company Manual A–5 to A–6, A–214. A corporation may act as its own transfer agent but then it must have an independent registrar.

[17] For a typical time schedule see Wheat and Blackstone, Guideposts for a First

importance of "due diligence" on the part of all those who will be involved in the registration process. This is best done through a general description of the duties and potential civil and criminal liabilities imposed by Section 11 of the Securities Act of 1933 as well as by other provisions of the 1933 and 1934 Acts[18] for negligence in preparing registration statements or for failure to abide by the other requirements of the securities laws.[19] Needless to say, similar liabilities may result from analogous violations of state Blue Sky or securities laws. Although the arrangement may vary with the particular financing, it is generally the responsibility of counsel for the underwriter to see that the issue is properly "Blue Skyed" or qualified under the securities laws of the various states in which the offering will be made. Overall supervision of the financing and coordination of the work involved in preparing the registration statement may be the task of special counsel for the issuer, with various portions of the registration statement being initially prepared by those company officials who are most conversant with the particular topics to be covered. Even though responsibility is thus delegated

Public Offering, 15 Bus. Law. 556–558 (1960), reprinted in ABA, Selected Articles on Federal Securities Law 1, 18–20 (Wander and Grienenberger eds. 1968). See also the sample Time Schedule which appears as Appendix C at the end of this volume, as well as Appendix D, a typical "Closing Memorandum."

[18] See Securities Act of 1933, 15 U.S.C. §§77a–77aa, 48 Stat. 74 (hereinafter referred to as the Securities Act of 1933), and Securities Exchange Act of 1934, 15 U.S.C. §§78a–78hh, 48 Stat. 881 (hereinafter referred to as the Securities Exchange Act of 1934). The most significant civil liability provisions of the Securities Act of 1933 are Section 11 (defective registration statements), Section 12 (sales or offers in violation of Section 5 of the Act and fraudulent sales), Section 15 (liabilities of controlling persons) and Section 17 (an antifraud prohibition). Among the most significant civil liability provisions of the Securities Exchange Act of 1934 are Section 9 (manipulation of security prices), Section 10 and particularly the Commission's rule 10b–5, 17 C.F.R. §240.10b–5 (prohibiting fraudulent or deceitful practices, including so-called half-truths, and certain forms of negligence in the preparation of financial statements, etc. (see Ch. VI, text accompanying notes 229–265)), Section 14 (false or misleading proxy materials), Section 16 (reports of directors, officers and principal shareholders of securities transactions and so-called short-swing trading), Section 15 (liabilities of brokers and dealers), Section 18 (liabilities for false or misleading reports or documents filed with the Commission) and Section 20 (liabilities of controlling persons). The criminal penalties for wilful violations of the Securities Act of 1933 are specified by Section 24 of the Act as a maximum fine of $5000 or five years imprisonment or both. Section 32 of the Securities Exchange Act of 1934 provides for criminal penalties of a fine of not more than $10,000 (in the case of individuals) and imprisonment for not more than two years or both.

[19] The most recent dramatic exposition of the extent of possible liability under Section 11 of the Securities Act of 1933 is Escott v. Bar Chris Constr. Corp., 283 F. Supp. 643 (S.D.N.Y. 1968). Among the exhaustive discussions of the *Bar Chris* case are Proceedings, ABA Natl. Inst., "The Bar Chris Case": Prospectus Liability, 24 Bus. Law. 523 (1969); Folk, Civil Liabilities Under the Federal Securities Acts: The Bar Chris Case, 55 Va. L. Rev. (Part I) 1 and (Part II) 199 (1969); See also Comments, 68 Colum. L. Rev. 1411 (1968); 82 Harv. L. Rev. 908 (1969); 21 Stan. L. Rev. 171 (1968). For a panel discussion of the various ramifications of the case, see Bar Chris: A Dialogue on a Bad Case Making Hard Law, 57 Geo. L.J. 221 (1968) (Heller, moderator, with Israels, Schwartz and Weiss).

to various members of a working group or "team," the utmost care should be taken that each member of the group not only be diligent in the performance of his own tasks but be alert to inadequacies or discrepancies which may appear in the work submitted by others. Thus counsel for the issuer or underwriter may not blindly rely upon statements made by company officers if they have reason to believe that such statements are false or inaccurate and if independent verification of the statements is possible through examining the issuer's minute books and other records.[20]

Another important problem which should be considered is that of prefiling publicity. Since the Securities Act of 1933 prohibits any "offer" of a security prior to the date on which a registration statement is filed with the Commission (the "filing date"),[21] every precaution must be taken that news releases, speeches of corporate officials and other activities do not in substance amount to an informal offer prohibited under the terms of the statute. This is the problem known to securities experts as "jumping the gun." [22] Although it is difficult, if not impossible, to draw a hard and fast line between various types of news releases and other activities and specify with absolute certainty those which amount to an informal, unlawful offer of securities, it is generally safe to say that a corporation which contemplates a public offering may continue to engage in those activities which are a normal part of its business routine, such as issuing regular reports to shareholders and timely disclosures to the news media and stock exchanges of important corporate developments. Anything beyond this, however, particularly conferences with securities analysts and speeches by corporate officers and public relations personnel, should be cleared in advance with corporate counsel and preferably with special counsel in charge of the registration process in order to prevent inadvertent violations of the securities laws.[23] The gun-jumping problem has become particularly sensitive due to a possible conflict between the "early disclosure" philosophy of rule 10b–5 under the Securities Exchange Act of 1934 (i.e., the need for prompt public disclosure of material corporate developments as highlighted by such leading cases as *SEC v. Texas Gulf Sulphur Co.*[24]) and the problem of avoiding premature disclosure or unlawful "conditioning of the market" for

---

[20] See Escott v. Bar Chris Constr. Corp., 283 F. Supp. 643 (S.D.N.Y. 1968), and the various commentaries cited in note 19 *supra*.

[21] Securities Act of 1933, §5(c).

[22] See In the Matter of Carl M. Loeb, Rhoades & Co. and Dominick & Dominick, 38 S.E.C. 843 (1959); 1 L. Loss, Securities Regulation 215–221 (1961); Demmler, Problems Inherent in Pre-Filing Publicity, 15 Bus. Law. 132 (1959), reprinted in ABA, Selected Articles on Federal Securities Law 81 (Wander and Grienenberger eds. 1968). The basic thinking of the Commission on this problem is set forth in SEC Securities Act Release No. 3844 (1957), which provides useful illustrations of various situations where press releases, speeches of company officers, etc., will or will not amount to "gun jumping."

[23] See note 22 *supra* and particularly SEC Securities Act Release No. 3844 (1957).

[24] 401 F.2d 833 (2d Cir. 1968) (*en banc*, two dissents), *cert. denied*, 394 U.S. 976 (1969).

a forthcoming registration of securities under the Securities Act of 1933. For example, in *Chris-Craft Industries, Inc. v. Bangor Punta Corp.*,[25] a press release which announced the terms of a proposed merger and exchange of securities, accompanied by optimistic projections of future sales for the consolidated corporations and an estimate of the worth of a package of shares to be offered by the acquiring corporation, was held to violate the gun-jumping prohibition, despite the company's argument that the rules of the New York Stock Exchange[26] and SEC rule 10b–5 required prompt disclosure of the information it distributed to the public. The Commission shortly thereafter issued a clarifying statement of policy emphasizing that a press release will not violate the gun-jumping prohibition if it is purely factual in content and does not include predictions or opinions.[27]

9.3 THE REGISTRATION PROCEDURE

The basic approach of the Securities Act of 1933 is to require public disclosure through filing a registration statement with the Commission and the distribution of prospectuses to all those who purchase securities in a public offering made through the mails or any means or instrumentality of interstate commerce, such as a national securities exchange or the over-the-counter market. As previously indicated, no offer of a security to the public may be made prior to the date a registration statement is filed with the Commission. The Securities Act of 1933 provides that a registration statement becomes "effective" and securities may be sold after the expiration of twenty days from the date the registration statement is filed,[28] but since the registration statement must, as a practical matter, be amended to provide further information, such as the offering price, the underwriting discount and estimated expenses of the offering, as well as to correct any deficiencies referred to in the Commission's "letter of comment" (formerly known as the "deficiency letter"), any amendment will start the statutory twenty-day "waiting period" running all over again. Since, especially in the case of a firm commitment underwriting in a rapidly fluctuating market, the underwriting syndicate will be unwilling to commit itself to a definite offering price until a day or two before the date when the securities may be lawfully

---

[25] 426 F.2d 569 (2d Cir. 1970), *rev'g* Chris-Craft Industries, Inc. v. Piper Aircraft Corp., 303 F. Supp. 191 (S.D.N.Y. 1969). In an earlier proceeding brought by the Commission, another District Court had determined that the gun-jumping rules had been violated, SEC v. Bangor Punta Corp., CCH Fed. Sec. L. Rep. ¶92, 428 (D.D.C. 1969).

[26] N.Y. Stock Exchange Company Manual A–19. The various Canadian securities exchanges have also adopted similar policies. See Wall Street Journal (Midwest ed.) Oct. 1, 1968, at 4, cols. 3, 4. In March of 1970, the American Stock Exchange adopted a policy. See N.Y. Times, Mar. 23, 1970, at 59, col. 8.

[27] See SEC Securities Act Release No. 5009 (1969).

[28] Securities Act of 1933 §8(a).

sold (the so-called effective date of the registration statement) a "pricing" amendment to the registration statement is necessary at the last moment. Since this technically advances the effective date by another twenty days, the problem is handled from a practical standpoint by filing with the Commission a "request for acceleration" of the effective date when the final pricing amendment to the registration statement is filed. If all goes well, and if the Commission staff is satisfied that the registration statement and prospectus are not deficient, acceleration will normally be granted, thus permitting the offering to be made in accordance with the contemplated time schedule. If the offering is successful, all the securities may be sold, or as underwriting parlance puts it, "go out the window," within a matter of hours after Commission clearance has been obtained. Needless to say, appropriate clearances must also be obtained from the various state Blue Sky officials before the securities may be sold in particular jurisdictions.[29] All of this requires a high degree of organizational teamwork and precise timing. This emphasizes the need for experienced counsel wherever a company goes public for the first time.

Although during the "waiting period" (the period between the date the registration statement is filed and its effective date) securities may not be sold (i.e., no one may enter into a binding commitment to purchase or sell the securities covered by the registration statement), the securities may yet be offered if care is taken that no offer may be accepted prior to the date the registration statement becomes effective. The Commission's rules permit offerings to be made through a so-called preliminary prospectus (sometimes referred to as a "red herring" because of the conspicuous legend in red which appears on its left margin indicating that the securities may not lawfully be sold until the registration statement has become effective).[30] Also, certain types of so-called summary prospectuses[31] or newspaper notices colloquially termed "tombstone ads"[32] may be used if the Commission's rules are strictly complied with.

In summary, then, the Securities Act of 1933 prohibits an offer of securities to the public until the filing of a registration statement, but after the filing date it permits offers, but not sales, and the use of certain materials such as preliminary prospectuses, summary prospectuses and tombstone ad-

[29] This process has been greatly simplified in jurisdictions which have adopted the Uniform Securities Act, which provides for registration of securities by "coordination" when such securities have also been filed for registration under federal law. In general the state filing requirements can be fulfilled by filing with the state securities commission copies of the documents which have been filed with the SEC. Unless the state securities commissioner raises some objection or requests additional information, the offering becomes automatically effective for state securities law purposes when the federal registration statement becomes effective. See also Uniform Securities Act §303; L. Loss and E. Cowett, Blue Sky Law 290–299 (1958). See text accompanying note 135 *infra*.

[30] SEC rule 433.

[31] Id. rules 434 and 434A.

[32] Id. rule 134.

vertisements. After the registration statement has become effective, the securities may be sold, but even here there is a prohibition against sending a security through the mail unless it is accompanied or preceded by a prospectus which meets the minimum disclosure requirements of the statute and regulations. In practical effect this means that a prospective investor may not receive a written communication from the offeror or seller without at the same time receiving a prospectus, either a preliminary prospectus if the communication takes place during the waiting period, or a definitive prospectus if it takes place after the effective date of the registration statement. In no event may he receive the security itself through the mails or any other means or instrumentality of interstate commerce unless the security is accompanied by or has been preceded by a prospectus.[33]

Despite all these precautions, however, it is still possible to sell a security (over the telephone, for example) and deliver it *along with* the prospectus. The net result is that an investor may never see the prospectus, which, aside from the registration statement (publicly on file in Washington, D.C.), is intended to be the basic disclosure document, until he has purchased the securities. Thus his reading the prospectus may do little more than inform him that he has, in effect, purchased a lawsuit.[34] Although the other civil and criminal liability provisions of the securities acts may give the purchaser a right to rescind the transaction or sue for damages,[35] it seems preferable that he not be put to the burden of litigating his rights but that he be adequately informed as to what he is buying before the sale is made. It is for this reason that the Commission has proposed a new rule which would, in effect, require the delivery of preliminary prospectuses a reasonable time (forty-eight hours) prior to the effective date to all persons to whom confirmations of sale are proposed to be sent.[36] Such a rule will give prospective purchasers an opportunity to revoke a purchase order prior to the effective date.

[33] This regulatory scheme is achieved through the interrelationship between the prohibitions of Section 5 of the Act and the definition of the term "prospectus" in Section 2 (10) of the Act to include "any prospectus, notice, circular, advertisement, letter, or communication, written or by radio or television, which offers any security for sale or confirms the sale of any security . . . [with certain specified exceptions]." Since Section 10 of the Act and its accompanying regulations specify the minimal contents for a prospectus, it follows that the sending of any writing which does not meet the statutory or regulatory requirements constitutes a violation of the Act.

[34] See 1 L. Loss, Securities Regulation 246–247 (1961). See also Cohen, "Truth in Securities" Revisited, 79 Harv. L. Rev. 1340, 1350–1351 (1966).

[35] See note 18 *supra*.

[36] See proposed SEC rule 460, which resulted from the Commission's Disclosure Policy Study, authorized by SEC Securities Act Release No. 4885 (1967), made publicly available in March of 1969 (hereinafter referred to as the Wheat Report, the study having been conducted under the supervision of former SEC Commissioner Francis M. Wheat).

9.4   PREPARING A REGISTRATION STATEMENT

The actual preparation of a registration statement is a complex and time-consuming matter, requiring both skill and considerable patience. At a very minimum the statutory and regulatory requirements must be closely read and adhered to. To assist in this there are several commercially available loose-leaf multi-volume securities laws reporters, which have a utility and importance analogous to the loose-leaf services used by tax consultants. In addition, the Commission has from time to time issued general guides for the preparation and filing of registration statements, the most recent of these being one published on December 9, 1968.[37] Copies of the various registration forms may readily be obtained not only from the Commission but also from the various commercial printing companies which specialize in this type of work. The forms, with explanatory comments, are also available in the various loose-leaf services.

Despite this wealth of material there is still a considerable body of unwritten learning, sometimes referred to as "filing cabinet law," which consists largely in various interpretive rulings of the Commission and various staff members on specific factual situations which may never have been made publicly available.[38] This is an unavoidable consequence of the interrelationship of an administrative agency with a highly skilled securities regulation "bar" of practitioners continually preoccupied with the business of public financing, thereby widening the gap between ill-informed and inexperienced counsel and those firms which specialize in securities work. Despite these disadvantages, however, there is no reason why a normally conscientious and competent attorney cannot guide his client through the somewhat arduous process of going public. In addition to the various published materials which have already been mentioned, there are numerous handbooks, treatises and guides[39] as well as sample forms on file with the

[37] See SEC Securities Act Release No. 4936 (1968), available from the Commission in pamphlet form. See also id. No. 4666 (1964).

[38] The Commission is reported to be giving active study to making information of this type available in published form or by request. Very recently the Commission announced that it would implement this disclosure program with respect to "no-action" requests received after December 1, 1970. See SEC Securities Act Release No. 5098 (1970).

[39] The definitive work in this area is L. Loss, Securities Regulation (2d ed. 1961), a three-volume work supplemented in 1969 by three additional volumes. For those who wish a less intensive but still thorough guide to the Securities Act of 1933 and its registration procedures, see H. Sowards, The Federal Securities Act (1965). For a somewhat older and yet valuable discussion see When Corporations Go Public (Israels and Duff eds. 1962). A very useful anthology of law review and other materials has been published by the American Bar Association, Selected Articles on Federal Securities Law (Wander and Grienenberger eds. 1968). See also R. Jennings and H. Marsh, Securities Regulation—Cases and Materials (2d ed. 1968).

offices of the Commission (both in Washington, D.C., and in the regional office libraries) which may serve as a guide in drafting documents such as prospectuses, registration statements, underwriting agreements, bond indentures and so forth. It is common knowledge that few lawyers start from scratch, as it were, when it comes to drafting. They almost always use one or more forms from prior situations either in their own practices or in the practices of friends or associates. The skillful use of such forms, the choice of those which are most appropriate to the situation at hand and the intelligent modification of language or "boilerplate" to accommodate the needs of the client are among the primary talents of the successful practitioner.

If there is doubt regarding the need to disclose a particular item of information or it is necessary to ascertain the interpretation of the Commission or its staff on some aspect of the statute or regulations, it is generally wise for counsel to take the matter up informally either by letter or telephone with an appropriate Commission staff member. The Commission has stated that it

> has a long established policy of holding its staff available for conferences with prospective registrants or their representatives in advance of filing a registration statement. These conferences may be held for the purpose of discussing generally the problems confronting a registrant in effecting registration or to resolve specific problems of an unusual nature which are sometimes presented by involved or complicated financial transactions.[40]

Thus, although there may be situations where a registrant or its counsel does not consider it wise to take the Commission into its confidence by a prefiling inquiry or conference, great difficulty can sometimes be avoided by candor and sensitivity to the reactions of the Commission staff members to the particular problem involved. Although it would be improper for the issuer's counsel not to be discreet in protecting his client's interests and naive to advise that he should always take the Commission into his confidence, it would be equally misleading to recommend that he always assume the role of an adversary dealing at arm's length with a potentially hostile administrative antagonist. In such a subtle balancing of the various factors involved resides much of the art of the truly skilled securities practitioner. At times counsel may find it prudent to submit a draft of a proposed registration statement to the Commission staff for a prefiling "review." In this regard perhaps it is best to refer again to the Commission's release which has already been quoted:

> Occasionally a registrant will request a pre-filing review of a registration statement, but such a review has been refused since it would delay the examination of material which has already been filed and would favor certain issuers at the expense of others. Registrants or their representatives also occasionally consult the staff to draft a paragraph or other statement which will comply with some requirement or request for disclosure. The

40 SEC Securities Act Release No. 4936, *supra* note 37.

staff cannot undertake to prepare material for filing but limits itself to stating the kind of disclosure required, leaving the actual drafting to the registrant and its representatives.[41]

Within the confines of a brief discussion such as this it is difficult, if not impossible, and it is certainly unwise to attempt to summarize the many things which must be disclosed in an issuer's registration statement and prospectus and the manner in which they should be disclosed in order to meet Commission requirements. As has already been mentioned, scrupulous attention must be paid to the statute, the regulations and the particular form which is applicable to the offering. Although the standard registration form is Form S-1, there are numerous other forms which may apply, such as Form S-2 (which applies to cash offerings of newly formed issuers which have not had substantial gross returns from the sale of products or services or any substantial net income from any source for five years); Form S-3 (offerings of mining companies in the promotional stage); Form S-7 (a short-form registration for issues of certain so-called seasoned securities); Form S-8 (securities offered to employees pursuant to certain benefit plans); Form S-9 (high-grade debt securities); Form S-10 (oil or gas interests or rights); Form S-11 (securities of certain real estate companies); Form S-13 (voting trust certificates); and Form S-14 (securities acquired in mergers and consolidations).[42]

At the risk of some superficiality it may yet be appropriate to indicate briefly some of the things which go into a typical registration statement. It is composed of two parts: a prospectus, bound into the registration statement and incorporated by reference into it, and other information which is not required to be in the prospectus. The information required by each item of the applicable form must be supplied and a cross-reference sheet must appear at the beginning of the registration statement to indicate those headings in the prospectus under which the information called for by each item in the form may be found. The whole document, consisting of the registration statement and prospectus, is printed in the proper form, number of copies and type style required by the Commission's rules,[43] with which financial printers who customarily perform this type of work are generally familiar. The front page of the registration statement, as well as the facing page of the prospectus, identifies the offering and sets forth in tabular form the offering price per share—and in the case of the registration statement, the amount being registered and the amount of the registration fee—along with the approximate date of the proposed sale to the public.

[41] Ibid.
[42] The list is merely representative and does not purport to be inclusive. The forms are frequently revised and reference to one or more of the loose-leaf services for the precise text of the form and its instructions is essential. For a discussion of the rules relating to Form S-14, applicable to mergers, asset sales, consolidations and other forms of corporate combinations, see text accompanying note 128 *infra*.
[43] SEC rules 401–404.

The prospectus, in red herring[44] or preliminary form, also contains spaces for inserting the offering price, underwriting discounts and proceeds to the issuer (or selling shareholders) as well as additional information relating to issuance of options, warrants or additional shares to underwriters, and an estimate of the expenses of selling the issue, such as legal, printing and accounting fees. Some of this information must be supplied in the pricing amendment filed immediately before the effective date.[45] Consistent with the philosophy of the securities acts that the primary purpose is one of disclosure and not one of preventing public sale of unsuitable investments, filing of these documents with the Commission is no guarantee either that the investments are sound or even that the statutory disclosure requirements have been met. Thus the Commission by rule[46] requires that the cover page of every prospectus bear the following statement in bold roman type:

THESE SECURITIES HAVE NOT BEEN APPROVED OR DISAP-PROVED BY THE SECURITIES AND EXCHANGE COMMISSION NOR HAS THE COMMISSION PASSED UPON THE ACCURACY OR ADEQUACY OF THIS PROSPECTUS. ANY REPRESENTA-TION TO THE CONTRARY IS A CRIMINAL OFFENSE

The preliminary prospectus also bears a legend, in red ink, required by rule:[47]

A registration statement relating to these securities has been filed with the Securities and Exchange Commission but has not yet become effective. These securities may not be sold nor may offers to buy be accepted prior to the time the registration statement becomes effective. This (communication) shall not constitute an offer to sell or the solicitation of an offer to buy nor shall there be any sale of these securities in any State in which such offer, solicitation or sale would be unlawful prior to registration or qualification under the securities laws of any such state.

Although it is possible to comply literally with the disclosure require-ments of the particular forms by supplying the information in a disorgan-ized, confusing and perhaps unreadable manner,[48] it is far better, not only in the interests of achieving prompt clearance of the materials from the Commission but also from the standpoint of the reaction of prospective investors, brokers, dealers and investment advisors, that the prospectus be clearly written—as easily understood as possible under the circumstances—and that it be in a format which is easy to follow. The Commission has stressed the avoidance of "prolix or technical expression and unnecessary detail." [49] Thus a prospectus should be readable and easily understood and

---

[44] See text accompanying note 30 *supra.*
[45] See id. note 28 *supra.*
[46] SEC rule 425.
[47] Id. rule 134(b)(1).
[48] See 1 L. Loss, Securities Regulation 261–265 (1961).
[49] See SEC Securities Act Release No. 4936, *supra* note 37. This problem was also discussed in the Wheat Report at 77–80. The Commission's rule 460(f) states

yet contain all of the material required by the statute and the regulations.

Occasionally an overly zealous issuer or its officers may exert considerable pressure upon those who are responsible for drafting the prospectus to give it the tone of a "selling document," describing the company, its officers and the earnings prospects in glowing terms. Although this is understandable not only because of pride or ego but also because of a natural willingness (one should not say "greed") to insure that the offering goes well, it should be discouraged in that a prospectus is not designed to be a *selling* document; it is, rather, designed to be a document of *disclosure*.[50] Although the corporate client, upon reading the first draft of the prospectus, is likely to remark "There's no life in this thing . . . How can we sell a stock with a prospectus like this?"[51] and even display a distressing lack of confidence in the ability of his counsel to appreciate what he considers to be the realities of the stock market, the attorney should as tactfully as possible stick to his guns. After all it is his fee which will be in jeopardy if something misfires and he may be personally liable to investors for negligence or misstatements, although, perhaps fortunately for the attorney, the precise extent of his liability to investors is thus far unclear.[52] However, since the liability of the corporation, its directors and officers is, to put it mildly, considerably clearer than that of the attorney, they would do well to listen to his advice when it comes to preparing the prospectus, registration statement and other accompanying materials, and restrain their natural enthusiasm to "sell" the stock, their company and themselves.

Another matter which is likely to be of some concern (one might almost say consternation) to the client is the Commission's practice of requiring a prospectus to set forth a so-called introductory statement immediately following the cover page which sets forth:

> a carefully organized series of short, concise paragraphs, under subcaptions where appropriate, summarizing the principal factors which make the offering one of high risk or speculative. These factors may be due to such matters as an absence of an operating history of the registrant, an absence of profitable operations in recent periods, an erratic financial history, the financial position of the registrant, or the nature of the business in which

---

that in passing upon requests for acceleration of the effective date of a registration statement "the Commission will consider whether there has been a bona fide effort to make the prospectus reasonably concise and readable, so as to facilitate an understanding of the information required or permitted to be contained in the prospectus."

[50] See Wheat and Blackstone, Guideposts for a First Public Offering, 15 Bus. Law. 560–562 (1960), reprinted in ABA, Selected Articles on Federal Securities Law 22–24 (Wander and Grienenberger eds. 1968).

[51] Ibid.

[52] See Escott v. Bar Chris Constr. Corp., 283 F. Supp. 643 (S.D.N.Y. 1968), and other authorities cited *supra* note 19. For a discussion of the attorney's liability, under Section 11 of the Securities Act of 1933, as a so-called expert, see Proceedings, ABA Natl. Inst., "The Bar Chris Case": Prospectus Liability, 24 Bus. Law. 636–637 (1969) (remarks of Milton V. Freeman, Esq.). See also 3 L. Loss, Securities Regulation 1740–1742 (1961).

the registrant is engaged or proposes to engage. In this connection see In the Matter of Universal Camera Corporation, 19 S.E.C. 648 (1945) and Doman Helicopter, Inc., 41 S.E.C. 431 (1963).

Where there is substantial disparity between the public offering price and the effective cash cost to officers, directors, promoters, and affiliated persons for shares acquired by them in a transaction which is currently significant, or which they have a right to acquire, there should be included a comparison of the public contribution under the proposed offering and the effective cash contribution of such persons. In such cases, and in other instances where the extent of the dilution makes it appropriate, the following shall be given: (a) the net tangible book value per share before and after the distribution; (b) the amount of the increase in such net tangible book value per share attributable to the cash payments made by purchasers of the shares being offered; and (c) the amount of the immediate dilution from the public offering price which will be absorbed by such purchasers.[53]

Such a disclosure of the extent of dilution inherent in the offering, as well as commissions and other arrangements made with underwriters, promoters and the like, is not only required under the federal law but may raise even greater difficulties under certain state securities or Blue Sky laws. Thus the rules of some state securities commissioners may limit the underwriting spread or discount, the amount of so-called cheap or discount stock sold to underwriters and others, and the extent of the dilution inherent in the offering.[54] This highlights the importance of keeping in mind, when setting the terms of the offering, not only the federal disclosure requirements but also the statutory or regulatory requirements of those states in which the securities are proposed to be offered. The disclosure requirement may be troublesome enough, but it may be even more troublesome if the securities cannot be offered at all in some state because they fail to qualify under local rules. In such a case, if the number of potential offerees is relatively modest, it may be preferable to eliminate that particular state from the list of those in which the securities will be sold rather than restructure the terms of the deal to meet specialized state requirements.

The federal or state disclosure requirements may sometimes require the issuer to notify the investor in bold-faced type on the cover page of the

[53] SEC Securities Act Release No. 4936, *supra* note 37.

[54] For a good summary of the various requirements imposed under local securities laws, see L. Loss and E. Cowett, Blue Sky Law 67–79 (1958). In some states the requirements are spelled out by statute or rule; in others they are merely applied informally as a species of "filing cabinet law." See text accompanying note 38 *supra*. In still others the statutes themselves are so vaguely worded as to give the Commissioner what amounts to *carte blanche* to make his own determination of whether the securities should be qualified for registration. See, e.g., Mo. Sec. Laws §409.306-(E) (1968) which gives the Commissioner the power to issue a stop order or suspend or revoke the effectiveness of any registration statement if he finds that "(i) the offering has worked or tended to work a fraud upon purchasers or would so operate; or (ii) any aspect of the offering is *substantially unfair, unjust, unequitable* or *oppressive,* or (iii) the enterprise or business of the issuer is based upon *unsound business principles* [emphasis supplied]."

prospectus that "These securities are being offered as a speculation." [55] Dismaying as this may seem to those who have in mind the selling potentialities of the prospectus, this language has been known to have a tempting effect on certain investor types, particularly in a so-called hot-issue market. Thus the requirement may cut both ways.

The overall emphasis of the prospectus should be upon disclosure of pertinent or material *facts* and should avoid an *evaluation* of those facts, particularly such areas as projections of earnings, "possible" mineral or oil reserves and glowing descriptions of processes which are still in the experimental stage or not even on the drawing board. In matters such as these not only must the Commission's rules themselves be kept in mind (i.e., what must, may or may not be disclosed) but also it is vital that the offerors be aware that, *regardless* of what the Commission's rules say, they may be exposed to civil liability to those who invest in reliance upon a representation which has been fraudulently or even negligently made. Although good faith reliance upon a rule of the Commission may be a defense in a civil case, [56] it is far better not to run the risk at all. All that is being said here is that those who sell securities should not assume that compliance with the Commission's rules, much less Commission "clearance" of the registration statement, is an infallible guarantee that they might not subsequently be held liable in a civil action or at least exposed to extensive litigation, which is both costly and time consuming. To put the matter differently, the emphasis should be upon *disclosure* to the investor of those *basic* facts [57] which are pertinent to a reasonably well-informed decision to purchase, and not upon an *evaluation* of those facts or their presentation in a manner which is calculated to induce him to purchase.

It has already been said that registration involves time (three to six

---

[55] See D. Herwitz, Business Planning 227, 236 (1966). (Offering Circulars of Kilbanon Corporation and Chomerics, Inc.)

[56] See Securities Exchange Act of 1934, §23(a).

[57] Cf. SEC v. Texas Gulf Sulphur Co., 401 F.2d 833, 864 (2d Cir. 1968) (*en banc*, two dissents), a leading case involving, among other things, possible corporate liability for an allegedly false or misleading press release in violation of SEC rule 10b–5. There the majority opinion stated that despite whatever uncertainties the company may have had about the extent of its exploration work "it would have obviously been better to have specifically described the known drilling progress as of April 10 by stating the *basic facts*. Such an explicit disclosure would have permitted the investing public to evaluate the 'prospect' of a mine at Timmins without having to read between the lines to understand that preliminary indications were favorable—in itself an understatement [emphasis supplied]." For a critique of the majority's assumption that disclosure of the "basic facts" is always wise or even possible, see the dissent of Judge Moore (concurred in by Judge Lumbard), 401 F.2d at 875 and 881. As the dissenters point out, the disclosure of basic facts in the form of a mass of technical data may be both meaningless and confusing to the average investor. It may, in fact, produce the opposite of disclosure, as indicated in discussing the problem of the unreadable prospectus. See text accompanying note 48 *supra*.

months or more),[58] extensive work (often at nighttime or other inconvenient hours), distraction of energies of company personnel from other tasks which they would normally be pursuing, profound risks of civil and possible criminal liability and always considerable expense. The latter item (expense) is particularly difficult to predict since it will necessarily vary with the character of the securities being sold, the nature of the company (e.g., whether it is a first offering by a highly promotional enterprise), the total amount being sold and the complexity of the transaction, including the preparation of complicated documents such as trust indentures, listing agreements and forms for qualifying the securities for sale in various states. Yet is still possible to make a rough estimate in a given situation. For example, in one hypothetical case involving a first offering of $1.5 million in stock, one commentator estimated the expenses of the offering (other than the

[58] Market conditions which result in large numbers of new offerings of securities greatly increase the work load of the Commission and, because of budgetary and other problems, the result is a substantial increase in the time between the date a registration statement is filed and the date it becomes effective. Although the Commission has adopted temporary procedures for processing registrations which to some extent reduce the burden on its staff, the processing time, particularly with new issues of unseasoned securities, is still likely to be a matter of many months. For a description of the temporary procedures for processing registration statements, see SEC Securities Act Release No. 4934 (1968), CCH Fed. Sec. L. Rep. ¶77,627 (1967–1969 transfer binder). Under these procedures a division officer makes a cursory review of the registration statement and classifies it into one of three categories: (1) The registration statement has been so poorly prepared or otherwise presents problems which are so serious that no further review will be made. Oral or written comments will not be issued, for to do so "would delay the review of other registration statements which do not appear to contain comparable disclosure problems." Counsel for the disappointed registrant will, however, be notified. (2) Counsel for the registrant shall be advised that the Commission staff has made only a "cursory review" of the registration statement; no oral or written comments will be provided; and "review by the staff, whether extensive as is customary or cursory as in this case, may not be relied upon in any degree to indicate that the registration is true, complete or accurate." The Commission requests, particularly with respect to companies which have not previously been subject to the registration process, that counsel furnish, as supplemental information, letters from the chief executive officer of the issuer, the auditors, and the managing underwriter. The letters must include representations that these persons are aware that the Commission staff has made only a cursory and not a customary review of the registration statement, which may not be relied upon in any degree to indicate that the registration statement is true, complete or accurate and the letter must also indicate that these various persons are aware of their statutory responsibilities under the Securities Act. (In this regard it is significant that the Commission's release expressly refers to Escott v. Bar Chris Constr. Corp. 283 F. Supp. 643 (S.D.N.Y. 1968).) And (3) the registration statement will be subject to the regular review process because it does not fall within either of the first two classifications. It is obvious that registration of a new issue, if it falls within the third category, can be expected to take an unusually long period of time and the client should be so informed by its counsel. The time schedule and other details of the offering can then be revised or prepared to take the delay into account. Regardless of the category into which the registration statement happens to fall, counsel should not file it without a careful reading of the above-mentioned release, which sets forth other matters which should be kept in mind when the filing is made. As has already been mentioned, careful adherence to the Commission's rules and forms is a *sine qua non* and in this regard the work of all concerned should be painstaking.

underwriting discount and omitting liability insurance, often a necessary item) at approximately $35,000.[59] In times of inflation such an estimate may be overly optimistic. If the work is done by one of the larger metropolitan firms, which may bill the time of partners at an hourly rate of $75 to $100 and the time of associates at hourly rates of $35 to $75, it is all too apparent that even the legal costs involved in a project which may continue for several months may be impressive and even staggering, particularly to an unsophisticated client. One solution to this problem is merely to increase the size of the offering—i.e., sell more stock or securities. This assumes that the offering is attractive and that the investors will pay the cost of the venture. Another alternative is to explore the possibility of raising the funds without registration. Thus we come to the matter of determining ways in which an offering may be made exempt.

9.5   EXEMPT SECURITIES AND TRANSACTIONS

The Securities Act of 1933 has two types of exemptions. The first deals with so-called exempt securities and the second with exempt transactions. Although these terms are descriptive, they can be misleading. As we shall see, several of the so-called securities exemptions (principally those in Subsections 3(a)(9)–3(a)(11) and Subsection 3(b) of the Act) are in reality transaction exemptions in that the exemption depends not on the type of securities being sold but upon the circumstances under which they are sold (i.e., on the transaction). Additional subtleties arise from the fact that the Commission has acted pursuant to its statutory power to define technical and trade names used in the Act[60] to provide for other exemptions, such as rule 133, dealing with mergers, asset sales, consolidations and the like.

Rather than become enmeshed in a prolonged discussion of all the possible exempt securities and transactions, it seems best to highlight a few of those which are likely to be of particular use in financing a closely held corporation.

(a)   OFFERINGS WHICH ARE NOT TO THE PUBLIC—PRIVATE
       PLACEMENTS

Section 4(2) of the Act exempts "transactions by an issuer not involving any public offering." This is a frequently used financing technique and has several significant advantages. Needless to say, it avoids the cost, burden and confusion often associated with a full-fledged registration. It tends to be

---

[59] See Wheat and Blackstone, Guideposts for a First Public Offering, 15 Bus. Law. 550–552 (1960), reprinted in ABA, Selected Articles on Federal Securities Law, 12–14 (Wander and Grienenberger eds. 1968).

[60] See Securities Act of 1933, §19(a).

relatively simple, since few purchasers are involved, and it may frequently be performed expeditiously, with none of the costly delay encountered with new issues filed with the Commission. Moreover, a factor which is often overlooked is that a private financing may enable the various parties to agree upon special terms which might not be acceptable if the financing were a public offering. In other words they may be able to get a tailor-made deal whereas if the securities were sold to the public the financing might have to conform to some more conventional mold. An additional advantage of private financing is that the issuer may employ what has come to be called "letter stock." This is generally stock sold to designated individuals or more commonly to institutional investors, such as insurance companies and mutual and pension funds, on the basis of an "investment letter." [61] The function of the latter is to document the purchaser's intention that he is purchasing for investment and not for resale. It also commonly provides that any resale by the purchaser of the securities shall be conditioned upon a receipt of a satisfactory opinion of counsel either to the effect that registration of the securities under the Securities Act of 1933 is not required for the resale or, if registration is required, then that the securities have been effectively registered. Such registration is customarily at the expense of the issuer on whose behalf they were first privately "placed" if pursuant to the terms of the private placement it entered into a covenant to bear subsequent registration costs on a resale of the securities. Alternatively the reseller of the securities may be given the right to have them registered in what has been called a "piggyback" registration—i.e., have the securities included along with others which the issuer intends to register in a registration statement filed as part of a separate financing.

The investment letter, which has at times been referred to by the Commission as a "self-serving" document,[62] amounts to a representation by the purchaser that he is purchasing the stock for his own account "for investment and with no present intention of distributing the same" and yet it is also made clear that "the disposition of your property shall at all times be within your control." Occasionally counsel for the issuer may insert a clause whereby the investor states that he has been given "unlimited access" to all the books and records of the corporation and that he has obtained or has had

---

[61] For a good description of the letter stock phenomenon, of relatively recent origin, see "Bargain" Securities—Issues of "Letter Stock," Not Readily Disposable, Increase but Draw Fire, Wall Street Journal (Midwest ed.), Nov. 18, 1969, at 1, col. 6. The seriousness of the problem was highlighted by an administrative proceeding against Mates Financial Services, Inc., which was subsequently settled. See CCH Fed. Sec. L. Rep. ¶77,721 (1969), and SEC Securities Act Release No. 8836, CCH Fed. Sec. L. Rep. ¶77,790 (1970). Also the Commission has issued guidelines for investment companies to follow in valuing letter stock held in portfolios. See Accounting Series Release No. 113, Investment Companies Act Release No. 5847 (1969), 4 CCH Fed. Sec. L. Rep. ¶72,135 (1969).

[62] See SEC Securities Act Release No. 4552 (1962), which should be consulted by anyone wishing to rely on the "private placement" exemption, for a comprehensive description of the Commission's views on the availability of the exemption.

access to all the information which is necessary for him to make an informed decision to purchase the shares.[63] Needless to say this "bootstrapping" technique cannot effectively be used to avoid the fundamental issue —namely, is the situation one in which a registration statement is required because the offeree does not have access to the type of information which would normally be provided in a registration statement? This is, in fact, the test used by the leading case dealing with the question of what is a public offering for the purposes of the Securities Act of 1933, *SEC v. Ralston Purina Co.*[64] There a corporation sold nearly $2 million of its stock to relatively large numbers of its employees over a period of several years. The number of employees who purchased varied with the particular year. Thus, in 1947 there were 243 employees who bought stock; in 1948 there were 20 employees who purchased; in 1949 the number of purchasers rose to 414; and in 1950 the number purchasing stock was 411. Although the company purported to make the offering available only to what it termed "key employees," its definition of that term was broad enough to include most, if not all, of its employees. Among the various purchasers of stock were employees having such duties as artist, bakeshop foreman, chow-loading foreman, clerical assistant, copyrighter, electrician, stock clerk, mill office clerk, order credit trainee, production trainee, stenographer and veterinarian, some of whom were in annual salary brackets as low as $2435. The issuer claimed that the offering was exempt because it was not open to the public and was confined to key employees. Both the District Court and the Court of Appeals upheld this contention, the latter emphasizing that the issuer was engaging in an "offering, without solicitation, of common stock to a selected group of key employees of the issuer, most of whom are already stockholders when the offering is made, with the sole purpose of enabling them to secure a proprietary interest in the company or to increase the interest already held by them." [65] In reversing both the District Court and the Circuit Court, the Supreme Court indicated that the test of what is or is not a "public offering" is essentially a factual one, based on a functional view of the purposes of the Act, namely, to provide disclosure to investors. Thus the number of purchasers or offerees is not necessarily determinative.[66] Although the number of offerees is not *irrelevant* (to the extent that numbers are relevant here, it is the number of *offerees*—not merely the number who

---

[63] See, e.g., Custer v. Channel Wing Corp., 247 F. Supp. 481 (D. Md. 1965), *aff'd*, 376 F.2d 675 (4th Cir. 1967), *cert. denied*, 389 U.S. 850 (1967).

[64] 346 U.S. 119 (1953).

[65] SEC v. Ralston Purina Co., 200 F.2d 85, 91 (8th Cir. 1952), *rev'd*, 346 U.S. 119 (1953).

[66] SEC v. Ralston Purina Co., 346 U.S. 119, 125 (1953), citing Nash v. Lynde [1929] A.C. 158, 169, wherein Viscount Sumner observed that "The word 'public' . . . is of course a general word. No particular numbers are prescribed. Anything from two to infinity may serve: perhaps even one, if he is intended to be the first of a series of subscribers, but makes further proceedings needless by himself subscribing the whole."

ultimately purchase the shares), one must also look to the character of the offerees—i.e., whether they need the protection that would be afforded by registration of the securities. To put the matter differently, the Supreme Court conceded that "some employee offerings may come within . . . [the nonpublic offering exemption], e.g., one made to executive personnel who because of their position have access to the same kind of information that the Act would make available in the form of a registration statement." [67]

From all of this one may conclude that the determination of what is a public offering is best resolved by looking to at least two things: first, the *number* of offerees and second, *who* the offerees are. Although the matter, as previously stated, may not be resolved exclusively in terms of numbers, the fewer the number of offerees the greater the likelihood that no public offering is involved. In securities practice it has been traditional to speak in terms of twenty-five offerees as an appropriate dividing line. This probably originated in an early opinion from the office of the Commission's General Counsel that "under ordinary circumstances" an offering to not more than approximately twenty-five persons "presumably" does not involve a public offering.[68] Although this general guideline continues to have some vitality in the investment community, it has become clear that it is no sense a "magic" number, since a test based exclusively on the number of offerees has been expressly repudiated by the Commission.[69] Moreover there have been some holdings that a public offering can be made to less than twenty-five persons and that an exemption might be available for offerings to a greater number of persons if they are so situated that they have access[70] to the kind of information which would be available in a registration statement. For example, an offering to thirty-five or forty large institutional investors who are not only relatively sophisticated and able to fend for themselves but are in a bargaining position with the issuer such that they can (and normally do) require substantial amounts of information as to the issuer's financial affairs as a prerequisite to purchasing the securities, is probably exempt as a "private placement" *if* all those who purchase the securities do so with the intent to hold them for investment and not for resale. Thus the "investment intent" of those who purchase becomes rele-

[67] SEC v. Ralston Purina Co., 346 U.S. 119, 125–126 (1953).

[68] Op. Gen. Counsel, SEC Securities Act Release No. 285 (1935).

[69] See SEC Securities Act Release No. 4552 (1962), *supra* note 62, wherein the Commission, after referring to the Supreme Court's *Ralston Purina* holding, 346 US. 119 (1953), stated that "It should be emphasized, therefore, that the number of persons to whom the offering is extended is relevant only to the question whether they have the requisite association with and knowledge of the issuer which make the exemption available."

[70] It is fairly obvious that the "access" test is not satisfied merely by the issuer's *volunteering* to give the requisite information to the offerees, or by the latter's agreement that they have been furnished with such information or have been given access to it, since to permit this would effectively subvert the requirement that an issuer which is not exempt must file a registration statement. See Custer v. Channel Wing Corp., 247 F. Supp. 481 (D. Md. 1965). For discussion of the various holdings see 1 L. Loss, Securities Regulation 656–665 (1961).

vant (one might well say crucial) to the availability of the exemption. If, for example, one of the thirty-five institutional investors purchased with intent to resell its allotment of securities to others, or even to place the securities in various discretionary accounts which it maintained for customers (as in the case of a brokerage firm), then we must look to the number of "actual" purchasers and the institutional investor or brokerage firm which did not have the requisite investment intent would be considered a mere conduit or intermediary.[71] If the number of persons to whom the securities were resold was relatively modest and the purchasers were themselves so situated that they would have access to the type of information that would be in a registration statement, then the private placement exemption might yet be available (as, for example, a resale by one institutional investor to five other institutional investors). However, in most circumstances a resale by one of those with whom securities have been privately placed is highly dangerous and may destroy the exemption not only as regards the issuer's sale to the institutional investor who "stepped out of line," as it were, in violating its commitment not to resell but also as regards the entire offering (i.e., that part of the offering which was made to the other institutional investors who purchased with the requisite investment intent). The consequences of all of this—i.e., the extent of the issuer's liability and the rights of other institutional purchasers who had no notice that one of their group did not have the requisite investment intent, are not at all clear from the cases or administrative rulings. Perhaps the best that can be said is that the issuer may be liable for violating the Act if it knew or had reason to know that one of the purchasers intended to resell the securities publicly.

Finally, to complicate an already confused picture, the Commission has indicated that an investor is permitted to resell securities if there has been an "unforeseen change of circumstances." This generally is taken to refer to a change not in the issuer's circumstances but in the circumstances of the holder of the securities or prospective reseller. The clearest case might be personal bankruptcy or some unforeseen situation arising in the affairs of the reseller that necessitate disposal of the securities in order to achieve liquidity. Short of that, it is unclear what amounts to a change of circumstances.[72] The only clarity in the Commission's position is that the change of circumstances must relate to the person who is doing the reselling and not to the affairs of the issuer. Thus a purchaser who resells because the issuer's operating results have not turned out as expected or because the price of the issuer's stock has not reached a hoped-for level, or for any other

---

[71] As a technical matter, the reselling investor would fall within the statutory definition of the term "underwriter" in Section 2(2) of the Act, since it would have "purchased from an issuer with a view to . . . the distribution of any security. . . ." If the offering were a public offering, the exemption in Section 4(1) of the Act of "transactions by any person other than an issuer, underwriter, or dealer" would not apply, since the reselling investor would technically be an "underwriter." If a registration statement were not filed, such an offering would therefore violate Section 5 of the Act.

[72] For a discussion see 1 L. Loss, id. at 671–672.

reason pertaining to the issuer's financial picture, does not qualify under the change of circumstances test.[73] It is ironic, however, that most purchasers, particularly institutional investors, even when they do in fact purchase for investment, almost always contemplate a later resale if, due to market conditions or changes in the issuer's financial affairs, things do not turn out as originally expected. Thus arose the shopworn adage that the investor should "cut his losses and ride with his gains." [74] The upshot of this is that if the Commission's interpretation of change of circumstances be strictly followed, then few if any investors would qualify. It is not surprising, then, that some practical stress has been placed on the *period* for which the securities have been held. Although here, as with the supposedly magic number of twenty-five offerees, it seems fairly clear, at least as far as the Commission is concerned, that the length of the holding period is not conclusive on the matter and is but a factor which should be determined in ascertaining the purchaser's initial investment intent,[75] a relatively early opinion of the Commission's General Counsel indicated that a "strong inference" of investment intent should be drawn from a holding of the securities for one year.[76] Beyond that, one authority has surmised that a holding of a year or more should create "something of an inference" of original investment intent and that a holding for two years or more should be "well-nigh conclusive" on the matter.[77]

Since these concepts of investment intent, change of circumstances, and public offering are so elusive, ambiguous and unreliable, most issuers who rely upon a private placement exemption are not even content with the customary investment letter supported by an opinion of counsel that registration is not required. It is better practice to put a stock transfer restriction on the securities themselves, with a legend indicating the nature of the restriction being stamped on each stock certificate, informing the holder that the securities have not been registered under the Securities Act of 1933 and may not be offered for sale in the absence of a registration statement or an opinion of counsel satisfactory to the issuer that such registration is not required.[78] Although there may be some doubt about the validity of such a restriction under the laws of some states which have traditionally

[73] See SEC Securities Act Release No. 4552 (1962), *supra* note 62. See also Crowell-Collier Publ. Co., SEC Securities Act Release No. 3825 (1957); Gilligan, Will & Co. v. SEC, 267 F.2d 461 (2d Cir. 1959), *cert. denied,* 361 U.S. 896 (1959).

[74] A marketplace maxim which might be as useful as the tongue-in-cheek advice that an investor should always strive to purchase at the lowest possible price and to sell at the highest price.

[75] See SEC Securities Act Release No. 4552 (1962), *supra* note 62.

[76] Op. Gen. Counsel, SEC Securities Act Release No. 1862 (1938).

[77] See 1 L. Loss, id. at 671–672.

[78] See Israels, Checklist re Use of "Stop Transfer Procedures," 18 Bus. Law. 97 (1962). For another good discussion of the problem by the same author see Israels, Some Commercial Overtones of Private Placement, 45 Va. L. Rev. 851, 861–868 (1959), reprinted in ABA, Selected Articles on Federal Securities Law, 135–142 (Wander and Grienenberger eds. 1968).

required restrictions to be "reasonable" and have generally prohibited "absolute" restraints on transfer even for a relatively limited period of time,[79] some of the more recent statutory revisions expressly provide for restraints of this type.[80] Even in the absence of such legislation it is probable that this form of restraint, functionally justified by a need to comply with the federal securities laws, would be reasonable as a matter of state law. Finally, to "backstop" the stock transfer restriction and further implement its enforceability, it is customary for the issuer to place what is known as a "transfer stop" on the transfer books, which indicates, in much the same language as the stock transfer restriction, that the transfer agent may not transfer the shares without an opinion of counsel either that the shares have been registered or that, under the circumstances of the proposed transfer, registration is not required.[81]

Fortunately some of the doubt in this area will be alleviated by the Commission's adoption of substantial reforms in its rules, which are largely an outgrowth of the recommendations of the Wheat Report already referred to.[82] Briefly, the rule revisions eliminate the troublesome problem of determining whether there has been investment intent or a change of circumstances. The effect of the revised rules is to permit certain issuers, known as "qualified" issuers, to place privately issues of their securities, and such securities may then be resold publicly[83] after the expiration of one year from

[79] See Ch. III, text accompanying note 16.
[80] See Ch. XI, text accompanying notes 87–102.
[81] See Israels, *supra.*
[82] See note 36 *supra.*
[83] The securities could be resold in any event under one or more of the statutory exemptions to registration, such as another private placement, an intrastate offering under Section 3(a)(11) of the Act or a Regulation A offering under Section 3(b), all of which are discussed later in this chapter. After the text of this discussion had been set in type the Commission proposed a further suggestion, namely proposed rule 144, SEC Securities Act Release No. 5087 (1970), which in many respects deviates from and is meant to supplant the various proposed rules discussed herein. Very generally speaking, the approach of proposed rule 144 would be to extend the holding period for privately placed securities to 18 months, instead of the one-year period applicable to privately placed securities of "qualified" issuers contemplated by the Commission's earlier proposals. In proposing the new rule, the Commission expressed its view that it felt the one-year holding period contemplated by the earlier proposal to be too short and would result in the sale of large amounts of unregistered securities to the public. In addition, it did not believe that it had the requisite staff available within the Commission to maintain and keep current an adequate list of "qualified" issuers, such as was contemplated by the earlier proposal. In the absence of such a list the burden would then be upon those who seek to take advantage of the procedures under proposed rule 144 to establish that adequate current information concerning the issuer is publicly available. If the issuer files reports under Sections 13 or 15(d) of the Securities Exchange Act, there would be a presumption that adequate current information is publicly available, but, in any case, the burden of showing this appears to be placed on the issuer. In view of the controversial character of proposed rule 144 and the likelihood that numerous objections and further suggestions will be submitted to the Commission by interested parties, it seems wise to retain the discussion which follows concerning the Commission's other proposals in its so-called "160 Series."

the date of purchase within certain limitations. These limitations are as follows:

(1) if the security is traded only otherwise than on a securities exchange, then the amount resold may (when added to all other sales of the same security by the same offeror within the preceding six months, excepting sales in nonpublic offerings) not exceed approximately 1 percent of the shares of such security outstanding at the time the broker receives the order to execute the transaction; or

(2) if the security is admitted to trading on a securities exchange, then the amount resold may (when added to all other sales of the same security by the same offeror within the preceding six months, excepting sales in nonpublic offerings) not exceed the lesser of

(i) 1 percent of the shares of such security outstanding at the time the broker receives the order to execute the transaction, or

(ii) the largest aggregate reported volume of trading on securities exchanges during any one week within the four calendar weeks preceding the receipt of the order.[84]

A qualified issuer is a company which is required to file periodic reports under Section 13 or Section 15(d) of the Securities Exchange Act of 1934.[85] The reasoning behind this specialized treatment for resale of securities of qualified issuers is that since they are already subject to the reporting requirements imposed by the Securities Exchange Act of 1934, the need for registration statement disclosure under the Securities Act of 1933 is not as acute as it is for other companies ("nonqualified" issuers) which are not subject to the periodic reporting requirements and whose financial affairs may to a large extent be unknown to the investing public. Such nonqualified issuers may still place their securities privately but such securities may not be publicly resold without the filing by the issuer of a registration statement (unless some other exemption of the Securities Act of 1933 is available, such as the exemption for "intrastate" offerings, discussed below). However, if the security is held for five consecutive years during each of which the issuer has had annual gross revenues from operations amounting

---

[84] See the Commission's proposed rule 162(a)(4) in SEC Securities Act Release No. 4997 (1969). In addition, the offering must be made through a broker who acts as agent for the offeror and who only executes the order to sell (in contrast to soliciting orders to buy), receives no more than a designated minimum commission, and makes no payment in connection with executing the transaction to any other person. See proposed rule 162(a)(3).

[85] See the Commission's proposed rule 163 in SEC Securities Act Release No. 4997 (1969). Generally such corporations will include (1) those having a security listed on a national securities exchange, or (2) corporations having assets in excess of $1 million and a class of equity security held of record by five hundred or more persons or (3) an issuer which has already filed a registration statement in a public offering of its securities pursuant to the Securities Act of 1933 and has undertaken to file periodic reports of its affairs under Section 15(d) of the Securities Exchange Act of 1934.

to at least $250,000, then the security no longer falls within the definition of a "restricted security," [86] and it may be publicly resold, unless a registration statement is required because the person on whose behalf the sale is made is in a "controlling" position with regard to the issuer (i.e., unless the distribution is a "secondary distribution").[87]

Although the revised rules do not eliminate the problem of determining what is a public offering and the general test of the *Ralston Purina* case, already discussed,[88] is still controlling, they do, as already indicated, clear up many of the problems which arise after it has been determined that securities have been privately sold, namely, when may the securities be resold or how long must they be held before resale. If the securities are those of a qualified issuer, then they may be resold publicly within the percentage limits already described, after the passage of one year from their purchase. If they are not securities of a qualified issuer, then they may not be publicly resold without the filing of a registration statement unless five years have elapsed from the date of their purchase and the issuer, during each of the five years, has met the $250,000 annual gross operating revenues test. Even then a public resale of the securities would require a registration statement if the person on whose behalf the resale is made is in control of the issuer.

The revised rules consist largely in a redefinition of the term "distribution" as used in Section 2(11) of the Securities Act so as to permit certain resales of securities without their amounting to a "distribution" and so be subject to the registration requirements.[89] A key definition in the new rules is that of a "restricted security," a term which has already been mentioned. This is defined as a security "acquired directly or indirectly from its issuer, or from an affiliate of its issuer, in a transaction or chain of transactions none of which was a public offering or other public disposition." [90]

Thus a restricted security is one which has been acquired by private placement. We have already seen the conditions under which such securities may be resold. Resale without meeting the conditions may subject those

[86] See the Commission's proposed rule 161. The concept of a restricted security corresponds generally to that of a security which has been sold in a private placement (i.e., sold as part of an offering which was not to the public). See text accompanying note 90 *infra*.

[87] See id. note 12 *supra*.

[88] See id. note 64 *supra*.

[89] The key to this in the proposed rules is rule 162 in SEC Securities Act Release No. 4997 (1969), which defines the term "distribution" as any public offering of a security with the exceptions which have been already discussed—i.e., an offering of a security by a qualified issuer through a broker who has complied with the restrictions applicable to permitted brokerage transactions (see note 84 *supra*) where the offering is within the maximum amounts permitted under subdivision (4) of rule 162(a) (see text accompanying note 84 *supra*), and where the security is restricted security if it has been held for at least one year. See text accompanying note 83 *supra* and proposed rule 162(c).

[90] See the Commission's proposed rule 161(a) in SEC Securities Act Release No. 4997 (1969).

involved in the resale, as well as the issuer, to the liabilities of the Act. Therefore the Commission has urged that the fact that a security is restricted be conspicuously indicated by a legend to that effect on the face of the stock certificate.[91] Use of such a legend, as well as a stop order on the books of the transfer agent, has already been discussed.[92] These will continue to be valuable policing devices and the Commission has indicated that it will "regard the presence or absence of such legend upon certificates or other instruments evidencing restricted securities as a significant indication of whether the circumstances surrounding an offering are consistent with exemption under Section 4(2) of the Act." [93]

(b) EXEMPTION FOR INTRASTATE OFFERINGS

Perhaps the most easily misunderstood and hazardous exemption is that pertaining to offerings of securities within a single state. In part this is due to the relatively narrow manner in which the exemption has been construed by the Commission. As far as the statute is concerned, the exemption applies to "Any security which is a part of an *issue offered and sold only* to persons *resident* within a single State or Territory, where the *issuer* of such security is a person *resident and doing business* within, or, *if a corporation, incorporated by and doing business within,* such State or Territory." [94] Proper use of the exemption requires that scrupulous attention be given to the statutory language, particularly the portions italicized in the above passage.

As the statute provides, the issue must be offered and sold only to residents of a single state or territory. The term "issue" is a word of art and refers to an entire issue in the sense of a plan of financing.[93] For example, a question may arise as to whether a prior offer or sale of securities pursuant to a private placement exemption is "integrated" with a subsequent offer of securities pursuant to the intrastate exemption. If the two offerings are, in fact, integrated so as to comprise a single plan of financing, then there can be no reliance upon the intrastate exemption unless *all* of the securities offered and sold pursuant to the private placement were offered and sold exclusively to residents of the same state as that to which the intrastate offering pertains. This is because a single offer (not merely a sale) to an out-of-state resident destroys the exemption for the *entire issue.*[96] It thus becomes crucial to determine whether two financings are in fact integrated with one another and here there is no easy test, the matter being essentially

[91] See SEC Securities Act Release No. 4997 (1969).
[92] See text accompanying notes 78–81 *supra.*
[93] See SEC Securities Act Release No. 4997 (1969).
[94] Securities Act of 1933, §3(a)(11) (emphasis supplied).
[95] For a comprehensive discussion of the issue concept see 1 L. Loss, Securities Regulation 591–595 (1961).
[96] See SEC Securities Act Release No. 4434 (1961). Professor Loss, id. at 593, indicates that the exemption is destroyed even though the offer to the out-of-state resident is made without using the mails or any facilities of interstate commerce.

one of fact. Among the factors to be considered are whether the two offerings are part of a single plan of financing, involve the same class of security, are made at or about the same time, are for the same type of consideration (e.g., cash or some other security) or are made for the same general purposes.[97] Two offerings are not necessarily integrated if they happen to share one or two of the foregoing characteristics, but the more factors they have in common the greater is the risk that there will be integration. For example, common stock could be sold to promoters upon the formation of a corporation on the basis of a private placement exemption and more common stock could be sold to the public several months later under an intrastate exemption if the two financings differed in other respects, such as the form of consideration (the promotors paying for their shares with property other than cash and the public paying cash) and the use of proceeds (the property received from the promotors being assets which are essential for the operation of the business and the cash received from the public being used to increase working capital). However, since the question of integration is one of fact and its proper resolution vitally affects the availability of the intrastate exemption for the entire issue, it is well to seek a ruling or at least an informal comment from the Commission in any situation where there is substantial doubt.

From what has been said it should be apparent that the entire issue must not only be sold but *offered exclusively* to residents of a single state. It is thus vital to the exemption that there be no *offer* to an out-of-state resident, even though he should not have ultimately purchased. The term "resident" means domicile and thus the residence requirement is not satisfied by temporary presence in the state, as with the stationing of military personnel at a particular post.[98] Needless to say, the place of business of the offeree is entirely irrelevant, unless he should be so unusual as to dwell where he works.

Equally important is that the entire issue be sold to residents of a single state. Although this requirement may seem fairly easy to comply with, it may become exceedingly elusive, as where a resident of the state in which the securities were issued purchases with the intent to resell to someone who resides without the state. If the purchase was for resale rather than for investment, then the immediate purchaser is viewed as merely a conduit or, technically speaking, an underwriter in the statutory sense,[99] in which case

[97] See SEC Securities Act Release No. 4434 (1961).

[98] Ibid. See also Owen, The Private Offering and Intrastate Exemptions Under the Securities Act of 1933, reprinted in ABA, Selected Articles on Federal Securities Law, 165, 174–175 (Wander and Grienenberger eds. 1968). For an argument that residence should not necessarily be equated with domicile, see 1 L. Loss, id. at 598–599. In the case of offerings of securities by controlling persons (i.e., secondary distributions), the offeror need not be a resident of the same state as the offerees provided that the issuer of the securities (i.e., the company itself) is incorporated within the state. SEC Securities Act Release No. 4434 (1961).

[99] See Securities Act of 1933, §2(11) for the definition of the term "underwriter." For further discussion see note 71 *supra*.

the sale is considered to have been made in substance to the out-of-state resident, disqualifying the exemption for the *entire* issue. It thus becomes vital for the issuer to assure itself of the investment intent of those to whom it sells. This can be done in several ways: First, the terms of the offering should clearly state that it is confined exclusively to residents of a particular state and that any offer or sale to nonresidents is unlawful. Secondly, the purchaser should be required to sign an affidavit of residence and affirm that he is purchasing the securities for investment and not for resale. Thirdly, resale of the securities may, if feasible, be subject to a restriction such as that employed in the private placement situation and this may be reinforced by placing a transfer "stop" on the books of the issuer.[100] In effect this gives the issuer control over any subsequent transfer to an out-of-state resident. Although, as we have seen, an intent to resell the securities one or two years later does not establish investment intent, since the intent must be "indefinite" in nature, a resale after that period of time will normally raise an inference that the initial purchase was with an intent to invest.[101] Therefore restrictions on resale or a stop on subsequent transfers need not be for an indefinite period of time. The crucial requirement is that all the securities "come to rest" within the state in which the offering was initially made.[102] Once this has happened, the restrictions may be lifted and there may even be active trading in the shares, although this would be somewhat unusual, since the number of purchasers in offerings relying upon this exemption is likely to be relatively small. Finally, it has been suggested [103] that the funds received from the intrastate offering should be placed in escrow along with the stock certificates until the offering has been completed, at which time the issuer should reconfirm that all the purchasers continue to reside solely within the state and that none of the securities have been resold in violation of the restriction. If the stock certificates are then issued with a legend giving proper notification of the restriction, as has already been suggested,[104] the likelihood of the shares being inadvertently or secretly resold to an unauthorized person is greatly diminished.

Assuming that the offer and sale of the shares is suitably confined to residents, there are further requirements which pertain to the issuer and its use of the proceeds of the offering. As the statute indicates, the issuer must be a resident or, if a corporation, incorporated within the state and doing business therein. The Commission has indicated that the "doing business" requirement is met only if the issuer is performing "substantial operational activities" in the state of incorporation and is not therefore satisfied merely

---

[100] For a discussion of such transfer restrictions see text accompanying notes 78–81 *supra*. A legend giving proper notice of the restriction should be placed on each stock certificate. See text accompanying notes 78 and 91 *supra*.

[101] See text accompanying note 76 *supra*.

[102] See SEC Securities Act Release No. 4434 (1961). See also Owen, *supra* at 173.

[103] See id. at 175.

[104] See note 100 *supra*.

by the performance of bookkeeping, stock record or similar clerical activi-ties.[105] The purchaser of the securities must obtain an interest in the is-suer's activities within the state. Thus an issuer selling undivided fractional oil and gas interests located in other states could not rely on the exemption even though it might conduct other business within the state where the offering is made, since the purchasers would acquire no interest in the is-suer's business within the state.[106] Furthermore, the proceeds of the offer-ing must be used primarily in connection with the issuer's business within the state. Where the proceeds are to be used to expand or diversify the issuer's out-of-state business, the exemption is not available.[107]

Finally it should be mentioned that the exemption, like most of the other exemptions, such as the exemption for "small offerings," now to be dis-cussed, only avoids the need for filing a registration statement and does not exempt the offeror from the antifraud provisions of Sections 12(2) and 17 of the Securities Act of 1933 and rule 10b-5 of the Securities Exchange Act of 1934, as well as of the criminal penalties which may be imposed for intentional violations of either Act.

(c) SMALL OFFERINGS UNDER REGULATION A

In view of the hazards of relying on the exemption for intrastate offer-ings, many issuers choose to take advantage of the exemption for "small offerings" of securities under Section 3(b) of the Act. Perhaps the most significant aspect of this exemption is that its availability depends entirely upon the rule-making power of the Commission. Thus the statute provides that

> The Commission may from time to time by its rules and regulations, and subject to such terms and conditions as may be prescribed therein, add any class of securities to the securities exempted as provided in this section, if it finds that the enforcement of this title with respect to such securities is not necessary in the public interest and for the protection of investors by reason of the small amount involved or the limited character of the public offering; but no issue of securities shall be exempted under this subsection where the aggregate amount at which such issue is offered to the public exceeds $300,000.[108]

[105] See SEC Securities Act Release No. 4434 (1961), and 1 L. Loss, Securities Regulation 601 (1961).

[106] Ibid.

[107] Ibid. See, e.g., SEC v. Truckee Showboat, Inc., 157 F. Supp. 824, 825 (S.D. Cal. 1957).

[108] Securities Act of 1933, §3(b). For discussion see 1 L. Loss, id. at 605; Demm-ler, Developments in Federal Regulation of Securities, 12 Bus. Law. 470, 477 (1957); Frank, The Processing of Small Issues of Securities Under Regulation A, [1962] Duke L.J. 507; Weiss, Regulation A Under the Securities Act of 1933—Highways and Byways, 8 N.Y.L.F. 1 (1962); Weiss, Highways and Byways Revisited, 15 N.Y.L.F. 218 (1969). The $300,000 limit will be increased to $500,000 by legisla-tion passed by the Congress and awaiting the President's signature. See Wall Street Journal (Midwest ed.), Dec. 8, 1970, cols. 3, 4.

From the foregoing it is clear that the Commission need not have provided for a small offerings exemption and may do so on its own terms. This highlights the importance of strict compliance with the Commission's regulations, and specifically with Regulation A, which deals with small offerings. If the regulation is not complied with, then the entire offering is subject to the formal registration requirements, unless protected by some other exemption, such as the one for intrastate offerings.[109] Although the following is a brief description of the main features of Regulation A, it should not serve as a substitute for a careful reading of the regulation by anyone seeking to rely thereon.

As suggested by the statute, the Commission has exempted offerings of securities if

> The aggregate offering price of all of the following securities of the issuer, its predecessors and all of its affiliates which were incorporated or organized, or became affiliates of the issuer, within the past two years, shall not exceed $300,000:
> (1) all securities of such persons presently being offered under . . . [Regulation A or] proposed to be so offered;
> (2) all securities of such persons previously sold pursuant to an offering under . . . [Regulation A] commenced within one year prior to the commencement of the proposed offering; and
> (3) all securities of such persons sold in violation of Section 5(a) of the Act within one year prior to the commencement of the proposed offering.[110]

The above-quoted passage then proceeds to specify that the aggregate offering price in secondary distributions (i.e., offerings by controlling persons) shall not exceed $100,000, except where the securities are being offered on behalf of the estate of a deceased person within two years after his death. Since the above-quoted passage limits the aggregate offering price of all securities of an issuer "presently being offered" under Regulation A to $300,000, whether or not offered by the issuer itself, the $300,000 limitation includes any secondary distributions currently being made under Regulation A or commenced within the preceding year. In other words, if a controlling shareholder were to offer $100,000 worth of securities in Jan-

---

[109] The Wheat Report, at 310, recommends that loss of the exemption for "technical" violations of Regulation A be prospective only. In other words, offerings prior to the technical violation would still be exempt, but Regulation A would not be available for subsequent offerings for a period of five years. See Wheat Report at 308–309, and rules 252(c)(2) and 261. As an example of such a technical violation, the report mentions an issuer's failure to file a report of the termination of the offering under rule 260.

[110] Rule 254. The reference to Section 5(a) of the Act in the third subdivision relates to securities which were sold in violation of the Act for failure to file a registration statement (i.e., securities sold in a public offering where none of the other exemptions from registration were available). Rule 251 defines the term "affiliate" as "a person controlling, controlled by or under common control with such issuer" and also specifies that an individual who controls the issuer is an affiliate. The term "predecessor" is also defined.

uary of any year, the issuer could offer only $200,000 worth of securities during the twelve-month period commencing with the date of the secondary distribution.[111]

Since the exemption turns upon whether $300,000 of securities have been offered in any one year, the determination of the amount of the offering is obviously crucial. Although rule 254 contains some guidelines on determining the offering price,[112] problems such as those discussed with respect to the private placement and intrastate offering exemptions may arise in the Regulation A area. Thus it may become important to determine whether a prior offering was of the same "issue" and should be integrated with the Regulation A offering. For example, a prior offering purportedly exempt as a private placement may in fact be integrated with a subsequent offering under Regulation A, in which case the two offerings may not in the aggregate exceed $300,000. The same is true with the intrastate exemption. Since, as we have seen, an offering of any part of the issue to an out-of-state resident destroys the intrastate exemption,[113] if the intrastate and Regulation A offerings are integrated with one another the two offerings may be exempt, if at all, only under Regulation A, and then only if the $300,000

[111] The twelve-month period need not be a calendar year. Note that more than $300,000 in securities may be actually *sold* under Regulation A within a twelve-month period since the rule refers to securities "sold pursuant to an offering . . . *commenced* within one year prior to the *commencement* of the proposed offering" (emphasis supplied). For example, an offering of $300,000 in securities could be commenced in January and terminated in December, with another offering being commenced in January of the following year. In such a situation more than $300,000 worth of securities might be sold during the period running from July of the preceding year to June in the year of the subsequent offering. See 1 L. Loss, id. at 613 n.221. The Wheat Report, at 301–304, recommends that certain secondary distributions, although restricted to the $100,000 limitation, should not diminish the issuer's ability to offer $300,000 worth of securities within the same year. However, the more liberal rule would not apply to offerings by holders of restricted securities of the issuer outstanding less than one year or individual holders of nonrestricted securities of the issuer who have been controlling persons for less than one year. Offerings by persons in these categories would not only be subject to the $100,000 limitation but would also reduce the $300,000 limitation applicable to offerings by the issuer in that particular year. For discussion of what is meant by the term "restricted" security, see text accompanying note 90 *supra*.

[112] The general rule is that the offering price is computed on the basis of the market value of the securities determined from transactions or quotations on a specified date within fifteen days prior to the date the notification covering the Regulation A offering is filed with the Commission, or the offering price to the public, whichever is higher. The aggregate gross proceeds received from the public cannot exceed the numerical maximum of $300,000 or $100,000, as the case may be. Rule 254(b). If the issuer's securities have no determinable market value and are offered in exchange for other securities, claims, property or services, the offering price is determined on the basis of the price of other securities of the same class if concurrently offered for cash, by bona fide sales of similar securities made within a reasonable time, or by the fair value of the consideration received for the securities (i.e., the property, services, etc.) as determined by some accepted standard. Rule 254(c).

[113] See text accompanying note 96 *supra*.

maximum is not exceeded.[114] The test for determining whether there is an integration of two or more issues is the same as that previously discussed.[115]

Another subtlety arises in determining the offering price where securities purchased under Regulation A are resold shortly thereafter. If the securities were not purchased for investment but for resale, then the investment intent concept previously discussed [116] may require that the offering price be that at which the securities were resold, because the person purchasing for resale is treated as merely a conduit or underwriter for the issuer. In other words, as with the private placement and intrastate exemptions, the situation must be viewed in terms of where the securities come to rest and, as far as Regulation A is concerned, it is the price paid by the ultimate purchaser which determines the offering price.[117]

Certain securities may not be offered and certain issuers may not make use of Regulation A. Fractional undivided interests in oil or gas rights or of any investment company registered under the Investment Company Act of 1940 cannot be sold under Regulation A.[118] And Regulation A is not available if the issuer, its predecessors or affiliates are subject to pending administrative proceedings, have been subject to a refusal order or stop order or have been convicted of certain criminal offenses, including postal fraud, involving the purchase or sale of securities within a period of five years prior to the proposed offering under Regulation A. Similar disqualifications exist if any of the issuer's directors, officers, principal security holders, promoters or underwriters (including any partner, director or officer of the underwriter) has been convicted of similar offenses, or is subject to similar judicial or administrative proceedings.[119]

Special provisions are applicable to offerings of so-called promotional issuers. These are defined as (1) issuers which were incorporated or organized within one year prior to the date of the filing of the form of notification for the Regulation A offering which have not had net income from operations or (2) issuers which were incorporated more than one year prior to such date which have not had a net income from operations for at least one of the last two fiscal years.[120] If the issuer falls within either category, no

---

[114] See 1 L. Loss, id. at 615–619.

[115] See text accompanying note 97 *supra.*

[116] See id. notes 71 and 99 *supra.*

[117] See Glavin and Purcell, Securities Offerings and Regulation A—Requirements and Risks, 13 Bus. Law. 303, 316 (1958).

[118] Rule 252(b).

[119] Rule 252(c)–(f). The Wheat Report, at 308–309, proposed that the rules on disqualification of the issuer be liberalized where the ground of disqualification is entirely due to actions of an underwriter, the issuer being entirely innocent.

[120] Rule 253(a). The Wheat Report, at 304–306, proposed that rule 253 be modified so as to apply only to the first category of promotional issuers (those which have been incorporated within one year prior to the offering and which have not had a net income from operations). The rule would thus apply only where the issuer has had less than one full year of continuous operations immediately prior to the filing of the notification.

secondary distribution of its securities may be made under Regulation A (i.e., only a distribution by the issuer itself, unless a registration statement is filed or there is some other exemption) and all offerings must be made by an offering circular. Furthermore, in computing the $300,000 limitation, securities issued to promoters and others, including directors, officers, underwriters, dealers, and security salesmen, or issued prior to the filing of the notification for assets or services, must be included unless an effective provision is made, generally by means of an escrow agreement, to assure that the securities will not be reoffered to the public within one year after the commencement of the Regulation A offering. In other words, if the securities issued to the promoters are suitably escrowed for the one-year period, they need not be included in computing the $300,000 maximum amount which may be offered under Regulation A.

As far as the filing requirements go, rules 255 and 256 of Regulation A provide for what is in effect a simplified or "short-form" version of the full-fledged registration. In lieu of a registration statement there is a simpler form, designated Form 1-A, financial statements of the issuer need not be certified and, instead of a prospectus, a simpler form of an offering circular is required, at least if the aggregate offering price exceeds $50,000 or if the issuer falls within the promotional category previously discussed.[121] The filing is with the regional office of the Commission instead of in Washington, as with registration statements, and the waiting period before sales can be made is only ten days, instead of twenty days if the offering is not under Regulation A. However, in contrast to an offering made under a registration statement, no offer (much less a sale) may be made during the waiting period. Thus underwriters may not make informal inquiries to seek out potential purchasers until the waiting period has elapsed. This makes Regulation A less attractive from the marketing standpoint. Furthermore, as we have seen in the case of registration statements, the waiting period is customarily extended due to amendments to cure defects pointed out in the Commission's letter of comment, and to provide pricing data if the latter is withheld until a date immediately prior to the actual offering.[122] The upshot of this is that a Regulation A offering will normally take considerably more than the ten-day period to process. This, together with the relatively high cost of preparing the materials, when compared with the modest amount of securities which may be sold under this exemption, may cause an issuer to reconsider the advisability of filing a registration statement, particularly if there is a reasonable possibility that its financial needs may exceed the $300,000 limitation or if Regulation A may have to be used again after twelve months have expired, resulting in duplication of effort.

As in full-fledged registrations, a form of tombstone advertisement is per-

---

[121] Rules 255–257. The Wheat Report, at 306–307, proposed that an offering circular should be required in all cases.
[122] See text accompanying note 28 *supra*.

mitted for Regulation A filings if it does no more than state from whom the offering circular may be obtained and identify the issuer, the security being offered, the offering price, the general type of business of the issuer and the general character and location of its property.[123] The offering circular must be revised if the offering is not completed within nine months (twelve months in the case of offerings under stock purchase, option or similar plans for employees),[124] and supplementary sales material must be filed also.[125] Finally, reports of sales of securities under Regulation A must be filed at the end of each six-month period following the date of the original offering circular and a final report of sales must be made upon completion or termination of the offering.[126] As previously indicated, failure to file such reports may lead to suspension of the exemption.[127] As with other exemptions from registration, offerings under Regulation A are still subject to the antifraud provisions, particularly Sections 12(2) and 17 of the Securities Act of 1933 and rule 10b-5 promulgated under the Securities Exchange Act of 1934.

9.6   MERGERS, ASSET SALES AND OTHER CORPORATE COMBINATIONS

In the preceding chapter we considered in some detail the corporate and tax aspects of various forms of corporate combination. It is now appropriate to consider the securities law aspects.

Prior to the revisions of the Commission's rule 133 which were recommended as a result of the Wheat Report, no registration of securities was required in connection with mergers, consolidations and sales of assets where the transaction was required by state or other applicable law to be submitted for approval by the shareholders and the vote of a required favorable majority would bind all shareholders except those who might be entitled to appraisal rights. The purported justification for this approach was the theory that since all shareholders were bound by the action taken at the shareholders' meeting, there was not a "sale" of securities in the ordinary sense of the term, the transaction being, in a sense, involuntary. Thus rule 133 came to be called the "no-sale rule." The rule was not only difficult to apply but had several exceptions, the primary one being to require registration of the securities if persons formerly in control of the acquired corporation disposed of more than a designated amount of securities in the open

---

[123] Rule 256(c). For a discussion of the tombstone advertisement see note 32 *supra.*

[124] Rule 256(e).

[125] Rule 258.

[126] Rule 260.

[127] See note 109 *supra.*

market.[128] Moreover, the underlying justification for the rule was open to doubt in that despite the compulsory effect of shareholder approval the solicitation of a shareholder's vote is similar to an offer of securities of the acquiring corporation and involves a volitional element since each shareholder is free to vote against the transaction. These and other anomalies, such as the fact that substantial blocks of stock could be disposed of by noncontrolling shareholders on the open market without registration, as well as the fact that exchange offers of securities (i.e., offers not submitted for formal shareholder approval) are subject to the registration requirements, led to the proposed revisions of rule 133. Under the revised rule, reclassifications, mergers, consolidations and asset sales are deemed to involve an offer of securities. However, in the case of asset sales this is so only if the plan or agreement of sale provides for dissolution of the selling corporation within one year after the shareholder vote authorizing the sale. To expedite registration of the securities of the acquiring corporation there is a simplified form of registration statement known as a "wrap around" registration (Form S-14), consisting of the proxy statement required to be filed by those companies subject to the Commission's proxy regulations, supplemented in certain respects. Filing of such a registration statement takes the place of the filing of proxy materials.[129]

Where the shares of the acquired corporation are held by relatively few individuals, the sale may amount to an offering which is not to the public, although the offer to them may result in a sale under the revised rules. In this respect proposed rule 181 provides that an offering to not more than twenty-five persons need not require registration.[130] The rule is not meant to be exclusive in that an offering to more than twenty-five persons may, under the facts of a particular situation, not be a public offering, applying the test of the *Ralston Purina* case previously discussed.[131] In applying the guideline and determining whether or not the offering is to more than twenty-five persons, proposed rule 181 provides that certain family members, such as an offeree's spouse, minor children and certain trusts, partnerships and corporations in which they have a substantial interest, are treated as a single offeree. Moreover the rule leaves open the possibility that an

---

[128] The formula setting the maximum amount which could be disposed of was similar to that set forth in the text accompanying note 84 *supra*. Among the most perplexing problems raised by the no-sale rule was whether it applied where, due to the concentration of share ownership in the hands of one or a few individuals, the shareholders' vote is little more than a formality. To put the matter differently, if a few people control the acquired corporation, then their consent is necessary to obtain the requisite shareholder majority and the transaction is, in that respect, a sale as to them, being voluntary in nature. For a discussion of the various positions taken by the Commission and its staff in the past on this matter, see Wheat Report at 262–266.

[129] See SEC Securities Act Release No. 5012 (1969), CCH Fed. Sec. L. Rep. ¶77,748.

[130] Ibid.

[131] See text accompanying note 64 *supra*.

offeree's resale of securities which were not acquired for investment may result in a public offering, in that the offeree who resells may be deemed an underwriter for the acquiring corporation in the statutory sense.[132] If the issuer of the securities (i.e., the acquiring corporation) is subject to the reporting requirements of the Securities Exchange Act of 1934, and is therefore on the Commission's list of qualified issuers promulgated pursuant to proposed rule 163, then proposed rule 162(c)(2) provides that restricted securities may be resold without registration if held for at least one year. The one-year period may be determined by "tacking" the period during which the person held the securities of the acquired corporation to the period during which he held the securities of the acquiring corporation received by him in the exchange,[133] but only if the acquired corporation had gross revenues of at least $250,000 during the immediately preceding twelve calendar months.

The revised rules also contain some relatively technical changes, such as a provision in revised rule 133 that the sending of a simple notice of the shareholders' meeting for the purpose of voting on the proposal of merger, asset sale, etc., is not an offer or sale of a security if a prospectus is given to the shareholders entitled to vote at least twenty days prior to the meeting. This is also true as to certain communications sent out in advance of a proxy statement, as permitted by rule 14a-12 under the Securities Exchange Act of 1934.

As a result of the amendments to the Commission's rules, registration of securities will generally be required for all corporate combinations, except those involving an offering which is not public, such as offerings to twenty-five or fewer persons, as previously discussed. This, along with the new legislation requiring disclosure in connection with cash tender offers and certain other acquisitions of shares,[134] will make more information available to investors so that they make an intelligent decision on whether to vote in

132 See SEC Securities Act Release No. 5012 (1969), CCH Fed. Sec. L. Rep. ¶77,748. See also text accompanying note 71 *supra.*

133 See the discussion of proposed rule 162, id. note 84 *supra.*

134 See 15 U.S.C.A. §§78 l, m, n (Supp. 1969), as amended by Pub. L. No. 90–439, 90th Cong., 2d Sess., 82 Stat. 454 (1968). Briefly this requires disclosure of specified items of information concerning the offeror, its plans regarding the offeree, its source of funds, its beneficial interest in the offeree and any contracts or other arrangements which the offeror may have with respect to the offeree's securities. Since disclosure is required only in connection with a tender offer for securities which are registered pursuant to Section 12 of the Securities Exchange Act of 1934 (i.e., securities listed on a national securities exchange or securities traded over-the-counter which have been issued by a company having total assets in excess of $1 million and which are held of record by 500 or more persons), the legislation does not apply to cash take-overs of closely held concerns. However, the antifraud provision of Section 14(e), added by the legislation, is not restricted to cash tender offers for registered shares and thus would apply to shares of closely held corporations, along with rule 10b–5. For a comprehensive discussion of the new legislation see A. Bromberg, Securities Law Fraud—SEC Rule 10b–5 §6.3 (1969). See also Hamilton, Some Reflections on Cash Tender Offer Legislation, 15 N.Y.L.F. 269 (1969).

favor of a proposed acquisition. This will be particularly meaningful in so-called hostile take-over attempts. Even in friendly take-overs more information is often beneficial to the shareholders in view of the gulf which sometimes develops between them and management.

9.7 STATE SECURITIES LAWS

Finally a brief word is necessary concerning state securities (Blue Sky) laws. Even though an offering might be exempt from registration under the federal securities laws, some form of registration may be required on the state level.

The general philosophy of many state securities laws tends to be more paternalistic than the disclosure philosophy of the federal securities laws. Mere disclosure is often not enough. Many states seek to determine whether investments fall below a minimum standard of quality. More specifically they regulate the terms of the offering, the amount of so-called cheap stock which may be sold to promoters and other insiders, the extent of dilution which may result from the sale of shares to the public at a higher price than that paid by promoters, and the amount of underwriter's compensation, including options, warrants and cheap stock. In addition, many states have fairly comprehensive schemes for regulating the distribution process, imposing license and bonding requirements for dealers and salesmen. Although some states used to merely prohibit fraud in connection with the offer or sale of securities, all states today have some form of securities registration or registration of dealers and salesmen or both. Many states have now adopted the Uniform Securities Act, promulgated in 1956 by the Commissioners on Uniform State Laws,[135] or at least have adopted many of its provisions. One of the outstanding features of the Uniform Act is a simplified procedure for registering securities by "coordination" if they are subject to the registration requirements of the federal securities laws.[136] Briefly this entails merely filing copies of the various documents which are required to be filed under the federal statute, such as the registration statement and prospectus, together with any amendments subsequently filed with the Commission. Unless the state securities administrator requires more information, this is generally sufficient and the registration becomes effective for state purposes on the same date that the federal registration statement becomes effective, unless the state securities administrator enters an order to the contrary. This greatly simplifies both filing and clearance. In those jurisdictions which have not yet adopted the Uniform Act, the filing requirements and application forms differ, complicating the problem of ob-

[135] See L. Loss and E. Cowett, Blue Sky Law (1950). Professor Loss and Mr. Cowett drafted the Uniform Securities Act.
[136] Uniform Securities Act §303.

taining the necessary clearance. Before the widespread adoption of the Uniform Act, "blue skying" an issue was a major undertaking, requiring several weeks of work by a skilled practitioner. If clearance was not obtained in a particular state by the time the federal registration statement became effective, the complications and difficulties were apt to multiply in that if one state refused to clear the issue, this might lead other states to take similar action in a domino-like fashion, entering the stop orders in situations where otherwise the issue might have been cleared with little difficulty. Although this continues to be so even with the adoption of the Uniform Act by many states, the simpler filing procedure makes the job of blue skying the issue less time-consuming and complex, and permits the practitioner to focus most of his attention on states whose laws are apt to present particular difficulties (such as California, Illinois and Ohio). Despite the simpler procedure, however, it is wise for the practitioner to arrange for each state securities administrator to send collect telegrams expressly authorizing the sale of the securities in his state on the date the registration statement becomes effective. Thus the issuer and underwriter may be protected against the possibility of some state's entering a stop order at the last moment.

Aside from registration by coordination, two other forms of registration, prevalent both in states which have adopted the Uniform Act and states which have not done so, are registration by qualification and registration by notification.[137] The former type of registration is by far the more comprehensive and is reserved for issues which are not "seasoned" and thus do not live up to certain investment standards. These are typically issues of newly formed or promotional enterprises, although many issuers which have been in business for a considerable period of time may not have the financial stability or earnings record to be entitled to registration by notification. Registration by notification tends to be simpler, requires less information and entails less risk that the issue will not be cleared for sale in a particular jurisdiction.

Many states have exemptions for offers or sales to small numbers of shareholders[138] or for what is termed an "isolated transaction." [139] Depending upon the interpretation given that term by state law or regulation, this may consist in a sale to a single individual or a relatively small number of persons. Further grounds for exemption may be the fact that a security is listed on one or more of the national securities exchanges or appears in one of the standard securities manuals, such as Moody's or Standard and

---

[137] Id. §§302, 304.

[138] Id. §402(b)(9).

[139] Id. §402(b)(1) (exemption for isolated non-issuer transactions). For a detailed discussion of various statutory patterns and interpretations of exemptions for isolated or small offerings, see L. Loss and E. Cowett, id. at 369–374. As the authors point out, this exemption is generally available only if the purchasers acquire the securities for investment and not for resale.

Poor's.[140] Also certain types of securities are commonly exempted, such as national or state bank securities, securities of federal or state building and loan associations, insurance company securities, and securities of credit unions, railroads and other common carriers, public utilities, charitable organizations, commercial paper and certain employee benefit plans.[141]

Violation of a state securities law may result in civil liability to the purchaser of the security[142] and various criminal or administrative penalties, including injunctions, fines or prison terms.[143] As with the federal securities law, if there is any doubt concerning the interpretation of a particular provision in the statute or regulations, it is wise to take the matter up informally with the state securities administrator. Otherwise an issuer runs the risk of having the administrator enter a stop order or bring a criminal or injunctive proceeding wherein the proper interpretation of the law is determined at considerable expense. The resulting delay may for all practical purposes make issuance of the securities unfeasible at least in that particular jurisdiction.

[140] Uniform Securities Act §§402(a)(8), 402(b)(2).
[141] Id. §402(a).
[142] Id. §410.
[143] Id. §§408, 409.

X Fringe Benefits for Employees of Closely Held Corporations

As we saw in Chapter I, one of the advantages of doing business in the corporate form is the greater flexibility and variety of fringe benefits available for corporate employees.[1] Among the principal fringe benefits are pension, profit-sharing and stock bonus plans, stock option and employee stock purchase plans, "restricted" stock and so-called phantom stock option plans, group life insurance, the $5000 death benefit exclusion, accident and health plans, salary continuation plans and deferred compensation arrangements of various types (funded and unfunded). In this chapter we shall consider these in some detail, although comprehensive treatment must necessarily be left to treatises and other intensive studies of this complicated subject.[2]

10.1 QUALIFIED PENSION PLANS

The advantages of "qualified" pension, profit-sharing and stock bonus plans have already been discussed and contrasted with similar but less favorable plans for self-employed individuals, such as members of a partnership.[3] As already indicated, deductions for contributions to pension plans for the self-employed are limited to the lesser of 10 percent of an individual's earned income from trade or business or $2500, there is no capital gain treatment for lump sum distributions and the latter are subject to a five-year

[1] See Ch. I, text accompanying note 25.
[2] For good discussions of this area see T. Ness and E. Vogel, Taxation of the Closely Held Corporation §§8.11–8.56 and 9.11–9.28 (1967); G. Washington and V. Rothschild, Compensating the Corporate Executive (3d ed. 1962). In addition the Bureau of National Affairs has several helpful portfolios in its Tax Management series.
[3] See Ch. I, text accompanying note 25. Although an election under Subchapter S of the Code does not disqualify a corporation from eligibility for a qualified pension plan (see Rev. Rul. 66–218, 1966–2 Cum. Bull. 120) under Section 1379(b) of the Code, added by the Tax Reform Act of 1969, a shareholder-employee of such a corporation must include in his income the contributions made by the corporation on his behalf which exceed 10 percent of his salary, or $2500, whichever is less, the limitation imposed on contributions to plans of self-employed persons.

averaging formula, in contrast to qualified pension plans for corporate employees, where the formula for computing deductions permits higher contributions and where, prior to the 1969 tax reforms, lump sum distributions from the employees' trust received capital gain treatment.[4] For these and other reasons, including the additional fringe benefits which have already been mentioned, various professional persons have been led to incorporate under professional corporation laws enacted in nearly all states. These expressly permit attorneys, physicians and some other professional persons to do business in the corporate form, subject to restrictions as to share ownership, qualifications of directors and officers, rendering of professional services, liabilities arising from relationships with clients or patients and confidentiality of communications. Although the subject will be considered in greater detail at a later point in this chapter,[5] it may suffice to say that despite the widespread enactment of these professional corporation laws the Treasury Department has until very recently steadfastly resisted attempts to equate such professional organizations with corporations of the more conventional variety and has challenged the right of professional corporations to adopt qualified pension plans and related employee benefit schemes. This in turn has led to confusion and uncertainty, although professional corporations continue to have considerable popularity.

Pension and profit-sharing plans serve different needs and are subject to different requirements, although the general rules for qualification of these and of stock bonus plans are set forth together in Section 401 of the Code. Before discussing the requirements for qualifying such plans, it may be well to mention some of the major differences between them. Pension plans assume that a specified benefit will accrue to the employee upon his retirement or the occurrence of a contingency such as his death. The benefit is thus predetermined—the employer's contribution is computed on the basis

---

[4] The Tax Reform Act of 1969 amended Section 402(a) of the Code so as to restrict capital gain treatment for lump sum distributions to benefits accrued by the employee prior to January 1, 1970, and benefits accruing thereafter which do not consist of the employee's allocable share of contributions by the employer to the trust. See Int. Rev. Code of 1954, §402(a)(5). These lump sum distributions allocable to employer contributions during 1970 and thereafter are treated as ordinary income, except that they are eligible for taxation under a special seven-year "forward" averaging formula. See id. §72(n)(4).

Amounts which are unpaid at the death of the employee, to the extent attributable to employer contributions, unless payable to the employee's estate, are exempt from estate tax under Section 2039(c) of the Code. An irrevocable election of survivorship benefits is exempt from the gift tax under Section 2517(a). Also a lump sum distribution qualifies for the $5000 death benefit exclusion under Section 101(b) of the Code. All of these benefits are in addition to the principal ones already discussed: deductibility of contributions to the employer, nontaxability of the employee at the time the contributions are made, nontaxability of the employee's trust, permitting income of the trust to accumulate and to be reinvested free of tax, and postponement of the tax impact on the employee until the distribution is received, at which time he is likely to be in a lower tax bracket. See Ch. I, text accompanying note 25.

[5] See text accompanying note 140 *infra*.

of the benefit and therefore tends to be relatively predictable. In sharp contrast, a profit-sharing plan provides for a benefit which is not predictable, since it depends upon the employer's contributions, which in turn depend upon corporate earnings. Pension plans provide security and permit the employee to plan his retirement program with the expectation of receiving a fixed amount. Profit-sharing plans serve as an incentive to increase corporate profits, permit employees to participate in higher earnings and yet postpone their receipt until the date of retirement. Although they play an important part in a retirement program, they do not afford the stability or certainty of a pension plan. On the other hand, they may result in significant monetary benefits since the higher the corporate profits, the greater the benefit under a profit-sharing plan. This is also true with a stock bonus plan, except that the benefit is geared to the value of shares which in turn may depend, at least in part, upon corporate profits.

Another important distinction between pension plans and profit-sharing plans relates to the vesting of benefits and whether or not past service may be taken into account when the plan is established. With pension plans, vesting of benefits may be postponed until retirement. Although this gives the employee less security, it may encourage him to stay with the employer, for if he leaves he will forfeit any benefits which have not vested. Profit-sharing plans are subject to stricter vesting requirements and in this respect are less desirable from the employer's standpoint. However, since contributions to the plan depend upon corporate profits, the cost of running the plan is not a fixed charge and is less burdensome to the employer when profits are low. From the employee's standpoint, the profit-sharing plan may constitute a "hedge" against inflation, assuming that corporate profits rise with the diminishing value of the dollar. An employee's past service may be taken into account in establishing a pension plan, in contrast to a profit-sharing plan, where past service may not, except to a limited extent, be taken into account. This may be a decided advantage to relatively elderly employees with many years of service who might otherwise receive only minimal advantages from a plan which is put into effect only a few years before they retire.

The rules relating to qualification of pension, profit-sharing and stock bonus plans are complex. For that reason it is wise to obtain advance clearance from the Internal Revenue Service before the plan is put into effect to assure that the plan meets all the requirements.[6] The plan may either employ a trust or be fully funded through an annuity or insurance contract. The rules on qualification of the plan are much the same in either case.[7] In

---

[6] See Rev. Proc. 69–4, 1969–1 Cum. Bull. 391. Helpful guides are a comprehensive revenue ruling, Rev. Rul. 69–421, 1969–2 Cum. Bull. 59, and various speeches of Isidore Goodman, Chief of the Internal Revenue Service Pension Trust Branch, reprinted in the pension and profit-sharing services of Prentice-Hall and Commerce Clearing House.

[7] See Int. Rev. Code of 1954, §§401, 404(a)(2).

any event the plan must be embodied in a definite written program which is communicated to the employees.[8]

The keynote of the qualification rules is set by two basic requirements, namely, that the terms of the plan must be such that

> it is impossible, at any time prior to the satisfaction of all liabilities with respect to employees and their beneficiaries under the trust, for any part of the corpus or income to be . . . used for, or diverted to, purposes other than for the exclusive benefit of . . . employees or their beneficiaries;[9]

and that the plan must not discriminate in favor of a particular category of personnel as regards its coverage, the manner of computing employer contributions and the way in which benefits payable under the plan are determined.[10]

The prohibition against diversion of the trust assets or income to nonemployee uses is best complied with by a provision in the trust instrument which repeats the statutory language verbatim. There is no absolute prohibition against any part of the trust assets reverting to the employer; rather, the prohibition is against such reversion "at any time prior to the satisfaction of all liabilities with respect to employees and their beneficiaries." Hence an employer may be entitled to a refund of amounts erroneously contributed to a pension trust due to an improper actuarial computation.[11] Care must also be taken as to how the trust assets are invested. Thus the Code prohibits certain transactions. A trust will not be exempt if, in dealings with the creator of the trust (i.e., the employer), it

> (1) lends any part of its income or corpus, without the receipt of adequate security, and a reasonable rate of interest . . .
> (2) pays any compensation, in excess of a reasonable allowance for salaries or other compensation for personal services actually rendered . . .
> (3) makes any part of its services available on a preferential basis . . .
> (4) makes any substantial purchase of securities or any other property, for more than adequate consideration in money or money's worth . . .
> (5) sells any substantial part of its securities or other property, for less than an adequate consideration in money or money's worth . . .
> (6) engages in any other transaction which results in a substantial diversion of its income or corpus. . . .[12]

As far as investments are concerned, the Internal Revenue Service has ruled that the investments must be "consistent with the purpose of the exclusive benefit of the employees," their cost may not exceed fair market value at the time of purchase, they must yield a fair return commensurate with the prevailing rate, they must have sufficient liquidity in order to permit distributions in accordance with the plan, and the investment policy

---

[8] Treas. Reg. §1.401–1(a)(2).
[9] Int. Rev. Code of 1954, §401(a)(2).
[10] Id. §401(a)(4).
[11] See Rev. Rul. 69–421, Part 3(d), *supra* note 6.
[12] Int. Rev. Code of 1954, §501(c).

must provide for safeguards and diversity such as those which would be demanded by a prudent investor.[13] Although this does not mean that a trust may not invest in securities issued by the employer, extreme care must be taken that the securities are purchased at and may be resold for a fair price and that their yield is reasonable. Further difficulties may arise in connection with shares in closely held corporations which may have no ready market other than the corporation, which may be subject to stock transfer restrictions and which may have a relatively low yield because of the shareholders' desire to plow back corporate earnings rather than have them distributed as dividends and taxed at ordinary income rates. In addition, the setting of an excessive valuation on the securities when they are sold to the pension trust may not only disqualify the trust but could create substantial problems with the gift or estate tax imposed on shareholders who may die or wish to give stock to relatives and others.[14]

Nondiscrimination in coverage of the plan is insured by two alternative tests set forth in Section 401 of the Code. The first is a formula test and the second, a more flexible one, depends upon whether a particular plan is "found by the Secretary or his delegate not to be discriminatory in favor of employees who are officers, shareholders, persons whose principal duties consist in supervising the work of other employees, or highly compensated employees;" [15] The formula test[16] sets up certain percentage requirements as to minimum coverage and eligibility of employees. A plan will qualify if it benefits 70 percent or more of all the employees (excluding employees in certain classifications mentioned below). If the plan does not benefit 70 percent of all employees, then it may still qualify if at least 70 percent of all employees (with the same exclusions) are *eligible* to benefit under the plan and, of those who are eligible to benefit, at least 80 percent of the eligible persons do in fact benefit under the plan. In practical effect this means that

[13] See Rev. Rul. 69–421, Part 2(k)(1), *supra* note 6. This provides that any investments in shares or securities of the employer or related or controlled entities must be reported to the District Director on Form 990–P, in order that the propriety of such investments can be determined. See also Rev. Rul. 69–494, 1969–2 Cum. Bull. 88.

[14] For a discussion of this problem see 2 G. Washington and V. Rothschild, Compensating the Corporate Executive 683–686 (3d ed. 1962). Normally the corporation will not realize gain on transferring shares to the trust. Int. Rev. Code of 1954, §1032. See 2 G. Washington and V. Rothschild, id. at 686. Also, as the authors point out, funding the plan through contributions of stock has significant advantages from the employer's standpoint in that little or no cash outlay is required. Id. at 685. On the other hand, the shareholders' equity is diluted if new shares are issued. The purchase of shares in the open market to contribute to the trust will, of course, involve cash expenditures, although this may result in an indirect benefit to the shareholders insofar as the purchasing supports the market price. The corporate purchaser must beware that its purchases do not have a manipulative effect on prices in violation of Sections 9 and 10 of the Securities Exchange Act of 1934. For discussion see A. Bromberg, Securities Law Fraud—SEC Rule 10b–5, §7.3(3) (1968); W. Painter, Federal Regulation of Insider Trading 326–328 (1968).

[15] Int. Rev. Code of 1954, §401(a)(3)(B).

[16] Id. §401(a)(3)(A).

the plan must in fact benefit at least 56 percent of all employees (i.e., 80 percent of 70 percent). Employees who may be excluded in determining whether the mathematical formula has been met are (1) those who have been employed not more than a minimum period prescribed by the plan, not exceeding five years, (2) employees whose customary employment is for not more than twenty hours in any one week, and (3) employees whose customary employment is for not more than five months in any calendar year. Despite the fact that such employees may be excluded and only 56 percent of the remaining employees must benefit under the plan, some corporations, particularly large ones, find that because of cost and other considerations it is unfeasible to adopt a plan broad enough to meet the formula test. Thus the plan must be submitted to the Internal Revenue Service for a determination as to whether it may still be found nondiscriminatory under the broader test, which essentially depends on the facts of each particular case. Here again the Code contains some provisions which are of some help:

> A classification shall not be considered discriminatory . . . merely because it excludes employees the whole of whose remuneration constitutes "wages" under section 3121(a)(1) (relating to the Federal Insurance Contributions Act) or merely because it is limited to salaried or clerical employees. Neither shall a plan be considered discriminatory . . . merely because the contributions or benefits of or on behalf of the employees under the plan bear a uniform relationship to the total compensation, or the basic or regular rate of compensation, of such employees, or merely because the contributions or benefits based on that part of an employee's remuneration which is excluded from "wages" by section 3121(a)(1) differ from the contributions or benefits based on employee's remuneration not so excluded, or differ because of any retirement benefits created under State or Federal law.[17]

This provision means that a plan is not discriminatory "merely" because it is limited to salaried or clerical employees or "merely" because it excludes employees whose total remuneration does not exceed the base earnings used for determining the social security tax. It then goes on to provide similar rules relating to contributions or benefits and permits these to bear a uniform relationship to total compensation (in effect allowing higher contributions and benefits to those who receive greater remuneration) and permits the plan to provide lower benefits (and thus require lower contributions) as to that part of an individual's earnings which does not exceed the base remuneration for social security tax purposes. In other words, a plan may be integrated with retirement benefits payable under social security, providing for reduced benefits because of other benefits payable under that program or a retirement program created under state law. Many employers take advantage of this provision because it substantially reduces the cost of funding the retirement plan.

[17] Id. §401(a)(5).

As has been said, Section 401(a)(5) of the Code provides that a plan is not discriminatory merely because it is confined to salaried or clerical employees. This language, on its surface, appears to legitimize all plans which are limited to salaried or clerical help, and yet it is apparent, especially with relatively small companies where few individuals may fall within this category, that a plan may be discriminatory because of the particular factual situation. Consider, for example, a company having only two or three salaried and clerical employees, with approximately seventeen other employees excluded from the plan because they fall within the hourly paid category. Such a plan would no doubt be discriminatory in its effect, particularly if those employees who were included in the plan were officers, shareholders, highly compensated employees or persons whose principal duties consisted in supervising the work of others.[18] Contrast this with a somewhat larger company, having one hundred and nine employees, eighty-three of whom are excluded from the plan because of being hourly paid persons; of the twenty-six remaining employees covered by the plan, only eleven are officers, shareholders, highly compensated persons or supervisory personnel. Since those included in the plan present a fair "cross section" of various types of salaried and clerical personnel and the balance is not weighted too heavily in favor of officers, etc., the plan would not be discriminatory.[19] This highlights the fact that a plan must be considered as to its total effect. Although it may not, on its face, appear discriminatory, it may work out that way in practice and effect a type of *de facto* discrimination. Thus, consider a plan which, although purportedly covering all employees regardless of length of service, in fact restricts benefits to persons with fifteen years of service who remain with the company until sixty-five years of age. If most of the company's employees are migratory or transient in character, the plan would, in its operation, have a discriminatory effect.[20]

A plan may be funded exclusively by employer contributions or it may be partially funded by contributions from employees. As regards the latter, the plan will qualify if the contribution required from employees is kept within "reasonable bounds," i.e., no more than 6 percent of the employee's compensation. If the employee is not *required* to contribute in order to receive benefits, the reasonableness test is satisfied if his contributions do not exceed 10 percent of his compensation.[21]

As already mentioned, the employer's contributions to the plan are deductible to it and are not taxable to the employee, whether or not his rights in the plan are vested, provided that the contributions meet the general test prescribed by Section 162 of the Code—that they, along with the employ-

[18] See Rev. Rul. 66–13, 1966–1 Cum. Bull. 73. See also Commissioner v. Pepsi-Cola Niagara Bottling Corp., 399 F.2d 390 (2d Cir. 1968); Ed and Jim Fleitz, Inc., 50 T.C. 384 (1968).

[19] See Rev. Rul. 66–12, 1966–1 Cum. Bull. 72.

[20] See Rev. Rul. 69–421, Part 4(i), *supra* note 6.

[21] Id. at Part 4(g).

ee's other compensation, are reasonable in relation to the value of his services and qualify as ordinary and necessary business expenses—and also that they do not exceed the following limits set forth in Section 404(a)(1) of the Code:

(A) an amount not in excess of 5 percent of the compensation otherwise paid or accrued during the taxable year to all employees under the trust . . . plus

(B) any excess over the . . . [foregoing amount] necessary to provide with respect to all of the employees under the trust the remaining unfunded cost of their past and current service credits distributed as a level amount, or a level percentage of compensation, over the remaining future service of each such employee . . . , or

(C) in lieu of . . . [the amounts in (A) and (B) above], an amount equal to the normal cost of the plan, as determined under regulations prescribed by the Secretary or his delegate, plus, if past service or other supplementary pension or annuity credits are provided by the plan, an amount not in excess of 10 percent of the cost which would be required to completely fund or purchase such pension or annuity credits as of the date when they are included in the plan. . . .

Employer contributions which exceed the deductible limits may be carried forward and deducted in subsequent years to the extent that they, along with other contributions subsequently made, qualify for deduction.[22] As previously indicated, the contributions and benefits provided under the plan may not discriminate in favor of employees who are officers, shareholders, supervisory personnel or highly compensated employees.[23]

As far as benefits are concerned, these must be definitely determinable. If any benefits are forfeited by employees who leave their employment when their rights are not vested, the benefits payable to other employees who remain in the plan cannot be increased; rather the forfeiture causes a reduction in the employer contributions.[24] Benefits may be based on an employee's compensation over a period prior to his retirement and may also take into account his length of service. In order to prevent discrimination in favor of highly paid employees who may receive substantial salary increases during their final years of service, the Internal Revenue Service requires that where benefits are determinable on the basis of a pay period, the period must consist of at least five years.[25] These need not, however, be the five years immediately prior to retirement. For example, the plan could provide that the benefits would be determined on the basis of the five highest paid consecutive years out of the ten years immediately prior to the employee's retirement.

The method of distribution may be in the form of a lump sum, an annuity of some type or a payment of a certain amount over a set period of years.

---

[22] Int. Rev. Code of 1954, §404(a)(1)(D).
[23] Id. §401(a)(4).
[24] Id. §401(a)(8).
[25] See Rev. Rul. 69–421, Part 5(j), *supra* note 6.

Unless the method of distribution is selected by the employee prior to his retirement, it should be determined by an administrative committee established pursuant to the plan, which may take into account the wishes and needs of the employee. This is necessary in order that the employee may not be considered as having "constructively" received the proceeds in the form of a lump sum, and then having reinvested them in the plan to be paid out to him in some other manner. If this were so he would, of course, be subject to tax on the entire amount in the year of constructive receipt. To safeguard against this, the plan could provide that the employee must make his election as to the type of benefits payable to him on or before a designated date prior to his retirement.[26] If he fails to do so, the election is made by the administrative committee.

A pension plan may be terminated or amended at any time, unless it provides to the contrary or the plan is subject to union negotiation.[27] However, to safeguard the rights of employees and to prevent discrimination which might result from early termination of a plan under which only highly paid employees have acquired rights, the Code and regulations require that the plan must contain certain restrictions. Section 401(a)(7) of the Code provides that

> A trust shall not constitute a qualified trust under this section unless the plan of which such trust is a part provides that, upon its termination or upon complete discontinuance of contributions under the plan, the rights of all employees to benefits accrued to the date of such termination or discontinuance, to the extent then funded, or the amounts credited to the employees' accounts, are nonforfeitable. This paragraph shall not apply to benefits or contributions which, under provisions of the plan adopted pursuant to regulations prescribed by the Secretary or his delegate to preclude the discrimination prohibited by paragraph (4) [i.e., discrimination in favor of officers, shareholder-employees and supervisory and highly compensated personnel] may not be used for designated employees in the event of early termination of the plan.

Regulations adopted pursuant to this provision are fairly complex but in general they impose various restrictions on the benefits payable to a person who is among the twenty-five highest paid employees at the time the plan is established and whose anticipated annual pension under the plan exceeds $1500. The restrictions apply in the event that the plan is terminated within ten years after its establishment, or if the benefits of an employee such as the one just described become payable within ten years after the plan is established or at a time when the full current costs of the plan for the first ten years have not been funded. In such a situation the employer contributions which may be used for the benefit of the employee may not

---

[26] See Rev. Rul. 57–260, 1957–1 Cum. Bull. 164.

[27] If a plan is terminated shortly after it is put into effect and without a justifiable business reason, there is a serious risk that the plan would be attacked as not having been a bona fide one and hence not entitled to treatment as a qualified plan. See Treas. Reg. §1.401–1(b)(2).

exceed the greater of $20,000 or 20 percent of the first $50,000 of the employee's annual compensation, multiplied by the number of years between the date the plan is established and the date the plan is terminated, or various other dates specified in the regulations.[28] These restrictions could create particular difficulties with respect to highly paid or senior personnel who retire within ten years after the plan is established, except that the regulations provide an escape hatch which permits the payment of additional benefits if the full current costs of the plan have been met or if the aggregate of such supplemental payments for all employees in the restricted category does not exceed the aggregate employer contributions already made under the plan in the year in which the payments are made.[29]

10.2 QUALIFIED PROFIT-SHARING AND STOCK BONUS PLANS

The rules regarding qualification of profit-sharing and stock bonus plans are much the same as those already described with respect to pension plans. The profit-sharing plan must be funded [30] and employer contributions to the fund are not taxable to the employee when made. They are deductible to the employer if not in excess of 15 percent of the compensation otherwise paid during the taxable year to all employees under the plan[31] and, as with pension plan contributions, if the contribution, taken together with the employees' other compensation, is within the limits of reasonableness.[32] The contributions must be allocated among the various participants in accordance with a definite formula,[33] and care should be taken that the manner of allocation does not discriminate in favor of highly paid personnel, officers, shareholder-employees, supervisory personnel, etc. The same formula should be used to allocate amounts which result from forfeitures due to employees leaving the plan. Unlike the pension plan situation, forfeitures may be used to increase the benefits payable to those remaining in a profit-sharing plan. Under this scheme, the longer a person is in the plan the more his benefits are likely to increase from forfeitures resulting from turnover of other personnel. Since officers and highly paid and supervisory personnel are likely to remain in the plan longer than other employees, relatively speaking, discrimination in benefits will probably result unless some provision is made for vesting of benefits after a person has been with the plan a certain number of years. Thus many plans provide for vesting after ten or fifteen years of service, although there is no express requirement

---

28 Id. §1.401–4(c)(1)–(2).
29 Id. §1.401–4(c)(4)(iii).
30 See Rev. Rul. 69–421, Part 2(b), *supra* note 6.
31 Int. Rev. Code of 1954, §404(a)(3).
32 See text accompanying note 21 *supra*.
33 See Rev. Rul. 69–421, Part 2(t), *supra* note 6.

for vesting in the Code or regulations other than that benefits must vest at retirement or on termination of the plan.[34] As with a pension plan, an employee may make his own contributions to a profit-sharing plan, except that these must be kept within reasonable bounds in order to avoid discrimination.[35]

Due to the obvious complexities of the pension and profit-sharing area and the expertise required to prepare a plan which survives scrutiny by the Internal Revenue Service and results in a favorable determination letter, some businesses, particularly small ones which cannot afford specialized counsel, may benefit from a simplified procedure of adopting a so-called master or prototype plan in accordance with procedures set forth in Revenue Procedure 68–45, issued December 30, 1968.[36] A standardized form and also a "variable" form of plan may be adopted, the variable form permitting the employer to elect among several alternative arrangements as to coverage, contributions, benefits and vesting. Although this procedure reduces the expense of drafting otherwise complex plan provisions, and lessens the likelihood of failure to qualify the plan, it also has a certain rigidity and, in the words of one commentator, may appeal only to "small corporations with vastly outnumbered non-stockholder-employees." [37] Accordingly, many corporations may find it worthwhile to pay the cost of preparing an individualized plan better suited to their particular needs if the standard forms cannot be readily adapted to their requirements.

10.3 STOCK OPTIONS, STOCK PURCHASE PLANS, RESTRICTED STOCK, ETC.

Stock options have several advantages as a fringe benefit. They provide a convenient way for employees to acquire an interest in the business at a "bargain" price, resulting in increased incentive which comes from being a part owner of the enterprise. As the business prospers the shares rise in value, and if the options have not been exercised, they too increase in worth, providing a tangible reward for the employee's contribution towards the growth of the business. As far as the corporation is concerned, there need be no cash outlay, as compared with other types of fringe benefits, such as contributions to pension funds or bonuses. The only cost is the dilution of shareholder's equity which comes from the exercise of options when shares are purchased for less than their fair value. This, at least, is the classical justification for stock options. Whether it works out that way in practice is

---

[34] Id. at Parts 5(c) and 6(a).

[35] See text accompanying note 21 *supra*.

[36] 1968–2 Cum. Bull. 957.

[37] Meyer, The Master Plan and Prototype Procedure for Corporate Qualified Employee Benefit Plans, 23 Sw. L.J. 417, 437 (1969). For further discussion see Goodman, Streamlined Pension and Profit-Sharing Tax Procedures, 47 Taxes 270 (1969).

another matter. For example, if the shares have a market, employees may dispose of shares purchased under options exercised at a prior date in order to finance the exercise of subsequent options, thereby defeating the purpose of the option insofar as it may have been intended to increase the employee's proprietary interest. Viewed in this light, the option becomes merely a vehicle for enabling the employees to receive increased compensation, the cost of doing so being imposed directly upon the shareholders rather than being paid out of the corporate till. On the other hand, if the shares are not marketable, the employees, although receiving a proprietary interest, are minority shareholders and are unlikely to hold enough shares to vote for even one director of their own choosing even if there be cumulative voting, unless the board of directors is inordinately large and all directors are reelected annually. If dividends on the shares are relatively modest, as may be so where those in control of the corporation wish to plow back earnings in order to finance expansion or avoid taxation of dividends at ordinary rates (earnings which are withdrawn being paid out in the form of tax-deductible salaries), the rewards of being part owner of the business may be relatively elusive, particularly in view of the cost of acquiring the shares through exercise of options. Although the shares so acquired will grow in value if earnings are reinvested in the business, the employee is unlikely to enjoy the benefits of this unless the corporation or the other shareholders agree to repurchase his shares, which may be only when he retires or dies. If the purchase price is fair, then the benefit is ultimately received, but the understanding may be that the shares must be resold at "book" value, excluding good will [38] or even at cost.[39] If this is the case, the stock option is less a fringe benefit and more a device whereby the corporation may, at minimal cost to it, have the use of the employee's cash resources.

It is for these reasons that the stock option device is less popular in closely held corporations than in publicly held ones. In addition, if the main advantages of stock options are thought to be tax advantages which result from qualifying the options under Sections 421–425 of the Code, such options become even less attractive for closely held concerns, at least if the shares are difficult to value as is so often the case. This is because qualification of the options for favorable tax treatment depends upon the option price being a certain percentage of the fair market value of the shares at the time the options are granted (100 percent in the case of options granted solely to officers, key employees, etc.).[40] If qualification depends upon value

[38] See, e.g., Lawson v. Household Finance Corp., 17 Del. Ch. 343, 152 Atl. 723 (Sup. Ct. 1930), discussed in Ch. III, text accompanying note 28.

[39] See Allen v. Biltmore Tissue Corp., 2 N.Y.2d 534, 141 N.E.2d 812, 161 N.Y.S.2d 418 (1957). See also In re Estate of Mather, 410 Pa. 361, 189 A.2d 586 (1963). See Ch. III, text accompanying note 12.

[40] Int. Rev. Code of 1954, §422(b)(4). For discussion see Havighurst, The Continuing Inutility of Employee Stock Options in Closely Held Business, 18 Fla. L.

and value is difficult to determine, this constitutes a continuing uncertainty and a source of potential litigation with the Internal Revenue Service. Accordingly, qualified stock options find their major appeal with those corporations whose shares are publicly traded and thus easily valued. Indeed, as to the latter the benefit is likely to be excessive in that, especially with a growth company whose shares may rapidly climb in value in a brief period of time, officers and other highly placed employees may receive what amounts to a fortune for services which, although valuable, are hardly worth the total benefit. The stock option thus becomes a controversial way of benefiting the few at the expense of the many—i.e., the shareholders. This is particularly apparent when it is remembered that if the option is qualified for favorable tax treatment as far as the employee is concerned, the corporation loses its right to deduct the benefit as a business expense. The only advantages received by the corporation are the services of the optionee. If the latter are indispensible and if his services cannot be had without the incentive of the option, then the cost is probably justified. Stock options are a popular method of inducing a person to leave the employ of another (perhaps larger and more stable) concern to go with a smaller company whose future is more speculative. However, even from the employee's standpoint, the stock option may not be a completely satisfactory solution in that it necessarily entails his committing personal funds to finance the option at a time when his cash reserves may be low and when borrowing may be difficult. In other words, he may decide to forego the potential gains and tax benefits of the options in order to receive the "bird in the hand" that increased compensation provides. This does not mean that he may not receive both a high wage, bonuses, etc., and stock options. It is only to point out that stock options may not have all the appeal that they purport to have and that an employee, if offered a choice, may elect fewer options in favor of increased compensation or greater benefits under a retirement program or deferred compensation arrangement, which entails little or no expenditure of his personal funds.

Notwithstanding the above limitations of stock options, particularly insofar as closely held corporations are concerned, it is still worthwhile to summarize briefly the various characteristics of qualified stock options and employee stock purchase plans, as well as the tax treatment which may result from options which do not qualify for special benefits under the Code.

Except for a specialized provision governing so-called restricted stock options[41] (i.e., "grandfather" clause treatment for certain options granted during the period running from February 26, 1945, to January 1, 1964), the

---

Rev. 251 (1965); Rothschild, The New Stock Option: Problems of the Smaller Company, 33 Fordham L. Rev. 393 (1965). For extensive discussion of corporate and other aspects see Vernava, Stock Options: Corporate, Regulatory and Related Tax Aspects, 30 U. Pitt. L. Rev. 197 (1968).

[41] Int. Rev. Code of 1954, §424.

Code provides for two types of options which may be qualified for special tax advantages. The first is the so-called qualified stock option and the second the employee stock purchase plan. The main difference between the two is that options granted pursuant to the latter must be made available to *all* employees (except persons who have been employed less than two years, those whose customary employment is for twenty hours or less per week, employees who work for not more than five months per year and officers, supervisory personnel and highly compensated employees).[42] Moreover, all employees covered by the plan must have the same rights or privileges, except that the amount of stock optioned to each employee may bear a uniform relationship to his total compensation.[43] The net result of these provisions is that an employee stock purchase plan may not be made available only to a few highly placed officers and is thus unsuitable as an incentive plan for key management. The proper vehicle to accomplish the latter objective is the qualified stock option plan,[44] which is subject to more restrictive provisions than the employee stock purchase plan.

Assuming that an option qualifies under one plan or the other, the tax treatment for the employer and employee is the same—i.e., no income results at the time the option is exercised,[45] the employer receives no deduction and is not taxable on the amount received from the employee (the transaction being treated like any other purchase of shares), and the employee, provided that he holds the shares for the prescribed period,[46] receives capital gains or loss treatment on any sale or exchange of the shares. The basis for determining gain or loss is the price paid for the shares. If the employee dies after having purchased the shares but before disposing of them, then his estate receives a new basis for the shares, the fair value at the date of death or on the alternate valuation date one year later. It is rather obvious that an employee may receive what amounts to a substantial benefit and pay a tax, if at all, only at capital gains rates.

As has been said, the qualified stock option, appropriate for officers and

---

[42] Id. §423(b)(4).

[43] Id. §423(b)(5).

[44] Id. §422.

[45] Id. §421(a)(1). There are two exceptions: In the case of a qualified stock option where there is a good faith error in computing the fair market value of the shares subject to the option, ordinary income may result to a limited extent when the option is exercised. See text accompanying note 49 *infra.* Secondly, Section 56 of the Code, added by the Tax Reform Act of 1969, imposes a minimum tax on certain items of "tax preference" income, among which is the amount by which the fair market value of shares subject to a qualified or restricted stock option exceeds the option price at the time the option is exercised. The tax is imposed only if the tax preference income for the year exceeds $30,000. Options granted under Section 423 of the Code (employee stock purchase plans) remain unaffected.

[46] Section 422(a)(1) of the Code requires that shares acquired pursuant to a qualified stock option be held for at least three years. Under Section 423(a)(1), shares acquired pursuant to an employee stock purchase plan must be held for at least two years after the date the option was granted or six months after their purchase, whichever is longer.

other key employees, is subject to the more restrictive requirements.[47] The shares must be held for three years following exercise of the option. The option cannot be exercised unless the optionee is an employee (except that he may do so within three months after ceasing to be an employee, if this is permitted by the plan). The plan must receive shareholder approval; the option must be granted within ten years from the date the plan is adopted (or the date of shareholder approval, whichever is earlier); it cannot be exercised after five years from the date the option is granted; and the option price must be no less than the fair market value of the shares on the date of the grant. Other restrictions include a provision requiring an optionee, who holds options granted to him at different times, to exercise them in the priority in which they were granted (i.e., the earliest first), a prohibition against transfer of the option otherwise than by will or by operation of law, and a prohibition against granting options to those who own more than 5 percent of the total combined voting power or value of all classes of stock of the employer corporation, or any parent or subsidiary.[48]

Since the option price must equal or exceed the fair market value of the shares, much depends upon the accuracy with which the shares are valued. As has been pointed out, this presents difficulties with shares of closely held corporations which are not generally traded. The Code provides for partial tax relief in the event the option fails to qualify "because there was a failure, made in good faith," to set an appropriate value on the shares. If this happens, although the full difference between the option price and the value of the shares on the date of exercise is not ordinary income, as would normally be the case if the option failed to qualify, the optionee is required to include as ordinary income an amount equal to the lesser of (1) 150 percent of the difference between the option price and the fair market value of the shares at the time the option was granted, or (2) the difference between the option price and the fair market value of the shares at the date of exercise.[49] Suppose, for example, that an optionee receives the right to purchase 100 shares at $100 per share, and that the employer in good faith determined that the fair value of the shares was $100 on the date the options were granted. If, in fact, the value of the shares was $125 and if the options were later exercised when the shares were worth $200 each, then

[47] See generally Int. Rev. Code of 1954, §422.

[48] Id. §422(b)(7). However, if the equity capital of the corporation, determined at the time the option is granted, is less than $2 million, then in applying the 5 percent limitation there is added to the 5 percent figure a percentage, not higher than 5 percent, which bears the same ratio to 5 percent as the difference between the corporation's equity capital and $2 million bears to $1 million. Section 422(c)(3) defines the term "equity capital" as the sum of a corporation's cash and other property, in an amount equal to its adjusted basis for determining gain, less the amount of its indebtedness, other than indebtedness to shareholders. Note, also, that to determine ownership the attribution rules of Section 425(d) of the Code must be taken into account. Thus an individual is deemed to own shares held by his spouse, brothers, sisters, ancestors and lineal descendants, and also (proportionately) shares held by a corporation, partnership, estate or trust in which he has an interest.

[49] Id. §422(c)(1).

the optionee would be required to include as ordinary income the lesser of $37.50 (150 percent of the difference between the option price—$100— and the value at the date of grant—$125) and $100 (the difference between the option price and the value at the date of exercise). Thus, instead of ordinary income of $100 for each share, ordinary income treatment would be limited to $37.50 for each share, or $3750 for the 100 shares. The basis of the shares purchased would be increased by the amount included as ordinary income. Thus the basis would consist in the $100 purchase price plus $37.50 or $137.50 for each share. The remainder of the gain would be taxed at capital gains rates when the shares were sold, provided, of course, that they were held for at least three years after their purchase.

Although the tax treatment just discussed provides some relief for an erroneous calculation of the value of the shares, the uncertainties, the potential tax impact at ordinary rates and the expense of litigating the proper method of determining value, as well as the other disadvantages discussed earlier, make qualified stock options of limited appeal for closely held corporations. Moreover, the regulations point out that care must be taken in determining the option price to take into account the possible effect of imputed interest which may arise under Section 483 of the Code if stock is to be paid for over a period lasting for more than one year, since that part of the payment which is attributable to imputed interest is not part of the option price.[50] In other words, if the stock is to be paid for over more than one year, the total amount payable must include the imputed interest plus an amount equal to at least the market value of the shares at the time of the grant of the option. The imputed interest provisions may be avoided by (1) arranging for payment of the purchase price over a period of one year or less,[51] (2) keeping the purchase price below $3000,[52] (3) specifying that interest on the contract shall be payable at a rate not less than 4 percent,[53] or, perhaps the best approach, (4) limiting the number of shares which may be purchased under the option so that they are paid for in full at the time the option is exercised. The latter approach may be better from the standpoint of corporate law, since statutes commonly require that shares be paid for in cash, property or services actually performed and prohibit the issuance of shares for a promissory note.[54]

Employee stock purchase options resemble qualified stock options except that they are subject to less restrictive provisions. As previously mentioned, the plan must provide for the granting of options to all employees, with certain exceptions, and the amount of stock purchased under options may

[50] Treas. Reg. §1.422–2(e)(2)(ii).
[51] Int. Rev. Code of 1954, §483(c)(1)(A).
[52] See id. §483(f)(1).
[53] Id. §483(c)(1). The regulations under this provision provide for interest to be imputed at the rate of 5 percent and the Code permits a contract to specify interest at a rate one percentage point lower (i.e., 4 percent) without any additional interest being imputed. See Treas. Reg. §1.483–1(d)(2).
[54] See, e.g., Model Bus. Corp. Act §19. But see §17, which permits shares to be paid for in installments under a subscription agreement.

bear a uniform relationship to total compensation.[55] The plan cannot, therefore, be made available only to key management employees, nor can officers and others receive more than their proportionate share of stock, based on the amount of compensation they are paid. The minimum holding period for shares purchased pursuant to the plan is less than that applicable to qualified stock options. Thus shares may not be disposed of within two years after the date the option is granted, nor within six months after the option is exercised.[56] The plan must receive shareholder approval within twelve months before or after the date the plan is adopted.[57] The option price may be determined in either of two ways: (1) an amount not less than 85 percent of the fair market value of the shares at the time the option is *granted*, or (2) an amount which may not be less that 85 percent of the fair market value of the shares at the time the option is exercised.[58] If the former method is chosen, the plan must provide that the option cannot be exercised after the expiration of twenty-seven months; if the latter method is used, the option may be exercisable up to five years from the date it was granted.[59] No employee may be granted an option if he owns stock possessing 5 percent or more of the total combined voting power or value of all classes of stock of the employer, its parent corporation or a subsidiary.[60] Also no employee may be granted an option which permits him to accrue rights to purchase more than $25,000 worth of stock of the employer, parent corporation or subsidiary for each calendar year.[61] Finally, as in the case of

[55] See text accompanying note 42 *supra*. Extreme care must be taken that the plan covers *all* employees (with the permitted exceptions) and that the amount which may be purchased is determined on a uniform basis. If a plan inadvertently leaves out a single employee who should have been covered, then none of the options under the plan may qualify for special tax treatment. See Treas. Reg. §1.423–2(a)(2).

[56] Int. Rev. Code of 1954, §423(a)(1).

[57] Id. §423(b)(2).

[58] Id. §423(b)(6). Both methods may be used. Thus the option price could be set at 85 percent of the fair market value of the shares at the date the option is granted or at the date the option is exercised, whichever is less. The option may also provide for purchase at the lesser of a fixed price or a percentage (not less than 85 percent) of the value of the shares at the date the option is exercised. However, in this situation the fixed price must be not less than 85 percent of the fair market value of the shares at the date the option is granted. See Treas. Reg. §1.423–2(g)(2).

[59] Int. Rev. Code of 1954, §423(b)(7).

[60] Id. §423(b)(3). As with the case of qualified stock options, the attribution rules of Section 425(d) of the Code apply in determining the amount of stock ownership. See note 48 *supra*. Note, however, that unlike qualified stock options there is no provision which requires the limit to be raised above 5 percent in the case of certain small corporations, i.e., those with equity capital of less than $2 million. See id. §422(b)(7), discussed in note 48 *supra*.

[61] Id. §423(b)(8). This limitation applies only to shares purchased under employee stock purchase plans and thus does not limit the amount which may be purchased under a qualified stock option plan. See Treas. Reg. §1.423–2(i)(2). The limitation applies on a cumulative basis. Thus, if an employee does not exercise his option during the first calendar year that it becomes exercisable, he may purchase up to $50,000 worth of stock the following calendar year.

qualified stock options, the option is not transferable other than by will or by the laws of descent and distribution, and is exercisable, during the optionee's lifetime, only by him.[62]

As already indicated, no income results to the employee on exercise of the employee stock purchase option, nor does the employer receive any deduction, and the employee is then taxed at capital gains rates only when he disposes of the shares. However, a special rule applies where the option price is between 85 and 100 percent of the value of the shares at the date the option was granted. If he disposes of the shares (assuming that he holds them for the minimum period [63]) or at his death, there is included in his income as compensation (i.e., as ordinary and not capital gain) an amount equal to the lesser of (1) the excess of the fair market value of the share at the time it was sold or at the optionee's death over the amount paid for it, or (2) the excess of the fair market value of the share at the date the option was granted over the option price. The basis of the share is correspondingly increased by the amount included as compensation and any further gain is taxed at capital gains rates.[64] Thus suppose that the option price was $95 and the fair market value of the share on the date the option was granted was $100. Suppose further that the share was subsequently sold for $150. The optionee would realize ordinary income to the extent of $5 on the sale of the share and the basis would be increased from $95 to $100, with the $50 remaining gain being taxed at capital gains rates. Notwithstanding the taxation of the $5 to the optionee at ordinary rates in the year he disposes of the shares, the employer would not be entitled to a deduction.[65]

Both in the case of qualified stock options and employee stock purchase plans, care must be taken if for any reason it is necessary to make any change in the terms of an option after it has been granted. If the change gives the employee any additional benefits under the option, such as an extension of the period during which the option may be exercised, or a reduction of the price at which the shares may be purchased,[66] this is considered as the granting of a new option, in which case the option must again meet the various tests which have already been described, such as the requirement, in the case of qualified stock options, that the option price be equal to the fair market value of the shares at the date the option is granted (i.e., the date of the modification). To determine qualification of an option in the event of its modification, Section 425(h)(2) of the Code provides (with certain exceptions) that the fair market value of the shares at the date the option is granted shall be considered as the highest of the following:

62 Int. Rev. Code of 1954, §423(b)(9).
63 See text accompanying note 56 *supra*.
64 Int. Rev. Code of 1954, §423(c).
65 See Treas. Reg. §1.423–2(k)(3), Ex. (1).
66 See Int. Code of 1954, §425(h)(3).

(i) the fair market value of such stock on the date of the original granting of the option,

(ii) the fair market value of such stock on the date of the making of such modification, extension, or renewal, or

(iii) the fair market value of such stock at the time of the making of any intervening modification, extension, or renewal.

Thus if an option were granted to purchase at $100 shares worth $100 and the option were subsequently modified when the shares were worth $125 so as to extend the period within which the option could be exercised, the option would not qualify unless the option price were adjusted upwards to $125, at least if the option purported to be a qualified stock option pursuant to Section 422 of the Code. In view of the technicalities of the problem of what constitutes a modification of existing options and what changes must be made in the plan so that it may continue to qualify, it may often be advisable to avoid modifying an existing plan, cancel any outstanding options and grant new ones, starting in with a clean slate as it were. If this is done, care must be taken that the outstanding options are in fact cancelled. Otherwise, the grant of a new option may be considered as in substance a modification of an existing one, with consequent confusion, uncertainty and possible loss of tax benefits.

A brief word is necessary concerning the tax treatment of options which fail to qualify under the various provisions previously discussed. If this happens, the general rule is that the employee is taxable at ordinary rates (i.e., receives compensation income) equal to the difference between the price he pays for the stock and its fair market value at the date he acquires it (i.e., on the date he exercises the option).[67] However, there is a possibility that the tax may be imposed at an earlier date, namely, when the option is granted. This would happen if the option has a readily ascertainable market value and if the recipient is free to sell the option.[68] The regulations carry out this theme and provide that an option does not "ordinarily" have a readily ascertainable fair market value unless it is actively traded on an established market.[69] However, if the option is not actively traded, the fair market value of the option is not readily ascertainable unless the taxpayer can show that all of the following conditions exist:

(a) The option is freely transferable by the optionee;

(b) The option is exercisable immediately in full by the optionee;

(c) The option or the property subject to the option is not subject to any restriction or condition (other than a lien or other condition to secure the payment of the purchase price) which has a significant effect upon the fair market value of the option or such property;

(d) The fair market value of the option privilege is readily ascertainable. . . .[70]

[67] See, e.g., Commissioner v. LoBue, 351 U.S. 243 (1956).
[68] Id. at 249 (dictum), citing Commissioner v. Smith, 324 U.S. 177, 181–182 (1945).
[69] Treas. Reg. §1.421–6(c)(2).
[70] Id. §1.421–6(c)(3)(i).

The regulations also observe that the option privilege may have a fair market value even though the option price be equivalent to the value of the shares subject to option on the date the option is granted. In other words, the option privilege includes the value of an opportunity to purchase shares at today's market price for some period of time, during which there is a reasonable probability that the value of the shares will rise. To determine whether the value of the option privilege can be readily ascertained, the following factors must be considered:

(a) Whether the value of the property subject to the option can be ascertained;

(b) The probability of any ascertainable value of such property increasing or decreasing; and

(c) The length of the period during which the option can be exercised.[71]

If, on the basis of the foregoing, it is found that the option itself has a readily ascertainable value, the employee realizes compensation income to the extent of the value of the *option* when it is *received* by him. Correspondingly, the employer receives a deduction for the compensation deemed to have been paid to the employee. If the option does not have a readily ascertainable value, then, as has been said, the employee is normally taxed on the difference between the value of the *shares* purchased by him and the price he pays, the tax being imposed when the option is exercised. As before, the employer receives a deduction in the amount of the compensation deemed to have been paid to the employee, assuming, of course, that it, along with the employee's other compensation, is reasonable in relation to his services. There is, however, one further possibility, namely, that when the option is exercised the fair market value of the *shares* so purchased cannot be readily ascertained. This would be so if the stock were subject to a restriction which had a significant effect on its value.

The tax treatment of such "restricted stock" has been a matter of some controversy. Prior to the enactment of Section 83 of the Code, added by the Tax Reform Act of 1969, the regulations provided that no tax was imposed in this situation until the restrictions lapsed or the stock was sold, and then only to the extent of the difference between the price paid for the stock and the *lesser* of either its fair market value at the time the stock was acquired (determined without regard to the restriction) or its fair market value at the time the restriction lapsed (or, if the shares were sold, the price received for them).[72] The effect of this was to permit the employee to avoid paying tax on any appreciation in the shares from the time he received them until the restriction lapsed. In 1968 the Treasury Department proposed new regulations which would impose a tax at the time the restriction lapsed on the difference between the price paid for the shares and their value at the date of the lapse.[73] In effect this would tax any appreciation in value of the

---

71 Id. §1.421–6(c)(3)(ii).
72 Id. §§1.61–2(d)(5) and 1.421–6(d)(2).
73 Proposed Treas. Reg. §1.421–6(d)(2)(i), 33 Fed. Reg. 15870 (1968). See

shares between the date of their acquisition and the lapse of the restriction.

This area has now been dealt with largely by the enactment of Section 83 of the Code. This provides, in part:

> If, in connection with the performance of services, property is transferred to any person other than the person for whom such services are performed, the excess of
>
> (1) the fair market value of such property (determined without regard to any restriction other than a restriction which by its terms will never lapse) at the first time the rights of the person having the beneficial interest in such property are transferable or are not subject to a substantial risk of forfeiture, whichever occurs earlier, over
>
> (2) the amount (if any) paid for such property, shall be included in the gross income of the person who performed such services in the first taxable year in which the rights of the person having the beneficial interest in such property are transferable or are not subject to a substantial risk of forfeiture, whichever is applicable. The preceding sentence shall not apply if such person sells or otherwise disposes of such property in an arm's length transaction before his rights in such property become transferable or not subject to a substantial risk of forfeiture.[74]

The employer receives a deduction in an amount corresponding to the amount included as compensation to the employee.[75]

In effect this brings the tax treatment of restricted stock into line with the proposed regulations relating to stock acquired pursuant to options and in that respect codifies the approach taken by the Treasury Department. The Code goes on to provide that the rights of a person in property are subject to a "substantial risk of forfeiture" if such person's rights to full enjoyment of the property "are conditioned upon the future performance of substantial services" by him.[76] It also permits the employee to elect to have the tax imposed at the date he receives the property, in which case the amount of compensation income is measured by the difference between the price paid for the property and its fair market value at the time the employee receives it, determined without regard to any restriction other than a restriction which, by its terms, will never lapse.[77] In the case of the latter type restriction (i.e., one which by its terms will never lapse), if the restriction is subsequently cancelled, a tax is imposed at the time of cancellation on the excess of the fair market value of the property (computed without regard to the restriction) at the time of cancellation over the sum of the

---

also 26 C.F.R. §1.421–6(d)(2)(i) (1970). For a discussion see Silbert and Rosenberg, Non-Statutory Stock Options and Restricted Stock—The New Proposed Regulations, N.Y.U. 27th Inst. on Fed. Tax. 51 (1969). The article was written before the enactment of Section 83 of the Code, added by Section 321 of the Tax Reform Act of 1969.

[74] Int. Rev. Code of 1954, §83(a).
[75] Id. §83(h).
[76] Id. §83(c)(1).
[77] Id. §83(b).

amount, if any, paid for the cancellation and the fair market value of the property (computed by taking the restriction into account) immediately before the cancellation. The tax may be avoided if the taxpayer is able to establish that the cancellation was not "compensatory" and if the employer is willing to forego any deduction to which he otherwise would be entitled.[78]

Section 83 is, by its terms, inapplicable to a transaction to which Section 421 applies (i.e., qualified options or employee stock purchase plans), a transfer pursuant to qualified trusts or annuity plans, the transfer of an option without a readily ascertainable fair market value, or the transfer of property pursuant to the exercise of an option with a readily ascertainable fair market value at the date of grant.[79] However, Section 83 does apply not only to restricted stock of the employer corporation but also to restricted shares of any corporation transferred in connection with the performance of services. In other words, an employer might choose to transfer to an employee shares of some other corporation, and subject the shares to a restriction pursuant to an agreement entered into with the employee recipient. Although this device had some popularity prior to the proposal to revise the regulations, and the enactment of Section 83 of the Code, it has become considerably less attractive since any appreciation in value of the shares is taxed to the employee at the time the restriction lapses. However, the employee continues to be able to defer the tax until the later date. For example, if the restriction continues until the employee retires, although he must pay a tax at that time, he is likely to be in a lower tax bracket. This deferral of tax may be achieved through other types of deferred compensation schemes, which will be discussed later in this chapter.

There is one other form of stock plan, sometimes referred to as a "phantom" plan, which is not, properly speaking, a stock option plan but more a retirement plan funded by a formula which depends upon the value of the employer's stock. This entails the creation of "deferred compensation units," which represent shares of the employer's stock. Each employee is credited with a number of units depending upon the level of his other compensation. Thereafter a separate ledger account is maintained for each employee wherein the number of units credited to him is recorded, along with additional amounts representing dividends which would have been received by him had he held the shares corresponding to the units with which he is credited. Upon retirement or death the value of the units in the employee's account is fixed either at the date of termination of employment or at an alternate valuation date, selected by the employee or his beneficiary. A three-year period is allowed for such selection and if no selection is made, the value of the unit is determined as of the third anniversary of the date the employment was terminated. If an employee selects a value, the value

[78] Id. §83(d).
[79] Id. §83(e).

so selected cannot exceed the highest price at which the employer's shares traded from the time the employee became a member of the plan until he retired. In other words, the employee is finally credited with an aggregate amount which represents the value of the shares initially credited to him plus any appreciation in the shares and any dividends which would have been paid thereon up until the valuation date. The total amount to which the employee thus becomes entitled is then paid out to him over a designated period of time. Such plans also commonly contain provisions requiring an employee to remain with the company for a minimum period following his award of units in the plan, to make himself available for consultation services at the request of his former employer at any time after retirement and not to compete with his employer during that time.

The validity of such plans as a matter of state law is a point on which courts have differed. In *Berkwitz v. Humphrey*[80] it was held that such a plan was invalid in that it failed to equate the value of the employee's services with the amount which he might receive under the plan. In other words, the plan resulted in compensation which would be measured by fluctuating stock prices, general economic conditions and other factors unrelated to the services rendered by the employee. However, the Delaware Supreme Court shortly thereafter held that such a plan was no more objectionable than a stock option plan and deferred to the judgment of the company's directors and its administrative committee to allocate units to reflect the value of employees' services. If this is done in a reasonable and relatively disinterested fashion (i.e., if there is little or no self-dealing), such a plan does not appear objectionable.[81]

Assuming that such plans can be validly established if carefully drafted, they have several advantages over conventional stock option plans. Since no shares are actually issued, there is no need for the employee to invest his own funds, thereby depleting his resources and exposing himself to the risk of a decline in the market value of the stock. He receives all the advantages of share ownership, except for voting rights, with no risk of his capital. The worst that can happen is that the value of his compensation unit may decline, in which case he merely receives less than he might otherwise receive. He loses nothing by way of personal investment. From the employer's standpoint, there is no need to worry about federal or state securities laws, registration or exemption procedures or other costs entailed in issuing

---

[80] 163 F. Supp. 78 (N.D. Ohio 1958) (plan adopted by Pittsburgh-Consolidation Coal Company).

[81] Lieberman v. Becker, 38 Del. Ch. 540, 155 A.2d 596 (Del. Sup. Ct. 1959). For discussion of these cases see 1 G. Washington and V. Rothschild, Compensating the Corporate Executive 153 (3d ed. 1962); Hancock, The Non-Qualified Stock Option Plan and the Shadow Stock Plan, 24 Bus. Law. 1245 (1969); Shelmerdine, Shadow Stock Deferred Compensation Arrangements, N.Y.U. 17th Inst. on Fed. Tax. 933 (1959); 1 B.C. Ind. & Com. L. Rev. 108 (1959); 76 Harv. L. Rev. 619 (1963); 35 N.Y.U.L. Rev. 838 (1960); 29 U. Cinn. L. Rev. 245 (1960); 108 U. Pa. L. Rev. 1066 (1960).

shares, nor is there dilution in the shareholders' equity, unless the plan is actually funded by the contribution of shares to a trust or other reserve. When the amounts due under the plan are finally paid, the employer will receive a deduction if the payment qualifies as a reasonable business expense—i.e., if it, along with the rest of the compensation paid to the employee, is reasonable in relation to his services.[82] Although the employee is taxed at ordinary rates when he receives the payments, the latter are spread out over a number of years, minimizing the tax impact. Also the tax is paid at a time when the employee is likely to be in a lower tax bracket (i.e., after his retirement).

Despite the above advantages of phantom stock plans, they do not appear particularly attractive for the closely held corporation whose shares are not traded in an active market. Although the value of the shares can be periodically determined by some formula, such as capitalization of earnings at an agreed rate, these plans seem more appropriate to publicly held corporations, the value of whose shares is readily determinable by consulting the financial pages. Closely held corporations can achieve similar advantages by deferred compensation plans of other types, or by qualified pension, profit-sharing or stock bonus plans, which have already been discussed.

10.4 GROUP LIFE INSURANCE

Section 79 of the Code permits an employee to exclude from his gross income amounts equal to the cost of group term insurance on the life of employees purchased by his employer to the extent of the cost of $50,000 worth of coverage. The insurance must be provided under a master policy taken out by the employer and must be term insurance rather than so-called ordinary life insurance, except that a group policy which permits the employee to convert, at his own cost, to ordinary life insurance upon leaving his employment may still qualify as group insurance.[83] The insurance protection cannot qualify for the exclusion if it is provided as an incidental benefit pursuant to a qualified pension or profit-sharing plan.[84] Although an insurance benefit may be provided to a limited extent under such a plan,[85] the employer's contribution toward the cost of such protection is taxable to the employees when made.[86] Thus a separate group policy is far better for the employee from a tax standpoint and may provide greater coverage. The group plan must comply with state insurance laws as to the maximum contribution which can be required of employees; if the em-

---

[82] For discussion of deferred compensation arrangements see text accompanying note 104 *infra*.

[83] Treas. Reg. §1.79–1(b)(1)(ii).

[84] Int. Rev. Code of 1954, §79(b)(3); Treas. Reg. §1.79–2(d).

[85] See Rev. Rul. 69–421, Part 2(n), *supra* note 6.

[86] Int. Rev. Code of 1954, §72(m)(3); Treas. Reg. §1.72–16(b)(2).

ployer chooses, he can, of course, pay the entire cost. In any event the plan must cover at least ten full-time employees unless some further restrictions, set forth in the regulations, are met.[87] The Code also excludes any payments towards coverage provided after an individual has terminated his employment, has reached retirement age or has become disabled, as well as payments on any coverage with respect to which the employer or a charitable organization is the beneficiary.[88]

Since Section 2042(2) of the Code provides that proceeds are not included in the gross estate of an insured for estate tax purposes if he assigns all the incidents of ownership in the policy to another person prior to his death, an employee should seriously consider the advantages of assigning, perhaps to his wife or children, all incidents in any group coverage maintained by his employer with respect to him. In doing this, care must be taken that *all* incidents of ownership are assigned, for otherwise the proceeds will be included in the employee's gross estate. For example, if the employee, by terminating his employment, can terminate the coverage, he retains incidents of ownership in that respect. Thus the policy must permit conversion of the coverage into individual insurance upon termination of employment and the employee must assign all rights in the policy, including the right to convert the coverage.[89] In effect this means that the assignee can continue the coverage, by converting the policy and paying premiums on it, after the employee has terminated his employment. If the employee retains an option *not* to convert, the proceeds are includible in his gross estate. The assignee may, of course, elect not to convert the policy, in which case the coverage terminates.

The cost of group term insurance is relatively low in that it has no cash value. Also most group policies provide coverage without the need for an employee's taking a physical examination, at least if he elects to be included in the plan within a certain time after coverage is offered to him. The coverage lasts as long as the insured remains an employee. Thus the coverage continues even though a person might become uninsurable due to an illness or physical disability. This is particularly advantageous to older employees who might find the cost of coverage prohibitive if they were to seek insurance on their own.

Notwithstanding the exclusion from the income of the employee (to the extent of $50,000 of coverage) of premiums paid by the employer, the latter may receive a deduction if the premiums qualify as ordinary and necessary business expenses and are compensatory in nature, and assuming that the employee's other compensation is reasonable in amount in relation to his

[87] Id. §1.79–1(b)(iii)(d).

[88] Int. Rev. Code of 1954, §79(b).

[89] See Rev. Rul. 69–54, 1969–1 Cum. Bull. 221. An employee's right to terminate his employment is not an incident of ownership of a group policy where he has assigned all his other rights, including his right to convert the policy to individual coverage by continuing payment of premiums. Landorf v. United States, 408 F.2d 461 (Ct. Cl. 1969).

services. However, the deduction will be disallowed if the employer is directly or indirectly a beneficiary under the policy[90] or if the insurance is not true employee group insurance but is designed to benefit certain shareholders rather than employees generally, regardless of share ownership.[91]

Prior to 1964, a scheme known as "split-dollar" insurance received considerable attention, but the promulgation of Revenue Ruling 64–328, revoking an earlier favorable ruling, may limit its effectiveness considerably.[92] Briefly, the split-dollar scheme involves the employer's payment of that part of the net premium on an insurance policy on an employee's life which represents the annual increase in cash value of the policy, with the employee paying the remainder. The insured may designate a beneficiary who is entitled to receive that part of the policy proceeds which exceeds the cash surrender value. The earlier revenue ruling held that the arrangement constituted in substance a series of interest-free loans made by the employer to the employee to the extent of the periodic increase in the cash surrender value and that the employer's payment of the premiums did not therefore constitute income to the employee. This position was subsequently repudiated and the Internal Revenue Service indicated that it would tax the employee on an amount equal to the annual cost of the declining term coverage, less any portion of the premium paid by him. For that reason, although the split-dollar plan may continue to have some appeal from a business standpoint, it has little or no tax advantages.[93] This is also true from the employers standpoint, since, due to its being a beneficiary of the policy to the extent of its cash surrender value, premium payments by it are not deductible.[94]

10.5 THE DEATH BENEFIT EXCLUSION

Section 101(b) of the Code provides for a death benefit exclusion of $5000 for amounts paid by an employer to the beneficiaries or estate of an employee "by reason of the death of the employee." The exclusion has a

---

[90] Int. Rev. Code of 1954, §264(a)(1). Furthermore, payment of premiums by the employer would not qualify for exclusion from the employee's income. See text accompanying note 88 *supra*.

[91] In this event the payment would not be compensatory in nature in that it would be unrelated to services performed. Furthermore the payment would not qualify for exclusion from the shareholder-employee's income. See Treas. Reg. §1.79–1(b)(1)-(iii)(b), which requires that the plan include all employees or a class of employees determined on the basis of factors which preclude individual selection or selection on the basis of factors unrelated to employment, such as share ownership.

[92] Rev. Rul. 64–328, 1964–2 Cum. Bull. 11, revoking Rev. Rul. 55–713, 1955–2 Cum. Bull. 23.

[93] For further discussion of split-dollar insurance schemes, see 2 G. Washington and V. Rothschild, Compensating the Corporate Executive 715 (3d ed. 1962). See also 34–2 Bureau of National Affairs Tax Management Portfolio: Life Insurance —Corporate Business Use, at A–27 and A–34.

[94] Int. Rev. Code of 1954, §264(a)(1).

number of exceptions. The main exceptions relate to (1) amounts with respect to which the employee possessed, immediately before his death, a nonforfeitable right to receive while living, and (2) amounts received by a surviving annuitant under a joint and survivor's annuity contract if payments thereunder commenced prior to the employee's death. The first of these exceptions also has an exception, namely, lump sum distributions from a qualified stock bonus, pension or profit-sharing trust, or a qualified annuity plan. In other words, such lump sum distributions are entitled to the $5000 exclusion.

The operation of the exclusion can be best appreciated by a few examples: Suppose that an employer voluntarily makes a payment of $10,000 to the widow of a deceased employee. The payment does not represent unpaid compensation or any amount to which the employee might have been entitled had he lived. There is, first of all, the possibility that some courts would hold that the payment, being voluntary in nature, was a gift and so was fully exempt from tax.[95] Even if the payment were not a gift, it would still qualify for the death benefit exclusion to the extent of $5000, since the regulations provide that the payment need not be made pursuant to a contractual obligation.[96]

Suppose that an employee was a participant in a pension plan, that after his retirement he became entitled to monthly payments of $100 for his life or for at least 120 months, and that he died after having received ten payments. Although his widow, beneficiary or estate would be entitled to the remaining 110 payments, no part of the payments would qualify for the death benefit exclusion since the deceased possessed, at his death, a nonforfeitable right to receive them during his life.[97] On the other hand, if the employee had been a member of a noncontributory qualified retirement plan and his widow elected to receive in a lump sum the present value ($6000) of an annuity to which the employee would have become entitled had he not died prior to retirement, $5000 of the $6000 payment would qualify for the exclusion.[98]

As already indicated, certain amounts paid out as an annuity may qualify for the exclusion. Here the rules are fairly complex. In the case of a joint and survivor's annuity, the exclusion does not apply if payment of the annuity has commenced prior to the employee's death.[99] Thus it would only be where the employee died before receiving annuity payments and where

---

[95] *Compare* Smith v. Commissioner, 305 F.2d 778 (3d Cir. 1962), *cert. denied,* 371 U.S. 904 (1962), *with* Poyner v. Commissioner, 301 F.2d 287 (4th Cir. 1962), and Kuntz v. Commissioner, 300 F.2d 849 (6th Cir. 1962), *cert. denied,* 371 U.S. 903 (1960). Cf. Commissioner v. Duberstein, 363 U.S. 278 (1960) (determination of whether or not a gift is present is essentially one of fact). For general discussion see [1961] Ill. L.F. 179; 49 Va. L. Rev. 74 (1963). See also Annot. 95 A.L.R.2d 520 (1964).

[96] Treas. Reg. §1.101–2(a).

[97] See id. §1.101–2(d)(2), Ex. (1).

[98] See id. §1.101–2(d)(3)(ii), Ex. (1).

[99] Int. Rev. Code of 1954, §101(b)(2)(C).

the payments were received by his widow or other beneficiary that they would qualify for the exclusion. Also the exclusion would not apply to amounts with respect to which the employee possessed, immediately before his death, a nonforfeitable right, nor to amounts contributed by the employee to the retirement or annuity plan. This means, in effect, that the present value of the annuity which is payable to the beneficiary must be determined and from that must be subtracted any amounts representing employee contributions or amounts with respect to which the employee possessed a nonforfeitable interest. Any remaining amount qualifies for the exclusion.[100] Suppose, for example, that the widow of an employee became entitled to receive an annuity of $2000 per year during her life and that her child was also entitled to receive $1000 per year for fifteen years. Suppose, further, that the employee made no contributions to the plan and died while still employed, having received no payments under the annuity. We shall also assume that at the date of his death the amount in his account was $18,000, and that under the terms of the plan this amount would have been distributable to him on account of voluntary termination of employment. Since the $18,000 constitutes an amount with respect to which the employee possessed a nonforfeitable interest, only that much of the annuity which exceeded $18,000 would be eligible for the exclusion. The regulations provide for the calculation of the present value of these annuities on the basis of tables and, assuming that the widow is fifty-five years old when she becomes entitled to the payments, value an annuity such as the one described at $37,761.[101] Since this exceeds the $18,000 which is not eligible for the exclusion, the widow is entitled to the full exclusion of $5000. She and her child receive the benefit of the exclusion over the period when the payments are being made by an adjustment to the so-called exclusion ratio which governs the taxation of annuity payments.[102] Under the exclusion ratio approach, the annuitant is entitled to exclude that part of each payment which bears the same ratio to the payment as the so-called investment in the contract bears to the so-called expected return under the annuity. The latter is an estimate of the total amount which is likely to be paid under the annuity, on the basis of actuarial tables. The former may be recouped over the life of the annuity free of tax. Normally the investment in the contract would correspond to whatever amount the employee had contributed toward its cost. Section 101(b)(2)(D) of the Code, therefore, provides that the $5000 death benefit exclusion shall be treated as additional consideration paid by the employee. In other words, the $5000 or whatever lesser amount the beneficiary becomes entitled to exclude, is added to the investment in the contract and the exclusion ratio is correspondingly increased. The effect of this is to prorate the exclusion over the period when the payments are being made.

[100] See Treas. Reg. §1.101–2(e).
[101] Id. §1.101–2(e)(2), Ex. (1).
[102] Int. Rev. Code of 1954, §72(b).

10.6   COMPENSATION FOR INJURIES OR SICKNESS; WAGE CONTINUATION OR SICK PAY EXCLUSION

Sections 104 and 105 of the Code provide that certain payments received by an employee due to an injury or a sickness may be excluded from his gross income. Section 104 relates to amounts received under workmen's compensation acts, damages received (either as a result of a court judgment or from a settlement) for personal injuries or sickness, and amounts received from accident or health insurance which the employee has himself purchased. Section 105 provides an exclusion for certain amounts paid from accident or health insurance purchased with employer contributions. In this category are amounts paid to reimburse the employee for expenses incurred by him for the medical care of himself, his spouse and his dependents and also payments for the permanent loss or loss of use of a member or function of the body or the permanent disfigurement of the employee, his spouse or a dependent. Neither the Section 104 nor Section 105 exclusion is available if the taxpayer was allowed a deduction in any prior taxable year for the medical expense involved. Suppose, for example, that an employee incurs $500 in medical expense and is allowed a deduction for that amount under Section 213 of the Code. If, in the following year, he receives either from accident or health insurance which he has himself purchased (Section 104) or from insurance purchased by his employer (Section 105) a payment to reimburse him for the medical expense, the payment is taxable to him in the year of receipt. If, on the other hand, he did not claim the item as a medical expense in the prior year but elected to take the standard deduction, the payment qualifies for exclusion in the following year.

Section 105 also provides for a limited exclusion for certain amounts (referred to as "sick pay") received by an employee as wages or in lieu of wages (i.e., as a "wage continuation") while he is absent from work on account of personal injuries or sickness. The exclusion is limited to $100 per week. Moreover, there is a waiting period of thirty days during which the employee is not eligible for the exclusion if he receives more than 75 percent of his regular weekly wage. If he receives 75 percent or less of his regular wage, then he may exclude up to $75 per week if he is hospitalized for at least one day. If he is not hospitalized for at least one day, then the $75 weekly exclusion applies after he has been absent from work because of injuries or sickness for seven days. If the employee is absent for more than thirty days the exclusion is raised to $100 per week.

The sick pay exclusion also applies to payments made to an employee who is forced to retire prior to his normal retirement age because of sickness or other disability. Thus the employee is not taxed on the first $100 of each weekly amount received from a disability pension, with the exclusion continuing until the first date at which he might have elected to retire had he not been disabled.[103]

10.7 DEFERRED COMPENSATION ARRANGEMENTS

We have seen how closely held corporations may run into difficulty in qualifying a stock option plan for preferential tax treatment.[104] Although they may adopt qualified pension, profit-sharing or stock bonus plans, these must be funded and the employer may find the cost of such a plan to be excessively high, inasmuch as the plan must be broad enough to be nondiscriminatory (i.e., the plan cannot usually be designed to include only a few key officers or employees).[105] For these and other reasons employers often find it advantageous to adopt deferred compensation arrangements, either as a substitute for a qualified pension plan or as a supplement.

A deferred compensation arrangement is precisely what its name implies. The employee agrees to be paid at a later date for services performed at an earlier time. What has been thought a major advantage of such an agreement from the employee's standpoint is the opportunity to defer payment of a tax on the deferred compensation until the year in which it is paid to him, at which time he may be in a lower tax bracket. If this happens, the total tax cost of his receiving the compensation is lessened. Counterbalanced against this possible advantage are several disadvantages:

(1) The employee cannot be certain that his tax bracket will be lower in the year he receives the deferred compensation. He may have substantially more income-producing property as a result of the death of relatives and others, as well as the very real possibility in many growth-oriented corporations that the value of shares he owns in the corporation may have increased substantially, producing more income and greater capital gains if the shares are disposed of. He must also take into account the tax on any payments which he receives from a retirement program. In view of all this the tax savings may not be as great as expected. In addition, the maximum tax rate applicable to earned income effected by Section 1348 of the Code, added by the Tax Reform Act of 1969, further lessens the likelihood that there will be a substantial difference between the rate at which earnings are taxed if paid in the year the services are performed and the rate of tax imposed on deferred compensation paid in later years. The new provision taxes earned income at a maximum rate of 60 percent in 1971, and 50 percent in 1972 and thereafter, with the benefit being reduced to the extent that the tax-

---

[103] See Rev. Rul. 68–385, 1968–2 Cum. Bull. 53. But see Winter v. Commissioner, 303 F.2d 150 (3d Cir. 1962), holding that the exclusion applies up until the customary or mandatory retirement age and does not terminate at an earlier date merely because the employee might have voluntarily retired had he continued to work.

[104] See text accompanying note 49 *supra*.

[105] See id. notes 15–20 *supra*.

payer has tax preference income in excess of $30,000.[106] At 1970 tax rates, married persons filing joint returns would pay a tax at a rate less than 50 percent on the first $44,000 of taxable income. For unmarried individuals, other than a surviving spouse or a head of a household, this is so unless the taxable income exceeds $32,000. In other words, deferral of the tax will represent a saving (assuming that an earlier payment would have qualified for taxation at the 50 percent maximum rate) only if the post-retirement taxable income of the employee is less than the above limits.[107] Moreover, if the tax rate which would have been imposed on income received in an earlier year would have been *less* than 50 percent, the potential tax saving is even less. Finally, one must also take into account the fact that deferred compensation is not considered to be earned income for the purpose of the 50 percent limitation in Section 1348.[108] In other words, deferred compensation will be taxed at the regular rates which, depending upon the employee's tax bracket in the year of payment, may exceed 50 percent, the maximum rate which might have been imposed had he received the income in the years the services were performed.

(2) One must also take into account the fact that receipt of the income is *deferred*, i.e., that the employee must forego use of the funds until a later date. If the funds were received in an earlier year, the tax paid and the residue invested, the yield on the investment might be expected to equal or exceed 8 percent, depending upon whether the funds are invested in industrial bonds, municipal bonds or quality growth stock, and upon general economic conditions, including prevailing interest rates. If the yield on such investments is itself reinvested (and especially if, in the case of municipal bonds or other obligations, it is tax free), the total amount of capital which may be accumulated may well exceed the amount which would have been paid under the deferred method, even taking into account the tax advantage, if any, of having the payments taxed at lower rates in later years.

(3) Since, as we shall see, most deferred compensation arrangements are, for tax and other reasons, unfunded, the employee does not have the relative security of a qualified retirement plan. First, he must rely solely upon the promise of his employer to pay the benefit, a promise which might not be carried out if the employer were to experience severe financial difficulty in later years, or if it were acquired by some other enterprise by a method, such as an asset purchase, whereby the acquiring corporation were able to repudiate its liability on the obligation.[109] The employee is thus, for a protracted period of time, exposed to the vicissitudes of the marketplace.

---

[106] See Int. Rev. Code of 1954, §1348(b)(2). See also Section 56 of the Code, also added by the Tax Reform Act of 1969 and discussed in note 45 *supra*, imposing a minimum tax on so-called tax preference income.

[107] In the interests of simplicity this calculation does not consider the effect of the retirement income credit. This further reduces the tax cost of receiving retirement income, but only to a relatively minor extent.

[108] Int. Rev. Code of 1954, §1348(b)(1).

[109] See Ch. VIII, text accompanying note 21.

Added to this are the uncertainties which arise from various covenants which are commonly inserted in deferred compensation contracts, such as a requirement that the employee render a specified number of years of faithful service, that he make himself available after retirement for consultation services, if required, and that he not compete with his former employer. Hence the employee's rights are often forfeitable; if there is a falling out between the parties, the deferred compensation may never be paid.

(4) Finally, since deferred compensation is not considered as compensation for the purpose of determining benefits or contributions under a qualified retirement plan,[110] an employee with substantial deferred compensation and relatively modest current compensation may find that his benefits under the qualified plan are correspondingly modest. This also illustrates how a deferred compensation arrangement may be used by an employer to reduce the cost of funding a qualified plan.

In view of all this one might well wonder why deferred compensation plans have any popularity. It would be misleading, however, to neglect some very real advantages:

(1) From the employee's standpoint the advantages stem mainly from the differential between the tax rates in years of service and years of retirement. We have seen that the difference may be less than that commonly supposed, but it would also be wrong to assume that it may not, in specific instances, be substantial. *If* he also receives substantial tax preference income, thereby reducing the extent to which he may qualify for the 50 percent maximum tax on earned income, or *if* his tax rate in the years following retirement is substantially less than 50 percent, deferral of the tax may represent a savings, despite his loss of the use of the funds for investment purposes in the interim. Also, the disadvantages which result from loss of use of the funds prior to retirement may be alleviated through various formula-type arrangements, whereby the employee is credited not only with the deferred compensation but also with interest at an agreed rate of return or, as in the case of the phantom stock plan already discussed,[111] with hypothetical appreciation in the value of stock, either of the employer or of one or more other corporations, together with dividends that would have been paid had the funds been invested in an assumed manner. The main disadvantage of such a scheme from the employee's standpoint is that it may lack a certain flexibility and, of course, places the funds beyond his control as far as investment decisions are concerned. On the other hand, if the plan is wisely administered, the investment value of the deferred benefit may be greater than what might be expected from investments made by an inexperienced employee.

(2) From the employer's standpoint there are some very real advantages. If the plan is unfunded, the cost of the plan is restricted to the amounts which are in fact paid to employees. The employer receives the employee's

---

[110] See Rev. Rul. 68–454, 1968–2 Cum. Bull. 164.
[111] See text accompanying note 80 *supra*.

services now and pays for them at a later date, holding down costs in a period when the enterprise may need to plow back earnings for expansion and increased working capital. This also highlights the fact that the employer is in effect permitted the use of the employee's funds for a substantial period of time. If the funds are considered as having been reinvested in the enterprise at a favorable rate of return, the resulting benefit to the employer can be substantial. During the period prior to retirement, when the employer thus has the investment value of the funds which otherwise would have been paid to the employee, he may be assured of the latter's continued faithfulness, for if employment is terminated, the employee will generally lose his right to the deferred compensation, since the benefit is not vested. The employer's "hold" on the employee continues even after the latter's retirement to the extent that the employee may be required to refrain from competition or stand ready to render "consulting" services as a prerequisite to receiving benefits.

In summary, although the benefits for both employer and employee are real enough in this area, they may or may not be substantial, depending upon the employee's other circumstances and the precise nature of the deferred compensation agreement. In view of this one may consider deferred compensation as a supplementary type of fringe benefit, increasing the attractiveness of a scheme which also embodies adequate current compensation, together with at least some retirement benefits under a qualified pension, profit-sharing or stock bonus plan.

The tax aspects of deferred compensation arrangements are not as complex as other types of fringe benefits, particularly qualified pension, profit-sharing and stock bonus plans, qualified stock option plans and employee stock purchase plans. At the risk of some oversimplification, they can be summarized in a few words. If the arrangement is unfunded, as it generally is, the employee receives no taxable income until the latter is paid to him or otherwise made subject to his immediate right of withdrawal. This is so even though, prior to the time he receives the payments (i.e., in the period before his retirement), his rights to eventual payment are fixed and nonforfeitable.[112] Correspondingly, where the plan is unfunded, the employer receives a deduction for payments made to the former employee in the year of payment, provided that the amount, together with the other compensation previously paid to the employee, qualifies under the test of reasonableness imposed by Section 162 of the Code.[113] If the plan is funded and yet has not been qualified for special tax treatment under Section 401 of the Code and related provisions (a somewhat unusual situation), the employer receives a deduction only in the year contributions are made to the fund and then only if the employee's rights in the fund are nonforfeitable.[114]

[112] The basic ruling on this is Rev. Rul. 60–31, 1960–1 Cum. Bull. 174, as modified by Rev. Rul. 64–279, 1964–2 Cum. Bull. 121.

[113] Ibid. See also Int. Rev. Code of 1954, §404(a)(5), and Treas. Reg. §1.404-(a)–12.

[114] Int. Rev. Code of 1954, §404(a)(5).

Also, as before, the deduction is qualified by the pervasive requirement that the benefit be a reasonable one in relation to the employee's services and other compensation. If the employer does not qualify for a deduction because the employee's rights are forfeitable, it is the position of the Internal Revenue Service that the deduction is not available at a later date, whether it be the date when the benefits become nonforfeitable or the date they are actually paid to the employee.[115] This somewhat dogmatic view has been questioned in the courts which have tended to permit a deduction in the year of payment, if not before.[116] Finally, as regards the tax consequences to the employee in a funded nonqualified plan, if his rights are nonforfeitable at the time of the employer's contribution, he is required to include such amount in his income, regardless of whether or not the employer qualifies for a deduction (i.e., irrespective of whether the payment is a reasonable business expense).[117] If the employee's rights are forfeitable, he is taxed on the amount when it is paid to him, whether or not his rights may have become nonforfeitable at an earlier date.[118] In other words, the employee is not required to include the amount in income until the year of receipt if his rights were forfeitable when the contribution was made; no tax arises merely from the vesting of the rights after the contribution and prior to payment.

At the risk of oversimplification, the above tax effects may be diagramed as follows:

Plan Funded or Unfunded?	Vesting at Date of Contribution?	Vesting Later?	Employer Deduction?*	Employee Inclusion?
Unfunded	Yes		Year of payment	Year of payment
	No	Yes	Same	Same
	No	No	Same	Same
Funded	Yes		Year of contribution	Year of contribution
	No	Yes	No deduction at any time?	Year of payment
	No	No	Same	Year of payment

* Employer's deduction is always qualified by the requirement that the amount be reasonable under Section 162 of the Code.

[115] Treas. Reg. §1.404(a)–12.

[116] See Buttrey Stores, Inc. v. United States, 375 F.2d 799 (Ct. Cl. 1967); Mississippi River Fuel Corp. v. United States, 314 F.2d 953 (Ct. Cl. 1963); Russell Mfg. Co. v. United States, 175 F. Supp. 159 (Ct. Cl. 1959). Contra: Wesley Heat Treating Co. v. Commissioner, 267 F.2d 853 (7th Cir. 1959).

[117] Treas. Reg. §§1.402(b)–1 and 1.403(c)–1.

[118] Id. §1.402(b)–1(a)(1).

The above chart illustrates that a funded nonqualified deferred compensation arrangement has no tax advantages for the employee as well as some tax disadvantages for the employer, i.e., the possibility, at least if the regulations are upheld by a court, that the employer may lose its deduction entirely unless the employee's rights are nonforfeitable at the time the contribution is made. Thus the employer may not impose conditions on the employee's right to receive the payments, other than the general requirement that he wait until retirement in order to receive the benefit.[119] From the employee's standpoint the arrangement is distasteful in that although the employer will probably give him vested rights in order to insure deductibility of the contribution, the employee must pay a tax at the time of contribution on amounts which he will receive only at some time in the future. In this respect he pays now and enjoys later, which is likely to be the precise opposite of his preferred philosophy of life.

It is therefore more fruitful to concentrate our attention in the remainder of this discussion on the unfunded deferred compensation arrangement. Among the various tax problems which may arise is that of so-called constructive receipt. This is described in the regulations as follows:

> Income although not actually reduced to a taxpayer's possession is constructively received by him in the taxable year during which it is credited to his account, set apart for him, or otherwise made available so that he may draw upon it at any time, or so that he could have drawn upon it during the taxable year if notice of intention to withdraw had been given. However, income is not constructively received if the taxpayer's control of its receipt is subject to substantial limitations or restrictions.[120]

An illustration of this principle is *Richard R. Deupree*.[121] There the president of a corporation had been paid additional compensation for a number of years in cash. However, in 1938 he directed the company to purchase a single premium annuity for his benefit, which was not assignable and which had no cash surrender value. The Tax Court held that since he could have received the cash and instead elected to have the company purchase the annuity in lieu of cash, he should be treated as having constructively received the cash and having reinvested it in the annuity. On the other hand, where the taxpayer, *prior* to the time he becomes legally entitled to receive a designated amount, agrees that the amount will be paid to him at some later date, the constructive receipt doctrine will not apply if the agreement is binding and at arm's length and not merely a formalistic attempt to disguise the fact that the amount is subject to the effective control of the recipient but that he chooses not to receive it when it is within his power to

---

119 Id. §1.402(b)–1(a)(2)(iii), stating that the mere fact that an employee may not live to retirement or may live only a short time thereafter and thus may not be able to enjoy the benefit does not make his beneficial interest forfeitable.

120 Id. §1.451–2(a).

121 1 T.C. 113 (1942). For other cases involving constructive receipt as well as a good discussion of the area see, 1 G. Washington and V. Rothschild, Compensating the Corporate Executive 119 n.55 and 124–136 (3d ed. 1962).

do so. For example, in *Commissioner v. Oates*,[122] a general agent of an insurance company was entitled to receive commissions on renewal premiums as they were collected during the nine years subsequent to his retirement. This would have resulted in his receiving a relatively large amount of commissions during the first year of his retirement, with lesser amounts being paid in later years. In order to provide greater regularity in payment amounts, the taxpayer and the insurance company entered into an agreement whereby he could elect to have the payments made either on the existing basis or in equal monthly installments over a period not to exceed fifteen years. The election, once made, was binding on both parties and could not be modified. The taxpayer elected to have the commissions paid over the fifteen-year period and the company credited the agent's account with the commissions due him as they were collected but paid him lesser amounts in accordance with a schedule of payments to run over the fifteen years. Both the Tax Court and the Court of Appeals rejected the Commissioner's attempt to charge the taxpayer with the full amount of the commissions collected on his behalf in the year they were credited to his account, and gave effect to the contract which spread them out over the lengthier period, saying that the arrangement amounted to a novation whereby the original obligation was extinguished and replaced by the different one. The Commissioner at first refused to acquiesce in this decision,[123] but subsequently, in a basic statement of policy,[124] reversed his earlier position and acquiesced. Among the illustrative situations referred to in the revenue ruling was that of an author and a publisher who had entered into an agreement whereby the former was to receive royalties based on semiannual statements of the sales of a book. On the same day that the contract was signed another agreement was entered into whereby, notwithstanding the first agreement, the publisher would pay the taxpayer not more than a designated amount in any one calendar year, with any excess amounts which otherwise would have been due under the earlier agreement being carried over to succeeding payment periods. The publisher was not required to pay interest on the amounts held in the taxpayer's account or to segregate such amounts from his general funds. In giving effect to the second contract and permitting deferral of the tax until the amounts were actually received, it was emphasized that the supplemental agreement was made before the royalties were earned. From this one might infer that had the amounts become due under the first contract before the second was signed, such amounts would have been taxable to the author under the doctrine of constructive receipt. These agreements will therefore be given effect only if they are entered into before the taxpayer has an unqualified right to receive the amounts in question.[125]

[122] 207 F.2d 711 (7th Cir. 1953).
[123] See 1952–2 Cum. Bull. 5.
[124] Rev. Rul. 60–31, 1960–1 Cum. Bull. 174, 180.
[125] For a more recent statement of the Service's position on these arrangements,

Problems may arise in a closely held corporation when an executive, who also controls a majority of the shares and thus the board of directors, enters into an agreement with the corporation whereby payment of compensation is deferred. In this situation one might well question whether there can ever be a true arm's-length agreement which would effectively bind the taxpayer in that it is always within his power to cause the board of directors to surrender its rights under the agreement and pay the amounts in accordance with the needs and desires of the controlling shareholder. The point was raised in *Casale v. Commissioner*,[126] wherein the chief executive officer and 98 percent shareholder of a corporation entered into an agreement whereby the latter would purchase an insurance policy on the taxpayer's life under which monthly payments were to be made to him after he reached the age of sixty-five. The policy was purchased by the company incident to a deferred compensation agreement between it and the taxpayer whereby it would be obligated to make similar payments to him after the age of sixty-five but only if the taxpayer did not leave his employment against the company's wishes before reaching retirement and only if he refrained from accepting employment with any competitor after retirement. The Tax Court, following the Commissioner's suggestion, included in the taxpayer's income the premiums which the corporation paid to obtain the insurance, refusing to recognize the separate identity of the corporation or the significance of the compensation agreement, since the corporation was totally subservient to the taxpayer's wishes. This was reversed by the Second Circuit Court of Appeals, which chose to respect the separate identity of the corporation and the fact that it and not the taxpayer was the owner of the policy, pointing out that the taxpayer, under the deferred compensation agreement, assumed the risk that the company, although almost wholly owned by him, might become insolvent.

A concept which is easily confused with constructive receipt is that of economic benefit. The difference between the two is that constructive re-

---

see Rev. Rul. 69–649, 1969–2 Cum. Bull. 106, and Rev. Rul. 69–650, 1969–2 Cum. Bull. 106. In the first of these, a deferred compensation arrangement was entered into during the year when the services were performed. However, selection of the employees who might be entitled to participate in the plan and the amount of the bonus was fixed by a committee of the company's board of directors, who were neither officers nor employees of the company nor any of its affiliates. The committee had sole discretion as to whether to defer any part of the bonus and to specify the time of payment. Although the agreement was entered into in the year the employee rendered the services for which the bonus served as compensation, deferral of the tax was obtained because the arrangement was under the control of a disinterested committee and not subject to the direction of the employee. The second ruling presents an easier case, in that the employee's election to defer receipt of the benefits until a later year had to be made prior to the year in which the amounts were earned. Presumably an arrangement of this type would not require the supervision of an executive committee and the amount and timing of the payment could be specified by the employee, provided that the election is binding and irrevocable.

[126] 247 F.2d 440 (2d Cir. 1957). For discussion of this area see 1 G. Washington and V. Rothschild, id. at 134–136.

ceipt relates to the problem of *when* a taxable item must be included in the income of a cash basis taxpayer; economic benefit relates not to *when* (i.e., the particular year of inclusion) but to *whether* a noncash item should be considered as taxable to a cash basis taxpayer because it results in a distinct benefit to him.[127] Thus in *Renton K. Brodie*,[128] an employer's purchase of a paid-up retirement annuity, unconditionally transferred to the taxpayer, resulted in an economic benefit, the value of which was taxed to him, even though the annuity was neither assignable nor had cash surrender value. And where an employer transfers funds to an irrevocable trust for the taxpayer's benefit, the amount so transferred is taxable to him in the year the contribution is made, unless the trust is established pursuant to a qualified pension, profit-sharing or stock bonus plan.[129] This does not involve constructive receipt since the tax is not imposed because of the taxpayer's control over property or right to receive it. Rather, the tax results from the presence of a benefit which is sufficiently definite that a tax should be imposed although the taxpayer cannot immediately receive cash.

As has been stated, a taxable economic benefit results from an employer's funding of amounts to which the employee has a nonforfeitable right, but the more perplexing question has been whether an unfunded promise by an employer to pay a benefit at some future time might result in a taxable economic benefit even to a cash basis taxpayer if the promise were unconditional. The matter would be particularly troublesome if there were little, if any, risk that the employer might become insolvent or otherwise unable to fulfill the promise. Suppose, for example, that an insurance company or other similar institution were to promise its own employees deferred compensation, without funding the obligation in any way. If the obligation were funded through the purchase of an annuity policy from another insurer, a tax could justifiably be imposed.[130] Is the situation any different where, instead of purchasing a policy, the insurer substitutes its own promise to pay without funding the promise? Although state insurance laws require insurers to maintain adequate reserves to fund their obligations under life, annuity and other policies, the likelihood of an insurer's not being able to meet its obligations to its own employees merely because their rights are based on an unfunded promise may be negligible in the case of large, well established insurers.

Notwithstanding this, it seems fairly well accepted, as expressed by one of the basic rulings on the subject, that "A mere promise to pay, not represented by notes or secured in any way, is not regarded as a receipt of income within the intendment of the cash receipts and disbursements method." [131]

[127] See id. at 119.

[128] 1 T.C. 275 (1942).

[129] See E. T. Sproull, 16 T.C. 244 (1951), *aff'd per curiam*, 194 F.2d 541 (6th Cir. 1952). See also Int. Rev. Code of 1954, §404(a)(5).

[130] See Renton K. Brodie, 1 T.C. 275 (1942).

[131] Rev. Rul. 60–31, 1960–1 Cum. Bull. 174, 177.

This would be so despite the solvency or stability of the promisor and the fact that the employee's rights are nonforfeitable. In one of the illustrative cases mentioned in the ruling, an employer credited specified amounts to a bookkeeping reserve each year with the understanding that payments from the reserve would commence after the employee's retirement, his becoming a part-time employee or his becoming partially or totally incapacitated. Despite the presence of a bookkeeping reserve, there was no arrangement for segregating the amounts in trust or otherwise. The employee's rights in the reserve were nonforfeitable. The only provision relating to possible loss of benefits was one which would relieve the employer from making *further* credits to the reserve if the employee should fail or refuse to perform his duties. In other words the employee would always be entitled to amounts already credited to his account, but only after his retirement or upon the occurrence of the other contingencies. This arrangement was held to result in no tax to the employee until the payments were made to him.

Despite the Internal Revenue Service's continuing to take the view that an unfunded promise to pay does not itself result in a taxable economic benefit even where the promise is unconditional and the employee's rights nonforfeitable, there is always a risk that this position may be changed some time in the future. For that reason it is common practice to insert various covenants in deferred compensation agreements which subject the employer's promise to pay to a number of contingencies, thus rendering the employee's rights forfeitable. Again, it should be emphasized that such covenants are probably not necessary at the present time to postpone taxability and yet they are inserted as a safeguard against the possibility that the law may change.[132] Furthermore, they also serve a number of other purposes, such as increasing the likelihood that the employee will remain with his employment, that he will perform his duties faithfully and efficiently and that, after retirement, he will not enter into any competing business. Certain covenants, such as one to stand ready to render consulting services, may pose a threat that the receipt of payments might impair the employee's eligibility to receive social security benefits, although this is relatively unlikely except for the period during which such services are in fact rendered and then only to the extent of the fair value of the services, rather than the total amount received as deferred compensation.[133]

[132] For a useful discussion of the need for such covenants, as well as for sample provisions which might be used, see Jacobson, Deferred Income Contracts—Nonqualified Pension Plans, N.Y.U. 27th Inst. on Fed. Tax. 69, 89–92 (1969).

[133] For cases and rulings dealing with the question of what are "earnings" for the purpose of reducing social security benefits, see 1 P-H Soc. Sec. Tax Serv. ¶32,653. The question is resolved primarily on the facts of each situation. The taxpayer in a closely held corporation might be particularly sensitive to attack on this ground in that he might continue to give advice, at least informally, to management subsequent to his retirement. An additional problem arises from the fact that the Internal Revenue Service considers that a consulting contract is an "interest" in the corporation for the purpose of compliance with Section 302(c)(2) as regards the waiver of the

As with forfeiture provisions, which are not needed to effect deferral of tax if the employer's promise remains unfunded, a nonassignability of benefits provision, although not strictly necessary, is nonetheless advisable to establish conclusively that the employee is receiving no immediate economic benefit. There is thus no possibility that he could assign or pledge his rights and receive cash.[134]

An important disadvantage with deferred compensation arrangements as opposed to qualified pension, profit-sharing or stock bonus plans relates to the estate tax consequences. With deferred compensation arrangements a decedent employee's gross estate includes the value of an annuity or other payment receivable by any beneficiary by reason of surviving the decedent if, under the contract, an annuity or other payment was payable to the decedent or he possessed the right to receive the annuity or payment either for his life, for any period not ascertainable without reference to his death or for any period which does not in fact end before his death.[135] Whether or not the right to the payments was forfeitable is immaterial if, at the time of his death, the decedent either was receiving payments or had complied with all his obligations under the contract up to the time of his death and so, at that time, could be said to have had an enforceable right to receive payments sometime in the future had he lived.[136] If, on the other hand, an annuity or other amount is payable from a *qualified* pension, profit-sharing or stock bonus plan to any beneficiary other than the decedent's estate, it is not subject to estate tax except to the extent that the payment represents contributions or payments made by the decedent. Thus employer contributions are excluded from the estate tax.[137]

As far as the gift tax is concerned, no tax will be due unless the employee possesses nonforfeitable rights under the deferred compensation contract and has made an irrevocable designation of his beneficiary.[138] In other words, if his rights are forfeitable, or if he may change the beneficiary, there is no completed gift and no tax is due.

As previously indicated, a death benefit exclusion of $5000 is available for income tax purposes where the decedent's rights were forfeitable at the time of his death. This would also be so in the case of payments made under a joint and survivor annuity if the decedent died prior to the annuity starting date.[139]

The rules as to gift tax and death benefit exclusion are a further reason

---

"family" attribution rules with respect to stock redemptions. See Ch. VI, note 69, and Rev. Rul. 70–104, 1970–10 I.R.B. 9.

[134] See Jacobson, *supra* at 93.

[135] Int. Rev. Code of 1954, §2039(a), (b).

[136] Treas. Reg. §20.2039–1(b), Ex. (3).

[137] Int. Rev. Code of 1954, §2039(c).

[138] See Treas. Reg. §25.2511–1(h)(10). For the exclusion from gift tax of employer contributions under qualified pension, profit-sharing or stock bonus plans, see Int. Rev. Code of 1954, §2517.

[139] See text accompanying notes 95–102 *supra*.

why deferred compensation contracts should contain clauses providing for forfeiture of the employee's rights. Also, as we have seen, such provisions, aside from their tax aspects, insure that the employer will receive the employee's continued faithful and efficient service and that he will not engage in a competing business after his retirement.

10.8 PROFESSIONAL CORPORATIONS

The advantages of corporate life, both from the standpoint of fringe benefits and other aspects such as estate planning, have led many professional persons to take advantage of the so-called professional corporation laws which have now been adopted in virtually every state. Their efforts to do so have, until now, been subject to what could only be termed a negative attitude on the part of the Internal Revenue Service which, under its so-called Kintner Regulations,[140] has continually questioned and litigated the right of professional persons to corporate advantages, despite their attaining corporate status under local law. The overall approach of the Service's attack has been the argument that despite the formal designation under local law of a professional service organization as a "corporation," it lacks the essential attributes of corporate life for federal income tax purposes. These are (1) continuity of life, (2) centralization of management, (3) limited liability (i.e., the liability of the owners for corporate debts is limited to corporate property) and (4) free transferability of interests.[141] To qualify as an "association" or "corporation" for tax purposes, an organization must have more corporate characteristics than noncorporate characteristics. In determining this, all characteristics which are common to both types of organizations (i.e., corporations and partnerships) are not to be considered. Thus a limited partnership may have free transferability of interests and centralized management, but if it lacks continuity of life and limited liability (except for limited partners), it is not an association or corporation for tax purposes.[142]

The regulations proceed to examine in detail the characteristics of professional service organizations and conclude that despite the corporate nomenclature authorized under local law, they lack the characteristics of corporateness in that they do not have the requisite continuity of life, centralized management, limited liability and free transferability of interests that are ordinarily identified with the corporate form.[143] For example, the right to share in the profits of a professional corporation is nearly always conditioned upon a member's continuing to perform services. If a physician

[140] Treas. Reg. §301.7701–2. The name is derived from a leading case, United States v. Kintner, 216 F.2d 418 (9th Cir. 1954).

[141] Ibid.

[142] Treas. Reg. §301.7701–2(a)(3).

[143] Id. §301.7701–2(h).

or an attorney retires, he is usually required to sell his interest back to the firm. Although local law may view the enterprise as a continuing one, the organization, according to the regulations, resembles more a partnership than a corporation.[144] This is also true as regards free transferability of interests. In other words, despite the existence of a first refusal type restriction, if ownership in the enterprise is inextricably intertwined with the performance of services and if the remaining members of the firm have exclusive control over the selection of future members, such a modified form of transferability of interests does not, the regulations say, qualify as a corporate characteristic.[145] The regulations also contain similar observations regarding centralized management and limited liability. Although certain administrative details may be delegated to one or more persons, the actual details, policies and procedures involved in the handling of clients are necessarily left to individual physicians and attorneys. This, according to the regulations, is so different from the centralized management which exists in an ordinary business corporation that it does not qualify for determining corporateness for tax purposes.[146] And where, under local law, a mutual agency relationship exists between members of a professional service organization which is similar to that of an ordinary professional partnership, the organization lacks the corporate characteristic of limited liability.[147]

It would be of doubtful utility to recapitulate in detail the battle which has been so vigorously fought over this territory, either by recounting the numerous cases which the Internal Revenue Service has lost and which have invalidated the Kintner Regulations,[148] or by recapitulating the voluminous commentary which this litigation has generated.[149] It should suffice to say that on August 8, 1969, the Internal Revenue Service announced that it would not continue to litigate the question,[150] but it also announced its intention to seek legislative reform. This is where the matter now stands. Physicians and attorneys may incorporate, but they may not be assured that the rules will remain unchanged. There is, in fact, every expectation that the Internal Revenue Service, having lost its battle in the courts, will eventually resume the fight in Congress.

[144] Id. §301.7701–2(h)(2).
[145] Id. §301.7701–2(h)(5).
[146] Id. §301.7701–2(h)(3).
[147] Id. §301.7701–2(h)(4).
[148] For a collection of most of the cases see Troyer, Prescriptions for Professionals by Doctors Kintner and Keogh: The Current State of the Therapy, and Some Observations on Prognosis, N.Y.U. 27th Inst. on Fed. Tax. 1279 (1969).
[149] For bibliography see id. at 1288 n.32. See also 66 Mich. L. Rev. 779, 781 n.6 (1968). A recent exhaustive discussion is Fox, The Maximum Scope of the Association Concept, 25 Tax L. Rev. 311 (1970).
[150] See Rev. Rul 70–101, 1970–9 I.R.B. 13.

XI Close Corporation Legislation

In Chapter III we saw how many troublesome problems arise because most corporation statutes are better accommodated to the needs of publicly held corporations than closely held ones. For example, most statutes require that a corporation have a board of directors elected by the shareholders, and that such a board exercise its "discretion" in managing the company's business.[1] The directors elect officers and exercise their discretion as to who the officers shall be and what salaries they shall be paid. All of this seems unnecessarily formalistic, if not incongruous, in a closely held corporation where the same persons generally elect themselves directors and appoint themselves officers. We are told that as shareholders they may not enter into agreements binding their discretion when they act as directors.[2] Thus they may not provide minimum salaries in the bylaws or in a shareholders' agreement, nor specify that various individuals are to be retained in corporate offices; such matters are left up to the directors and their discretion must be unimpeded lest the shareholders (often the same persons) or creditors suffer (even though shareholders may often be personally liable on individual guarantees of the indebtedness of a closely held concern). Where all the shares are held by a single individual, he may find that he must still have at least three directors, all elected by himself. The result is that the board consists of the sole shareholder and two "dummy" directors, who have little or no discretion to exercise, or act in peril of being ousted from the board or not being reelected. In a similar vein some states require that there be at least two officers.[3] Where the corporation is owned by a single individual, it is he who is normally elected president; the other corporate office, often a corporate secretary, is filled by whoever acts as counsel or advisor to the sole shareholder and in effect serves at his pleasure. Unless the statute otherwise

[1] E.g., Ill. Bus. Corp. Act §33 (1957). For further discussion see Ch. III, text accompanying notes 167–182.

[2] Ibid.

[3] E.g., Mo. Gen. & Bus. Corp. Law §351.360 (1965) (president and secretary; no person may occupy both offices, although the same person may hold two or more other offices). See also Model Bus. Corp. Act §50 (president, one or more vice-presidents, secretary and treasurer; any two or more offices may be held by the same person except the offices of president and secretary).

provides, there must be meetings of shareholders and directors.[4] In the context of a closely held concern, the requirement of a formal meeting is often incongruous and not easily understood by the client, for he customarily confers with his associates in the course of normal business activities and a meeting merely formalizes what has already been decided among them.

One could enumerate other inconveniences and uncertainties which arise when a closely held concern must operate under a statute which is more appropriate for a publicly held one. Thus, as we have seen, there may be difficulties as to how shareholder agreements are enforced (entirely apart from their validity insofar as they purport to restrict the discretion of directors).[5] There are uncertainties as to the enforceability of irrevocable proxy arrangements and the unclear requirement that a proxy, to be irrevocable, must be "coupled with an interest." [6] There are uncertainties as to various stock transfer restrictions, arising from a policy against "unreasonable" restraints on alienation of personal property, and the accompanying difficulty of determining when a given restriction is unreasonable.[7] Finally (this list being merely illustrative and not exhaustive) there are problems which result from the fact that a corporation is less flexible and less easily dissolved than a partnership. Any member of a partnership may dissolve the firm at any time although in doing so he may be liable in damages for breach of the partnership agreement.[8] As we have seen, a corporation is not as easily dissolved. In many states a so-called voluntary dissolution requires the vote of at least a majority of the outstanding shares entitled to vote,[9] and a so-called involuntary dissolution requires a judicial determination that the corporation is deadlocked, that the shareholders are unable to break the deadlock, that irreparable injury to the corporation is being suffered or is threatened thereby, that the acts of the directors or those in control of the corporation are illegal, oppressive or fraudulent, or that the corporate assets are being misapplied or wasted.[10] We have seen that courts may be reluctant to dissolve a solvent going concern even though the statutory grounds for dissolution are shown to exist.[11]

All of the foregoing difficulties complicate the job of business planning for the closely held corporation, particularly in protecting the interests of the minority shareholders who have a legitimate concern in not being

[4] A number of states, however, provide that action may be taken by shareholders or directors without a meeting if unanimous consent to the action to be taken is obtained. See, e.g., id. §§44, 145.

[5] See Ch. III, text accompanying notes 116–155, and particularly the discussion of Ringling v. Ringling Bros.–Barnum & Bailey Combined Shows, Inc., at note 128.

[6] See Ch. III, text accompanying notes 156–166.

[7] See id., text accompanying notes 1–39.

[8] See Uniform Partnership Act §31(2). See also J. Crane and A. Bromberg, Partnership §75 (1968).

[9] See, e.g., Model Bus. Corp. Act §84(c).

[10] See, e.g., id. §97(a).

[11] See Ch. VII, text accompanying notes 71–76.

"squeezed out," "frozen out" or "diluted out" at some future time.[12] Hence it is to be expected that some state laws have been revised to accommodate them more precisely to the needs of the closely held corporation. However, it is puzzling that only a relatively few states have thus far enacted appreciable amounts of legislation in this respect. The states which have done so, for the most part, have been the eastern, industrially oriented states rather than the more rural states which may yet have a vital interest in the relatively small, closely held concern as opposed to the large, publicly held one.

The reasons for resistance to legislation of this type are not entirely clear. Professor O'Neal has surmised that there may be a fear that separate legislation for closely held corporations would impede their growth and discourage their evolution into publicly held concerns.[13] In addition, he has suggested that some members of the corporate bar may have discouraged such legislation because of a fear that separate statutory provisions for the closely held concern would politically isolate large, publicly held concerns and prevent their being grouped with the smaller closely held corporations which may have considerable political power.[14] Whether or not such fears exist or are well-founded is even more difficult to determine. Perhaps the experience of those states where close corporation legislation has been adopted will provide more information along these lines, from the standpoint of what types of legislation are desirable and feasible and what their political, economic and other effects will be.

Another possible reason for reluctance to enact close corporation legislation is the difficulty of defining precisely what is meant by a close corporation. The draftsmen of the New York statute, for example, abandoned any attempt to delineate the difference between a close corporation and a publicly held one.[15] On the other hand, the Delaware and Pennsylvania statutes define a close corporation as one in which all the corporation's stock of all classes, exclusive of treasury shares, is held of record by not more than a specified number of persons, not to exceed thirty, as set forth in its certificate of incorporation. In addition, all of the shares must be subject to one or more restrictions on transfer and the corporation may not make any public offering of its shares, as defined in the Securities Act of 1933.[16] The Flor-

[12] See generally Ch. IV.

[13] See 1 F. O'Neal, Close Corporations: Law and Practice §1.13 at 28 (1958).

[14] Ibid. See also Hetherington, Special Characteristics, Problems, and Needs of the Close Corporation, [1969] Ill. L.F. 1, discussing many of the recently enacted statutory provisions.

[15] See Joint Legislative Committee to Study Revision of Corporation Laws, (First) Interim Report to 1957 Session of New York State Legislature, 1957 N.Y. Legislation Docket No. 17, at 115. See also Hoffman, New Horizons for the Close Corporation in New York Under Its New Business Corporation Law, 28 Brooklyn L. Rev. 1, 2 (1961). But see N.Y. Bus. Corp. Law §620 (1965), discussed *infra* note 18. Cf. Md. Gen. Corp. Law §100 (1967), which merely defines a close corporation as one whose charter contains a statement that it is a close corporation.

[16] Del. Gen. Corp. Law §342 (1967); Pa. Bus. Corp. Law §372 (1968).

ida statute, on the other hand, applies to any corporation whose shares are not "generally traded in the markets maintained by securities dealers or brokers." [17] Both New York[18] and South Carolina[19] have somewhat similar criteria as to the applicability of provisions relating to various agreements between shareholders. Thus the New York provision applies to any corporation whose shares are not *listed* on a national securities exchange or regularly *quoted* in an over-the-counter market by one or more members of a national or affiliated securities association. South Carolina, on the other hand, applies its provision as long as the shares are not *traded* on a national securities exchange or "regularly traded" in any over-the-counter market maintained by "one or more brokers or dealers in securities," a test similar to that adopted in Florida and somewhat vaguer than the New York one. Due to the difficulties of determining when shares are regularly traded or regularly quoted in an over-the-counter market, the draftsmen of the Delaware statute adopted an approach modeled after that of the "private company," formerly in the English statute.[20] This seems sound not only in view of the difficulty of determining when the trading or quotation of shares is regular but also in view of the possibility that shareholders who wish to avoid their commitments might seize upon a period of sporadic trading in a company's securities as a reason for repudiating an otherwise valid agreement.

Legislative reform in this area has taken a number of forms. A handful of eastern states, Delaware, Florida, Maryland and Pennsylvania, have passed statutes that have separate sets of close corporation provisions.[21] Several other states, without enacting a separate subdivision of the statute applica-

[17] Fla. Gen. Corp. Law §608.0100(2) (1963). See also Ga. Bus. Corp. Code §22–611 (1969).

[18] N.Y. Bus. Corp. Law §620 (1965). See also N.J. Bus. Corp. Act §14A:5–21(3)(b) (1968).

[19] S.C. Bus. Corp. Act §12–16.22(c) (1962).

[20] The membership of a "private corporation" was limited to fifty, the right to transfer shares was restricted and public offerings were prohibited. See L. Gower, The Principles of Modern Company Law 13 (1954). For further discussion see Folk, Corporation Statutes: 1959–1966, [1966] Duke L.J. 875, 946, and 1 F. O'Neal, Close Corporations §§1.02, 1.13 (1958). However, the Jenkins Committee on Company Law Reform recommended that the distinction between public and private companies be eliminated. See Report of the Company Law Committee, Cmd. No. 1749, ¶¶63, 67 (1962). This was done in the 1967 Companies Act, Part I, cl. 2. See Thompson, The Companies Act 1967, [1968] J. Bus. Law 7, 9.

[21] See Del. Gen. Corp. Law §341–356 (1967); Fla. Gen. Corp. Law §§608.0100–608.0107 (1963); Md. Gen. Corp. Law §§100–111 (1967); Pa. Bus. Corp. Law §§371–386 (1968). For discussion of these statutes see Bradley, A Comparative Evaluation of the Delaware and Maryland Close Corporation Statutes, [1968] Duke L.J. 425; Bradley, Toward a More Perfect Close Corporation—The Need for More and Improved Legislation, 54 Geo. L.J. 1145 (1966); E. Folk, The New Delaware Corporation Law 27 (1967); Folk, Corporation Statutes: 1959–1966, [1966] Duke L.J. 875, 926; Hall, The New Maryland Close Corporation Law, 27 Md. L. Rev. 341 (1967); Hetherington, Special Characteristics, Problems and Needs of the Close Corporation, [1969] Ill. L.F. 1; Kessler, Drafting a Shareholders' Agreement for a New York Close Corporation, 35 Fordham L. Rev. 625 (1967); O'Neal, Developments in the Regulation of the Close Corporation, 50 Cornell L. Rev. 641 (1965); Comment, 75 Harv. L. Rev. 852 (1962). See also note 74 *infra*.

ble exclusively to closely held corporations, have adopted specific provisions designed to meet the needs of close corporations, an approach which from a practical standpoint more or less amounts to the same thing.[22] Other states, without adopting such relatively progressive legislation, have at least entered upon the path of reform by abolishing the need for more than one incorporator,[23] providing that the number of directors need be no greater than the number of shareholders[24] and permitting informal action by directors and shareholders in lieu of a meeting[25]—in effect allowing a "one-man" corporation.[26] These provisions, as well as others, permitting so-called veto powers (higher than majority quorum or voting rights for directors' or shareholders' meetings),[27] broadening the grounds upon which a deadlocked corporation may be dissolved,[28] and defining with greater precision the scope of preemptive rights[29] as well as permissible stock transfer restrictions[30]—these will now be discussed in greater detail.

11.1 STATUTORY PROVISION FOR SHAREHOLDERS' AGREEMENTS

It has already been said that troublesome problems arise in enforcing shareholders' agreements. First, although shareholders may generally agree as to how they will vote their shares (short of the prohibition against vote selling),[31] it is uncertain whether such agreements may be specifically enforced, particularly with the lack of judicial definition of when an irrevocable proxy is coupled with a sufficient interest. Secondly, there are uncer-

---

[22] See, e.g., Conn. Stock Corp. Act §33–339 (1959); Ga. Bus. Corp. Code §22–611 (1969); La. Bus. Corp. Law §12:29 (1968); Mass. Bus. Corp. Law §54 (1965); N.J. Bus. Corp. Act §14A:5–21 (1968); N.Y. Bus. Corp. Law §620 (1965); N.C. Bus. Corp. Act §55–73 (1955); S.C. Bus. Corp. Act §12–16.22 (1962); Tenn. Gen. Corp. Law §48–7.14 (1968); Tex. Bus. Corp. Act art. 2.30 (1955); Wyo. Bus. Corp. Act §31 (1961).

[23] Over half the states have done this. See 1 P-H Corp. Serv. ¶¶9001–9051.

[24] A little less than half of the states have done this. See ibid.

[25] See, e.g., Del. Gen. Corp. Law §228 (1970); Ga. Bus. Corp. Code §22–603 (1969); Mich. Gen. Corp. Act §21.13 (1948); N.J. Bus. Corp. Act §14A:5–6 (1969); Pa. Bus. Corp. Law §513 (1968). See also Model Bus. Corp. Act §§44, 145. See text accompanying notes 61–66 *infra*.

[26] See N.C. Bus. Corp. Act §55–3.1 (1955), providing that the existence of a corporation is not to be impaired by the acquisition by one person of all the shares. The statute was apparently enacted in response to a judicial implication to the contrary in Park Terrace v. Phoenix Indemnity Co., 243 N.C. 595, 91 S.E.2d 584 (1956). See also Mo. Gen. & Bus. Corp. Law §351.050 (1965). See Latty, A Conceptualistic Tangle and the One or Two-Man Corporation, 34 N.C.L. Rev. 471 (1956).

[27] See text accompanying notes 67–75 *infra*. See also Ch. III, text accompanying notes 183–201.

[28] See text accompanying notes 103–116 *infra*.

[29] See id. notes 76–86 *infra*.

[30] See id. notes 87–102 *infra*.

[31] See Ch. III, text accompanying notes 119–124.

tainties as to whether shareholders may agree on how, as directors, they will vote on certain matters falling within their discretion. Thirdly, it is unclear whether shareholders may directly assume some of the powers otherwise within the province of a board of directors (such as the setting of salaries, appointment of officers, establishing minimum rates of dividend payment, etc.), or whether they may do away with a board of directors and operate the corporation by a method analogous to a partnership. This is unlawful except in those states having statutory provisions expressly permitting this technique to be used. It is now appropriate to consider various statutory solutions to these three problems arising in connection with shareholders' agreements.

11.2 ENFORCING AGREEMENTS AS TO VOTING SHARES; IRREVOCABLE PROXIES

Two of the most popular provisions relating to the validity of "pooling agreements" among shareholders and the manner in which they may be enforced are those adopted by New York and Delaware. Section 620(a) of the New York Business Corporation Law provides:

> An agreement between two or more shareholders, if in writing and signed by the parties thereto, may provide that in exercising any voting rights, the shares held by them shall be voted as therein provided, or as they may agree, or as determined in accordance with a procedure agreed upon by them.

Section 609(f)(5) of the New York Business Corporation Law supplements this by providing that a proxy may state that it is irrevocable and may be enforced as such if it is held by one or more individuals acting in certain capacities,[32] including "a person designated by or under an agreement under paragraph (a) of section 620." Georgia, New Jersey and Tennessee[33] have adopted statutory provisions very similar to that of New York.

The Delaware provision[34] was modeled after its New York counterpart, contains essentially the same language except for minor variations, and goes on to provide that the agreement is limited to a ten-year period, except that, at any time within two years prior to its expiration, it may be extended for as many additional ten-year periods as the parties may desire. Delaware, like New York, provides for the enforceability of irrevocable proxies, but, unlike the New York statute, there is no express reference to proxies given to persons designated under a shareholders' voting agreement. Rather, the

---

[32] A pledgee, a person who has purchased the shares or has agreed to do so, a creditor of the corporation, and a person who has contracted to perform services as an officer of the corporation, if a proxy is required by the contract of employment.

[33] See Ga. Bus. Corp. Code §§22–610, 22–611 (1969); N.J. Bus. Corp. Act §14A:5–21 (1968); Tenn. Gen. Corp. Law §§48–7.06, 48–7.14 (1968).

[34] Del. Gen. Corp. Law §218(c) (1969).

Delaware statute contains the classic requirement that the proxy, to be irrevocable, must be "coupled with an interest sufficient in law to support an irrevocable power" but clarifies this by stating that "A proxy may be made irrevocable regardless of whether the interest with which it is coupled is an interest in the stock itself or an interest in the corporation generally." [35] This language would support a holding that an irrevocable proxy, given by shareholders to one another pursuant to a valid pooling agreement, would be enforceable even if no shareholder were to have a legal or equitable interest in the shares of any other shareholder, such as a first-refusal option or a cross-purchase agreement. Also it is highly likely that the Delaware courts will now hold that mutual promises given pursuant to a valid pooling agreement are sufficient to make a proxy irrevocable, since each shareholder has the necessary "interest in the corporation generally." [36] Finally, the Delaware provision, which also contains the requirements for a valid voting trust, now provides that "This section shall not be deemed to invalidate any voting or other agreement among stockholders or any irrevocable proxy which is not otherwise illegal." [37] Thus, in the words of one of the draftsmen of the provision, "the similarity to a voting trust is no longer a ground, as it was under prior case law, to strike down an arrangement which complies with the relevant statute." [38]

Connecticut has a provision which follows, in general, the New York pattern (i.e., validating pooling agreements and making irrevocable a proxy given in connection with a pooling agreement) and, like the Delaware provision, limits the agreement to ten years, subject to extension for an additional ten-year period.[39] A similar ten-year limitation is imposed by the Texas and South Carolina statutes.[40] Georgia limits the agreement to twenty years.[41] Some states, such as Connecticut and Texas, require the voting agreement to be deposited with the corporation and made subject to inspection rights by any shareholder in a manner similar to a shareholder's right to inspect corporate books and records, and also require that the existence of the agreement be noted on the certificates of shares covered by the agreement.[42] As one commentator has pointed out,[43] this approach subjects shareholder pooling agreements to requirements similar to those imposed on voting trusts, whereas in other states, such as New York, South Carolina

---

[35] Id. §212(c) (1969).

[36] See Ch. III, text accompanying notes 146–149 and 157–166.

[37] Del. Gen. Corp. Law §218(e) (1969).

[38] See E. Folk, The New Delaware Corporation Law 27 (1967). See also Ch. III text accompanying note 92, and Abercombie v. Davies, 36 Del. Ch. 371, 130 A.2d 338 (Sup. Ct. 1957).

[39] Conn. Stock Corp. Act §33–339 (1959).

[40] Tex. Bus. Corp. Act art. 2.30 (1955); S.C. Bus. Corp. Act 12–16.15 (1962).

[41] Ga. Bus. Corp. Code §22–611(c) (1969).

[42] See statutes in notes 39–40 *supra*.

[43] Folk, Corporation Statutes: 1959–1966, [1966] Duke L.J. 875, 926.

and Wyoming, such an agreement is more akin to the common law version of a pooling agreement.[44]

Other states, such as Louisiana and Maryland,[45] also have provisions specifically permitting shareholder pooling agreements.

As to the enforceability of pooling agreements, the New York provision is fairly representative of the general approach, i.e., specifying that the agreement may provide how the shares shall be voted or that the shares shall be voted "as determined in accordance with a procedure agreed upon by [the parties to the agreement]," [46] and then specifically authorizing irrevocable proxies given pursuant to the agreement. This, at least, provides for machinery whereby specific enforcement may be obtained. The Wyoming and Maryland statutes, however, are considerably more explicit. For example, Wyoming provides:

> In an action by a shareholder who is a party to such an agreement a court of competent jurisdiction may enjoin another party or parties to such agreement from voting his or their shares in violation thereof, and the court may, in an action to which the corporation is a party, by appropriate decree set aside an election of directors or other action resulting from the voting of shares in violation of such agreement, and in addition the court may grant such other or further relief as is appropriate under the circumstances for the enforcement of such agreement.[47]

Other states, such as Texas and South Carolina,[48] provide for enforcement, although not in as comprehensive terms as those of the Wyoming and Maryland provisions.

11.3 SHAREHOLDER AGREEMENTS WHICH IMPEDE THE EXERCISE OF DIRECTORS' DISCRETION

Several states have provisions which permit the shareholders, either by an agreement or by a provision in the articles of incorporation or bylaws, to bind themselves as to various matters which would otherwise fall within the discretion of the board of directors. Although most of the statutes merely state that the agreement, or provision in the articles of incorporation,

---

[44] See N.Y. Bus. Corp. Law §620(a) (1965); S.C. Bus. Corp. Act §12–16.15 (1962); Wyo. Bus. Corp. Act §31 (1961).

[45] La. Bus. Corp. Law §12:29 (1968); Md. Gen. Corp. Law §104 (1967); cf. also Pa. Bus. Corp. Law §385 (1968) (shareholders of closely held corporations may enter into agreement to "operate corporation as a partnership," and in doing so may agree as to the election of directors or officers).

[46] See N.Y. Bus. Corp. Law §620(a) (1965), quoted in text accompanying note 32 *supra*.

[47] See Wyo. Bus. Corp. Act §31 (1961). See also Md. Gen. Corp. Law §104 (1967).

[48] See note 40 *supra*.

is not invalid, as between the parties to the agreement or the shareholders of the corporation, on the ground that it so relates to the conduct of the business and affairs of the corporation as to restrict or interfere with the discretion or powers of the board of directors[49]

some statutes, such as that in Maryland,[50] spell out the various topics which an agreement of this type might cover (the following list, however, not purporting to be an exhaustive one).

(1) The management of the business and the affairs of the corporation
(2) Restrictions on the transfer of stock
(3) The right of one or more stockholders to dissolution of the corporation at will or upon the occurrence of a specified event or contingency
(4) The exercise or division of voting power
(5) The terms and conditions of the employment of any officer or employee regardless of the length of the period of such employment
(6) The persons who shall be directors and officers of the corporation
(7) The payment of dividends or divisions of profits

A number of states require that if the provision is not in the bylaws or articles of incorporation, then it must be in an agreement to which *all* the shareholders are parties.[51] Some states, however, permit such agreements between less than all of the shareholders (i.e., between a majority) [52] and at least four states permit persons who are not shareholders (e.g., creditors) to be parties to the agreement.[53] In any event, such agreements are commonly valid only if the corporation qualifies as a close corporation, i.e., if its shares are not listed, or regularly traded or quoted in an over-the-counter market[54] and the agreement is often limited to a ten- or twenty-year period, subject to extension as in the case of shareholder voting agreements.[55]

[49] Pa. Bus. Corp. Law §381 (1968). See also Del. Gen. Corp. Law §350 (1967).
[50] Md. Gen. Corp. Law §104 (1967). See also Fla. Gen. Corp. Law §608.0105 (1963) for a similar listing.
[51] E.g., Ga. Bus. Corp. Code §22–611(b) (1969); La. Bus. Corp. Law §12:29 (1968); Md. Gen. Corp. Law §104 (1967); N.J. Bus. Corp. Act §14A:5–21 (1968) (must be in certificate of incorporation); N.Y. Bus. Corp. Law §620(b) (1965) (must be in certificate of incorporation); S.C. Bus. Corp. Act §12–16.22 (1962) (must be in articles of incorporation); cf. Mass. Bus. Corp. Law §54 (1965) (articles of incorporation or bylaws may reserve to shareholders powers normally held by directors).
[52] Del. Gen. Corp. Law §350 (1967); Fla. Gen. Corp. Law §608.0105(3) (1963); N.C. Bus. Corp. Act §55–73(c) (1955); Pa. Bus. Corp. Law §381 (1968); Tenn. Gen. Corp. Law §48–7.14 (1968).
[53] Del. Gen. Corp. Law §350 (1967); Fla. Gen. Corp. Law §608.0105(3) (1963); Pa. Bus. Corp. Law §381 (1968); Tenn. Gen. Corp. Law §48–7.14 (1968).
[54] Fla. Gen. Corp. Law §608.0105 (1963); Ga. Bus. Corp. Code §22–611(b) (1969); N.J. Bus. Corp. Act §14A:5–21 (1968); N.Y. Bus. Corp. Law §620(b) (1965); N.C. Bus. Corp. Act §55–73(b); Pa. Bus. Corp. Law §381 (1968); S.C. Bus. Corp. Act §12–16.22 (1962).
[55] E.g., Ga. Bus. Corp. Code §22–611(b) (1969) (twenty years); S.C. Bus. Corp. Act §12–16.22 (1962) (ten years).

Furthermore, the stock certificates must contain a notice of the agreement in order to bind transferees who have no actual knowledge of it.[56] Where the shareholders have agreed to assume some or all of the powers of the directors, it is common to provide that the directors shall to that extent be relieved of liability for managerial acts or omissions which otherwise would be imposed by law on directors, and that such liabilities shall be imposed upon those shareholders who are parties to the agreement.[57]

11.4 SHAREHOLDERS' ASSUMPTION OF DIRECTORS' POWERS: ABOLISHING THE BOARD OF DIRECTORS; OPERATION OF A CORPORATION AS A PARTNERSHIP

In contrast to an agreement whereby shareholders seek to bind themselves as to how they shall vote as directors, a more thoroughgoing approach, generally appropriate only where all the shareholders are directors, is to do away with any requirement that there be a board of directors and to have the shareholders run the corporation themselves as they would if they were members of a partnership. Several statutes permit this technique but generally limit it to close corporations, i.e., corporations whose shares are held by no more than a specified number of persons, or whose shares are not listed or regularly traded or quoted in an over-the-counter market.[58] If this approach is used, then a meeting of shareholders is equivalent to a directors' meeting and the liability that would normally be imposed on directors is imposed on the shareholders.[59] Where the shareholders assume all the directors' powers, and dispense with a board of directors, then each shareholder becomes, in a sense, a *de facto* director and subject to a director's duties and liabilities. This should not mean, however, that because as a matter of internal organization the corporation is run "as a partnership" the shareholders are liable to outsiders as partners, unless they have represented themselves to be such and thus have become partners by estoppel.[60] In

---

[56] E.g., Ga. Bus. Corp. Code §22–611(b) (1969); La. Bus. Corp. Law §12:29 (1968); N.J. Bus. Corp. Act §14A:5–21 (1968); N.Y. Bus. Corp. Law §620(b) (1965); S.C. Bus. Corp. Act §12–16.22 (1962).

[57] Del. Gen. Corp. Law §350 (1967); Fla. Gen. Corp. Law §608.0105(3) (1963); Ga. Bus. Corp. Code §22–611(b) (1969); N.J. Bus. Corp. Act §14A:5–21 (1968); N.Y. Bus. Corp. Law §620(b) (1965); Pa. Bus. Corp. Law §381 (1968); S.C. Bus. Corp. Act §12–16.22 (1962); Tenn. Gen. Corp. Law §48–7.14 (1968).

[58] E.g., Del. Gen. Corp. Law §§351, 354 (1967); Fla. Gen. Corp. Law §608.0102 (1967); Md. Gen. Corp. Law §105 (1970); Pa. Bus. Corp. Law §§382, 385 (1968); cf. Ga. Bus. Corp. Code §22–611(b) (1969); N.J. Bus. Corp. Act §14A:5–21(2) (1968); N.C. Bus. Corp. Act §55–73(b) (1955); S.C. Bus. Corp. Act. §12–16.22(a) (1962).

[59] E.g., Del. Gen. Corp. Law §351 (1967); Fla. Gen. Corp. Law §608.0102 (1967); Md. Gen. Corp. Law §105 (1970); Pa. Bus. Corp. Law §382 (1968).

[60] See Uniform Partnership Act §16.

other words, even though a corporation may have elected to be operated as a partnership for the purpose of having its affairs run directly by the shareholders instead of indirectly through a board of directors, it is still a corporation as a matter of law and its shareholders are entitled to the limited liability which usually pertains to shareholder status.

11.5   INFORMAL ACTION BY SHAREHOLDERS AND DIRECTORS

Many states permit directors or shareholders to authorize various corporate acts without holding a formal meeting, provided that either all or at least a majority of those who would otherwise be entitled to vote file a written consent to the proposed action and that such a procedure is authorized by the articles of incorporation or the bylaws. As previously indicated, this makes sense in a closely held concern, since the directors and the shareholders are frequently the same people and at least a majority of them are generally involved with the active conduct of the business, although this is not invariably so, since some investors may play a relatively passive role, and yet it is still likely that those who hold a majority interest in the corporation will take an active part in running the business.

In the case of informal action by the directors, it is generally required that the consent of all the directors be obtained for the action proposed to be taken and that the consent be filed with the minutes of directors' meetings. Thus informal action cannot be taken with the consent of only a majority of the board.[61]

The North and South Carolina statutes contain somewhat unusual provisions permitting directors to take informal action without obtaining a written consent from each director if the directors are "accustomed" to take informal action and this custom is "generally known" to the shareholders, and if the directors know of the action in question and no director makes prompt objection thereto. Even if the foregoing conditions are not met, the action is also valid if all of the shareholders know of the action in question and do not promptly object.[62] Although such complete freedom from formality might be convenient in many closely held concerns, it presents difficult problems of proof since there is no written record of consents by shareholders or directors to the action proposed to be taken. A factual inquiry must be made as to whether there was a "custom" to operate the corporation in this fashion, whether the custom was "generally known" to shareholders, whether either directors or shareholders made a "prompt" objection, etc.

[61] See Del. Gen. Corp. Law §141(f) (1970); Ga. Bus. Corp. Code §22–710 (1969); Mich. Gen. Corp. Act §21.13(c) (1948); Nev. Gen. Corp. Law §78.315 (1959); Pa. Bus. Corp. Law §402(7) (1968); Model Bus. Corp. Act §44.
[62] N.C. Bus. Corp. Act §55–29 (1959); S.C. Bus. Corp. Act §12–18.12 (1962).

Where shareholder action is concerned, although some states require that the consent of all the shareholders be obtained,[63] several states permit informal action to be taken with the consent of only a majority of shareholders, or at least the holders of that percentage of the outstanding shares which would be required to authorize the action in question if a meeting were held.[64] As one commentator has pointed out, such a procedure presents serious questions of fairness unless all the shareholders receive notice of the proposed action and the fact that written consents to it have been obtained.[65] Otherwise, minority shareholders could be kept in ignorance of important corporate developments of which, but for the informal procedure, they would have been notified prior to a meeting. Accordingly, some states require that those shareholders who did not consent to the proposed action receive notice of it,[66] and even in the absence of such a requirement it would seem wise to notify minority shareholders in order to lessen the likelihood of litigation at some future date based on fraud or intentional concealment.

11.6 HIGHER THAN MAJORITY QUORUM OR VOTING REQUIREMENTS FOR SHAREHOLDERS' OR DIRECTORS' MEETINGS—VETO POWERS

Although so-called veto powers have already been discussed in considerable detail,[67] some further discussion of the statutory provisions and other aspects may still be appropriate. As we have seen, most of the difficulties in this area stem from the leading New York case *Benintendi v. Kenton Hotel*,[68] which invalidated an agreement requiring unanimity for shareholder or director action. We have also seen how the New York legislature was quick to repeal the *Benintendi* case by enacting Section 9 of the New York Stock Corporation Law,[69] the forerunner of similar legislation enacted in numerous other states.[70] Occasionally a statute may permit the

---

[63] Ga. Bus. Corp. Code §22–603(d) (1969); Mich. Gen. Corp. Act §21.39(1) (1967); Model Bus. Corp. Act §145.

[64] Del. Gen. Corp. Law §228 (1969); N.J. Bus. Corp. Act §14A:5–6(2) (1969); Nev. Gen. Corp. Law §78.320 (1959); N.Y. Bus. Corp. Law §615(a) (1961); Pa. Bus. Corp. Law §513 (1968). The Pennsylvania statute requires the consent of a percentage not less than "the larger of (1) two-thirds of the total number of votes which all shareholders of the corporation or of a class of shareholders are entitled by the articles to cast upon such action or (2) the minimum percentage of the vote required by [the Pennsylvania statute] for the proposed corporate action."

[65] See Folk, Corporation Statutes: 1959–1966, [1966] Duke L.J. 875, 917.

[66] N.J. Bus. Corp. Act §14A:5–6(2) (1969); Pa. Bus. Corp. Law §513 (1968).

[67] See Ch. III, text accompanying notes 183–201.

[68] 294 N.Y. 112, 60 N.E.2d 829 (1945). See Ch. III, text accompanying note 183.

[69] N.Y. Stock Corp. Law §9 (1948). The present New York provisions are found in N.Y. Bus. Corp. Law §§616, 709 (1961).

[70] See Model Bus. Corp. Act §§32,40. See generally 1 F. O'Neal, Close Corporations §§4.14–4.17 (1958).

bylaws or articles of incorporation to specify not only that *more* than a majority may be required for a quorum of directors or shareholders but that *less* than a majority is also permissible. However, if the latter alternative is chosen, it is sometimes specified that a quorum in no case shall be less than a designated percentage of the directors[71] or shareholders.[72] Also, as we have seen,[73] a high quorum or voting requirement in the articles of incorporation or bylaws must be protected from being "amended out" and thus rendered ineffective. This may be done by a provision in the articles or bylaws requiring a high percentage vote for amending the clause containing the high quorum or vote requirement. An alternative is for the statute to specify that the clause may not be amended or eliminated without the vote of a designated percentage of the shareholders.[74] Finally, it should be reiterated that despite the usefulness of these so-called veto powers, they should be employed with caution, lest the corporation be unduly hampered in its activities and be inflexible or deadlocked. A careful study should therefore be made of the various types of corporate action which should be subjected to a high quorum or vote requirement, leaving normal or routine corporate matters to be decided by a simple majority.[75]

11.7 STATUTORY PROVISIONS RELATING TO PREEMPTIVE RIGHTS

As we saw in an earlier discussion,[76] the shareholder's preemptive right is largely a common law doctrine which, along with general equity concepts of fairness and injunctive relief against fraudulent stock issues, protects the shareholder from having his interest diluted. In this sense it resembles the right of a partner not to have additional persons admitted as members of the firm without his consent, unless the partnership agreement provides

[71] See Del. Gen. Corp. Law §141(b) (1970) (no less than one third of the total number of directors, except that where there is only one director then one director shall constitute a quorum).

[72] Model Bus. Corp. Act §32 (no less than one third of the shares entitled to vote at the meeting). But see Iowa Bus. Corp. Act §31 (apparently permitting the articles of incorporation to establish any quorum requirement, no matter how low). For a criticism of this approach, see Folk, Corporation Statutes: 1959–1966, [1966] Duke L.J. 914–915.

[73] See Ch. III, text accompanying note 199.

[74] For a discussion of the various statutory approaches to this problem, see Folk, Corporation Statutes: 1959–1966, [1966] Duke L.J. 875, 919–920. For discussion of these problems with reference to particular jurisdictions, see Dykstra, Molding the Utah Corporation: Survey and Commentary, 7 Utah L. Rev. 1, 6 (1960); Kessler, Certificate of Incorporation for a New York Close Corporation: A Form, 34 Fordham L. Rev. 541, 563 (1965); Logan, Methods to Control the Closely Held Kansas Corporation, 7 Kan. L. Rev. 405, 428–429 (1959).

[75] For discussion see Ch. III, text accompanying note 191.

[76] See Ch. IV, text accompanying notes 12–18.

to the contrary.[77] However, we have seen that the common law preemptive right is severely limited. It attaches only to a *new* issue of shares for *cash* and thus does not relate to sales of treasury shares or shares issued for a noncash consideration, such as property, services or in connection with a merger or reorganization.[78] Accordingly it was suggested that if the minority shareholders are to be fully protected, some thought should be given to broadening the preemptive right by a suitable provision in the articles of incorporation. Enlarging the preemptive right is generally permitted under state laws,[79] and some statutes expressly provide for an expanded preemptive right as to close corporations.[80] Other statutes clarify some of the exceptions to the preemptive right and permit the articles of incorporation to broaden the right to eliminate one or more of the exceptions. Thus the New York Business Corporation law states that, unless otherwise provided in the certificate of incorporation, no preemptive right shall attach to shares if they

(1) Are to be issued by the board to effect a merger or consolidation or offered or subjected to rights or options for consideration other than cash;

(2) Are to be issued or subjected to rights or options [to purchase shares or where such rights or options have been issued to directors, officers and employees];

(3) Are to be issued to satisfy conversion or option rights theretofore granted by the corporation;

(4) Are treasury shares;

(5) Are part of the shares or other securities of the corporation authorized in its original certificate of incorporation and are issued, sold or optioned within two years from the date of filing such certificate; or

(6) Are to be issued under a plan of reorganization approved in a proceeding under any applicable act of congress relating to reorganization of corporations.[81]

The New York statute also contains rather elaborate provisions clarifying the right of shareholders of one class of stock to receive shares of another class.

In view of the possibility that those who draft the articles of incorporation may not focus upon the problem of protecting minority shareholder rights by broadening them in the manner suggested, a statutory provision

[77] See Uniform Partnership Act §18(g).

[78] See Ch. IV, text accompanying notes 14–17.

[79] See 1 F. O'Neal, Close Corporations 121 n.87 (1958).

[80] See Pa. Bus. Corp. Law §379 (1968).

[81] N.Y. Bus. Corp. Law §622(e) (1961). For a similar listing of exceptions to the preemptive right, see Md. Gen. Corp. Law §30 (1967); Ga. Bus. Corp. Law §22–602(d) (1969). See also Model Bus. Corp. Act §26A, limiting preemptive rights to holders of common shares, denying holders of common shares preemptive rights to issues of preferred shares (other than convertible preferred), denying holders of nonvoting common shares preemptive rights to purchase voting common and denying all preemptive rights to purchase shares issued for other than cash—unless otherwise provided in the articles of incorporation.

such as that adopted in Pennsylvania automatically broadening the preemptive rights of shareholders who elect to be covered by the Pennsylvania close corporation provisions seems highly desirable. The Pennsylvania law states that

> Unless otherwise provided in its articles, the holders of any class of voting shares of a close corporation shall have a preemptive right to subscribe for or purchase any voting shares (or any option rights or securities having conversion or option rights with respect to any voting shares) issued or sold by the corporation for any form of consideration from its treasury or otherwise; but this section shall not apply to any issue of voting shares (or of any option rights or securities having conversion or option rights with respect to such voting shares) pursuant to a plan to which section 515 of this act [relating to dissenters' appraisal rights] is applicable.[82]

Such a statute, although allowing the articles of incorporation to "otherwise provide," automatically extends the preemptive right to such areas as the issue of shares (whether or not a part of the "original issue") for property, services or any other form of consideration, and also includes sales of treasury stock. In the case of mergers, consolidations and other organic changes, the preemptive right is denied if the shareholder is entitled to appraisal rights. Thus, if he objects to the transaction, he has an opportunity to be bought out at a fair price. This Pennsylvania approach seems better than that of the Delaware statute, which provides that preemptive rights must be expressly specified in the articles of incorporation, thus eliminating common law preemptive rights, except those in existence when the Delaware amendment took effect (July 3, 1967).[83] One of the draftsmen of this provision stated that the old law, which preserved the common law preemptive right unless specifically denied in the articles of incorporation, was always "hard to define" and that the effect of the Delaware change has been to produce greater certainty.[84] Although it may be safe to assume that closely held corporations desiring preemptive rights will often "spell out the situations in which they wish to have them" [85] it is also possible that the problem may be overlooked by incautious counsel or, perhaps, intentionally left unmentioned by counsel who acts primarily to protect the interests of the majority shareholders. This places an undesirable burden on the minority shareholders: first, to be aware of the need to provide expressly for preemptive rights, and secondly, to insist upon their inclusion in the articles of incorporation before making any financial commitment to the corporation. In many situations ill-informed minority shareholders may overlook the problem or assume that to raise it is to overemphasize a technicality. Pennsylvania has adopted the Delaware approach as to corporations which are

[82] Pa. Bus. Corp. Law §379 (1968).
[83] See Del. Gen. Corp. Law §102(b)(3) (1969).
[84] See E. Folk, The New Delaware Corporation Law 3 (1967).
[85] Ibid.

not closely held. In that respect it has eliminated preemptive rights (unless specified in the articles) except for certain unlisted corporations having preemptive rights at the time the Pennsylvania law became effective.[86] Thus Pennsylvania has used the Delaware technique for publicly held corporations while preserving a different approach for those which are closely held.

11.8   STOCK TRANSFER RESTRICTIONS

As pointed out in a prior discussion, the validity of certain stock transfer restrictions is unclear, particularly those which prohibit the transfer of shares without the consent of the directors or other shareholders or those which prohibit all transfers for a designated period of time, such as one or two years.[87] This is because of a supposed public policy against "unreasonable" restraints on the alienation of personal property. Several statutory attempts have been made to deal with this problem. Although some states merely codify the existing case law, with its attendant confusions,[88] others are more helpful and enumerate in differing degrees of detail various restrictions which are lawful. Texas, for example, permits not only so-called first-refusal restrictions but also buy-and-sell agreements, limiting the latter to situations where there are no more than twenty shareholders of record in the class of stock subject to the agreement.[89] The Wyoming statute is patterned along the lines of the Texas provision and seems more satisfactory in that it also permits consent-type restrictions, but again only where all the shares are owned beneficially and of record by no more than twenty shareholders.[90]

A statute which appears to be having considerable influence on law reform in other states is that of Delaware.[91] This enumerates a wide variety of restrictions which may be imposed in the certificate of incorporation, the bylaws or an agreement between any number of shareholders or between the shareholders and the corporation. The restriction cannot be enforced, except as against a person having actual knowledge of it, unless it is noted conspicuously on the stock certificate.[92] Moreover, the restriction is not binding with respect to securities issued prior to its adoption unless the

---

[86] Pa. Bus. Corp. Law §611 (1968).

[87] See Ch. III, text accompanying notes 1–39.

[88] Ark. Gen. Corp. Act §64–211 (1965); Conn. Stock Corp. Act §33–306a (1961).

[89] Tex. Bus. Corp. Act art. 2.22 (1967).

[90] Wyo. Bus. Corp. Act §32 (1961).

[91] Del. Gen. Corp. Law §202 (1968).

[92] Ibid. This is a codification of similar requirements in Section 8–204 of the Uniform Commercial Code and its predecessor, Section 15 of the Uniform Stock Transfer Act. See Ch. III, text accompanying notes 20–22.

holders of the securities are parties to the agreement, or, if it is in the bylaws or the certificate of incorporation, unless they voted in favor of it.[93] The specific restrictions permitted by the Delaware provision are as follows:

(c) A restriction on the transfer of securities of a corporation is permitted by this section if it:

(1) Obligates the holder of the restricted securities to offer to the corporation or to any other holders of securities of the corporation or to any other person or to any combination of the foregoing, a prior opportunity, to be exercised within a reasonable time, to acquire the restricted securities; or

(2) Obligates the corporation or any holder of securities of the corporation or any other person or any combination of the foregoing, to purchase the securities which are the subject of an agreement respecting the purchase and sale of the restricted securities; or

(3) Requires the corporation or the holders of any class of securities of the corporation to consent to any proposed transfer of the restricted securities or to approve the proposed transferee of the restricted securities; or

(4) Prohibits the transfer of the restricted securities to designated persons or classes of persons, and such designation is not manifestly unreasonable.

(d) Any restriction on the transfer of the shares of a corporation for the purpose of maintaining its status as an electing small business corporation under subchapter S of the United States Internal Revenue Code is conclusively presumed to be for a reasonable purpose.

(e) Any other lawful restriction on transfer or registration of transfer of securities is permitted by this section.[94]

A similar listing may be found in several other states.[95]

The New Jersey statute[96] sets forth the procedure to be followed if a stock transfer restriction is held unenforceable due to its being unreasonable. If this happens, then the corporation is given a right to purchase the shares at a price to be agreed upon or at their fair value as determined by an appraisal proceeding:

(4) If a restriction on transfer of shares or other securities having conversion or option rights is held not to be authorized by the law of this State, the corporation shall nevertheless have an option for a period of 30 days after the judgment setting aside the restriction becomes final, to acquire the restricted securities at a price to be agreed upon by the parties, or if no agreement is reached as to price, then at their fair value as determined by any court having jurisdiction. In order to determine fair value, the court may appoint an appraiser to receive evidence and report to the court his findings and recommendations as to fair value. The appraiser shall

[93] For similar provisions in other states see Conn. Stock Corp. Act §33–306a (1961); N.J. Bus. Corp. Act §14A:7–12 (1968); Nev. Gen. Corp. Law §78.240 (1969); Pa. Bus. Corp. Law §613.1 (1968); Wyo. Bus. Corp. Act §32 (1961).

[94] Del. Gen. Corp. Law §202(c) (1968).

[95] N.J. Bus. Corp. Act §14A:7–12 (1968); Nev. Gen. Corp. Law §78.240 (1969); Pa. Bus. Corp. Law §613.1 (1968).

[96] N.J. Bus. Corp. Act §14A:7–12 (1968).

have such powers and shall proceed so far as applicable, in the same manner as an appraiser appointed under section 14A:11–8.

The comments of the Corporation Law Revision Commission state that it was thought that this procedure would "enable untested restrictions to be employed more freely by reducing the severity of the sanction in case they are held unreasonable." Although this approach may have a certain appeal, if the corporation is given an option to purchase the shares when a transfer restriction is invalid, then there seems to be little reason for the requirement that a restriction must be reasonable. To put the matter differently, a provision of this type in effect enforces an unreasonable restraint, but only enforces it as a first-refusal option, giving the corporation a right to purchase at fair value as determined by an appraisal proceeding. This comes very close to saying that all stock transfer restrictions are valid regardless of reasonableness. In view of the rather tenuous basis for the American (as opposed to English) doctrine on stock transfer restrictions and the doubtful analogy between restraints on alienation of stock and restraints on personal property,[97] it might be more candid to say that no restriction freely entered into in a contractual sense should be unenforceable.

Finally, Maryland has a somewhat unusual provision which is worthy of mention. Shares in a close corporation[98] may not be transferred[99] without the written consent of all the shareholders of the corporation.[100] If the shareholders fail to consent to the transfer, then the person whose efforts to transfer the shares are thereby frustrated has an option to dissolve the corporation, in accordance with the following provision:

> (b) Unless otherwise provided by a stockholders' agreement authorized by Section 104 of this Article, a stockholder of a close corporation shall have the right to require dissolution of the corporation, which right shall be enforceable by petition to a court of equity of the county in which the principal office of the corporation is located, when (i) he has made written request for stockholder consent to a proposed bona fide transfer pursuant to subsection (a)(1) of this section, specifying the proposed transferee or transferees and the consideration, and such consent has not been re-

---

[97] See Ch. III, text accompanying notes 1–9.

[98] A "close corporation" is defined as a corporation which has elected to be such by a provision to that effect in its articles of incorporation. Md. Gen. Corp. Law §100 (1967).

[99] The term "transfer" is defined in id. §101(c) (1970) as follows: "(c) For purposes of this section, transfer means all transfers of any interest in the stock of a close corporation other than (i) a transfer by operation of law to an executor, administrator, trustee in bankruptcy, receiver, guardian, conservator or similar legal representative, (ii) the acquisition of a lien or power of sale pursuant to an attachment, levy or similar procedure, and (iii) the creation or assignment of a security interest. A foreclosure sale or other transfer by a person who acquired his interest or power in a transaction described in the foregoing clauses (i), (ii) and (iii) shall be a transfer subject to all the provisions of this section, and the person effecting such foreclosure sale or other transfer shall be treated as and have the rights of a holder of the stock under this section in connection with such transfer."

[100] Id. §101(a)(1) (1970).

ceived by him within thirty days after the date of the request, or (ii) another party to a stockholders' agreement authorized by Section 104 of this Article has defaulted in an obligation set forth in or arising under such agreement to purchase or cause to be purchased stock of such stockholder and such default has not been cured within thirty days after the date for performance of such obligation. A petition for dissolution pursuant to this subsection must be filed within two months after the date of the request or the default, as the case may be. A proceeding for dissolution pursuant to this subsection shall be in accordance with the provisions of Sections 109(b) and (c) of this Article.[101]

The threat of dissolution should provide a definite stimulus for the parties to come to some form of agreement. However, dissolution may be too potent a remedy, particularly when the tax effects are considered. A better approach might be a buy-out pursuant to a judicially approved fair appraisal price, as in the New Jersey statute already discussed.[102]

11.9 STATUTORY DEVICES FOR RESOLVING DEADLOCKS

Since this matter has already been discussed to a considerable extent,[103] it is appropriate merely to summarize and supplement what has already been said regarding various statutory procedures for dealing with the problem of the deadlocked corporation. We have seen how deadlocks may be resolved through various types of buy-out agreements,[104] arbitration[105] through the appointment of a so-called provisional director in states permitting that device,[106] appointment of a "custodian" to manage the corporate affairs pending a resolution of the deadlock[107] or appointment of a receiver, either to manage the business temporarily or to assist in winding up its affairs.[108] Finally, we have seen that numerous states have provisions permitting one or more shareholders or directors to bring a proceeding for judicial dissolution of a corporation on the ground that it is hopelessly deadlocked, that the acts of those in control are illegal, oppressive or fraudulent or that its assets are being misapplied or wasted.[109]

One further remedy deserves some mention. In several states the shareholders may enter into an agreement, or adopt a provision in the articles of incorporation or bylaws, which permits a nonjudicial dissolution of the corporation upon the occurrence of a specified event, such as deadlock or at the

---

[101] Id. §101(b) (1970).
[102] *Supra* note 96.
[103] See Ch. VII, text accompanying notes 1–76.
[104] Id. at notes 7–19.
[105] Id. at notes 20–48.
[106] Id. at notes 49–56.
[107] Id. at note 57.
[108] Id. at notes 57–64.
[109] Id. at notes 65–76.

petition of any shareholder.[110] For example, the Delaware General Corporation Law provides:

> The certificate of incorporation of any close corporation may include a provision granting to any stockholder, or to the holders of any specified number or percentage of shares of any class of stock, an option to have the corporation dissolved at will or upon the occurrence of any specified event or contingency. Whenever any such option to dissolve is exercised, the stockholders exercising such option shall give written notice thereof to all other stockholders. After the expiration of 30 days following the sending of such notice, the dissolution of the corporation shall proceed as if the required number of stockholders having voting power had consented in writing to dissolution of the corporation. . . .[111]

If such a provision has been adopted, notice to that effect must appear on the face of each stock certificate.[112] Several states permit such provisions only for close corporations;[113] others, such as New York and New Jersey,[114] although permitting any corporation to adopt such a provision, recognize that arrangements of this type are feasible only where a corporation is closely held.[115] These provisions authorize the shareholders to agree that any shareholder, or a specified percentage of the shareholders, may dissolve the corporation *at will,* as well as upon the occurrence of a designated contingency. If a corporation may be dissolved at will, then it resembles a partnership. Therefore it is perhaps no coincidence that several of the states which have adopted these provisions also permit a corporation to be run like a partnership, i.e., directly by the shareholders without the intervention of a board of directors.[116]

[110] E.g., Del. Gen. Corp. Law §355 (1968); Md. Gen. Corp. Law §104 (1967); N.J. Bus. Corp. Act §14A:12–5 (1968); N.Y. Bus. Corp. Law §1002 (1961); N.C. Bus. Corp. Act §55–125(3) (1959); Pa. Bus. Corp. Law §386 (1968); S.C. Bus. Corp. Act §12–22.14 (1962).

[111] Del. Gen. Corp. Law §355(a) (1968).

[112] Id. §355(c) (1968).

[113] E.g., Del. Gen. Corp. Law §355 (1968); Md. Gen. Corp. Law §104 (1967); Pa. Bus. Corp. Law §386 (1968); S.C. Bus. Corp. Act §12–22.14 (1962).

[114] N.J. Bus. Corp. Act §14A:12–5 (1968); N.Y. Bus. Corp. Law §1002 (1961).

[115] See comments of the Law Revision Commissions of these two states following each statutory provision in 4 P-H Corp. Serv. at 678 and N234–B, respectively.

[116] See note 58 *supra.*

Appendixes

Appendix A
The Decision to Incorporate—Tax and Nontax Aspects

TAX ASPECTS

Sole Proprietorship

Income taxable to owner.

Partnership

Income taxable to partners on distributable shares, whether or not received.

Corporation

Dividends taxable to extent of corporate earnings and profits.

Double taxation avoided through use of salaries, interest (beware of "thinness"), lease payments and Subchapter S.

Corporation tax rate often lower.

Capital gain distributed does not retain original character.

Losses deductible by owner.

Losses deductible by partners to extent of basis in partnership. Basis computed

Losses deductible by corporation. But see Subchapter S giving pass-through

Sole Proprietorship	Partnership	Corporation
	according to basis of property, including money, contributed plus income taxed but unreceived, less losses. Also elective method of computing basis.	treatment for net operating losses (but not capital losses).
	Partner may sell or lease property to firm, but beware of disallowance of losses between partner and 50 percent owned partnership. Also ordinary gain on transfer between partner and 80 percent owned partnership. Step up in basis available. May lease property to firm.	Beware of Section 267, disallowing losses, and Section 1239, creating ordinary gain for transfers to controlled corporation. Step up in basis available. May lease property to corporation.
Loss on investment is ordinary loss.	All partnership losses pass through.	Loss on investment is capital loss (Section 165(g)). But see Section 1244.
Sale of business gives rise to gain or loss depending on assets transferred. Williams v. McGowen, 152 F.2d 570 (2d Cir. 1945).	Same. But sale of interest in partnership gives capital gain except for Section 751. Watch Section 751 also on disproportionate distributions.	Same. But sale of stock gives capital gain.
	H.R. 10 (limited to 10 percent of earned income or $2500).	Fringe benefits. Section 401 plans, stock options, sick pay plans, insurance plans, employee death benefits, etc. 85 percent dividends received credit. 100 percent for affiliated corporations. Corporation can "time" its distributions of income to shareholders.

Sole Proprietorship	Partnership	Corporation
Amounts may be transferred in and out with little tax effect.	Same. Capital gain on distribution of any money in excess of basis. See also Section 751.	Tax on excess accumulations, personal holding companies and collapsible corporations.
		Less flexible. Liquidation provisions produce capital gain or loss except for Section 333 one-month liquidation provisions. Section 351 permits tax-free formation.

SUMMARY

Businesses with small profits, relatively few employees (see fringe benefits), or losses which can be passed through should not incorporate. See, however, Subchapter S. Also where owners are in relatively low tax brackets, incorporation is less advisable. Do *not* incorporate solely for tax reasons.

NONTAX ASPECTS

Sole Proprietorship	Partnership	Corporation
Simplicity of operation, but task may become too complex for owner.	Partner has less control over way business is run except for partnership agreement, but benefits in having skills, etc., of co-partners.	Control is in directors with residual control in shareholders. Pyramidal organization structure helps in fixing responsibility.
No need to prepare articles of incorporation, bylaws, etc. Ease and informality of operation.	Must prepare partnership agreement—still a flexible way in which to do business.	Formalities more complex. Shareholders' and directors' meetings. Cost factor—organization expenses, at-

Sole Proprietorship	Partnership	Corporation
		torney's fees, SEC and state Blue Sky, qualifications to do business in other states, taxes, etc.
Individual assets exposed to business risks. But insurance can be obtained.	Unlimited personal liability. But insurance can be obtained.	Limited liability. Shareholders may have to guarantee corporate borrowing. Insurance is probably necessary despite limited liability.
Often hard to finance if individual credit rating is poor.	Can finance only through bank loans, etc., and sale of limited partnerships.	Greater ease of financing.
Business may terminate on death unless a buyer can be found or someone in the family is willing to continue.	Partnership technically terminates on death or retirement of a partner, but in fact may continue if provided in partnership agreement.	Corporation may have perpetual life.
	Partner may transfer his right to receive profits and his rights on liquidation, but not his membership.	Shareholders may freely transfer stock except for reasonable stock transfer restrictions.
	Estate planning difficulties encountered with partner's death. Complexity of probate where partnership properties are located in several jurisdictions.	More flexible for estate planning purposes. Use of preferred stock. Avoidance of probate problems or ancillary proceedings where business properties are located in several jurisdictions.

Sole Proprietorship	*Partnership*	*Corporation*
	Partnership may be more easily dissolved than corporation in the event of deadlock.	Corporation may be more difficult to dissolve in the event of deadlock.

SUMMARY

If a business is small, involves relatively few people, has modest profits and little need for extensive financing, sole proprietorship or partnership may be indicated.

Appendix B
Selling the Business—Tax and Nontax Aspects

SELLING THE BUSINESS

I. *Tax Aspects*

  A. *Should the transaction be set up so as to be taxable or nontaxable? (The answer to the problem should not depend solely on tax aspects.)*
    1. *Seller's viewpoint*
      a. If nontaxable, no gain need be recognized (unless boot—property other than stock or securities—is received). Stock or securities received in the transaction can be held and, under existing law, basis will be stepped up at date of death.
      b. However, seller may want cash or marketable assets, or wish to recognize loss, rather than receive a large block of stock in the purchaser. If so, then the transaction should be taxable.
    2. *Purchaser's viewpoint*
      a. Factors favoring a nontaxable transaction.
        (1) Purchaser may wish a carry-over of seller's tax attributes (such as a loss carry-over).
        (2) Purchaser may not wish to expend cash.
      b. Factors favoring a taxable transaction.
        (1) If taxable, purchaser is able to obtain a stepped-up basis for assets acquired from seller.
        (2) Purchaser may not wish to issue additional stock.

  B. *Alternative methods of setting up transaction*
    1. Purchase of stock.
    2. Purchase of assets.
    3. Purchase of stock followed by liquidation.

  C. *Tax-free reorganizations*
    1. Merger or consolidation
      a. Continuity of interest requirement must be met. Revenue Procedure 66–34 indicates that 50 percent continuity by way of equity is enough.

b. Bonds or notes may thus be issued. Caveat—make sure the notes are securities (i.e., over 10 years preferably). Otherwise boot results.

c. Preferred or nonvoting common may be issued. These qualify for the continuity of interest test. However, beware of redeeming preferred before five years have elapsed.

d. Watch dispositions of stock by shareholders of merging corporation. Stock of acquiring corporation should be held for five years to be absolutely safe. Watch preexisting commitments to sell stock to others.

e. Recent changes in the Code now permit so-called triangular mergers—i.e., mergers with a subsidiary of a controlling parent corporation—if the subsidiary issues to the shareholders of the acquired corporation *either* its own shares *or* shares of its parent (but *not both* its own shares and its parent's shares). See Code §§368(a)(2)(D) and 368(b)(2).

2. Acquisition by one corporation *solely* for all or part of its voting stock (or voting stock of parent) of stock in another corporation, if control requirement is met immediately after.

a. Must be *solely* for voting stock.

b. Receipt of *any* additional consideration will result in tax of the *entire* transaction (not merely the additional consideration).

c. Danger in acquiring corporation paying expenses of acquired corporation. This may be considered payment of additional consideration.

d. Acquiring corporation may acquire gradual or "creeping" control of acquired corporation but must beware of "step transaction" doctrine.

3. Acquisition by one corporation *solely* for all or part of its voting stock (or voting stock of parent) of *substantially* all properties of another corporation.

a. Must be *solely* for voting stock (liabilities assumed are not counted). But where exchange is not *solely* for voting stock (i.e., there is other consideration), then transaction still qualifies if 20 percent or less in fair value of property of acquired corporation is purchased through use of other consideration (i.e., not voting stock). In determining the 20 percent "leeway" here, liabilities *are* taken into account.

b. Must be "substantially all." See Rev. Proc. 66–34. (The test is satisfied if there is a transfer of assets representing at least 90 percent of the fair value of the *net* assets and at least 70 percent of the fair value of the *gross* assets of the acquiring corporation.)

c. Acquiring corporation may have difficulty with "creeping control" concept of the Bausch and Lomb doctrine, discussed in Ch. VIII, text accompanying note 159.

II. *Nontax Aspects*

A. Mergers or consolidations

Advantages	*Disadvantages*
Relative simplicity of transfer of assets, i.e., by operation of law.	Approval by shareholders of *both* companies usually required, except in certain states, such as Delaware (Gen. Corp. Law §251(f)), where vote of shareholders of surviving corporation is not required unless merger results in increase of more than 15 percent of outstanding shares.
Usually no sales taxes or other transfer taxes.	
Flexibility, particularly from tax standpoint, in issuing various types of consideration for shares, i.e., bonds, debentures, notes, etc. (See tax checklist.)	
"Short-form" mergers are often possible between parent corporation and 90 or 95 percent owned subsidiary. (See Del. Gen. Corp. Law §253). No shareholder approval required and minority shareholders may be paid off in cash rather than shares.	Shareholders of both corporations are usually entitled to appraisal rights, except in certain states, such as Delaware (Gen. Corp. Law §262(k)), where shares are registered on a national securities exchange or held of record by 2000 or more shareholders or, in the case of a surviving corporation's shareholders, where shareholder approval was not required.
No requirement for SEC registration of shares of surviving corporation issued to merging corporation's shareholders if SEC Rule 133 is complied with. But Wheat Report proposals may change this.	Surviving corporation assumes all liabilities of merging corporation, whether unknown or contingent, by operation of law.
	Difficulties are occasionally encountered in merging enterprises incorporated in two different states. Consent of corporations commissioner or public service commission may be required. Sometimes this may result in a "reverse" merger, i.e., B merges into A instead of A into B. Similar problems are encountered where local franchises, etc., are not transferable.
	Necessity for qualifying surviving corporation to do business in various states in which merging corporation did business.

B. Sale of stock

Advantages	Disadvantages
Simplicity.	Transfer of shares may give rise to local transfer taxes.
No need for shareholder approval unless approval by shareholders of purchasing corporation is required under N.Y.S.E. rules or to authorize additional shares.	If less than 100 percent of the shares are purchased the parent corporation must face the problems of dealing with minority shareholders of its subsidiary (Possible solution—to "merge them out" through paying cash in a short-form merger, if permitted by state law. See checklist on mergers *supra*.)
No dissenter's appraisal rights, unless than transaction is deemed to be a "de facto" merger.	
Purchasing corporation does not subject itself to immediate liability for liabilities of acquired company (although it remains indirectly responsible for these since the acquired company is its subsidiary).	Possible (although not probable) liability to acquired company's minority shareholders if controlling shares are purchased at a premium.
	Inflexibility from tax standpoint: Only voting common stock may be issued. (See tax checklist.)
	SEC registration problems if there are numerous shareholders of the acquired corporation and the acquisition is by means of shares of the acquiring corporation. Cash tender offer may dispense with registration requirement, but not for need to disclose material facts if required by recent amendments to §§13 and 14 of Securities Exchange Act.

C. Asset sales

Advantages	Disadvantages
Purchasing corporation may limit its liabilities by appropriate choice of assets to be purchased; avoid contingent liabilities, etc.	Liabilities may yet arise due to failure to comply with Bulk Sales Act, where applicable, and also for transferee liability in certain transfers in fraud of creditors, particularly if consideration for sale is in shares of purchasing corporation and is transmitted directly to shareholders of selling corporation.
No approval by shareholders of purchasing corporation required, unless required under N.Y.S.E. rules or unless to authorize issuance of additional shares. Similarly, pur-	

Advantages	*Disadvantages*

chasing corporation's shareholders have no appraisal rights.

No SEC registration required if transaction qualifies under SEC Rule 133. But Wheat Report proposals may change this.

Need for preparing complicated instruments of transfer, securing releases or waivers from lien holders, lessors, etc.

Applicability of sales taxes, transfer taxes, etc.

Approval by shareholders of selling corporation normally required if sale is not in usual and regular course of business. Dissenting shareholders may have appraisal rights. In de facto mergers, merger rules (see above) will apply.

Relative inflexibility from tax standpoint. Only voting common shares may be issued, except for 20 percent leeway rule of Code §368-(a)(2)(B). Transfer must be of "substantially all" assets. See tax checklist *supra*.

Appendix C
Time Schedule

Date	Steps to Be Taken
March 19	Make list of persons whose assistance will be required in preparation of registration statement and what work will be required of each. Consult with appropriate company officer with regard to retention of experts and, in particular, independent accountants, in order to expedite preparation of certified financial statements.

March 19 — Consult with company and underwriter arrangements for appointing counsel to carry out "Blue Sky" investigation, preparation of "Blue Sky" memorandum and qualification of securities in states where necessary, as well as dealer registration.

Consult with company and underwriter arrangements for preparation of stock certificates, particularly if engraved certificates are necessary; discuss possibility of facsimile signatures.

March 20 — Initial meeting of company officers, representatives of underwriter (including counsel for underwriter), company counsel (and special counsel where required) and independent accountants.

General discussion of underwriting and assignment of work (assignments to be completed by no later than April 3).

Work assigned as follows:

PRESIDENT OF COMPANY TO PREPARE DRAFTS
Item 3*—Use of Proceeds
Item 4—Description of Organization and Business
Item 8—Promoters, Directors and Officers

TREASURER OF COMPANY TO PREPARE DRAFTS
Item 5—Description of Property
Item 9—Remuneration of Officers and Directors
Item 11—Principal Security Holders

* Item references are to SEC Form S-2.

Date *Steps to Be Taken*

> *Item 12*—Interest of Management and Others in Certain Transactions
>
> *Item 14*—Other Expenses of Registration and Distribution

COUNSEL FOR UNDERWRITER TO PREPARE
> *Item 1*—Distribution Spread
>
> *Item 2*—Plan of Distribution

In addition, counsel for the underwriter is to prepare underwriting contract, agreement among underwriters and Blue Sky memorandum.

INDEPENDENT ACCOUNTANTS TO PREPARE
> *Item 13*—Financial Statements

COMPANY COUNSEL TO PREPARE
> *Item 6*—Material Litigation
>
> *Item 7*—Shares Being Registered
>
> *Item 10*—Options to Purchase Securities of Registrant
>
> *Item 15*—Interest of Experts Named in Registration Statement
>
> *Item 16*—Recent Sales of Unregistered Securities
>
> *Item 17*—Indemnification of Directors and Officers
>
> *Item 18*—Exhibits Filed

In addition, company counsel is to obtain and advise with respect to any title search required by Item 5 and to advise with respect to any deed or encumbrance specified in Item 5; to complete the facing page of the prospectus, signature page, etc.; to arrange for obtaining consents of experts and all exhibits other than those to be furnished by counsel for underwriter.

March 23   Underwriters', directors' and officers' questionnaires to be mailed.

March 27   Hold meeting of board of directors of company to recommend amendment of certificate of incorporation to increase authorized shares (or, if upon organization of company, meeting of incorporators, directors, stockholders, etc.); call special stockholders' meeting; authorize filing of registration statement; ratify retention of independent accountants and special counsel (if needed); appoint agent for service of notices and other SEC communications; adopt Blue Sky resolutions; approve underwriting agreement; and authorize its execution and delivery.

April 3   Work assigned to working group to be delivered to company counsel for collating.

Date	*Steps to Be Taken*
April 6	Informal conference of working group to correct deficiencies.
April 10	Collated and corrected material to be sent to printer, with directions to furnish each member of working group with desired number of proofs.
April 16	Prefiling conference with SEC staff. First proofs should have been received.
April 17	First proof meeting of working group for discussion of proofs and decisions with respect to corrections and revisions.
April 20	Corrected and revised proofs, etc., to be sent to printer.
April 22	Special stockholders' meeting (if required) to approve amendment of certificate of incorporation, etc.
April 23	Amended certificate of incorporation filed with Secretary of State, etc. Second proof meeting of working group to verify corrections and revisions of first proof.
April 27	Registration statement filed with SEC.
May 18* (approx.)	Receipt of Letter of Comment from SEC.
May 19	Meeting of working group to discuss deficiencies if any in registration statement; preparation of revisions and corrections.
May 22	Filing of amendment to registration statement with SEC to reflect changes required by Letter of Comment, with request for acceleration.
June 1	Execution of underwriting agreement and underwriter's "due diligence" meeting.
June 2	Filing of price amendment with SEC with request for acceleration; effective date of registration statement; obtain Blue Sky clearances, etc.
June 3	Counsel for company and counsel for underwriter to prepare closing agenda; counsel for company to arrange for delivery of requisite numbers and denominations of stock certificates, registered as requested by underwriter. Counsel for company to obtain documents, certificates, etc., required at closing.
June 16	Closing.
June 17	Counsel for company to prepare closing memorandum.

* The date is probably overly optimistic in view of the SEC's workload. See page 374 *supra.*

Appendix D
Closing Memorandum

SPACE SCIENCES, INC.

CLOSING MEMORANDUM

60,000 Shares Class A Voting Stock
65,000 Shares Class B Voting Stock

The closing of the sale to the public through underwriters of 60,000 shares of Class A Voting Common Stock, and the sale privately of 65,000 shares of Class B Voting Common Stock of Space Sciences, Inc. (hereinafter called the "Company"), was held at the office of the First National Bank of Langdell, Ames, on Tuesday, June 16, 1970 at 10:30 A.M., Daylight Saving Time.

I. *Action Prior to Closing*

Corporate Action

At a meeting held on March 27, 1970, the Board of Directors of the Company recommended the amendment of the Company's certificate of incorporation so as to authorize the issuance of the Class A and Class B Voting Common Stock, called a Special Meeting of Stockholders of the Company to be held on April 22, 1970, to adopt such amendment, authorized the preparation and filing of a registration statement with the Securities and Exchange Commission (hereinafter called the "SEC"), ratified the retention of independent accountants, appointed agents for services of notices and other communications by the SEC, adopted resolutions pertaining to the qualification of the Class A and Class B stock under the securities laws of the several states in which the offering was to be made and approved the underwriting agreement and authorized its execution and delivery.

A Special Meeting of Stockholders of the Company was held on April 22, 1970, whereat the amendment to the Company's certificate of incorporation was adopted by the requisite majority. Such amendment was filed, on April 23, 1970, with the Secretary of State of Ames and a certified copy thereof recorded in the office of the recorder of Maguire County, where the Company's principal place of business is located.

Registration Under the Securities Act of 1933

The Registration Statement on Form S-2 was filed with the SEC on April 27, 1970. The contents of the SEC's letter of comments dated May 15, 1970, was received on May 18, 1970. Amendment No. 1 to the Company's registration statement, reflecting the comments of the SEC, was filed with the SEC on May 22, 1970. Amendment No. 2 to the Company's registration statement was filed with the SEC on June 2, 1970 and the registration statement became effective at noon on the same date.

Underwriting Arrangements

After a meeting between the underwriters and the officers of the Company on June 1, 1970, the underwriting agreement and agreement among underwriters was executed and delivered.

II.   The Closing

(All steps listed below were deemed to take place simultaneously.)

Unless otherwise indicated, copies or counterparts of each document were delivered one each to representatives of the Company, counsel for the Company, representatives of the underwriter and counsel for the underwriter.

1.   *Corporate Organization and Standing of the Company*

1.01   Certificate of Incorporation of the Company and all amendments thereto, certified, as of a recent date, by the Secretary of State of the State of Ames, accompanied by a copy of a certificate of the Recorder of Maguire County as to the recording thereof, such certificate to state that the attached copies of the Certificate of Incorporation and any amendments thereto constitute all of the corporate records of the Company on file and of record in his office.

1.02   Certificate of the Secretary of State of the State of Ames, as of a recent date, stating that the Company is in good standing.

1.03   Telegram from the Secretary of State of the State of Ames, dated June 16, 1970, as to the good standing of the Company.

1.04   Certificate of the Secretary of the Company, dated June 16, 1970, that no corporate documents affecting the Company have been filed with the Secretary of State of the State of Ames since the date of the certification referred to in Item 1.01, and that all corporate documents affecting the Company which have been filed with the Recorder of Maguire County and which are required by law to be filed with the Secretary of State of the State of Ames, have been filed with the Secretary of State of the State of Ames.

1.05   Letter from the Department of Revenue of the State of Ames, dated near the closing date, as to the payment of franchise taxes.

1.06   Copy of the Bylaws of the Company, certified by the Secretary of the Company as in effect on June 2, 1970, and thereafter to and including the closing date.

2. *Authorization of Class A and Class B Common Stock*

    2.01   Certificate of the Secretary of the Company dated June 16, 1970, that the attached copy of the resolutions of the Board of Directors of the Company, at a meeting held March 27, 1970, authorizing the amendment to the Company's Certificate of Incorporation, calling a Special Meeting of Stockholders, and taking other necessary action so as to authorize the creation and issuance of the Class A and Class B Common Stock, were duly adopted at such meeting and are in full force and effect.

    2.02   Certificate of the Secretary of the Company, dated June 16, 1970, that the attached specimen certificates for the Company's Class A and Class B Common Stock are in the forms approved by the Directors.

    2.03   Certificate of the Secretary of the Company, dated June 16, 1970, as to the election, qualification, incumbency and signatures of the signing officers of the Company.

3. *Underwriting Agreement*

    3.01   Executed counterparts of the Underwriting Agreement and the Agreement Among Underwriters.

    3.02   Certificate of the Secretary of the Company, dated June 16, 1970, that the attached conformed copy of the Underwriting Agreement, as executed on June 1, 1970, is in the form approved by the Company's Board of Directors.

    3.03   Certificate of the President of the Company, dated June 16, 1970, as to the matters referred to in the Underwriting Agreement.

    3.04   Certificate of Accountants, dated June 16, 1970, pursuant to the Underwriting Agreement.

    3.05   Opinion of Counsel to the Underwriters, pursuant to the Underwriting Agreement.

4. *Registration Under Securities Act of 1933*

    4.01   Executed counterpart of registration statement as filed with the SEC on April 27, 1970.

    4.02   Executed counterpart of Amendment No. 1 to registration statement as filed with the SEC on May 22, 1970.

    4.03   Executed counterpart or conformed copy of Amendment No. 2, filed with the SEC on June 2, 1970.

    4.04   Copies of correspondence between the Company, Counsel for the Company and the SEC relating to the Company's filing of the registration statement.

    4.05   Telegram from the SEC to the Company, dated June 2, 1970, declaring the Company's registration statement to be effective.

    4.06   Telegram from the SEC to the Company, dated June 15, 1970, stating that no "Stop Order" has been issued as of the date thereof.

5. *Blue Sky Qualification of Class A and Class B Common Stock*
    5.01   Blue Sky Memorandum, as delivered to the Underwriter by Counsel for the Underwriter.
    5.02   Copies of telegrams from Securities Commissioners of the several states wherein the offering is to be made, dated June 2, 1970, granting requisite permission to offer the Class A and Class B Common Stock.
    5.03   Opinion of Counsel to the Underwriter, dated June 16, 1970, that no action has been taken by any of the states referred to in Item 5.02 since June 2, 1970, which would adversely affect the offering of the Class A and Class B Common Stock.

6. *Special Meeting of Stockholders*
    6.01   Certificate of the Secretary of the Company, dated June 16, 1970, that the attached copy of the resolutions of the stockholders of the Company were duly adopted at a meeting held on April 22, 1970, and are in full force and effect.

7. *Closing Under the Underwriting Agreement*
    7.01   Certificate of Transfer Agent for the Company as to countersignature and registration of the certificates of Class A and Class B Common Stock, and as to payment of stock transfer and issuance taxes.
    7.02   Certificates for Class A and Class B Common Stock of the Company.
    7.03   Certified or bank cashier's check of the Underwriter in payment for the Class A Common Stock and for the portion of Class B Common Stock purchased by the Underwriter.
    7.04   Receipt of the Company for the funds referred to in Item 7.03, countersigned by the Underwriter to indicate receipt by the latter of the stock certificates referred to in Item 7.02.
    7.05   Opinion of Counsel to the Company, addressed to the Company and dated June 16, 1970.
    7.06   Opinion of Counsel to the Company, addressed to the Underwriters and dated June 16, 1970, pursuant to the Underwriting Agreement.

Table of Cases

Table of Rulings and Regulations

Index